Rail Guide 2020

Colin J. Marsden

Crécy Publishing Ltd

First published 2010
Reprinted 2010,
Revised editions 2011, 2012, 2013, 2014, 2015, 2016, 2017, 2018, 2019
This Eleventh Edition published 2020 by Crécy Publishing

ISBN 978 1 9108 09594

Printed in Malta by Gutenberg Press Ltd

Crécy Publishing Ltd
1a Ringway Trading Estate
Shadowmoss Road
Manchester
M22 5LH
Tel +44 (0) 161 499 0024

www.crecy.co.uk

Front cover top: *In 2019, First TransPennine Express commenced the roll-out of Mk5 CAF-built stock including driving cab cars. A five-car formation with a cab-car leading is seen at Scarborough.* **CJM**

Front cover bottom: *Greater Anglia-operated, Stadler-built Class 745/0 12-car 'Intercity' set No. 745005 is seen at speed at Brantham on 2 October 2019 with the 09.03 Norwich Crown Point to London Liverpool Street test run.* **Paul Biggs**

Back cover top: *On the Isle of Man Steam Railway Manx Northern Railway No. 4* Caledonia *is seen with a Douglas to Port Erin service at Castletown on 2 August 2019.* **CJM**

Back cover bottom: *In summer 2019, Porterbrook unveiled a major advance in traction technology, with the roll-out of Class 799 No. 799001 (rebuilt from a Class 319), powered by a Hydrogen Fuel Cell. The set is seen at Long Marston.* **CJM**

Rail Guide information is correct to 1 February 2020

Acknowledgement – The Author would like to record his thanks to the many railway staff who have provided invaluable information for the production of this book. Also to the many photographers, especially Antony Christie, Nathan Williamson, Cliff Beeton and John Binch, for providing many of the images. I would also like to express my thanks to Keith Ewins and Antony Christie for reading the updated manuscript. **CJM**

Welcome to the fully updated and revised 2020 edition of *ABC Rail Guide*. The only title published giving a complete overview of UK railways.

During 2019, huge changes have taken place on the rail scene, with many new classes entering service and several of the older fleets being withdrawn, most notable the 1972-design Class 313 and 314s with major inroads also made to the Class 315 fleet. After many years of promises, the first withdrawals of Class 142 'Pacer' stock took place, and by summer 2020 the entire fleets of Class 142, 143 and 144 should be history working on the main line.

Many new classes have taken to the road, including Class 195 diesel and 331 electric sets built by CAF for the Northern franchise. In Scotland, the full Hitachi AT200 Class 385 fleet was introduced. While on Greater Anglia, the Stadler bi-mode Class 755 sets have been introduced on branch line routes radiating from Norwich, allowing a cascade of stock. On the Anglia main line, the first 12-car Class 745 articulated EMUs entered service in the first week of 2020, paving the way for the withdrawal of Class 90 and Mk3 stock. Sadly, the introduction of Bombardier Class 720s on local services has been heavily delayed.

In the London area, the long-awaited introduction of the Bombardier Class 710s on the Gospel Oak-Barking and Euston-Watford routes took place. On the Elizabeth Line (Crossrail), the full fleet of 70 Class 345s was delivered, but only a handful were in service operating Liverpool Street-Shenfield and Paddington-Reading services. The full Elizabeth line is now unlikely to open until 2021.

The most significant news in terms of fleet change came in summer 2019, when First Great Western was able to withdraw its entire fleet of full-length HSTs, following the commissioning of Class 800 and 802 stock. A number of these vehicles were cascaded to Abellio Scotrail for use on their Inter7City services, but a large number went to store and face scrap. FGW continued to introduce short 2+4 HST sets on Cardiff-Bristol-Taunton to the West Country route. From the start of 2020 all were refurbished with sliding passenger doors and retention toilet systems.

On the East Coast LNER route, Class 800 and 801 'Azuma' stock was introduced, leading to the entire LNER HST fleet being stood down by the end of 2019. A number of Class 91/Mk4 sets were withdrawn, with many coaches being broken up.

Hitachi-built five-car Class 802 sets were also introduced on TransPennine Express and Hull Trains routes, allowing older stock to be cascaded, in terms of Hull Trains, the displaced Class 180s passing to East Midlands Railway.

CAF-built Mk5 passenger stock was introduced on the entire Serco-Caledonian Sleeper network, allowing old Mk2 and Mk3 fleets to be withdrawn. CAF also successfully introduced five-car rakes of Mk5 stock, including a remote cab-car, on TransPennine services, with power provided by Class 68s leased from DRS.

TransPennine Express has also taken delivery of CAF 'Civity' EMUs for Anglo-Scottish services, classified 397, these should go into passenger service in the first quarter of 2020.

At the end of 2019 two new fleets were under advanced construction; Class 777s for Merseyrail, with two sets delivered by Stadler to the Wildenrath test track for dynamic testing, with the first set arriving in the UK in January 2020. The first few Bombardier Class 701 sets for South Western Railway were also completed, with one set going to the test track at Velim in the Czech Republic.

The first of the new West Midlands Class 196 sets from CAF was delivered for testing.

Development of Porterbrooks Class 769 *Flex* project has been ongoing, but no trains were in traffic by the end of 2019. The innovative Vivarail Class 230 project, using rebuilt London Underground 'D' stock, continued with three sets entering service on the Bedford-Bletchley route, further deliveries have been delayed, but an additional order was announced to replace vintage stock on the Isle of Wight.

Turning to the freight business, DB-C has seen a reduction in work and locos, while GBRf has expanded its fleet, adding extra Class 66s from Mainland Europe and officially ordering 10 Class 69s from Progress Rail, these being Class 56 bodyshells rebuilt with EMD prime movers.

DRS, although speculated to be about to order new locos, took on a long-term lease of a small batch of spare Class 66s from DB-C.

Specialist operator Rail Operations Group (ROG) continues to grow, taking on more locos and winning new contracts for the transfer of stock around the network.

The UK light rail systems continue to provide a valuable service, no new stock was introduced in 2019, but a major order is about to be announced to replace the entire Tyne & Wear fleet. In Birmingham, the West Midlands Metro expanded operations further into the City Centre, using battery technology, eliminating the need for overhead wires. Extra trams have also been ordered for the Birmingham system to cope with major route expansion.

Preserved railways continue to play an important part of the economy, with most lines reporting a good operating year. Further modern traction locos and multiple units have entered preservation and the number of fully restored and operational vehicles continues to rise. It is pleasing to record that the pioneer production HST power car No. 43002 has been saved for preservation and is currently on display at the National Railway Museum, York.

The Editor and Publisher of *ABC Rail Guide* hope you continue to enjoy this product, any reader with additional information is welcome to submit to the publishers' address.

Colin J. Marsden
Editor
February 2020

Train Operators, The Rail Operations Group, and Network Rail welcome rail enthusiasts and photographers, but in today's safety-led railway and with the continued concerns about possible transport terrorism, guidelines are very important and we encourage all to follow these published guidelines as much as possible. They are available to view and download from the National Rail and ROG websites, but are reproduced in full below to assist you with this information. ■

The Official Railway Enthusiasts Guidelines

■ Network Rail welcomes rail enthusiasts to our stations.

■ The following guidelines are designed to help you to have a safe and enjoyable experience. Please keep them with you when you are at Network Rail-managed stations.

■ You may also wish to take a copy of the Railway by-laws which are available from the Office of Public Sector Information website.

Before you enter the platform

■ When you arrive at a station, please let the staff at the Network Rail Reception Desk know that you are on the station. This will help keep station staff informed so that they can go about their duties without concern as to your reasons for being there.

■ You may require a platform ticket to allow access to platforms.

While you are on the platform

■ You need to act safely and sensibly at all times.

- Stay clear of the platform edge and stay behind the yellow lines where they are provided.
- Be aware of your surroundings.

Please DO NOT:

- Trespass on to the tracks or any other part of the railway that is not available to passengers.
- Use flash photography because it can distract train drivers and train despatch staff and so is potentially very dangerous.
- Climb on any structure or interfere with platform equipment.
- Obstruct any signalling equipment or signs which are vital to the safe running of the railway.
- Wear anything which is similar in colour to safety clothing, such as high-visibility jackets, as this could cause confusion to drivers and other railway employees.
- Gather together in groups at busy areas of the platform (e.g. customer information points, departure screens, waiting areas, seating etc.) or where this may interfere with the duties of station staff.

■ If possible, please try to avoid peak hours which are Monday – Friday 6:00am (06.00) – 10:30am (10.30) and 3:30pm (15.30) – 7:30pm (19.30).

Extra eyes and ears

■ If you see anything suspicious or notice any unusual behaviour or activities, please tell a member of staff immediately.

■ For emergencies and serious incidents, either call:

The British Transport Police on 0800 40 50 40. Or text a message to 61016.
The Police on 999, or 101.

■ Your presence at a station can be very helpful to us as extra 'eyes and ears' and can have a positive security benefit.

Photography

■ You can take photographs at stations provided you do not sell them. However, you are not allowed to take photographs of security-related equipment, such as CCTV cameras.

■ Flash photography on platforms is not allowed at any time. It can distract train drivers and train despatch staff and so is potentially very dangerous.

■ Tripod legs must be kept away from platform edges and behind the yellow lines. On busy stations, you may not be allowed to use a tripod because it could be a dangerous obstruction to passengers.

Railway by-laws

For safety and ease of travel on the railway system (which includes passengers, staff, property and equipment), the by-laws must be observed by everyone. A copy of the by-laws can be obtained at stations or downloaded from the Office of Public Sector Information website.

General

Train operators must put the safety of their passengers and staff first. You may very occasionally be asked by station staff to move to another part of the station or to leave the station altogether. Station staff should be happy to explain why this is necessary. If you are travelling by train, they may ask you to remain in the normal waiting areas with other passengers. If this occurs, please follow their instructions with goodwill as staff have many things to consider, including the safety and security of all passengers, and are authorised to use judgement in this regard.

Below: *The modernisation of our railways, with the introduction of new stock will continue through 2020, with many new classes introduced throughout the country. The year should see the completion of the delivery of Bombardier Class 710 sets to Transport for London. These four- and five-car sets are part of the growing 'Aventra' family, and many problems have surrounded the introduction of this design with different operators. Set No. 710263 is seen passing Gospel Oak in May 2019.* **CJM**

Passenger Train Operating Companies – P8 – 179

Freight Operating Companies – P180 – 212

Infrastructure Companies – P213 – 226

Train Engineering Companies – P227 – 232

Reconditioned Loco Suppliers – P233 – 234

Rolling Stock Hire Companies – P235 – 241

Private Train Operators & Support Coaches – P242 – 253

Off-Lease Rolling Stock – P254 – 256

Ex-BR Industrial Locos – P257

UK Exported Motive Power – P258 – 261

Irish Railways – P262 – 269

Transport For London (TFL) London Underground – P270 – 285

Transport For London (TFL) Trams – P286 – 288

Below: *Operated by GB Railfreight, Class 66s Nos. 66743 and 66746 are painted in Royal Scotsman maroon and gold livery to match the colours of the Royal Scotsman luxury land cruise train. When not required for VIP train use, the pair share duties within the general GBRf Class 66 roster. On 9 July 2019, the pair lead the Royal Scotsman, through the Powderham Estate in Devon.* **CJM**

Avanti West Coast

Address: 85 Smallbrook Queensway, Birmingham, B5 4HA
info@avantiwestcoast.co.uk
0845 000 8000
www.avantiwestcoast.co.uk

Managing Director: Phil Whittingham

Franchise Dates: 8 December 2019 - 2031

Principal Routes: London Euston - Birmingham, Holyhead, Manchester Liverpool, Glasgow and Edinburgh

Depots: Edge Hill§ (LL), Longsight§ (MA), Oxley (OY), Wembley§ (WB), Central Rivers (CZ)
§ Operated by Alstom

Parent Company: First Group (70%), Trenitalia (30%)

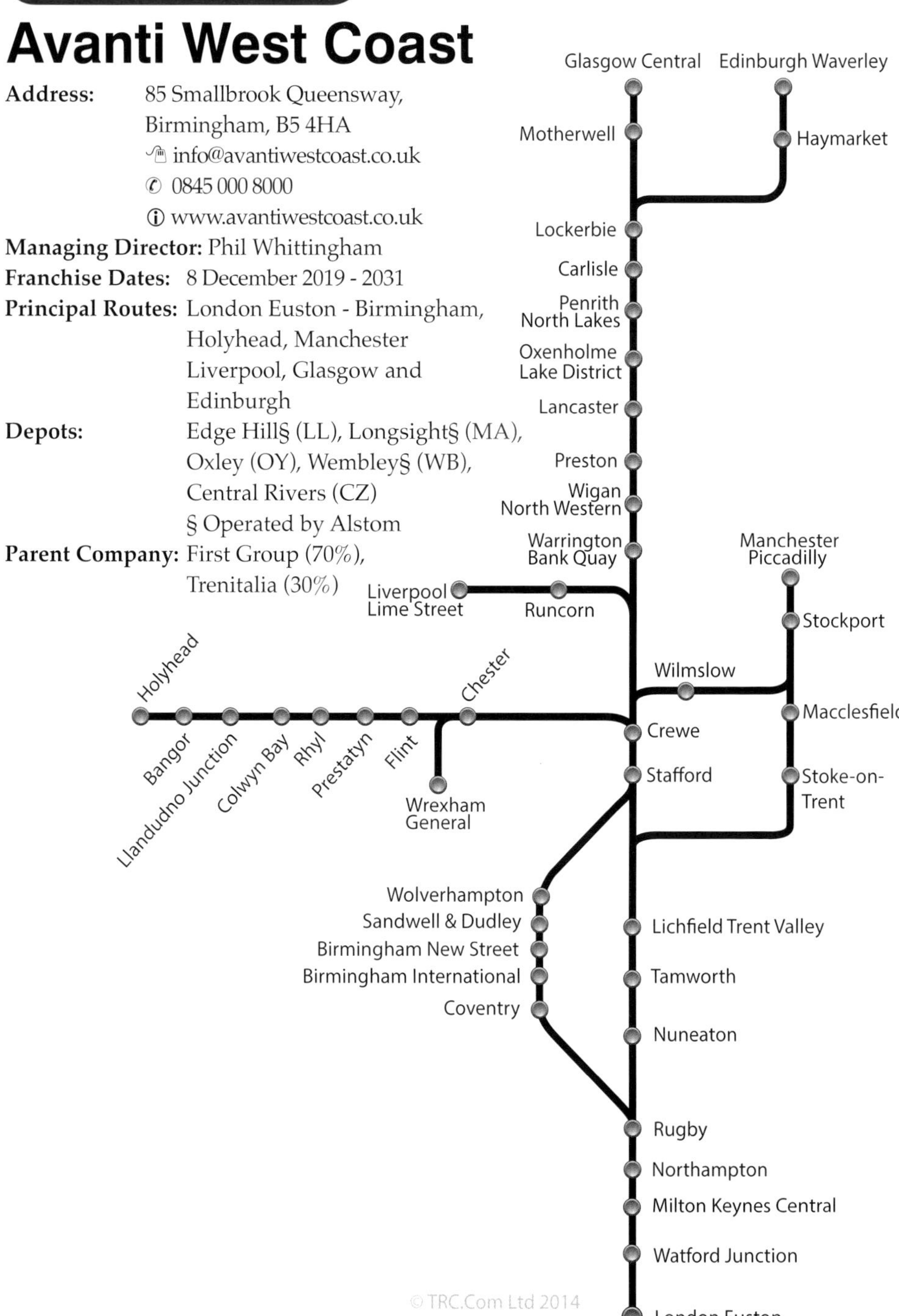

The new West Coast 'Avanti' franchise from December 2019 will see many changes to the route. The Class 390 Pendolino fleet will be refurbished with new seats and decor including extra luggage space. The 'Super Voyager' Class 221s with be withdrawn by 2022, replaced by 23 new train sets, 10 seven-car electric sets for London, West Midlands and Liverpool use and 13 five-car bi-mode sets for use on North Wales - London services. These new sets will be variants of the Hitachi Class 800 and 801 design, funded by Rock Rail West, built at Newton Aycliffe and based at Oxley.

Class 221
Super Voyager

Vehicle Length: 77ft 6in (23.62m)
Height: 12ft 4in (3.75m)
Width: 8ft 11in (2.73m)
Engine: 1 x Cummins 750hp per vehicle
Horsepower: 5-car - 3,750hp (2,796kW). 4-car - 3,000hp (2,237kW)
Seats (total/car): 26F/214S 42S/60S/60S/52S/26F (*not in 4-car set)*

Number	*Formation* DMS+MS+MS+MSRMB+DMF	*Depot*	*Livery*	*Owner*	*Operator*
221101	60351+60951+60851+60751+60451	CZ	AWC	BEA	AWC
221102	60352+60952+60852+60752+60452	CZ	AWW	BEA	AWC
221103	60353+60953+60853+60753+60453	CZ	AWW	BEA	AWC
221104	60354+60954+60854+60754+60454	CZ	AWW	BEA	AWC
221105	60355+60955+60855+60755+60455	CZ	AWW	BEA	AWC
221106	60356+60956+60856+60756+60456	CZ	AWW	BEA	AWC
221107	60357+60957+60857+60757+60457	CZ	AWW	BEA	AWC
221108	60358+60958+60858+60758+60458	CZ	AWW	BEA	AWC
221109	60359+60959+60859+60759+60459	CZ	AWW	BEA	AWC
221110	60360+60960+60860+60760+60460	CZ	AWW	BEA	AWC
221111	60361+60961+60861+60761+60461	CZ	AWW	BEA	AWC
221112	60362+60962+60862+60762+60462	CZ	AWW	BEA	AWC
221113	60363+60963+60863+60763+60463	CZ	AWW	BEA	AWC
221114	60364+60964+60864+60764+60464	CZ	AWW	BEA	AWC
221115	60365+60965+60865+60765+60465	CZ	AWW¤	BEA	AWC
221116	60366+60966+60866+60766+60466	CZ	AWW	BEA	AWC
221117	60367+60967+60867+60767+60467	CZ	AWW	BEA	AWC
221118	60368+60968+60868+60768+60468	CZ	AWW	BEA	AWC
221142	60392+60992+60986+60792+60492	CZ	AWW	BEA	AWC
221143	60393+60993+60994+60793+60493	CZ	AWW	BEA	AWC

¤ One driving car carries Bombardier branding.

Below: *From the franchise change at the end of 2019, the Virgin branding was quickly removed from the red and silver liveried Class 221 fleet, with ugly scars left on the front ends and sides. Avanti branding will be applied and no major repaint/ brand plans have been announced. Set No. 221114 is seen in an unbranded condition at Kidsgrove.* **Cliff Beeton**

Avanti West Coast

Class 390
Pendolino

Vehicle Length (Driving): 75ft 6in (23.01m)
Height: 11ft 6in (3.50m)
Width: 8ft 11in (2.71m)

Horsepower: 6,840hp (5,100kW)
Seats (total/car): 147F/300S, 18F/39F/44F/46F/74S/76S/76S/66S/48S/64S/46S
35 sets are now formed of 11 vehicles 147F/450S

Number	Formation DMRFO+MFO+PTFO+MFO[MSO]*+(TSO+MSO)+TSO+MSO+PTSRMB+MSO+DMSO	Depot	Livery	Owner	Operator	Name
390001	69101+69401+69501+69601*+68801+69701+69801+69901+69201	MA	AWW	ANG	AWC	*Bee Together*
390002	69102+69402+69502+69602*+68802+69702+69802+69902+69202	MA	AWW	ANG	AWC	*Stephen Sutton*
390103	69103+69403+69503+69603+65303+68903+68803+69703+69803+69903+69203	MA	AWW	ANG	AWC	*Virgin Hero*
390104	69104+69404+69504+69604+65304+68904+68804+69704+69804+69904+69204	MA	AWW	ANG	AWC	*Alstom Pendolino*
390005	69105+69405+69505+69605*+68805+69705+69805+69905+69205	MA	AWW	ANG	AWC	*City of Wolverhampton*
390006	69106+69406+69606*+68806+69706+69806+69906+69206	MA	AWW	ANG	AWC	*Rethink Mental Illness*
390107	69107+69407+69507+69607+65307+68907+68807+69707+69807+69907+69207	MA	AWW	ANG	AWC	
390008	69108+69408+69508+69608*+68808+69708+69808+69908+69208	MA	AWW	ANG	AWC	*Charles Rennie Mackintosh*
390009	69109+69409+69509+69609*+68809+69709+69809+69909+69209	MA	AWW	ANG	AWC	*Treaty of Union*
390010	69110+69410+69510+69610*+68810+69710+69810+69910+69210	MA	AWW	ANG	AWC	*Cumbrian Spirit*
390011	69111+69411+69511+69611*+68811+69711+69811+69911+69211	MA	AWW	ANG	AWC	*City of Lichfield*
390112	69112+69412+69512+69612+65312+68912+68812+69712+69812+69912+69212	MA	AWW	ANG	AWC	*Virgin Star*
390013	69113+69413+69513+69613*+68813+69713+69813+69913+69213	MA	AWW	ANG	AWC	*Blackpool Belle*
390114	69114+69414+69514+69614+65314+68914+68814+69714+69814+69914+69214	MA	AWW	ANG	AWC	*City of Manchester*
390115	69115+69415+69515+69615+65315+68915+68815+69715+69815+69915+69215	MA	AWW	ANG	AWC	*Virgin Crusader*
390016	69116+69416+69516+69616*+68816+69716+69816+69916+69216	MA	AWW	ANG	AWC	
390117	69117+69417+69517+69617+65317+68917+68817+69717+69817+69917+69217	MA	AWW	ANG	AWC	*Blue Peter*
390118	69118+69418+69518+69618+65318+68918+68818+69718+69818+69918+69218	MA	AWW	ANG	AWC	*Virgin Princess*
390119	69119+69419+69519+69619+65319+68919+68819+69719+69819+69919+69219	MA	AWW	ANG	AWC	*Unkown Soldier*
390020	69120+69420+69520+69620*+68820+69720+69820+69920+69220	MA	AWW	ANG	AWC	*Crewe - All Change (Alison)*
390121	69121+69421+69521+69621+65321+68921+68821+69721+69821+69921+69221	MA	AWW	ANG	AWC	*Virgin Dream*
390122	69122+69422+69522+69622+65322+68922+68822+69722+69822+69922+69222	MA	AWW	ANG	AWC	*Penny the Pendolino*
390123	69123+69423+69523+69623+69323+68923+68823+69723+69823+69923+69223	MA	AWW	ANG	AWC	*Virgin Glory*
390124	69124+69424+69524+69624+65324+68924+68824+69724+69824+69924+69224	MA	AWW	ANG	AWC	*Virgin Venturer*
390125	69125+69425+69525+69625+65325+68925+68825+69725+69825+69925+69225	MA	AWW	ANG	AWC	*Virgin Stagecoach*
390126	69126+69426+69526+69626+65326+68926+68826+69726+69826+69926+69226	MA	AWW	ANG	AWC	*Virgin Enterprise*
390127	69127+69427+69527+69627+65327+68927+68827+69727+69827+69927+69227	MA	AWW	ANG	AWC	*Virgin Buccaneer*
390128	69128+69428+69528+69628+65328+68928+68828+69728+69828+69928+69228	MA	AWW	ANG	AWC	*City of Preston*
390129	69129+69429+69529+69629+65329+68929+68829+69729+69829+69929+69229	MA	AWW	ANG	AWC	*City of Stoke-on-Trent*
390130	69130+69430+69530+69630+65330+68930+68830+69730+69830+69930+69230	MA	AWW	ANG	AWC	*City of Edinburgh*
390131	69131+69431+69531+69631+65331+68931+68831+69731+69831+69931+69231	MA	AWW	ANG	AWC	*City of Liverpool*
390132	69132+69432+69532+69632+65332+68932+68832+69732+69832+69932+69232	MA	AWW	ANG	AWC	*City of Birmingham*
390134	69134+69434+69534+69634+65334+68934+68834+69734+69834+69934+69234	MA	AWW	ANG	AWC	*City of Carlisle*
390135	69135+69435+69535+69635+65335+68935+68835+69735+69835+69935+69235	MA	AWW	ANG	AWC	*City of Lancaster*
390136	69136+69436+69536+69636+65336+68936+68836+69736+69836+69936+69236	MA	AWW	ANG	AWC	*City of Coventry*
390137	69137+69437+69537+69637+65337+68937+68837+69737+69837+69937+69237	MA	AWW	ANG	AWC	*Virgin Difference*
390138	69138+69438+69538+69638+65338+68938+68838+69738+69838+69938+69238	MA	AWW	ANG	AWC	*City of London*
390039	69139+69439+69539+69639*+68839+69739+69839+69939+69239	MA	AWW	ANG	AWC	*Virgin Quest*
390040	69140+69440+69540+69640*+68840+69740+69840+69940+69240	MA	AWW	ANG	AWC	*Virgin Radio Star*

390141	69141+69441+69541+69641+65341+68941+68841+69741+69841+69941+69241	MA	AWW	ANG	AWC	*City of Chester*
390042	69142+69442+69542+69642*+68842+69742+69842+69942+69242	MA	AWW	ANG	AWC	
390043	69143+69443+69543+69643*+68843+69743+69843+69943+69243	MA	AWW	ANG	AWC	
390044	69144+69444+69544+69644*+68844+69744+69844+69944+69244	MA	AWW	ANG	AWC	*Virgin Lionheart*
390045	69145+69445+69545+69645*+68845+69745+69845+69945+69245	MA	AWW	ANG	AWC	*Virgin Pride*
390046	69146+69446+69546+69646*+68846+69746+69846+69946+69246	MA	AWW	ANG	AWC	*Virgin Soldiers*
390047	69147+69447+69547+69647*+68847+69747+69847+69947+69247	MA	AWW	ANG	AWC	
390148	69148+69448+69548+69648+65348+68948+68848+69748+69848+69948+69248	MA	AWW	ANG	AWC	*Flying Scouseman*
390049	69149+69449+69549+69649*+68849+69749+69849+69949+69249	MA	AWW	ANG	AWC	
390050	69150+69450+69550+69650*+68850+69750+69850+69950+69250	MA	AWW	ANG	AWC	
390151	69151+69451+69551+69651+65351+68951+68851+69751+69851+69951+69251	MA	AWW	ANG	AWC	*Virgin Ambassador*
390152	69152+69452+69552+69652+65352+68952+68852+69752+69852+69952+69252	MA	AWW	ANG	AWC	*Alison Waters*
390153	69153+69453+69553+69653+65353+68953+68853+69753+69853+69953+69253	MA	AWW	ANG	AWC	*Mission Accomplished*
390154	69154+69454+69554+69654+65354+68954+68854+69754+69854+69954+69254	MA	AWW	ANG	AWC	*Matthew Flinders*
390155	69155+69455+69555+69655+68355+68955+68855+69755+69855+69955+69255	MA	AWC	ANG	AWC	*Pride and Prosperity*
390156	69156+69456+69556+69656+68356+68956+68856+69756+69856+69956+69256	MA	AWC	ANG	AWC	
390157	69157+69457+69557+69657+68357+68957+68857+69757+69857+69957+69257	MA	AWC	ANG	AWC	*Chad Varah*

■ Vehicles 69133 and 69833 have been rebuilt as static training vehicles for use at the West Coast training school in Crewe. Nos. 69933 and 69733 are in use at the fire training school in Moreton-in-Marsh. These coaches came from collision-damaged and withdrawn set No. 390033.

Left: *Nine-car Class 390/1 No. 390155 displaying the new Avanti West Coast livery is seen at Crewe on the first day Avanti operations on 9 December 2019, forming the 15.47 Liverpool Lime Street to London Euston.* **Antony Christie**

c2c - Essex/East Thameside

Address: ✉ 2nd Floor, Cutlers Court, 115 Houndsditch, London, EC3A 7BR
contact@c2crail.co.uk
✆ 03457 444422
ⓘ www.c2c-online.co.uk

Managing Director: Julian Drury
Franchise Dates: 26 May 1996 - 8 November 2029
Principal Routes: London Fenchurch Street - Shoeburyness
Barking - Pitsea via Purfleet
Ockendon branch
London Liverpool Street - Barking (limited service)
Depots: East Ham (EM), Shoeburyness*
* Stabling point
Parent Company: Trenitalia

Note: Under the terms of the c2c East Thameside franchise, a fleet of six ten-car Bombardier 'Aventra' Class 720/6 units were ordered in late 2017 for delivery in 2021. These sets will be funded by Porterbrook. When delivered, the existing Class 387 sets will be taken off lease. The Class 720s will be numbered 720601-720606.

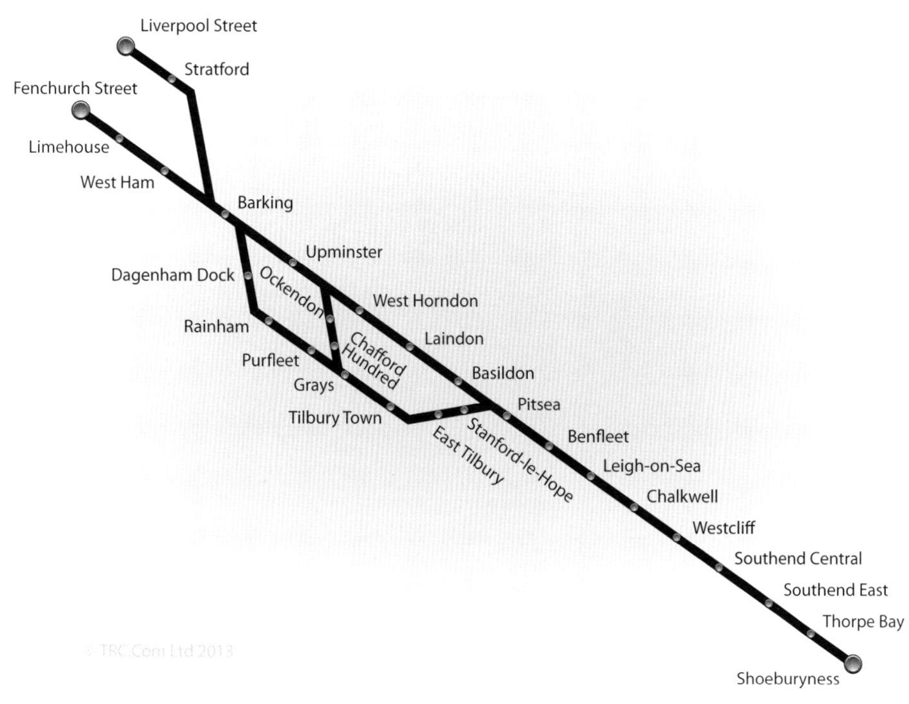

Class 357/0
Electrostar

Vehicle Length: (Driving) 68ft 1in (20.75m) (Inter) 65ft 11½in (20.10m)
Height: 12ft 4½in (3.78m)
Width: 9ft 2½in (2.80m)
Horsepower: 2,011hp (1,500kW)
Seats (total/car): 282S, 71S/78S/62S/71S

Number	*Formation* DMSO(A)+MSO+PTSO+DMSO(B)	*Depot*	*Livery*	*Owner*	*Op'r*	*Name*
357001	67651+74151+74051+67751	EM	C2C	PTR	c2c	*Barry Flaxman*
357002	67652+74152+74052+67752	EM	C2C	PTR	c2c	*Arthur Lewis Stride 1841-1922*
357003	67653+74153+74053+67753	EM	C2C	PTR	c2c	*Southend City on Sea*
357004	67654+74154+74054+67754	EM	C2C	PTR	c2c	*Tony Amos*
357005	67655+74155+74055+67755	EM	C2C	PTR	c2c	*Southend : 2017 Alternative City of Culture*
357006	67656+74156+74056+67756	EM	C2C	PTR	c2c	*Diamond Jubilee 1952 - 2012*
357007	67657+74157+74057+67757	EM	C2C	PTR	c2c	*Sir Andrew Foster*
357008	67658+74158+74058+67758	EM	C2C	PTR	c2c	
357009	67659+74159+74059+67759	EM	C2C	PTR	c2c	
357010	67660+74160+74060+67760	EM	C2C	PTR	c2c	
357011	67661+74161+74061+67761	EM	C2C	PTR	c2c	*John Lowing*
357012	67662+74162+74062+67762	EM	C2C	PTR	c2c	
357013	67663+74163+74063+67763	EM	C2C	PTR	c2c	
357014	67664+74164+74064+67764	EM	C2C	PTR	c2c	
357015	67665+74165+74065+67765	EM	C2C	PTR	c2c	
357016	67666+74166+74066+67766	EM	C2C	PTR	c2c	
357017	67667+74167+74067+67767	EM	C2C	PTR	c2c	
357018	67668+74168+74068+67768	EM	C2C	PTR	c2c	*Remembering the Fallen 88 1914-1918*
357019	67669+74169+74069+67769	EM	C2C	PTR	c2c	
357020	67670+74170+74070+67770	EM	C2C	PTR	c2c	
357021	67671+74171+74071+67771	EM	C2C	PTR	c2c	
357022	67672+74172+74072+67772	EM	C2C	PTR	c2c	
357023	67673+74173+74073+67773	EM	C2C	PTR	c2c	
357024	67674+74174+74074+67774	EM	C2C	PTR	c2c	
357025	67675+74175+74075+67775	EM	C2C	PTR	c2c	
357026	67676+74176+74076+67776	EM	C2C	PTR	c2c	
357027	67677+74177+74077+67777	EM	C2C	PTR	c2c	
357028	67678+74178+74078+67778	EM	C2C	PTR	c2c	*London, Tilbury & Southend Railway 1854-2004*
357029	67679+74179+74079+67779	EM	C2C	PTR	c2c	*Thomas Whitelegg 1840-1922*
357030	67680+74180+74080+67780	EM	C2C	PTR	c2c	*Robert Harben Whitelegg 1871-1957*
357031	67681+74181+74081+67781	EM	C2C	PTR	c2c	
357032	67682+74182+74082+67782	EM	C2C	PTR	c2c	
357033	67683+74183+74083+67783	EM	C2C	PTR	c2c	
357034	67684+74184+74084+67784	EM	C2C	PTR	c2c	

Below: *A fleet of 46 four-car Class 357/0 'Electrostar' units are allocated to East Ham for c2c services, the sets operate alongside members of Class 357/2 and 357/3. Sets are painted in white livery, with blue passenger doors with c2c and Trenitalia bodyside branding. No. 357021 is seen passing Shadwell.* **CJM**

c2c

357035	67685+74185+74085+67785	EM	C2C	PTR	c2c
357036	67686+74186+74086+67786	EM	C2C	PTR	c2c
357037	67687+74187+74087+67787	EM	C2C	PTR	c2c
357038	67688+74188+74088+67788	EM	C2C	PTR	c2c
357039	67689+74189+74089+67789	EM	C2C	PTR	c2c
357040	67690+74190+74090+67790	EM	C2C	PTR	c2c
357041	67691+74191+74091+67791	EM	C2C	PTR	c2c
357042	67692+74192+74092+67792	EM	C2C	PTR	c2c
357043	67693+74193+74093+67793	EM	C2C	PTR	c2c
357044	67694+74194+74094+67794	EM	C2C	PTR	c2c
357045	67695+74195+74095+67795	EM	C2C	PTR	c2c
357046	67696+74196+74096+67796	EM	C2C	PTR	c2c

Class 357/2 & 357/3
Electrostar

Vehicle Length: (Driving) 68ft 1in (20.75m) (Inter) 65ft 11½in (20.10m)
Height: 12ft 4½in (3.78m)
Width: 9ft 2½in (2.80m)
Horsepower: 2,011hp (1,500kW)
Seats (total/car): 282S, 71S/78S/62S/71S
Class 357/3 sets are fitted with revised interiors using 2+2 low-density layout with total seating for 223S passengers

Number	*Formation* DMSO(A)+MSO+PTSO+DMSO(B)	*Depot*	*Livery*	*Owner*	*Operator*	*Name*
357201	68601+74701+74601+68701	EM	C2C	ANG	c2c	*Ken Bird*
357202	68602+74702+74602+68702	EM	C2C	ANG	c2c	*Kenny Mitchell*
357203	68603+74703+74603+68703	EM	C2C	ANG	c2c	*Henry Pumfrett*
357204	68604+74704+74604+68704	EM	C2C	ANG	c2c	*Derek Flowers*
357205	68605+74705+74605+68705	EM	C2C	ANG	c2c	*John D'Silva*
357206	68606+74706+74606+68706	EM	C2C	ANG	c2c	*Martin Aungier*
357207	68607+74707+74607+68707	EM	C2C	ANG	c2c	*John Page*
357208	68608+74708+74608+68708	EM	C2C	ANG	c2c	*Dave Davis*
357209	68609+74709+74609+68709	EM	C2C	ANG	c2c	*James Snelling*
357210	68610+74710+74610+68710	EM	C2C	ANG	c2c	
357211	68611+74711+74611+68711	EM	C2C	ANG	c2c	
357312 (357212)	68612+74712+74612+68712	EM	C2C	ANG	c2c	
357313 (357213)	68613+74713+74613+68713	EM	C2C	ANG	c2c	*Upminster IECC*
357314 (357214)	68614+74714+74614+68714	EM	C2C	ANG	c2c	
357315 (357215)	68615+74715+74615+68715	EM	C2C	ANG	c2c	
357316 (357216)	68616+74716+74616+68716	EM	C2C	ANG	c2c	
357317 (357217)	68617+74717+74617+68717	EM	C2C	ANG	c2c	*Allan Burnell*
357318 (357218)	68618+74718+74618+68718	EM	C2C	ANG	c2c	
357319 (357219)	68619+74719+74619+68719	EM	C2C	ANG	c2c	
357320 (357220)	68620+74720+74620+68720	EM	C2C	ANG	c2c	
357321 (357221)	68621+74721+74621+68721	EM	C2C	ANG	c2c	
357322 (357222)	68622+74722+74622+68722	EM	C2C	ANG	c2c	
357323 (357223)	68623+74723+74623+68723	EM	C2C	ANG	c2c	
357324 (357224)	68624+74724+74624+68724	EM	C2C	ANG	c2c	
357325 (357225)	68625+74725+74625+68725	EM	C2C	ANG	c2c	
357326 (357226)	68626+74726+74626+68726	EM	C2C	ANG	c2c	
357327 (357227)	68627+74727+74627+68727	EM	C2C	ANG	c2c	*Southend United*
357328 (357228)	68628+74728+74628+68728	EM	C2C	ANG	c2c	

Left: *A follow-on order for 28 Class 357/2 'Electrostar' sets followed, these were identical to the Class 357/0s, but were funded by Angel Trains. A number of these sets are named, with cast plates fitted just inward of the cab door at cant rail height. No. 357202* Kenny Mitchell *is illustrated.* **CJM**

Right: *To increase c2c route accommodation, under the previous franchise owner National Express, a fleet of 17 Class 357/2s were modified with 'Metro' interiors, having reduced seating and increased standing space, especially in the door areas. Straps were also installed for standees to hold if needed. Re-classified as 357/3s, externally the sets carried 'Metro' branding and revised numbers. The last two digits of the number remained as in Class 357/2 days. Set No. 357314 is seen at Limehouse.* **CJM**

Class 387
Electrostar

Vehicle Length: (Driving) 66ft 9in (20.3m) Width: 9ft 2in (2.79m)
(Inter) 65ft 6in (19.96m) Horsepower: 2,012hp (1,500kW)
Height: 12ft 4in (3.75m) Seats (total/car): 223S. 56S/62S/45S/60S

Number	*Formation* DMSO(A)+MSO+TSO+DMSO(B)	*Depot*	*Livery*	*Owner*	*Operator*
387301	**421301+422301+423301+424301**	**EM**	**C2C**	**PTR**	**c2c**
387302	**421302+422302+423302+424302**	**EM**	**C2C**	**PTR**	**c2c**
387303	**421303+422303+423303+424303**	**EM**	**C2C**	**PTR**	**c2c**
387304	**421304+422304+423304+424304**	**EM**	**C2C**	**PTR**	**c2c**
387305	**421305+422305+423305+424305**	**EM**	**C2C**	**PTR**	**c2c**
387306	**421306+422306+423306+424306**	**EM**	**C2C**	**PTR**	**c2c**

Below: *Provision of adequate seating on the busy c2c route was a major problem and to provide a short term fix until extra stock was ordered, six four-car Class 387/3 sets were leased from Porterbrook in 2016 until new 'Adventra' sets are delivered in 2020-2021. The sets were part of a speculative order made by Porterbrook and will move to a new operator when the ordered Class 720/6s enter traffic. Set No. 378305 is illustrated, sets are finished in base white, with purple passenger doors and standard c2c and Trenitalia branding.* **CJM**

Chiltern Railways

Address: ✉ 2nd floor, Western House, Rickfords Hill, Aylesbury, Buckinghamshire, HP20 2RX

Via website (www.chilternrailways.co.uk)

✆ 08456 005165 ⓘ www.chilternrailways.co.uk

Managing Director: Dave Penney

Franchise Dates: 21 July 1996 - 21 December 2021

Principal Routes: London Marylebone - Birmingham Snow Hill

London Marylebone - Aylesbury

London Marylebone - Stratford-upon-Avon

Depots: Aylesbury (AL), Wembley* * Stabling point

Parent Company: Deutsche Bahn AG (DB Regio)

Class 165/0 (2-car)
Networker Turbo

Vehicle Length: (Driving) 75ft 2½in (22.91m), (Inter) 74ft 6½in (22.72m)
Height: 12ft 5¼in (3.79m)
Width: 9ft 2½in (2.81m)
Seats (total/car): 183S, 89S/94S
Engine: 1 x Perkins 2006 TWH of 350hp per vehicle
Horsepower: 700hp (522kW)

Number	Formation DMSL+DMS	Depot	Livery	Owner	Operator
165001	58801+58834	AL	CRW	ANG	CRW
165002	58802+58835	AL	CRR	ANG	CRW
165003	58803+58836	AL	CRR	ANG	CRW
165004	58804+58837	AL	CRR	ANG	CRW
165005	58805+58838	AL	CRR	ANG	CRW
165006	58806+58839	AL	CRR	ANG	CRW
165007	58807+58840	AL	CRR	ANG	CRW
165008	58808+58841	AL	CRW	ANG	CRW
165009	58809+58842	AL	CRR	ANG	CRW
165010	58810+58843	AL	CRW	ANG	CRW
165011	58811+58844	AL	CRW	ANG	CRW
165012	58812+58845	AL	CRW	ANG	CRW
165013	58813+58846	AL	CRR	ANG	CRW
165014	58814+58847	AL	CRW	ANG	CRW
165015	58815+58848	AL	CRW	ANG	CRW
165016	58816+58849	AL	CRW	ANG	CRW
165017	58817+58850	AL	CRW	ANG	CRW
165018	58818+58851	AL	CRW	ANG	CRW
165019	58819+58852	AL	CRW	ANG	CRW
165020	58820+58853	AL	CRW	ANG	CRW
165021	58821+58854	AL	CRW	ANG	CRW
165022	58822+58855	AL	CRW	ANG	CRW
165023	58873+58867	AL	CRR	ANG	CRW
165024	58874+58868	AL	CRW	ANG	CRW
165025	58875+58869	AL	CRW	ANG	CRW
165026	58876+58870	AL	CRW	ANG	CRW
165027	58877+58871	AL	CRR	ANG	CRW
165028	58878+58872	AL	CRW	ANG	CRW

Right: *Ordered in the days of Network SouthEast as part of the Chiltern and Thames modernisation, Chiltern Railways currently operate a fleet of 28 two-car 'Networker Turbo' sets. Sets have been refurbished and now sport air conditioning and meet the latest requirements in terms of displays and access. Painted in the latest Chiltern Railways livery, set No. 165008 is shown at Leamington Spa.* **CJM**

Class 165/0 (3-car)
Networker Turbo

Vehicle Length: (driving) 75ft 2½in (22.91m), (Inter) 74ft 6½in (22.72m)
Height: 12ft 5¼in (3.79m)
Width: 9ft 2½in (2.81m)
Seats (total/car): 289S, 89S/106S/94S
Engine: 1 x Perkins 2006 TWH of 350hp per vehicle
Horsepower: 1,050hp (783kW)

Number	Formation DMSL+MS+DMS	Depot	Livery	Owner	Operator
165029	58823+55404+58856	AL	CRW	ANG	CRW
165030	58824+55405+58857	AL	CRW	ANG	CRW
165031	58825+55406+58858	AL	CRW	ANG	CRW
165032	58826+55407+58859	AL	CRW	ANG	CRW
165033	58827+55408+58860	AL	CRW	ANG	CRW
165034	58828+55409+58861	AL	CRW	ANG	CRW
165035	58829+55410+58862	AL	CRR	ANG	CRW
165036	58830+55411+58863	AL	CRW	ANG	CRW
165037	58831+55412+58864	AL	CRR	ANG	CRW
165038	58832+55413+58865	AL	CRW	ANG	CRW
165039	58833+55414+58866	AL	CRR	ANG	CRW

Right: *Operating alongside the two-car 'Networker Turbo' fleet are 11 three-car sets, these now carry the latest Chiltern livery. The two and three car sets are fitted with 'trip-cock' equipment to allow operation over London Underground signalled lines, the equipment being installed on the non-driving side of the leading bogie. Set No. 165035 is seen at Amersham.* **Antony Christie**

Chiltern Railways

Class 168/0
Turbostar

Vehicle Length: 77ft 6in (23.62m)
Height: 12ft 4½in (3.77m)
Width: 8ft 10in (2.69m)
Engine: 1 x MTU 6R 183TD13H pf 422hp per vehicle
Horsepower: 1,688hp (1,259kW)
Seats (total/car): 278S, 60S/73S/77S/68S

Number	Formation DMSL(A)+MSL+MS+DMSL(B)	Depot	Livery	Owner	Operator
168001	58151+58651+58451+58251	AL	CRG	PTR	CRW
168002	58152+58652+58452+58252	AL	CRG	PTR	CRW
168003	58153+58653+58453+58253	AL	CRG	PTR	CRW
168004	58154+58654+58454+58254	AL	CRG	PTR	CRW
168005	58155+58655+58455+58255	AL	CRG	PTR	CRW

Left: *The original batch of Adtranz-designed 'Turbostar' stock was ordered by Chiltern Railways directly after privatisation, being introduced in 1997. These original five sets have a slightly different front end design. When built these were three car sets, quickly being increased to four-car formations to meet passenger growth. Sets are currently painted in Chiltern 'Main Line' silver grey and white livery. Set No. 168005 is seen at Leamington Spa.* **CJM**

Class 168/1
Turbostar

Vehicle Length: 77ft 6in (23.62m)
Height: 12ft 4½in (3.77m)
Width: 8ft 10in (2.69m)
Engine: 1 x MTU 6R 183TD13H of 422hp per vehicle
Horsepower: 3/4-car 1,266hp (944kW)/1,688hp (1,259kW)
Seats (total/car): 3-car - 208S, 59S/73S/76S, 4-car - 284S, 59S/73S/76S/76S

Number	Formation DMSL(A)+MS+MS+DMSL(B)	Depot	Livery	Owner	Operator	Notes
168106	58156+58756§+58456+58256	AL	CRG	PTR	CRW	§ is a MSL vehicle
168107	58157+58457+58757§+58257	AL	CRG	PTR	CRW	§ is a MSL vehicle
168108	58158+58458+58258	AL	CRG	PTR	CRW	
168109	58159+58459+58259	AL	CRG	PTR	CRW	
168110	58160+58460+58260	AL	CRG	PTR	CRW	
168111	58161+58461+58261	AL	CRG	EVL	CRW	58461 was originally 58661
168112	58162+58462+58262	AL	CRG	EVL	CRW	58462 was originally 58662
168113	58163+58463+58263	AL	CRG	EVL	CRW	58463 was originally 58663

Below: *Follow-on orders for the 'Turbostar' design quickly followed, but these incorporated what became the standard 'Turbostar' front end design. Classified as 168/1, a total of 26 vehicles were constructed, which are currently formed into two four-car and six three-car units. All are allocated to Aylesbury and operate in a common '168' pool. Three-car set No. 168110 is shown.* **CJM**

Class 168/2 *Turbostar*

Vehicle Length: 77ft 6in (23.62m)
Height: 12ft 4½in (3.77m)
Width: 8ft 10in (2.69m)
Engine: 1 x MTU 6R 183TD13H of 422hp per vehicle
Horsepower: 3/4-car 1,266hp (944kW)/1,688hp (1,259kW)
Seats (total/car): 3-car - 204S, 59S/76S/69S, 4-car - 277S, 59S/73S/76S/69S

Number	*Formation* DMSL(A)+MS+MS+DMSL(B)	*Depot*	*Livery*	*Owner*	*Operator*
168214	**58164+58464+58264**	**AL**	**CRG**	**PTR**	**CRW**
168215	**58165+58465+58365+58265**	**AL**	**CRG**	**PTR**	**CRW**
168216	**58166+58466+58366+58266**	**AL**	**CRG**	**PTR**	**CRW**
168217	**58167+58467+58367+58267**	**AL**	**CRG**	**PTR**	**CRW**
168218	**58168+58468+58268**	**AL**	**CRG**	**PTR**	**CRW**
168219	**58169+58469+58269**	**AL**	**CRG**	**PTR**	**CRW**

Right: *Introduced between 2003 and 2006 was a fleet of near identical Class 168/2 sets, but these incorporated a slightly revised front lamp cluster with large headlights and joint tail/marker lights. A total of 21 vehicles of this sub class were built, presently formed as three three-car and three four-car units. Set No. 165219 is illustrated. All sets carry the Chiltern 'Main Line' silver/grey and white colours.* **CJM**

Class 168/3 *Turbostar*

Vehicle Length: 77ft 6in (23.62m)
Height: 12ft 4½in (3.77m)
Width: 8ft 10in (2.69m)
Engine: 1 x MTU 6R 183TD13H of 422hp per vehicle
Horsepower: 844hp (629kW)
Seats (total/car): 8F/108S 8F-43S/65S

Number	*Formation* DMCL+DMS	*Depot*	*Livery*	*Owner*	*Operator*
168321	**50301+79301**	**AL**	**CRG**	**PTR**	**CRW**
168322	**50302+79302**	**AL**	**CRG**	**PTR**	**CRW**
168323	**50303+79303**	**AL**	**CRG**	**PTR**	**CRW**
168324	**50304+79304**	**AL**	**CRG**	**PTR**	**CRW**
168325	**50305+79305**	**AL**	**CRG**	**PTR**	**CRW**
168326	**50306+79306**	**AL**	**CRG**	**PTR**	**CRW**
168327	**50307+79307**	**AL**	**CRG**	**PTR**	**CRW**
168328	**50308+79308**	**AL**	**CRG**	**PTR**	**CRW**
168329	**50399+79399**	**AL**	**CRG**	**PTR**	**CRW**

Previously numbered 170301 - 170309 and operated by South West Trains and First TransPennine

Below: *Previously used by South West Trains and First TransPennine as Class 170s, Nine two-car sets were taken over by Chiltern in 2015-2016 and modified as Class 168/3s. In terms of style, the sets were very similar to the Class 168/1 breed. Set No. 168322 is shown, this was previously set No. 170302.* **CJM**

Chiltern Railways

Class 172/1 *Turbostar*

Vehicle Length: 73ft 4in (22.37m)
Height: 12ft 4½in (3.77m)
Width: 8ft 8in (2.69m)
Engine: MTU 6H1800 of 360kW
Horsepower: 965hp (720kW)
Seats (total/car): 121S, 53S/68S

Number	Formation DMS+DMS	Depot	Livery	Owner	Operator
172101	**59111+59211**	**AL**	**CRW**	**ANG**	**CRW**
172102	**59112+59212**	**AL**	**CRW**	**ANG**	**CRW**
172103	**59113+59213**	**AL**	**CRW**	**ANG**	**CRW**
172104	**59114+59214**	**AL**	**CRW**	**ANG**	**CRW**

Left: *In 2010 the demand for extra trains for the Chiltern route, saw four two-car Class 172/1s added to the fleet, leased from Angel Trains. These four units display Chiltern Railways white and blue livery and are usually restricted to shorter distance operation. They are not fitted with 'trip-cock' equipment due to their bogie design. Set No. 172103 is illustrated passing South Ruislip.* **CJM**

Class 68 'UK Light'

Vehicle Length: 67ft 3in (20.5m)
Height: 12ft 6½in (3.82m)
Speed: 100mph (161km/h)
Engine: Caterpillar C175-16
Horsepower: 3,750hp (2,800kW)
Electrical Equipment: ABB

Number	Depot	Pool	Livery	Owner	Operator
68010	**CR**	**XHVE**	**CRG**	**BEA**	**DRS/CRW**
68011	**CR**	**XHVE**	**CRG**	**BEA**	**DRS/CRW**
68012	**CR**	**XHVE**	**CRG**	**BEA**	**DRS/CRW**
68013	**CR**	**XHVE**	**CRG**	**BEA**	**DRS/CRW**
68014	**CR**	**XHVE**	**CRG**	**BEA**	**DRS/CRW**
68015	**CR**	**XHVE**	**CRG**	**BEA**	**DRS/CRW**

Name applied - **68010** ***Oxford Flyer***

Above: *Chiltern Main Line services linking London Marylebone and Birmingham are formed of Mk3 stock, powered by hired-in Class 68s from Direct Rail Services. Six locos, Nos. 68010-68015 are painted in Chiltern two-tone grey. The locos are usually formed at the north end of trains. No. 68012 is seen at Leamington Spa.* **CJM**

Mk3 Hauled Stock (Passenger)

Vehicle Length: 75ft 0in (22.86m)
Height: 12ft 9in (3.88m) Width: 8ft 11in (2.71m)
Bogie Type: BT10

AJ1F - GFW *Seating 30F (Catering out of use)*

Number		Depot	Livery	Owner
10271	(10236/10018)	AL	CRG	DBR
10272	(10208/40517)	AL	CRG	DBR
10273	(10230/10021)	AL	CRG	DBR
10274	(10255/11010)	AL	CRG	DBR

AC2G - TSO/TSOL* *Seating 72S*

Number		Depot	Livery	Owner
11029		AL	CRG	DBR
11031		AL	CRG	DBR
12017		AL	CRG	DBR
12036		AL	CRG	DBR
12043		AL	CRG	DBR
12094		AL	CRG	DBR
12119		AL	CRG	DBR
12602	(12072)	AL	CRG	DBR
12603*	(12053)	AL	CRG	DBR
12604	(12131)	AL	CRG	DBR
12605*	(11040)	AL	CRG	DBR
12606	(12048)	AL	CRG	DBR
12607*	(12038)	AL	CRG	DBR
12608	(12069)	AL	CRG	DBR
12609*	(12014)	AL	CRG	DBR
12610	(12117)	AL	CRG	DBR
12613*	(12173/11042)	AL	CRG	DBR
12614	(12145)	AL	CRG	DBR
12615*	(12059)	AL	CRG	DBR
12616	(12127)	AL	CRG	DBR
12617*	(12174/11050)	AL	CRG	DBR
12618	(12169)	AL	CRG	DBR
12619*	(12175/11052)	AL	CRG	DBR
12620	(12124)	AL	CRG	DBR
12621	(11046)	AL	CRG	DBR
12623	(11019)	AL	CRG	DBR
12625	(11030)	AL	CRG	DBR
12627	(11054)	AL	CRG	DBR

Above: *Chiltern Railways Main Line loco-hauled services are operated by a fleet of 32 refurbished Mk3s and six Mk3 Driving Van Trailers. These are usually marshalled in six passenger vehicle formations, with a DVT at the London end. All are painted in Chiltern Main Line two-tone grey. The DVTs carry an auxiliary generator for train supply purposes. A southbound train is seen arriving at Leamington Spa, led by DVT No. 82305.* **CJM**

Mk3 Hauled Stock (NPCCS)

Vehicle Length: 75ft 0in (22.86m)
Height: 12ft 9in (3.88m)
Width: 8ft 11in (2.71m)
Bogie Type: BT7

NZAG - DVT

Number	Depot	Livery	Owner
82301 (82117)	AL	CRG	DBR
82302 (82151)	AL	CRG	DBR
82303 (82135)	AL	CRG	DBR
82304 (82130)	AL	CRG	DBR
82305 (82134)	AL	CRG	DBR
82309 (82104)	AL	CRG	DBR

Class 01.5 (0-6-0)

Number	Depot	Pool	Livery	Owner	Operator	Name
01509 (433) RH468043	AL	MBDL	BLU	CRW	CRW	*Lesley*

CrossCountry Trains

Address: ✉ Cannon House, 18 The Priory, Queensway, Birmingham, B4 6BS
info@crosscountrytrains.co.uk
✆ 0870 0100084
ⓘ www.crosscountrytrains.co.uk

Managing Director: Tom Joyner

Franchise Dates: 11 November 2007 - December 2024

Principal Routes: Penzance / Paignton - Manchester / Edinburgh / Aberdeen
Bournemouth - Manchester / Edinburgh / Aberdeen
Birmingham - Stansted
Nottingham - Cardiff

Depots: Central Rivers (CZ), Tyseley (TS), Laira (LA)

Parent Company: Deutsche Bahn AG (DB Regio) / Arriva

Class 43 – HST

Vehicle Length: 58ft 5in (18.80m)
Height: 12ft 10in (3.90m)
Width: 8ft 11in (2.73m)
Engine: MTU 16V4000 R41R
Horsepower: 2,250hp (1,680kW)
Electrical Equipment: Brush

Number	Depot	Pool	Livery	Owner	Operator
43207 (43007)	LA	EHPC	AXC	ANG	AXC
43285 (43085)	LA	EHPC	AXC	PTR	AXC
43301 (43101)	LA	EHPC	AXC	PTR	AXC
43303 (43103)	LA	EHPC	AXC	PTR	AXC
43304 (43104)	LA	EHPC	AXC	ANG	AXC
43321 (43121)	LA	EHPC	AXC	PTR	AXC
43357 (43157)	LA	EHPC	AXC	PTR	AXC
43366 (43166)	LA	EHPC	AXC	ANG	AXC
43378 (43178)	LA	EHPC	AXC	ANG	AXC
43384 (43184)	LA	EHPC	AXC	ANG	AXC

Right: *The CrossCountry HST fleet is now operated from Plymouth Laira depot, where the 2019 allocation of 10 Class 43s are based. This number may increase in 2020 as it is proposed to transfer in some off lease sets. All vehicles carry standard XC livery and usually six train-sets are in traffic each day, sets are frequently changed over during the day at Plymouth. No. 43304 is illustrated at Totnes.* **Nathan Williamson**

Nos. 43208 and 43239 reported to be transferring to CrossCountry in spring 2020.

HST passenger fleet

Vehicle Length: 75ft 0in (22.86m)
Height: 12ft 9in (3.88m)
Width: 8ft 11in (2.71m)
Bogie Type: BT10
Fitted with sliding doors

GH1G - TF *Seating 40F*

Number	Depot	Livery	Owner	
41026	LA	AXC	ANG	
41035	LA	AXC	ANG	
41193 (11060)	LA	AXC	PTR	
41194 (11016)	LA	AXC	PTR	
41195¤ (11020)	LA	AXC	PTR	¤ = TFD

GH2G - TS *Seating 82S*

Number	Depot	Livery	Owner	
42036	LA	AXC	ANG	
42037	LA	AXC	ANG	
42038	LA	AXC	ANG	
42051	LA	AXC	ANG	
42052	LA	AXC	ANG	
42053	LA	AXC	ANG	
42097	LA	AXC	ANG	
42234	LA	AXC	PTR	
42290	LA	AXC	PTR	
42342 (44082)	LA	AXC	ANG	
42366 (12007)	LA	AXC	PTR	
42367 (12025)	LA	AXC	PTR	
42368 (12028)	LA	AXC	PTR	
42369 (12050)	LA	AXC	PTR	
42370 (12086)	LA	AXC	PTR	
42371 (12052)	LA	AXC	PTR	
42372 (12055)	LA	AXC	PTR	
42373 (12071)	LA	AXC	PTR	
42374 (12075)	LA	AXC	PTR	
42375 (12113)	LA	AXC	PTR	
42376 (12085)	LA	AXC	PTR	
42377 (12102)	LA	AXC	PTR	
42378 (12123)	LA	AXC	PTR	
42379* (41036)	LA	AXC	ANG	*=TSD
42380* (41025)	LA	AXC	ANG	*=TSD

GJ2G - TGS *Seating 67S*

Number	Depot	Livery	Owner
44012	LA	AXC	ANG
44017	LA	AXC	ANG
44021	LA	AXC	ANG
44052	LA	AXC	PTR
44072	LA	AXC	PTR

GH3G - TCC *Seating 30F/10S*

Number	Depot	Livery	Owner
45001 (12004)	LA	AXC	PTR
45002 (12106)	LA	AXC	PTR
45003 (12076)	LA	AXC	PTR
45004 (12077)	LA	AXC	PTR
45005 (12080)	LA	AXC	PTR

CrossCountry Trains

Above: *The 80 strong HST Mk3 fleet has recently been overhauled at Wabtec, Doncaster and fitted with sliding passenger doors, the doors are finished in pink and body mounted controls are provided by each door. All vehicles carry standard XC colours. A number of CrossCountry Mk3s are rebuilds from loco-hauled stock, as at the time of their introduction, insufficient HST vehicles were available. Sliding door fitted standard class vehicle No. 42036 is illustrated.* **Nathan Williamson**

Class 170/1
Turbostar

Vehicle Length: 77ft 6in (23.62m)
Height: 12ft 4½in (3.77m)
Width: 8ft 10in (2.69m)
Engine: 1 x MTU 6R 183TD13H of 422hp per vehicle
Horsepower: 1,266hp (944kW)
Seats (total/car): 9F/191S 52S/80S/9F-59S

Number	*Formation* DMS+MS+DMCL	*Depot*	*Livery*	*Owner*	*Operator*
170101	50101+55101+79101	TS	AXC	PTR	AXC
170102	50102+55102+79102	TS	AXC	PTR	AXC
170103	50103+55103+79103	TS	AXC	PTR	AXC
170104	50104+55104+79104	TS	AXC	PTR	AXC
170105	50105+55105+79105	TS	AXC	PTR	AXC
170106	50106+55106+79106	TS	AXC	PTR	AXC
170107	50107+55107+79107	TS	AXC	PTR	AXC
170108	50108+55108+79108	TS	AXC	PTR	AXC
170109	50109+55109+79109	TS	AXC	PTR	AXC
170110	50110+55110+79110	TS	AXC	PTR	AXC

Left: *A sizeable fleet of Class 170 'Turbostar' sets operate on the east-west CrossCountry routes, these are based at Tyseley. A batch of 10 three-car Class 170/0s, which were originally introduced for Midland Main Line operations, are in service. These have nine first class seats in one driving car (the DMCL). Set No. 170107 is captured heading south at Stenson Junction.* **CJM**

Vehicle Length: 77ft 6in (23.62m)
Height: 12ft 4½in (3.77m)
Width: 8ft 10in (2.69m)
Engine: 1 x MTU 6R 183TD13H of 422hp per vehicle
Horsepower: 844hp (629kW)
Seats (total/car): 9F-111S 59S/9F-52S

Number	*Formation* DMS+DMCL	*Depot*	*Livery*	*Owner*	*Operator*
170111*	50111+79111	TS	AXC	PTR	AXC
170112	50112+79112	TS	AXC	PTR	AXC
170113	50113+79113	TS	AXC	PTR	AXC
170114	50114+79114	TS	AXC	PTR	AXC
170115	50115+79115	TS	AXC	PTR	AXC
170116	50116+79116	TS	AXC	PTR	AXC
170117	50117+79117	TS	AXC	PTR	AXC

* Fitted with passenger counters

Right: *Seven two-car Class 170/0s are also in service, these were again originally used on Midland Main Line services. These sets, together with the entire Class 170 fleet, have all been refurbished to the same style, with the fleet operating as a common pool. Viewed from its first class seating end, set No. 170111 heads north at Stenson Junction.* **CJM**

Class 170/3
Turbostar

Vehicle Length: 77ft 6in (23.62m)
Height: 12ft 4½in (3.77m)
Width: 8ft 10in (2.69m)
Engine: 1 x MTU 6R 183TD13H of 422hp per vehicle
Horsepower: 1,266hp (944kW)
Seats (total/car): 9F-191S 59S/80S/9F-52S

Number	*Formation* DMSL+MS+DMCL	*Depot*	*Livery*	*Owner*	*Operator*
170397	50397+56397+79397	TS	AXC	PTR	AXC
170398	50398+56398+79398	TS	AXC	PTR	AXC

Class 170/5
Turbostar

Vehicle Length: 77ft 6in (23.62m)
Height: 12ft 4½in (3.77m)
Width: 8ft 10in (2.69m)
Engine: 1 x MTU 6R 183TD13H of 422hp per vehicle
Horsepower: 844hp (629kW)
Seats (total/car): 9F-111S 59S/9F-52S

Number	*Formation* DMSL+DMCL	*Depot*	*Livery*	*Owner*	*Operator*
170518	50518+79518	TS	AXC	PTR	AXC
170519	50519+79519	TS	AXC	PTR	AXC
170520	50520+79520	TS	AXC	PTR	AXC
170521	50521+79521	TS	AXC	PTR	AXC
170522	50522+79522	TS	AXC	PTR	AXC
170523	50523+79523	TS	AXC	PTR	AXC

Right: *The six members of the two-car formed Class 170/5 and the four three-car Class 170/6s have slightly revised front end design, with a less bulky valance. Set No. 170523 is seen from its Driving Motor Standard Lavatory end.* **CJM**

Class 170/6
Turbostar

Vehicle Length: 77ft 6in (23.62m)
Height: 12ft 4½in (3.77m)
Width: 8ft 10in (2.69m)
Engine: 1 x MTU 6R 183TD13H of 422hp per vehicle
Horsepower: 1,266hp (944kW)
Seats (total/car): 9F-191S 59S/80S/9F-52S

Number	*Formation* DMSL+MS+DMCL	*Depot*	*Livery*	*Owner*	*Operator*
170636	50636+56636+79636	TS	AXC	PTR	AXC
170637	50637+56637+79637	TS	AXC	PTR	AXC
170638	50638+56638+79638	TS	AXC	PTR	AXC
170639	50639+56639+79639	TS	AXC	PTR	AXC

CrossCountry Trains

Class 220
Voyager

Vehicle Length: 77ft 6in (23.62m)
Height: 12ft 4in (3.75m)
Width: 8ft 11in (2.73m)
Engine: 1 x Cummins of 750hp per vehicle
Horsepower: 3,000hp (2,237kW)
Seats (total/car): 26F/174S 42S/66S/66S/26F

Number	Formation DMS+MS+MS+DMF	Depot	Livery	Owner	Operator
220001	60301+60701+60201+60401	CZ	AXC	BEA	AXC
220002	60302+60702+60202+60402	CZ	AXC	BEA	AXC
220003	60303+60703+60203+60403	CZ	AXC	BEA	AXC
220004	60304+60704+60204+60404	CZ	AXC	BEA	AXC
220005	60305+60705+60205+60405	CZ	AXC	BEA	AXC
220006	60306+60706+60206+60406	CZ	AXC	BEA	AXC
220007	60307+60707+60207+60407	CZ	AXC	BEA	AXC
220008	60308+60708+60208+60408	CZ	AXC	BEA	AXC
220009	60309+60709+60209+60409	CZ	AXC	BEA	AXC
220010	60310+60710+60210+60410	CZ	AXC	BEA	AXC
220011	60311+60711+60211+60411	CZ	AXC	BEA	AXC
220012	60312+60712+60212+60412	CZ	AXC	BEA	AXC
220013	60313+60713+60213+60413	CZ	AXC	BEA	AXC
220014	60314+60714+60214+60414	CZ	AXC	BEA	AXC
220015	60315+60715+60215+60415	CZ	AXC	BEA	AXC
220016	60316+60716+60216+60416	CZ	AXC	BEA	AXC
220017	60317+60717+60217+60417	CZ	AXC	BEA	AXC
220018	60318+60718+60218+60418	CZ	AXC	BEA	AXC
220019	60319+60719+60219+60419	CZ	AXC	BEA	AXC
220020	60320+60720+60220+60420	CZ	AXC	BEA	AXC
220021	60321+60721+60221+60421	CZ	AXC	BEA	AXC
220022	60322+60722+60222+60422	CZ	AXC	BEA	AXC
220023	60323+60723+60223+60423	CZ	AXC	BEA	AXC
220024	60324+60724+60224+60424	CZ	AXC	BEA	AXC
220025	60325+60725+60225+60425	CZ	AXC	BEA	AXC
220026	60326+60726+60226+60426	CZ	AXC	BEA	AXC
220027	60327+60727+60227+60427	CZ	AXC	BEA	AXC
220028	60328+60728+60228+60428	CZ	AXC	BEA	AXC
220029	60329+60729+60229+60429	CZ	AXC	BEA	AXC
220030	60330+60730+60230+60430	CZ	AXC	BEA	AXC
220031	60331+60731+60231+60431	CZ	AXC	BEA	AXC
220032	60332+60732+60232+60432	CZ	AXC	BEA	AXC
220033	60333+60733+60233+60433	CZ	AXC	BEA	AXC
220034	60334+60734+60234+60434	CZ	AXC	BEA	AXC

Below: *The core CrossCountry fleet is made up of two fleets of 'Voyager' stock, introduced as replacement for loco-hauled sets after privatisation. The sets are disliked by most passengers and the fleet is likely to have a short life. A fleet of 34 non-tilt four-car sets classified 220 are based at Central Rivers and operate on all main XC routes. Seen from its standard class end, set No. 220028 arrives at Doncaster on 29 March 2019.* **CJM**

Class 221
Super Voyager

Vehicle Length: 77ft 6in (23.62m)
Height: 12ft 4in (3.75m)
Width: 8ft 11in (2.73m)

Engine: 1 x Cummins of 750hp per vehicle
Horsepower: 3,750hp (2,796kW)
Seats (total/car): 26F/236S 42S/66S/66S/62S/26F

Originally fitted with tilt system to allow higher speeds over curves. Equipment now isolated.

Number	*Formation* DMS+MS+MS+MS+DMF	*Depot*	*Livery*	*Owner*	*Operator*	
221119	60369+60769+60969+60869+60469	CZ	AXC	BEA	AXC	
221120	60370+60770+60970+60870+60470	CZ	AXC	BEA	AXC	
221121	60371+60771+60971+60871+60471	CZ	AXC	BEA	AXC	
221122	60372+60772+60972+60872+60472	CZ	AXC	BEA	AXC	
221123	60373+60773+60973+60873+60473	CZ	AXC	BEA	AXC	
221124	60374+60774+60974+60874+60474	CZ	AXC	BEA	AXC	
221125	60375+60775+60975+60875+60475	CZ	AXC	BEA	AXC	
221126	60376+60776+60976+60876+60476	CZ	AXC	BEA	AXC	
221127	60377+60777+60977+60877+60477	CZ	AXC	BEA	AXC	
221128	60378+60778+60978+60878+60478	CZ	AXC	BEA	AXC	
221129	60379+60779+60979+60879+60479	CZ	AXC	BEA	AXC	
221130	60380+60780+60980+60880+60480	CZ	AXC	BEA	AXC	
221131	60381+60781+60981+60881+60481	CZ	AXC	BEA	AXC	
221132	60382+60782+60982+60882+60482	CZ	AXC	BEA	AXC	
221133	60383+60783+60983+60883+60483	CZ	AXC	BEA	AXC	
221134	60384+60784+60984+60884+60484	CZ	AXC	BEA	AXC	
221135	60385+60785+60985+60885+60485	CZ	AXC	BEA	AXC	
221136	60386+60786+-+60886+60486	CZ	AXC	BEA	AXC	*(four-car set)*
221137	60387+60787+60987+60887+60487	CZ	AXC	BEA	AXC	
221138	60388+60788+60988+60888+60488	CZ	AXC	BEA	AXC	
221139	60389+60789+60989+60889+60489	CZ	AXC	BEA	AXC	
221140	60390+60790+-+60890+60490	CZ	AXC	BEA	AXC	*(four-car set)*
221141	60391+60791+60991+-+60491	CZ	AXC	BEA	AXC	*(four-car set)*
221144	60394+60794+60990+-+60494	CZ	AXC	BEA	AXC	*(four-car set)*

Below: *A fleet of 24 Class 221 'Super Voyager' sets are on the books of CrossCountry. These were originally built with tilting capability, but this has now been isolated. Of the 24 sets, 20 are five-car formation and four are four-car. The sets operate in a common pool with the Class 220 stock and can be found operating throughout the main north-south CrossCountry network. On 14 May 2019, set No. 221122 passes below Rockstone footbridge on the Dawlish Sea Wall.* **CJM**

Elizabeth Line (CrossRail)

Address: ✉ 6th Floor, St Mary Axe, London, EC3A 8NH
helpdesk@crossrail.co.uk
✆ 03432 2211234
ⓘ http://www.crossrail.co.uk

Managing Director: Steve Murphy

Principal Routes: Present - Liverpool Street - Shenfield
Paddington - Hayes and Harlington
Future - Reading to Shenfield / Abbey Wood, Heathrow spur

Depots: Ilford (IL), Old Oak Common (OC)

Parent Company: MTR Corporation (Crossrail) Limited
Transport for London

Through services due to commence in mid-2021.

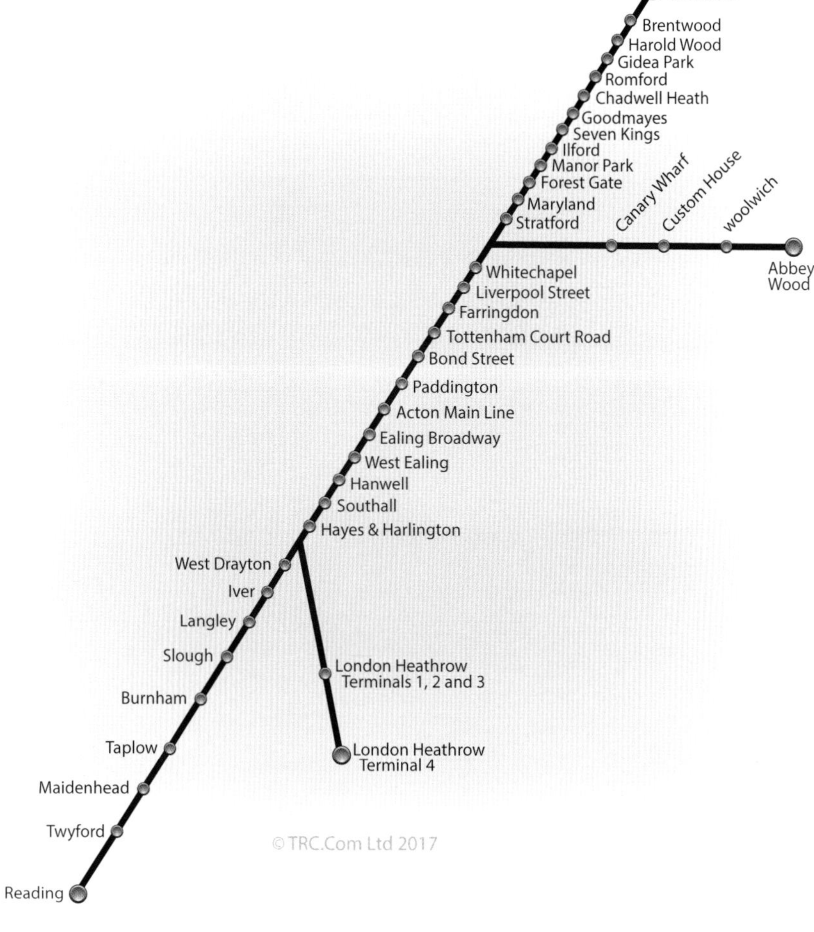

Class 315

Vehicle Length: (Driving) 64ft 11½in (19.80m) (Inter) 65ft 4½in (19.92m)
Height: 11ft 6½in (3.58m)
Width: 9ft 3in (2.82m)
Horsepower: 880hp (656kW)
Seats (total/car): 318S, 74S/86S/84S/74S

Number	Formation DMSO(A)+TSO+PTSO+DMSO(B)	Depot	Livery	Owner	Operator	Name
315818	64495+71298+71406+64496	IL	CRO	EVL	CRO	
315819	64497+71299+71407+64498	IL	CRO	EVL	CRO	
315820	64499+71300+71408+64500	IL	CRO	EVL	CRO	
315824	64507+71304+71412+64508	IL	CRO	EVL	CRO	
315826	64511+71306+71414+64512	IL	CRO	EVL	CRO	
315827	64513+71307+71415+64514	IL	CRO	EVL	LOG	*(On loan to London Overground)*
315829	64517+71309+71417+64518	IL	CRO	EVL	CRO	***London Borough of Havering Celebrating 40 Years***
315830	64519+71310+71418+64520	IL	CRO	EVL	CRO	
315831	64521+71311+71419+64522	IL	CRO	EVL	LOG	*(On loan to London Overground)*
315834	64527+71314+71422+64528	IL	CRO	EVL	CRO	
315836	64531+71316+71424+64532	IL	CRO	EVL	LOG	*(On loan to London Overground)*
315837	64533+71317+71425+64534	IL	CRO	EVL	CRO	
315838	64535+71318+71426+64536	IL	CRO	EVL	CRO	
315839	64537+71319+71427+64538	IL	CRO	EVL	CRO	
315843	64545+71323+71431+64546	IL	CRO	EVL	CRO	
315844	64547+71324+71432+64548	IL	CRO	EVL	CRO	
315847	64553+71327+71435+64554	IL	CRO	EVL	CRO	
315848	64540+71328+71436+64556	IL	CRO	EVL	CRO	
315849	64557+71329+71437+64558	IL	CRO	EVL	CRO	
315851	64561+71331+71439+64562	IL	CRO	EVL	CRO	
315852	64563+71332+71440+64564	IL	CRO	EVL	CRO	
315853	64565+71333+71441+64566	IL	CRO	EVL	CRO	
315854	64567+71334+71442+64568	IL	CRO	EVL	CRO	
315856	64571+71336+71444+64572	IL	CRO	EVL	CRO	
315857	64573+71337+71445+64574	IL	CRO	EVL	CRO	

Right: *Now some of the oldest suburban trains in operation, the Ilford-based four-car Class 315s are in the process of being replaced by Elizabeth Line Class 345s. However, their introduction has been delayed and the '315s' will remain in service for many months. Painted in white and blue Transport for London livery, set No. 315851 is seen at Stratford operating on a Liverpool Street to Shenfield service.* **CJM**

Class 345
Aventra

Train Length: (Driving) - 7-car - 524ft (159.74m) - 9-car - 673ft (205m)
Weight: - 7-car - 252.7t 9-car - 327.1t
Width: - 9ft 2in (2.78m)
Max Speed: 90mph (145km/h)
Seats (total/car): 9-car - 406S (7-car - 314S) 46S/46S/46S/46S/38S/46S/46S/46S/46S

Many sets have been delivered as seven-car units to allow operation on Shenfield - Liverpool Street and Hayes & Harlington to Paddington services until platform extension and software work is complete. From December 2019 sets were introduced on the Reading to Paddington route. A full Elizabeth Line service is scheduled to open in mid-2021.

Number	Formation DMSO(A)+PMSO(A)+MSO+MSO+TSO+MSO+MSO+PMSO+DMSO(B)	Depot	Livery	Owner	Operator
345001	340101+340201+340301+*340401*+340501+*340601*+340701+340801+340901	OC	CRO	3RL	CRO
345002	340102+340202+340302+*340402*+340502+*340602*+340702+340802+340902	OC	CRO	3RL	CRO
345003	340103+340203+340303+*340403*+340503+*340603*+340703+340803+340903	OC	CRO	3RL	CRO
345004	340104+340204+340304+*340404*+340504+*340604*+340704+340804+340904	OC	CRO	3RL	CRO
345005	340105+340205+340305+*340405*+340505+*340605*+340705+340805+340905	OC	CRO	3RL	CRO
345006	340106+340206+340306+*340406*+340506+*340606*+340706+340806+340906	OC	CRO	3RL	CRO

CrossRail

345007	340107+340207+340307+*340407*+340507+*340607*+340707+340807+340907	OC	CRO	3RL	CRO
345008	340108+340208+340308+*340408*+340508+*340608*+340708+340808+340908	OC	CRO	3RL	CRO
345009	340109+340209+340309+*340409*+340509+*340609*+340709+340809+340909	OC	CRO	3RL	CRO
345010	340110+340210+340310+*340410*+340510+*340610*+340710+340810+340910	OC	CRO	3RL	CRO
345011	340111+340211+340311+*340411*+340511+*340611*+340711+340811+340911	OC	CRO	3RL	CRO
345012	340112+340212+340312+*340412*+340512+*340612*+340712+340812+340912	OC	CRO	3RL	CRO
345013	340113+340213+340313+*340413*+340513+*340613*+340713+340813+340913	OC	CRO	3RL	CRO
345014	340114+340214+340314+*340414*+340514+*340614*+340714+340814+340914	OC	CRO	3RL	CRO
345015	340115+340215+340315+*340415*+340515+*340615*+340715+340815+340915	OC	CRO	3RL	CRO
345016	340116+340216+340316+340416+340516+340616+340716+340816+340916	OC	CRO	3RL	CRO
345017	340117+340217+340317+340417+340517+340617+340717+340817+340917	OC	CRO	3RL	CRO
345018	340118+340218+340318+340418+340518+340618+340718+340818+340918	OC	CRO	3RL	CRO
345019	340119+340219+340319+340419+340519+340619+340719+340819+340919	OC	CRO	3RL	CRO
345020	340120+340220+340320+*340420*+340520+*340620*+340720+340820+340920	OC	CRO	3RL	CRO
345021	340121+340221+340321+340421+340521+340621+340721+340821+340921	OC	CRO	3RL	CRO
345022	340122+340222+340322+340422+340522+340622+340722+340822+340922	OC	CRO	3RL	CRO
345023	340123+340223+340323+340423+340523+340623+340723+340823+340923	OC	CRO	3RL	CRO
345024	340124+340224+340324+340424+340524+340624+340724+340824+340924	OC	CRO	3RL	CRO
345025	340125+340225+340325+340425+340525+340625+340725+340825+340925	OC	CRO	3RL	CRO
345026	340126+340226+340326+340426+340526+340626+340726+340826+340926	OC	CRO	3RL	CRO
345027	340127+340227+340327+340427+340527+340627+340727+340827+340927	OC	CRO	3RL	CRO
345028	340128+340228+340328+*340428*+340528+*340628*+340728+340828+340928	OC	CRO	3RL	CRO
345029	340129+340229+340329+*340429*+340529+*340629*+340729+340829+340929	OC	CRO	3RL	CRO
345030	340130+340230+340330+340430+340530+340630+340730+340830+340930	OC	CRO	3RL	CRO
345031	340131+340231+340331+340431+340531+340631+340731+340831+340931	OC	CRO	3RL	CRO
345032	340132+340232+340332+340432+340532+340632+340732+340832+340932	OC	CRO	3RL	CRO
345033	340133+340233+340333+340433+340533+340633+340733+340833+340933	OC	CRO	3RL	CRO
345034	340134+340234+340334+340434+340534+340634+340734+340834+340934	OC	CRO	3RL	CRO
345035	340135+340235+340335+340435+340535+340635+340735+340835+340935	OC	CRO	3RL	CRO
345036	340136+340236+340336+340436+340536+340636+340736+340836+340936	OC	CRO	3RL	CRO
345037	340137+340237+340337+340437+340537+340637+340737+340837+340937	OC	CRO	3RL	CRO
345038	340138+340238+340338+*340438*+340538+*340638*+340738+340838+340938	OC	CRO	3RL	CRO
345039	340139+340239+340339+*340439*+340539+*340639*+340739+340839+340939	OC	CRO	3RL	CRO
345040	340140+340240+340340+*340440*+340540+*340640*+340740+340840+340940	OC	CRO	3RL	CRO
345041	340141+340241+340341+340441+340541+340641+340741+340841+340941	OC	CRO	3RL	CRO
345042	340142+340242+340342+*340442*+340542+*340642*+340742+340842+340942	OC	CRO	3RL	CRO
345043	340143+340243+340343+340443+340543+340643+340743+340843+340943	OC	CRO	3RL	CRO
345044	340144+340244+340344+*340444*+340544+*340644*+340744+340844+340944	OC	CRO	3RL	CRO
345045	340145+340245+340345+340445+340545+340645+340745+340845+340945	OC	CRO	3RL	CRO
345046	340146+340246+340346+340446+340546+340646+340746+340846+340946	OC	CRO	3RL	CRO
345047	340147+340247+340347+*340447*+340547+*340647*+340747+340847+340947	OC	CRO	3RL	CRO
345048	340148+340248+340348+340448+340548+340648+340748+340848+340948	OC	CRO	3RL	CRO
345049	340149+340249+340349+*340449*+340549+*340649*+340749+340849+340949	OC	CRO	3RL	CRO
345050	340150+340250+340350+340450+340550+340650+340750+340850+340950	OC	CRO	3RL	CRO
345051	340151+340251+340351+*340451*+340551+*340651*+340751+340851+340951	OC	CRO	3RL	CRO
345052	340152+340252+340352+*340452*+340552+*340652*+340752+340852+340952	OC	CRO	3RL	CRO
345053	340153+340253+340353+340453+340553+340653+340753+340853+340953	OC	CRO	3RL	CRO
345054	340154+340254+340354+340454+340554+340654+340754+340854+340954	OC	CRO	3RL	CRO
345055	340155+340255+340355+*340455*+340555+*340655*+340755+340855+340955	OC	CRO	3RL	CRO
345056	340156+340256+340356+*340456*+340556+*340656*+340756+340856+340956	OC	CRO	3RL	CRO
345057	340157+340257+340357+*340457*+340557+*340657*+340757+340857+340957	OC	CRO	3RL	CRO
345058	340158+340258+340358+340458+340558+340658+340758+340858+340958	OC	CRO	3RL	CRO
345059	340159+340259+340359+*340459*+340559+*340659*+340759+340859+340959	OC	CRO	3RL	CRO
345060	340160+340260+340360+340460+340560+340660+340760+340860+340960	OC	CRO	3RL	CRO
345061	340161+340261+340361+340461+340561+340661+340761+340861+340961	OC	CRO	3RL	CRO
345062	340162+340262+340362+340462+340562+340662+340762+340862+340962	OC	CRO	3RL	CRO
345063	340163+340263+340363+*340463*+340563+*340663*+340763+340863+340963	OC	CRO	3RL	CRO
345064	340164+340264+340364+*340464*+340564+*340664*+340764+340864+340964	OC	CRO	3RL	CRO
345065	340165+340265+340365+340465+340565+340665+340765+340865+340965	OC	CRO	3RL	CRO
345066	340166+340266+340366+340466+340566+340666+340766+340866+340966	OC	CRO	3RL	CRO
345067	340167+340267+340367+340467+340567+340667+340767+340867+340967	OC	CRO	3RL	CRO
345068	340168+340268+340368+340468+340568+340668+340768+340868+340968	OC	CRO	3RL	CRO
345069	340169+340269+340369+340469+340569+340669+340769+340869+340969	OC	CRO	3RL	CRO
345070	340170+340270+340370+340470+340570+340670+340770+340870+340970	OC	CRO	3RL	CRO

Above: *The new Class 345 Bombardier 'Aventra' sets which will operate the Elizabeth Line when fully commissioned are currently operating limited services in the east between Liverpool Street and Shenfield and in the west between Paddington and Reading. Sets are mainly seven-car formation, but some nine-car sets are in operation on Paddington routes. Set No. 345007 is captured approaching Hanwell with a West Drayton to Paddington service on 16 April 2019.* **CJM**

Class 360/2
Desiro

Vehicle Length: 66ft 9in (20.4m)
Height: 12ft 1½in (3.7m)
Width: 9ft 2in (2.79m)
Horsepower: 1,341hp (1,000kW)
Seats (total/car): 340S, 63S/66S/74S/74S/63S (360205 - 280S using 2+2 seats)

Number	*Formation* DMSO(A)+PTSO+TSO+TSO+DMSO(B)	*Depot*	*Livery*	*Owner*	*Operator*
360201	**78431+63421+72431+72421+78441**	**OH**	**HEC**	**BAA**	**TfL**
360202	**78432+63422+72432+72422+78442**	**OH**	**HEC**	**BAA**	**TfL**
360203	**78433+63423+72433+72423+78443**	**OH**	**HEC**	**BAA**	**TfL**
360204	**78434+63424+72434+72424+78444**	**OH**	**HEC**	**BAA**	**TfL**
360205	**78435+63425+72435+72425+78445**	**OH**	**HEL**	**BAA**	**TfL**

■ Class 360/2 sets due off-lease following introduction of Class 345 stock.

Above: *Until the full Cross-Rail 'Elizabeth Line service is introduced, The Heathrow Connect service, operated by TfL will use five Class 360 'Desiro sets. These five-car units, operate on the semi-fast services linking London Paddington with Heathrow Airport and are also used on the Airport terminal shuttle service. Set No. 360201 is seen at Hanwell and Elthorne bound for Paddington.* **CJM**

East Midlands Railway

Address: ✉ 1 Prospect Place, Millennium Way, Pride Park, Derby, DE24 8HG
contact@eastmidlandsrailway.co.uk ✆ 03457 125 678
ⓘ www.eastmidlandsrailways.co.uk

Managing Director: Will Rogers
Franchise Dates: 18 August 2019 - August 2027
Principal Routes: St Pancras - Sheffield / York / Leeds / Nottingham
Norwich / Skegness / Cleethorpes - Nottingham / Crewe / Liverpool and Matlock
Depots: Derby (DY), Nottingham (NM), Neville Hill (NL)
Parent Company: Abellio Group

A fleet of 33 five-car Hitachi-built Class 800 sets are on order for delivery in 2021-2022
21 Class 360s will transfer from Greater Anglia by August 2020 for Corby services

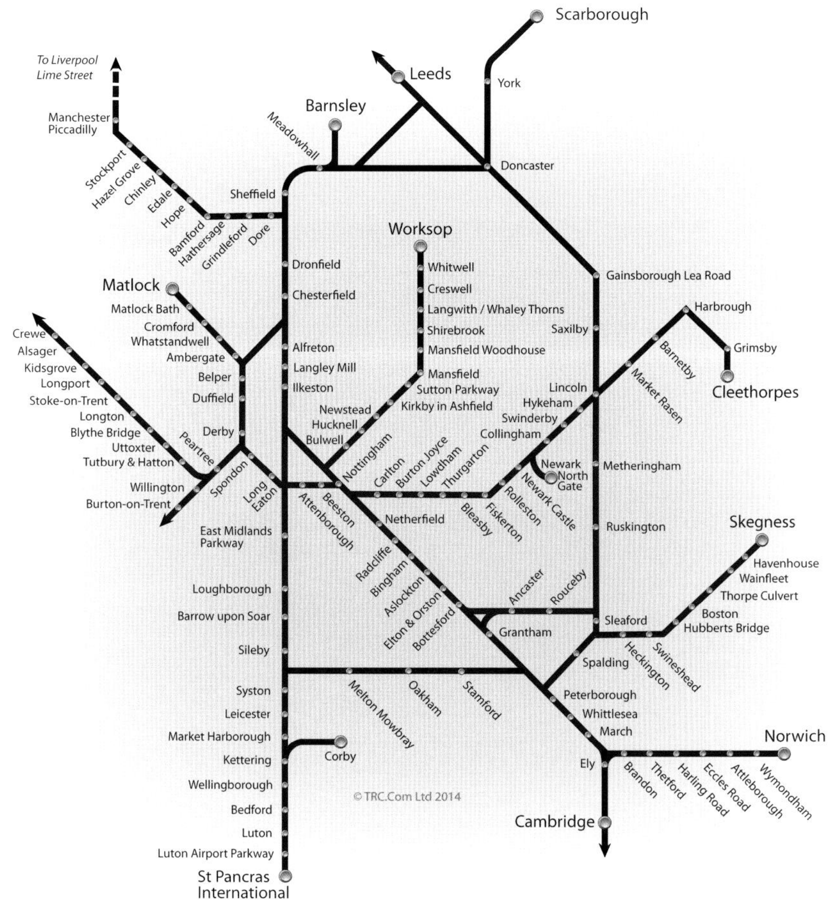

Class 08

Vehicle Length: 29ft 3in (8.91m)
Height: 12ft 8⅝in (3.87m)
Width: 8ft 6in (2.59m)
Engine: English Electric 6K
Horsepower: 400hp (298kW)
Electrical Equipment: English Electric

Number	Depot	Pool	Livery	Owner	Operator	Name
08405	NL	EMSL	RSS	RSS	EMR	
08525	NL	EMSL	EMT	EMT	EMR	*Duncan Bedford*
08690	NL	EMSL	EMT	EMT	EMR	*David Thirkill*
08899	DY	EMSL	MAR	EMT	EMR	*Midland Counties Railway 175 1839-2014*
08908	DY	EMSL	EMT	EMT	EMR	
08950	NL	EMSL	EMT	EMT	EMR	*David Lightfoot*

Class 43/0 – HST

Vehicle Length: 58ft 5in (18.80m)
Height: 12ft 10in (3.90m)
Width: 8ft 11in (2.73m)
Engine: Paxman VP185
Horsepower: 2,100hp (1,565kW)
Electrical Equipment: Brush

Number	Depot	Pool	Livery	Owner	Operator
43043	NL	EMPC	SCE	PTR	EMR
43044	NL	EMPC	SCE	PTR	EMR
43045	NL	EMPC	SCE	PTR	EMR
43046	NL	EMPC	SCE	PTR	EMR
43047	NL	EMPC	SCE	PTR	EMR
43048	NL	EMPC	SCE	PTR	EMR
43049	NL	EMPC	SCE	PTR	EMR
43050	NL	EMPC	SCE	PTR	EMR
43052	NL	EMPC	SCE	PTR	EMR
43054	NL	EMPC	SCE	PTR	EMR
43055	NL	EMPC	SCE	PTR	EMR
43058	NL	EMPC	SCE	PTR	EMR
43059	NL	EMPC	SCE	PTR	EMR
43060	NL	EMPC	SCE	PTR	EMR
43061(S)	NL	EMPC	SCE	PTR	EMR
43064	NL	EMPC	SCE	PTR	EMR
43066	NL	EMPC	SCE	PTR	EMR
43073	NL	EMPC	SCE	PTR	EMR
43075(S)	NL	EMPC	SCE	PTR	EMR
43076	NL	EMPC	SCE	PTR	EMR
43081	NL	EMPC	SCE	PTR	EMR
43082	NL	EMPC	SCE	PTR	EMR
43083	NL	EMPC	SCE	PTR	EMR
43089	NL	EMPC	SCE	PTR	EMR

Names applied

43045	*EMT Customer Service Week #TrainWatch*
43048	*T. C. B. Miller MBE*
43049	*Neville Hill*
43055	*The Sheffield Star 125 Years*
43076	*In Support of Help for Heroes*
43082	*Railway Children Fighting for Street Children*

Class 43/4 – HST

Vehicle Length: 58ft 5in (18.80m)
Height: 12ft 10in (3.90m)
Width: 8ft 11in (2.73m)
Engine: MTU 16V4000 R41R
Horsepower: 2,250hp (1,680kW)
Electrical Equipment: Brush

Number	Depot	Pool	Livery	Owner	Operator
43423 (43123)	DY	EMPC	EMB	ANG	EMR
43465 (43065)	DY	EMPC	EMB	ANG	EMR
43467 (43067)	DY	EMPC	EMB	ANG	EMR
43468 (43068)	DY	EMPC	EMB	ANG	EMR
43480 (43080)	DY	EMPC	EMB	ANG	EMR
43484 (43084)	DY	EMPC	SCF	ANG	EMR

Names applied

43423	*'Valenta' 1972 - 2010*
43467	*Nottinghamshire Fire and Rescue service / British Transport Police Nottingham*
43480	*West Hampstead PSB*

Right: *The new East Midlands Railway franchise will see major changes over the next few years. The HST and Class 222 fleets will be replaced by 33 five-car 24m vehicle length, Hitachi AT300s, of similar design to the Class 800s. In addition, Class 360s will be introduced on St Pancras to Corby services and a number of Class 170s will cascaded to replace existing DMUs. The HST fleet will be phased out from 2022-2023. In 2020 a fleet of 30 Class 43s were on the EMR roster, 24 standard Class 43/0s fitted with a Paxman engines and six Class 43/4s (previously with Grand Central), fitted with MTU engines. The fleet carries the previous operator's Stagecoach blue with EMR branding. PC No. 43468 is seen at Nottingham. EMR operates as three business units - InterCity, Regional and Electric.* **Antony Christie**

HST fleet changes

To meet 2020 legislation for for Persons with Reduced Mobility (PRM), the EMR franchise will, from spring 2020, be replacing its current HST fleet with cascaded sets from LNER, replaced by the introduction of Azuma stock. When we closed for press, the following former LNER Class 43s were scheduled to transfer to EMR operation - 43238, 43251, 43257, 43272, 43274, 43277, 43290, 43295, 43296, 43299, 43302, 43305, 43306, 43307, 43308, 43309, 43310, 43316, 43317, 43318, 43319, 43320. These will operate with rakes of former LNER HST Mk3 stock.

Class 153

Vehicle Length: 76ft 5in (23.29m)
Height: 12ft $3\frac{1}{8}$in (3.75m)
Width: 8ft 10in (2.70m)

Engine: 1 x NT855R5 of 285hp
Horsepower: 285hp (213kW)
Seats (total/car): 66S

Number	Formation DMSL	Depot	Livery	Owner	Operator
153302	52302	NM	EMR	ANG	EMR
153308	52308	NM	EMR	ANG	EMR
153311	52311	NM	EMR	PTR	EMR
153318	52318	NM	EMR	ANG	EMR
153319	52319	NM	EMR	ANG	EMR
153355	57355	NM	EMR	ANG	EMR
153357	57357	NM	EMR	ANG	EMR
153368	52368	NM	EMR	ANG	EMR
153372	52372	NM	EMR	ANG	EMR
153374	57374	NM	EMR	ANG	EMR
153376	57376	NM	EMR	PTR	EMR
153379	57379	NM	EMR	PTR	EMR
153381	57381	NM	EMR	PTR	EMR
153382	52382	NM	EMR	ANG	EMR
153383	57383	NM	EMR	PTR	EMR
153384	57384	NM	EMR	PTR	EMR
153385	57385	NM	EMR	PTR	EMR

Names applied

153376	***X-24 Expeditious***
153383	***Ecclesbourne Valley Railway 150 years***

Left: *In 2020 a fleet of 21 single car Class 153s were on the EMR Regional roster, based at Nottingham Eastcroft. The vehicles displayed the previous operators livery with EMR Regional branding, shown on set No. 153376 at Longport.* **Cliff Beeton**

Class 156

Vehicle Length: 75ft 6in (23.03m)
Height: 12ft 6in (3.81m)
Width: 8ft 11in (2.73m)

Engine: 1 x Cummins NT855R5 of 285hp
Horsepower: 570hp (425kW)
Seats (total/car): 148S, 72S/76S

Number	Formation DMSL+DMS	Depot	Livery	Owner	Operator
156401	52401+57401	NM	EMR	PTR	EMR
156403	52403+57403	NM	EMR	PTR	EMR
156404	52404+57404	NM	EMR	PTR	EMR
156405	52405+57405	NM	EMR	PTR	EMR
156406	52406+57406	NM	EMR	PTR	EMR
156408	52408+57408	NM	EMR	PTR	EMR
156410	52410+57410	NM	EMR	PTR	EMR
156411	52411+57411	NM	EMR	PTR	EMR
156413	52413+57413	NM	EMR	PTR	EMR
156414	52414+57414	NM	BLU	PTR	EMR
156415	52415+57415	NM	EMR	PTR	EMR
156470	52470+57470	NM	EMR	PTR	EMR
156473	52473+57473	NM	EMR	PTR	EMR
156497	52497+57497	NM	EMR	PTR	EMR
156498	52498+57498	NM	EMR	PTR	EMR

As above, except - Seats (total/car): 136S, 62S/74S

Number	Formation DMSL+DMS	Depot	Livery	Owner	Operator
156902	52402+57402	DY	EMR	PTR	EMR
156907	52407+57407	DY	EMR	PTR	EMR
156909	52409+57409	DY	EMR	PTR	EMR
156912	52412+57412	DY	EMR	PTR	EMR
156916	52416+57416	DY	EMR	PTR	EMR
156917	52417+57417	DY	EMR	PTR	EMR
156918	52418+57418	DY	EMR	PTR	EMR
156919	52419+57419	DY	EMR	PTR	EMR
156922	52422+57422	DY	EMR	PTR	EMR

1569xx sets renumbered from 1504xx series due to modifications upon transfer from Greater Anglia.

Left: *At the start of 2020 a fleet of 24 Class 156s were operated by East Midlands Railway, including nine recently transferred from Great Anglia. These two-car sets operate on the longer domestic services. Set No. 156497 with EMR Regional branding is seen at Loughborough.* **Antony Christie**

Class 158

Vehicle Length: 76ft 1¾in (23.21m)
Height: 12ft 6in (3.81m)
Width: 9ft 3¼in (2.82m)
Engine: 158770-813, 889 - 1 x Cummins NT855R5 of 350hp
Horsepower: 700hp (522kW)
Engine: 158846-862 - 1 x Perkins 2006TWH of 350hp
Horsepower: 700hp (522kW)
Engine: 158863-866 - 1 x Cummins NT855R5 of 400hp
Horsepower: 800hp (597kW)
Seats (total/car): 146S - 74S, 72S

Number	Formation DMSL+DMSL	Depot	Livery	Owner	Operator
158770	52770+57770	NM	SCE	PTR	EMR
158773	52773+57773	NM	WHT	PTR	EMR
158774	52774+57774	NM	WHT	PTR	EMR
158777	52777+57777	NM	SCE	PTR	EMR
158780	52780+57780	NM	SCE	ANG	EMR
158783	52783+57783	NM	SCE	ANG	EMR
158785	52785+57785	NM	SCE	ANG	EMR
158788	52788+57788	NM	SCE	ANG	EMR
158799	52799+57799	NM	SCE	PTR	EMR
158806	52806+57806	NM	SCE	PTR	EMR
158810	52810+57810	NM	SCE	PTR	EMR
158812	52812+57812	NM	SCE	PTR	EMR
158813	52813+57813	NM	SCE	PTR	EMR
158846	52846+57846	NM	SCE	ANG	EMR
158847	52847+57847	NM	SCE	ANG	EMR
158852	52852+57852	NM	SCE	ANG	EMR
158854	52854+57854	NM	SCE	ANG	EMR
158856	52856+57856	NM	SCE	ANG	EMR
158857	52857+57857	NM	SCE	ANG	EMR
158858	52858+57858	NM	SCE	ANG	EMR
158862	52862+57862	NM	SCE	ANG	EMR
158863	52863+57863	NM	SCE	ANG	EMR
158864	52864+57864	NM	SCE	ANG	EMR
158865	52865+57865	NM	SCE	ANG	EMR
158866	52866+57866	NM	SCE	ANG	EMR
158889	52808+57808	NM	SCE	PTR	EMR§

Names applied
158847 ***Lincoln Castle Explorer***
158854 ***The Station Volunteer***
158864 ***ELR50 - visit Lincolnshire in 2020***

§ On loan from SWR

Right: *For longer distance Regional services a fleet of Class 158s are operated, these are based at Nottingham Eastcroft and carry the old Stagecoach white livery now with EMR Regional branding. Set No. 158812 displays this class and livery.* **Antony Christie**

■ The four former First Hull Trains operated Class 180 sets are scheduled to transfer to East Midlands Railway in 2020 to replace some of the HST sets. At the start of 2020 the sets were receiving attention prior to transfer.

Class 180
Adelante

Vehicle Length: (Driving) 75ft 7in (23.71m), (Inter) 75ft 5in (23.03m)
Height: 12ft 4in (3.75m)
Width: 9ft 2in (2.80m)
Engine: 1 x Cummins OSK19 of 750hp per vehicle
Horsepower: 3,750hp (2,796kW)
Seats (total/car): 42F/226S, 46S/42F/68S/56S/56S

Number	Formation DMSL(A)+MFL+MSF+MSLRB+DMSL(B)	Depot	Livery	Owner	Operator
180109	50909+54909+55909+56909+59909	DY	FHT	ANG	EMR
180110	50910+54910+55910+56910+59910	DY	FHT	ANG	EMR
180111	50911+54911+55911+56911+59911	DY	FHT	ANG	EMR
180113	50913+54913+55909+56913+59913	DY	FHT	ANG	EMR

Class 222

Vehicle Length: 77ft 6in (23.62m)
Height: 12ft 4in (3.75m)
Width: 8ft 11in (2.73m)
Engine: 1 x Cummins OSK9R of 750hp per vehicle
Horsepower: 5,250hp (3,914kW)
Seats (total/car): 106F/236S
38S/68S/68S/62S/42F/42F/22F

Number	Formation DMS+MS+MS+MSRMB+MF+MF+DMRFO	Depot	Livery	Owner	Op'r	Name
222001	60161+60551+60561+60621+60341+60445+60241	DY	SCE	EVL	EMR	*The Entrepreneur Express*
222002	60162+60544+60562+60622+60342+60346+60242	DY	SCE	EVL	EMR	*The Cutlers' Company*
222003	60163+60553+60563+60623+60343+60446+60243	DY	SCE	EVL	EMR	*Tornado*
222004	60164+60554+60564+60624+60344+60345+60244	DY	SCE	EVL	EMR	*Childrens Hospital Sheffield*
222005	60165+60555+60565+60625+60443+60347+60245	DY	SCE	EVL	EMR	
222006	60166+60556+60566+60626+60441+60447+60246	DY	SCE	EVL	EMR	*The Carbon Cutter*

Vehicle Length: 77ft 6in (23.62m)
Height: 12ft 4in (3.75m)
Width: 8ft 11in (2.73m)
Engine: 1 x Cummins OSK9R of 750hp per vehicle
Horsepower: 3,750hp (2,796kW)
Seats (total/car): 50F/190S
38S/68S/62S/28F-22S/22F

Number	Formation DMS+MS+MSRMB+MC+DMRFO	Depot	Livery	Owner	Operator	Name
222007	60167+60567+60627+60442+60247	DY	SCE	EVL	EMR	
222008	60168+60545+60628+60918+60248	DY	SCE	EVL	EMR	Derby Etches Park
222009	60169+60557+60629+60919+60249	DY	SCE	EVL	EMR	
222010	60170+60546+60630+60920+60250	DY	SCE	EVL	EMR	
222011	60171+60531+60631+60921+60251	DY	SCE	EVL	EMR	Sheffield City Battalion 1914 - 1918
222012	60172+60532+60632+60922+60252	DY	SCE	EVL	EMR	
222013	60173+60536+60633+60923+60253	DY	SCE	EVL	EMR	
222014	60174+60534+60634+60924+60254	DY	SCE	EVL	EMR	
222015	60175+60535+60635+60925+60255	DY	SCE	EVL	EMR	175 Years of Derby's Railways 1839-2014
222016	60176+60533+60636+60926+60256	DY	SCE	EVL	EMR	
222017	60177+60537+60637+60927+60257	DY	SCE	EVL	EMR	Lions Clubs International Centenary 1917-2017
222018	60178+60444+60638+60928+60258	DY	SCE	EVL	EMR	
222019	60179+60547+60639+60929+60259	DY	SCE	EVL	EMR	
222020	60180+60543+60640+60930+60260	DY	SCE	EVL	EMR	
222021	60181+60552+60641+60931+60261	DY	SCE	EVL	EMR	
222022	60182+60542+60642+60932+60262	DY	SCE	EVL	EMR	Invest in Nottingham
222023	60183+60541+60643+60933+60263	DY	SCE	EVL	EMR	

Left: *Until the deployment of new AT300 stock, the Bombardier Class 222s will form the core IC fleet. A fleet of six seven-car and 17-five-car sets are allocated to Derby Etches Park and currently carry the former Stagecoach white livery now with EMR InterCity branding, as displayed on five-car set No. 222010 passing Duffield.* **Antony Christie**

Class 222/1

Vehicle Length: 77ft 6in (23.62m)
Height: 12ft 4in (3.75m)
Width: 8ft 11in (2.73m)
Engine: 1 x Cummins OSK9R of 750hp per vehicle
Horsepower: 3,000hp (2,237kW)
Seats (total/car): 33F/148S
22F/11F-46S/62S/40S

Number	Formation DMF+MC+MSRMB+DMS	Depot	Livery	Owner	Operator
222101	60271+60571+60681+60191	DY	SCE	EVL	EMR
222102	60272+60572+60682+60192	DY	SCE	EVL	EMR
222103	60273+60573+60683+60193	DY	SCE	EVL	EMR
222104	60274+60574+60684+60194	DY	EMR	EVL	EMR

Left: *For the official launch of the new Abellio franchise of East Midlands Railway, one Class 222/1 No. 222104 was decorated in the new house colours of deep purple, off-set by grey passenger doors and a standard yellow end. On the side of each vehicle is the EMR InterCity brand name. The set is seen at Nottingham.* **Antony Christie**

HST Passenger Fleet

Vehicle Length: 75ft 0in (22.86m) Width: 8ft 11in (2.71m)
Height: 12ft 9in (3.88m) Bogie Type: BT10

GN1G - TRFB *Seating 23F*

Number	Depot	Livery	Owner
40204	DY	SCE	ANG
40205	DY	SCE	ANG
40221	DY	SCE	ANG

GK1G - TRFB *Seating 17F*

Number	Depot	Livery	Owner
40700	NL	SCE	PTR
40728	NL	SCE	PTR
40730	NL	SCE	PTR
40741§	NL	SCE	PTR
40746	NL	SCE	PTR
40749	NL	SCE	PTR
40753	NL	SCE	PTR
40754	NL	SCE	PTR
40756	NL	SCE	PTR

GH1G - TF *Seating 46F*

Number	Depot	Livery	Owner
41041	NL	SCE	PTR
41046	NL	SCE	PTR
41057	NL	SCE	PTR
41061	NL	SCE	PTR
41063	NL	SCE	PTR
41064	NL	SCE	PTR
41067§	NL	SCE	PTR
41069	NL	SCE	PTR
41070	NL	SCE	PTR
41071	NL	SCE	PTR
41072	NL	SCE	PTR
41075	NL	SCE	PTR
41076	NL	SCE	PTR
41077	NL	SCE	PTR
41079	NL	SCE	PTR
41084	NL	SCE	PTR
41111	NL	SCE	PTR
41113	NL	SCE	PTR
41117	NL	SCE	PTR
41156	NL	SCE	PTR

GH1G - TF *Seating 48F*

Number	Depot	Livery	Owner
41204 (11023)	DY	SCE	ANG
41205 (11036)	DY	SCE	ANG
41206 (11055)	DY	SCE	ANG
41207 (42403)	DY	SCE	ANG
41208 (42406)	DY	SCE	ANG
41209 (42409)	DY	SCE	ANG

GH2G - TS *Seating 74S*

Number	Depot	Livery	Owner
42100	NL	SCE	PTR
42111	NL	SCE	PTR
42113	NL	SCE	PTR
42119§	NL	SCE	PTR
42120	NL	SCE	PTR
42121	NL	SCE	PTR
42124	NL	SCE	PTR
42131	NL	SCE	PTR
42132	NL	SCE	PTR
42133	NL	SCE	PTR
42135	NL	SCE	PTR
42136	NL	SCE	PTR
42137	NL	SCE	PTR
42139	NL	SCE	PTR
42140	NL	SCE	PTR
42141	NL	SCE	PTR
42148	NL	SCE	PTR
42149	NL	SCE	PTR
42151	NL	SCE	PTR
42152	NL	SCE	PTR
42153	NL	SCE	PTR
42155	NL	SCE	PTR
42156	NL	SCE	PTR
42157	NL	SCE	PTR
42164	NL	SCE	PTR
42165	NL	SCE	PTR
42220	NL	SCE	PTR
42230	NL	SCE	PTR
42327	NL	SCE	PTR
42328	NL	SCE	PTR
42329	NL	SCE	PTR
42331	NL	SCE	PTR
42337	NL	SCE	PTR
42339	NL	SCE	PTR
42341	NL	SCE	PTR
42384¤	NL	SCE	PTR

¤ Modified from 41078

GH2G - TS *Seating 64S*
**TSD Seating 60S*

Number	Depot	Livery	Owner
42401 (12149)	DY	SCE	ANG
42402 (12155)	DY	SCE	ANG
42404 (12152)	DY	SCE	ANG
42405 (12136)	DY	SCE	ANG
42407 (12044)	DY	SCE	ANG
42408 (12121)	DY	SCE	ANG

Number	Depot	Livery	Owner
42584 (41201)	DY	SCE	ANG
42585 (41202)	DY	SCE	ANG
42586 (41203)	DY	SCE	ANG

GJ2G - TGS *Seating 63S*

Number	Depot	Livery	Owner
44041	NL	SCE	PTR
44044	NL	SCE	PTR
44046	NL	SCE	PTR
44047	NL	SCE	PTR
44048	NL	SCE	PTR
44051	NL	SCE	PTR
44054	NL	SCE	PTR
44070	NL	SCE	PTR
44071	NL	SCE	PTR
44085	NL	SCE	PTR

Right: *A fleet of 94 HST Mk3s make up the HST passenger fleet, these are mainly owned by Porterbrook, with the vehicles coming from Grand Central being owned by Angel Trains. Angel Trains owned TRFB No. 40204 is illustrated.* **Antony Christie**

§ For preservation by 125 Group

Former East Coast HST stock being introduced on EMR in 2020

EC51	ANG	41120 41150	40748	42091	42146	42150	42154	44094
EC52	ANG	41039 41040	40725	42189	42057	42058	42059	44019
EC53	ANG	41090 41044	40737	42127	42063	42064	42065	44045
EC57	ANG	41151 41152	40740	42128	42182	42186	42190	44080
EC58	ANG	41097 41098	40750	42238	42191	42192	42193	44061
EC59	ANG	41099 41100	40711	42239	42240	42198	42199	44063
EC61	PTR	41115 41165	40702	42159	42160	42109	42110	44057
EC62	PTR	41185 41095	40701	42326	42330	42237	42307	44075
EC63	PTR	41159 41083	40708	42286	42228	42130	42322	44050

At the time of going to press, major changes to the East Midlands HST fleet was ongoing, with their original fleet being withdrawn and replaced by former East Coast vehicles which meet the latest group standards. The HST stock is scheduled for early replacement by new stock. The vehicles and formations are shown in the green panel left.

Eurostar

Address: ✉ Eurostar, Times House, Bravingtons Walk, Regent Quarter, London, N1 9AW

new.comments@eurostar.com

✆ 08701 606 600

ⓘ www.eurostar.com

CEO: Mike Cooper

Principal Routes: St Pancras International - Brussels and Paris, also serving Disneyland Paris, and a winter sport service to Bourg St Maurice

Owned Stations: St Pancras International, Stratford International, Ebbsfleet

Depots: Temple Mills [UK] (TI), Forest [Belgium] (FF), Le Landy [France] (LY)

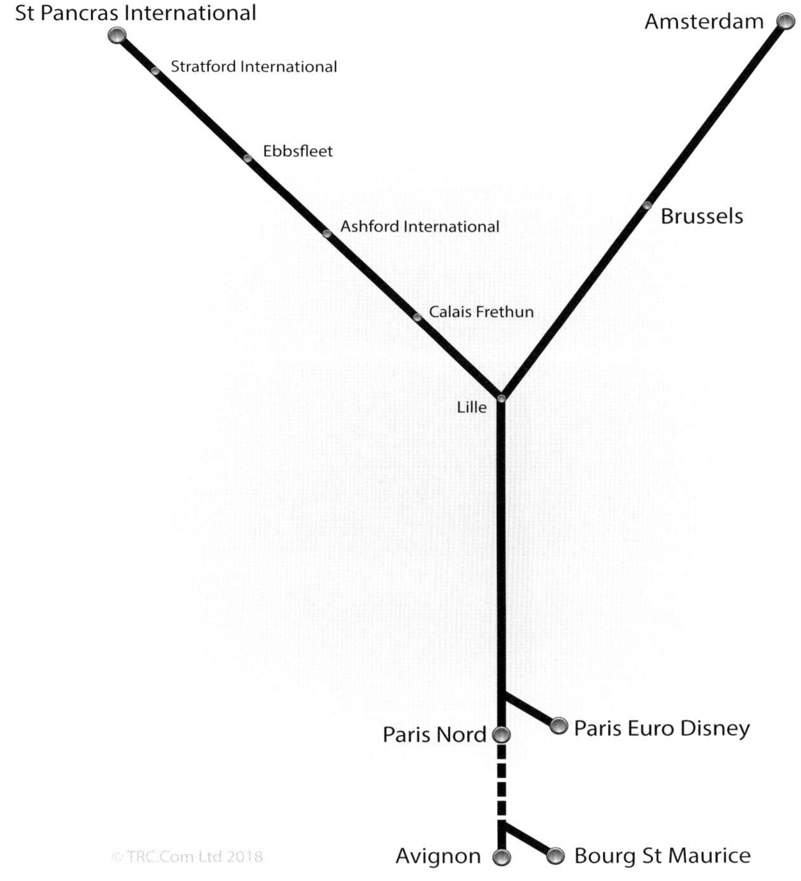

Class 373 (e300)

Vehicle Length: (DM) 72ft 8in (22.15m), (MS) 71ft 8in (21.84m)
(TS, RB, TF, TBF) 61ft 4in (18.70m)
Height: 12ft 4½in (3.77m)
■ *Modified for 1500V dc operation*

Width: 9ft 3in (2.81m)
Horsepower: 16,400hp (12,249kW)
Seats (total/car): 102F/272S, 0/48S/56S/56S/56S/56S/0/39F/39F/24F

Number	*Formation* DM+MSO+TSO+TSO+TSO+TSO+RB+TFO+TFO+TBFO	*Depot*	*Livery*	*Owner*	*Operator*	*Name*
UK sets (Class 373/0)						
373007	3730070+3730071+3730072+3730073+3730074+3730075+3730076+3730077+3730078+3730079	TI	EUB	EUS	EUS	*Waterloo Sunset*
373008	3730080+3730081+3730082+3730083+3730084+3730085+3730086+3730087+3730088+3730089	TI	EUB	EUS	EUS	*Waterloo Sunset*
373015	3730150+3730151+3730152+3730153+3730154+3730155+3730156+3730157+3730158+3730159	TI	EUB	EUS	EUS	
373016	3730160+3730161+3730162+3730163+3730164+3730165+3730166+3730167+3730168+3730169	TI	EUB	EUS	EUS	
373021§	3730210+3730211+3730212+3730213+3730214+3730215+3730216+3730217+3730218+3730219	TI	EUS	EUS	EUS	
373022§	3730220+3730221+3730222+3730223+3730224+3730225+3730226+3730227+3730228+3730229	TI	EUS	EUS	EUS	
French sets (Class 373/2)						
373205	3732050+3732051+3732052+3732053+3732054+3732055+3732056+3732057+3732058+3732059	LY	EUB	SNF	EUS	
373206	3732060+3732061+3732062+3732063+3732064+3732065+3732066+3732067+3732068+3732069	LY	EUB	SNF	EUS	
373209	3732090+3732091+3732092+3732093+3732094+3732095+3732096+3732097+3732098+3732099	LY	EUB	SNF	EUS	
373210	3732100+3732101+3732102+3732103+3732104+3732105+3732106+3732107+3732108+3732109	LY	EUB	SNF	EUS	
373211	3732030+3732031+3732032+3732033+3732034+3732035+3732036+3732037+3732038+3732039	LY	EUB	SNF	EUS	
373212	3732040+3732041+3732042+3732043+3732044+3732045+3732046+3732047+3732048+3732049	LY	EUB	SNF	EUS	
373213●	3732130+3732131+3732132+3732133+3732134+3732135+3732136+3732137+3732138+3732139	LY	IZY	SNF	EUS	
373214§	3732140+3732141+3732142+3732143+3732144+3732145+3732146+3732147+3732148+3732149	LY	EUS	SNF	EUS	
373215§	3732150+3732151+3732152+3732153+3732154+3732155+3732156+3732157+3732158+3732159	LY	EUB	SNF	EUS	
373216§	3732160+3732161+3732162+3732163+3732164+3732165+3732166+3732167+3732168+3732169	LY	EUB	SNF	EUS	
373217	3732170+3732171+3732172+3732173+3732174+3732175+3732176+3732177+3732178+3732179	LY	EUS	SNF	EUS	
373218	3732180+3732181+3732182+3732183+3732184+3732185+3732186+3732187+3732188+3732189	LY	EUS	SNF	EUS	
373219	3732190+3732191+3732192+3732193+3732194+3732195+3732196+3732197+3732198+3732199	LY	EUB	SNF	EUS	
373220	3732200+3732201+3732202+3732203+3732204+3732205+3732206+3732207+3732208+3732209	LY	EUB	SNF	EUS	
373221	3732210+3732211+3732212+3732213+3732214+3732215+3732216+3732217+3732218+3732219	LY	EUB	SNF	EUS	
373222	3732220+3732221+3732222+3732223+3732224+3732225+3732226+3732227+3732228+3732229	LY	EUB	SNF	EUS	
373223§	3732230+3732231+3732232+3732233+3732234+3732235+3732236+3732237+3732238+3732239	LY	EUS	SNF	EUS	
373224●	3732240+3732241+3732242+3732243+3732244+3732245+3732246+3732247+3732248+3732249	LY	ISY	SNF	EUS	
373229	3732290+3732291+3732292+3732293+3732294+3732295+3732296+3732297+3732298+3732299	LY	EUS	SNF	EUS	*The Da Vinci Code*
373230	3732300+3732301+3732302+3732303+3732304+3732305+3732306+3732307+3732308+3732309	LY	EUS	SNF	EUS	*The Da Vinci Code*

§ Scheduled for early withdrawal.
● For use by Thalys on Paris to Brussells route for low cost Izy services

Spare Driving Motor

Number		*Depot*	*Livery*	*Owner*	*Operator*
3999	(Spare vehicle used as required to cover for maintenance.)	TI	EUB	EUS	EUS

Eurostar

Left: *From their introduction in the mid-1990s, launching international train operation from the UK, the Class 373 or e300 fleet has seen a lot of changes. The recent refurbishment of sets to remain in operation alongside the newer Class 374 sets has seen units outshopped in the latest blue, white and grey colours. A set, led by French power-car No. (37)3229 is seen traversing HS1 in Kent at the line speed of 186mph (300km/h).* **Howard Lewsey**

Class 374 (e320)

Vehicle Length: Car 1 - 26.075m, Car 2-8 - 24.775m.
Height: 3.77m, Width: 2.82m, Train length (8-car) 199.46m
Horsepower: 25kV ac operation - 21,000hp (16,000kW) 3,000V dc, 1,500V dc
Seats (total/car): 107F/336S. 40F/36F/31F/76S/76S/76S/76S/32S (half train)
Electrical Equipment: Siemens

Set No.	DMFO / TBFO / MFO / TSO / TSO MSO / TSO / MSORB
374001	93 70 3740 011+93 70 3740 012+93 70 3740 013+93 70 3740 014+93 70 3740 015+ 93 70 3740 016+93 70 3740 017+93 70 3740 018
374002	93 70 3740 021+93 70 3740 022+93 70 3740 023+93 70 3740 024+93 70 3740 025+ 93 70 3740 026+93 70 3740 027+93 70 3740 028
374003	93 70 3740 031+93 70 3740 032+93 70 3740 033+93 70 3740 034+93 70 3740 035+ 93 70 3740 036+93 70 3740 037+93 70 3740 038
374004	93 70 3740 041+93 70 3740 042+93 70 3740 043+93 70 3740 044+93 70 3740 045+ 93 70 3740 046+93 70 3740 047+93 70 3740 048
374005	93 70 3740 051+93 70 3740 052+93 70 3740 053+93 70 3740 054+93 70 3740 055+ 93 70 3740 056+93 70 3740 057+93 70 3740 058
374006	93 70 3740 061+93 70 3740 062+93 70 3740 063+93 70 3740 064+93 70 3740 065+ 93 70 3740 066+93 70 3740 067+93 70 3740 068
374007	93 70 3740 071+93 70 3740 072+93 70 3740 073+93 70 3740 074+93 70 3740 075+ 93 70 3740 076+93 70 3740 077+93 70 3740 078
374008	93 70 3740 081+93 70 3740 082+93 70 3740 083+93 70 3740 084+93 70 3740 085+ 93 70 3740 086+93 70 3740 087+93 70 3740 088
374009	93 70 3740 091+93 70 3740 092+93 70 3740 093+93 70 3740 094+93 70 3740 095+ 93 70 3740 096+93 70 3740 097+93 70 3740 098
374010	93 70 3740 101+93 70 3740 102+93 70 3740 103+93 70 3740 104+93 70 3740 105+ 93 70 3740 106+93 70 3740 107+93 70 3740 101
374011	93 70 3740 111+93 70 3740 112+93 70 3740 113+93 70 3740 114+93 70 3740 115+ 93 70 3740 116+93 70 3740 117+93 70 3740 118
374012	93 70 3740 121+93 70 3740 122+93 70 3740 123+93 70 3740 124+93 70 3740 125+ 93 70 3740 126+93 70 3740 127+93 70 3740 128
374013	93 70 3740 131+93 70 3740 132+93 70 3740 133+93 70 3740 134+93 70 3740 135+ 93 70 3740 136+93 70 3740 137+93 70 3740 138
374014	93 70 3740 141+93 70 3740 142+93 70 3740 143+93 70 3740 144+93 70 3740 145+ 93 70 3740 146+93 70 3740 147+93 70 3740 148
374015	93 70 3740 151+93 70 3740 152+93 70 3740 153+93 70 3740 154+93 70 3740 155+ 93 70 3740 156+93 70 3740 157+93 70 3740 158
374016	93 70 3740 161+93 70 3740 162+93 70 3740 163+93 70 3740 164+93 70 3740 165+ 93 70 3740 166+93 70 3740 167+93 70 3740 168
374017	93 70 3740 171+93 70 3740 172+93 70 3740 173+93 70 3740 174+93 70 3740 175+ 93 70 3740 176+93 70 3740 177+93 70 3740 178
374018	93 70 3740 181+93 70 3740 182+93 70 3740 183+93 70 3740 184+93 70 3740 185+ 93 70 3740 186+93 70 3740 187+93 70 3740 188
374019	93 70 3740 191+93 70 3740 192+93 70 3740 193+93 70 3740 194+93 70 3740 195+ 93 70 3740 196+93 70 3740 197+93 70 3740 198
374020	93 70 3740 201+93 70 3740 202+93 70 3740 203+93 70 3740 204+93 70 3740 205+ 93 70 3740 206+93 70 3740 207+93 70 3740 208

374021 93 70 3740 211+93 70 3740 212+93 70 3740 213+93 70 3740 214+93 70 3740 215+
93 70 3740 216+93 70 3740 217+93 70 3740 218
374022 93 70 3740 221+93 70 3740 222+93 70 3740 223+93 70 3740 224+93 70 3740 225+
93 70 3740 226+93 70 3740 227+93 70 3740 228
374023 93 70 3740 231+93 70 3740 232+93 70 3740 233+93 70 3740 234+93 70 3740 235+
93 70 3740 236+93 70 3740 237+93 70 3740 238
374024 93 70 3740 241+93 70 3740 242+93 70 3740 243+93 70 3740 244+93 70 3740 245+
93 70 3740 246+93 70 3740 247+93 70 3740 248
374025 93 70 3740 251+93 70 3740 252+93 70 3740 253+93 70 3740 254+93 70 3740 255+
93 70 3740 256+93 70 3740 257+93 70 3740 258
374026 93 70 3740 261+93 70 3740 262+93 70 3740 263+93 70 3740 264+93 70 3740 265+
93 70 3740 266+93 70 3740 267+93 70 3740 268
374027 93 70 3740 271+93 70 3740 272+93 70 3740 273+93 70 3740 274+93 70 3740 275+
93 70 3740 276+93 70 3740 277+93 70 3740 278
374028 93 70 3740 281+93 70 3740 282+93 70 3740 283+93 70 3740 284+93 70 3740 285+
93 70 3740 286+93 70 3740 287+93 70 3740 288
374029 93 70 3740 291+93 70 3740 292+93 70 3740 293+93 70 3740 294+93 70 3740 295+
93 70 3740 296+93 70 3740 297+93 70 3740 298
374030 93 70 3740 301+93 70 3740 302+93 70 3740 303+93 70 3740 304+93 70 3740 305+
93 70 3740 306+93 70 3740 307+93 70 3740 308
374031 93 70 3740 311+93 70 3740 312+93 70 3740 313+93 70 3740 314+93 70 3740 315+
93 70 3740 316+93 70 3740 317+93 70 3740 318
374032 93 70 3740 321+93 70 3740 322+93 70 3740 323+93 70 3740 324+93 70 3740 325+
93 70 3740 326+93 70 3740 327+93 70 3740 328
374033 93 70 3740 331+93 70 3740 332+93 70 3740 333+93 70 3740 334+93 70 3740 335+
93 70 3740 336+93 70 3740 337+93 70 3740 338
374034 93 70 3740 341+93 70 3740 342+93 70 3740 343+93 70 3740 344+93 70 3740 345+
93 70 3740 346+93 70 3740 347+93 70 3740 348

Above: *The 17 Class 374 e320 double-sets, built by Siemens, now form the backbone of Eurostar services. Based at Temple Mills in east London, the sets carry the latest Eurostar livery. No.(37)4028 is seen passing Harrietsham on HS1.* **CJM**

Class 08

Vehicle Length: 29ft 3in (8.91m)
Height: 12ft 8⅝in (3.87m)
Width: 8ft 6in (2.59m)

Engine: English Electric 6K
Horsepower: 400hp (298kW)
Electrical Equipment: English Electric

Number	*Depot*	*Pool*	*Livery*	*Owner*	*Operator*
08948	TI	GPSS	TTG	EUS	EUS

First Great Western Railway

Address: ✉ Milford House, 1 Milford Street, Swindon, SN1 1HL

gwrfeedback@gwr.com

✆ 08457 000125 ⓘ www.gwr.com

Managing Director: Matthew Golton (intrim)

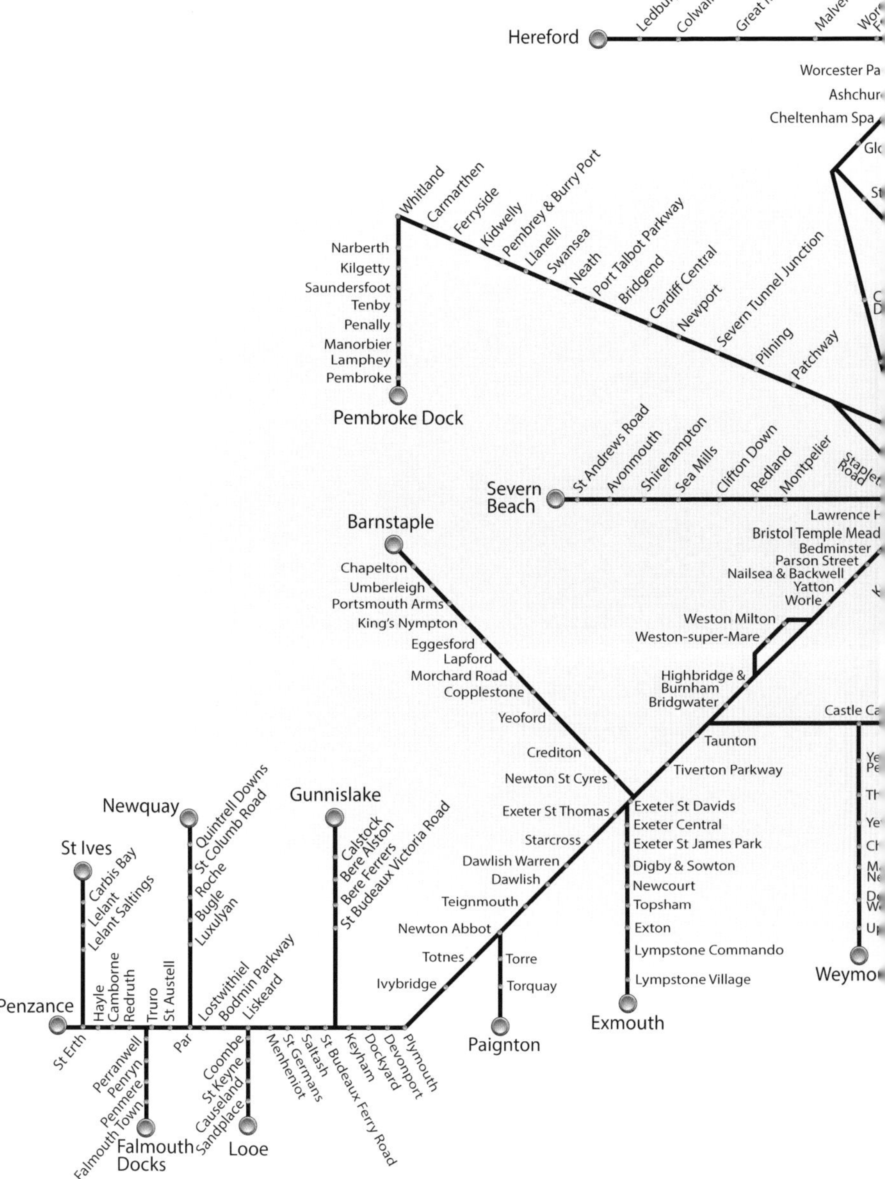

Franchise Dates: 1 April 2006 - Open extension

Principal Routes: Paddington - Penzance/Paignton, Bristol, Swansea
Thames Valley local lines, to Worcester, Hereford and Gloucester
Local lines in Bristol, Exeter, Plymouth and Cornwall
Bristol - Weymouth, Portsmouth/Brighton/Great Malvern

Depots: Exeter (EX) Laira (LA), St Philip's Marsh (PM), Penzance (PZ), Reading (RG), North Pole (NP) Stoke Gifford (ST)

Parent Company: First Group PLC

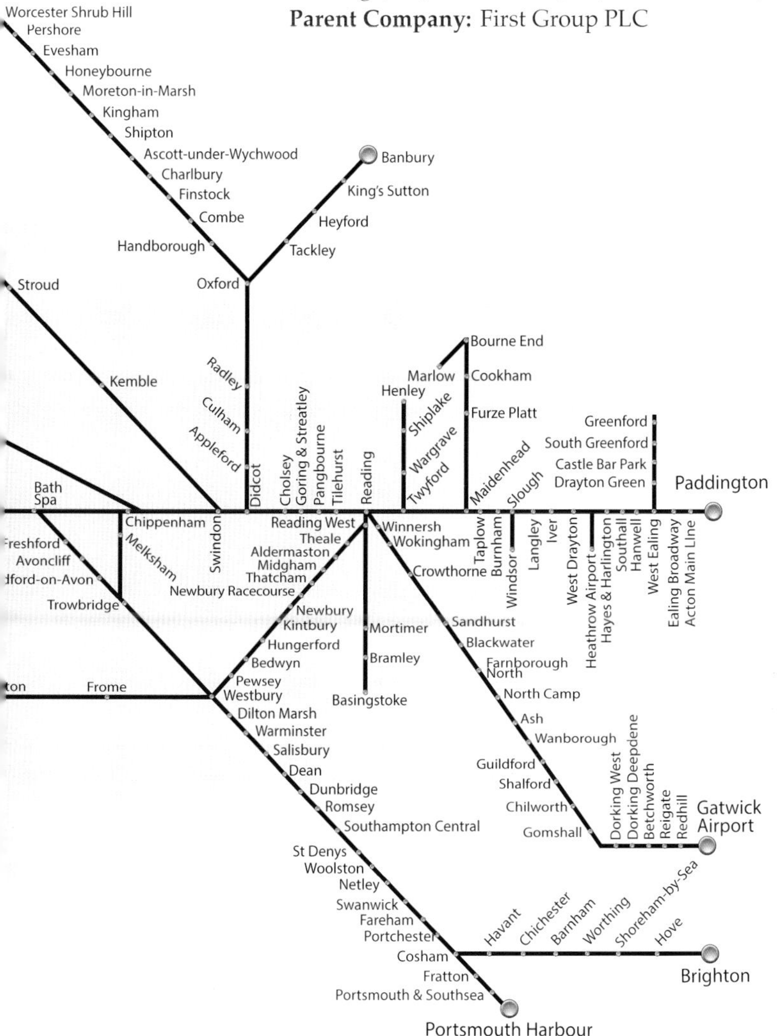

Great Western Railway

Class 08

Vehicle Length: 29ft 3in (8.91m)	Engine: English Electric 6K
Height: 12ft 8⅝in (3.87m)	Horsepower: 400hp (298kW)
Width: 8ft 6in (2.59m)	Electrical Equipment: English Electric

Number	Depot	Pool	Livery	Owner	Operator
08410§	LA	EFSH	GRN	FGP	-
08483§	LA	EFSH	BLK	FGP	-
08641	LA	EFSH	BLU	FGP	GWR
08644	PZ	EFSH	BLU	FGP	GWR
08645	PZ	EFSH	SPL	FGP	GWR
08822	PM	EFSH	ICS	FGP	GWR
08836	RG	EFSH	GWG	FGP	GWR

§ Advertised for sale in January 2020, reported sold in February 2020

	Names applied
08641	*Pride of Laira*
08644	*Laira Diesel Depot 50 years 1962-2012*
08645	*St. Piran*
08822	*Dave Mills*

Left: *The requirement for shunting locos has hugely reduced since the introduction of Class 800 and 802 stock, with little loco work at depots apart from Plymouth Laira and Penzance Long Rock. Restored to 1960s Rail Blue, No. 08644* Laira Diesel Depot 50 Years 1962 - 2012, *shunts at Laira depot on 25 September 2019.* **Antony Christie**

Class 43 – HST

Vehicle Length: 58ft 5in (18.80m)	Engine: MTU 16V4000 R41R
Height: 12ft 10in (3.90m)	Horsepower: 2,250hp (1,680kW)
Width: 8ft 11in (2.73m)	Electrical Equipment: Brush

Number	Depot	Pool	Livery	Owner	Operator	Names applied
43004	LA	EFPC	GWG	ANG	GWR	*Caerphilly Castle*
43005	LA	EFPC	GWG	ANG	GWR	
43016	LA	EFPC	GWG	ANG	GWR	
43040	LA	EFPC	GWG	ANG	GWR	
43041	LA	EFPC	GWG	ANG	GWR	*St Catherine's Castle*
43042	LA	EFPC	GWG	ANG	GWR	*Tregenna Castle*
43092	LA	EFPC	GWG	FGP	GWR	*Cromwell's Castle*
43093	LA	EFPC	SPL	FGP	GWR	*Old Oak Common HST Depot 1976-2018*
43094	LA	EFPC	GWG	FGP	GWR	*St Mawes Castle*
43097	LA	EFPC	GWG	FGP	GWR	*Environment Agency*
43098	LA	EFPC	GWG	FGP	GWR	*Walton Castle*
43122	LA	EFPC	GWG	FGP	GWR	*Dunster Castle*
43153	LA	EFPC	GWG	FGP	GWR	*Chun Castle*
43154	LA	EFPC	GWG	FGP	GWR	*Compton Castle*
43155	LA	EFPC	GWG	FGP	GWR	
43158	LA	EFPC	GWG	FGP	GWR	*Kingswear Castle*
43170	LA	EFPC	GWG	ANG	GWR	*Chepstow Castle*
43186	LA	EFPC	GWG	ANG	GWR	*Taunton Castle*
43187	LA	EFPC	GWG	ANG	GWR	
43188	LA	EFPC	GWG	ANG	GWR	
43189	LA	EFPC	GWG	ANG	GWR	*Launceston Castle*
43192	LA	EFPC	GWG	ANG	GWR	
43194	LA	EFPC	GWG	FGP	GWR	*Okehampton Castle*
43198	LA	EFPC	GWG	FGP	GWR	*Driver Brian Cooper 15 June 1947 - 5 October 1999* (side B) *Driver Stan Martin 25 June 1960 - 6 November 2004* (side A)

43088, 43156, 43160, 43162 and 43195 are owned by Great Western Group for spares or further use.

Right: *After full introduction of Class 800 and 802 stock on Great Western services, culminating in the final standard HST set operating in summer 2019, most Class 43s have been sent for either reworking for use in Scotland, or stored, with a very uncertain future. However, Great Western retain 24 Class 43s to operate with 11 'Castle' 2+4 sets. Based at Laira, most are painted in Great Western green and carry 'Castle class' cast nameplates. No. 43189* Launceston Castle *is seen at Plymouth.*
Antony Christie

Class 57/6

Vehicle Length: 63ft 6in (19.38m)
Height: 12ft 10 1/8in (3.91m)
Width: 9ft 2in (2.79m)
Engine: EMD 645-12E3
Horsepower: 2,500hp (1,860kW)
Electrical Equipment: Brush

Number	*Depot*	*Pool*	*Livery*	*Owner*	*Operator*	*Name*
57602 (47337)	PZ	EFOO	GWG	PTR	GWR	*Restormel Castle*
57603 (47349)	PZ	EFOO	GWG	PTR	GWR	*Tintagel Castle*
57604 (47209)	PZ	EFOO	GWR	PTR	GWR	*Pendennis Castle*
57605 (47206)	PZ	EFOO	GWG	PTR	GWR	*Totnes Castle*

Right: *Based at Penzance for use on the 'Night Riviera' sleeper service between London and Penzance, are four Class 57/6s, rebuilds with GM power of Class 47s. The locos are seldom seen on other work. Three locos are painted in First Great Western green, while No. 57604 carried Great Western Railway 1940s green livery. All locos carry cast nameplates after west country castles. No. 57603* Tintagel Castle *is seen at Dawlish Warren.* **CJM**

HST Passenger Fleet

Vehicle Length: 75ft 0in (22.86m)
Height: 12ft 9in (3.88m)
Width: 8ft 11in (2.71m)
Bogie Type: BT10

Castle Stock

TS- *Seating 84S*

Number	*Depot*	*Livery*	*Owner*
48101 (48111, 42093)	LA	GWG	FGP
48102 (42218)	LA	GWG	FGP
48103 (48101, 42168)	LA	GWG	FGP
48104 (42365)	LA	GWG	FGP
48105 (42266)	LA	GWG	FGP
48106 (42258)	LA	GWG	PTR
48107 (42101)	LA	GWG	FGP
48108 (42174)	LA	GWG	FGP
48109 (42085)	LA	GWG	FGP
48110 (42315)	LA	GWG	FGP
48111 (42224)	LA	GWG	FGP
48112 (42222)	LA	GWG	FGP
48113 (48102, 42177)	LA	GWG	FGP
48114 (42317)	LA	GWG	FGP
48115 (42285)	LA	GWG	FGP
48116 (42273)	LA	GWG	ANG
48117 (42271)	LA	GWG	ANG
48118 (42073)	LA	GWG	ANG
48119 (42204)	LA	GWG	ANG
48120 (42201)	LA	GWG	ANG
48121 (42027)	LA	GWG	ANG
48122 (42214)	LA	GWG	ANG
48123 (-)	LA	GWG	ANG
48124 (42212)	LA	GWG	ANG
48125 (42203)	LA	GWG	ANG
48126 (42138)	LA	GWG	ANG
48127 (42349)	LA	GWG	ANG
48128 (-)	LA	GWG	ANG
48129 (42008)	LA	GWG	ANG
48130 (-)	LA	GWG	ANG
48131 (42102)	LA	GWG	FGP
48132 (-)	LA	GWG	ANG
48133 (-)	LA	GWG	ANG
48134 (-)	LA	GWG	ANG
48135 (42251)	LA	GWG	ANG

TGS- *Seating 71S*

Number	*Depot*	*Livery*	*Owner*
49101 (44055)	LA	GWG	FGP
49102 (44083)	LA	GWG	FGP
49103 (44097)	LA	GWG	FGP
49104 (44101)	LA	GWG	FGP

Great Western Railway

49105 (44090)	LA	GWG	FGP
49106 (44033)	LA	GWG	ANG
49107 (44064)	LA	GWG	ANG
49108 (44067)	LA	GWG	ANG
49109 (44003)	LA	GWG	ANG
49110 (44014)	LA	GWG	ANG
49111 (44036)	LA	GWG	ANG
49112 (44079)	LA	GWG	FGP
49113 (44034)	LA	GWG	ANG

Numbers in light type are the *proposed* renumbering order

Castle Stock Formations

Number	*Formation* DMSO(A)+MSO+TSO+DMSO(B)	*Depot*	*Livery*	*Owner*	*Operator*
GW01	48103+48102+48101+49101	LA	GWG	FGP	GWR
GW02	48106+48105+48104+49102	LA	GWG	FGP	GWR
GW03	48109+48108+48107+49103	LA	GWG	FGP	GWR
GW04	48112+48111+48110+49104	LA	GWG	FGP	GWR
GW05	48115+48114+48113+49105	LA	GWG	FGP	GWR
GW06	48118+48117+48116+49106	LA	GWG	ANG	GWR
GW07	48121+48120+48119+49107	LA	GWR	ANG	GWR
GW08	48124+48123+48122+49108	LA	GWR	ANG	GWR
GW09	48127+48126+48125+49109	LA	GWR	ANG	GWR
GW10	48130+48129+48128+49110	LA	GWR	ANG	GWR
GW11	48133+48132+48131+49111	LA	GWR	ANG	GWR

Left: *The Great Western 'Castle' HST sets, formed as 2+4 sets and based at Laira have all been refurbished by Wabtec, Doncaster and fitted with sliding doors, as well as retention toilet systems. Trailer Guards Standard No. 49106 from set GW06 is illustrated from the saloon end, this vehicle was rebuilt from No. 44033.* **CJM**

Class 143
Pacer

Vehicle Length: 51ft 0½in (15.55m)
Height: 12ft 2¼in (3.73m)
Width: 8ft 10½in (2.70m)
Engine: 1 x Cummins LTA10-R per vehicle
Horsepower: 460hp (343kW)
Seats (total/car): 92S, 48S/44S

Number	*Formation* DMS+DMSL	*Depot*	*Livery*	*Owner*	*Operator*
143603	55658+55689	EX	GWG	PTR	FGW
143611	55652+55677	EX	GWG	PTR	FGW
143612	55653+55678	EX	GWG	PTR	FGW
143617	55644+55683	EX	GWG	PTR	FGW
143618	55659+55684	EX	GWG	PTR	FGW
143619	55660+55685	EX	GWG	PTR	FGW
143620	55661+55686	EX	GWG	PTR	FGW
143621	55662+55687	EX	GWG	PTR	FGW

Left: *Under original plans, the Exeter-based Great Western Class 143 'Pacer' sets should have been withdrawn by the end of 2019, however, this has not been possible and the sets remain in service until summer 2020. All eight sets are confined to the Exeter to Barnstaple, Exmouth and Paignton routes, they can operate in multiple with Class 150 and 158 units. All eight are painted in Great Western green. Set No. 143617 is seen arriving at Dawlish, working with a Class 150/2 set on 11 May 2019.* **CJM**

FGW Class 143s are scheduled to be withdrawn by summer 2020.

Class 150/0
Sprinter

Vehicle Length: (Driving) 65ft 9¾in (20.05m), (Inter) 66ft 2½in (20.18m)
Height: 12ft 4½in (3.77m)
Width: 9ft 3⅛in (2.82m)
Engine: 1 x Cummins NT855R4 of 285hp per vehicle
Horsepower: 855hp (638kW)
Seats (total/car): 240S, 72S/92S/76S

Number	Formation DMSL+MS+DMS	Depot	Livery	Owner	Op'r
150001	55200+55400+55300	EX	GWG	ANG	GWR
150002	55201+55401+55301	EX	GWG	ANG	GWR

Right: *The original BR Provincial sector prototype BREL three-car second generation DMUs of Class 150/0 are now on the books of Great Western and are based at Exeter working Devon and Cornwall local services, as well as being seen from time to time in the Bristol area. The two three-car non-gangway sets display full GW green livery, set No. 150002 is seen on a Paignton to Exmouth service traversing the Dawlish sea wall.* **CJM**

Class 150/2
Sprinter

Vehicle Length: 64ft 9¾in (19.74m)
Height: 12ft 4½in (3.77m)
Width: 9ft 3⅛in (2.82m)
Engine: 1 x NT855R5 of 285hp per vehicle
Horsepower: 570hp (425kW)
Seats (total/car): 116S, 60S/56S
*Refurbished * 108S 50S/58S*

Number	Formation DMSL+DMS	Depot	Livery	Owner	Op'r
150202	52202+57202	EX	GWG	ANG	GWR
150207	52207+57207	EX	GWG	ANG	GWR
150216	52216+57216	EX	GWG	ANG	GWR
150219	52219+57219	EX	FGB	PTR	GWR
150221	52221+57221	EX	GWG	PTR	GWR
150232	52232+57232	EX	GWG	PTR	GWR
150233	52233+57233	EX	GWG	PTR	GWR
150234	52234+57234	EX	GWG	PTR	GWR
150238	52238+57238	EX	FGB	PTR	GWR
150239	52239+57239	EX	GWG	PTR	GWR
150243	52243+57243	EX	GWG	PTR	GWR
150244	52244+57244	EX	GWG	PTR	GWR
150246	52246+57246	EX	GWG	PTR	GWR
150247	52247+57247	EX	GWG	PTR	GWR
150248	52248+57248	EX	GWG	PTR	GWR
150249	52249+57249	EX	GWG	PTR	GWR
150261	52261+57261	EX	GWG	PTR	GWR
150263	52263+57263	EX	GWG	PTR	GWR
150265	52265+57265	EX	GWG	PTR	GWR
150266	52266+57266	EX	GWG	PTR	GWR

Right: *Great Western operates a fleet of 20 two-car Class 150/2 gangway fitted sets, based at Exeter. These sets not only operate in Devon and Cornwall, but can frequently be found working from Bristol on routes to Weymouth, Westbury and Gloucester. All but two sets (Nos. 150219/238) sport GW green livery, the two exceptions carrying First Great Western blue. All sets, except two (150202/216) have 2+2 seating, these exceptions still have 2+3 high-density seats. Set No. 150233 is viewed at St Erth.* **CJM**

Great Western Railway

Class 158/0 (2-car)

Vehicle Length: 76ft 1¾in (23.21m)
Height: 12ft 6in (3.81m)
Width: 9ft 3¾in (2.82m)
Engine: 1 x Cummins NTA855R of 350hp per vehicle
Horsepower: 700hp (522kW)
Seats (total/car): 134S, 66S/68S

Number	Formation DMSL+DMSL	Depot	Livery	Owner	Operator
158745	52745+57745	EX	GWR	PTR	GWR
158747	52747+57747	EX	GWR	PTR	GWR
158749	52749+57749	EX	GWG	PTR	GWR
158751	52751+57751	EX	GWG	PTR	GWR
158760	52760+57760	EX	GWG	PTR	GWR
158761	52761+57761	EX	GWG	PTR	GWR
158762	52762+57762	EX	GWG	PTR	GWR
158763	52763+57763	EX	GWG	PTR	GWR
158764	52764+57764	EX	GWG	PTR	GWR
158765	52765+57765	EX	GWG	PTR	GWR
158766	52766+57766	EX	GWG	PTR	GWR
158767	52767+57767	EX	GWG	PTR	GWR
158769	52769+57769	EX	GWG	PTR	GWR

Class 158/0 (3-car)

Vehicle Length: 76ft 1¾in (23.21m)
Height: 12ft 6in (3.81m)
Width: 9ft 3¼in (2.82m)
Engine: 1 x Cummins NTA855R of 350hp per vehicle
Horsepower: 1,050hp (783kW)
Seats (total/car): 158798 - 200S, 66S/66S/68S
158956-959 - 204S, 66S/70S/68S

Number	Formation DMSL+MSL+DMSL	Depot	Livery	Owner	Operator
158798	52798+58715+57798	PM	GWG	PTR	GWR

Number		Formation DMSL+DMSL+DMSL	Depot	Livery	Owner	Operator
158956	(158748/768)	57748+52768+57768	PM	GWG	PTR	GWR
158957	(158748/771)	52748+52771+57771	PM	GWG	PTR	GWR
158958	(158746/776)	57746+52776+57776	PM	GWG	PTR	GWR
158959	(158746/778)	52746+52778+57778	PM	GWG	PTR	GWR

Left: *A number of Class 158s are operated by Great Western, based at Bristol St Philips Marsh depot. Until recently these have been the main power for longer distance services from Bristol and Cardiff to such places as Portsmouth, but following introduction of Class 165/166 stock to these routes, the '158s' have commenced work in the West Country. At the time of writing most of the three-car sets are being reformed as two-car units. Fixed three-car set No. 158798 is still operated by Great Western and is illustrated at Southampton Central.* **CJM**

Class 165/1 (3-car)
Networker Turbo

Vehicle Length: (Driving) 75ft 2½in (22.91m), (Inter) 74ft 6½in (22.72m)
Height: 12ft 5¼in (3.79m)
Width: 9ft 5½in (2.81m)
Engine: 1 x Perkins 2006TWH of 350hp per car
Horsepower: 1,050hp (783kW)
Seats (total/car): 286S, 82S/106S/98S

Number	Formation DMSL+MS+DMS	Depot	Livery	Owner	Operator
165101	58953+55415+58916	RG	GWG	ANG	GWR
165102	58954+55416+58917	RG	GWG	ANG	GWR
165103	58955+55417+58918	RG	GWG	ANG	GWR
165104	58956+55418+58919	RG	GWG	ANG	GWR
165105	58957+55419+58920	RG	GWG	ANG	GWR
165106	58958+55420+58921	RG	GWG	ANG	GWR
165107	58959+55421+58922	RG	GWG	ANG	GWR
165108	58960+55422+58923	RG	GWG	ANG	GWR
165109	58961+55423+58924	RG	GWG	ANG	GWR
165110	58962+55424+58925	RG	GWG	ANG	GWR
165111	58963+55425+58926	RG	GWG	ANG	GWR
165112	58964+55426+58927	PM	GWG	ANG	GWR
165113	58965+55427+58928	RG	GWG	ANG	GWR
165114	58966+55428+58929	RG	GWG	ANG	GWR
165116	58968+55430+58931	PM	GWG	ANG	GWR
165117	58969+55431+58932	RG	GWG	ANG	GWR

Class 165/1 (2-car)
Networker Turbo

Vehicle Length: 75ft 2½in (22.91m)
Height: 12ft 5¼in (3.79m)
Width: 9ft 5½in (2.81m)
Engine: 1 x Perkins 2006TWH of 350hp per car
Horsepower: 700hp (522kW)
Seats (total/car):186S, 88S/98S

Number	Formation DMSL+DMS	Depot	Livery	Owner	Operator
165118	58879+58933	PM	GWG	ANG	GWR
165119	58880+58934	PM	GWG	ANG	GWR
165120	58881+58935	PM	GWG	ANG	GWR
165121	58882+58936	RG	GWG	ANG	GWR
165122	58883+58937	PM	GWG	ANG	GWR
165123	58884+58938	RG	GWG	ANG	GWR
165124	58885+58939	RG	GWG	ANG	GWR
165125	58886+58940	RG	GWG	ANG	GWR
165126	58887+58941	RG	GWG	ANG	GWR
165127	58888+58942	PM	GWG	ANG	GWR
165128	58889+58943	RG	GWG	ANG	GWR
165129	58890+58944	PM	GWG	ANG	GWR
165130	58891+58945	RG	GWG	ANG	GWR
165131	58892+58946	RG	GWG	ANG	GWR
165132	58893+58947	PM	GWG	ANG	GWR
165133	58894+58948	RG	GWG	ANG	GWR
165134	58895+58949	PM	GWG	ANG	GWR
165135	58896+58950	RG	GWG	ANG	GWR
165136	58897+58951	RG	GWG	ANG	GWR
165137	58898+58952	PM	GWG	ANG	GWR

Right: *Introduced as part of the NSE Thames route modernisation, the Class 165 sets are now found operating from Bristol and even into the West Country. Some sets still operate on non-electrified services in the London area and are based at Reading. The final two-car set of the class, No. 165137, is seen departing from Westbury with a stopping service to Bristol on 23 July 2019.* **CJM**

Class 166
Networker Turbo Express

Vehicle Length: (Driving) 75ft 2½in (22.91m), (Inter) 74ft 6½in (22.72m)
Height: 12ft 5¼in (3.79m)
Width: 9ft 5½in (2.81m)
Engine: 1 x Perkins 2006TWH of 350hp per car
Horsepower: 1,050hp (783kW)
Seats (total/car): 274S, 90S/96S/88S

Number	Formation DMSL+MS+DMSL	Depot	Livery	Owner	Operator	Name
166201	58101+58601+58122	PM	FGB	ANG	GWR	
166202	58102+58602+58123	PM	FGB	ANG	GWR	
166203	58103+58603+58124	PM	FGB	ANG	GWR	
166204	58104+58604+58125	PM	GWG	ANG	GWR	*Norman Topsom MBE*
166205	58105+58605+58126	PM	GWG	ANG	GWR	
166206	58106+58606+58127	PM	GWG	ANG	GWR	
166207	58107+58607+58128	PM	FGB	ANG	GWR	
166208	58108+58608+58129	PM	GWG	ANG	GWR	
166209	58109+58609+58130	PM	FGB	ANG	GWR	
166210	58110+58610+58131	PM	GWG	ANG	GWR	
166211	58111+58611+58132	PM	FGB	ANG	GWR	
166212	58112+58612+58133	PM	GWG	ANG	GWR	
166213	58113+58613+58134	PM	GWG	ANG	GWR	
166214	58114+58614+58135	PM	GWG	ANG	GWR	
166215	58115+58615+58136	PM	FGB	ANG	GWR	
166216	58116+58616+58137	PM	GWG	ANG	GWR	
166217	58117+58617+58138	PM	GWG	ANG	GWR	
166218	58118+58618+58139	PM	GWG	ANG	GWR	
166219	58119+58619+58140	PM	GWG	ANG	GWR	
166220	58120+58620+58141	PM	GWG	ANG	GWR	*Roger Walkins - The GWR Master Train Planner*
166221	58121+58621+58142	PM	FGB	ANG	GWR	*Reading Train Care Depot*

Left: *A fleet of 21 'Networker Turbo Express' Class 166 sets are now based at Bristol St Philips Marsh for longer distance routes such as Bristol to Portsmouth, Weymouth and Worcester. These sets are in the process of being repainted into GW green and receiving interior modifications to meet new 2020 restrictions of disabled access. Set No. 166219 is viewed at Millbrook working a Portsmouth service.* **CJM**

Class 332

Vehicle Length: (Driving) 77ft 10¾in (23.74m) (Inter) 75ft 11in (23.143m) Height: 12ft 1½in (3.70m)
Width: 9ft 1in (2.75m) Horsepower: 1,876hp (1,400kW) Seats 4-car (total/car): 26F-148S, 26F/56S/44S/48S 5-car (total/car): 26F-204S, 26F/56S/44S/56S/48S

Number	Formation DMFO+TSO+PTSO+(TSO)+DMSO	Depot	Livery	Owner	Operator
332001	78400+72412+63400+ - +78401	OH	HEX	BAA	HEX
332002	78402+72409+63406+ - +78403	OH	HEX	BAA	HEX
332003	78404+72407+63402+ - +78405	OH	HEX	BAA	HEX
332004	78406+72405+63403+ - +78407	OH	HEX	BAA	HEX
332005	78408+72411+63404+72417+78409	OH	HEX	BAA	HEX
332006	78410+72410+63405+72415+78411	OH	HEX	BAA	HEX
332007	78412+72401+63401+72414+78413	OH	HEX	BAA	HEX

Vehicle Length: (Driving) 77ft 10¾in (23.74m) (Inter) 75ft 11in (23.143m) Height: 12ft 1½in (3.70m)
Width: 9ft 1in (2.75m) Horsepower: 1,876hp (1,400kW) Seats 4-car (total/car): 14F-148S, 48S/56S/44S/14F 5-car (total/car): 14F-204S, 48S/56S/44S/56S/14F

Number	Formation DMSO+TSO+PTSO+(TSO)+DMFLO	Depot	Livery	Owner	Operator
332008	78414+72413+63407+72418+78415	OH	HEX	BAA	HEX
332009	78416+72400+63408+72416+78417	OH	HEX	BAA	HEX
332010	78418+72402+63409+ - +78419	OH	HEX	BAA	HEX
332011	78420+72403+63410+ - +78421	OH	HEX	BAA	HEX
332012	78422+72404+63411+ - +78423	OH	HEX	BAA	HEX
332013	78424+72408+63412+ - +78425	OH	HEX	BAA	HEX
332014	78426+72406+63413+ - +78427	OH	HEX	BAA	HEX

The 14 Class 332 sets which have operated the Heathrow Express service between Paddington and Heathrow Airport since the service commenced operation in the 1990s are scheduled to be replaced by modified Class 387 stock from early 2020. The Class 332s will then go off-lease, they could be sold for further use or scrapped.

Class 387
Electrostar

Vehicle Length: (Driving) 66ft 9in (20.3m) (Inter) 65ft 6in (19.96m) Height: 12ft 4in (3.75m)
Width: 9ft 2in (2.79m) Horsepower: 2,012hp (1,500kW) Seats (total/car): 223S. 56S/62S/45S/60S

Number	Formation DMSO(A)+MSO+TSO+DMSO(B)	Depot	Livery	Owner	Operator
387130§	421130+422130+423130+424130	RG	HEX	PTR	GWR
387131§	421131+422131+423131+424131	RG	HEX	PTR	GWR
387132§	421132+422132+423132+424132	RG	HEX	PTR	GWR
387133§	421133+422133+423133+424133	RG	HEX	PTR	GWR
387134§	421134+422134+423134+424134	RG	HEX	PTR	GWR
387135§	421135+422135+423135+424135	RG	HEX	PTR	GWR
387136§	421136+422136+423136+424136	RG	HEX	PTR	GWR
387137§	421137+422137+423137+424137	RG	HEX	PTR	GWR
387138§	421138+422138+423138+424138	RG	HEX	PTR	GWR
387139§	421139+422139+423139+424139	RG	HEX	PTR	GWR
387140§	421140+422140+423140+424140	RG	HEX	PTR	GWR
387141§	421141+422141+423141+424141	RG	HEX	PTR	GWR

Right: *Electrification of the GW main line from Paddington has seen the use of Class 387 'Electrostar' sets on lines from Paddington to Newbury and Didcot, soon to be extending to Swindon. The sets, painted in GW green livery have 2+3 interiors and are based at Reading, operating as four-, eight- or twelve-car trains. Set No. 387158 leads an eight-car formation through Hanwell and Elthorne bound for Paddington.* **CJM**

387142	421142+422142+423142+424142	RG	GWG	PTR	GWR
387143	421143+422143+423143+424143	RG	GWG	PTR	GWR
387144	421144+422144+423144+424144	RG	GWG	PTR	GWR
387145	421145+422145+423145+424145	RG	GWG	PTR	GWR
387146	421146+422146+423146+424146	RG	GWG	PTR	GWR
387147	421147+422147+423147+424147	RG	GWG	PTR	GWR
387148	421148+422148+423148+424148	RG	GWG	PTR	GWR
387149	421149+422149+423149+424149	RG	GWG	PTR	GWR
387150	421150+422150+423150+424150	RG	GWG	PTR	GWR
387151	421151+422151+423151+424151	RG	GWG	PTR	GWR
387152	421152+422152+423152+424152	RG	GWG	PTR	GWR
387153	421153+422153+423153+424153	RG	GWG	PTR	GWR
387154	421154+422154+423154+424154	RG	GWG	PTR	GWR
387155	421155+422155+423155+424155	RG	GWG	PTR	GWR
387156	421156+422156+423156+424156	RG	GWG	PTR	GWR
387157	421157+422157+423157+424157	RG	GWG	PTR	GWR
387158	421158+422158+423158+424158	RG	GWG	PTR	GWR
387159	421159+422159+423159+424159	RG	GWG	PTR	GWR
387160	421160+422160+423160+424160	RG	GWG	PTR	GWR
387161	421161+422161+423161+424161	RG	GWG	PTR	GWR
387162	421162+422162+423162+424162	RG	GWG	PTR	GWR
387163	421163+422163+423163+424163	RG	GWG	PTR	GWR
387164	421164+422164+423164+424164	RG	GWG	PTR	GWR
387165	421165+422166+423165+424165	RG	GWG	PTR	GWR
387166	421166+422166+423166+424166	RG	GWG	PTR	GWR
387167	421167+422167+423167+424167	RG	GWG	PTR	GWR
387168	421168+422168+423168+424168	RG	GWG	PTR	GWR
387169	421169+422169+423169+424169	RG	GWG	PTR	GWR
387170	421170+422170+423170+424170	RG	GWG	PTR	GWR
387171	421171+422171+423171+424171	RG	GWG	PTR	GWR
387172	421172+422172+423172+424172	RG	GWG	PTR	GWR
387173	421173+422173+423173+424173	RG	GWG	PTR	GWR
387174	421174+422174+423174+424174	RG	GWG	PTR	GWR

§ Heathrow Express modified, revised seating and ETCS

Right: *The first 12 of the Class 387 fleet are now dedicated to the Heathrow Express operation linking Paddington with Heathrow Airport. They took over from Siemens/CAF Class 332s in January. Still based at Reading, the sets sport a Heathrow Express livery and revised seating with extra luggage space. Set No. 387130 is seen at Reading depot, soon after return from conversion at Bombardier, Ilford.* **Darren Ford**

Great Western Railway

Class 769 Flex

Vehicle Length: (Driving) 65ft 0¾in (19.83m) (Inter) 65ft 4¼in (19.92m)
Height: 11ft 9in (3.58m)
Width: 9ft 3in (2.82m)
Horsepower: 1,326hp (990kW)
Seats (total/car):

Number	Formation DTSO+MSO+TSO+DTSO	Depot	Livery	Owner	Operator
769422	77333+62912+71793+77332	RG	GWG	PTR	GWR
769423	77335+62913+71794+77334	RG	GWG	PTR	GWR
769425	77339+62915+71796+77338	RG	GWG	PTR	GWR
769427	77343+62917+71798+77342	RG	GWG	PTR	GWR
769428	77345+62918+71799+77344	RG	GWG	PTR	GWR
769430	77349+62920+71801+77348	RG	GWG	PTR	GWR
769432	77353+62922+71803+77352	RG	GWG	PTR	GWR
769435	77359+62925+71806+77358	RG	GWG	PTR	GWR
769436	77361+62926+71807+77360	RG	GWG	PTR	GWR
769437	77363+62927+71808+77362	RG	GWG	PTR	GWR
769438	77365+62928+71809+77364	RG	GWG	PTR	GWR
769439	77367+62929+71810+77366	RG	GWG	PTR	GWR
769440	77369+62930+71811+77368	RG	GWG	PTR	GWR
769443	77375+62933+71814+77374	RG	GWG	PTR	GWR
769445	77379+62935+71816+77378	RG	GWG	PTR	GWR
769447	77431+62961+71866+77430	RG	GWG	PTR	GWR
769449	77435+62963+71868+77434	RG	GWG	PTR	GWR
769452	77441+62966+71871+77440	RG	GWG	PTR	GWR
769459	77455+62973+71878+77454	RG	GWG	PTR	GWR

These are tri-mode former Class 319 sets, able to operate from 750V DC third rail, 25kV AC overhead as well as from an on-board diesel engine below each driving vehicle. The last three digits of the 769 numbers are the same as their previous Class 319 identities.

Mk3 Hauled Stock

Vehicle Length: 75ft 0in (22.86m)
Height: 12ft 9in (3.88m)
Width: 8ft 11in (2.71m)
Bogie Type: BT10

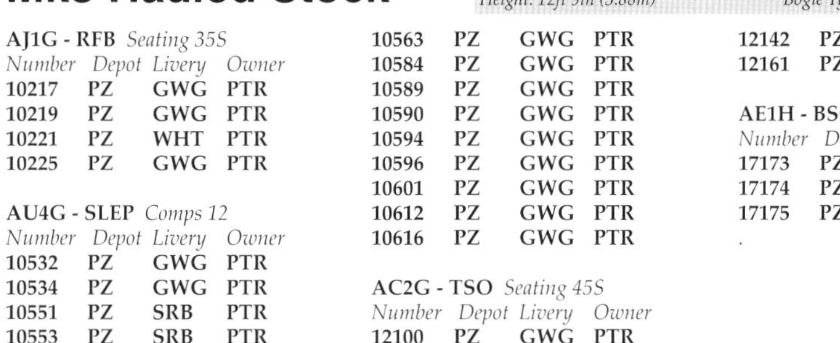

AJ1G - RFB *Seating 35S*

Number	Depot	Livery	Owner
10217	PZ	GWG	PTR
10219	PZ	GWG	PTR
10221	PZ	WHT	PTR
10225	PZ	GWG	PTR

AU4G - SLEP *Comps 12*

Number	Depot	Livery	Owner
10532	PZ	GWG	PTR
10534	PZ	GWG	PTR
10551	PZ	SRB	PTR
10553	PZ	SRB	PTR
10563	PZ	GWG	PTR
10584	PZ	GWG	PTR
10589	PZ	GWG	PTR
10590	PZ	GWG	PTR
10594	PZ	GWG	PTR
10596	PZ	GWG	PTR
10601	PZ	GWG	PTR
10612	PZ	GWG	PTR
10616	PZ	GWG	PTR

AC2G - TSO *Seating 45S*

Number	Depot	Livery	Owner
12100	PZ	GWG	PTR
12142	PZ	GWG	PTE
12161	PZ	FGW	PTR

AE1H - BSO *Seating 55U*

Number	Depot	Livery	Owner
17173	PZ	GWG	PTR
17174	PZ	GWG	PTR
17175	PZ	GWG	PTR

Left: *First Great Western Mk3 SLEP No. 10563 is illustrated at Newton Abbot from its corridor side. Note the electric tail lights fitted to the sleeper vehicles.* **Antony Christie**

Right: *Long Rock depot in Penzance is the home of 21 Mk3 loco-hauled vehicles, used on the Night Riviera service which operates six days a week between London and Penzance in both directions. The Mk3 fleet is a mix of day, sleeper and catering vehicles, all painted in GW green livery. Brake Standard Open (BSO) No. 17174 is seen from the saloon end. Reduced lighting is installed in the day saloons to improve the travelling experience.* **CJM**

Service Stock

HST Barrier Vehicles

Number	*Depot*	*Livery*	*Owner*	*Former Identity*
6330	LA	FGB	ANG	BFK - 14084
6336	PM	FGB	ANG	BG - 81591/92185
6338	LA	FGB	ANG	BG - 81581/92180
6348	PZ	FGB	ANG	BG - 81233/92963

Right: *Currently Great Western have four HST barrier vehicles on their books, but this number may reduce following the reduction of Mk3 buck-eye fitted vehicles with the operator. The vehicles are likely to be retained for use in other areas. Vehicle 6330 is shown, this is a convert from BFK No. 14084. It retains its brake compartment, but all other items have been removed.* **CJM**

Class 800/0 Bi-Mode 'IET' stock

5-car sets

Vehicle Length: (Driving) 85ft 4in (26m)
Height: 11ft 8¾in (3.62m)
Engine: MTU 12V 1600R80L of 750hp (560kW) x 3
Width: 8ft 10in (2.7m)
Horsepower: Electric 3,636hp (2,712kW)
Seats (total/car): 36F/290S - 18F, 18F/58S, 88S, 88S, 56F

Number	*Formation* DTRBFO+MC+MS+MS+DTSO	*Depot*	*Livery*	*Owner*	*Operator*	*Name*
800001*	811001+812001+813001+814001+815001§	NP	GWG	AGT	GWR	
800002*	811002+812002+813002+814002+815002§	NP	GWG	AGT	GWR	
800003*	811003+812003+813003+814003+815003	NP	GWG	AGT	GWR	(Queen Elizabeth II / Queen Victoria)
800004*	811004+812004+813004+814004+815004	NP	GWG	AGT	GWR	(Sir Daniel Gooch / Isambard Kingdom Brunel)
800005	811005+812005+813005+814005+815005	NP	GWG	AGT	GWR	
800006	811006+812006+813006+814006+815006	NP	GWG	AGT	GWR	
800007	811007+812007+813007+814007+815007	NP	GWG	AGT	GWR	
800008	811008+812008+813008+814008+815008	NP	GWG	AGT	GWR	
800009	811009+812009+813009+814009+815009	NP	GWG	AGT	GWR	Sir Gareth Edwards / John Charles
800010	811010+812010+813010+814010+815010	NP	GWG	AGT	GWR	Michael Bond / Paddington Bear
800011	811011+812011+813011+814011+815011	NP	GWG	AGT	GWR	
800012	811012+812012+813012+814012+815012	NP	GWG	AGT	GWR	
800013	811013+812013+813013+814013+815013	NP	GWG	AGT	GWR	

800014	811014+812014+813014+814014+815014	NP	GWG	AGT	GWR	*Edith New / Meghan Lloyd George*
800015	811015+812015+813015+814015+815015	NP	GWG	AGT	GWR	
800016	811016+812016+813016+814016+815016	NP	GWG	AGT	GWR	
800017	811017+812017+813017+814017+815017	NP	GWG	AGT	GWR	
800018	811018+812018+813018+814018+815018	NP	GWG	AGT	GWR	
800019	811019+812019+813019+814019+815019	NP	GWG	AGT	GWR	*Jonny Johnson MBE DFM / Joy Lofthouse*
800020	811020+812020+813020+814020+815020	NP	GWG	AGT	GWR	*Bob Woodward / Elizabeth Ralph*
800021	811021+812021+813021+814021+815021	NP	GWG	AGT	GWR	
800022	811022+812022+813022+814022+815022	NP	GWG	AGT	GWR	
800023	811023+812023+813023+814023+815023	NP	GWG	AGT	GWR	*Kathryn Osmond / Firefighter Fleur Lombard*
800024	811024+812024+813024+814024+815024	NP	GWG	AGT	GWR	
800025	811025+812025+813025+814025+815025	NP	GWG	AGT	GWR	*Don Cameron*
800026	811026+812026+813026+814026+815026	NP	GWG	AGT	GWR	
800027	811027+812027+813027+814027+815027	NP	GWG	AGT	GWR	
800028	811028+812028+813028+814028+815028	NP	GWG	AGT	GWR	
800029	811029+812029+813029+814029+815029	NP	GWG	AGT	GWR	
800030	811030+812030+813030+814030+815030	NP	GWG	AGT	GWR	
800031	811031+812031+813031+814031+815031	NP	GWG	AGT	GWR	
800032	811032+812032+813032+814032+815032	NP	GWG	AGT	GWR	
800033	811033+812033+813033+814033+815033	NP	GWG	AGT	GWR	
800034	811034+812034+813034+814034+815034	NP	GWG	AGT	GWR	
800035	811035+812035+813035+814035+815035	NP	GWG	AGT	GWR	
800036	811036+812036+813036+814036+815036	NP	GWG	AGT	GWR	

Left: *A fleet of 36 five-car Class 800/0 sets are allocated to North Pole and operate GW InterCity on all routes. They seldom operate west of Exeter, as this is the domain of Class 802s. Sets operate in either five- or ten vehicle formations and if possible the first class end is operated towards London. Running as a five car set on a Bedwyn to Paddington service on 17 September 2019, set No. 800018 is seen at Newbury.* **CJM**

Class 800/3 Bi-Mode 'IET' stock

9-car sets

Vehicle Length: (Driving) 85ft 4in (26m)
Height: 11ft 8¾in (3.62m)
Engine: MTU 12V 1600R80L of 750hp (560kW) x 5
Width: 8ft 10in (2.7m)
Horsepower: Electric 6,061hp (4,520kW)
Seats (total/car): 93F/534S - 56S, 88S, 88S, 88S, 88S, 88S,30F/38S, 48F, 15F

Number	*Formation* DTRBFO+MF+MC+TS+MS+TS+MS+MS+DTSO	*Depot*	*Livery*	*Owner*	*Operator*
800301	821001+822001+823001+824001+825001+826001+827001+828001+829001	NP	GWG	AGT	GWR
800302*	821002+822002+823002+824002+825002+826002+827002+828002+829002	NP	GWG	AGT	GWR
800303*	821003+822003+823003+824003+825003+826003+827003+828003+829003	NP	GWG	AGT	GWR
800304	821004+822004+823004+824004+825004+826004+827004+828004+829004	NP	GWG	AGT	GWR
800305	821005+822005+823005+824005+825005+826005+827005+828005+829005	NP	GWG	AGT	GWR
800306	821006+822006+823006+824006+825006+826006+827006+828006+829006	NP	GWG	AGT	GWR
800307	821007+822007+823007+824007+825007+826007+827007+828007+829007	NP	GWG	AGT	GWR
800308	821008+822008+823008+824008+825008+826008+827008+828008+829008	NP	GWG	AGT	GWR
800309	821009+822009+823009+824009+825009+826009+827009+828009+829009	NP	GWG	AGT	GWR
800310	821010+822010+823010+824010+825010+826010+827010+828003+829010	NP	GWG	AGT	GWR
800311	821011+822011+823011+824011+825011+826011+827011+828011+829011§	NP	GWG	AGT	GWR

800312	821012+822012+823012+824012+825012+826012+827012+828012+829012§	NP	GWG	AGT	GWR
800313	821013+822013+823013+824013+825013+826013+827013+828013+829013	NP	GWG	AGT	GWR
800314	821014+822014+823014+824014+825014+826014+827014+828014+829014	NP	GWG	AGT	GWR
800315	821015+822015+823015+824015+825015+826015+827015+828015+829015	NP	GWG	AGT	GWR
800316	821016+822016+823016+824016+825016+826016+827016+828016+829016	NP	GWG	AGT	GWR
800317	821017+822017+823017+824017+825017+826017+827017+828017+829017	NP	GWG	AGT	GWR
800318	821018+822018+823018+824018+825018+826018+827018+828018+829018	NP	GWG	AGT	GWR
800319	821019+822019+823019+824019+825019+826019+827019+828019+829019	NP	GWG	AGT	GWR
800320	821020+822020+823020+824020+825020+826020+827020+828020+829020	NP	GWG	AGT	GWR
800321	821021+822021+823021+824021+825021+826021+827021+828021+829021	NP	GWG	AGT	GWR

* Built in Japan, delivered to the UK
§ 829011 and 829012 previously 815001 and 815002 from sets No. 800001/002

Names Applied. *800306 Allan Leonard Lewis VC / Harold Day DSC*

Right: *North Pole depot, London is the home for 21 nine-car Class 800/3 sets. These operate in the same pool as double Class 800/0 sets, as well as on some Paddington to Paignton services. At weekends they can often be found working services to the far west including Penzance. Set No. 800306 is seen near Bedwyn carrying 'Poppy' branding.* **Antony Christie**

Class 802 Bi-Mode 'IET' stock

'West of England' sets

5-car sets 802/0

Vehicle Length: (Driving) 85ft 4in (26m) — *Width: 8ft 10in (2.7m)*
Height: 11ft 8¾in (3.62m) — *Horsepower: Electric 3,636hp (2,712kW)*
Engine: MTU 12V 1600R80L of 940hp (700kW) x 3 — *Diesel 2,820hp (2,100kW)*
Seats (total/car): 36F/290S -18F, 18F/58S, 88S, 88S, 56F

Number	*Formation* DTRBFO+MC+MS+MS+DTSO	*Depot*	*Livery*	*Owner*	*Operator*	*Name*
802001*	831001+832001+833001+834001+835001	NP	GWG	EVL	GWR	
802002*	832002+832002+833002+834002+835002	NP	GWG	EVL	GWR	
802003	833003+832003+833003+834003+835003	NP	GWG	EVL	GWR	
802004	834004+832004+833004+834004+835004	NP	GWG	EVL	GWR	
802005	835005+832005+833005+834005+835005	NP	GWG	EVL	GWR	
802006	836006+832006+833006+834006+835006	NP	GWG	EVL	GWR	
802007	837007+832007+833007+834007+835007	NP	GWG	EVL	GWR	
802008	838008+832008+833008+834008+835008	NP	GWG	EVL	GWR	*RNLB Solomon Brown Penlee Lifeboat / Rick Rescorla*
802009	839009+832009+833009+834009+835009	NP	GWG	EVL	GWR	
802010	840010+832010+833010+834010+835010	NP	GWG	EVL	GWR	
802011	841011+832011+833011+834011+835011	NP	GWG	EVL	GWR	*Sir Joshua Reynolds PRA / Capt. Robert Falcon Scott RN CVO*
802012	842012+832012+833012+834012+835012	NP	GWG	EVL	GWR	
802013	843013+832013+833013+834013+835013	NP	GWG	EVL	GWR	*Michael Eavis*
802014	844014+832014+833014+834014+835014	NP	GWG	EVL	GWR	
802015	845015+832015+833015+834015+835015	NP	GWG	EVL	GWR	
802016	846016+832016+833016+834016+835016	NP	GWG	EVL	GWR	
802017	847017+832017+833017+834017+835017	NP	GWG	EVL	GWR	
802018	848018+832018+833018+834018+835018	NP	GWG	EVL	GWR	
802019	849019+832019+833019+834019+835019	NP	GWG	EVL	GWR	
802020	850020+832020+833020+834020+835020	NP	GWG	EVL	GWR	
802021	851021+832021+833021+834021+835021	NP	GWG	EVL	GWR	
802022	852022+832022+833022+834022+835022	NP	GWG	EVL	GWR	

Great Western Railway

Right: *Following the DfT order for IET (Class 800 and 801) stock, Great Western in partnership with Eversholt Leasing obtained 22 five-car Class 802/0 and 14 nine-car Class 802/1s. These were structurally the same as the '800s' but had some equipment differences, making the sets more suitable for operation over the steeply graded West of England route. The class is booked to operate all Devon and Cornwall services, with the exception of a few Paignton duties. Set No. 802021 is seen at Totnes on 21 May 2019.* **Nathan Williamson**

9-car sets 802/1

Vehicle Length: (Driving) 85ft 4in (26m)
Height: 11ft 8¾in (3.62m)
Engine: MTU 12V 1600R80L of 940hp (750kW) x 5
Seats (total/car): 101F/526S, 15F, 56F, 30F/38S 88S, 88S, 88S, 88S, 88S, 48S
Width: 8ft 10in (2.7m)
Horsepower: Electric 6,061hp (4,520kW)
Diesel 4,700hp (3,500kW)

Number	*Formation* DTRBFO+MF+MC+TS+MS+TS+MS+MS+DTSO	*Depot*	*Livery*	*Owner*	*Operator*
802101*	831101+832101+833101+834101+835101+836101+837101+838101+839101	NP	GWG	EVL	GWR
802102	831102+832102+833102+834102+835102+836102+837102+838102+839102	NP	GWG	EVL	GWR
802103	831103+832103+833103+834103+835103+836103+837103+838103+839103	NP	GWG	EVL	GWR
802104	831104+832104+833104+834104+835104+836104+837104+838104+839104	NP	GWG	EVL	GWR
802105	831105+832105+833105+834105+835105+836105+837105+838105+839105	NP	GWG	EVL	GWR
802106	831106+832106+833106+834106+835106+836106+837106+838106+839106	NP	GWG	EVL	GWR
802107	831107+832107+833107+834107+835107+836107+837107+838107+839107	NP	GWG	EVL	GWR
802108	831108+832108+833108+834108+835108+836108+837108+838108+839108	NP	GWG	EVL	GWR
802109	831109+832109+833109+834109+835109+836109+837109+838109+839109	NP	GWG	EVL	GWR
802110	831110+832110+833110+834110+835110+836110+837110+838110+839110	NP	GWG	EVL	GWR
802111	831111+832111+833111+834111+835111+836111+837111+838111+839111	NP	GWG	EVL	GWR
802112	831112+832112+833112+834112+835112+836112+837112+838112+839112	NP	GWG	EVL	GWR
802113	831113+832113+833113+834113+835113+836113+837113+838113+839113	NP	GWG	EVL	GWR
802114	831114+832114+833114+834114+835114+836114+837114+838114+839114	NP	GWG	EVL	GWR

* Built in Japan

Name applied
802101 ***Nancy Astor CH***

The 14 nine-car sets tend to operate the main services on the Penzance-Plymouth-Paddington route, providing some 526 standard class and plus 101 first class seats per train. First class seating is identified by a grey band at cant rail height and a light grey surround to the high-level marker light on the cab end, thus announcing to passengers and staff which end the first class accommodation is located as a train arrives at a station. With its first class branding visible, set No. 802104 is seen near Powderham. **CJM**

First Hull Trains

Address: ✉ Europa House, 184 Ferensway, Kingston-upon-Hull, HU1 3UT
customer.services@hulltrains.co.uk
✆ 0345 071 0222 ⓘ www.hulltrains.co.uk

Managing Director: Louise Cheeseman
Franchise Dates: Private Open Access Operator, agreement to December 2029
Principal Route: London King's Cross - Hull **Depots:** Crofton (XW)
Parent Company: First Group PLC

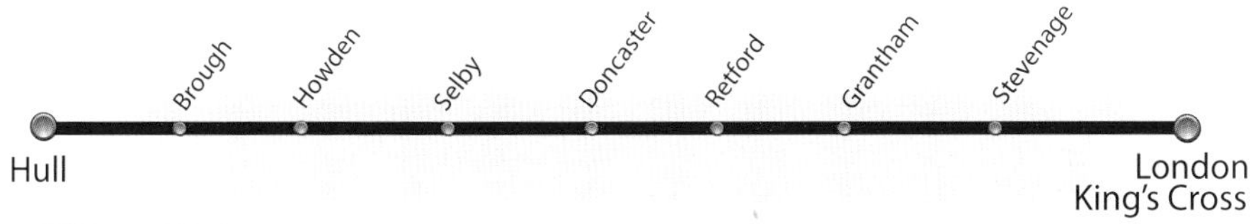

Class 802/3

Paragon

Vehicle Length: (Driving) 85ft 4in (26m)
Height: 11ft 8¾in (3.62m)
Engine: MTU 12V 1600R80L of 940hp (700kW) x 3
Seats (total/car): Awaited
Width: 8ft 10in (2.7m)
Horsepower: Electric 3,636hp (2,712kW)
Diesel 2,820hp (2,100kW)

Number	*Formation* DTRBFO+MSO+MSO+MSO+PDTSO	*Depot*	*Livery*	*Owner*	*Operator*
802301	**831301+832301+833301+834001+835001**	**BN**	**FHN**	**ANG**	**FHT**
802302	**831302+832302+833302+834002+835002**	**BN**	**FHN**	**ANG**	**FHT**
802303	**831303+832303+833303+834003+835003**	**BN**	**FHN**	**ANG**	**FHT**
802304	**831304+832304+833304+834004+835004**	**BN**	**FHN**	**ANG**	**FHT**
802305	**831305+832305+833305+834005+835005**	**BN**	**FHN**	**ANG**	**FHT**

Below: *In early 2020, five new five-car Class 802/3 'Paragon' sets took over from HST and Class 180s on Hull Trains open access services. The sets are finished in Hull dark blue livery with bodyside branding and do not sport a yellow warning end. Set No. 802302 is seen passing Doncaster on 19 December 2019.* **Antony Christie**

First TransPennine Express

Address: ✉ Floor 7, Bridgewater House, 60 Whitworth Street, Manchester, M1 6LT
tpecustomer.relations@firstgroup.com ✆ 0845 600 1671
ⓘ www.tpexpress.co.uk

Managing Director: Leo Goodwin
Franchise Dates: 1 February 2004 - 31 March 2023
Principal Routes: Newcastle, Middlesbrough, Scarborough, Hull, Cleethorpes to Manchester, Liverpool, Barrow, Carlisle, Edinburgh and Glasgow
Depots: Ardwick (AK), York (YK), Crofton (XW), Manchester (MA)
Parent Company: First Group PLC

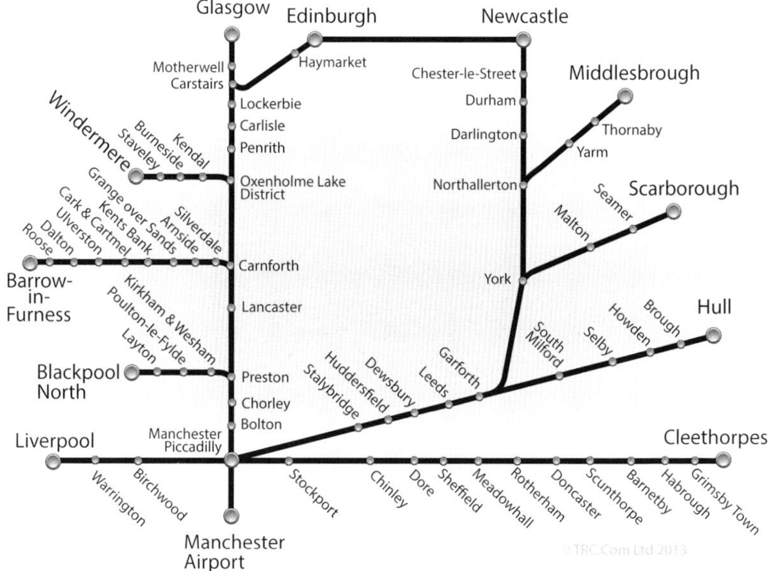

Class 68 'UK Light'

Vehicle Length: 67ft 3in (20.5m)
Height: 12ft 6½in (3.82m)
Speed: 100mph (161km/h)
Engine: Caterpillar C175-16
Horsepower: 3,750hp (2,800kW)
Electrical Equipment: ABB

Number	*Depot*	*Pool*	*Livery*	*Owner*	*Operator*	*Name*
68019	LG	TPEX	FTN	BEA	DRS/TPE	*Brutus*
68020	LG	TPEX	FTN	BEA	DRS/TPE	*Reliance*
68021	LG	TPEX	FTN	BEA	DRS/TPE	*Tireless*
68022	LG	TPEX	FTN	BEA	DRS/TPE	*Resolution*
68023	LG	TPEX	FTN	BEA	DRS/TPE	*Achilles*
68024	LG	TPEX	FTN	BEA	DRS/TPE	*Centaur*
68025	LG	TPEX	FTN	BEA	DRS/TPE	*Superb*
68026	LG	TPEX	FTN	BEA	DRS/TPE	*Enterprise*
68027	LG	TPEX	FTN	BEA	DRS/TPE	*Splendid*
68028	LG	TPEX	FTN	BEA	DRS/TPE	*Lord President*
68029	LG	TPEX	FTN	BEA	DRS/TPE	*Courageous*
68030	LG	TPEX	FTN	BEA	DRS/TPE	*Black Douglas*
68031	LG	TPEX	FTN	BEA	DRS/TPE	*Felix*
68032	LG	TPEX	FTN	BEA	DRS/TPE	*Destroyer*

Above: *From the autumn of 2019, Class 68s and CAF-built Mk5 stock has been introduced on some longer distance First TransPennine services. The '68s' owned by Beacon Rail and operated by DRS and sub-leased to TPE and carry their distinctive livery. No. 68025* Superb *is seen with a Mk5 rake at Crewe.* **Cliff Beeton**

Class 185
Desiro

Vehicle Length: (Driving) 77ft 11in (23.76m), (Inter) 77ft 10½in (23.75m)
Height: 12ft 4in (3.75m)
Width: 9ft 3in (2.81m)
Engine: 1 x Cummins OSK19 of 750hp per vehicle
Horsepower: 2,250hp (1,680kW)
Seats (total/car): 15F/154S, 15F-18S/72S/64S

Number	*Formation* DMCL+MSL+DMS	*Depot*	*Livery*	*Owner*	*Operator*
185101	51101+53101+54101	AK	FTP	EVL	FTP
185102	51102+53102+54102	AK	FTN	EVL	FTP
185103	51103+53103+54103	AK	FTN	EVL	FTP
185104	51104+53104+54104	AK	FTN	EVL	FTP
185105	51105+53105+54105	AK	FTN	EVL	FTP
185106	51106+53106+54106	AK	FTN	EVL	FTP
185107	51107+53107+54107	AK	FTN	EVL	FTP
185108	51108+53108+54108	AK	FTN	EVL	FTP
185109	51109+53109+54109	AK	FTN	EVL	FTP
185110	51110+53110+54110	AK	FTN	EVL	FTP
185111	51111+53111+54111	AK	FTN	EVL	FTP
185112	51112+53112+54112	AK	FTP	EVL	FTP
185113	51113+53113+54113	AK	FTN	EVL	FTP
185114	51114+53114+54114	AK	FTN	EVL	FTP
185115	51115+53115+54115	AK	FTN	EVL	FTP
185116	51116+53116+54116	AK	FTP	EVL	FTP
185117	51117+53117+54117	AK	FTN	EVL	FTP
185118	51118+53118+54118	AK	FTN	EVL	FTP
185119	51119+53119+54119	AK	FTN	EVL	FTP
185120	51120+53120+54120	AK	FTP	EVL	FTP
185121	51121+53121+54121	AK	FTN	EVL	FTP
185122	51122+53122+54122	AK	FTP	EVL	FTP
185123	51123+53123+54123	AK	FTN	EVL	FTP
185124	51124+53124+54124	AK	FTN	EVL	FTP
185125	51125+53125+54125	AK	FTN	EVL	FTP
185126	51126+53126+54126	AK	FTN	EVL	FTP
185127	51127+53127+54127	AK	FTN	EVL	FTP
185128	51128+53128+54128	AK	FTN	EVL	FTP
185129	51129+53129+54129	AK	FTP	EVL	FTP
185130	51130+53130+54130	AK	FTN	EVL	FTP
185131	51131+53131+54131	AK	FTN	EVL	FTP
185132	51132+53132+54132	AK	FTN	EVL	FTP
185133	51133+53133+54133	AK	FTN	EVL	FTP

First TransPennine Express

■ Following introduction of new stock, 22 Class 185s may be taken off lease, this depends on proposed franchise changes.

Left: *The 51 strong fleet of Siemens Class 185s all sport the multi-coloured FTPE livery and are based at Ardwick depot in Manchester. With its DMS vehicle nearest the camera, set No. 185110 is seen at York.* **CJM**

185134	51134+53134+54134	AK	FTN	EVL	FTP
185135	51135+53135+54135	AK	FTN	EVL	FTP
185136	51136+53136+54136	AK	FTP	EVL	FTP
185137	51137+53137+54137	AK	FTP	EVL	FTP
185138	51138+53138+54138	AK	FTN	EVL	FTP
185139	51139+53139+54139	AK	FTN	EVL	FTP
185140	51140+53140+54140	AK	FTN	EVL	FTP
185141	51141+53141+54141	AK	FTN	EVL	FTP
185142	51142+53142+54142	AK	FTA	EVL	FTP
185143	51143+53143+54143	AK	FTN	EVL	FTP
185144	51144+53144+54144	AK	FTN	EVL	FTP
185145	51145+53145+54145	AK	FTN	EVL	FTP
185146	51146+53146+54146	AK	SPL	EVL	FTP
185147	51147+53147+54147	AK	FTN	EVL	FTP
185148	51148+53148+54148	AK	FTN	EVL	FTP
185149	51149+53149+54149	AK	FTN	EVL	FTP
185150	51150+53150+54150	AK	FTN	EVL	FTP
185151	51151+53151+54151	AK	FTP	EVL	FTP

Class 397
'Civity' Nova 2

Vehicle Length: End-24.03m / Int-23.35m
Height: 3.80m
Width: 2.71m

Output: Total 2,640kW
Seats (total/car): 24F/264S
24F/76S/68S/76S/44S

Number	*Formation* *DMF+PTS(A)+MS+PTS(B)+DMS*	*Depot*	*Livery*	*Owner*	*Operator*
397001	471001+472001+473001+474001+475001	MA	FTN	EVL	FTP
397002	471001+472002+473002+474002+475002	MA	FTN	EVL	FTP
397003	471003+472003+473003+474003+475003	MA	FTN	EVL	FTP
397004	471004+472004+473004+474004+475004	MA	FTN	EVL	FTP
397005	471005+472005+473005+474005+475005	MA	FTN	EVL	FTP
397006	471006+472006+473006+474006+475006	MA	FTN	EVL	FTP
397007	471007+472007+473007+474007+475007	MA	FTN	EVL	FTP
397008	471008+472008+473008+474008+475008	MA	FTN	EVL	FTP
397009	471009+472009+473009+474009+475009	MA	FTN	EVL	FTP
397010	471010+472010+473010+474010+475010	MA	FTN	EVL	FTP
397011	471011+472011+473011+474011+475011	MA	FTN	EVL	FTP
397012	471012+472012+473012+474012+475012	MA	FTN	EVL	FTP

Left: *A fleet of 12 CAF-built Class 397 Nova 2 sets were entering service at the start of 2020, replacing Class 350 stock on FTPE West Coast services. These five-car streamlined units are part of the CAF 'Civity' platform. Set No. 397003 is recorded passing Penrith.* **Gordon Kirkby**

Class 802 Bi-Mode IET stock

5-car sets - *Nova 1*

Vehicle Length: (Driving) 85ft 4in (26m)
Height: 12ft 4in (3.75m)
Engine: MTU 12V 1600R80L of 750hp (560kW) x 3
Width: 8ft 10in (2.7m)
Horsepower: Electric 3,636hp (2,712kW)
Seats (total/car): 24F/318S

Number	*Formation* DTRBFO+MSO+MSO+MSO+PDTSO	*Depot*	*Livery*	*Owner*	*Operator*
802201*	831201+832201+833201+834201+835201	DN	GRY	ANG	FTP
802202*	831202+832202+833202+834202+835202	DN	FTN	ANG	FTP
802203	831203+832203+833203+834203+835203	DN	FTN	ANG	FTP
802204	831204+832204+833204+834204+835204	DN	FTN	ANG	FTP
802205	831205+832205+833205+834205+835205	DN	FTN	ANG	FTP
802206	831206+832206+833206+834206+835206	DN	FTN	ANG	FTP
802207	831207+832207+833207+834207+835207	DN	FTN	ANG	FTP
802208	831208+832208+833208+834208+835208	DN	FTN	ANG	FTP
802209	831209+832209+833209+834209+835209	DN	FTN	ANG	FTP
802210	831210+832210+833210+834210+835210	DN	FTN	ANG	FTP
802211	831211+832211+833211+834211+835211	DN	GRY	ANG	FTP
802212	831212+832212+833212+834212+835212	DN	FTN	ANG	FTP
802213	831213+832213+833213+834213+835213	DN	FTN	ANG	FTP
802214	831214+832214+833214+834214+835214	DN	FTN	ANG	FTP
802215	831215+832215+833215+834215+835215	DN	FTN	ANG	FTP
802216	831216+832216+833216+834216+835216	DN	FTN	ANG	FTP
802217	831217+832217+833217+834217+835217	DN	FTN	ANG	FTP
802218	831218+832218+833218+834218+835218	DN	FTN	ANG	FTP
802219	831219+832219+833219+834219+835219	DN	FTN	ANG	FTP

* Built in Japan, remainder built in Pistoia, Italy

Below: *In September 2019, the first of 19 five-car Class 802/2 sets entered service with First TransPennine Express on Liverpool to North-East services. Introduction will continue to mid 2020 and will slowly replace Class 185 stock. Class 802/2s are painted in the new standard FTPE livery. Set No. 802206 is illustrated.* **Nathan Williamson**

First TransPennine Express

Mk5a Hauled Stock
Nova 3

Vehicle Length: DTS/TF 22.37m, TS 22.2m
Width: 2.75m
Bogie Type: CAF
Seats: DTS 64S, T2(TS) 59S, T3 (TS) 69S, T1 (TF) 30F Total: 261S, 30F

Set Number	Formation DTS+T2(TS)+T3-1(TS)+T3-2(TS)+T1(TF)+Loco	Depot	Livery	Owner	Operator
TP01	12801+12703+12702+12701+11501	MA	FTN	BEA	S
TP02	12802+12706+12705+12704+11502	MA	FTN	BEA	S
TP03	12803+12709+12708+12707+11503	MA	FTN	BEA	S
TP04	12804+12712+12711+12710+11504	MA	FTN	BEA	FTP
TP05	12805+12715+12714+12713+11505	MA	FTN	BEA	S
TP06	12806+12718+12717+12716+11506	MA	FTN	BEA	FTP
TP07	12807+12721+12720+12719+11507	MA	FTN	BEA	FTP
TP08	12808+12724+12723+12722+11508	MA	FTN	BEA	FTP
TP09	12809+12727+12726+12725+11509	MA	FTN	BEA	FTP
TP10	12810+12730+12729+12728+11510	MA	FTN	BEA	FTP
TP11	12811+12733+12732+12731+11511	MA	FTN	BEA	FTP
TP12	12812+12736+12735+12734+11512	MA	FTN	BEA	FTP
TP13	12813+12739+12738+12737+11513	MA	FTN	BEA	FTP
Spare	12814	MA	FTN	BEA	FTP

Left and Below: *First TransPennine Mk5 stock, built by CAF in Spain has now entered service. A fleet of 13 five-car sets, with one spare driving car are allocated to Manchester and operate with leased Class 68 locos. On the left is T1 (TF) No. 11506 from set TP006 with seats for 30 in the 2+1 style Below is a T3-1 TS with seating for 69 in the 2+2 layout. Both:* **CJM**

Below: *To drive from the remote end of the TPE Mk5 sets a fleet of 14 Driving Trailer Standard (DTS) vehicles are in service. These have a cab layout similar to a Class 68. They have standard end draw-gear and provide seating for 64 standard class passengers. All passenger stock carries TPE grey, blue and mauve colours without yellow warning ends on locos and DTS coaches. No. 12812 is illustrated at Scarborough.* **CJM**

Grand Central

Address: ✉ River House, 17 Museum Street, York, YO1 7DJ
info@grandcentral.com
✆ 0845 603 4852
ⓘ www.grandcentral.co.uk

Managing Director: Richard McLean

Franchise Dates: Open Access Operator, to December 2026

Principal Routes: London King's Cross - Sunderland / Bradford

Depots: Heaton (HT)

Parent Company: Arriva PLC

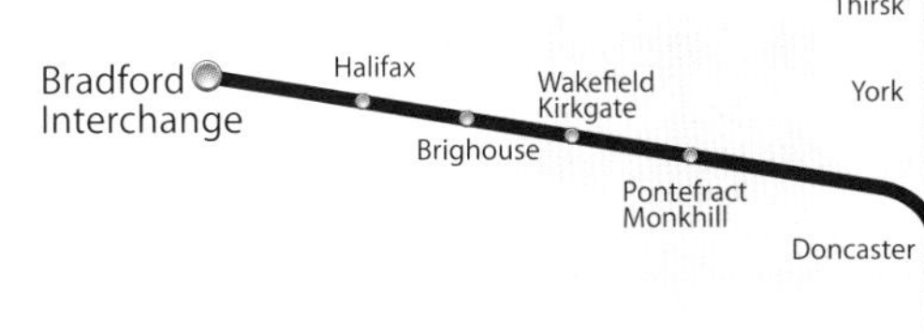

Below: *Grand Central operates a fleet of 10 refurbished Class 180 sets on its Open Access routes between London and Sunderland/Bradford. The five-car sets are based at Heaton and carry the pleasing black and orange GC livery. Set No. 180103 is seen departing from Doncaster in May 2019.* **CJM**

Class 180
Zephyr

Vehicle Length: (Driving) 75ft 7in (23.71m), (Inter) 75ft 5in (23.03m)
Height: 12ft 4in (3.75m)
Width: 9ft 2in (2.80m)
Engine: 1 x Cummins OSK19 of 750hp per vehicle
Horsepower: 3,750hp (2,796kW)
Seats (total/car): 42F/226S, 46S/42F/68S/56S/56S

Number	*Formation* DMSL(A)+MFL+MSL+MSLRB+DMSL(B)	*Depot*	*Livery*	*Owner*	*Operator*	*Name*
180101	50901+54901+55901+56901+59901	HT	GTO	ANG	GTL	
180102	50902+54902+55902+56902+59902	HT	GTO	ANG	GTL	
180103	50903+54903+55903+56903+59903	HT	GTO	ANG	GTL	
180104	50904+54904+55904+56904+59904	HT	GTO	ANG	GTL	
180105	50905+54905+55905+56905+59905	HT	GTO	ANG	GTL	*The Yorkshire Artist Ashley Jackson*
180106	50906+54906+55906+56906+59906	HT	GTO	ANG	GTL	
180107	50907+54907+55907+56907+59907	HT	GTO	ANG	GTL	*Hart of the North*
180108	50908+54908+55908+56908+59908	HT	GTO	ANG	GTL	*William Shakespeare*
180112	50912+54912+55912+56912+59912	HT	GTO	ANG	GTL	*James Herriot Celebrating 100 Years 1916-2016*
180114	50914+54914+55914+56914+59914	HT	GTO	ANG	GTL	*Kirkgate Calling*

Grand Central have been given authorisation to operate a new Open Access service between Euston and Blackpool North, starting summer 2020. Trains will be formed of hired Class 90s from DB with five car rakes of Mk4 passenger stock and a DVT (displaced from LNER). As we closed for press the first passenger set was identified - 82228, 11327, 10319, 12321, 12471, 12227. Others will follow.

Greater Anglia

Address: ✉ 1 Ely Place, London, EC1N 6RY
contactcentre@greateranglia.co.uk
✆ 0345 600 7245
ⓘ www.greateranglia.co.uk

Managing Director: Jamie Burles
Franchise Dates: 1 February 2012 - October 2025
Principal Routes: London Liverpool Street to Norwich, Cambridge, Enfield Town, Hertford East, Upminster, Southend Victoria, Southminster, Braintree, Sudbury, Clacton, Walton, Harwich Town, Felixstowe, Lowestoft, Great Yarmouth, Sheringham, Stansted Airport, Kings Lynn and Peterborough
Depots: Ilford (IL), Norwich (NC), Clacton (CC)
Parent Company: Abellio (60%), Mitsui (40%)

Class 90/0

Vehicle Length: 61ft 6in (18.74m) *Power Collection: 25kV ac overhead*
Height: 13ft 0¼in (3.96m) *Horsepower: 7,860hp (5,860kW)*
Width: 9ft 0in (2.74m) *Electrical Equipment: GEC*

Number	*Depot*	*Pool*	*Livery*	*Owner*	*Operator*	*Name*
90001	NC	IANA	AWT	PTR	GAR	*Crown Point*
90002	NC	IANA	AWT	PTR	GAR	*Eastern Daily Press 1870-2010 Serving Norfolk for 140 years*
90003	NC	IANA	AWT	PTR	GAR	
90004	NC	IANA	AWT	PTR	GAR	*City of Chelmsford*
90005	NC	IANA	AWT	PTR	GAR	*Vice-Admiral Lord Nelson*
90006	NC	IANA	AWT	PTR	GAR	*Roger Ford / Modern Railways Magazine*
90007	NC	IANA	AWT	PTR	GAR	*Sir John Betjeman*
90008	NC	IANA	AWT	PTR	GAR	*The East Anglian*
90009	NC	IANA	AWT	PTR	GAR	
90010	NC	IANA	AWT	PTR	GAR	*Bressingham Steam and Gardens*
90011	NC	IANA	AWT	PTR	GAR	*East Anglian Daily Times Suffolk & Proud*
90012	NC	IANA	AWT	PTR	GAR	*Royal Anglian Regiment*
90013	NC	IANA	AWT	PTR	GAR	*The Evening Star*
90014	NC	IANA	AWT	PTR	GAR	*Norfolk and Norwich Festival*
90015	NC	IANA	AWT	PTR	GAR	*Colchester Castle*

Below: *Soon to be displaced by Stadler Class 745 EMU sets, the Class 90s continue to provide good service on the London Liverpool Street to Norwich route powering Mk3 stock. All locos carry Greater Anglia white livery. After displacement from GE duties, Nos. 90001/002 are scheduled to go to Loco Services Ltd at Crewe and the remainder will transfer to Freightliner in pool DFGI. No. 90007 is shown at Stratford.* **CJM**

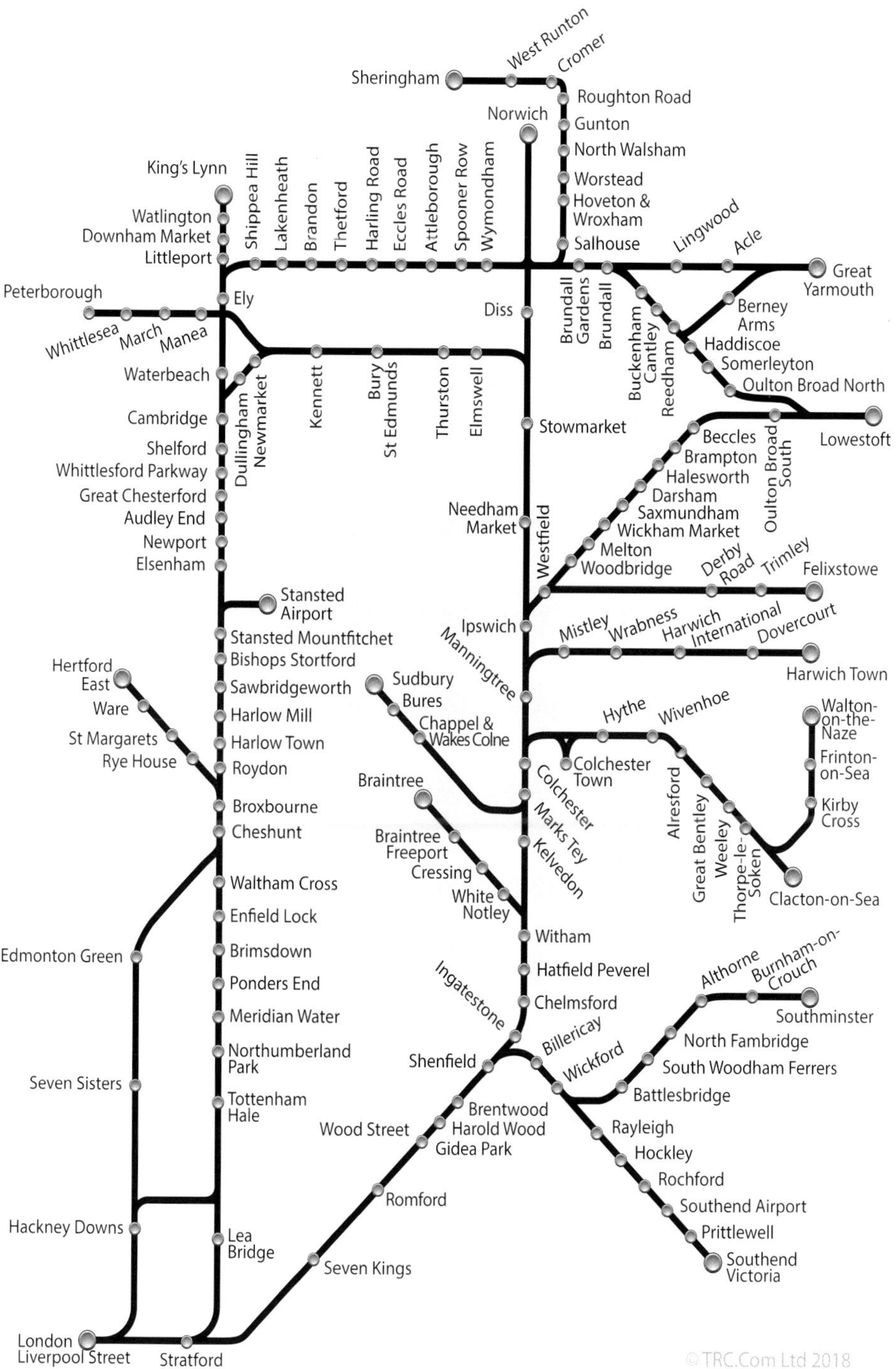
Sheringham
West Runton
Cromer
Roughton Road
Gunton
North Walsham
Worstead
Hoveton & Wroxham
Salhouse
Norwich
King's Lynn
Watlington
Downham Market
Littleport
Shippea Hill
Lakenheath
Brandon
Thetford
Harling Road
Eccles Road
Attleborough
Spooner Row
Wymondham
Lingwood
Acle
Great Yarmouth
Peterborough
Whittlesea
March
Manea
Ely
Diss
Brundall Gardens
Brundall
Buckenham
Cantley
Reedham
Berney Arms
Haddiscoe
Somerleyton
Oulton Broad North
Waterbeach
Cambridge
Dullingham
Newmarket
Kennett
Bury St Edmunds
Thurston
Elmswell
Stowmarket
Lowestoft
Beccles
Brampton
Halesworth
Darsham
Saxmundham
Wickham Market
Melton
Woodbridge
Oulton Broad South
Shelford
Whittlesford Parkway
Great Chesterford
Audley End
Newport
Elsenham
Needham Market
Westfield
Derby Road
Trimley
Felixstowe
Stansted Airport
Stansted Mountfitchet
Bishops Stortford
Ipswich
Manningtree
Mistley
Wrabness
Harwich International
Dovercourt
Harwich Town
Hertford East
Ware
St Margarets
Rye House
Sawbridgeworth
Harlow Mill
Harlow Town
Roydon
Sudbury
Bures
Chappel & Wakes Colne
Hythe
Wivenhoe
Colchester Town
Walton-on-the-Naze
Frinton-on-Sea
Kirby Cross
Braintree
Colchester
Marks Tey
Kelvedon
Alresford
Great Bentley
Weeley
Thorpe-le-Soken
Clacton-on-Sea
Broxbourne
Cheshunt
Braintree Freeport
Cressing
White Notley
Waltham Cross
Enfield Lock
Brimsdown
Ponders End
Meridian Water
Northumberland Park
Tottenham Hale
Edmonton Green
Seven Sisters
Witham
Hatfield Peverel
Chelmsford
Ingatestone
Shenfield
Billericay
Wickford
Althorne
Burnham-on-Crouch
Southminster
North Fambridge
South Woodham Ferrers
Battlesbridge
Brentwood
Harold Wood
Gidea Park
Wood Street
Rayleigh
Hockley
Rochford
Southend Airport
Prittlewell
Southend Victoria
Romford
Hackney Downs
Lea Bridge
Seven Kings
London Liverpool Street
Stratford

Mk3 Hauled Stock

Vehicle Length: 75ft 0in (22.86m) Width: 8ft 11in (2.71m)
Height: 12ft 9in (3.88m) Bogie Type: BT10

AN2G - TSOB *Seating 52S*			
10401 (12168)	NC	AWT	PTR
10402 (12010)	NC	AWT	PTR
10403 (12135)	NC	AWT	PTR
10404 (12068)	NC	AWT	PTR
10405 (12137)	NC	AWT	PTR
10406 (12020)	NC	AWT	PTR
10411 (10200)	NC	AWT	PTR
10412 (10203)	NC	AWT	PTR
10413 (10214)	NC	AWT	PTR
10414 (10216)	NC	AWT	PTR
10415 (10223)	NC	AWT	PTR
10416 (10228)	NC	AWT	PTR
10417 (10247)	NC	AWT	PTR

AD1G - FO, *FOD *Seating 48F/37F**			
11066	NC	AWT	PTR
11067	NC	AWT	PTR
11068	NC	AWT	PTR
11069	NC	AWT	PTR
11070	NC	AWT	PTR
11072*	NC	AWT	PTR
11073*	NC	AWT	PTR
11075	NC	AWT	PTR
11076	NC	AWT	PTR
11077	NC	AWT	PTR
11078*	NC	AWT	PTR
11080	NC	AWT	PTR
11081(S)	NC	AWT	PTR
11082	NC	AWT	PTR
11085*	NC	AWT	PTR
11087*	NC	AWT	PTR
11088*	NC	AWT	PTR
11090*	NC	AWT	PTR
11091*	NC	AWT	PTR
11092	NC	AWT	PTR
11093*	NC	AWT	PTR
11094*	NC	AWT	PTR
11095*	NC	AWT	PTR
11096*	NC	AWT	PTR
11098*	NC	AWT	PTR
11099*	NC	AWT	PTR
11100*	NC	AWT	PTR
11101*	NC	AWT	PTR

AC2G - TSO *Seating 80S*			
12005(S)	NC	AWT	PTR
12009	NC	AWT	PTR
12012	NC	AWT	PTR
12013	NC	AWT	PTR
12015(S)	NC	AWT	PTR
12016	NC	AWT	PTR
12019	NC	AWT	PTR
12021(S)	NC	AWT	PTR
12024	NC	AWT	PTR
12026	NC	AWT	PTR
12027	NC	AWT	PTR
12030	NC	AWT	PTR
12031	NC	AWT	PTR
12032	NC	AWT	PTR
12034	NC	AWT	PTR
12035	NC	AWT	PTR
12037(S)	NC	AWT	PTR
12040	NC	AWT	PTR
12041(S)	NC	AWT	PTR
12042(S)	NC	AWT	PTR
12046	NC	AWT	PTR
12049	NC	AWT	PTR
12051	NC	AWT	PTR
12056	NC	AWT	PTR
12057	NC	AWT	PTR
12060	NC	AWT	PTR
12061	NC	AWT	PTR
12062	NC	AWT	PTR
12064	NC	AWT	PTR
12066	NC	AWT	PTR
12067	NC	AWT	PTR
12073	NC	AWT	PTR
12079	NC	AWT	PTR
12081	NC	AWT	PTR
12082(S)	NC	AWT	PTR
12084(S)	NC	AWT	PTR
12089(S)	NC	AWT	PTR
12090	NC	AWT	PTR
12091	NC	AWT	PTR
12093	NC	AWT	PTR
12097	NC	AWT	PTR
12098	NC	AWT	PTR
12099	NC	AWT	PTR
12103	NC	AWT	PTR
12105	NC	AWT	PTR
12107(S)	NC	AWT	PTR
12108	NC	AWT	PTR
12109	NC	AWT	PTR
12110	NC	AWT	PTR
12111	NC	AWT	PTR
12114	NC	AWT	PTR
12115	NC	AWT	PTR
12116	NC	AWT	PTR
12118	NC	AWT	PTR
12120	NC	AWT	PTR
12125	NC	AWT	PTR
12126	NC	AWT	PTR
12129(S)	NC	AWT	PTR
12130	NC	AWT	PTR
12132	NC	AWT	PTR
12137	NC	AWT	PTR
12139	NC	AWT	PTR
12141	NC	AWT	PTR
12143(S)	NC	AWT	PTR
12146	NC	AWT	PTR
12147	NC	AWT	PTR
12148	NC	AWT	PTR
12150	NC	AWT	PTR
12151	NC	AWT	PTR
12153	NC	AWT	PTR
12154	NC	AWT	PTR
12159	NC	AWT	PTR
12164	NC	AWT	PTR
12166	NC	AWT	PTR
12167	NC	AWT	PTR
12170(S)	NC	AWT	PTR
12171	NC	AWT	PTR

NZAH - DVT			
82102	NC	AWT	PTR
82103§	NC	AWT	PTR
82105	NC	AWT	PTR
82107	NC	AWT	PTR
82112	NC	AWT	PTR
82114	NC	AWT	PTR
82118	NC	AWT	PTR
82121	NC	AWT	PTR
82127	NC	AWT	PTR
82132	NC	AWT	PTR
82133	NC	AWT	PTR
82136	NC	AWT	PTR
82139	NC	AWT	PTR
82143	NC	AWT	PTR
82152	NC	AWT	PTR

§ Fitted with de-icing equipment

Left: *Until full introduction of Class 745 sets on InterCity London-Norwich services, Mk3 stock will be used, operating in semi-permanient formations with a Mk3 DVT at the Norwich end. First Open Disabled (FOD) No 11087 is shown. The first class area on this fleet is identified by the traditional yellow can rail band.* **Antony Christie**

Class 317/3

Vehicle Length: (Driving) 65ft 0¾in (19.83m) (Inter) 65ft 4¼in (19.92m) Height: 12ft 1½in (3.58m) Width: 9ft 3in (2.82m) Horsepower: 1,000hp (746kW) Seats (total/car): 22F/269S, 74S/79S/22F-46S/70S

Number	Formation DTSO+MSO+TCO+DTSO	Depot	Livery	Owner	Operator	Name
317337	77036+62671+71613+77084	IL	TLK	ANG	GAR	
317338	77037+62698+71614+77085	IL	TLK	ANG	GAR	
317339	77038+62699+71615+77086	IL	TLK	ANG	GAR	
317340	77039+62700+71616+77087	IL	TLK	ANG	GAR	
317341	77040+62701+71617+77088	IL	AWT	ANG	GAR	
317342	77041+62702+71618+77089	IL	TLK	ANG	GAR	
317343	77042+62703+71619+77090	IL	TLK	ANG	GAR	
317344	77029+62690+71620+77091	IL	AWT	ANG	GAR	
317345	77044+62705+71621+77092	IL	AWT	ANG	GAR	*Driver John Webb*
317346	77045+62706+71622+77093	IL	AWT	ANG	GAR	
317347	77046+62707+71623+77094	IL	AWT	ANG	GAR	
317348	77047+62708+71624+77095	IL	TLK	ANG	GAR	*Richard A. Jenner*

Right: *Soon to be replaced by Class 720 'Aventra' stock, which has been heavily delayed, the former 'Bed-Pan' Class 317 is still the core power for the West Anglia routes. Set No. 317342 in un-branded white livery with sky blue passenger doors is seen at Bethnal Green.* **CJM**

Class 317/5

Vehicle Length: (Driving) 65ft 0¾in (19.83m) (Inter) 65ft 4¼in (19.92m) Height: 12ft 1½in (3.58m) Width: 9ft 3in (2.82m) Horsepower: 1,000hp (746kW) Seats (total/car): 291S, 74S/79S/68S/70S

Number	Former Number	Formation DTSO(A)+MSO+TCO+DTSO(B)	Depot	Livery	Owner	Operator	Name
317501	(317301)	77024+62661+71577+77048	IL	AWT	ANG	GAR	
317502	(317302)	77001+62662+71578+77049	IL	AWT	ANG	GAR	
317503	(317303)	77002+62663+71579+77050	IL	AWT	ANG	GAR	
317504	(317304)	77003+62664+71580+77051	IL	AWT	ANG	GAR	
317505	(317305)	77004+62665+71581+77052	IL	AWT	ANG	GAR	
317506	(317306)	77005+62666+71582+77053	IL	AWT	ANG	GAR	
317507	(317307)	77006+62667+71583+77054	IL	AWT	ANG	GAR	*University of Cambridge 800 years 1209-2009*
317508	(317311)	77010+62697+71587+77058	IL	AWT	ANG	GAR	
317509	(317312)	77011+62672+71588+77059	IL	AWT	ANG	GAR	
317510	(317313)	77012+62673+71589+77060	IL	AWT	ANG	GAR	
317511	(317315)	77014+62675+71591+77062	IL	AWT	ANG	GAR	
317512	(317316)	77015+62676+71592+77063	IL	AWT	ANG	GAR	
317513	(317317)	77016+62677+71593+77064	IL	AWT	ANG	GAR	
317514	(317318)	77017+62678+71594+77065	IL	AWT	ANG	GAR	
317515	(317320)	77019+62680+71596+77067	IL	AWT	ANG	GAR	

Right: *The 15 members of Class 317/5 are refurbished Class 317/3s. The standard class only sets operate on the West Anglia routes and are based at Ilford. Set No. 317502 carries white Abellio Greater Anglia livery with contrasting orange passenger doors. These sets will soon be displaced by Class 720 'Aventra' stock.* **CJM**

Greater Anglia

Class 317/6

Vehicle Length: (Driving) 65ft 0¾in (19.83m) (Inter) 65ft 4¼in (19.92m)
Height: 12ft 1½in (3.58m)
Width: 9ft 3in (2.82m)
Horsepower: 1,000hp (746kW)
Seats (total/car): 24F/244S, 64S/70S/62S/24F-48S

Number	Former Number	Formation DTSO+MSO+TSO+DTCO	Depot	Livery	Owner	Operator	Name
317649	(317349)	77200+62846+71734+77220	IL	AWT	ANG	GAR	
317650	(317350)	77201+62847+71735+77221	IL	AWT	ANG	GAR	
317651	(317351)	77202+62848+71736+77222	IL	AWT	ANG	GAR	
317652	(317352)	77203+62849+71739+77223	IL	AWT	ANG	GAR	
317653	(317353)	77204+62850+71738+77224	IL	AWT	ANG	GAR	
317654	(317354)	77205+62851+71737+77225	IL	AWT	ANG	GAR	*Richard Wells*
317655	(317355)	77206+62852+71740+77226	IL	AWT	ANG	GAR	
317656	(317356)	77207+62853+71742+77227	IL	AWT	ANG	GAR	
317657	(317357)	77208+62854+71741+77228	IL	NXU	ANG	GAR	
317658	(317358)	77209+62855+71743+77229	IL	AWT	ANG	GAR	
317659	(317359)	77210+62856+71744+77230	IL	AWT	ANG	GAR	
317660	(317360)	77211+62857+71745+77231	IL	AWT	ANG	GAR	
317661	(317361)	77212+62858+71746+77232	IL	AWT	ANG	GAR	
317662	(317362)	77213+62859+71747+77233	IL	AWT	ANG	GAR	
317664	(317364)	77215+62861+71749+77235	IL	AWT	ANG	GAR	
317665	(317365)	77216+62862+71750+77236	IL	AWT	ANG	GAR	
317666	(317366)	77217+62863+71752+77237	IL	NXU	ANG	GAR	
317667	(317367)	77218+62864+71751+77238	IL	AWT	ANG	GAR	
317668	(317368)	77219+62865+71753+77239	IL	AWT	ANG	GAR	
317670	(317370)	77281+62887+71763+77285	IL	AWT	ANG	GAR	
317671	(317371)	77282+62888+71764+77286	IL	AWT	ANG	GAR	
317672	(317372)	77283+62889+71765+77287	IL	AWT	ANG	GAR	

Left: *The Class 317/6 sets are facelifted phase 2 sets, built with the rounded roof profile above the driving cab. Displaying Greater Anglia white livery, with deep blue passenger doors, set No. 317651 is seen at Cheshunt.* **CJM**

Class 317/8

Vehicle Length: (Driving) 65ft 0¾in (19.83m) (Inter) 65ft 4¼in (19.92m)
Height: 12ft 1½in (3.58m)
Width: 9ft 3in (2.82m)
Horsepower: 1,000hp (746kW)
Seats (total/car): 20F/265S, 74S/79S/20F-42S/70S

Number	Former Number	Formation DTSO(A)+MSO+TCO+DTSO(B)	Depot	Livery	Owner	Operator
317881	(317321)	77020+62681+71597+77068	IL	AWT	ANG	GAR
317882	(317324)	77023+62684+71600+77071	IL	NXU	ANG	GAR
317883	(317325)	77000+62685+71601+77072	IL	AWT	ANG	GAR
317884	(317326)	77025+62686+71602+77073	IL	AWT	ANG	GAR
317885	(317327)	77026+62687+71603+77074	IL	AWT	ANG	GAR
317886	(317328)	77027+62688+71604+77075	IL	AWT	ANG	GAR

Class 321/3

Vehicle Length: (Driving) 65ft 0¾in (19.83m) (Inter) 65ft 4¼in (19.92m)
Height: 12ft 4¾in (3.78m)
Width: 9ft 3in (2.82m)
Horsepower: 1,328hp (996kW)
Seats (total/car): 16F/292S, 16F-57S/82S/75S/78S

Number	Formation DTCO+MSO+TSO+DTSO	Depot	Livery	Owner	Operator	Name
321301	78049+62975+71880+77853	IL	GAZ	EVL	GAR	
321302	78050+62976+71881+77854	IL	GAZ	EVL	GAR	
321303	78051+62977+71882+77855	IL	GAZ	EVL	GAR	

Right: *Another class of Greater Anglia stock which will soon be phased out of service are the Class 321s, which form the backbone of outer suburban services. As yet, no indication has been given as to the future of these vehicles. Displaying Greater Anglia white with branding on the driving cars and orange passenger doors, set No. 321364 is seen arriving at Stratford heading to Liverpool Street.* **CJM**

321304	78052+62978+71883+77856	IL	GAZ	EVL	GAR	
321305	78053+62979+71884+77857	IL	GAZ	EVL	GAR	
321306	78054+62980+71885+77858	IL	GAZ	EVL	GAR	
321307	78055+62981+71886+77859	IL	GAZ	EVL	GAR	
321308	78056+62982+71887+77860	IL	GAZ	EVL	GAR	
321309	78057+62983+71888+77861	IL	GAZ	EVL	GAR	
321310	78058+62984+71889+77862	IL	GAZ	EVL	GAR	
321311	78059+62985+71890+77863	IL	GAZ	EVL	GAR	
321312	78060+62986+71891+77864	IL	GAZ	EVL	GAR	
321313	78061+62987+71892+77865	IL	GAZ	EVL	GAR	
321314	78062+62988+71893+77866	IL	GAZ	EVL	GAR	
321315	78063+62989+71894+77867	IL	GAZ	EVL	GAR	
321316	78064+62990+71895+77868	IL	GAZ	EVL	GAR	
321317	78065+62991+71896+77869	IL	GAZ	EVL	GAR	
321318	78066+62992+71897+77870	IL	GAZ	EVL	GAR	
321319	78067+62993+71898+77871	IL	GAZ	EVL	GAR	
321320	78068+62994+71899+77872	IL	GAZ	EVL	GAR	
321321	78069+62995+71900+77873	IL	GAZ	EVL	GAR	*NSPCC Essex Full Stop*
321322	78070+62996+71901+77874	IL	GAZ	EVL	GAR	
321323	78071+62997+71902+77875	IL	GAZ	EVL	GAR	
321324	78072+62998+71903+77876	IL	GAZ	EVL	GAR	
321325	78073+62999+71904+77877	IL	GAZ	EVL	GAR	
321326	78074+63000+71905+77878	IL	GAZ	EVL	GAR	
321327	78075+63001+71906+77879	IL	GAZ	EVL	GAR	
321328	78076+63002+71907+77880	IL	GAZ	EVL	GAR	
321329	78077+63003+71908+77881	IL	GAZ	EVL	GAR	
321330	78078+63004+71909+77882	IL	GAR	EVL	GAR	
321331	78079+63005+71910+77883	IL	NXU	EVL	GAR	
321332	78080+63006+71911+77884	IL	NXU	EVL	GAR	
321333	78081+63007+71912+77885	IL	NXU	EVL	GAR	*Amsterdam*
321334	78082+63008+71913+77886	IL	NXU	EVL	GAR	
321335	78083+63009+71914+77887	IL	NXU	EVL	GAR	*Geoffrey Freeman Allen*
321336	78084+63010+71915+77888	IL	NXU	EVL	GAR	
321337	78085+63011+71916+77889	IL	NXU	EVL	GAR	
321338	78086+63012+71917+77890	IL	NXU	EVL	GAR	
321339	78087+63013+71918+77891	IL	NXU	EVL	GAR	
321340	78088+63014+71919+77892	IL	NXU	EVL	GAR	
321341	78089+63015+71920+77893	IL	NXU	EVL	GAR	
321342	78090+63016+71921+77894	IL	NXU	EVL	GAR	*R Barnes*
321343	78091+63017+71922+77895	IL	NXU	EVL	GAR	
321344	78092+63018+71923+77896	IL	NXU	EVL	GAR	
321345	78093+63019+71924+77897	IL	NXU	EVL	GAR	
321346	78094+63020+71925+77898	IL	NGU	EVL	GAR	
321347	78131+63105+71991+78280	IL	NXU	EVL	GAR	
321348	78132+63106+71992+78281	IL	NXU	EVL	GAR	
321349	78133+63107+71993+78282	IL	NGE	EVL	GAR	
321350	78134+63108+71994+78283	IL	NXU	EVL	GAR	*Gurkha*
321351	78135+63109+71995+78284	IL	NXU	EVL	GAR	*London Southend Airport*
321352	78136+63110+71996+78285	IL	NXU	EVL	GAR	
321353	78137+63111+71997+78286	IL	NXU	EVL	GAR	
321354	78138+63112+71998+78287	IL	NXU	EVL	GAR	
321355	78139+63113+71999+78288	IL	NXU	EVL	GAR	
321356	78140+63114+72000+78289	IL	NGU	EVL	GAR	
321357	78141+63115+72001+78290	IL	NGE	EVL	GAR	

Greater Anglia

321358	78142+63116+72002+78291	IL	NXU	EVL	GAR	
321359	78143+63117+72003+78292	IL	AWT	EVL	GAR	
321360	78144+63118+72004+78293	IL	NXU	EVL	GAR	*Phoenix*
321361	78145+63119+72005+78294	IL	AWT	EVL	GAR	
321362	78146+63120+72006+78295	IL	AWT	EVL	GAR	
321363	78147+63121+72007+78296	IL	AWT	EVL	GAR	
321364	78148+63122+72008+78297	IL	AWT	EVL	GAR	
321365	78149+63123+72009+78298	IL	AWT	EVL	GAR	
321366	78150+63124+72010+78299	IL	AWT	EVL	GAR	

Class 321/4

Vehicle Length: (Driving) 65ft 0¾in (19.83m) (Inter) 65ft 4¼in (19.92m)
Height: 12ft 4¾in (3.78m)
Width: 9ft 3in (2.82m)
Horsepower: 1,328hp (996kW)
Seats (total/car): 16F/283S, 16F-52S/79S/74S/78S

Number	*Formation* DTCO+MSO+TSO+DTSO	*Depot*	*Livery*	*Owner*	*Operator*	*Name/Note*
321403	78097+63065+71950+77945	IL	BLU	EVL	GAR	
321405	78099+63067+71953+77947	IL	BLU	EVL	GAR	
321406	78100+63068+71954+77948	IL	BLU	EVL	GAR	
321407	78101+63069+71955+77949	IL	BLU	EVL	GAR	
321408	78102+63070+71956+77959	IL	BLU	EVL	GAR	
321409	78103+63071+71957+77960	IL	BLU	EVL	GAR	*Dame Alive Owen's School 400 Years of Learning*
321410	78104+63072+71958+77961	IL	BLU	EVL	GAR	
321419	78113+63081+71969+77963	IL	BLU	EVL	GAR	
321421	78115+63083+71969+77963	IL	NXU	EVL	GAR	
321422	78116+63084+71970+77964	IL	NXU	EVL	GAR	
321423	78117+63085+71971+77965	IL	NXU	EVL	GAR	
321424	78118+63086+71972+77966	IL	GAR	EVL	GAR	
321425	78119+63087+71973+77967	IL	AWT	EVL	GAR	
321426	78120+63088+71974+77968	IL	GAR	EVL	GAR	
321427	78121+63089+71975+77969	IL	GAR	EVL	GAR	
321428	78122+63090+71976+77970	IL	AWT	EVL	GAR	*The Essex Commuter*
321429	78123+62091+71977+77971	IL	GAR	EVL	GAR	
321430	78124+63092+71978+77972	IL	GAR	EVL	GAR	
321431	78151+63125+72011+78300	IL	GAR	EVL	GAR	
321432	78152+63126+72012+78301	IL	NXU	EVL	GAR	
321433	78153+63127+72013+78302	IL	NXU	EVL	GAR	
321434	78154+63128+72014+78303	IL	NXU	EVL	GAR	
321435	78155+63129+72015+78304	IL	NXU	EVL	GAR	
321436	78156+63130+72016+78305	IL	NXU	EVL	GAR	
321437	78157+63131+72017+78306	IL	NXU	EVL	GAR	
321438	78158+63132+72018+78307	IL	AWT	EVL	GAR	
321439	78159+63133+72019+78308	IL	AWT	EVL	GAR	
321440	78160+63134+72020+78309	IL	AWT	EVL	GAR	
321441	78161+63135+72021+78310	IL	AWT	EVL	GAR	
321442	78162+63136+72022+78311	IL	AWT	EVL	GAR	*Crouch Valley 1889-2014*
321443	78125+63099+71985+78274	IL	AWT	EVL	GAR	
321444	78126+63100+71986+78275	IL	AWT	EVL	GAR	*Essex Lifeboats*
321445	78127+63101+71987+78276	IL	AWT	EVL	GAR	
321446	78128+63102+71988+78277	IL	AWT	EVL	GAR	*George Mullings*
321447	78129+63103+71989+78278	IL	AWT	EVL	GAR	
321448§	78130+63104+71990+78279	IL	ADV	EVL	-	

§ Eversholt development train consisting of two vehicles with Metro interior and two with suburban, seating 246 passengers and allocated to Ilford for demonstration. Stored.

Class 360/1
Desiro

Vehicle Length: 66ft 9in (20.4m)
Height: 12ft 1½in (3.7m)
Width: 9ft 2in (2.79m)
Horsepower: 1,341hp (1,000kW)
Seats (total/car): 16F/265S, 8F-59S/69S/78S/8F-59S

Number	*Formation* DMCO(A)+PTSO+TSO+DMCO(B)	*Depot*	*Livery*	*Owner*	*Operator*
360101	65551+72551+74551+68551	IL	FNA	ANG	GAR
360102	65552+72552+74552+68552	IL	FNA	ANG	GAR
360103	65553+72553+74553+68553	IL	FNA	ANG	GAR
360104	65554+72554+74554+68554	IL	FNA	ANG	GAR

360105	65555+72555+74555+68555	IL	FNA	ANG	GAR
360106	65556+72556+74556+68556	IL	FNA	ANG	GAR
360107	65557+72557+74557+68557	IL	FNA	ANG	GAR
360108	65558+72558+74558+68558	IL	FNA	ANG	GAR
360109	65559+72559+74559+68559	IL	FNA	ANG	GAR
360110	65560+72560+74560+68560	IL	FNA	ANG	GAR
360111	65561+72561+74561+68561	IL	FNA	ANG	GAR
360112	65562+72562+74562+68562	IL	FNA	ANG	GAR
360113	65563+72563+74563+68563	IL	FNA	ANG	GAR
360114	65564+72564+74564+68564	IL	FNA	ANG	GAR
360115	65565+72565+74565+68565	IL	FNA	ANG	GAR
360116	65566+72566+74566+68566	IL	FNA	ANG	GAR
360117	65567+72567+74567+68567	IL	FNA	ANG	GAR
360118	65568+72568+74568+68568	IL	FNA	ANG	GAR
360119	65569+72569+74569+68569	IL	FNA	ANG	GAR
360120	65570+72570+74570+68570	IL	FNA	ANG	GAR
360121	65571+72571+74571+68571	IL	FNA	ANG	GAR

Right: *The 21 Class 360/1 'Desiro' sets, introduced in 2002-2003 will soon be replaced by new stock. At one time their future looked bleak, but in autumn 2019 it was announced that the sets will be transferring via refurbishment to East Midland Railways to operate the electrified St Pancras to Corby commuter services, operating under the EMR Electric title. Painted in all-over blue with white bands and Greater Anglia branding, set No. 360106 is recorded on an outbound service at Stratford.* **CJM**

Class 379
Electrostar

Vehicle Length: (Driving) 66ft 9in (20.40m)
(Inter) 65ft 6in (19.99m)
Height: 12ft 4in (3.77m)
Width: 9ft 2in (2.80m)
Horsepower: 2,010hp (1,500kW)
Seats (total/car): 20F/189S, 60S/62S/43S/20F-24S

Number	*Formation* DMSO(A)+MSO+TSO+DMCO	*Depot*	*Livery*	*Owner*	*Operator*	*Name*
379001	61201+61701+61901+62101	IL	NXU	MAG	GAR	
379002	61202+61702+61902+62102	IL	NXU	MAG	GAR	
379003	61203+61703+61903+62103	IL	NXU	MAG	GAR	
379004	61204+61704+61904+62104	IL	NXU	MAG	GAR	
379005	61205+61705+61905+62105	IL	NXU	MAG	GAR	*Stansted Express*
379006	61206+61706+61906+62106	IL	NXU	MAG	GAR	
379007	61207+61707+61907+62107	IL	NXU	MAG	GAR	
379008	61208+61708+61908+62108	IL	NXU	MAG	GAR	
379009	61209+61709+61909+62109	IL	NXU	MAG	GAR	
379010	61210+61710+61910+62110	IL	NXU	MAG	GAR	
379011	61211+61711+61911+62111	IL	NXU	MAG	GAR	*Ely Cathedral*
379012	61212+61712+61912+62112	IL	NXU	MAG	GAR	*The West Anglian*
379013	61213+61713+61913+62113	IL	NXU	MAG	GAR	
379014	61214+61714+61914+62114	IL	NXU	MAG	GAR	
379015	61215+61715+61915+62115	IL	NXU	MAG	GAR	*City of Cambridge*
379016	61216+61716+61916+62116	IL	NXU	MAG	GAR	
379017	61217+61717+61917+62117	IL	NXU	MAG	GAR	
379018	61218+61718+61918+62118	IL	NXU	MAG	GAR	
379019	61219+61719+61919+62119	IL	NXU	MAG	GAR	
379020	61220+61720+61920+62120	IL	NXU	MAG	GAR	
379021	61221+61721+61921+62121	IL	NXU	MAG	GAR	
379022	61222+61722+61922+62122	IL	NXU	MAG	GAR	
379023	61223+61723+61923+62123	IL	NXU	MAG	GAR	
379024	61224+61724+61924+62124	IL	NXU	MAG	GAR	
379025	61225+61725+61925+62125	IL	NXU	MAG	GAR	*Go Discover*
379026	61226+61726+61926+62126	IL	NXU	MAG	GAR	

Greater Anglia

379027	61227+61727+61927+62127	IL	NXU	MAG	GAR
379028	61228+61728+61928+62128	IL	NXU	MAG	GAR
379029	61229+61729+61929+62129	IL	NXU	MAG	GAR
379030	61230+61730+61930+62130	IL	NXU	MAG	GAR

Left: *The 30 strong fleet of Class 379 'Electrostar' units used on the Greater Anglia Stansted Airport route will be replaced by new twelve-car Class 745/1 stock in 2020. The future for the Class 379s is uncertain, but being relatively modern sets only introduced in 2010-2011 a new operator is likely to be found, or the sets could be exported. No. 379013 is shown passing Bethnal Green. These sets carry both Greater Anglia and Stansted Express branding.* **CJM**

Class 720/1
Aventra

Vehicle Length: Driving: 24.47m
Int: 24.21m
Seats (total/car): awaited
Horsepower: 16 x 265kW = 4,240kW
Height: 3.71m
Width: 2.79m

10-car sets

Number	*Formation* *DMSO+PMSOL+MSO+MSO+TSO+MSO+PMSOL+MSO+MSO+DTSOL* *DT+M3L+M2+PM+EMLW* I *ET+M3+M2+PML+DM*	*Depot*	*Livery*	*Owner*	*Op'r*
720101	450101+451101+452101+453101+454101+455101+456101+457101+458101+459101	IL	GAR	ANG	GAR
720102	450102+451102+452102+453102+454102+455102+456102+457102+458102+459102	IL	GAR	ANG	GAR
720103	450103+451103+452103+453103+454103+455103+456103+457103+458103+459103	IL	GAR	ANG	GAR
720104	450104+451104+452104+453104+454104+455104+456104+457104+458104+459104	IL	GAR	ANG	GAR
720105	450105+451105+452105+453105+454105+455105+456105+457105+458105+459105	IL	GAR	ANG	GAR
720106	450106+451106+452106+453106+454106+455106+456106+457106+458106+459106	IL	GAR	ANG	GAR
720107	450107+451107+452107+453107+454107+455107+456107+457107+458107+459107	IL	GAR	ANG	GAR
720108	450108+451108+452108+453108+454108+455108+456108+457108+458108+459108	IL	GAR	ANG	GAR
720109	450109+451109+452109+453109+454109+455109+456109+457109+458109+459109	IL	GAR	ANG	GAR
720110	450110+451110+452110+453110+454110+455110+456110+457110+458110+459110	IL	GAR	ANG	GAR
720111	450111+451111+452111+453111+454111+455111+456111+457111+458111+459111	IL	GAR	ANG	GAR
720112	450112+451112+452112+453112+454112+455112+456112+457112+458112+459112	IL	GAR	ANG	GAR
720113	450113+451113+452113+453113+454113+455113+456113+457113+458113+459113	IL	GAR	ANG	GAR
720114	450114+451114+452114+453114+454114+455114+456114+457114+458114+459114	IL	GAR	ANG	GAR
720115	450115+451115+452115+453115+454115+455115+456115+457115+458115+459115	IL	GAR	ANG	GAR
720116	450116+451116+452116+453116+454116+455116+456116+457116+458116+459116	IL	GAR	ANG	GAR
720117	450117+451117+452117+453117+454117+455117+456117+457117+458117+459117	IL	GAR	ANG	GAR
720118	450118+451118+452118+453118+454118+455118+456118+457118+458118+459118	IL	GAR	ANG	GAR
720119	450119+451119+452119+453119+454119+455119+456119+457119+458119+459119	IL	GAR	ANG	GAR
720120	450120+451120+452120+453120+454120+455120+456120+457120+458120+459120	IL	GAR	ANG	GAR
720121	450121+451121+452121+453121+454121+455121+456121+457121+458121+459121	IL	GAR	ANG	GAR
720122	450122+451122+452122+453122+454122+455122+456122+457122+458122+459122	IL	GAR	ANG	GAR

Class 720/5
Aventra

Vehicle Length: Driving: 24.47m
Int: 24.21m
Seats (total/car): awaited
Horsepower: 8 x 265kW = 2,120kW
Height: 3.71m
Width: 2.79m

5-car sets

Number	*Formation* *DMSO+PMSOL+MSO+MSO+DTSOL* *DTLW+M3+M2+PML+DM*	*Depot*	*Livery*	*Owner*	*Operator*
720501	450501+451501+452501+453501+459501	IL	GAR	ANG	GAR
720502	450502+451502+452502+453502+459502	IL	GAR	ANG	GAR
720503	450503+451503+452503+453503+459503	IL	GAR	ANG	GAR
720504	450504+451504+452504+453504+459504	IL	GAR	ANG	GAR
720505	450505+451505+452505+453505+459505	IL	GAR	ANG	GAR
720506	450506+451506+452506+453506+459506	IL	GAR	ANG	GAR
720507	450507+451507+452507+453507+459507	IL	GAR	ANG	GAR

720508	450508+451508+452508+453508+459508	IL	GAR	ANG	GAR
720509	450509+451509+452509+453509+459509	IL	GAR	ANG	GAR
720510	450510+451510+452510+453510+459510	IL	GAR	ANG	GAR
720511	450511+451511+452511+453511+459511	IL	GAR	ANG	GAR
720512	450512+451512+452512+453512+459512	IL	GAR	ANG	GAR
720513	450513+451513+452513+453513+459513	IL	GAR	ANG	GAR
720514	450514+451514+452514+453514+459514	IL	GAR	ANG	GAR
720515	450515+451515+452515+453515+459515	IL	GAR	ANG	GAR
720516	450516+451516+452516+453516+459516	IL	GAR	ANG	GAR
720517	450517+451517+452517+453517+459517	IL	GAR	ANG	GAR
720518	450518+451518+452518+453518+459518	IL	GAR	ANG	GAR
720519	450519+451519+452519+453519+459519	IL	GAR	ANG	GAR
720520	450520+451520+452520+453520+459520	IL	GAR	ANG	GAR
720521	450521+451521+452521+453521+459521	IL	GAR	ANG	GAR
720522	450522+451522+452522+453522+459522	IL	GAR	ANG	GAR
720523	450523+451523+452523+453523+459523	IL	GAR	ANG	GAR
720524	450524+451524+452524+453524+459524	IL	GAR	ANG	GAR
720525	450525+451525+452525+453525+459525	IL	GAR	ANG	GAR
720526	450526+451526+452526+453526+459526	IL	GAR	ANG	GAR
720527	450527+451527+452527+453527+459527	IL	GAR	ANG	GAR
720528	450528+451528+452528+453528+459528	IL	GAR	ANG	GAR
720529	450529+451529+452529+453529+459529	IL	GAR	ANG	GAR
720530	450530+451530+452530+453530+459530	IL	GAR	ANG	GAR
720531	450531+451531+452531+453531+459531	IL	GAR	ANG	GAR
720532	450532+451532+452532+453532+459532	IL	GAR	ANG	GAR
720533	450533+451533+452533+453533+459533	IL	GAR	ANG	GAR
720534	450534+451534+452534+453534+459534	IL	GAR	ANG	GAR
720535	450535+451535+452535+453535+459535	IL	GAR	ANG	GAR
720536	450536+451536+452536+453536+459536	IL	GAR	ANG	GAR
720537	450537+451537+452537+453537+459537	IL	GAR	ANG	GAR
720538	450538+451538+452538+453538+459538	IL	GAR	ANG	GAR
720539	450539+451539+452539+453539+459539	IL	GAR	ANG	GAR
720540	450540+451540+452540+453540+459540	IL	GAR	ANG	GAR
720541	450541+451541+452541+453541+459541	IL	GAR	ANG	GAR
720542	450542+451542+452542+453542+459542	IL	GAR	ANG	GAR
720543	450543+451543+452543+453543+459543	IL	GAR	ANG	GAR
720544	450544+451544+452544+453544+459544	IL	GAR	ANG	GAR
720545	450545+451545+452545+453545+459545	IL	GAR	ANG	GAR
720546	450546+451546+452546+453546+459546	IL	GAR	ANG	GAR
720547	450547+451547+452547+453547+459547	IL	GAR	ANG	GAR
720548	450548+451548+452548+453548+459548	IL	GAR	ANG	GAR
720549	450549+451549+452549+453549+459549	IL	GAR	ANG	GAR
720550	450550+451550+452550+453550+459550	IL	GAR	ANG	GAR
720551	450551+451551+452551+453551+459551	IL	GAR	ANG	GAR
720552	450552+451552+452552+453552+459552	IL	GAR	ANG	GAR

Right: *The assembly of the Class 720 'Aventra' sets for Greater Anglia is being undertaken at the Bombardier factory in Litchurch Lane, Derby. Dynamic testing has been undertaken at the Old Dalby test site. Construction and testing has been a protracted operation, with many issues surrounding the build, seriously delaying the project. No. 720503 is seen at the Old Dalby test site.* **Antony Christie**

Greater Anglia

720553	450553+451553+452553+453553+459553	IL	GAR	ANG	GAR
720554	450554+451554+452554+453554+459554	IL	GAR	ANG	GAR
720555	450555+451555+452555+453555+459555	IL	GAR	ANG	GAR
720556	450556+451556+452556+453556+459556	IL	GAR	ANG	GAR
720557	450557+451557+452557+453557+459557	IL	GAR	ANG	GAR
720558	450558+451558+452558+453558+459558	IL	GAR	ANG	GAR
720559	450559+451559+452559+453559+459559	IL	GAR	ANG	GAR
720560	450560+451560+452560+453560+459560	IL	GAR	ANG	GAR
720561	450561+451561+452561+453561+459561	IL	GAR	ANG	GAR
720562	450562+451562+452562+453562+459562	IL	GAR	ANG	GAR
720563	450563+451563+452563+453563+459563	IL	GAR	ANG	GAR
720564	450564+451564+452564+453564+459564	IL	GAR	ANG	GAR
720565	450565+451565+452565+453565+459565	IL	GAR	ANG	GAR
720566	450566+451566+452566+453566+459566	IL	GAR	ANG	GAR
720567	450567+451567+452567+453567+459567	IL	GAR	ANG	GAR
720568	450568+451568+452568+453568+459568	IL	GAR	ANG	GAR
720569	450569+451569+452569+453569+459569	IL	GAR	ANG	GAR
720570	450570+451570+452570+453570+459570	IL	GAR	ANG	GAR
720571	450571+451571+452571+453571+459571	IL	GAR	ANG	GAR
720572	450572+451572+452572+453572+459572	IL	GAR	ANG	GAR
720573	450573+451573+452573+453573+459573	IL	GAR	ANG	GAR
720574	450574+451574+452574+453574+459574	IL	GAR	ANG	GAR
720575	450575+451575+452575+453575+459575	IL	GAR	ANG	GAR
720576	450576+451576+452576+453576+459576	IL	GAR	ANG	GAR
720577	450577+451577+452577+453577+459577	IL	GAR	ANG	GAR
720578	450578+451578+452578+453578+459578	IL	GAR	ANG	GAR
720579	450579+451579+452579+453579+459579	IL	GAR	ANG	GAR
720580	450580+451580+452580+453580+459580	IL	GAR	ANG	GAR
720581	450581+451581+452581+453581+459581	IL	GAR	ANG	GAR
720582	450582+451582+452582+453582+459582	IL	GAR	ANG	GAR
720583	450583+451583+452583+453583+459583	IL	GAR	ANG	GAR
720584	450584+451584+452584+453584+459584	IL	GAR	ANG	GAR
720585	450585+451585+452585+453585+459585	IL	GAR	ANG	GAR
720586	450586+451586+452586+453586+459586	IL	GAR	ANG	GAR
720587	450587+451587+452587+453587+459587	IL	GAR	ANG	GAR
720588	450588+451588+452588+453588+459588	IL	GAR	ANG	GAR
720589	450589+451589+452589+453589+459589	IL	GAR	ANG	GAR

Class 745
Flirt

Vehicle Length:
Height:
Width:
Horsepower:
Seats (total/car):

Class 745/0 - InterCity main line sets

Number	*Formation* *DMF+PTF+TS(A)+TS(B)+TS(C)+MS(A)+MS(B)+TS(D)+TS(E)+TS(F)+PTS+DMS*	*Depot*	*Livery*	*Owner*	*Operator*
745001	413001+426001+332001+343001+341001+301001+ 302001+342001+344001+346001+322001+312001	NC	GAR	ROK	GAR
745002	413002+426002+332002+334002+341002+301002+ 302002+342002+344002+346002+322002+312002	NC	GAR	ROK	GAR
745003	413003+426003+332003+343003+341003+301003+ 302003+342003+344003+346003+322003+312003	NC	GAR	ROK	GAR
745004	413004+426004+332004+343004+341004+301004+ 302004+342004+344004+346004+322004+312004	NC	GAR	ROK	GAR
745005	413005+426005+332005+343005+341005+301005+ 302005+342005+344005+346005+322005+312005	NC	GAR	ROK	GAR
745006	413006+426006+332006+343006+341006+301006+ 302006+342006+344006+346006+322006+312006	NC	GAR	ROK	GAR
745007	413007+426007+332007+343007+341007+301007+ 302007+342007+344007+346007+322007+312007	NC	GAR	ROK	GAR
745008	413008+426008+332008+343008+341008+301008+ 302008+342008+344008+346008+322008+312008	NC	GAR	ROK	GAR
745009	413009+426009+332009+343009+341009+301009+ 302009+342009+344009+346009+322009+312009	NC	GAR	ROK	GAR
745010	413010+426010+332010+343010+341010+301010+ 302010+342010+344010+346010+322010+312010	NC	GAR	ROK	GAR

Class 745/1 - Airport Express sets

Number	*Formation* DMS+PTS+TS(A)+TS(B)+TS(C)+MS(A)+MS(B)+TS(D)+TS(E)+TS(F)+PTS+DMS	*Depot*	*Livery*	*Owner*	*Operator*
745101	313001+326101+332101+343101+341101+301101+ 302101+342101+344101+346101+322101+312101	IL	GAR	ROK	GAR
745102	313002+326102+332102+343102+341102+301102+ 302102+342102+344102+346102+322102+312102	IL	GAR	ROK	GAR
745103	313003+326103+332103+343103+341103+301103+ 302103+342103+344103+346103+322103+312103	IL	GAR	ROK	GAR
745104	313004+326104+332104+343104+341104+301104+ 302104+342104+344104+346104+322104+312104	IL	GAR	ROK	GAR
745105	313005+326105+332105+343105+341105+301105+ 302105+342105+344105+346105+322105+312105	IL	GAR	ROK	GAR
745106	313006+326106+332106+343106+341106+301106+ 302106+342106+344106+346106+322106+312106	IL	GAR	ROK	GAR
745107	313007+326107+332107+343107+341107+301107+ 302107+342107+344107+346107+322107+312107	IL	GAR	ROK	GAR
745108	313008+326108+332108+343108+341108+301108+ 302108+342108+344108+346108+322108+312108	IL	GAR	ROK	GAR
745109	313009+326109+332109+343109+341109+301109+ 302109+342109+344109+346109+322109+312109	IL	GAR	ROK	GAR
745110	313010+326110+332110+343110+341110+301110+ 302110+342110+344110+346110+322110+312110	IL	GAR	ROK	GAR

Right: *The modernisation of Greater Anglia will see a total fleet replacement. The main line route between Liverpool Street and Norwich is to be operated by a fleet of 10 high-specification Class 745/0 sets built by Stadler. Each twelve-car train is formed of six vehicle pairs with an articulated bogie between coaches. Each train will have two first and ten standard class coaches providing accommodation for 80 first and 624 standard class passengers. Set No. 745005 is seen at Norwich Crown Point depot.* **Antony Christie**

Class 755/3
Flirt - Bi-Mode

Train Length: 65m
TPP Length: 6.69m
Width (pass): 2.72m, (PP) 2.82m
Output Electric: 2,600kW, Diesel: 960kW
Seats (total/car): 136S 60S/-/32S/52S

3-car sets

Number	*Formation* DMS(1)+ PP+PTSW+DMS(2)	*Depot*	*Livery*	*Owner*	*Operator*
755325	911325+971325+981325+912325	NC	GAR	ROK	GAR
755326	911326+971326+981326+912326	NC	GAR	ROK	GAR
755327	911327+971327+981327+912327	NC	GAR	ROK	GAR
755328	911328+971328+981328+912328	NC	GAR	ROK	GAR
755329	911329+971329+981329+912329	NC	GAR	ROK	GAR
755330	911330+971330+981330+912330	NC	GAR	ROK	GAR
755331	911331+971331+981331+912331	NC	GAR	ROK	GAR
755332	911332+971332+981332+912332	NC	GAR	ROK	GAR
755333	911333+971333+981333+912333	NC	GAR	ROK	GAR
755334	911334+971334+981334+912334	NC	GAR	ROK	GAR
755335	911335+971335+981335+912335	NC	GAR	ROK	GAR
755336	911336+971336+981336+912336	NC	GAR	ROK	GAR
755337	911337+971337+981337+912337	NC	GAR	ROK	GAR
755338	911338+971338+981338+912338	NC	GAR	ROK	GAR

Greater Anglia

Class 755/4
Flirt - Bi-Mode

Train Length: 80.7m
TPP Length: 6.69m
Width (pass): 2.72m, (PP) 2.82m
Output Electric: 2,600kW, Diesel: 1,920kW
Seats (total/car): 196S 60S/56S/-/32S/52S

4-car sets

Number	*Formation* *DMS(1)+PTS+PP+PTSW+DMS(2)*	*Depot*	*Livery*	*Owner*	*Operator*
755401	911401+961401+971401+981401+912401	NC	GAR	ROK	GAR
755402	911402+961402+971402+981402+912402	NC	GAR	ROK	GAR
755403	911403+961403+971403+981403+912403	NC	GAR	ROK	GAR
755404	911404+961404+971404+981404+912404	NC	GAR	ROK	GAR
755405	911405+961405+971405+981405+912405	NC	GAR	ROK	GAR
755406	911406+961406+971406+981406+912406	NC	GAR	ROK	GAR
755407	911407+961407+971407+981407+912407	NC	GAR	ROK	GAR
755408	911408+961408+971408+981408+912408	NC	GAR	ROK	GAR
755409	911409+961409+971409+981409+912409	NC	GAR	ROK	GAR
755410	911410+961410+971410+981410+912410	NC	GAR	ROK	GAR
755411	911411+961411+971411+981411+912411	NC	GAR	ROK	GAR
755412	911412+961412+971412+981412+912412	NC	GAR	ROK	GAR
755413	911413+961413+971413+981413+912413	NC	GAR	ROK	GAR
755414	911414+961414+971414+981414+912414	NC	GAR	ROK	GAR
755415	911415+961415+971415+981415+912415	NC	GAR	ROK	GAR
755416	911416+961416+971416+981416+912416	NC	GAR	ROK	GAR
755417	911417+961417+971417+981417+912417	NC	GAR	ROK	GAR
755418	911418+961418+971418+981418+912418	NC	GAR	ROK	GAR
755419	911419+961419+971419+981419+912419	NC	GAR	ROK	GAR
755420	911420+961420+971420+981420+912420	NC	GAR	ROK	GAR
755421	911421+961421+971421+981421+912421	NC	GAR	ROK	GAR
755422	911422+961422+971422+981422+912422	NC	GAR	ROK	GAR
755423	911423+961423+971423+981423+912423	NC	GAR	ROK	GAR
755424	911424+961424+971424+981424+912424	NC	GAR	ROK	GAR

Left and Below: *A fleet of 14 three-car and 24 four-car bi-mode Class 755 sets are currently entering service on Greater Anglia to replace Class 153, 156 and 170 stock working from Norwich. The Stadler 'Flirt' sets are articulated and each set contained a 'power pack' vehicle housing the diesel engines. Owned by Rock Rail and based at Crown Point, each vehicle has just one pair of bi-parting passenger doors on each side. The interiors are of a very high standard. On the left set No. 755409 is seen at Norwich, while below is articulated Pantograph Trailer Standard No. 981413.*
Both: **Antony Christie**

Island Line

Address: ✉ Ryde St Johns Road Station, Ryde, Isle of Wight, PO33 2BA

info@island-line.co.uk ✆ 01983 812591 ⓘ www.island-line.co.uk

General Manager: Andy Naylor

Franchise Dates: Part of SWR franchise until August 2023

Route: Ryde Pier Head - Shanklin

Owned Stations: All **Depot:** Ryde St Johns Road (RY)

Parent Company: First Group (70%), MTR (30%)

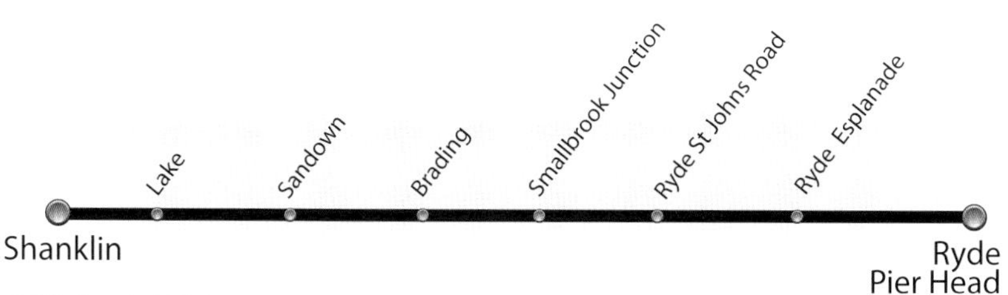

Class 483

Vehicle Length: 52ft 4in (15.95m)
Height: 9ft $5^{1}/_{2}$in (2.88m)
Width: 8ft $8^{1}/_{2}$in (2.65m)
Horsepower: 670hp (500kW)
Seats (total/car): 82S, 40S/42S

Number	*Formation DMSO+DMSO*	*Depot*	*Livery*	*Owner*	*Operator*
(483)002	122+222	RY	LUL	SWR	SWR §
(483)004	124+224	RY	LUL	SWR	SWR
(483)006	126+226	RY	LUL	SWR	SWR
(483)007	127+227	RY	LUL	SWR	SWR
(483)008	128+228	RY	LUL	SWR	SWR
(483)009	129+229	RY	LUL	SWR	SWR §

§ Stored out of service

■ In September 2019, a major upgrade of the Isle of Wight railway was announced, when an order for five Class 484 two-car electric sets was placed with Vivarail for delivery in 2020-2021. These will be rebuilds of former London Underground D-stock and the numbering will be 484001-484005. Delivery will be between 07/20-03/21.

Below: *The year 2020 should be the last year these 'old ladies', now in their 80s, will still be in service, as in September 2019 it was announced that five 'new' two car Class 484 sets, converted from ex-LUL 'D" stock would be introduced in 2020-2021. Carrying Island Line SWR branding, set No. 008 is seen at Sandown with a service for Shanklin on 26 August 2019.* **Antony Christie**

Govia Thameslink Railway

Address: Thameslink, Hertford House, 1 Cranwood Street, London, EC1V 9QS
icustomer service@thameslinkrailway.com ✆ 0345 0264700
ⓘ www.thameslinkrailway.com

Managing Director: Thameslink/GN - Tom Moran, Southern/Gatwick - Angie Doll

Franchise Dates: September 2014 - September 2021

Principal Routes: London Victoria/London Bridge to Brighton, 'Coastway' route, Uckfield/East Grinstead. Services to Surrey/Sussex, London King's Cross - King's Lynn, Peterborough/Cambridge, Moorgate - Hertford Loop/Letchworth, Bedford - Brighton/Sutton/Wimbledon

Depots: Bedford Cauldwell Walk (BF), Brighton (BI), Hornsey (HE), Selhurst (SU), Stewarts Lane (SL), Three Bridges (TB)

Parent Company: Govia

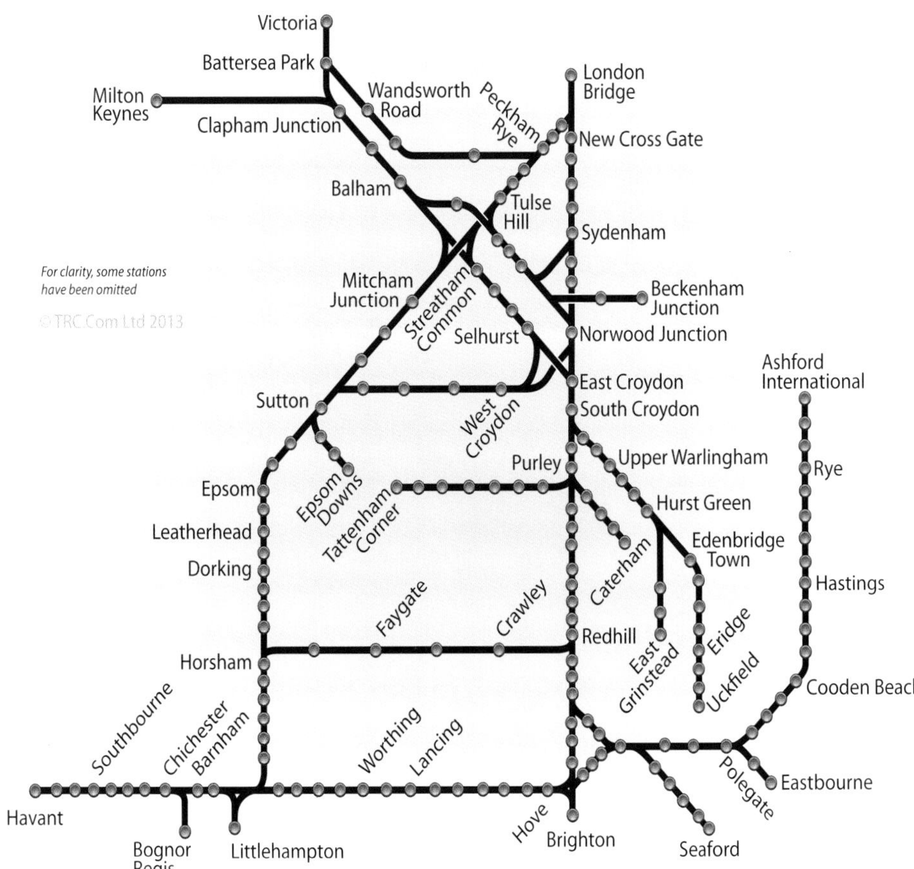

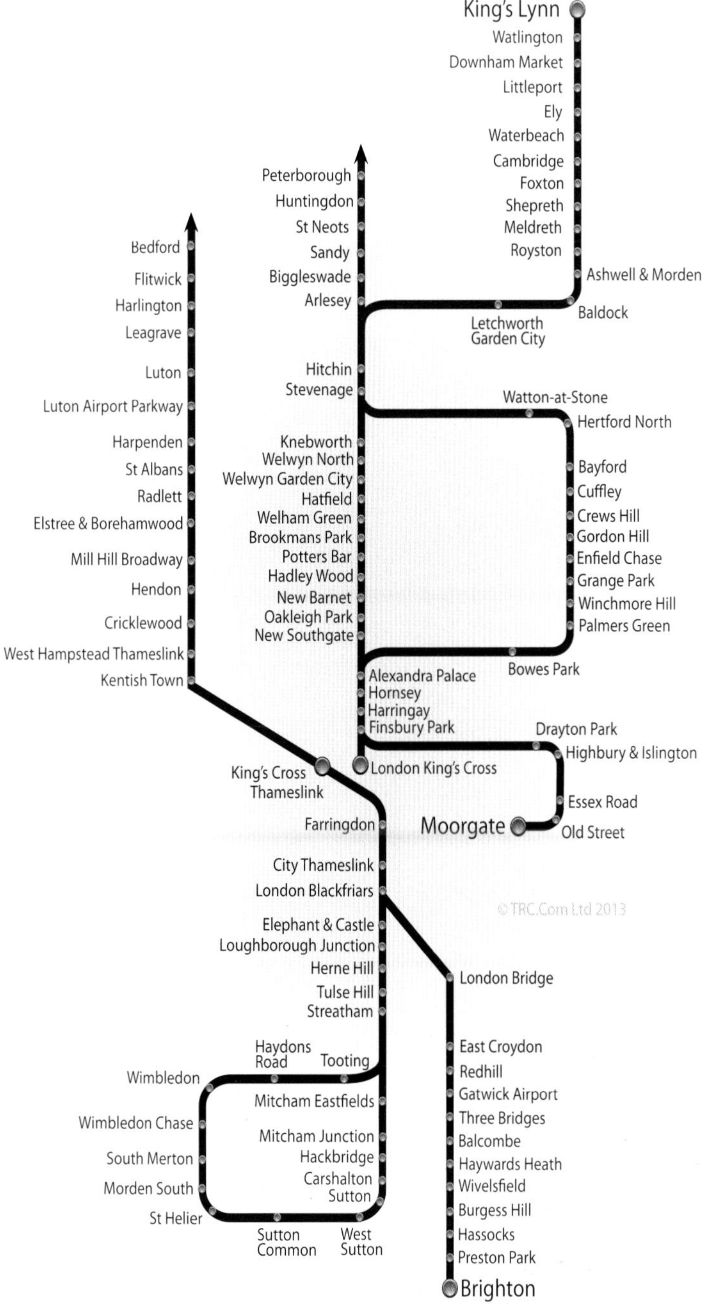
King's Lynn
Watlington
Downham Market
Littleport
Ely
Waterbeach
Cambridge
Foxton
Shepreth
Meldreth
Royston
Ashwell & Morden
Baldock
Letchworth Garden City
Peterborough
Huntingdon
St Neots
Sandy
Biggleswade
Arlesey
Hitchin
Stevenage
Watton-at-Stone
Hertford North
Bayford
Cuffley
Crews Hill
Gordon Hill
Enfield Chase
Grange Park
Winchmore Hill
Palmers Green
Bowes Park
Knebworth
Welwyn North
Welwyn Garden City
Hatfield
Welham Green
Brookmans Park
Potters Bar
Hadley Wood
New Barnet
Oakleigh Park
New Southgate
Alexandra Palace
Hornsey
Harringay
Finsbury Park
Drayton Park
Highbury & Islington
Essex Road
Old Street
Moorgate
London King's Cross
Bedford
Flitwick
Harlington
Leagrave
Luton
Luton Airport Parkway
Harpenden
St Albans
Radlett
Elstree & Borehamwood
Mill Hill Broadway
Hendon
Cricklewood
West Hampstead Thameslink
Kentish Town
King's Cross Thameslink
Farringdon
City Thameslink
London Blackfriars
Elephant & Castle
Loughborough Junction
Herne Hill
Tulse Hill
Streatham
Haydons Road
Tooting
Wimbledon
Wimbledon Chase
South Merton
Morden South
St Helier
Sutton Common
West Sutton
Mitcham Eastfields
Mitcham Junction
Hackbridge
Carshalton
Sutton
London Bridge
East Croydon
Redhill
Gatwick Airport
Three Bridges
Balcombe
Haywards Heath
Wivelsfield
Burgess Hill
Hassocks
Preston Park
Brighton
© TRC.Com Ltd 2013

Class 73/2

Vehicle Length: 53ft 8in (16.35m)
Height: 12ft $5^{5}/_{16}$in (3.79m)
Width: 8ft 8in (2.64m)
Power: 750V dc third rail or English Electric 6K
Horsepower: E/D - 1,600hp (1,193kW) / 600hp (447kW)
Electrical Equipment: English Electric

Number	*Depot*	*Pool*	*Livery*	*Owner*	*Operator*	*Name*
73202 (73137)	SL	MBED	SOU	PTR	GTR	*Graham Stenning*

Class 171/2 *Turbostar*

Vehicle Length: 77ft 6in (23.62m)
Height: 12ft $4^{1}/_{2}$in (3.77m)
Width: 8ft 10in (2.69m)
Engine: 1 x MTU 6R 183TD13H of 422hp per vehicle
Horsepower: 844hp (629kW)
Seats (total/car): 9F-107S 9F-43S/64S

Number	*Former Number*	*Formation DMCL+DMSL*	*Depot*	*Livery*	*Owner*	*Operator*
171201	(170421)	50421+79421	SU	SOU	EVL	GTR
171202	(170423)	50423+79423	SU	SOU	EVL	GTR

Class 171/4 *Turbostar*

Vehicle Length: 77ft 6in (23.62m)
Height: 12ft $4^{1}/_{2}$in (3.77m)
Width: 8ft 10in (2.69m)
Engine: 1 x MTU 6R 183TD13H of 422hp per vehicle
Horsepower: 1,688hp (1,259kW)
Seats (total/car): 9F-259S 9F-43S/76S/76S/64S

Number	*Former Number*	*Formation DMCL+MS+MS+DMSL*	*Depot*	*Livery*	*Owner*	*Operator*
171401	(170422)	50422+56421+56422+79422	SU	SOU	EVL	GTR
171402	(170424)	50424+56423+56424+79424	SU	SOU	EVL	GTR

Class 171/7 *Turbostar*

Vehicle Length: 77ft 6in (23.62m)
Height: 12ft $4^{1}/_{2}$in (3.77m)
Width: 8ft 10in (2.69m)
Engine: 1 x MTU 6R 183TD13H of 422hp per vehicle
Horsepower: 844hp (629kW)
Seats (total/car): 9F-107S 9F-43S/64S

Number	*Formation DMCL+DMSL*	*Depot*	*Livery*	*Owner*	*Operator*
171721	50721+79721	SU	SOU	PTR	GTR
171722	50722+79722	SU	SOU	PTR	GTR
171723	50723+79723	SU	SOU	PTR	GTR
171724	50724+79724	SU	SOU	PTR	GTR
171725	50725+79725	SU	SOU	PTR	GTR
171726	50726+79726	SU	SOU	PTR	GTR
171727	50727+79727	SU	SOU	PTR	GTR
171728	50728+79728	SU	SOU	PTR	GTR
171729	50729+79729	SU	SOU	PTR	GTR
171730	50392+79392	SU	SOU	PTR	GTR

171730 previously numbered 170392

Class 171/8 *Turbostar*

Vehicle Length: 77ft 6in (23.62m)
Height: 12ft $4^{1}/_{2}$in (3.77m)
Width: 8ft 10in (2.69m)
Engine: 1 x MTU 6R 183TD13H of 422hp per vehicle
Horsepower: 1,688hp (1,259kW)
Seats (total/car): 18F-241S 9F-43S/74S/74S/9F-50S

Number	*Formation DMCL(A)+MS+MS+DMCL(B)*	*Depot*	*Livery*	*Owner*	*Operator*
171801	50801+54801+56801+79801	SU	SOU	PTR	GTR
171802	50802+54802+56802+79802	SU	SOU	PTR	GTR
171803	50803+54803+56803+79803	SU	SOU	PTR	GTR
171804	50804+54804+56804+79804	SU	SOU	PTR	GTR
171805	50805+54805+56805+79805	SU	SOU	PTR	GTR
171806	50806+54806+56806+79806	SU	SOU	PTR	GTR

Left: *GTR currently operates a fleet of 18 Class 171 'Turbostar' sets in either two or four-car formations. The sets are scheduled to be transferred away from GTR in September 2021 and operate for East Midlands Railway. On GTR the sets are allocated to Selhurst and operate the few remaining non-electrified routes. Four car set No. 171801 is seen on the rear of an eight car formation passing Honor Oak Park. Slight front end detail differences exist on some sets. Members of Class 171/2 and 171/4 were previously Class 170s operating for ScotRail.* **CJM**

Class 313/2

Vehicle Length: (Driving) 64ft 11½in (20.75m) (Inter) 65ft 4½in (19.92m)
Height: 11ft 9in (3.58m)
Width: 9ft 3in (2.82m)
Horsepower: 880hp (656kW)
Seats (total/car): 202S, 66S/70S/66S

Number	*Formation* DMSO+PTSO+BDMSO	*Depot*	*Livery*	*Owner*	*Operator*
313201 (313001/101)	62529+71213+62593	BI	BLG	BEA	GTR
313202 (313002/102)	62530+71214+62594	BI	SOU	BEA	GTR
313203 (313003/103)	62531+71215+62595	BI	SOU	BEA	GTR
313204 (313004/104)	62532+71216+62596	BI	SOU	BEA	GTR
313205 (313005/105)	62533+71217+62597	BI	SOU	BEA	GTR
313206 (313006/106)	62534+71218+62598	BI	SOU	BEA	GTR
313207 (313007/107)	62535+71219+62599	BI	SOU	BEA	GTR
313208 (313008/108)	62536+71220+62600	BI	SOU	BEA	GTR
313209 (313009/109)	62537+71221+62601	BI	SOU	BEA	GTR
313210 (313010/110)	62538+71222+62602	BI	SOU	BEA	GTR
313211 (313011/111)	62539+71223+62603	BI	SOU	BEA	GTR
313212 (313012/112)	62540+71224+62604	BI	SOU	BEA	GTR
313213 (313013/113)	62541+71225+62605	BI	SOU	BEA	GTR
313214 (313014/114)	62542+71226+62606	BI	SOU	BEA	GTR
313215 (313015/115)	62543+71227+62607	BI	SOU	BEA	GTR
313216 (313016/116)	62544+71228+62608	BI	SOU	BEA	GTR
313217 (313017/117)	62545+71229+61609	BI	SOU	BEA	GTR
313219 (313019/119)	62547+71231+61611	BI	SOU	BEA	GTR
313220 (313020/120)	62548+71232+61612	BI	SOU	BEA	GTR

Right: *Following withdrawal of the GTR Class 313/0 and 313/1 sets used on GN electrified services in 2019, the only remaining Class 313s are the 19 sets based at Brighton for 'Coastway' services. These sets, painted in route specific 'Southern' colours are refurbished and sport 2+2 seating. The sets ac power equipment is no longer maintained. Set No. 313215 shows the pictogram branding applied in the middle of each vehicle, showing images of the Coastway route.*
Nathan Williamson

Class 365
Networker Express

Vehicle Length: (Driving) 68ft 6½in (20.89m) (Inter) 65ft 9¼in (20.89m)
Height: 12ft 4½in (3.77m)
Width: 9ft 2½in (2.81m)
Horsepower: 1,684hp (1,256kW)
Seats (total/car): 24F/239S, 12F-56S/59S/68S/12F-56S

Number	*Formation* DMCO(A)+TSO+PTSO+DMCO(B)	*Depot*	*Livery*	*Owner*	*Operator*	*Name*
365502	65895+72243+72242+65936	HE	TLK	DFT	GTR	
365504	65897+72247+72246+65938	HE	TLK	DFT	GTR	
365506	65899+72251+72250+65940	HE	TLK	DFT	GTR	
365508	65901+72255+72254+65942	HE	TLK	DFT	GTR	
365510	65903+72259+72258+65944	HE	TLK	DFT	GTR	
365511	65904+72261+72260+65945	HE	TLK	DFT	GTR	
365512	65905+72263+72262+65946	HE	TLK	DFT	GTR	
365514	65907+72267+72266+65948	HE	TLK	DFT	GTR	
365516	65909+72271+72270+65950	HE	TLK	DFT	GTR	
365518	65911+72275+72274+65952	HE	TLK	DFT	GTR	
365520	65913+72279+72278+65954	HE	TLK	DFT	GTR	
365522	65915+72283+72282+65956	HE	TLK	DFT	GTR	
365524	65917+72287+72286+65958	HE	TLK	DFT	GTR	
365528	65921+72295+72294+65962	HE	TLK	DFT	GTR	
365530	65923+72299+72298+65964	HE	TLK	DFT	GTR	
365532	65925+72303+72302+65966	HE	TLK	DFT	GTR	
365534	65927+72307+72306+65968	HE	TLK	DFT	GTR	
365536	65929+72311+72310+65970	HE	TLK	DFT	GTR	
365538	65931+72315+72314+65972	HE	TLK	DFT	GTR	

Govia Thameslink Railway

365539	65932+72317+72316+65973	HE	TLK	DFT	GTR
365540	65933+72319+72318+65974	HE	TLK	DFT	GTR

Left: *Now officially owned by the Department for Transport, with a number of sets off-lease and stored, 21 sets are still on GTRs books based at Hornsey and operate mainly peak hour services on the GN route from King's Cross. Set No. 365502 is illustrated passing Alexandra Palace heading towards King's Cross. The sets carry GTR white livery with Great Northern branding.* **Nathan Williamson**

Class 377/1
Electrostar

Vehicle Length: (Driving) 66ft 9in (20.3m) (Inter) 65ft 6in (19.96m) Height: 12ft 4in (3.75m) Width: 9ft 2in (2.79m) Horsepower: 2,012hp (1,500kW) Seats (total/car): 24F-210S or 244S 12F-48S(56S)/62S(70S)/52S(62S)/12F-48S(56S)

Number	*Formation* DMCO(A)+MSO+TSO+DMCO(B)	*Depot*	*Livery*	*Owner*	*Operator*
377101	78501+77101+78901+78701	SU	SOU	PTR	GTR
377102	78502+77102+78902+78702	SU	SOU	PTR	GTR
377103	78503+77103+78903+78703	SU	SOU	PTR	GTR
377104	78504+77104+78904+78704	SU	SOU	PTR	GTR
377105	78505+77105+78905+78705	SU	SOU	PTR	GTR
377106	78506+77106+78906+78706	SU	SOU	PTR	GTR
377107	78507+77107+78907+78707	SU	SOU	PTR	GTR
377108	78508+77108+78908+78708	SU	SOU	PTR	GTR
377109	78509+77109+78909+78709	SU	SOU	PTR	GTR
377110	78510+77110+78910+78710	SU	SOU	PTR	GTR
377111	78511+77111+78911+78711	SU	SOU	PTR	GTR
377112	78512+77112+78912+78712	SU	SOU	PTR	GTR
377113	78513+77113+78913+78713	SU	SOU	PTR	GTR
377114	78514+77114+78914+78714	SU	SOU	PTR	GTR
377115	78515+77115+78915+78715	SU	SOU	PTR	GTR
377116	78516+77116+78916+78716	SU	SOU	PTR	GTR
377117	78517+77117+78917+78717	SU	SOU	PTR	GTR
377118	78518+77118+78918+78718	SU	SOU	PTR	GTR
377119	78519+77119+78919+78719	SU	SOU	PTR	GTR
377120	78520+77120+78920+78720	SU	SOU	PTR	GTR
377121	78521+77121+78921+78721	SU	SOU	PTR	GTR
377122	78522+77122+78922+78722	SU	SOU	PTR	GTR
377123	78523+77123+78923+78723	SU	SOU	PTR	GTR
377124	78524+77124+78924+78724	SU	SOU	PTR	GTR
377125	78525+77125+78925+78725	SU	SOU	PTR	GTR
377126	78526+77126+78926+78726	SU	SOU	PTR	GTR
377127	78527+77127+78927+78727	SU	SOU	PTR	GTR
377128	78528+77128+78928+78728	SU	SOU	PTR	GTR
377129	78529+77129+78929+78729	SU	SOU	PTR	GTR
377130	78530+77130+78930+78730	SU	SOU	PTR	GTR
377131	78531+77131+78931+78731	SU	SOU	PTR	GTR
377132	78532+77132+78932+78732	SU	SOU	PTR	GTR
377133	78533+77133+78933+78733	SU	SOU	PTR	GTR
377134	78534+77134+78934+78734	SU	SOU	PTR	GTR
377135	78535+77135+78935+78735	SU	SOU	PTR	GTR
377136	78536+77136+78936+78736	SU	SOU	PTR	GTR
377137	78537+77137+78937+78737	SU	SOU	PTR	GTR
377138	78538+77138+78938+78738	SU	SOU	PTR	GTR
377139	78539+77139+78939+78739	SU	SOU	PTR	GTR
377140	78540+77140+78940+78740	SU	SOU	PTR	GTR

377141	78541+77141+78941+78741	SU	SOU	PTR	GTR
377142	78542+77142+78942+78742	SU	SOU	PTR	GTR
377143	78543+77143+78943+78743	SU	SOU	PTR	GTR
377144	78544+77144+78944+78744	SU	SOU	PTR	GTR
377145	78545+77145+78945+78745	SU	SOU	PTR	GTR
377146	78546+77146+78946+78746	SU	SOU	PTR	GTR
377147	78547+77147+78947+78747	SU	SOU	PTR	GTR
377148	78548+77148+78948+78748	SU	SOU	PTR	GTR
377149	78549+77149+78949+78749	SU	SOU	PTR	GTR
377150	78550+77150+78950+78750	SU	SOU	PTR	GTR
377151	78551+77151+78951+78751	SU	SOU	PTR	GTR
377152	78552+77152+78952+78752	SU	SOU	PTR	GTR
377153	78553+77153+78953+78753	SU	SOU	PTR	GTR
377154	78554+77154+78954+78754	SU	SOU	PTR	GTR
377155	78555+77155+78955+78755	SU	SOU	PTR	GTR
377156	78556+77156+78956+78756	SU	SOU	PTR	GTR
377157	78557+77157+78957+78757	SU	SOU	PTR	GTR
377158	78558+77158+78958+78758	SU	SOU	PTR	GTR
377159	78559+77159+78959+78759	SU	SOU	PTR	GTR
377160	78560+77160+78960+78760	SU	SOU	PTR	GTR
377161	78561+77161+78961+78761	SU	SOU	PTR	GTR
377162	78562+77162+78962+78762	SU	SOU	PTR	GTR
377163	78563+77163+78963+78763	RE	SOU	PTR	SET (on hire)
377164	78564+77164+78964+78764	RE	SOU	PTR	SET (on hire)

Right: *Main line traction operating on GTR Southern services are in the hands of various sub-classes of Class 377 'Electrostar' stock. All sets are of the same appearance, but many minor detail differences can be found, including seating and front end design with different types of light clusters. A total of 64 Class 377/1s are in service, Southern operates 62 sets with two on loan to SouthEastern at Ramsgate. Set No. 377142 leads an eight-car formation south through Honor Oak Park.* **CJM**

Class 377/2
Electrostar

Vehicle Length: (Driving) 66ft 9in (20.3m)
(Inter) 65ft 6in (19.96m)
Height: 12ft 4in (3.75m)
Width: 9ft 2in (2.79m)
Horsepower: 2,012hp (1,500kW)
Seats (total/car): 24F-222S, 12F-48S/69S/57S/12F-48S

Number	*Formation* DMCO(A)+MSO+PTSO+DMCO(B)	*Depot*	*Livery*	*Owner*	*Operator*
377201	78571+77171+78971+78771	SU	SOU	PTR	GTR
377202	78572+77172+78972+78772	SU	SOU	PTR	GTR
377203	78573+77173+78973+78773	SU	SOU	PTR	GTR
377204	78574+77174+78974+78774	SU	SOU	PTR	GTR
377205	78575+77175+78975+78775	SU	SOU	PTR	GTR
377206	78576+77176+78976+78776	SU	SOU	PTR	GTR
377207	78577+77177+78977+78777	SU	SOU	PTR	GTR
377208	78578+77178+78978+78778	SU	SOU	PTR	GTR
377209	78579+77179+78979+78779	SU	SOU	PTR	GTR
377210	78580+77180+78980+78780	SU	SOU	PTR	GTR
377211	78581+77181+78981+78781	SU	SOU	PTR	GTR
377212	78582+77182+78982+78782	SU	SOU	PTR	GTR
377213	78583+77183+78983+78783	SU	SOU	PTR	GTR
377214	78584+77184+78984+78784	SU	SOU	PTR	GTR
377215	78585+77185+78985+78785	SU	SOU	PTR	GTR

Govia Thameslink Railway

Left: *The 15 strong Class 377/2 fleet are dual voltage sets, able to operate from either 750V dc third rail or 25kV ac overhead. The sets are thus used on cross London services by way of Kensington Olympia on the Croydon-Milton Keynes route. Set No. 377207 leads another unit past South Kenton.* **CJM**

Class 377/3
Electrostar

Vehicle Length: (Driving) 66ft 9in (20.3m) (Inter) 65ft 6in (19.96m)
Height: 12ft 4in (3.75m)
Width: 9ft 2in (2.79m)
Horsepower: 2,012hp (1,500kW)
Seats (total/car): 12F-163S, 60S/56S/12F-48S

Number	*Formation* DMSO+TSO+DMCO	*Depot*	*Livery*	*Owner*	*Operator*
377301 (375311)	68201+74801+68401	SU	SOU	PTR	GTR
377302 (375312)	68202+74802+68402	SU	SOU	PTR	GTR
377303 (375313)	68203+74803+68403	SU	SOU	PTR	GTR
377304 (375314)	68204+74804+68404	SU	SOU	PTR	GTR
377305 (375315)	68205+74805+68405	SU	SOU	PTR	GTR
377306 (375316)	68206+74806+68406	SU	SOU	PTR	GTR
377307 (375317)	68207+74807+68407	SU	SOU	PTR	GTR
377308 (375318)	68208+74808+68408	SU	SOU	PTR	GTR
377309 (375319)	68209+74809+68409	SU	SOU	PTR	GTR
377310 (375320)	68210+74810+68410	SU	SOU	PTR	GTR
377311 (375321)	68211+74811+68411	SU	SOU	PTR	GTR
377312 (375322)	68212+74812+68412	SU	SOU	PTR	GTR
377313 (375323)	68213+74813+68413	SU	SOU	PTR	GTR
377314 (375324)	68214+74814+68414	SU	SOU	PTR	GTR
377315 (375325)	68215+74815+68415	SU	SOU	PTR	GTR
377316 (375326)	68216+74816+68416	SU	SOU	PTR	GTR
377317 (375327)	68217+74817+68417	SU	SOU	PTR	GTR
377318 (375328)	68218+74818+68418	SU	SOU	PTR	GTR
377319 (375329)	68219+74819+68419	SU	SOU	PTR	GTR
377320 (375330)	68220+74820+68420	SU	SOU	PTR	GTR
377321 (375331)	68221+74821+68421	SU	SOU	PTR	GTR
377322 (375332)	68222+74822+68422	SU	SOU	PTR	GTR
377323 (375333)	68223+74823+68423	SU	SOU	PTR	GTR
377324 (375334)	68224+74824+68424	SU	SOU	PTR	GTR
377325 (375335)	68225+74825+68425	SU	SOU	PTR	GTR
377326 (375336)	68226+74826+68426	SU	SOU	PTR	GTR
377327 (375337)	68227+74827+68427	SU	SOU	PTR	GTR
377328 (375338)	68228+74828+68428	SU	SOU	PTR	GTR

Left: *A fleet of 28 three-car Class 377/3s are based at Selhurst and either operate lightly used routes or work in formations of three or four sets to form longer trains or operate with four car sets to form seven or ten car trains. The sets carry standard Southern livery and have first class accommodation in one driving car, located directly behind the driving cab. Set No. 377323 is seen at Clapham Junction.* **Antony Christie**

Class 377/4
Electrostar

Vehicle Length: (Driving) 66ft 9in (20.3m)
(Inter) 65ft 6in (19.96m)
Height: 12ft 4in (3.75m)
Width: 9ft 2in (2.79m)
Horsepower: 2,012hp (1,500kW)
Seats (total/car): 20F-221S, 10F-48S/69S/56S/10F-48S

Number	*Formation* DMCO(A)+MSO+TSO+DMCO(B)	*Depot*	*Livery*	*Owner*	*Operator*
377401	73401+78801+78601+73801	SU	SOU	PTR	GTR
377402	73402+78802+78602+73802	SU	SOU	PTR	GTR
377403	73403+78803+78603+73803	SU	SOU	PTR	GTR
377404	73404+78804+78604+73804	SU	SOU	PTR	GTR
377405	73405+78805+78605+73805	SU	SOU	PTR	GTR
377406	73406+78806+78606+73806	SU	SOU	PTR	GTR
377407	73407+78807+78607+73807	SU	SOU	PTR	GTR
377408	73408+78808+78608+73808	SU	SOU	PTR	GTR
377409	73409+78809+78609+73809	SU	SOU	PTR	GTR
377410	73410+78810+78610+73810	SU	SOU	PTR	GTR
377411	73411+78811+78611+73811	SU	SOU	PTR	GTR
377412	73412+78812+78612+73812	SU	SOU	PTR	GTR
377413	73413+78813+78613+73813	SU	SOU	PTR	GTR
377414	73414+78814+78614+73814	SU	SOU	PTR	GTR
377415	73415+78815+78615+73815	SU	SOU	PTR	GTR
377416	73416+78816+78616+73816	SU	SOU	PTR	GTR
377417	73417+78817+78617+73817	SU	SOU	PTR	GTR
377418	73418+78818+78618+73818	SU	SOU	PTR	GTR
377419	73419+78819+78619+73819	SU	SOU	PTR	GTR
377420	73420+78820+78620+73820	SU	SOU	PTR	GTR
377421	73421+78821+78621+73821	SU	SOU	PTR	GTR
377422	73422+78822+78622+73822	SU	SOU	PTR	GTR
377423	73423+78823+78623+73823	SU	SOU	PTR	GTR
377424	73424+78824+78624+73824	SU	SOU	PTR	GTR
377425	73425+78825+78625+73825	SU	SOU	PTR	GTR
377426	73426+78826+78626+73826	SU	SOU	PTR	GTR
377427	73427+78827+78627+73827	SU	SOU	PTR	GTR
377428	73428+78828+78628+73828	SU	SOU	PTR	GTR
377429	73429+78829+78629+73829	SU	SOU	PTR	GTR
377430	73430+78830+78630+73830	SU	SOU	PTR	GTR
377431	73431+78831+78631+73831	SU	SOU	PTR	GTR
377432	73432+78832+78632+73832	SU	SOU	PTR	GTR
377433	73433+78833+78633+73833	SU	SOU	PTR	GTR
377434	73434+78834+78634+73834	SU	SOU	PTR	GTR
377435	73435+78835+78635+73835	SU	SOU	PTR	GTR
377436	73436+78836+78636+73836	SU	SOU	PTR	GTR
377437	73437+78837+78637+73837	SU	SOU	PTR	GTR
377438	73438+78838+78638+73838	SU	SOU	PTR	GTR
377439	73439+78839+78639+73839	SU	SOU	PTR	GTR
377440	73440+78840+78640+73840	SU	SOU	PTR	GTR
377441	73441+78841+78641+73841	SU	SOU	PTR	GTR
377342	73442+78642+73842	SU	SOU	PTR	GTR (Temp reduced to three car)
377443	73443+78843+78643+73843	SU	SOU	PTR	GTR
377444	73444+78844+78644+73844	SU	SOU	PTR	GTR
377445	73445+78845+78645+73845	SU	SOU	PTR	GTR
377446	73446+78846+78646+73846	SU	SOU	PTR	GTR
377447	73447+78847+78647+73847	SU	SOU	PTR	GTR
377448	73448+78848+78648+73848	SU	SOU	PTR	GTR
377449	73449+78849+78649+73849	SU	SOU	PTR	GTR
377450	73450+78850+78650+73850	SU	SOU	PTR	GTR
377451	73451+78851+78651+73851	SU	SOU	PTR	GTR
377452	73452+78852+78652+73852	SU	SOU	PTR	GTR
377453	73453+78853+78653+73853	SU	SOU	PTR	GTR
377454	73454+78854+78654+73854	SU	SOU	PTR	GTR
377455	73455+78855+78655+73855	SU	SOU	PTR	GTR
377456	73456+78856+78656+73856	SU	SOU	PTR	GTR
377457	73457+78857+78657+73857	SU	SOU	PTR	GTR
377458	73458+78858+78658+73858	SU	SOU	PTR	GTR

377459	73459+78859+78659+73859	SU	SOU	PTR	GTR
377460	73460+78860+78660+73860	SU	SOU	PTR	GTR
377461	73461+78861+78661+73861	SU	SOU	PTR	GTR
377462	73462+78862+78662+73862	SU	SOU	PTR	GTR
377463	73463+78863+78663+73863	SU	SOU	PTR	GTR
377464	73464+78864+78664+73864	SU	SOU	PTR	GTR
377465	73465+78865+78665+73865	SU	SOU	PTR	GTR
377466	73466+78866+78666+73866	SU	SOU	PTR	GTR
377467	73467+78867+78667+73867	SU	SOU	PTR	GTR
377468	73468+78868+78668+73868	SU	SOU	PTR	GTR
377469	73469+78869+78669+73869	SU	SOU	PTR	GTR
377470	73470+78870+78670+73870	SU	SOU	PTR	GTR
377471	73471+78871+78671+73871	SU	SOU	PTR	GTR
377472	73472+78872+78672+73872	SU	SOU	PTR	GTR
377473	73473+78873+78673+73873	SU	SOU	PTR	GTR
377474	73474+78874+78674+73874	SU	SOU	PTR	GTR
377475	73475+78875+78675+73875	SU	SOU	PTR	GTR

Left: *The most numerous of the Class 377 builds is the Class 377/4 with 75 sets in service, based at Selhurst. Set No. 377453, operating on its own, passes through Honor Oak Park on the southbound main track.* **CJM**

Class 377/6
Electrostar

Vehicle Length: (Driving) 66ft 9in (20.3m) (Inter) 65ft 6in (19.96m)
Height: 12ft 4in (3.75m)
Width: 9ft 2in (2.79m)
Horsepower: 2,012hp (1,500kW)
Seats (total/car): 298S-60S/64S/46S/66S/62S

Number	*Formation* DMCO(A)+MSO+TSO+MSO+DMSO(B)	*Depot*	*Livery*	*Owner*	*Operator*
377601	70101+70201+70301+70401+70501	SU	SOU	PTR	GTR
377602	70102+70202+70302+70402+70502	SU	SOU	PTR	GTR
377603	70103+70203+70303+70403+70503	SU	SOU	PTR	GTR
377604	70104+70204+70304+70404+70504	SU	SOU	PTR	GTR
377605	70105+70205+70305+70405+70505	SU	SOU	PTR	GTR
377606	70106+70206+70306+70406+70506	SU	SOU	PTR	GTR
377607	70107+70207+70307+70407+70507	SU	SOU	PTR	GTR
377608	70108+70208+70308+70408+70508	SU	SOU	PTR	GTR
377609	70109+70209+70309+70409+70509	SU	SOU	PTR	GTR
377610	70110+70210+70310+70410+70510	SU	SOU	PTR	GTR
377611	70111+70211+70311+70411+70511	SU	SOU	PTR	GTR
377612	70112+70212+70312+70412+70512	SU	SOU	PTR	GTR
377613	70113+70213+70313+70413+70513	SU	SOU	PTR	GTR
377614	70114+70214+70314+70414+70514	SU	SOU	PTR	GTR
377615	70115+70215+70315+70415+70515	SU	SOU	PTR	GTR
377616	70116+70216+70316+70416+70516	SU	SOU	PTR	GTR
377617	70117+70217+70317+70417+70517	SU	SOU	PTR	GTR
377618	70118+70218+70318+70418+70518	SU	SOU	PTR	GTR
377619	70119+70219+70319+70419+70519	SU	SOU	PTR	GTR
377620	70120+70220+70320+70420+70520	SU	SOU	PTR	GTR
377621	70121+70221+70321+70421+70521	SU	SOU	PTR	GTR
377622	70122+70222+70322+70422+70522	SU	SOU	PTR	GTR
377623	70123+70223+70323+70423+70523	SU	SOU	PTR	GTR
377624	70124+70224+70324+70424+70524	SU	SOU	PTR	GTR
377625	70125+70225+70325+70425+70525	SU	SOU	PTR	GTR
377626	70126+70226+70326+70426+70526	SU	SOU	PTR	GTR

Right: *In 2013-2014 two fleets of five-car 'Electrostar' units were introduced in an attempt to reduce overcrowding. 26 dc only and 8 dual-voltage sets were built, the 377/6 sets being third rail only and the 377/7s being dual voltage. The final set of the Class 377/6 build No. 377626 with its DTC coach nearest the camera is seen at Forest Hill.* **CJM**

Class 377/7
Electrostar

Vehicle Length: (Driving) 66ft 9in (20.3m) Width: 9ft 2in (2.79m)
(Inter) 65ft 6in (19.96m) Horsepower: 2,012hp (1,500kW)
Height: 12ft 4in (3.75m) Seats (total/car): 298S-60S/64S/46S/66S/62S
Dual-voltage sets

Number	*Formation* DMSO(A)+MSO+TSO+MSO+DMSO(B)	*Depot*	*Livery*	*Owner*	*Operator*
377701	65201+70601+65601+70701+65401	SU	SOU	PTR	GTR
377702	65202+70602+65602+70702+65402	SU	SOU	PTR	GTR
377703	65203+70603+65603+70703+65403	SU	SOU	PTR	GTR
377704	65204+70604+65604+70704+65404	SU	SOU	PTR	GTR
377705	65205+70605+65605+70705+65405	SU	SOU	PTR	GTR
377706	65206+70606+65606+70706+65406	SU	SOU	PTR	GTR
377707	65207+70607+65607+70707+65407	SU	SOU	PTR	GTR
377708	65208+70608+65608+70708+65408	SU	SOU	PTR	GTR

Class 387/1
Electrostar

Vehicle Length: (Driving) 66ft 9in (20.3m) Width: 9ft 2in (2.79m)
(Inter) 65ft 6in (19.96m) Horsepower: 2,012hp (1,500kW)
Height: 12ft 4in (3.75m) Seats (total/car): 22F/201S, 22F/34S/62S/45S/60S

Number	*Formation* DMCO+MSO+TSO+DMSO	*Depot*	*Livery*	*Owner*	*Operator*
387101	421101+422101+423101+424101	HE	TMK	PTR	GTR
387102	421102+422102+423102+424102	HE	TMK	PTR	GTR
387103	421103+422103+423103+424103	HE	TMK	PTR	GTR
387104	421104+422104+423104+424104	HE	TMK	PTR	GTR
387105	421105+422105+423105+424105	SL	TMK	PTR	GTR (working for GatEx)
387106	421106+422106+423106+424106	HE	TMK	PTR	GTR
387107	421107+422107+423107+424107	HE	TMK	PTR	GTR
387108	421108+422108+423108+424108	HE	TMK	PTR	GTR
387109	421109+422109+423109+424109	HE	TMK	PTR	GTR
387110	421110+422110+423110+424110	HE	TMK	PTR	GTR
387111	421111+422111+423111+424111	HE	TMK	PTR	GTR
387112	421112+422112+423112+424112	HE	TMK	PTR	GTR
387113	421113+422113+423113+424113	HE	TMK	PTR	GTR
387114	421114+422114+423114+424114	HE	TMK	PTR	GTR
387115	421115+422115+423115+424115	HE	TMK	PTR	GTR
387116	421116+422116+423116+424116	HE	TMK	PTR	GTR
387117	421117+422117+423117+424117	HE	TMK	PTR	GTR

Right: *In 2014-2015 a fleet of 29 four-car Class 387/1 'Electrostar' sets were introduced and are now deployed on GTR Great Northern services, to locations such as Peterborough and Kings Lynn. Based at Hornsey, the sets have limited first class accommodation in one driving car. No. 378121, in need of a wash, passes Wellham Green with a Kings Lynn bound service on 9 April 2019.* **CJM**

387118	421118+422118+423118+424118	HE	TMK	PTR	GTR
387119	421119+422119+423119+424119	HE	TMK	PTR	GTR
387120	421120+422120+423120+424120	HE	TMK	PTR	GTR
387121	421121+422121+423121+424121	HE	TMK	PTR	GTR
387122	421122+422122+423122+424122	HE	TMK	PTR	GTR
387123	421123+422123+423123+424123	HE	TMK	PTR	GTR
387124	421124+422124+423124+424124	HE	TMK	PTR	GTR
387125	421125+422125+423125+424125	HE	TMK	PTR	GTR
387126	421126+422126+423126+424126	HE	TMK	PTR	GTR
387127	421127+422127+423127+424127	HE	TMK	PTR	GTR
387128	421128+422128+423128+424128	HE	TMK	PTR	GTR
387129	421129+422129+423129+424129	HE	TMK	PTR	GTR

Class 387/2
Electrostar

Vehicle Length: (Driving) 66ft 9in (20.3m)
(Inter) 65ft 6in (19.96m)
Height: 12ft 4in (3.75m)
Width: 9ft 2in (2.79m)
Horsepower: 2,012hp (1,500kW)
Seats (total/car): 201S/22F

Number	*Formation* DMCO+MSO+PTSO+DMSO	*Depot*	*Livery*	*Owner*	*Operator*
387201	421201+422201+423201+424201	SL	GAT	PTR	GTR
387202	421202+422202+423202+424202	SL	GAT	PTR	GTR
387203	421203+422203+423203+424203	SL	GAT	PTR	GTR
387204	421204+422204+423204+424204	SL	GAT	PTR	GTR
387205	421205+422205+423205+424205	SL	GAT	PTR	GTR
387206	421206+422206+423206+424206	SL	GAT	PTR	GTR
387207	421207+422207+423207+424207	SL	GAT	PTR	GTR
387208	421208+422208+423208+424208	SL	GAT	PTR	GTR
387209	421209+422209+423209+424209	SL	GAT	PTR	GTR
387210	421210+422210+423210+424210	SL	GAT	PTR	GTR
387211	421211+422211+423211+424211	SL	GAT	PTR	GTR
387212	421212+422212+423212+424212	SL	GAT	PTR	GTR
387213	421213+422213+423213+424213	SL	GAT	PTR	GTR
387214	421214+422214+423214+424214	SL	GAT	PTR	GTR
387215	421215+422215+423215+424215	SL	GAT	PTR	GTR
387216	421216+422216+423216+424216	SL	GAT	PTR	GTR
387217	421217+422217+423217+424217	SL	GAT	PTR	GTR
387218	421218+422218+423218+424218	SL	GAT	PTR	GTR
387219	421219+422219+423219+424219	SL	GAT	PTR	GTR
387220	421220+422220+423220+424220	SL	GAT	PTR	GTR
387221	421221+422221+423221+424221	SL	GAT	PTR	GTR
387222	421222+422222+423222+424222	SL	GAT	PTR	GTR
387223	421223+422223+423223+424223	SL	GAT	PTR	GTR
387224	421224+422224+423224+424224	SL	GAT	PTR	GTR
387225	421225+422225+423225+424225	SL	GAT	PTR	GTR
387226	421226+422226+423226+424226	SL	GAT	PTR	GTR
387227	421227+422227+423227+424227	SL	GAT	PTR	GTR

Left: *The important Gatwick Express operation, linking London Victoria with Gatwick Airport every 13 minutes, is operated by a dedicated fleet of 27 Class 378/2s, based at Stewarts Lane. The sets are painted in bright red with grey passenger doors and Gatwick Express branding. The sets are standard 'Electrostar' units. Set No. 378217 leads a train bound for Gatwick Airport through Clapham Junction.* **Antony Christie**

Class 455/8

Vehicle Length: (Driving) 65ft 0½in (19.83m)
(Inter) 65ft 4½in (19.92m)
Height: 12ft 1½in (3.79m)
Width: 9ft 3¼in (2.82m)
Horsepower: 1,000hp (746kW)
Seats (total/car): 310S, 74S/78S/84S/74S

Number	Formation DTSO(A)+MSO+TSO+DTSO(B)	Depot	Livery	Owner	Operator
455801	77627+62709+71657+77580	SL	SOU	EVL	GTR
455802	77581+62710+71664+77582	SL	SOU	EVL	GTR
455803	77583+62711+71639+77584	SL	SOU	EVL	GTR
455804	77585+62712+71640+77586	SL	SOU	EVL	GTR
455805	77587+62713+71641+77588	SL	SOU	EVL	GTR
455806	77589+62714+71642+77590	SL	SOU	EVL	GTR
455807	77591+62715+71643+77592	SL	SOU	EVL	GTR
455808	77637+62716+71644+77594	SL	SOU	EVL	GTR
455809	77623+62717+71648+77602	SL	SOU	EVL	GTR
455810	77597+62718+71646+77598	SL	SOU	EVL	GTR
455811	77599+62719+71647+77600	SL	SOU	EVL	GTR
455812	77595+62720+71645+77626	SL	SOU	EVL	GTR
455813	77603+62721+71649+77604	SL	SOU	EVL	GTR
455814	77605+62722+71650+77606	SL	SOU	EVL	GTR
455815	77607+62723+71651+77608	SL	SOU	EVL	GTR
455816	77609+62724+71652+77633	SL	SOU	EVL	GTR
455817	77611+62725+71653+77612	SL	SOU	EVL	GTR
455818	77613+62726+71654+77632	SL	SOU	EVL	GTR
455819	77615+62727+71637+77616	SL	SOU	EVL	GTR
455820	77617+62728+71656+77618	SL	SOU	EVL	GTR
455821	77619+62729+71655+77620	SL	SOU	EVL	GTR
455822	77621+62730+71658+77622	SL	SOU	EVL	GTR
455823	77601+62731+71659+77596	SL	SOU	EVL	GTR
455824	77593+62732+71660+77624	SL	SOU	EVL	GTR
455825	77579+62733+71661+77628	SL	SOU	EVL	GTR
455826	77630+62734+71662+77629	SL	SOU	EVL	GTR
455827	77610+62735+71663+77614	SL	SOU	EVL	GTR
455828	77631+62736+71638+77634	SL	SOU	EVL	GTR
455829	77635+62737+71665+77636	SL	SOU	EVL	GTR
455830	77625+62743+71666+77638	SL	SOU	EVL	GTR
455831	77639+62739+71667+77640	SL	SOU	EVL	GTR
455832	77641+62740+71668+77642	SL	SOU	EVL	GTR
455833	77643+62741+71669+77644	SL	SOU	EVL	GTR
455834	77645+62742+71670+77646	SL	SOU	EVL	GTR
455835	77647+62738+71671+77648	SL	SOU	EVL	GTR
455836	77649+62744+71672+77650	SL	SOU	EVL	GTR
455837	77651+62745+71673+77652	SL	SOU	EVL	GTR
455838	77653+62746+71674+77654	SL	SOU	EVL	GTR
455839	77655+62747+71675+77656	SL	SOU	EVL	GTR
455840	77657+62748+71676+77658	SL	SOU	EVL	GTR
455841	77659+62749+71677+77660	SL	SOU	EVL	GTR
455842	77661+62750+71678+77662	SL	SOU	EVL	GTR
455843	77663+62751+71679+77664	SL	SOU	EVL	GTR
455844	77665+62752+71680+77666	SL	SOU	EVL	GTR
455845	77667+62753+71681+77668	SL	SOU	EVL	GTR
455846	77669+62754+71682+77670	SL	SOU	EVL	GTR

Right: *Southern local or Metro services operating from Victoria or London Bridge are formed of Class 455 stock, with 46 four car sets allocated to Stewarts Lane. These high-density sets have all been refurbished, during which their original front end gangways were removed in favour of installing cab air conditioning. Sets are painted in standard GTR Southern white and green livery. Set No. 455808 is seen at Forest Hill.* **CJM**

Govia Thameslink Railway

Class 700
Desiro City

Vehicle Length: (Driving) 20m
(Inter) 20m
Height: 3.79m
Seats (total/car): 8-car - 52F/375S, 18F,26S/54S/64S/56S/40S/64S/54S/28F, 16S
12-car 52F/614S, 26F, 20S/54S/60S/56S/64S/56S/38S/64S/56S/60S/54S/26F, 20S
Weight: 278tonne/410 tonne
Power output: 3.3/5.0MW

Left: *The impressive Thameslink operation linking north and south London via Blackfriars and tunnels below London, is operated by a fleet of Class 700s, sixty sets are eight-car formations, known as Reduced Length Units (RLU), classified as 700/0. The Siemens Desiro City sets are based at Three Bridges. No. 700054 pulls into St Pancras International (Thameslink) with a service travelling south. From late 2019 trains have been operated through the 'core' section using Automatic Train Operation (ATO).* **CJM**

Number	*Formation (RLU - Reduced Length Units)* *DMCO+PTSO+MSO+TSO+TSO+MSO+PTSO+DMCO*	*Depot*	*Livery*	*Owner*	*Operator*
700001	401001+402001+403001+406001+407001+410001+411001+412001	TB	TMK	UKG	GTR
700002	401002+402002+403002+406002+407002+410002+411002+412002	TB	TMK	UKG	GTR
700003	401003+402003+403003+406003+407003+410003+411003+412003	TB	TMK	UKG	GTR
700004	401004+402004+403004+406004+407004+410004+411004+412004	TB	TMK	UKG	GTR
700005	401005+402005+403005+406005+407005+410005+411005+412005	TB	TMK	UKG	GTR
700006	401006+402006+403006+406006+407006+410006+411006+412006	TB	TMK	UKG	GTR
700007	401007+402007+403007+406007+407007+410007+411007+412007	TB	TMK	UKG	GTR
700008	401008+402008+403008+406008+407008+410008+411008+412008	TB	TMK	UKG	GTR
700009	401009+402009+403009+406009+407009+410009+411009+412009	TB	TMK	UKG	GTR
700010	401010+402010+403010+406010+407010+410010+411010+412010	TB	TMK	UKG	GTR
700011	401011+402011+403011+406011+407011+410011+411011+412011	TB	TMK	UKG	GTR
700012	401012+402012+403012+406012+407012+410012+411012+412012	TB	TMK	UKG	GTR
700013	401013+402013+403013+406013+407013+410013+411013+412013	TB	TMK	UKG	GTR
700014	401014+402014+403014+406014+407014+410014+411014+412014	TB	TMK	UKG	GTR
700015	401015+402015+403015+406015+407015+410015+411015+412015	TB	TMK	UKG	GTR
700016	401016+402016+403016+406016+407016+410016+411016+412016	TB	TMK	UKG	GTR
700017	401017+402017+403017+406017+407017+410017+411017+412016	TB	TMK	UKG	GTR
700018	401018+402018+403018+406018+407018+410018+411018+412018	TB	TMK	UKG	GTR
700019	401019+402019+403019+406019+407019+410019+411019+412019	TB	TMK	UKG	GTR
700020	401020+402020+403020+406020+407020+410020+411020+412020	TB	TMK	UKG	GTR
700021	401021+402021+403021+406021+407021+410021+411021+412021	TB	TMK	UKG	GTR
700022	401022+402022+403022+406022+407022+410022+411022+412022	TB	TMK	UKG	GTR
700023	401023+402023+403023+406023+407023+410023+411023+412023	TB	TMK	UKG	GTR
700024	401024+402024+403024+406024+407024+410024+411024+412024	TB	TMK	UKG	GTR
700025	401025+402025+403025+406025+407025+410025+411025+412025	TB	TMK	UKG	GTR
700026	401026+402026+403026+406026+407026+410026+411026+412026	TB	TMK	UKG	GTR
700027	401027+402027+403027+406027+407027+410027+411027+412027	TB	TMK	UKG	GTR
700028	401028+402028+403028+406028+407028+410028+411028+412028	TB	TMK	UKG	GTR
700029	401029+402029+403029+406029+407029+410029+411029+412029	TB	TMK	UKG	GTR
700030	410030+402030+403030+406030+407030+410030+411030+412030	TB	TMK	UKG	GTR
700031	401031+402031+403031+406031+407031+410031+411031+412031	TB	TMK	UKG	GTR
700032	401032+402032+403032+406032+407032+410032+411032+412032	TB	TMK	UKG	GTR
700033	401033+402033+403033+406033+407033+410033+411033+412033	TB	TMK	UKG	GTR
700034	401034+402034+403034+406034+407034+410034+411034+412034	TB	TMK	UKG	GTR
700035	401035+402035+403035+406035+407035+410035+411035+412035	TB	TMK	UKG	GTR
700036	401036+402036+403036+406036+407036+410036+411036+412036	TB	TMK	UKG	GTR
700037	401037+402037+403037+406037+407037+410037+411037+412037	TB	TMK	UKG	GTR
700038	401038+402038+403038+406038+407038+410038+411038+412038	TB	TMK	UKG	GTR
700039	401039+402039+403039+406039+407039+410039+411039+412039	TB	TMK	UKG	GTR
700040	401040+402040+403040+406040+407040+410040+411040+412040	TB	TMK	UKG	GTR
700041	401041+402041+403041+406041+407041+410041+411041+412041	TB	TMK	UKG	GTR

700042	401042+402042+403042+406042+407042+410042+411042+412042	TB	TMK	UKG	GTR
700043	401043+402043+403043+406043+407043+410043+411043+412043	TB	TMK	UKG	GTR
700044	401044+402044+403044+406044+407044+410044+411044+412044	TB	TMK	UKG	GTR
700045	401045+402045+403045+406045+407045+410045+411045+412045	TB	TMK	UKG	GTR
700046	401046+402046+403046+406046+407046+410046+411046+412046	TB	TMK	UKG	GTR
700047	401047+402047+403047+406047+407047+410047+411047+412047	TB	TMK	UKG	GTR
700048	401048+402048+403048+406048+407048+410048+411048+412048	TB	TMK	UKG	GTR
700049	401049+402049+403049+406049+407049+410049+411049+412049	TB	TMK	UKG	GTR
700050	401050+402050+403050+406050+407050+410050+411050+412050	TB	TMK	UKG	GTR
700051	401051+402051+403051+406051+407051+410051+411051+412051	TB	TMK	UKG	GTR
700052	401052+402052+403052+406052+407052+410052+411052+412052	TB	TMK	UKG	GTR
700053	401053+402053+403053+406053+407053+410053+411053+412053	TB	TMK	UKG	GTR
700054	401054+402054+403054+406054+407054+410054+411054+412054	TB	TMK	UKG	GTR
700055	401055+402055+403055+406055+407055+410055+411055+412055	TB	TMK	UKG	GTR
700056	401056+402056+403056+406056+407056+410056+411056+412056	TB	TMK	UKG	GTR
700057	401057+402057+403057+406057+407057+410057+411057+412057	TB	TMK	UKG	GTR
700058	401058+402058+403058+406058+407058+410058+411058+412058	TB	TMK	UKG	GTR
700059	401059+402059+403059+406059+407059+410059+411059+412059	TB	TMK	UKG	GTR
700060	401060+402060+403060+406060+407060+410060+411060+412060	TB	TMK	UKG	GTR

Right: *A fleet of 55 Class 700/1 12-vehicle sets, know as Full Length Units (FLUs) are also in operation, deployed on busier services, with each set offering in excess of 600 standard class seats. Both driving cars on Class 700 sets are composite vehicles with first and standard class seating. FLU No. 700152 passes Wellham Green with a service bound for Cambridge.* **CJM**

Number	*Formation (FLU - Full Length Units)* *DMCO+PTSO+MSO+MSO+TSO+TSO+* *TSO+TSO+MSO+MSO+PTSO+DMCO*	*Depot*	*Livery*	*Owner*	*Operator*
700101	401101+402101+403101+404101+405101+406101+ 407101+408101+409101+410101+411101+412101	TB	TMK	UKG	GTR
700102	401102+402102+403102+404102+405102+406102+ 407102+408102+409102+410102+411102+412102	TB	TMK	UKG	GTR
700103	401103+402103+403103+404103+405103+406103+ 407103+408103+409103+410103+411103+412103	TB	TMK	UKG	GTR
700104	401104+402104+403104+404104+405104+406104+ 407104+408104+409104+410104+411104+412104	TB	TMK	UKG	GTR
700105	401105+402105+403105+404105+405105+406105+ 407105+408105+409105+410105+411105+412105	TB	TMK	UKG	GTR
700106	401106+402106+403106+404106+405106+406106+ 407106+408106+409106+410106+411106+412106	TB	TMK	UKG	GTR
700107	401107+402107+403107+404107+405107+406107+ 407107+408107+409107+410107+411107+412107	TB	TMK	UKG	GTR
700108	401108+402108+403108+404108+405108+406108+ 407108+408108+409108+410108+411108+412108	TB	TMK	UKG	GTR
700109	401109+402109+403109+404109+405109+406109+ 407109+408109+409109+410109+411109+412109	TB	TMK	UKG	GTR
700110	401110+402110+403110+404110+405110+406110+ 407110+408110+409110+410110+411110+412110	TB	TMK	UKG	GTR
700111	401111+402111+403111+404111+405111+406111+ 407111+408111+409111+410111+411111+412111	TB	TMK	UKG	GTR
700112	401112+402112+403112+404112+405112+406112+ 407112+408112+409112+410112+411112+412112	TB	TMK	UKG	GTR
700113	401113+402113+403113+404113+405113+406113+ 407113+408113+409113+410113+411113+412113	TB	TMK	UKG	GTR
700114	401114+402114+403114+404114+405114+406114+ 407114+408114+409114+410114+411114+412114	TB	TMK	UKG	GTR
700115	401115+402115+403115+404115+405115+406115+ 407115+408115+409115+410115+411105+412115	TB	TMK	UKG	GTR

Govia Thameslink Railway

700116	401116+402116+403116+404116+405116+406116+ 407116+408116+409116+410116+411116+412116	TB	TMK	UKG	GTR
700117	401117+402117+403117+404117+405117+406117+ 407117+408117+409117+410117+411107+412117	TB	TMK	UKG	GTR
700118	401118+402118+403118+404118+405118+406118+ 407118+408118+409118+410118+411108+412118	TB	TMK	UKG	GTR
700119	401119+402119+403119+404119+405119+406119+ 407119+408119+409119+410119+411109+412119	TB	TMK	UKG	GTR
700120	401120+402120+403120+404120+405120+406120+ 407120+408120+409120+410120+411120+412120	TB	TMK	UKG	GTR
700121	401121+402121+403121+404121+405121+406121+ 407121+408121+409121+410121+411121+412121	TB	TMK	UKG	GTR
700122	401122+402122+403122+404122+405122+406122+ 407122+408122+409122+410122+411122+412122	TB	TMK	UKG	GTR
700123	401123+402123+403123+404123+405123+406123+ 407123+408123+409123+410123+411123+412123	TB	TMK	UKG	GTR
700124	401124+402124+403124+404124+405124+406124+ 407124+408124+409124+410124+411124+412124	TB	TMK	UKG	GTR
700125	401125+402125+403125+404125+405125+406125+ 407125+408125+409125+410125+411125+412125	TB	TMK	UKG	GTR
700126	401126+402126+403126+404126+405126+406126+ 407126+408126+409126+410126+411126+412126	TB	TMK	UKG	GTR
700127	401127+402127+403127+404127+405127+406127+ 407127+408127+409127+410127+411127+412127	TB	TMK	UKG	GTR
700128	401128+402128+403128+404128+405128+406128+ 407128+408128+409128+410128+411128+412128	TB	TMK	UKG	GTR
700129	401129+402129+403129+404129+405129+406129+ 407129+408129+409129+410129+411129+412129	TB	TMK	UKG	GTR
700130	401130+402130+403130+404130+405130+406130+ 407130+408130+409130+410130+411130+412130	TB	TMK	UKG	GTR
700131	401131+402131+403131+404131+405131+406131+ 407131+408131+409131+410131+411131+412131	TB	TMK	UKG	GTR
700132	401132+402132+403132+404132+405132+406132+ 407132+408132+409132+410132+411132+412132	TB	TMK	UKG	GTR
700133	401133+402133+403133+404133+405133+406133+ 407133+408133+409133+410133+411133+412133	TB	TMK	UKG	GTR
700134	401134+402134+403134+404134+405134+406134+ 407134+408134+409134+410134+411134+412134	TB	TMK	UKG	GTR
700135	401135+402135+403135+404135+405135+406135+ 407135+408135+409135+410135+411135+412135	TB	TMK	UKG	GTR
700136	401136+402136+403136+404136+405136+406136+ 407136+408136+409136+410136+411136+412136	TB	TMK	UKG	GTR
700137	401137+402137+403137+404137+405137+406137+ 407137+408137+409137+410137+411137+412137	TB	TMK	UKG	GTR
700138	401138+402138+403138+404138+405138+406138+ 407138+408138+409138+410138+411138+412138	TB	TMK	UKG	GTR
700139	401139+402139+403139+404139+405139+406139+ 407139+408139+409139+410139+411139+412139	TB	TMK	UKG	GTR
700140	401140+402140+403140+404140+405140+406140+ 407140+408140+409140+410140+411140+412140	TB	TMK	UKG	GTR
700141	401141+402141+403141+404141+405141+406141+ 407141+408141+409141+410141+411141+412141	TB	TMK	UKG	GTR
700142	401142+402142+403142+404142+405142+406142+ 407142+408142+409142+410142+411142+412142	TB	TMK	UKG	GTR
700143	401143+402143+403143+404143+405143+406143+ 407143+408143+409143+410143+411143+412143	TB	TMK	UKG	GTR
700144	401144+402144+403144+404144+405144+406144+ 407144+408144+409144+410144+411144+412144	TB	TMK	UKG	GTR
700145	401145+402145+403145+404145+405145+406145+ 407145+408145+409145+410145+411145+412145	TB	TMK	UKG	GTR
700146	401146+402146+403146+404146+405146+406146+ 407146+408146+409146+410146+411146+412146	TB	TMK	UKG	GTR
700147	401147+402147+403147+404147+405147+406147+ 407147+408147+409147+410147+411147+412147	TB	TMK	UKG	GTR
700148	401148+402148+403148+404148+405148+406148+ 407148+408148+409148+410148+411148+412148	TB	TMK	UKG	GTR

700149	401149+402149+403149+404149+405149+406149+ 407149+408149+409149+410149+411149+412149	TB	TMK	UKG	GTR
700150	401150+402150+403150+404150+405150+406150+ 407150+408150+409150+410150+411150+412150	TB	TMK	UKG	GTR
700151	401151+402151+403151+404151+405151+406151+ 407151+408151+409151+410151+411151+412151	TB	TMK	UKG	GTR
700152	401152+402152+403152+404152+405152+406152+ 407152+408152+409152+410152+411152+412152	TB	TMK	UKG	GTR
700153	401153+402153+403153+404153+405153+406153+ 407153+408153+409153+410153+411153+412153	TB	TMK	UKG	GTR
700154	401154+402154+403154+404154+405154+406154+ 407154+408154+409154+410154+411154+412154	TB	TMK	UKG	GTR
700155	401155+402155+403155+404155+405155+406155+ 407155+408155+409155+410155+411155+412155	TB	SPL	UKG	GTR

Class 717
Desiro City

Vehicle Length: (Driving) 20m
(Inter) 20m
Height: 3.79m

Weight:
Power output:
Seats (total/car):

Number	*Formation* DMS+TS+TS+MS+PTS+DMS	*Depot*	*Livery*	*Owner*	*Operator*
717001	451001+452001+453001+454001+455001+456001	HE	TLK	RKR	GTR
717002	451002+452002+453002+454002+455002+456002	HE	TLK	RKR	GTR
717003	451003+452003+453003+454003+455003+456003	HE	TLK	RKR	GTR
717004	451004+452004+453004+454004+455004+456004	HE	TLK	RKR	GTR
717005	451005+452005+453005+454005+455005+456005	HE	TLK	RKR	GTR
717006	451006+452006+453006+454006+455006+456006	HE	TLK	RKR	GTR
717007	451007+452007+453007+454007+455007+456007	HE	TLK	RKR	GTR
717008	451008+452008+453008+454008+455008+456008	HE	TLK	RKR	GTR
717009	451009+452009+453009+454009+455009+456009	HE	TLK	RKR	GTR
717010	451010+452010+453010+454010+455010+456010	HE	TLK	RKR	GTR
717011	451011+452011+453011+454011+455011+456011	HE	TLK	RKR	GTR
717012	451012+452012+453012+454012+455012+456012	HE	TLK	RKR	GTR
717013	451013+452013+453013+454013+455013+456013	HE	TLK	RKR	GTR
717014	451014+452014+453014+454014+455014+456014	HE	TLK	RKR	GTR
717015	451015+452015+453015+454015+455015+456015	HE	TLK	RKR	GTR
717016	451016+452016+453016+454016+455016+456016	HE	TLK	RKR	GTR
717017	451017+452017+453017+454017+455017+456017	HE	TLK	RKR	GTR
717018	451018+452018+453018+454018+455018+456018	HE	TLK	RKR	GTR
717019	451019+452019+453019+454019+455019+456019	HE	TLK	RKR	GTR
717020	451020+452020+453020+454020+455020+456020	HE	TLK	RKR	GTR
717021	451021+452021+453021+454021+455021+456021	HE	TLK	RKR	GTR
717022	451022+452022+453022+454022+455022+456022	HE	TLK	RKR	GTR
717023	451023+452023+453023+454023+455023+456023	HE	TLK	RKR	GTR
717024	451024+452024+453024+454024+455024+456024	HE	TLK	RKR	GTR
717025	451025+452025+453025+454025+455025+456025	HE	TLK	RKR	GTR

Below: *The replacement stock for the Great Northern local services, previously operated by Class 313 stock, is a fleet of 25 six-car Class 717 Siemens Desiro City sets, fitted with emergency end gangway doors. These sets do not have yellow warning ends and are finished in grey and white livery and carry Great Northern branding. Set No. 717002 is captured passing Wellham Green with a Moorgate bound train in April 2019.* **CJM**

London Overground

Address: ✉ 125 Finchley Road, London, NW3 6H
overgroundinfo@tfl.gov.uk, ✆ 0845 601 4867, ⓘ www.tfl.gov.uk/overground

Managing Director: Steve Murphy

Principal Routes: Clapham Junction - Willesden, Richmond - Stratford, Gospel Oak - Barking, Euston - Watford, East London and Dalston - West Croydon, GE local services from Liverpool Street

Depots: Willesden (WN), New Cross Gate (NG), Ilford (IL),

Parent Company: Transport for London (TfL), operated by Arriva

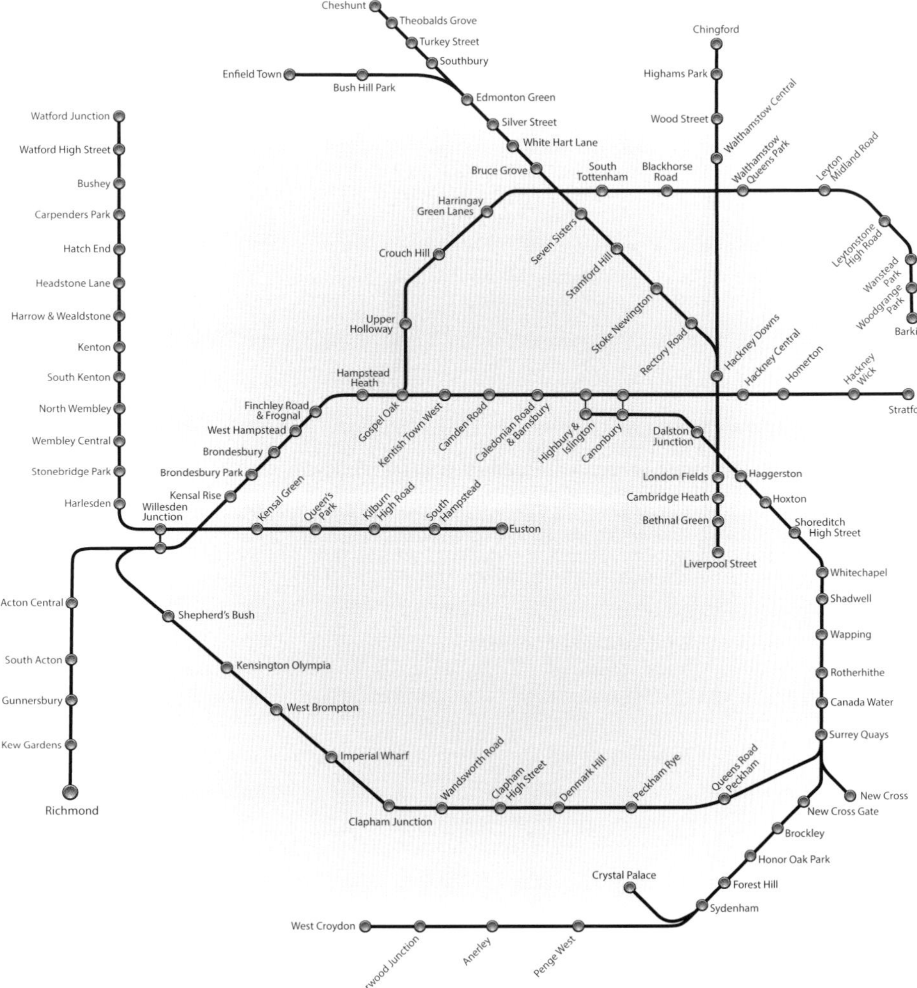

Class 09/0

Vehicle Length: 29ft 3in (8.91m)
Height: 12ft 8⅝in (3.87m)
Width: 8ft 6in (2.59m)
Engine: English Electric 6K
Horsepower: 400hp (298kW)
Electrical Equipment: English Electric

Number	Depot	Pool	Livery	Owner	Operator
09007 (D3671)	WN	-	GRN	LOG	LOG

Right: *The expanding London Overground operation, which is set to increase in size in the coming years, operates one diesel loco, Class 09 No. 09007 (which carries its 1957 identity of D3671). The loco is based at Willesden depot and used for shunting stock when power is unable to be collected from the overhead or third rail.* **Antony Christie**

Class 315

Vehicle Length: (Driving) 64ft 11½in (19.80m)
(Inter) 65ft 4½in (19.92m)
Height: 11ft 6½in (3.58m)
Width: 9ft 3in (2.82m)
Horsepower: 880hp (656kW)
Seats (total/car): 318S, 74S/86S/84S/74S

Right: *Until replaced by Bombardier 'Aventra' Class 710s, London Overground services from Liverpool Street to Chingford, Cheshunt and Enfield Town are in the hands of Class 315 sets. However some are getting in poor condition and a consideration is being given of transferring some from Great Eastern services to this route in 2020. Set No. 315808 in TfL livery is illustrated at Bethnal Green.* **CJM**

Number	Formation DMSO(A)+TSO+PTSO+DMSO(B)	Depot	Livery	Owner	Operator	Name
315801	64461+71281+71389+64462	IL	TFL	EVL	LOG	
315802	64463+71282+71390+64464	IL	TFL	EVL	LOG	
315803	64465+71283+71391+64466	IL	TFL	EVL	LOG	
315805	64469+71285+71393+64470	IL	TFL	EVL	LOG	
315806	64471+71286+71394+64472	IL	TFL	EVL	LOG	
315807	64473+71287+71395+64474	IL	TFL	EVL	LOG	
315808	64475+71288+71396+64476	IL	TFL	EVL	LOG	
315809	64477+71289+71397+64478	IL	TFL	EVL	LOG	
315810	64479+71290+71398+64480	IL	TFL	EVL	LOG	
315811	64481+71291+71399+64482	IL	TFL	EVL	LOG	
315812	64483+71292+71400+64484	IL	TFL	EVL	LOG	
315815	64489+71295+71403+64490	IL	TFL	EVL	LOG	
315816	64491+71296+71404+64492	IL	TFL	EVL	LOG	
315817	64493+71297+71405+64494	IL	TFL	EVL	LOG	*Transport for London*

Sets 315822/825/827/831/836 on loan to LOG from CrossRail

Class 317/7

Vehicle Length: (Driving) 65ft 0¾in (19.83m)
(Inter) 65ft 4¼in (19.92m)
Height: 12ft 1½in (3.58m)
Width: 9ft 3in (2.82m)
Horsepower: 1,000hp (746kW)
Seats (total/car): 22F/172S, 52S/62S/42S/22F-16S

Number	Former Number	Formation DTSO+MSO+TSO+DTCO	Depot	Livery	Owner	Operator
317708	(317308)	77007+62668+71584+77055	IL	TFL	ANG	LOG
317709	(317309)	77008+62669+71585+77056	IL	TFL	ANG	LOG
317710	(317310)	77009+62670+71586+77057	IL	TFL	ANG	LOG
317714	(317314)	77013+62674+71590+77061	IL	TFL	ANG	LOG
317719	(317319)	77018+62679+71595+77066	IL	TFL	ANG	LOG
317723	(317323/393)	77022+62683+71599+77070	IL	TFL	ANG	LOG
317729	(317329)	77028+62689+71605+77076	IL	TFL	ANG	LOG
317732	(317332)	77031+62692+71608+77079	IL	TFL	ANG	LOG

Left: *The eight Class 317/7s which sport a modified front end design, with a streamlined cab roof and revised light clusters are operated by London Overground. These structural changes came as part of a refurbishing project for Stansted Express stock. Displaying London Overground white and blue, set No. 317723 departs from Hackney Downs.* **Antony Christie**

Class 317/8

Vehicle Length: (Driving) 65ft 0¾in (19.83m) (Inter) 65ft 4¼in (19.92m)
Height: 12ft 1½in (3.58m)
Width: 9ft 3in (2.82m)
Horsepower: 1,000hp (746kW)
Seats (total/car): 20F/265S, 74S/79S/20F-42S/70S

317887	(317330)	77043+62704+71606+77077	IL	TFL	ANG	LOG	
317888	(317331)	77030+62691+71607+77078	IL	TFL	ANG	LOG	
317889	(317333)	77032+62693+71609+77080	IL	TFL	ANG	LOG	
317890	(317334)	77033+62694+71610+77081	IL	TFL	ANG	LOG	
317891	(317335)	77034+62695+71611+77082	IL	TFL	ANG	LOG	
317892	(317336)	77035+62696+71612+77083	IL	TFL	ANG	LOG	*Ilford Depot*

Left: *Six phase 1 Class 317s, classified 317/8 also operate London Overground services. These are fully refurbished sets and carry standard London Overground livery. No. 317889, a rebuild from original set No. 317333 departs from Bethnal Green.* **Antony Christie**

Class 378/1
Capitalstar

Vehicle Length: (Driving) 20.46m, (Inter) 20.14m
Height: 11ft 9in (3.58m)
750V dc sets
Width: 9ft 2in (2.80m)
Horsepower: 2,010hp (1,500kW)
Seats (total/car): 146S, 36S/40S/34S/36S

Number	*Formation* DMSO+MSO+TSO+MSO+DMSO	*Depot*	*Livery*	*Owner*	*Operator*	*Name*
378135	38035+38235+38335+38435+38135	NG	LON	QWR	LOG	*Daks Hamilton*
378136	38036+38236+38336+38436+38136	NG	LON	QWR	LOG	

Left: *The entire fleet of Class 387 Bombardier 'Capitalstar' five-car sets are operated by London Overground. The sets are Metro style units with longitudinal seating and large stand back areas. The 20 members of Class 378/1 are fitted for third rail operation only. The sets are allocated to New Cross Gate depot. Set No. 378147, painted in the new livery style with numbers applied to the cab side rather than the front is shown.* **Antony Christie**

378137	38037+38237+38337+38437+38137	NG	LOG	QWR	LOG
378138	38038+38238+38338+38438+38138	NG	LOG	QWR	LOG
378139	38039+38239+38339+38439+38139	NG	LOG	QWR	LOG
378140	38040+38240+38340+38440+38140	NG	LOG	QWR	LOG
378141	38041+38241+38341+38441+38141	NG	LOG	QWR	LOG
378142	38042+38242+38342+38442+38142	NG	LOG	QWR	LOG
378143	38043+38243+38343+38443+38143	NG	LOG	QWR	LOG
378144	38044+38244+38344+38444+38144	NG	LOG	QWR	LOG
378145	38045+38245+38345+38445+38145	NG	LOG	QWR	LOG
378146	38046+38246+38346+38446+38146	NG	LOG	QWR	LOG
378147	38047+38247+38347+38447+38147	NG	LON	QWR	LOG
378148	38048+38248+38348+38448+38148	NG	LOG	QWR	LOG
378149	38049+38249+38349+38449+38149	NG	LOG	QWR	LOG
378150	38050+38250+38350+38450+38150	NG	LON	QWR	LOG
378151	38051+38251+38351+38451+38151	NG	LOG	QWR	LOG
378152	38052+38252+38352+38452+38152	NG	LOG	QWR	LOG
378153	38053+38253+38353+38453+38153	NG	LOG	QWR	LOG
378154	38054+38254+38354+38454+38154	NG	LOG	QWR	LOG

Class 378/2
Capitalstar

Vehicle Length: (Driving) 20.46m, (Inter) 20.14m
Height: 11ft 9in (3.58m)
Dual voltage - 750V dc third rail and 25kV ac overhead
Width: 9ft 2in (2.80m)
Horsepower: 2,010hp (1,500kW)
Seats (total/car): 146S, 36S/40S/34S/36S

Sets built as three-car units as Class 378/0, MSO added and reclassified as 378/2

Number	*Formation* DMSO+MSO+PTSO+MSO+DMSO	*Depot*	*Livery*	*Owner*	*Operator*	*Name*
378201 (378001)	38001+38201+38301+38401+38101	NG	LOG	QWR	LOG	
378202 (378002)	38002+38202+38302+38402+38102	NG	LOG	QWR	LOG	
378203 (378003)	38003+38203+38303+38403+38103	NG	LOG	QWR	LOG	
378204 (378004)	38004+38204+38304+38404+38104	NG	LOG	QWR	LOG	*Professor Sir Peter Hall*
378205 (378005)	38005+38205+38305+38405+38105	NG	LOG	QWR	LOG	
378206 (378006)	38006+38206+38306+38406+38106	NG	LOG	QWR	LOG	**(4-car set for Goblin)**
378207 (378007)	38007+38207+38307+38407+38107	NG	LOG	QWR	LOG	
378208 (378008)	38008+38208+38308+38408+38108	NG	LOG	QWR	LOG	
378209 (378009)	38009+38209+38309+38409+38109	NG	LOG	QWR	LOG	
378210 (378010)	38010+38210+38310+38410+38110	NG	LOG	QWR	LOG	**(4-car set for Goblin)**
378211 (378011)	38011+38211+38311+38411+38111	NG	LOG	QWR	LOG	
378212 (378012)	38012+38212+38312+38412+38112	NG	LOG	QWR	LOG	
378213 (378013)	38013+38213+38313+38413+38113	NG	LOG	QWR	LOG	
378214 (378014)	38014+38214+38314+38414+38114	NG	LOG	QWR	LOG	
378215 (378015)	38015+38215+38315+38415+38115	NG	LOG	QWR	LOG	
378216 (378016)	38016+38216+38316+38416+38116	NG	LOG	QWR	LOG	
378217 (378017)	38017+38217+38317+38417+38117	NG	LOG	QWR	LOG	
378218 (378018)	38018+38218+38318+38418+38118	NG	LOG	QWR	LOG	
378219 (378019)	38019+38219+38319+38419+38119	NG	LOG	QWR	LOG	
378220 (378020)	38020+38220+38320+38420+38120	NG	LOG	QWR	LOG	
378221 (378021)	38021+38221+38321+38421+38121	NG	LOG	QWR	LOG	
378222 (378022)	38022+38222+38322+38422+38122	NG	LOG	QWR	LOG	
378223 (378023)	38023+38223+38323+38423+38123	NG	LOG	QWR	LOG	
378224 (378024)	38024+38224+38324+38424+38124	NG	LOG	QWR	LOG	

Sets 378216-378220 fitted with de-icing equipment

Number	*Formation* DMSO+MSO+TSO+MSO+DMSO	*Depot*	*Livery*	*Owner*	*Operator*	*Name/Note*
378225	38025+38225+38325+38425+38125	NG	LOG	QWR	LOG	
378226	38026+38226+38326+38426+38126	NG	LOG	QWR	LOG	
378227	38027+38227+38327+38427+38127	NG	LOG	QWR	LOG	
378228	38028+38228+38328+38428+38128	NG	LOG	QWR	LOG	
378229	38029+38229+38329+38429+38129	NG	LOG	QWR	LOG	
378230	38030+38230+38330+38430+38130	NG	LOG	QWR	LOG	
378231	38031+38231+38331+38431+38131	NG	LOG	QWR	LOG	
378232	38032+38232+38332+38432+38132	NG	LON	QWR	LOG	**(4-car set for Goblin)**
378233	38033+38233+38333+38433+38133	NG	LOG	QWR	LOG	*Ian Brown CBE*
378234	38034+38234+38334+38434+38134	NG	LOG	QWR	LOG	
378255	38055+38255+38355+38455+38155	NG	LOG	QWR	LOG	
378256	38056+38256+38356+38456+38156	NG	LOG	QWR	LOG	
378257	38057+38257+38357+38457+38157	NG	LOG	QWR	LOG	

London Overground

Left: *A batch of 37 Class 378s are capable of dual voltage operation and classified as 378/2. These are usually deployed on the Richmond/Clapham Junction to Stratford corridor. The central section of the front end of these sets is an emergency door for tunnel working. Set No. 378219 is seen at Highbury and Islington with a Stratford service.* **CJM**

Class 710
Aventra

Vehicle Length: (Driving) 23.62m (Inter) 22.50m
Height: 3.87m
Width: 2.78m
Output: 4-car 2,170 kW, 5-car 2,650kW
Seats (total/car): 4-car 171S, 5-car 217S

Class 710/1 *AC sets*

Number	*Formation* *DMSO(S)+MSO+PMSO+DMSO(B)*	*Depot*	*Livery*	*Owner*	*Operator*
710101	**431101+431201+431301+431501**	**WN**	**LON**	**SML**	**LOG**
710102	**431102+431202+431302+431502**	**WN**	**LON**	**SML**	**LOG**
710103	**431103+431203+431303+431503**	**WN**	**LON**	**SML**	**LOG**
710104	**431104+431204+431304+431504**	**WN**	**LON**	**SML**	**LOG**
710105	**431105+431205+431305+431505**	**WN**	**LON**	**SML**	**LOG**
710106	**431106+431206+431306+431506**	**WN**	**LON**	**SML**	**LOG**
710107	**431107+431207+431307+431507**	**WN**	**LON**	**SML**	**LOG**
710108	**431108+431208+431308+431508**	**WN**	**LON**	**SML**	**LOG**
710109	**431109+431209+431309+431509**	**WN**	**LON**	**SML**	**LOG**
710110	**431110+431210+431310+431510**	**WN**	**LON**	**SML**	**LOG**
710111	**431111+431211+431311+431511**	**WN**	**LON**	**SML**	**LOG**
710112	**431112+431212+431312+431512**	**WN**	**LON**	**SML**	**LOG**
710113	**431113+431213+431313+431513**	**WN**	**LON**	**SML**	**LOG**
710114	**431114+431214+431314+431514**	**WN**	**LON**	**SML**	**LOG**
710115	**431115+431215+431315+431515**	**WN**	**LON**	**SML**	**LOG**
710116	**431116+431216+431316+431516**	**WN**	**LON**	**SML**	**LOG**
710117	**431117+431217+431317+431517**	**WN**	**LON**	**SML**	**LOG**
710118	**431118+431218+431318+431518**	**WN**	**LON**	**SML**	**LOG**
710119	**431119+431219+431319+431519**	**WN**	**LON**	**SML**	**LOG**
710120	**431120+431220+431320+431520**	**WN**	**LON**	**SML**	**LOG**
710121	**431121+431221+431321+431521**	**WN**	**LON**	**SML**	**LOG**
710122	**431122+431222+431322+431522**	**WN**	**LON**	**SML**	**LOG**
710123	**431123+431223+431323+431523**	**WN**	**LON**	**SML**	**LOG**
710124	**431124+431224+431324+431524**	**WN**	**LON**	**SML**	**LOG**
710125	**431125+431225+431325+431525**	**WN**	**LON**	**SML**	**LOG**
710126	**431126+431226+431326+431526**	**WN**	**LON**	**SML**	**LOG**
710127	**431127+431227+431327+431527**	**WN**	**LON**	**SML**	**LOG**
710128	**431128+431228+431328+431528**	**WN**	**LON**	**SML**	**LOG**
710129	**431129+431229+431329+431529**	**WN**	**LON**	**SML**	**LOG**
710130	**431130+431230+431330+431530**	**WN**	**LON**	**SML**	**LOG**

Left: *A fleet of 30 Bombardier 'Aventra' Class 710/1 sets are on delivery to replace older London Overground stock on routes from Liverpool Street to Chingford, Cheshunt and Enfield Town. The sets will be based at Ilford depot. These units should have been introduced in 2019-2020, but problems with software has seen a protracted delivery and commissioning. Set No. 710105 is viewed at Stratford on a test run.* **Antony Christie**

Class 710/2
AC/DC four-car sets

Number	Formation DMSO(S)+MSO+PMSO+DMSO(B)	Depot	Livery	Owner	Operator
710256	432156+432256+432356+432556	WN	LON	SML	LOG
710257	432157+432257+432357+432557	WN	LON	SML	LOG
710258	432158+432258+432358+432558	WN	LON	SML	LOG
710259	432159+432259+432359+432559	WN	LON	SML	LOG
710260	432160+432260+432360+432560	WN	LON	SML	LOG
710261	432161+432261+432361+432561	WN	LON	SML	LOG
710262	432162+432262+432362+432562	WN	LON	SML	LOG
710263	432163+432263+432363+432563	WN	LON	SML	LOG
710264	432164+432264+432364+432564	WN	LON	SML	LOG
710265	432165+432265+432365+432565	WN	LON	SML	LOG
710266	432166+432266+432366+432566	WN	LON	SML	LOG
710267	432167+432267+432367+432567	WN	LON	SML	LOG
710268	432168+432268+432368+432568	WN	LON	SML	LOG
710269	432169+432269+432369+432569	WN	LON	SML	LOG
710270	432170+432270+432370+432570	WN	LON	SML	LOG
710271	432171+432271+432371+432571	WN	LON	SML	LOG
710272	432172+432272+432372+432572	WN	LON	SML	LOG
710273	432173+432273+432373+432573	WN	LON	SML	LOG

Class 710/3
AC/DC five-car sets

Number	Formation DMSO(S)+MSO+PMSO+MSO+DMSO(B)	Depot	Livery	Owner	Operator
710274	432174+432274+432374+432474+432574	WN	LON	SML	LOG
710275	432175+432275+432375+432475+432575	WN	LON	SML	LOG
710276	432176+432276+432376+432476+432576	WN	LON	SML	LOG
710277	432177+432277+432377+432477+432577	WN	LON	SML	LOG
710278	432178+432278+432378+432478+432578	WN	LON	SML	LOG
710279	432179+432279+432379+432479+432579	WN	LON	SML	LOG

Above: *The first of the Class 710 breed to enter service were a handful of Class 710/2s on the Gospel Oak-Barking line, which saw the sets introduced a year behind schedule. By late 2019 the sets had taken over the route and were also being introduced on the London Euston to Watford route, replacing some Class 378 duties. Set No. 710269 is seen on the Gospel Oak-Barking route at Crouch Hill.* **CJM**

London North Eastern Railway

Address: East Coast House, 25 Skeldergate, York, YO1 6DH
customers@eastcoast.co.uk
08457 225225
www.eastcoast.co.uk

Managing Director: David Horne
Franchise Dates: 24 June 2018-UFN
Principal Routes: London King's Cross - Aberdeen/Inverness, Edinburgh, Glasgow Hull, Leeds, Bradford, Skipton and Harrogate
Depots: Bounds Green (BN), Craigentinny (EC), Doncaster (DR)

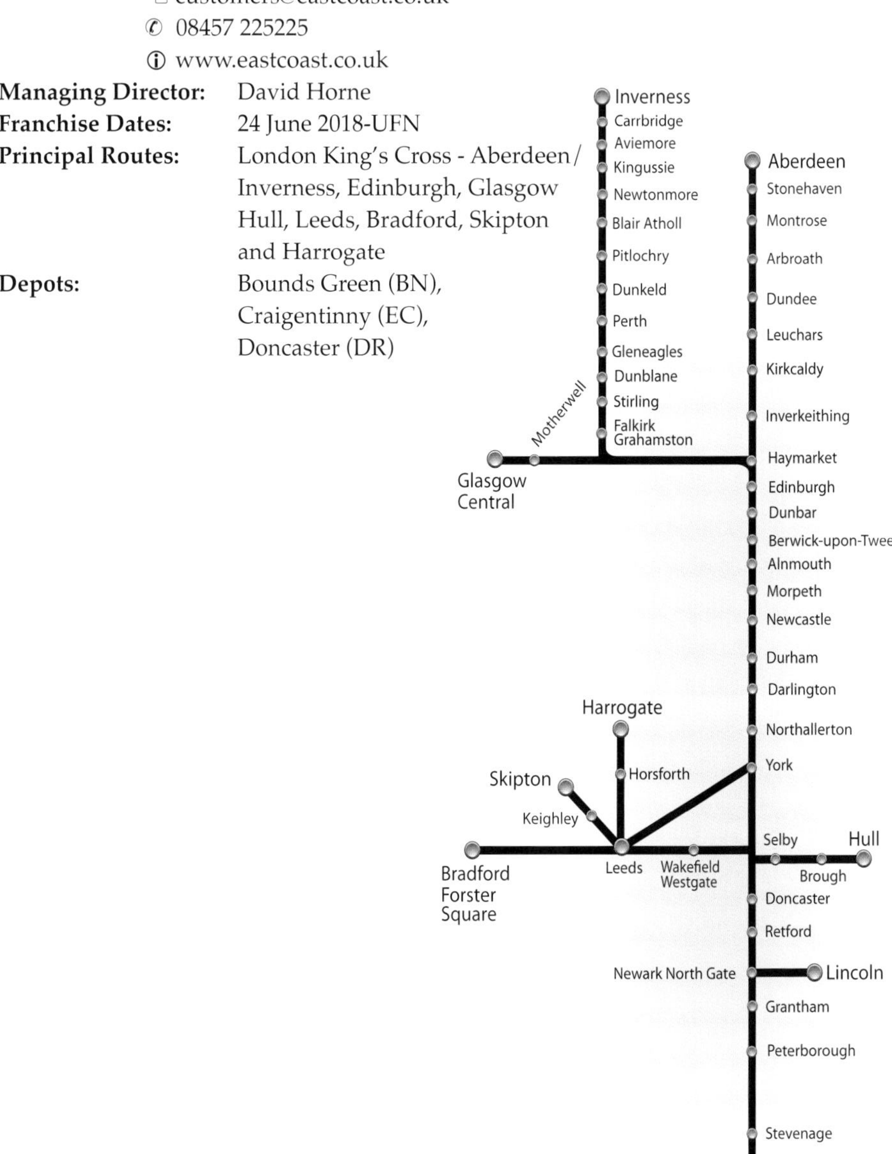

Class 91

Vehicle Length: 63ft 8in (19.40m)	Power Collection: 25kV ac overhead
Height: 12ft 4in (3.75m)	Horsepower: 6,300hp (4,700kW)
Width: 9ft 0in (2.74m)	Electrical Equipment: GEC

Number	Depot	Pool	Livery	Owner	Operator	Name
91101 (91001)	BN	IECA	SPL	EVL	LNE	*Flying Scotsman*
91104 (91004)	BN	IECA	LNR	EVL	LNE	
91105 (91005)	BN	IECA	LNR	EVL	LNE	
91106 (91006)	BN	IECA	LNR	EVL	LNE	
91107 (91007)	BN	IECA	LNR	EVL	LNE	*Skyfall*
91109 (91009)	BN	IECA	LNR	EVL	LNE	*Sir Bobby Robson*
91110 (91010)	BN	IECA	ADV	EVL	LNE	*Battle of Britain Memorial Flight - Spitfire Hurricane Lancaster Dakota*
91111 (91011)	BN	IECA	SPL	EVL	LNE	*For the Fallen*
91112 (91012)	BN	IECA	LNR	EVL	LNE	
91113 (91013)	BN	IECA	LNR	EVL	LNE	
91114 (91014)	BN	IECA	LNR	EVL	LNE	*Durham Cathedral*
91115 (91015)	BN	IECA	LNR	EVL	LNE	*Blaydon Races*
91116 (91016)	BN	IECA	LNR	EVL	LNE	
91118 (91018)	BN	IECA	LNR	EVL	LNE	*The Fusiliers*
91119 (91019)	BN	IECA	ICS	EVL	LNE	*Bounds Green Intercity Depot 1977-2017*
91121 (91021)	BN	IECA	LNR	EVL	LNE	
91124 (91024)	BN	IECA	LNR	EVL	LNE	
91125 (91025)	BN	IECA	LNR	EVL	LNE	
91126 (91026)	BN	IECA	LNR	EVL	LNE	*Darlington Hippodrome*
91127 (91027)	BN	IECA	LNR	EVL	LNE	
91129 (91029)	BN	IECA	LNR	EVL	LNE	
91130 (91030)	BN	IECA	LNR	EVL	LNE	*Lord Mayor of Newcastle*
91131 (91031)	BN	IECA	LNR	EVL	LNE	

Above: *As more Class 800 and 801 sets enter service, so the number of Class 91 and Mk 4 rakes reduces. A number of locos have been taken off-lease and the entire fleet will be gone during 2020. Some locos will find new work with other operators, mainly open access companies. InterCity-liveried No. 91119 is seen powering a Mk4 rake on the approaches to York.* **CJM**

■ In February 2020 it was announced that a small number of Class 91s and Mk4s will be retained until 2021-2022.

Mk4 Stock

Vehicle Length: 75ft 5in (23m)	Width: 8ft 11in (2.73m)
Height: 12ft 5in (3.79m)	Bogie Type: BT41

AJ2J - RSB *Seating 30S*

Number	Depot	Livery	Owner
10300	BN	LNR	EVL
10301	BN	LNR	EVL
10302	BN	LNR	EVL
10303	BN	LNR	EVL
10304	BN	LNR	EVL
10305	BN	LNR	EVL
10306	BN	LNR	EVL
10307	BN	LNR	EVL
10308	BN	LNR	EVL
10309	BN	LNR	EVL
10313	BN	LNR	EVL
10315	BN	LNR	EVL
10318	BN	LNR	EVL
10323	BN	LNR	EVL
10324	BN	LNR	EVL
10326	BN	LNR	EVL
10330	BN	LNR	EVL
10331	BN	LNR	EVL
10332	BN	LNR	EVL
10333	BN	LNR	EVL

AD1J - FO *Seating 46F*

Number	Depot	Livery	Owner
11201	BN	LNR	EVL
11219	BN	LNR	EVL
11229	BN	LNR	EVL
11244	BN	LNR	EVL
11277(12408)	BN	LNR	EVL
11278(12479)	BN	LNR	EVL
11279(12521)	BN	LNR	EVL
11280(12523)	BN	LNR	EVL
11281(12418)	BN	LNR	EVL

London North Eastern Railway

11282(12524)	BN	LNR	EVL
11283(12435)	BN	LNR	EVL
11284(12487)	BN	LNR	EVL
11285(12537)	BN	LNR	EVL
11286(12482)	BN	LNR	EVL
11287(12527)	BN	LNR	EVL
11288(12517)	BN	LNR	EVL
11289(12528)	BN	LNR	EVL
11290(12530)	BN	LNR	EVL
11291(12535)	BN	LNR	EVL
11298(12416)	BN	LNR	EVL
11299(12532)	BN	LNR	EVL

AL1J - FOD *Seating 42F*

Number	*Depot*	*Livery*	*Owner*
11301(11215)	BN	LNR	EVL
11302(11203)	BN	LNR	EVL
11303(11211)	BN	LNR	EVL
11304(11257)	BN	LNR	EVL
11305(11261)	BN	LNR	EVL
11306(11276)	BN	LNR	EVL
11307(11217)	BN	LNR	EVL
11308(11263)	BN	LNR	EVL
11309(11262)	BN	LNR	EVL
11310(11272)	BN	LNR	EVL
11311(11221)	BN	LNR	EVL
11312(11225)	BN	LNR	EVL
11313(11210)	BN	LNR	EVL
11314(11207)	BN	LNR	EVL
11315(11238)	BN	LNR	EVL
11316(11227)	BN	LNR	EVL
11317(11223)	BN	LNR	EVL
11318(11251)	BN	LNR	EVL
11319(11247)	BN	LNR	EVL
11320(11255)	BN	LNR	EVL
11321(11245)	BN	LNR	EVL
11322(11228)	BN	LNR	EVL
11324(11253)	BN	LNR	EVL

AD1J - FO *Seating 46F (55F*)*

Number	*Depot*	*Livery*	*Owner*
11401(11214)	BN	LNR	EVL*
11402(11216)	BN	LNR	EVL
11403(11258)	BN	LNR	EVL
11404(11202)	BN	LNR	EVL
11405(11204)	BN	LNR	EVL
11406(11205)	BN	LNR	EVL
11407(11256)	BN	LNR	EVL
11408(11218)	BN	LNR	EVL
11409(11259)	BN	LNR	EVL
11410(11260)	BN	LNR	EVL
11411(11240)	BN	LNR	EVL
11412(11209)	BN	LNR	EVL
11413(11212)	BN	LNR	EVL
11414(11246)	BN	LNR	EVL
11415(11208)	BN	LNR	EVL
11416(11254)	BN	LNR	EVL
11417(11226)	BN	LNR	EVL
11418(11222)	BN	LNR	EVL
11419(11250)	BN	LNR	EVL
11421(11220)	BN	LNR	EVL
11422(11232)	BN	LNR	EVL

AI2J - TSOE *Seating 76S*

Number	*Depot*	*Livery*	*Owner*
12200	BN	LNR	EVL
12201	BN	LNR	EVL
12202	BN	LNR	EVL
12203	BN	LNR	EVL
12205	BN	LNR	EVL
12207	BN	LNR	EVL
12208	BN	LNR	EVL
12209	BN	LNR	EVL
12210	BN	LNR	EVL
12211	BN	LNR	EVL
12212	BN	LNR	EVL
12213	BN	LNR	EVL
12214	BN	LNR	EVL
12215	BN	LNR	EVL
12222	BN	LNR	EVL
12223	BN	LNR	EVL
12226	BN	LNR	EVL
12228	BN	LNR	EVL
12229	BN	LNR	EVL
12230	BN	LNR	EVL
12232	BN	LNR	EVL

AL2J - TSOD *Seating 68S*

Number	*Depot*	*Livery*	*Owner*
12300	BN	LNR	EVL
12301	BN	LNR	EVL
12302	BN	LNR	EVL
12303	BN	LNR	EVL
12304	BN	LNR	EVL
12305	BN	LNR	EVL
12307	BN	LNR	EVL
12308	BN	LNR	EVL
12309	BN	LNR	EVL
12310	BN	LNR	EVL
12311	BN	LNR	EVL
12312	BN	LNR	EVL
12313	BN	LNR	EVL
12315	BN	LNR	EVL
12316	BN	LNR	EVL
12323	BN	LNR	EVL
12324	BN	LNR	EVL
12327	BN	LNR	EVL
12328	BN	LNR	EVL
12329	BN	LNR	EVL
12330	BN	LNR	EVL
12331(12531)	BN	LNR	EVL

Above: *The remote driving controls on Mk4 stock is provided by a fleet of Driving Van Trailers (DVTs). The inner end of the vehicle houses the guards office with the central section a luggage stowage area which today sees little use. The cab controls replicate those of the Class 91. No. 82225 is shown in LNER-branded Virgin red livery.* **CJM**

AC2J - TSO *Seating 76S*

Number	*Depot*	*Livery*	*Owner*
12400	BN	LNR	EVL
12401	BN	LNR	EVL
12402	BN	LNR	EVL
12404	BN	LNR	EVL
12405	BN	LNR	EVL
12406	BN	LNR	EVL
12407	BN	LNR	EVL
12409	BN	LNR	EVL
12410	BN	LNR	EVL
12411	BN	LNR	EVL
12414	BN	LNR	EVL
12415	BN	LNR	EVL
12417	BN	LNR	EVL
12419	BN	LNR	EVL
12420	BN	LNR	EVL
12421	BN	LNR	EVL
12422	BN	LNR	EVL
12423	BN	LNR	EVL
12424	BN	LNR	EVL
12426	BN	LNR	EVL
12427	BN	LNR	EVL
12428	BN	LNR	EVL
12430	BN	LNR	EVL
12431	BN	LNR	EVL
12432	BN	LNR	EVL
12433	BN	LNR	EVL
12434	BN	LNR	EVL
12436	BN	LNR	EVL
12437	BN	LNR	EVL
12441	BN	LNR	EVL
12442	BN	LNR	EVL
12443	BN	LNR	EVL
12444	BN	LNR	EVL
12445	BN	LNR	EVL
12448	BN	LNR	EVL
12450	BN	LNR	EVL
12452	BN	LNR	EVL
12453	BN	LNR	EVL
12459	BN	LNR	EVL
12460	BN	LNR	EVL
12461	BN	LNR	EVL
12467	BN	LNR	EVL
12468	BN	LNR	EVL
12469	BN	LNR	EVL
12470	BN	LNR	EVL
12473	BN	LNR	EVL
12476	BN	LNR	EVL
12478	BN	LNR	EVL
12480	BN	LNR	EVL
12481	BN	LNR	EVL
12483	BN	LNR	EVL
12484	BN	LNR	EVL
12485	BN	LNR	EVL
12486	BN	LNR	EVL
12488	BN	LNR	EVL
12489	BN	LNR	EVL
12513	BN	LNR	EVL
12514	BN	LNR	EVL
12515	BN	LNR	EVL
12518	BN	LNR	EVL
12520	BN	LNR	EVL
12522	BN	LNR	EVL
12526	BN	LNR	EVL

NZAJ - DVT

Number	*Depot*	*Livery*	*Owner*
82201	BN	LNR	EVL
82202	BN	LNR	EVL
82204	BN	LNR	EVL
82205	BN	LNR	EVL
82206	BN	LNR	EVL
82207	BN	LNR	EVL
82208	BN	LNR	EVL
82209	BN	LNR	EVL
82210	BN	LNR	EVL
82211	BN	LNR	EVL
82212	BN	LNR	EVL
82213	BN	LNR	EVL
82214	BN	LNR	EVL
82215	BN	LNR	EVL
82218	BN	LNR	EVL
82219	BN	LNR	EVL
82220	BN	LNR	EVL
82222	BN	LNR	EVL
82224	BN	LNR	EVL
82225	BN	LNR	EVL
82227	BN	LNR	EVL
82230	BN	LNR	EVL

Right: *When the Mk4 passenger stock is withdrawn from LNER use, it is hoped a number of vehicles will find further use. Transport for Wales are committed to taking some vehicles for use on their improved north-south Wales corridor. First Open (FO) No. 11229 with seats for 46 is seen at York.* **CJM**

Service Stock

HST and Mk4 Barrier Vehicles

Number	*Depot*	*Livery*	*Owner*	*Former Identity*
6340	EC	BLU	ANG	BCK - 21251
6344	EC	BLU	ANG	BG - 92080
6346	EC	BLU	ANG	BSO - 9422
6352	BN	HSB	HSB	SK - 19465
6353	BN	HSB	HSB	SK - 19478
9393	EC	PTR	PTR	BG - 92196
9394	EC	PTR	PTR	BG - 92906

Right: *A number of barrier vehicles are on the books of LNER, but these are more usually used by Rail Operations Group. These barriers are all rebuilds of former passenger or van stock, with brake vehicles retaining their brake equipment. Vehicle 6340 is shown, this was a rebuild from Mk1 Brake Composite Corridor (BCK) No. 21251. It is seen at Doncaster.* **CJM**

London North Eastern Railway

Class 800/1 Bi-Mode 'Azuma' IET stock

9-car sets

Vehicle Length: (Driving) 85ft 4in (26m)
Height: 11ft 8¾in (3.62m)
Engine: MTU 12V 1600R80L of 750hp (560kW) x 5
Width: 8ft 10in (2.7m)
Horsepower: Electric 6,061hp (4,520kW)
Seats (total/car): 101F/510S - 56S, 88S, 88S, 88S, 88S, 72S,30F/38S, 48F, 15F

Number	*Formation* DTRBFO+MF+MC+TSB+MS+TS+MS+MS+DTSO	*Depot*	*Livery*	*Owner*	*Operator*
800101 (T58)*	811101+812101+813101+814101+815101+816101+817101+818101+819101	DN	WHT	EVL	HIT
800102	811102+812102+813102+814102+815102+816102+817102+818102+819102	DN	LNE	EVL	LNE
800103*	811103+812103+813103+814103+815103+816103+817103+818103+819103	DN	LNE	EVL	LNE
800104	811104+812104+813104+814104+815104+816104+817104+818104+819104	DN	§	EVL	LNE
800105*	811105+812105+813105+814105+815105+816105+817105+818105+819105	DN	LNE	EVL	LNE
800106*	811106+812106+813106+814106+815106+816106+817106+818106+819106	DN	LNE	EVL	LNE
800107*	811107+812107+813107+814107+815107+816107+817107+818107+819107	DN	LNE	EVL	LNE
800108*	811108+812108+813108+814108+815108+816108+817108+818108+819108	DN	LNE	EVL	LNE
800109*	811109+812109+813109+814109+815109+816109+817109+818109+819109	DN	LNE	EVL	LNE
800110*	811110+812110+813110+814110+815110+816110+817110+818110+819110	DN	LNE	EVL	LNE
800111*	811111+812111+813111+814111+815111+816111+817111+818111+819111	DN	LNE	EVL	LNE
800112*	811112+812112+813112+814112+815112+816112+817112+818112+819112	DN	LNE	EVL	LNE
800113*	811113+812113+813113+814113+815113+816113+817113+818113+819113	DN	LNE	EVL	LNE

* *Built in Japan.* § *Celebrating Scotland livery*

Below: *Five and nine car, electric and bi-mode Class 800 and 801 'Azuma' stock is now the core traction for East Coast Services, painted in the distinctive white and red livery with both Azuma and LNER branding. Nine car bi-mode set No. 800111 is shown from its first class end, which is usually at the London end of formations.* **CJM**

Class 800/2 Bi-Mode 'Azuma' IET stock

5-car sets

Vehicle Length: (Driving) 85ft 4in (26m)
Height: 11ft 8¾in (3.62m)
Engine: MTU 12V 1600R80L of 750hp (560kW) x 3
Width: 8ft 10in (2.7m)
Horsepower: Electric 3,636hp (2,712kW)
Seats (total/car): 45F/270S - 56S, 88S, 88S, 30F/38S, 15F

Number	*Formation* DTRBFO+MC+MS+MS+DTSO	*Depot*	*Livery*	*Owner*	*Operator*
800201*	811201+812201+813201+814201+815201	DN	LNE	EVL	HIT
800202	811202+812202+813202+814202+815202	DN	LNE	EVL	LNE
800203	811203+812203+813203+814203+815203	DN	LNE	EVL	LNE
800204	811204+812204+813204+814204+815204	DN	LNE	EVL	LNE
800205	811205+812205+813205+814205+815205	DN	LNE	EVL	LNE
800206	811206+812206+813206+814206+815206	DN	LNE	EVL	LNE

800207	811207+812207+813207+814207+815207	DN	LNE	EVL	LNE
800208	811208+812208+813208+814208+815208	DN	LNE	EVL	LNE
800209	811209+812209+813209+814209+815209	DN	LNE	EVL	LNE
800210	811210+812210+813210+814210+815210	DN	WHT	EVL	LNE

Above and Left: *A fleet of 10 five-car bi-mode Class 800/2 sets are allocated to Doncaster and deployed on either lighter used services or in pairs on long distance duties. A single set, No. 800204 is seen at Peterborough on a Lincoln route service. On left a standard class vehicle interior is shown. Both:* **Antony Christie**

Class 801/1 Electric 'Azuma' IET stock

5-car sets

Vehicle Length: (Driving) 85ft 4in (26m)
Height: 12ft 4in (3.75m)
Engine: MTU 12V 1600R80L of 750hp (560kW) x 1
Width: 8ft 10in (2.7m)
Horsepower: 3,636hp (2,712kW)
Seats (total/car): 45F/270S - 56S, 88S, 88S, 30F/38S, 15F

Number	*Formation* DTRBFO+MC+MS+MS+DTSO	*Depot*	*Livery*	*Owner*	*Operator*
801101* (T71)	821101+822101+823101+824101+825101	DN	LNE	EVL	HIT
801102* (T72)	821102+822102+823102+824102+825102	DN	LNE	EVL	HIT
801103 (T73)	821103+822103+823103+824103+825103	DN	LNE	EVL	LNE
801104 (T74)	821104+822104+823104+824104+825104	DN	LNE	EVL	LNE
801105 (T75)	821105+822105+823105+824105+825105	DN	LNE	EVL	LNE
801106 (T76)	821106+822106+823106+824106+825106	DN	LNE	EVL	LNE
801107 (T77)	821107+822107+823107+824107+825107	DN	LNE	EVL	LNE
801108 (T78)	821108+822108+823108+824108+825108	DN	LNE	EVL	LNE
801109 (T79)	821109+822109+823109+824109+825109	DN	LNE	EVL	LNE
801110 (T80)	821110+822110+823110+824110+825110	DN	LNE	EVL	LNE
801111 (T81)	821111+822111+823111+824111+825111	DN	LNE	EVL	LNE
801112 (T82)	821112+822112+823112+824112+825112	DN	LNE	EVL	LNE

London North Eastern Railway

Above: *By the end of 2019, LNER had received a sufficient number of Class 800 and 801 sets in both five and nine car formations to withdraw their entire HST fleet and reduce the number of Class 91 duties. All electric set No. 801110 is seen from its standard class driving car at London Kings Cross.* **Antony Christie**

Below: *In normal service, the LNER Class 800 and 801 sets operate with their first class vehicles marshalled at the London end of trains. This can be identified by three blacked off passenger windows at the driving end of the leading vehicle, this is where the kitchen is located. Azuma set No. 801103 is seen heading south at Stevenage.* **Antony Christie**

Class 801/2 Electric 'Azuma' IET stock

9-car sets

Vehicle Length: (Driving) 85ft 4in (26m)
Height: 11ft 8¾in (3.62m)
Engine: MTU 12V 1600R80L of 750hp (560kW) x 1
Width: 8ft 10in (2.7m)
Horsepower: 6,061hp (4,520kW)
Seats (total/car): 101F/510S - 56S, 88S, 88S, 88S, 88S, 72S,30F/38S, 48F, 15F

Number	*Formation* DTRBFO+MF+MC+TSB+MS+TS+MS+MS+DTSO	*Depot*	*Livery*	*Owner*	*Operator*
801201*	821201+822201+823201+824201+825201+826201+827201+828201+829201	BN	LNE	EVL	LNE
801202	821202+822202+823202+824202+825202+826202+827202+828202+829202	BN	WHT	EVL	LNE
801203	821203+822203+823203+824203+825203+826203+827203+828203+829203	BN	LNE	EVL	LNE
801204	821204+822204+823204+824204+825204+826204+827204+828204+829204	BN	WHT	EVL	LNE
801205	821205+822205+823205+824205+825205+826205+827205+828205+829205	BN	LNE	EVL	LNE
801206	821206+822206+823206+824206+825206+826206+827206+828206+829206	BN	WHT	EVL	LNE
801207	821207+822207+823207+824207+825207+826207+827207+828207+829207	BN	LNE	EVL	LNE
801208	821208+822208+823208+824208+825208+826208+827208+828208+829208	BN	WHT	EVL	LNE
801209	821209+822209+823209+824209+825209+826209+827209+828209+829209	BN	LNE	EVL	LNE
801210	821210+822210+823210+824210+825210+826210+827210+828210+829210	BN	WHT	EVL	LNE
801211	821211+822211+823211+824211+825211+826211+827211+828211+829211	BN	LNE	EVL	LNE
801212	821212+822212+823212+824212+825212+826212+827212+828212+829212	BN	WHT	EVL	LNE
801213	821213+822213+823213+824213+825213+826213+827213+828213+829213	BN	LNE	EVL	LNE
801214	821214+822214+823214+824214+825214+826214+827214+828214+829214	BN	WHT	EVL	LNE
801215	821215+822215+823215+824215+825215+826215+827215+828215+829215	BN	LNE	EVL	LNE
801216	821216+822216+823216+824216+825216+826216+827216+828216+829216	BN	WHT	EVL	LNE
801217	821217+822217+823217+824217+825217+826217+827217+828217+829217	BN	LNE	EVL	LNE
801218	821218+822218+823218+824218+825218+826218+827218+828218+829218	BN	WHT	EVL	LNE
801219	821219+822219+823219+824219+825219+826219+827219+828219+829219	BN	LNE	EVL	LNE
801220	821220+822220+823220+824220+825220+826220+827220+828220+829220	BN	LNE	EVL	LNE
801221	821221+822221+823221+824221+825221+826221+827221+828221+829221	BN	LNE	EVL	LNE
801222	821222+822222+823222+824222+825222+826222+827222+828222+829222	BN	LNE	EVL	LNE
801223	821223+822223+823223+824223+825223+826223+827223+828223+829223	BN	WHT	EVL	LNE
801224	821224+822224+823224+824224+825224+826224+827224+828224+829224	BN	WHT	EVL	LNE
801225	821225+822225+823225+824225+825225+826225+827225+828225+829225	BN	WHT	EVL	LNE
801226	821226+822226+823226+824226+825226+826226+827226+828226+829226	BN	WHT	EVL	LNE
801227	821227+822227+823227+824227+825227+826227+827227+828227+829227	BN	WHT	EVL	LNE
801228	821228+822228+823228+824228+825228+826228+827228+828228+829228	BN	WHT	EVL	LNE
801229	821229+822229+823229+824229+825229+826229+827229+828229+829229	BN	WHT	EVL	LNE
801230	821230+822230+823230+824230+825230+826230+827230+828230+829230	BN	WHT	EVL	LNE

Below: *The fleet of 30 all-electric Class 801/2 nine-car Azuma sets are based at Bounds Green, north London and in early 2020 were in the final stage of delivery from Hitachi. Sets carry the standard Azuma livery and can be found throughout the LNER electrified area. Set No. 801209 is seen at Peterborough.* **Antony Christie**

Merseyrail

Address: ✉ Rail House, Lord Nelson Street, Liverpool, L1 1JF
comment@merseyrail.org
✆ 0151 702 2534
ⓘ www.merseyrail.org

Managing Director: Andy Heath
Franchise Dates: 20 July 2003 - 19 July 2028
Principal Routes: All non-main-line services in Liverpool area
Depots: Birkenhead North (BD) maintenance undertaken by Stadler Kirkdale (KK)
Parent Company: Serco / Abellio

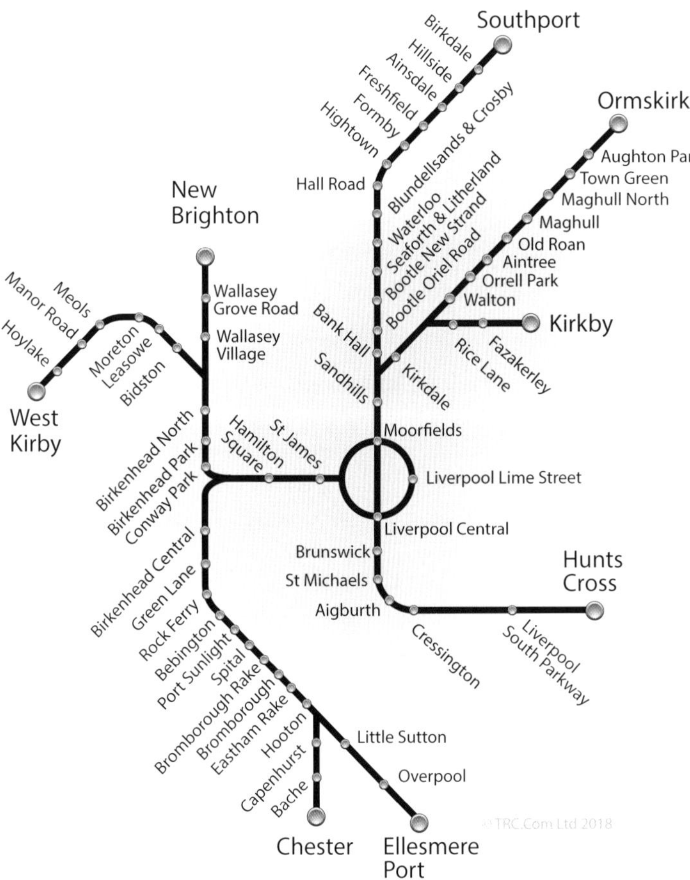

Right: *During 2020-2021 it is expected that the entire fleet of Class 507 and 508 stock on the Merseyside electrified system will be replaced by Stadler Class 777 stock. The 1972-desgn ex-BR sets being withdrawn and scrapped. Viewed from its yellow side, Class 507 No. 507005 is seen at Ormskirk.* **CJM**

Class 507

Vehicle Length: (Driving) 64ft 11½in (19.80m) (Inter) 65ft 4¼in (19.92m)
Height: 11ft 6½in (3.58m)
Width: 9ft 3in (2.82m)
Horsepower: 880hp (656kW)
Seats (total/car): 186S, 56S/74S/56S

Number	*Formation DMSO+TSO+DMSO*	*Depot*	*Livery*	*Owner*	*Operator*	*Name*
507001	64367+71342+64405	BD	MEY	ANG	MER	
507002	64368+71343+64406	BD	ADV	ANG	MER	
507003	64369+71344+64407	BD	MEY	ANG	MER	
507004	64388+71345+64408	BD	MEY	ANG	MER	*Bob Paisley*
507005	64371+71346+64409	BD	MEY	ANG	MER	
507006	64372+71347+64410	BD	MEY	ANG	MER	
507007	64373+71348+64411	BD	MEY	ANG	MER	
507008	64374+71349+64412	BD	MEY	ANG	MER	*Harold Wilson*
507009	64375+71350+64413	BD	MEY	ANG	MER	*Dixie Dean*
507010	64376+71351+64414	BD	MEY	ANG	MER	
507011	64377+71352+64415	BD	MEY	ANG	MER	
507012	64378+71353+64416	BD	MEY	ANG	MER	
507013	64379+71354+64417	BD	MEY	ANG	MER	
507014	64380+71355+64418	BD	MEY	ANG	MER	
507015	64381+71356+64419	BD	MEY	ANG	MER	
507016	64382+71357+64420	BD	MEY	ANG	MER	*Merseyrail - celebrating the first ten years 2003-2013*
507017	64383+71358+64421	BD	MEY	ANG	MER	
507018	64384+71359+64422	BD	MEY	ANG	MER	
507019	64385+71360+64423	BD	MEY	ANG	MER	
507020	64386+71361+64424	BD	MEY	ANG	MER	*John Peel*
507021	64387+71362+64425	BD	MEY	ANG	MER	*Red Rum*
507023	64389+71364+64427	BD	MEY	ANG	MER	*Operating Inspector Stuart Mason*
507024	64390+71365+64428	BD	MEY	ANG	MER	
507025	64391+71366+64429	BD	MEY	ANG	MER	
507026	64392+71367+64430	BD	MEY	ANG	MER	*Councillor George Howard*
507027	64393+71368+64431	BD	MEY	ANG	MER	
507028	64394+71369+64432	BD	MEY	ANG	MER	
507029	64395+71370+64433	BD	MEY	ANG	MER	
507030	64396+71371+64434	BD	MEY	ANG	MER	
507031	64397+71372+64435	BD	MEY	ANG	MER	
507032	64398+71373+64436	BD	MEY	ANG	MER	
507033	64399+71374+64437	BD	MEY	ANG	MER	

Class 508/1

Vehicle Length: (Driving) 64ft 11½in (19.80m) (Inter) 65ft 4¼in (19.92m) Height: 11ft 6½in (3.58m) Width: 9ft 3in (2.82m) Horsepower: 880hp (656kW) Seats (total/car): 186S, 56S/74S/56S

Number	Formation DMSO+TSO+DMSO	Depot	Livery	Owner	Operator	Name
508103	64651+71485+64694	BD	MEY	ANG	MER	
508104	64652+71486+64964	BD	MEY	ANG	MER	
508108	64656+71490+64699	BD	MEY	ANG	MER	
508110	64658+71492+64701	BD	MEY	ANG	MER	
508111	64659+71493+64702	BD	SPL	ANG	MER	*The Beatles*
508112	64660+71494+64703	BD	MEY	ANG	MER	
508114	64662+71496+64705	BD	MEY	ANG	MER	
508115	64663+71497+64708	BD	MEY	ANG	MER	
508117	64665+71499+64908	BD	MEY	ANG	MER	
508120	64668+71502+64711	BD	MEY	ANG	MER	
508122	64670+71504+64713	BD	MEY	ANG	MER	
508123	64671+71505+64714	BD	MEY	ANG	MER	*William Roscoe*
508124	64672+71506+64715	BD	MEY	ANG	MER	
508125	64673+71507+64716	BD	MEY	ANG	MER	
508126	64674+71508+64717	BD	MEY	ANG	MER	
508127	64675+71509+64718	BD	MEY	ANG	MER	
508128	64676+71510+64719	BD	MEY	ANG	MER	
508130	64678+71512+64721	BD	MEY	ANG	MER	
508131	64679+71513+64722	BD	MEY	ANG	MER	
508134(S)	64682+71516+64725	BD	MEY	ANG	-	
508136	64684+71518+64727	BD	MEY	ANG	MER	
508137	64685+71519+64728	BD	MEY	ANG	MER	
508138	64686+71520+64729	BD	MEY	ANG	MER	
508139	64687+71521+64730	BD	MEY	ANG	MER	
508140	64688+71522+64731	BD	MEY	ANG	MER	
508141	64689+71523+64732	BD	MEY	ANG	MER	
508143	64691+71525+64734	BD	MEY	ANG	MER	

left: *The Liverpool area operated Class 508s were originally used on BR Southern Region western section to replace 1936 SUB stock. The '508s' later transferred north. Modified from its original front end design with a high level marker light and modified light clusters, set No. 508140 is seen at Lime Street low level with a service to New Brighton.* **CJM**

Class 777

Vehicle Length: DMS 62ft 3in (19m) MS 44ft 7in (13.6m) Height: 12ft 6in (3.82m) Width: 9ft 2¼in (2.80m) Power supply: 750V dc, 25kV ac Horsepower: 2,800hp (2,088kW) Seats (total): 184S 53S/39S/39S/53S

Number	Formation DMS(A)+MS(A)+MS(B)+DMS(B)	Depot	Livery	Owner	Operator
777001	427001+428001+429001+430001	KK	NME	LIV	MER
777002	427002+428002+429002+430002	KK	NME	LIV	MER
777003	427003+428003+429003+430003	KK	NME	LIV	MER
777004	427004+428004+429004+430004	KK	NME	LIV	MER
777005	427005+428005+429005+430005	KK	NME	LIV	MER
777006	427006+428006+429006+430006	KK	NME	LIV	MER
777007	427007+428007+429007+430007	KK	NME	LIV	MER

777008	427008+428008+429008+430008	KK	NME	LIV	MER
777009	427009+428009+429009+430009	KK	NME	LIV	MER
777010	427010+428010+429010+430010	KK	NME	LIV	MER
777011	427011+428011+429011+430011	KK	NME	LIV	MER
777012	427012+428012+429012+430012	KK	NME	LIV	MER
777013	427013+428013+429013+430013	KK	NME	LIV	MER
777014	427014+428014+429014+430014	KK	NME	LIV	MER
777015	427015+428015+429015+430015	KK	NME	LIV	MER
777016	427016+428016+429016+430016	KK	NME	LIV	MER
777017	427017+428017+429017+430017	KK	NME	LIV	MER
777018	427018+428018+429018+430018	KK	NME	LIV	MER
777019	427019+428019+429019+430019	KK	NME	LIV	MER
777020	427020+428020+429020+430020	KK	NME	LIV	MER
777021	427021+428021+429021+430021	KK	NME	LIV	MER
777022	427022+428022+429022+430022	KK	NME	LIV	MER
777023	427023+428023+429023+430023	KK	NME	LIV	MER
777024	427024+428024+429024+430024	KK	NME	LIV	MER
777025	427025+428025+429025+430025	KK	NME	LIV	MER
777026	427026+428026+429026+430026	KK	NME	LIV	MER
777027	427027+428027+429027+430027	KK	NME	LIV	MER
777028	427028+428028+429028+430028	KK	NME	LIV	MER
777029	427029+428029+429029+430029	KK	NME	LIV	MER
777030	427030+428030+429030+430030	KK	NME	LIV	MER
777031	427031+428031+429031+430031	KK	NME	LIV	MER
777032	427032+428032+429032+430032	KK	NME	LIV	MER
777033	427033+428033+429033+430033	KK	NME	LIV	MER
777034	427034+428034+429034+430034	KK	NME	LIV	MER
777035	427035+428035+429035+430035	KK	NME	LIV	MER
777036	427036+428036+429036+430036	KK	NME	LIV	MER
777037	427037+428037+429037+430037	KK	NME	LIV	MER
777038	427038+428038+429038+430038	KK	NME	LIV	MER
777039	427039+428039+429039+430039	KK	NME	LIV	MER
777040	427040+428040+429040+430040	KK	NME	LIV	MER
777041	427041+428041+429041+430041	KK	NME	LIV	MER
777042	427042+428042+429042+430042	KK	NME	LIV	MER
777043	427043+428043+429043+430043	KK	NME	LIV	MER
777044	427044+428044+429044+430044	KK	NME	LIV	MER
777045	427045+428045+429045+430045	KK	NME	LIV	MER
777046	427046+428046+429046+430046	KK	NME	LIV	MER
777047	427047+428047+429047+430047	KK	NME	LIV	MER
777048	427048+428048+429048+430048	KK	NME	LIV	MER
777049	427049+428049+429049+430049	KK	NME	LIV	MER
777050	427050+428050+429050+430050	KK	NME	LIV	MER
777051	427051+428051+429051+430051	KK	NME	LIV	MER
777052	427052+428052+429052+430052	KK	NME	LIV	MER

Below: *In January 2020, the first of 52 four-car articulated Stadler-built Class 777 units was delivered to Mersey Rail at Kirkdale. The set, No. 777003 will be used for type test approval and training, before fleet deliveries commence in spring 2020. Set No. 777003 is seen at Crewe on its delivery run.* **Cliff Beeton**

Northern Rail

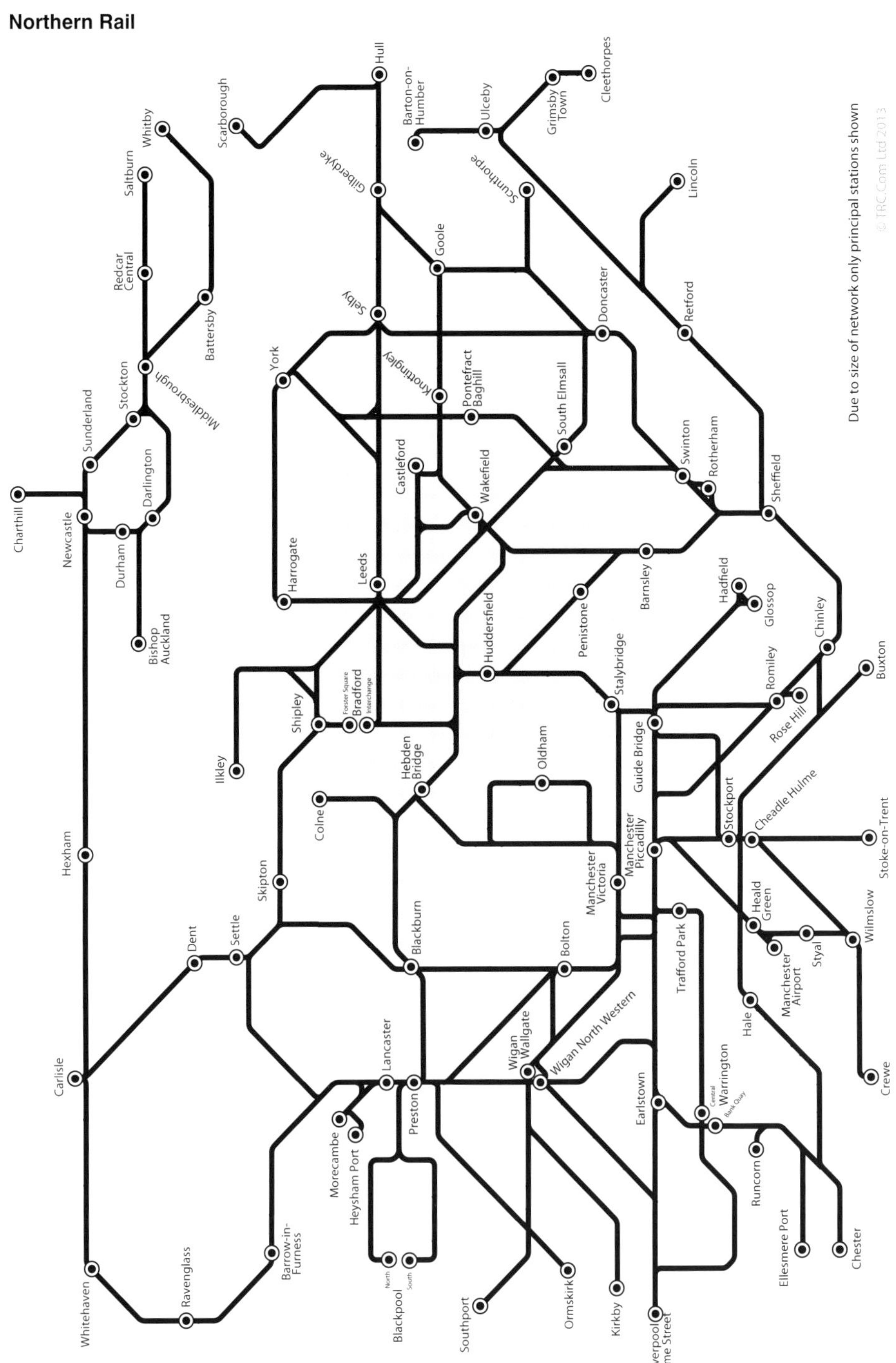

Northern Rail

Address: ✉ Northern House, 9 Rougier Street, York, YO1 6HZ
enquiries@northernrailway.co.ukg
✆ 0845 000125 ⓘ www.northernrailway.co.uk

Managing Director: David Brown
Franchise Dates: 12 December 2004 - March 2025
Principal Routes: Regional services in Merseyside, Greater Manchester, South / North Yorkshire, Lancashire, Cumbria and the North East
Depots: Newton Heath (NH), Heaton (HT), Longsight (LG), Neville Hill (NL), Allerton (AN)
Parent Company: Arriva Trains

Class 144
Pacer

Vehicle Length: 50ft 2in (15.25m)
Height: 12ft 2½in (3.73m)
Width: 8ft 10½in (2.70m)
Engine: 1 x Cummins LTA10-R per vehicle
Horsepower: 460hp (343kW)
Seats (total/car): 87S, 45S/42S

Number	*Formation DMS+DMSL*	*Depot*	*Livery*	*Owner*	*Operator*
144001	55801+55824	HT	NOR	PTR	NOR
144002	55802+55825	HT	NOR	PTR	NOR
144003	55803+55826	HT	NOR	PTR	NOR
144004	55804+55827	HT	NOR	PTR	NOR
144005	55805+55828	HT	NOR	PTR	NOR
144006	55806+55829	HT	NOR	PTR	NOR
144007	55807+55830	HT	NOR	PTR	NOR
144008	55808+55831	HT	NOR	PTR	NOR
144009	55809+55832	HT	NOR	PTR	NOR
144010	55810+55833	HT	NOR	PTR	NOR
144011	55811+55834	HT	NOR	PTR	NOR
144012§	55812+55835	HT	NOA	PTR	NOR
144013	55813+55836	HT	NOR	PTR	NOR

§ Set 144012 modified as '144evolution' train with new-style interior, seating and toilet. DMS seats 43S and DMSL 35S.

Name applied
144001 ***The Penistone Line Partnership***

Above: *Another 'Pacer' class which is due for early withdrawal are the Class 144 two and three-car sets. Usually operated on Metro services in the Sheffield/Doncaster area the sets sport Northern livery with the 'M' Metro logo on the bodyside. No. 144011 departs from Doncaster on a Hull service.* **CJM**

Northern Rail

Vehicle Length: 50ft 2in (15.25m)
Height: 12ft 2½in (3.73m)
Width: 8ft 10½in (2.70m)
Engine: 1 x Cummins LTA10-R per vehicle
Horsepower: 690hp (515kW)
Seats (total/car): 145S, 45S/58S/42S

Number	*Formation* DMS+MS+DMSL	*Depot*	*Livery*	*Owner*	*Operator*
144014	55814+55850+55837	HT	NOR	PTR	NOR
144015	55815+55851+55838	HT	NOR	PTR	NOR
144016	55816+55852+55839	HT	NOR	PTR	NOR
144017	55817+55853+55840	HT	NOR	PTR	NOR
144018	55818+55854+55841	HT	NOR	PTR	NOR
144019	55819+55855+55842	HT	NOR	PTR	NOR
144020	55820+55856+55843	HT	NOR	PTR	NOR
144021	55821+55857+55844	HT	NOR	PTR	NOR
144022	55822+55858+55845	HT	NOR	PTR	NOR
144023	55823+(55859)+55846	HT	NOR	PTR	NOR

Left: *The final 10 Class 144s, Nos. 144014-144023 are three car formations, with an intermediate Motor Standard (MS), the only non-driving 'Pacer' vehicle design. Set No. 144015 shows this design at Doncaster. The intermediate vehicles were painted all-over blue, with no mauve/grey decals.* **CJM**

Class 150/1
Sprinter

Vehicle Length: 64ft 9¾in (19.74m)
Height: 12ft 4½in (3.77m)
Width: 9ft 3⅛in (2.82m)
Engine: 1 x NT855R5 of 285hp per vehicle
Horsepower: 570hp (425kW)
Seats (total/car): 124S, 59S/65S

Number	*Formation* DMSL+DMS	*Depot*	*Livery*	*Owner*	*Operator*
150101	52101+57101	NH	NNR	ANG	NOR
150102	52102+57102	NH	NNR	ANG	NOR
150103	52103+57103	NH	NNR	ANG	NOR
150104	52104+57104	NH	NNR	ANG	NOR
150105	52105+57105	NH	LMI	ANG	NOR
150106	52106+57106	NH	NNR	ANG	NOR
150107	52107+57107	NH	LMI	ANG	NOR
150108	52108+57108	NH	NNR	ANG	NOR
150109	52109+57109	NH	NNR	ANG	NOR
150110	52110+57110	NH	NOR	ANG	NOR
150111	52111+57111	NH	NOR	ANG	NOR
150112	52112+57112	NH	NNR	ANG	NOR
150113	52113+57113	NH	NNR	ANG	NOR
150114	52114+57114	NH	NNR	ANG	NOR
150115	52115+57115	NH	NNR	ANG	NOR
150116	52116+57116	NH	NNR	ANG	NOR
150117	52117+57117	NH	NOR	ANG	NOR
150118	52118+57118	NH	NNR	ANG	NOR
150119	52119+57119	NH	NNR	ANG	NOR
150120	52120+57120	NH	NNR	ANG	NOR
150121	52121+57121	NH	NNR	ANG	NOR
150122	52122+57122	NH	FGB	ANG	NOR
150123	52123+57123	NH	NNR	ANG	NOR
150124	52124+57124	NH	NNR	ANG	NOR
150125	52125+57125	NH	NNR	ANG	NOR
150126	52126+57126	NH	NNR	ANG	NOR
150127	52127+57127	NH	NNR	ANG	NOR
150128	52128+57128	NH	NNR	ANG	NOR
150129	52129+57129	NH	NNR	ANG	NOR
150130	52130+57130	NH	NNR	ANG	NOR
150131	52131+57131	NH	NNR	ANG	NOR
150132	52132+57132	NH	NNR	ANG	NOR
150133	52133+57133	NH	NNR	ANG	NOR
150134	52134+57134	NH	NNR	ANG	NOR
150135	52135+57135	NH	NOR	ANG	NOR
150136	52136+57136	NH	NNR	ANG	NOR
150137	52137+57137	NH	NNR	ANG	NOR
150138	52138+57138	NH	NNR	ANG	NOR
150139	52139+57139	NH	NNR	ANG	NOR
150140	52140+57140	NH	NNR	ANG	NOR
150141	52141+57141	NH	NNR	ANG	NOR
150142	52142+57142	NH	NNR	ANG	NOR
150143	52143+57143	NH	NNR	ANG	NOR
150144	52144+57144	NH	NNR	ANG	NOR
150145	52145+57145	NH	NNR	ANG	NOR
150146	52146+57146	NH	NNR	ANG	NOR
150147	52147+57147	NH	NNR	ANG	NOR
150148	52148+57148	NH	NNR	ANG	NOR
150149	52149+57149	NH	NNR	ANG	NOR
150150	52150+57150	NH	NNR	ANG	NOR

Right: *The Northern franchise operates a considerable number of different DMU classes and sub-classes, the vast majority of which have now been refurbished and sport the latest Northern white and blue colours. The franchise has in recent years received all Class 150/1s from other operators. Set No. 150149 is recorded at Preston.* **CJM**

Class 150/2
Sprinter

Vehicle Length: 64ft 9¾in (19.74m)
Height: 12ft 4½in (3.77m)
Width: 9ft 3⅛in (2.82m)
Engine: 1 x NT855R5 of 285hp per vehicle
Horsepower: 570hp (425kW)
Seats (total/car): 132S, 62S/70S

Number	*Formation DMSL+DMS*	*Depot*	*Livery*	*Owner*	*Operator*
150201	52201+57201	NH	NOR	ANG	NOR
150203	52203+57203	NL	NNR	ANG	NOR
150204	52204+57204	NH	NNR	ANG	NOR
150205	52205+57205	NL	NNR	ANG	NOR
150206	52206+57206	NL	NNR	ANG	NOR
150209	57212+57209	NH	NNR	ANG	NOR
150210	52210+57210	NH	NOR	ANG	NOR
150211	52211+57211	NL	NNR	ANG	NOR
150214	52214+57214	NL	NNR	ANG	NOR
150215	52215+57215	NH	NNR	ANG	NOR
150218	52218+57218	NH	NOR	ANG	NOR
150220	52220+57220	NL	NNR	ANG	NOR
150222	52222+57222	NH	NNR	ANG	NOR
150223	52223+57223	NL	NNR	ANG	NOR
150224	52224+57224	NH	NNR	ANG	NOR
150225	52225+57225	NH	NNR	ANG	NOR
150226	52226+57226	NH	NOR	ANG	NOR
150228	52228+57228	NL	NNR	PTR	NOR
150268	52268+57268	NL	NNR	PTR	NOR
150269	52269+57269	NL	NNR	PTR	NOR
150270	52270+57270	NL	NNR	PTR	NOR
150271	52271+57271	NL	NNR	PTR	NOR
150272	52272+57272	NL	NNR	PTR	NOR
150273	52273+57273	NL	NNR	PTR	NOR
150274	52274+57274	NL	NNR	PTR	NOR
150275	52275+57275	NL	NNR	PTR	NOR
150276	52276+57276	NL	NNR	PTR	NOR
150277	52277+57277	NL	NNR	PTR	NOR

Name applied

150214 ***The Bentham Line - A Dementia-Friendly Railway***

Right: *Allocated to Neville Hill, Leeds and Heaton, Newcastle, Northern has a fleet of 28 Class 150/2s. Set No. 150205 in the latest Northern colours arrives at Manchester Piccadilly.* **Cliff Beeton**

Class 153

Vehicle Length: 76ft 5in (23.29m)
Height: 12ft 3⅛in (3.75m)
Width: 8ft 10in (2.70m)
Engine: 1 x NT855R5 of 285hp
Horsepower: 285hp (213kW)
Seats (total/car): 70S

Number	*Formation DMSL*	*Depot*	*Livery*	*Owner*	*Operator*
153301	52301	NL	NOR	ANG	NOR
153304	52304	NL	NOR	ANG	NOR
153307	52307	NL	NOR	ANG	NOR
153315	52315	NL	NOR	ANG	NOR
153316	52316	NL	NOR	PTR	NOR
153317	52317	NL	NOR	ANG	NOR
153324	52324	NL	NOR	PTR	NOR
153328	52328	NL	NOR	ANG	NOR
153330	52330	NL	NOR	PTR	NOR
153331	52331	NL	NOR	ANG	NOR
153332	52332	NL	NOR	ANG	NOR
153351	57351	NL	NOR	ANG	NOR
153352	57352	NL	NOR	ANG	NOR
153358	57358	NL	NOR	PTR	NOR

153359	57359	NL	NOR	PTR	NOR	153373	57373	NL	GWG	ANG	NOR
153360	57360	NL	NOR	PTR	NOR	153378	57378	NL	NOR	ANG	NOR
153363	57363	NL	NOR	PTR	NOR	153380	57380	NL	GWG	ANG	NOR

Name applied
153316 ***John 'Longitude' Harrison Inventor of the Marine Chronometer***

Left: *Over the last couple of years the ranks of Class 153s has increased, with several sets being transferred from other operators. In January 2020 the fleet size stood at 20, allocated to Leeds Neville Hill. Northern liveried No. 153378 is shown.* **CJM**

Class 155
Super Sprinter

Vehicle Length: 76ft 5in (23.29m)
Height: 12ft 3⅛in (3.75m)
Width: 8ft 10in (2.70m)
Engine: 1 x NT855R5 of 285hp per vehicle
Horsepower: 570hp (425kW)
Seats (total/car): 156S, 76S/80S

Number	*Formation DMSL+DMS*	*Depot*	*Livery*	*Owner*	*Operator*
155341	52341+57341	NL	NNR	PTR	NOR
155342	52342+57342	NL	NNR	PTR	NOR
155343	52343+57343	NL	NNR	PTR	NOR
155344	52344+57344	NL	NNR	PTR	NOR
155345	52345+57345	NL	NNR	PTR	NOR
155346	52346+57346	NL	NNR	PTR	NOR
155347	52347+57347	NL	NNR	PTR	NOR

Left: *Of the once large fleet of two-car Class 155s, built by Leyland, only seven sets remain, the others were split, rebuilt and now form Class 153. All Northern 155s, which are now scheduled to stay with the operator, are in the latest white and blue colours and have been refurbished. Set No. 155342 is seen at Colton Junction with a York-Hull service.* **CJM**

Class 156
Super Sprinter

Vehicle Length: 75ft 6in (23.03m)
Height: 12ft 6in (3.81m)
Width: 8ft 11in (2.73m)
Engine: 1 x Cummins NT855R5 of 285hp per car
Horsepower: 570hp (425kW)
Seats (total/car): 146S, 70/76S

Number	*Formation DMSL+DMS*	*Depot*	*Livery*	*Owner*	*Operator*
156420	52420+57420	NH	NNR	PTR	NOR
156421	52421+57421	HT	NNR	PTR	NOR
156423	52423+57423	NH	NNR	PTR	NOR
156424	52424+57424	NH	NNR	PTR	NOR
156425	52425+57425	NH	NOR	PTR	NOR
156426	52426+57426	NH	NOR	PTR	NOR
156427	52427+57427	NH	NNR	PTR	NOR
156428	52428+57428	NH	NNR	PTR	NOR
156429	52429+57429	NH	NOR	PTR	NOR
156438	52438+57438	HT	NNR	ANG	NOR
156440	52440+57440	NH	NNR	PTR	NOR
156441	52441+57441	HT	NNR	PTR	NOR
156443	52443+57443	HT	NNR	ANG	NOR
156444	52444+57444	HT	NNR	ANG	NOR
156447	52447+57447	HT	SRB	ANG	NOR
156448	52448+57448	HT	NNR	ANG	NOR
156449	52449+57449	HT	SRB	ANG	NOR
156451	52451+57451	HT	NNR	ANG	NOR
156452	52452+57452	NH	NNR	PTR	NOR
156454	52454+57454	HT	NNR	ANG	NOR
156455	52455+57455	NH	NNR	PTR	NOR
156459	52459+57459	NH	NNR	PTR	NOR

156460	52460+57460	NH	NOR	PTR	NOR
156461	52461+57461	NH	NOR	PTR	NOR
156463	52463+57463	HT	NOR	ANG	NOR
156464	52464+57464	NH	SPL	PTR	NOR
156465	52465+57465	HT	SRB	ANG	NOR
156466	52466+57466	NH	NNR	PTR	NOR
156468	52468+57468	HT	NNR	ANG	NOR
156469	52469+57469	HT	NNR	ANG	NOR
156471	52471+57471	HT	NNR	ANG	NOR
156472	52472+57472	HT	NNR	ANG	NOR
156475	52475+57475	HT	NNR	ANG	NOR
156479	52479+57479	HT	NNR	ANG	NOR
156480	52480+57480	HT	SPL	ANG	NOR
156481	52481+57481	HT	NNR	ANG	NOR
156482	52482+57482	HT	NNR	ANG	NOR
156483	52483+57483	HT	NNR	ANG	NOR
156484	52484+57484	HT	NNR	ANG	NOR
156485	52485+57485	HT	SRB	ANG	NOR
156486	52486+57486	HT	NNR	ANG	NOR
156487	52487+57487	HT	NNR	ANG	NOR
156488	52488+57488	HT	NNR	ANG	NOR
156489	52489+57489	HT	NNR	ANG	NOR
156490	52490+57490	HT	NNR	ANG	NOR
156491	52491+57491	HT	NNR	ANG	NOR
156496	52496+57496	HT	SCR	ANG	NOR

Names applied
156460 *Driver John Axon GC*
156464 *Lancashire DalesRail*
156469 *The Royal Northumberland Fusiliers (The Fighting Fifth)*
156480 *RAF 100 Spirit of The Royal Air Force*
156483 *William George 'Billy' Hardy 14/01/1903-10/03/1950*

Right: *Longer distance regional services operated by Northern are in the hands of a fleet of 47 two-car Class 156s, which operate from Heaton or Newton Heath depots. The majority of sets are now refurbished and sport Northern white livery, as shown on set No. 156427.* **CJM**

Class 158/0

Vehicle Length: 76ft 1¾in (23.21m)
Height: 12ft 6in (3.81m)
Width: 9ft 3¼in (2.82m)
Engine: 1 x Cummins NTA855R of 350hp per vehicle
Horsepower: 1,050hp (783kW)
Seats (total/car): 200S, 64S/68S/68S

Number	*Formation DMSL+MSL+DMSL*	*Depot*	*Livery*	*Owner*	*Op'r*
158752	52752+58716+57752	NL	NNR	PTR	NOR
158753	52753+58710+57753	NL	NNR	PTR	NOR
158754	52754+58708+57754	NL	NNR	PTR	NOR
158755	52755+58702+57755	NL	NNR	PTR	NOR
158756	52756+58712+57756	NL	NNR	PTR	NOR
158757	52757+58706+57757	NL	NNR	PTR	NOR
158758	52758+58714+57758	NL	NNR	PTR	NOR
158759	52759+58713+57759	NL	NNR	PTR	NOR

Below: *A fleet of eight three-car Class 158s are on the books of Neville Hill depot and operate longer distance services. All sets have been refurbished and meet the latest disability discrimination act regulations and have universal access toilets. Set No. 158759 stands at Preston with a Blackpool service.* **CJM**

Northern Rail

Class 158/0

Vehicle Length: 76ft 1¾in (23.21m)
Height: 12ft 6in (3.81m)
Width: 9ft 3¼in (2.82m)
Engine: 1 x Cummins NTA855R of 350hp per vehicle
Horsepower: 700hp (522kW)
Seats (total/car): 138S, 68S/70S (Refurb-66S / 72S)

Number	Formation DMSL+DMSL	Depot	Livery	Owner	Operator
158782	52782+57782	NL	NNR	ANG	NOR
158784	52784+57784	NL	NOR	ANG	NOR
158786	52786+57786	NL	NNR	ANG	NOR
158787	52787+57787	NL	NOR	ANG	NOR
158789	52789+57789	NL	NNR	ANG	NOR
158790	52790+57790	NL	NOR	ANG	NOR
158791	52791+57791	NL	NOR	ANG	NOR
158792	52792+57792	NL	NOR	ANG	NOR
158793	52793+57793	NL	NOR	ANG	NOR
158794	52794+57794	NL	NOR	ANG	NOR
158795	52795+57795	NL	NOR	ANG	NOR
158796	52796+57796	NL	NOR	ANG	NOR
158797	52797+57797	NL	NOR	ANG	NOR
158815	52815+57815	HT	NOR	ANG	NOR
158816	52816+57816	HT	NOR	ANG	NOR
158817	52817+57817	HT	NOR	ANG	NOR
158842	52842+57842	HT	NOR	ANG	NOR
158843	52843+57843	HT	NOR	ANG	NOR
158844	52844+57844	HT	NOR	ANG	NOR
158845	52845+57845	HT	NNR	ANG	NOR
158848	52848+57848	HT	NOR	ANG	NOR
158849	52849+57849	HT	NNR	ANG	NOR
158850	52850+57850	HT	NOR	ANG	NOR
158851	52851+57851	HT	NOR	ANG	NOR
158853	52853+57853	HT	NOR	ANG	NOR
158855	52855+57855	HT	NOR	ANG	NOR
158859	52859+57859	HT	NOR	ANG	NOR
158860	52860+57860	HT	NOR	ANG	NOR
158861	52861+57861	HT	NOR	ANG	NOR
158867	52867+57867	NL	NNR	ANG	NOR
158868	52868+57868	NL	NNR	ANG	NOR
158869	52869+57869	NL	NNR	ANG	NOR
158870	52870+57870	NL	NNR	ANG	NOR
158871	52871+57871	NL	NNR	ANG	NOR
158872	52872+57872	NL	NOR	ANG	NOR

Names applied
158784 ***Barbara Castle***
158791 ***County of Nottinghamshire***
158796 ***Fred Trueman - Cricketing Legend***
158797 ***Jane Tomlinson***
158860 ***Ian Dewhirst***
158861 ***Magna Carta 800 - Lincoln 800***
158910 ***William Wilberforce***

Left: *In 2020 a fleet of 35 two-car Class 158s were operated by Northern, allocated to either Neville Hill or Heaton depots. The sets carried a mix of new Northern or pictogram liveries. No. 158784* Barbara Castle *is shown in Manchester public transport pictogram livery.* **CJM**

Class 158/9

Vehicle Length: 76ft 1¾in (23.21m)
Height: 12ft 6in (3.81m)
Width: 9ft 3¼in (2.82m)
Engine: 1 x Cummins NTA855R of 350hp per vehicle
Horsepower: 700hp (522kW)
Seats (total/car): 142S, 70S/72S

Number	Formation DMSL+DMS	Depot	Livery	Owner	Operator
158901	52901+57901	NL	NNR	EVL	NOR
158902	52902+57902	NL	NNR	EVL	NOR
158903	52903+57903	NL	NNR	EVL	NOR
158904	52904+57904	NL	NNR	EVL	NOR
158905	52905+57905	NL	NNR	EVL	NOR
158906	52906+57906	NL	NNR	EVL	NOR
158907	52907+57907	NL	NNR	EVL	NOR
158908	52908+57908	NL	NNR	EVL	NOR
158909	52909+57909	NL	NNR	EVL	NOR
158910	52910+57910	NL	NNR	EVL	NOR

Left: *The ten members of Class 158/9 were originally sponsored by West Yorkshire PTE, but are now considered as part of the core Northern fleet. These sets carry a mix of new Northern colours and pictogram branding. Set No. 158901 shows a West Yorkshire travel pictogram livery.* **CJM**

Class 170/4
Turbostar

Vehicle Length: 77ft 6in (23.62m)
Height: 12ft 4½in (3.77m)
Width: 8ft 10in (2.69m)
Engine: 1 x MTU 6R 183TD13H of 422hp per vehicle
Horsepower: 1,266hp (944kW)
Seats: 200S, 57S/76S/67S

Number	*DMSL+MS+DMSL*	*Depot*	*Livery*	*Own'r*	*Op'r*
170453	50453+56453+79453	NL	NNR	PTR	NOR
170454	50454+56454+79454	NL	NNR	PTR	NOR
170455	50455+56455+79455	NL	NNR	PTR	NOR
170456	50456+56456+79456	NL	NNR	PTR	NOR
170457	50457+56457+79457	NL	NNR	PTR	NOR
170458	50458+56458+79458	NL	NNR	PTR	NOR
170459	50459+56459+79459	NL	NNR	PTR	NOR
170460	50460+56460+79460	NL	NNR	PTR	NOR
170461	50461+56461+79461	NL	NNR	PTR	NOR
170470	50470+56470+79470	NL	BLU	PTR	NOR
170471	50471+56471+79471	NL	BLU	PTR	NOR
170472	50472+56472+79472	NL	NNR	PTR	NOR
170473	50473+56473+79473	NL	NNR	PTR	NOR
170474	50474+56474+79474	NL	NNR	PTR	NOR
170475	50475+56475+79475	NL	NNR	PTR	NOR
170476	50476+56476+79476	NL	NNR	PTR	NOR
170477	50477+56477+79477	NL	NNR	PTR	NOR
170478	50478+56478+79478	NL	NNR	PTR	NOR

Right: *A recent addition to the Northern portfolio is a batch of Class 170s, displaced from ScotRail. The sets, allocated to Neville Hill, have been refurbished and now sport Northern white and blue colours, set No. 170474 departs from Doncaster on a Hull to Sheffield working.* **CJM**

Class 195
Civity

Vehicle Length: Driving - 24.03m
Inter - 23.35m
Height: 3.80m
Width: 2.55m
Engine: 1x MTU 6H 1800 R85L
Horsepower: 523hp
Seats (total/car): 2-car 108S, 45S/63S
3-car 184S, 45S/76S/63S

Number	*Formation DMSL+DMS*	*Depot*	*Livery*	*Owner*	*Op'r*
195001	101001+103001	NH	NNR	EVL	NOR
195002	101002+103002	NH	NNR	EVL	NOR
195003	101003+103003	NH	NNR	EVL	NOR
195004	101004+103004	NH	NNR	EVL	NOR
195005	101005+103005	NH	NNR	EVL	NOR
195006	101006+103006	NH	NNR	EVL	NOR
195007	101007+103007	NH	NNR	EVL	NOR
195008	101008+103008	NH	NNR	EVL	NOR
195009	101009+103009	NH	NNR	EVL	NOR
195010	101010+103010	NH	NNR	EVL	NOR
195011	101011+103011	NH	NNR	EVL	NOR
195012	101012+103012	NH	NNR	EVL	NOR
195013	101013+103013	NH	NNR	EVL	NOR
195014	101014+103014	NH	NNR	EVL	NOR
195015	101015+103015	NH	NNR	EVL	NOR
195016	101016+103016	NH	NNR	EVL	NOR
195017	101017+103017	NH	NNR	EVL	NOR
195018	101018+103018	NH	NNR	EVL	NOR
195019	101019+103019	NH	NNR	EVL	NOR
195020	101020+103020	NH	NNR	EVL	NOR
195021	101021+103021	NH	NNR	EVL	NOR
195022	101022+103022	NH	NNR	EVL	NOR
195023	101023+103023	NH	NNR	EVL	NOR
195024	101024+103024	NH	NNR	EVL	NOR
195025	101025+103025	NH	NNR	EVL	NOR

Number	*Formation DMSL+MS+DMS*	*Depot*	*Livery*	*Owner*	*Operator*	*Name*
195101	101101+102101+103101	NH	NNR	EVL	NOR	
195102	101102+102102+103102	NH	NNR	EVL	NOR	
195103	101103+102103+103103	NH	NNR	EVL	NOR	
195104	101104+102104+103104	NH	NNR	EVL	NOR	
195105	101105+102105+103105	NH	NNR	EVL	NOR	*Northern Powerhouse*
195106	101106+102106+103106	NH	NNR	EVL	NOR	
195107	101107+102107+103107	NH	NNR	EVL	NOR	
195108	101108+102108+103108	NH	NNR	EVL	NOR	
195109	101109+102109+103109	NH	NNR	EVL	NOR	*Deva Victrix*
195110	101110+102110+103110	NH	NNR	EVL	NOR	
195111	101111+102111+103111	NH	NNR	EVL	NOR	
195112	101112+102112+103112	NH	NNR	EVL	NOR	
195113	101113+102113+103113	NH	NNR	EVL	NOR	
195114	101114+102114+103114	NH	NNR	EVL	NOR	
195115	101115+102115+103115	NH	NNR	EVL	NOR	

195116	101116+102116+103116	NH	NNR	EVL	NOR	*Proud to be Northern*
195117	101117+102117+103117	NH	NNR	EVL	NOR	
195118	101118+102118+103118	NH	NNR	EVL	NOR	
195119	101119+102119+103119	NH	NNR	EVL	NOR	
195120	101120+102120+103120	NH	NNR	EVL	NOR	
195121	101121+102121+103121	NH	NNR	EVL	NOR	
195122	101122+102122+103122	NH	NNR	EVL	NOR	
195123	101123+102123+103123	NH	NNR	EVL	NOR	
195124	101124+102124+103124	NH	NNR	EVL	NOR	
195125	101125+102125+103125	NH	NNR	EVL	NOR	
195126	101126+102126+103126	NH	NNR	EVL	NOR	
195127	101127+102127+103127	NH	NNR	EVL	NOR	
195128	101128+102128+103128	NH	NNR	EVL	NOR	*Calder Champion*
195129	101129+102129+103129	NH	NNR	EVL	NOR	
195130	101130+102130+103130	NH	NNR	EVL	NOR	
195131	101131+102131+103131	NH	NNR	EVL	NOR	
195132	101132+102132+103132	NH	NNR	EVL	NOR	
195133	101133+102133+103133	NH	NNR	EVL	NOR	

Above: *The latest DMUs to enter service with Northern are a fleet of 25 two-car and 33 three-car CAF-built 'Civity' sets. The state-of-the-art sets entered passenger service in mid 2019 and the full fleet will be in traffic by mid 2020. The sets are being constructed in both Spain and CAFs new plant at Llanwern, Wales. Three-car set No. 195124 is seen at Preston.* **CJM**

Class 319

Vehicle Length: (Driving) 65ft 0¾in (19.83m) (Inter) 65ft 4¼in (19.92m)
Height: 11ft 9in (3.58m)
Width: 9ft 3in (2.82m)
Horsepower: 1,326hp (990kW)
Seats (total/car): 300S, 70S/78S/74S/78S

Number	*Formation* *DTCO+MSO+TSO+DTSO*	*Depot*	*Livery*	*Owner*	*Operator*
319361	77459+63043+71929+77458	AN	NNR	PTR	NOR
319363	77463+63045+71931+77462	AN	NNR	PTR	NOR
319365	77467+63047+71933+77466	AN	NNR	PTR	NOR
319366	77469+63048+71934+77468	AN	NNR	PTR	NOR
319367	77471+63049+71935+77470	AN	NNR	PTR	NOR
319368	77473+63050+71936+77472	AN	NNR	PTR	NOR
319369	77475+63051+71937+77474	AN	NNR	PTR	NOR
319370	77477+63052+71938+77476	AN	NNR	PTR	NOR
319372	77481+63054+71940+77480	AN	NNR	PTR	NOR
319374	77485+63056+71942+77484	AN	NNR	PTR	NOR
319375	77487+63057+71943+77486	AN	NNR	PTR	NOR
319378	77493+63060+71946+77492	AN	NNR	PTR	NOR
319379	77495+63061+71947+77494	AN	NNR	PTR	NOR
319381	77973+63093+71979+77974	AN	NNR	PTR	NOR
319383	77977+63096+71981+77978	AN	NNR	PTR	NOR
319385	77981+63097+71983+77982	AN	NNR	PTR	NOR
319386	77983+63098+71984+77984	AN	NNR	PTR	NOR
319446(S)	77381+62936+71817+77380	-	NNR	PTR	OLS

Set 319366 destined for Rail Operations Group 'Orion' service.

Right: *A fleet of 27 four-car ex-Thameslink Class 319s have been refurbished and currently operate north western area electrified services on the Blackpool/Preston to Manchester and Liverpool routes. In the long term, these will be replaced by cascaded Class 323s. In full Northern livery, set No. 319371 is seen arriving at Preston with a Blackpool bound service.* **CJM**

Class 321/9

Vehicle Length: (Driving) 65ft 0¾in (19.83m) (Inter) 65ft 4¼in (19.92m)
Height: 12ft 4¾in (3.78m)
Width: 9ft 3in (2.82m)
Horsepower: 1,328hp (996kW)
Seats (total/car): 288S, 52/79S/78S/79S

Number	Formation DTSOL+MSO+TSO+DTSO	Depot	Livery	Owner	Operator
321901(S)	77990+63153+72128+77993	-	NOE	EVL	Stored at Crewe
321902(S)	77991+63154+72129+77994	-	NOE	EVL	Stored at Crewe
321903	77992+63155+72130+77995	NL	NOE	EVL	NOR

Right: *Introduced in 1991 for the Doncaster-Leeds electrification, these three sets are likely to be stored and phased out of traffic soon, following replacement by Class 331s. Painted in Northern 'electric blue', set No. 321902 is seen at Ilkley.* **CJM**

Class 322

Vehicle Length: (Driving) 65ft 0¾in (19.83m) (Inter) 65ft 4¼in (19.92m)
Height: 12ft 4¾in (3.78m)
Width: 9ft 3in (2.82m)
Horsepower: 1,328hp (996kW)
Seats (total/car): 291S, 74S/83S/76S/58S

Number	Formation DTSOL+MSO+TSO+DTSO	Depot	Livery	Owner	Operator
322481	78163+63137+72023+77985	NL	NOR	EVL	NOR
322482	78164+63138+72024+77986	NL	NOR	EVL	NOR
322483	78165+63139+72025+77987	NL	NOR	EVL	NOR
322484	78166+63140+72026+77988	NL	NOR	EVL	NOR
322485	78167+63141+72027+77989	NL	NOR	EVL	NOR

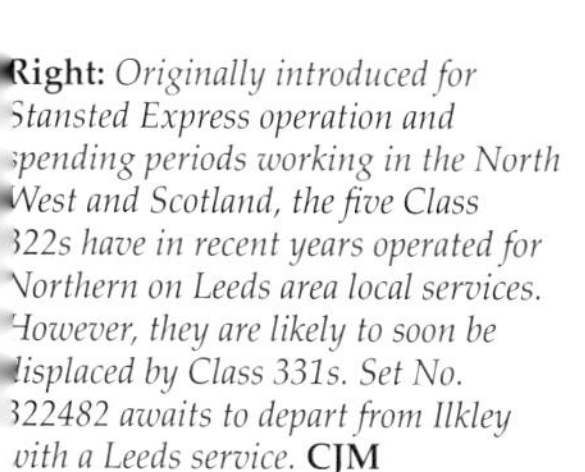

Right: *Originally introduced for Stansted Express operation and spending periods working in the North West and Scotland, the five Class 322s have in recent years operated for Northern on Leeds area local services. However, they are likely to soon be displaced by Class 331s. Set No. 322482 awaits to depart from Ilkley with a Leeds service.* **CJM**

Northern Rail

Class 323

Vehicle Length: (Driving) 76ft 8¼in (23.37m)
(Inter) 76ft 10¾in (23.44m)
Height: 12ft 4¾in (3.78m)
Width: 9ft 2¼in (2.80m)
Horsepower: 1,565hp (1,168kW)
Seats (total/car) 323223-225: 244S, 82S/80S/82S
323226-239: 284S, 98S/88S/98S

Number	Formation DMSO(A)+PTSO+DMSO(B)	Depot	Livery	Owner	Op'r
323223	64023+72223+65023	AN	NOR	PTR	NOR
323224	64024+72224+65024	AN	NOR	PTR	NOR
323225	64025+72225+65025	AN	NOR	PTR	NOR
323226	64026+72226+65026	AN	NNR	PTR	NOR
323227	64027+72227+65027	AN	NOR	PTR	NOR
323228	64028+72228+65028	AN	NOR	PTR	NOR
323229	64029+72229+65029	AN	NNR	PTR	NOR
323230	64030+72230+65030	AN	NOR	PTR	NOR
323231	64031+72231+65031	AN	NOR	PTR	NOR
323232	64032+72232+65032	AN	NOR	PTR	NOR
323233	64033+72233+65033	AN	NOR	PTR	NOR
323234	64034+72234+65034	AN	NNR	PTR	NOR
323235	64035+72235+65035	AN	NOR	PTR	NOR
323236	64036+72236+65036	AN	NOR	PTR	NOR
323237	64037+72237+65037	AN	NOR	PTR	NOR
323238	64038+72238+65038	AN	NNR	PTR	NOR
323239	64039+72239+65039	AN	NNR	PTR	NOR

Left: *In early 2020, Northern operated a fleet of 17 Class 323 three-car sets based at Allerton. After displacement by West Midlands, a further 17 sets will be transferred to Northern, which in time will replace the Class 319 sets, giving the operator a uniform fleet. In unbranded Northern colours, set No. 323236 is seen departing from Manchester Piccadilly.* **Antony Christie**

Class 331
Civity

Vehicle Length: (Driving) 77ft 10¾in (23.74m)
(Inter) 75ft 11in (23.14m)
Height: 12ft 1½in (3.79m)
Width: 9ft 0¼in (2.75m)
Horsepower: 1,475hp (1,100kW)
Seats (total/car): 3 Car - 203S, 51S/80S/72S
4 Car - 280S, 51S/80S/80S/72S

Number	Formation DMSL+PTS+DMS	Depot	Livery	Owner	Operator
331001	463001+464001+466001	AN	NNR	EVL	NOR
331002	463002+464002+466002	AN	NNR	EVL	NOR
331003	463003+464003+466003	AN	NNR	EVL	NOR
331004	463004+464004+466004	AN	NNR	EVL	NOR
331005	463005+464005+466005	AN	NNR	EVL	NOR
331006	463006+464006+466006	AN	NNR	EVL	NOR
331007	463007+464007+466007	AN	NNR	EVL	NOR
331008	463008+464008+466008	AN	NNR	EVL	NOR
331009	463009+464009+466009	AN	NNR	EVL	NOR
331010	463010+464010+466010	AN	NNR	EVL	NOR
331011	463011+464011+466011	AN	NNR	EVL	NOR
331012	463012+464012+466012	AN	NNR	EVL	NOR
331013	463013+464013+466013	AN	NNR	EVL	NOR
331014	463014+464014+466014	AN	NNR	EVL	NOR
331015	463015+464015+466015	AN	NNR	EVL	NOR
331016	463016+464016+466016	AN	NNR	EVL	NOR
331017	463017+464017+466017	AN	NNR	EVL	NOR
331018	463018+464018+466018	AN	NNR	EVL	NOR
331019	463019+464019+466019	AN	NNR	EVL	NOR
331020	463020+464020+466020	AN	NNR	EVL	NOR
331021	463021+464021+466021	AN	NNR	EVL	NOR
331022	463022+464022+466022	AN	NNR	EVL	NOR
331023	463023+464023+466023	AN	NNR	EVL	NOR
331024	463024+464024+466024	AN	NNR	EVL	NOR
331025	463025+464025+466025	AN	NNR	EVL	NOR

331026	463026+464026+466026	AN	NNR	EVL	NOR
331027	463027+464027+466027	AN	NNR	EVL	NOR
331028	463028+464028+466028	AN	NNR	EVL	NOR
331029	463029+464029+466029	AN	NNR	EVL	NOR
331030	463030+464030+466030	AN	NNR	EVL	NOR
331031	463031+464031+466031	AN	NNR	EVL	NOR

Number	*Formation* DMSL+PTS+TS+DMS	*Depot*	*Livery*	*Owner*	*Operator*	*Name*
331101	463101+464101+465101+466101	NL	NNR	EVL	NOR	
331102	463102+464102+465102+466102	AN	NNR	EVL	NOR	
331103	463103+464103+465103+466103	NL	NNR	EVL	NOR	
331104	463104+464104+465104+466104	AN	NNR	EVL	NOR	
331105	463105+464105+465105+466105	AN	NNR	EVL	NOR	
331106	463106+464106+465106+466106	AN	NNR	EVL	NOR	*Proud to be Northern*
331107	463107+464107+465107+466107	AN	NNR	EVL	NOR	
331108	463108+464108+465108+466108	NL	NNR	EVL	NOR	
331109	463109+464109+465109+466109	AN	NNR	EVL	NOR	
331110	463110+464110+465110+466110	NL	NNR	EVL	NOR	*Proud to be Northern*
331111	463111+464111+465111+466111	NL	NNR	EVL	NOR	
331112	463112+464112+465112+466112	NL	NNR	EVL	NOR	

Right: *A fleet of 31 three-car and 12 four-car Class 331 CAF-built 'Civity' EMUs are currently entering service with Northern, based at both Allerton and Neville Hill. The structural and interior design of these sets is very similar to the diesel Class 195s. Four-car set No. 331105 is seen in the Leeds bay at Doncaster.* **CJM**

Class 333

Vehicle Length: (Driving) 77ft 10¾in (23.74m)
(Inter) 75ft 11in (23.14m)
Height: 12ft 1½in (3.79m)
Width: 9ft 0¼in (2.75m)
Horsepower: 1,877hp (1,400kW)
Seats (total/car): 353S, 90S/73S/100S/90S

Number	*Formation* DMSO(A)+PTSO+TSO+DMSO(B)	*Depot*	*Livery*	*Owner*	*Op'r*
333001	78451+74461+74477+78452	NL	NNR	ANG	NOR
333002	78453+74462+74478+78454	NL	NNR	ANG	NOR
333003	78455+74463+74479+78456	NL	NNR	ANG	NOR
333004	78457+74464+74480+78458	NL	NNR	ANG	NOR
333005	78459+74465+74481+78460	NL	NOM	ANG	NOR
333006	78461+74466+74482+78462	NL	NOM	ANG	NOR
333007	78463+74467+74483+78464	NL	NNR	ANG	NOR
333008	78465+74468+74484+78466	NL	NNR	ANG	NOR
333009	78467+74469+74485+78468	NL	NNR	ANG	NOR
333010	78469+74470+74486+78470	NL	NNR	ANG	NOR
333011	78471+74471+74487+78472	NL	NNR	ANG	NOR
333012	78473+74472+74488+78474	NL	NNR	ANG	NOR
333013	78475+74473+74489+78476	NL	NNR	ANG	NOR
333014	78477+74474+74490+78478	NL	NNR	ANG	NOR
333015	78479+74475+74491+78480	NL	NNR	ANG	NOR
333016	78481+74476+74492+78482	NL	NOM	ANG	NOR

Right: *The 16 Aire Valley Class 333 CAF/Siemens sets based at Leeds are the backbone of services on the Leeds/Bradford to Ilkley and Skipton route. In 2019-2020 sets are being refurbished and emerging in the latest Northern white and blue livery. Set No. 333015 displays this colour scheme.* **CJM**

Northern Rail

Class 399
CityLink

Train Length: 122ft 0¾in (37.2m)
Width: 8ft 8½in (2.65m)
Power supply: 750V dc overhead (equipped for 25kV ac operation)
Power equipment: 6 x 145kW VEM traction motors
Seats (total/car): 88S, 22S/44S/22S

Number	Formation DMOSW+MOS+DMOSW	Depot	Livery	Owner	Operator	Name
399201 (201)*	**999001+999101+999201**	§	**SST**	**SST**	**SST**	
399202 (202)*	**999002+999102+999204**	§	**SST**	**SST**	**SST**	***Theo The Childrens Hospital Charity***
399203 (203)*	**999003+999103+999203**	§	**SST**	**SST**	**SST**	
399204 (204)*	**999004+999104+999202**	§	**SST**	**SST**	**SST**	
399205 (205)	**999005+999105+999205**	§	**SST**	**SST**	**SST**	
399206 (206)*	**999006+999106+999206**	§	**SST**	**SST**	**SST**	
399207 (207)	**999007+999107+999207**	§	**SST**	**SST**	**SST**	

* Authorised for TramTrain operation § - Sheffield Nunnery SST - Sheffield Super Tram

Left: *As part of the UK Government sponsored 'TramTrain' trial, Seven Vossloh three-section vehicles operate between Sheffield Cathedral and Rotherham Parkgate. The sets are owned and operated by Sheffield Super Tram and are included in this section as they operate over Northern infrastructure. The sets carry Stagecoach blue livery without a yellow front end. Set No. 399201 is seen passing the standard height platforms at Rotherham Central, the low-lever 'Tram Train' platform is at the far end.* **CJM**

Class 769
Flex

Vehicle Length: (Driving) 65ft 0¾in (19.83m)
(Inter) 65ft 4¼in (19.92m)
Height: 11ft 9in (3.58m)
Engine: MAN D2876, LUE631
Width: 9ft 3in (2.82m)
Horsepower: electric 1,326hp (990kW)
Horsepower: diesel 2x 523hp (390kW)
Seats (total/car): 300S, 70S/78S/74S/78S

Class 319 electric sets fitted with diesel engines in driving cars as dual power electro-diesel multiple units.

Number	Formation DMCO+MSO+TSO+DMSO	Depot	Livery	Owner	Operator
769424 (319424)	**77337+62914+71795+77336**	**AN**	**NNR**	**PTR**	*under conversion*
769431 (319431)	**77351+62921+71802+77350**	**AN**	**NNR**	**PTR**	**NOR**
769434 (319434)	**77357+62924+71805+77356**	**AN**	**NNR**	**PTR**	*under test*
769442 (319442)	**77373+62932+71813+77372**	**AN**	**NNR**	**PTR**	*under conversion*
769448 (319448)	**77433+62962+71867+77432**	**AN**	**NNR**	**PTR**	*under conversion*
769450 (319450)	**77437+62964+71869+77436**	**AN**	**NNR**	**PTR**	**NOR**
769456 (319456)	**77449+62970+71875+77448**	**AN**	**NNR**	**PTR**	*under test*
769458 (319458)	**77453+62972+71877+77452**	**AN**	**NNR**	**PTR**	**NOR**

Left: *The Porterbrook Leasing led conversion project of former Class 319 dual-voltage EMUs into bi-mode Class 769 sets by adding a diesel engine/ alternator raft below each driving car, has been a protracted affair. A number of sets have been converted but little operating had been done by the end of 2019. Northern are scheduled to have eight sets. Set No. 769450 (the former 319450) is shown.* **Cliff Beeton**

ScotRail

Address: ✉ Atrium Court, 50 Waterloo Street, Glasgow, G2 6HQ
customer.relations@scotrail.com, ✆ 0344 811 0141, ⓘ www.scotrail.com

Managing Director: Alex Haynes
Franchise Dates: 1 April 2015 - March 2022 (reduced from 2030)
Principal Routes: All Scottish services
Depots: Corkerhill (CK), Shields (GW), Haymarket (HA), Inverness (IS) Millerhill (ML)
Parent Company: Abellio

Class 43 – HST

Vehicle Length: 58ft 5in (18.80m)
Height: 12ft 10in (3.90m)
Width: 8ft 11in (2.73m)
Engine: MTU 16V4000 R41R
Horsepower: 2,250hp (1,680kW)
Electrical Equipment: Brush

Number	*Depot*	*Pool*	*Livery*	*Owner*	*Operator*
43003	HA	HPAC	SCI	ANG	ASR
43012	HA	HPAC	SCI	ANG	ASR
43015	HA	HPAC	SCI	ANG	ASR
43018	HA	-	BLU	ANG	(Spares)
43021	HA	HPAC	SCI	ANG	ASR
43026	HA	HPAC	SCI	ANG	ASR
43028	HA	HPAC	SCI	ANG	ASR
43030	HA	HPAC	SCI	ANG	ASR
43031	HA	HPAC	SCI	ANG	ASR
43032	HA	HPAC	SCI	ANG	ASR
43033	HA	HPAC	SCI	ANG	ASR
43034	HA	HPAC	SCI	ANG	ASR
43035	HA	HPAC	SCI	ANG	ASR
43036	HA	HPAC	SCI	ANG	ASR
43037	HA	HPAC	SCI	ANG	ASR
43124	HA	HPAC	SCI	ANG	ASR
43125	HA	HPAC	SCI	ANG	ASR
43126	HA	HPAC	SCI	ANG	ASR
43127	HA	HPAC	SCI	ANG	ASR
43128	HA	HPAC	SCI	ANG	ASR
43129	HA	HPAC	SCI	ANG	ASR
43130	HA	HPAC	SCI	ANG	ASR
43131	HA	HPAC	SCI	ANG	ASR
43132	HA	HPAC	SCI	ANG	ASR
43133	HA	HPAC	SCI	ANG	ASR
43134	HA	HPAC	SCI	ANG	ASR
43135	HA	HPAC	SCI	ANG	ASR
43136	HA	HPAC	SCI	ANG	ASR
43137	HA	HPAC	SCI	ANG	ASR
43138	HA	HPAC	SCI	ANG	ASR
43139	HA	HPAC	SCI	ANG	ASR
43140	HA	HPAC	SCI	ANG	ASR
43141	HA	HPAC	SCI	ANG	ASR
43142	HA	HPAC	SCI	ANG	ASR
43143	HA	HPAC	SCI	ANG	ASR
43144	HA	HPAC	SCI	ANG	ASR
43145	HA	HPAC	SCI	ANG	ASR
43146	HA	HPAC	SCI	ANG	ASR
43147	HA	HPAC	SCI	ANG	ASR
43148	HA	HPAC	SCI	ANG	ASR
43149	HA	HPAC	SCI	ANG	ASR
43150	HA	HPAC	SCI	ANG	ASR
43151	HA	HPAC	SCI	ANG	ASR
43152	HA	HPAC	SCI	ANG	ASR
43163	HA	HPAC	SCI	ANG	ASR
43164	HA	HPAC	SCI	ANG	ASR
43168	HA	HPAC	SCI	ANG	ASR
43169	HA	HPAC	SCI	ANG	ASR
43175	HA	HPAC	SCI	ANG	ASR
43176	HA	HPAC	SCI	ANG	ASR
43177	HA	HPAC	SCI	ANG	ASR
43179	HA	HPAC	SCI	ANG	ASR
43181	HA	HPAC	SCI	ANG	ASR
43182	HA	HPAC	SCI	ANG	ASR
43183	HA	HPAC	SCI	ANG	ASR

Below: *Abellio ScotRail are still in the process of introducing HST stock on Edinburgh/Glasgow '7City' main line services, with a fleet of 26 2+4 and 2+5 HST sets. The power cars, all former Great Western vehicles have been overhauled by Wabtec at Loughborough, while the stock has been overhauled at Wabtec Doncaster and Kilmarnock and fitted with sliding doors, retention toilets and new interiors. The power cars now sport a new ScotRail grey and blue livery, with a pictogram of the Scottish cities, which is different on either side. No. 43036 is shown.* **Antony Christie**

ScotRail

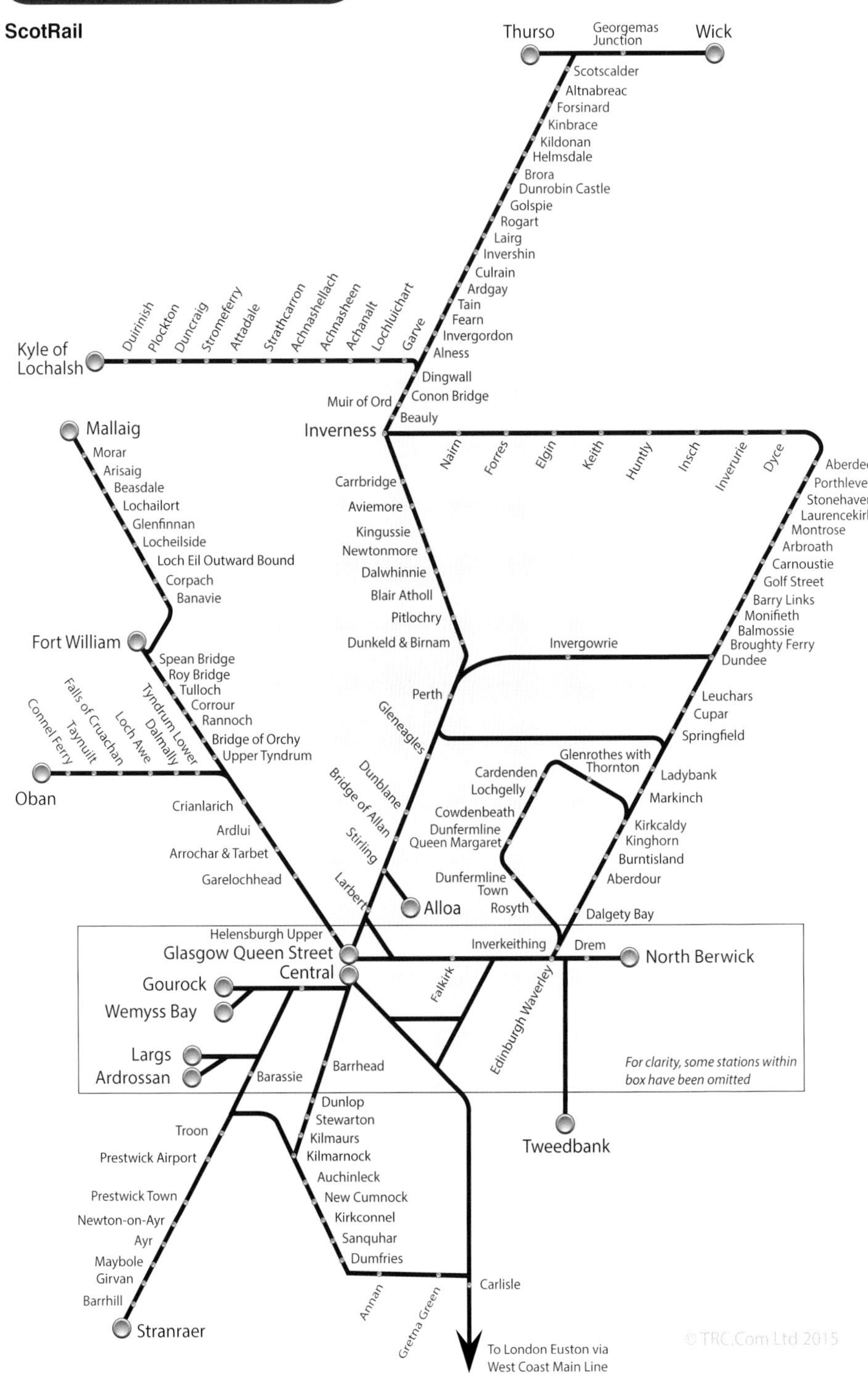

Thurso
Georgemas Junction
Wick
Scotscalder
Altnabreac
Forsinard
Kinbrace
Kildonan
Helmsdale
Brora
Dunrobin Castle
Golspie
Rogart
Lairg
Invershin
Culrain
Ardgay
Tain
Fearn
Invergordon
Alness
Kyle of Lochalsh
Duirinish
Plockton
Duncraig
Stromeferry
Attadale
Strathcarron
Achnashellach
Achnasheen
Achanalt
Lochluichart
Garve
Dingwall
Conon Bridge
Muir of Ord
Beauly
Inverness
Nairn
Forres
Elgin
Keith
Huntly
Insch
Inverurie
Dyce
Aberdeen
Porthleven
Stonehaven
Laurencekirk
Montrose
Arbroath
Carnoustie
Golf Street
Barry Links
Monifieth
Balmossie
Broughty Ferry
Dundee
Mallaig
Morar
Arisaig
Beasdale
Lochailort
Glenfinnan
Locheilside
Loch Eil Outward Bound
Corpach
Banavie
Fort William
Carrbridge
Aviemore
Kingussie
Newtonmore
Dalwhinnie
Blair Atholl
Pitlochry
Dunkeld & Birnam
Invergowrie
Perth
Spean Bridge
Roy Bridge
Tulloch
Corrour
Rannoch
Bridge of Orchy
Upper Tyndrum
Falls of Cruachan
Connel Ferry
Taynuilt
Loch Awe
Tyndrum Lower
Dalmally
Oban
Gleneagles
Leuchars
Cupar
Springfield
Glenrothes with Thornton
Cardenden
Lochgelly
Ladybank
Markinch
Cowdenbeath
Dunfermline Queen Margaret
Kirkcaldy
Kinghorn
Burntisland
Aberdour
Dunfermline Town
Rosyth
Dalgety Bay
Crianlarich
Ardlui
Arrochar & Tarbet
Garelochhead
Dunblane
Bridge of Allan
Stirling
Larbert
Alloa
Helensburgh Upper
Glasgow Queen Street
Central
Inverkeithing
Drem
North Berwick
Gourock
Wemyss Bay
Falkirk
Edinburgh Waverley
Largs
Ardrossan
Barassie
Barrhead
For clarity, some stations within box have been omitted
Dunlop
Stewarton
Kilmaurs
Kilmarnock
Tweedbank
Troon
Prestwick Airport
Auchinleck
New Cumnock
Kirkconnel
Sanquhar
Dumfries
Prestwick Town
Newton-on-Ayr
Ayr
Maybole
Girvan
Barrhill
Stranraer
Carlisle
Annan
Gretna Green
To London Euston via West Coast Main Line
© TRC.Com Ltd 2015

Class 153

Vehicle Length: 76ft 5in (23.29m)
Height: 12ft 3⅛in (3.75m)
Width: 8ft 10in (2.70m)
Engine: 1 x NT855R5 of 285hp
Horsepower: 285hp (213kW)
Seats (total/car): TBA

In 2020 ScotRail will be taking on five Class 153s to modify as cycle / baggage / catering cars for Scottish scenic route services.
Nos. 153373, 153380 to follow.

Number	Formation DML	Depot	Livery	Owner	Operator
153305	52305	-	ASR	ANG	ASR
153370	52370	-	ASR	ANG	ASR
153377	52377	-	ASR	ANG	ASR

Class 156
Super Sprinter

Vehicle Length: 75ft 6in (23.03m)
Height: 12ft 6in (3.81m)
Width: 8ft 11in (2.73m)
Engine: 1 x Cummins NT855R5 of 285hp per car
Horsepower: 570hp (425kW)
Seats (total/car): 142S, 70 or 72S

Number	Formation DMSL+DMS	Depot	Livery	Owner	Operator
156430	52430+57430	CK	SCR	ANG	ASR
156431	52431+57431	CK	SCR	ANG	ASR
156432	52432+57432	CK	SCR	ANG	ASR
156433	52433+57433	CK	SCR	ANG	ASR
156434	52434+57434	CK	SCR	ANG	ASR
156435	52435+57435	CK	SCR	ANG	ASR
156436	52436+57436	CK	SCR	ANG	ASR
156437	52437+57437	CK	SCR	ANG	ASR
156439	52439+57439	CK	SCR	ANG	ASR
156442	52442+57442	CK	SCR	ANG	ASR
156445	52445+57445	CK	SCR	ANG	ASR
156446	52446+57446	CK	SCR	ANG	ASR
156450	52450+57450	CK	SCR	ANG	ASR
156453	52453+57453	CK	SCR	ANG	ASR
156456	52456+57456	CK	SCR	ANG	ASR
156457	52457+57457	CK	SCR	ANG	ASR
156458	52458+57458	CK	SCR	ANG	ASR
156462	52462+57462	CK	SCR	ANG	ASR
156467	52467+57467	CK	SCR	ANG	ASR
156474	52474+57474	CK	SCR	ANG	ASR
156476	52476+57476	CK	SCR	ANG	ASR
156477	52477+57477	CK	SCR	ANG	ASR
156478§	52478+57478	CK	SCR	BRO	ASR
156492	52492+57492	CK	SCR	ANG	ASR
156493	52493+57493	CK	SCR	ANG	ASR
156494	52494+57494	CK	SCR	ANG	ASR
156495	52495+57495	CK	SCR	ANG	ASR
156499	52499+57499	CK	SRB	ANG	ASR
156500	52500+57500	CK	SCR	ANG	ASR
156501	52501+57501	CK	SCR	ANG	ASR
156502	52502+57502	CK	SCR	ANG	ASR
156503	52503+57503	CK	SCR	ANG	ASR
156504	52504+57504	CK	SCR	ANG	ASR
156505	52505+57505	CK	SCR	ANG	ASR
156506	52506+57506	CK	SCR	ANG	ASR
156507	52507+57507	CK	SCR	ANG	ASR
156508	52508+57508	CK	SCR	ANG	ASR
156509	52509+57509	CK	SCR	ANG	ASR
156510	52510+57510	CK	SCR	ANG	ASR
156511	52511+57511	CK	SCR	ANG	ASR
156512	52512+57512	CK	SCR	ANG	ASR
156513	52513+57513	CK	SCR	ANG	ASR
156514	52514+57514	CK	SCR	ANG	ASR

§ Owned by Brodie Engineering, prototype refurbished set.

Right: *ScotRail operates the largest fleet of Metro-Cammell built Class 156s, with 43 sets allocated to Corkerhill. The sets display Scottish Railways livery and operate longer-distance non-electrified services. No. 156504 is shown under the roof at Glasgow Central.* **Nathan Williamson**

Class 158

Vehicle Length: 76ft 1¾in (23.21m)
Height: 12ft 6in (3.81m)
Width: 9ft 3¼in (2.82m)
Engine: 1 x Cummins NTA855R of 350hp per vehicle
Horsepower: 700hp (522kW)
*Seats (total/car): 14F/116S, 14F-46S/70S, * 138S, 68S/70S*

Number	Formation DMCL/DMSL *+DMS	Depot	Livery	Owner	Operator
158701	52701+57701	IS	SCR	PTR	ASR
158702	52702+57702	IS	SCR	PTR	ASR
158703	52703+57703	IS	SCR	PTR	ASR
158704	52704+57704	IS	SCR	PTR	ASR
158705	52705+57705	IS	SCR	PTR	ASR
158706	52706+57706	IS	SCR	PTR	ASR
158707	52707+57707	IS	SCR	PTR	ASR
158708	52708+57708	IS	SCR	PTR	ASR
158709	52709+57709	IS	SCR	PTR	ASR
158710	52710+57710	IS	SCR	PTR	ASR
158711	52711+57711	IS	SCR	PTR	ASR
158712	52712+57712	IS	SCR	PTR	ASR
158713	52713+57713	IS	SCR	PTR	ASR
158714	52714+57714	IS	SCR	PTR	ASR
158715	52715+57715	IS	SCR	PTR	ASR

ScotRail

158716	52716+57716	IS	SCR	PTR	ASR
158717	52717+57717	IS	SCR	PTR	ASR
158718	52718+57718	IS	SCR	PTR	ASR
158719	52719+57719	IS	SCR	PTR	ASR
158720	52720+57720	IS	SCR	PTR	ASR
158721	52721+57721	IS	SCR	PTR	ASR
158722	52722+57722	IS	SCR	PTR	ASR
158723	52723+57723	IS	SCR	PTR	ASR
158724	52724+57724	IS	SCR	PTR	ASR
158725	52725+57725	IS	SCR	PTR	ASR
158726	52726+57726	CK	SCR	PTR	ASR
158727	52727+57727	IS	SCR	PTR	ASR
158728	52728+57728	IS	SCR	PTR	ASR
158729	52729+57729	CK	SCR	PTR	ASR
158730	52730+57730	CK	SCR	PTR	ASR
158731	52731+57731	CK	SCR	PTR	ASR
158732	52732+57732	CK	SCR	PTR	ASR
158733	52733+57733	CK	SCR	PTR	ASR
158734	52734+57734	CK	SCR	PTR	ASR
158735	52735+57735	CK	SCR	PTR	ASR
158736	52736+57736	CK	SCR	PTR	ASR
158737	52737+57737	CK	SCR	PTR	ASR
158738	52738+57738	CK	SCR	PTR	ASR
158739	52739+57739	CK	SCR	PTR	ASR
158740	52740+57740	CK	SCR	PTR	ASR
158741	52741+57741	CK	SCR	PTR	ASR

Names applied
158715 ***Haymarket***

Left: *Although in slightly reduced numbers, the Class 158s still feature prominently in ScotRail operations, with 41 sets in use at the start of 2020. Sets carry the stylish Scottish Railways blue livery, as displayed on set No. 158719 at Forres.* **Antony Christie**

Class 170/3
Turbostar

Vehicle Length: 77ft 6in (23.62m)
Height: 12ft 4½in (3.77m)
Width: 8ft 10in (2.69m)
Engine: 1 x MTU 6R 183TD13H of 422hp per vehicle
Horsepower: 1,266hp (944kW)
Seats (total/car): 197S, 57S/76S/64S

Number	*Formation* DMSL+MS+DMSL	*Depot*	*Livery*	*Owner*	*Operator*
170393	50393+56393+79393	HA	SCR	PTR	ASR
170394	50394+56394+79394	HA	SCR	PTR	ASR
170395	50395+56395+79395	HA	SCR	PTR	ASR
170396	50396+56396+79396	HA	SCR	PTR	ASR

Class 170/4
Turbostar

Vehicle Length: 77ft 6in (23.62m)
Height: 12ft 4½in (3.77m)
Width: 8ft 10in (2.69m)
Engine: 1 x MTU 6R 183TD13H of 422hp per vehicle
Horsepower: 1,266hp (944kW)
(170431/432 have 3 x 483hp engines giving 1,449hp)
Seats (total/car): 18F/168S 9F-43S/76S/9F-49S

Number	*Formation* DMCL+MS+DMCL	*Depot*	*Livery*	*Owner*	*Op'r*
170401	50401+56401+79401	HA	SCR	PTR	ASR
170402	50402+56402+79402	HA	SCR	PTR	ASR
170403	50403+56403+79403	HA	SCR	PTR	ASR
170404	50404+56404+79404	HA	SCR	PTR	ASR
170405	50405+56405+79405	HA	SCR	PTR	ASR
170406	50406+56406+79406	HA	SCR	PTR	ASR

Left: *Most longer distance services on ScotRail which are not formed of HST sets are operated by Class 170 three-car sets. Since the introduction of electric stock on the Edinburgh-Glasgow route, the complement has slightly declined, with in 2020 a fleet of 37 sets allocated to Edinburgh Haymarket depot. Set No. 170412, in full Scottish Railways livery is seen at Edinburgh Waverley.* **CJM**

170407	50407+56407+79407	HA	SCR	PTR	ASR
170408	50408+56408+79408	HA	SCR	PTR	ASR
170409	50409+56409+79409	HA	SCR	PTR	ASR
170410	50410+56410+79410	HA	SCR	PTR	ASR
170411	50411+56411+79411	HA	SCR	PTR	ASR
170412	50412+56412+79412	HA	SCR	PTR	ASR
170413	50413+56413+79413	HA	SCR	PTR	ASR
170414	50414+56414+79414	HA	SCR	PTR	ASR
170415	50415+56415+79415	HA	SCR	PTR	ASR
170416	50416+56416+79416	HA	SCB	EVL	ASR
170417	50417+56417+79417	HA	SCB	EVL	ASR
170418	50418+56418+79418	HA	SCB	EVL	ASR
170419	50419+56419+79419	HA	SCB	EVL	ASR
170420	50420+56420+79420	HA	SCB	EVL	ASR
170425	50425+56425+79425	HA	SCR	PTR	ASR
170426	50426+56426+79426	HA	SCR	PTR	ASR
170427	50427+56427+79427	HA	SCR	PTR	ASR
170428	50428+56428+79428	HA	SCR	PTR	ASR
170429	50429+56429+79429	HA	SCR	PTR	ASR
170430	50430+56430+79430	HA	SCR	PTR	ASR
170431	50431+56431+79431	HA	SCR	PTR	ASR
170432	50432+56432+79432	HA	SCR	PTR	ASR
170433	50433+56433+79433	HA	SCR	PTR	ASR
170434	50434+56434+79434	HA	SCR	PTR	ASR

Class 170/4
Turbostar

Vehicle Length: 77ft 6in (23.62m)
Height: 12ft 4½in (3.77m)
Width: 8ft 10in (2.69m)
Engine: 1 x MTU 6R 183TD13H of 422hp per vehicle
Horsepower: 1,266hp (944kW)
Seats: (total/car) 9F/180S, 55S/76S/9F,49S

Number	*Formation* DMSL+MS+DMCL	*Depot*	*Livery*	*Owner*	*Op'r*
170450	50450+56450+79450	HA	SCR	PTR	ASR
170451	50451+56451+79451	HA	SCR	PTR	ASR
170452	50452+56452+79452	HA	SCR	PTR	ASR

Right: *The Abellio ScotRail Class 170 fleet have various interior layouts. Set No. 170451 seen at Glasgow Queen Street, was originally built as a standard class only set, being retro-fitted with first class seating on the 79xxx driving car.* **CJM**

Class 318

Vehicle Length: (Driving) 65ft 0¾in (19.83m)
(Inter) 65ft 4¼in (19.92m)
Height: 12ft 1½in (3.70m)
Width: 9ft 3in (2.82m)
Horsepower: 1,328hp (996kW)
Seats (total/car): 216S, 66S/79S/71S

Number	*Formation* DTSO(A)+MSO+DTSO(B)	*Depot*	*Livery*	*Owner*	*Operator*
318250	77240+62866+77260	GW	SCR	EVL	ASR
318251	77241+62867+77261	GW	SCR	EVL	ASR
318252	77242+62868+77262	GW	SCR	EVL	ASR
318253	77243+62869+77263	GW	SCR	EVL	ASR
318254	77244+62870+77264	GW	SCR	EVL	ASR
318255	77245+62871+77265	GW	SCR	EVL	ASR
318256	77246+62872+77266	GW	SCR	EVL	ASR
318257	77247+62873+77267	GW	SCR	EVL	ASR
318258	77248+62874+77268	GW	SCR	EVL	ASR
318259	77249+62875+77269	GW	SCR	EVL	ASR
318260	77250+62876+77270	GW	SCR	EVL	ASR
318261	77251+62877+77271	GW	SCC	EVL	ASR
318262	77252+62878+77272	GW	SCR	EVL	ASR
318263	77253+62879+77273	GW	SCC	EVL	ASR
318264	77254+62880+77274	GW	SCR	EVL	ASR
318265	77255+62881+77275	GW	SCR	EVL	ASR
318266	77256+62882+77276	GW	SCR	EVL	ASR
318267	77257+62883+77277	GW	SCR	EVL	ASR
318268	77258+62884+77278	GW	SCR	EVL	ASR
318269	77259+62885+77279	GW	SCR	EVL	ASR
318270	77288+62890+77289	GW	SCR	EVL	ASR

ScotRail

Left: *Glasgow Shields Road depot is the base for 21 Class 318 three-car sets, deployed on Glasgow area local services. These sets were originally built with end gangways, but these were removed on refurbishment to improve the driving cab. All sets carry Scottish Railways blue livery, with set No. 318267 shown.* **Howard Lewsey**

Class 320/3

Vehicle Length: (Driving) 65ft 0¾in (19.83m) (Inter) 65ft 4¼in (19.92m)
Height: 12ft 4¾in (3.78m)
Width: 9ft 3in (2.82m)
Horsepower: 1,328hp (996kW)
Seats (total/car): 206S, 51S/78S/77S

Number	*Formation DTSO(A)+MSO+DTSO(B)*	*Depot*	*Livery*	*Owner*	*Operator*
320301	77899+63021+77921	GW	SCR	EVL	ASR
320302	77900+63022+77922	GW	SCR	EVL	ASR
320303	77901+63023+77923	GW	SCR	EVL	ASR
320304	77902+63024+77924	GW	SCR	EVL	ASR
320305	77903+63025+77925	GW	SCR	EVL	ASR
320306	77904+63026+77926	GW	SCR	EVL	ASR
320307	77905+63027+77927	GW	SCR	EVL	ASR
320308	77906+63028+77928	GW	SCR	EVL	ASR
320309	77907+63029+77929	GW	SCR	EVL	ASR
320310	77908+63030+77930	GW	SCR	EVL	ASR
320311	77909+63031+77931	GW	SCR	EVL	ASR
320312	77910+63032+77932	GW	SCR	EVL	ASR
320313	77911+63033+77933	GW	SCR	EVL	ASR
320314	77912+63034+77934	GW	SCR	EVL	ASR
320315	77913+63035+77935	GW	SCR	EVL	ASR
320316	77914+63036+77936	GW	SCR	EVL	ASR
320317	77915+63037+77937	GW	SCR	EVL	ASR
320318	77916+63038+77938	GW	SCR	EVL	ASR
320319	77917+63039+77939	GW	SCR	EVL	ASR
320320	77918+63040+77940	GW	SCR	EVL	ASR
320321	77919+63041+77941	GW	SCR	EVL	ASR
320322	77920+63042+77942	GW	SCR	EVL	ASR

Class 320/4

Vehicle Length: (Driving) 65ft 0¾in (19.83m) (Inter) 65ft 4¼in (19.92m)
Height: 12ft 4¾in (3.78m)
Width: 9ft 3in (2.82m)
Horsepower: 1,328hp (996kW)
Seats (total/car): 28F/197S, 28F-40S/79S//78S

Number	*Formation DTSO(A)+MSO+DTSO(B)*	*Depot*	*Livery*	*Owner*	*Operator*
320401 (321401)	78095+63063+77943	GW	SCR	EVL	ASR
320402 (321402)	78096+63064+77944	GW	SCR	EVL	ASR
320404 (321404)	78098+63066+77946	GW	SCR	EVL	ASR
320411 (321411)	78105+63073+77953	GW	SCR	EVL	ASR
320412 (321412)	78106+63074+77954	GW	SCR	EVL	ASR
320413 (321413)	78107+63075+77955	GW	SCR	EVL	ASR
320414 (321414)	78108+63076+77956	GW	SCR	EVL	ASR
320415 (321415)	78109+63077+77957	GW	SCR	EVL	ASR
320416 (321416)	78110+63078+77958	GW	SCR	EVL	ASR
320417 (321417)	78111+63079+77959	GW	SCR	EVL	ASR
320418 (321418)	78112+63080+77962	GW	SCR	EVL	ASR
320420 (321420)	78114+68032+77964	GW	SCR	EVL	ASR

Right: *Originally ScotRail operated a fleet of 22 three-car Class 320s, classified as 320/3, in the early 2010s, 12 redundant Class 321s were reduced to three-car formation and modified for Scottish use. The sets have a very slightly different interior. On transfer to Scotland the sets were reclassified as 320 and renumbered, retaining the last three digits of their original number. One of the original Class 320/3 sets No. 320317 is illustrated.*
Howard Lewsey

Class 334
Juniper

Vehicle Length: (Driving) 69ft 0¾in (21.04m)
(Inter) 65ft 4½in (19.93m)
Height: 12ft 3in (3.77m)
Width: 9ft 2¾in (2.80m)
Horsepower: 1,448hp (1,080kW)
Seats (total/car): 178S, 64S/55S/59S

Number	*Formation* DMSO(A)+PTSO+DMSO(B)	*Depot*	*Livery*	*Owner*	*Operator*
334001	64101+74301+65101	GW	SCR	EVL	ASR
334002	64102+74302+65102	GW	SCR	EVL	ASR
334003	64103+74303+65103	GW	SCR	EVL	ASR
334004	64104+74304+65104	GW	SCR	EVL	ASR
334005	64105+74305+65105	GW	SCR	EVL	ASR
334006	64106+74306+65106	GW	SCR	EVL	ASR
334007	64107+74307+65107	GW	SCR	EVL	ASR
334008	64108+74308+65108	GW	SCR	EVL	ASR
334009	64109+74309+65109	GW	SCR	EVL	ASR
334010	64110+74310+65110	GW	SCR	EVL	ASR
334011	64111+74311+65111	GW	SCR	EVL	ASR
334012	64112+74312+65112	GW	SCR	EVL	ASR
334013	64113+74313+65113	GW	SCR	EVL	ASR
334014	64114+74314+65114	GW	SCR	EVL	ASR
334015	64115+74315+65115	GW	SCR	EVL	ASR
334016	64116+74316+65116	GW	SCR	EVL	ASR
334017	64117+74317+65117	GW	SCR	EVL	ASR
334018	64118+74318+65118	GW	SCR	EVL	ASR
334019	64119+74319+65119	GW	SCR	EVL	ASR
334020	64120+74320+65120	GW	SCR	EVL	ASR
334021	64121+74321+65121	GW	SCR	EVL	ASR
334022	64122+74322+65122	GW	SCR	EVL	ASR
334023	64123+74323+65123	GW	SCR	EVL	ASR
334024	64124+74324+65124	GW	SCR	EVL	ASR
334025	64125+74325+65125	GW	SCR	EVL	ASR
334026	64126+74326+65126	GW	SCR	EVL	ASR
334027	64127+74327+65127	GW	SCR	EVL	ASR
334028	64128+74328+65128	GW	SCR	EVL	ASR
334029	64129+74329+65129	GW	SCR	EVL	ASR
334030	64130+74330+65130	GW	SCR	EVL	ASR
334031	64131+74331+65131	GW	SCR	EVL	ASR
334032	64132+74332+65132	GW	SCR	EVL	ASR
334033	64133+74333+65133	GW	SCR	EVL	ASR
334034	64134+74334+65134	GW	SCR	EVL	ASR
334035	64135+74335+65135	GW	SCR	EVL	ASR
334036	64136+74336+65136	GW	SCR	EVL	ASR
334037	64137+74337+65137	GW	SCR	EVL	ASR
334038	64138+74338+65138	GW	SCR	EVL	ASR
334039	64139+74339+65139	GW	SCR	EVL	ASR
334040	64140+74340+65140	GW	SCR	EVL	ASR

Left: *In the 1990s, ScotRail obtained a fleet of 40 three-car Alstom 'Juniper' sets, to augment services in the Glasgow area. The non-gangway units are allocated to Glasgow Shields Road and all sport Scottish Railways blue and white livery. No. 334022 is captured under the glazed roof at Edinburgh Waverley.* **Mark V. Pike**

Class 380/0
Desiro

Vehicle Length: 77ft 3in (23.57m)
Height: 12ft 1½in (3.7m)
Width: 9ft 2in (2.7m)
Horsepower: 1,341hp (1,000kW)
Seats (total/car): 191S, 70S/57S/64S

Number	*Formation* DMSO(A)+PTSO+DMSO(B)	*Depot*	*Livery*	*Owner*	*Operator*
380001	38501+38601+38701	GW	SCR	EVL	ASR
380002	38502+38602+38702	GW	SCR	EVL	ASR
380003	38503+38603+38703	GW	SCR	EVL	ASR
380004	38504+38604+38704	GW	SCR	EVL	ASR
380005	38505+38605+38705	GW	SCR	EVL	ASR
380006	38506+38606+38706	GW	SCR	EVL	ASR
380007	38507+38607+38707	GW	SCR	EVL	ASR
380008	38508+38608+38708	GW	SCR	EVL	ASR
380009	38509+38609+38709	GW	SCR	EVL	ASR
380010	38510+38610+38710	GW	SCR	EVL	ASR
380011	38511+38611+38711	GW	SCR	EVL	ASR
380012	38512+38612+38712	GW	SCR	EVL	ASR
380013	38513+38613+38713	GW	SCR	EVL	ASR
380014	38514+38614+38714	GW	SCR	EVL	ASR
380015	38515+38615+38715	GW	SCR	EVL	ASR
380016	38516+38616+38716	GW	SCR	EVL	ASR
380017	38517+38617+38717	GW	SCR	EVL	ASR
380018	38518+38618+38718	GW	SCR	EVL	ASR
380019	38519+38619+38719	GW	SCR	EVL	ASR
380020	38520+38620+38720	GW	SCR	EVL	ASR
380021	38521+38621+38721	GW	SCR	EVL	ASR
380022	38522+38622+38722	GW	SCR	EVL	ASR

Left: *Two fleets of Siemens 'Desiro' three and four-car units were delivered to ScotRail in 2010-2011. The sets are allocated to Glasgow Shields Road depot and operated medium and long distance electric services in the Edinburgh and Glasgow area. Four-car set No. 380103 is shown at Briech on a Glasgow to Edinburgh via Shotts service.* **Ian Lothian**

Class 380/1
Desiro

Vehicle Length: 77ft 3in (23.57m)
Height: 12ft 1½in (3.7m)
Width: 9ft 2in (2.7m)
Horsepower: 1,341hp (1,000kW)
Seats (total/car): 265S, 70S/57S/74S/64S

Number	*Formation* DMSO(A)+PTSO+MSO+DMSO(B)	*Depot*	*Livery*	*Owner*	*Operator*
380101	38551+38651+38851+38751	GW	SCR	EVL	ASR
380102	38552+38652+38852+38752	GW	SCR	EVL	ASR
380103	38553+38653+38853+38753	GW	SCR	EVL	ASR
380104	38554+38654+38854+38754	GW	SCR	EVL	ASR
380105	38555+38655+38855+38755	GW	SCR	EVL	ASR
380106	38556+38656+38856+38756	GW	SCR	EVL	ASR
380107	38557+38657+38857+38757	GW	SCR	EVL	ASR
380108	38558+38658+38858+38758	GW	SCR	EVL	ASR
380109	38559+38659+38859+38759	GW	SCR	EVL	ASR
380110	38560+38660+38860+38760	GW	SCR	EVL	ASR
380111	38561+38661+38861+38761	GW	SCR	EVL	ASR
380112	38562+38662+38862+38762	GW	SCR	EVL	ASR
380113	38563+38663+38863+38763	GW	SCR	EVL	ASR
380114	38564+38664+38864+38764	GW	SCR	EVL	ASR
380115	38565+38665+38865+38765	GW	SCR	EVL	ASR
380116	38566+38666+38866+38766	GW	SCR	EVL	ASR

Class 385/0
AT200

Vehicle Length: 77ft 3in (23.57m)
Height: awaited 12ft 2in (3.7m)
Width: 9ft 2in (2.74m)
Horsepower: 1,341hp (1,000kW)
Seats (total/car): 190S , 48S/80S/62S

Number	*Formation* DMSO(A)+PTSO+DMSO(B)	*Depot*	*Livery*	*Owner*	*Operator*
385001	441001+442001+444001	EC	SCR	SMB	ASR
385002	441002+442002+444002	EC	SCR	SMB	ASR
385003	441003+442003+444003	EC	SCR	SMB	ASR
385004	441004+442004+444004	EC	SCR	SMB	ASR
385005	441005+442005+444005	EC	SCR	SMB	ASR
385006	441006+442006+444006	EC	SCR	SMB	ASR
385007	441007+442007+444007	EC	SCR	SMB	ASR
385008	441008+442008+444008	EC	SCR	SMB	ASR
385009	441009+442009+444009	EC	SCR	SMB	ASR
385010	441010+442010+444010	EC	SCR	SMB	ASR
385011	441011+442011+444011	EC	SCR	SMB	ASR
385012	441012+442012+444012	EC	SCR	SMB	ASR
385013	441013+442013+444013	EC	SCR	SMB	ASR
385014	441014+442014+444014	EC	SCR	SMB	ASR
385015	441015+442015+444015	EC	SCR	SMB	ASR
385016	441016+442016+444016	EC	SCR	SMB	ASR
385017	441017+442017+444017	EC	SCR	SMB	ASR
385018	441018+442018+444018	EC	SCR	SMB	ASR
385019	441019+442019+444019	EC	SCR	SMB	ASR
385020	441020+442020+444020	EC	SCR	SMB	ASR
385021	441021+442021+444021	EC	SCR	SMB	ASR
385022	441022+442022+444022	EC	SCR	SMB	ASR
385023	441023+442023+444023	EC	SCR	SMB	ASR
385024	441024+442024+444024	EC	SCR	SMB	ASR
385025	441025+442025+444025	EC	SCR	SMB	ASR
385026	441026+442026+444026	EC	SCR	SMB	ASR
385027	441027+442027+444027	EC	SCR	SMB	ASR
385028	441028+442028+444028	EC	SCR	SMB	ASR
385029	441029+442029+444029	EC	SCR	SMB	ASR
385030	441030+442030+444030	EC	SCR	SMB	ASR
385031	441031+442031+444031	EC	SCR	SMB	ASR
385032	441032+442032+444032	EC	SCR	SMB	ASR
385033	441033+442033+444033	EC	SCR	SMB	ASR
385034	441034+442034+444034	EC	SCR	SMB	ASR
385035	441035+442035+444035	EC	SCR	SMB	ASR
385036	441036+442036+444036	EC	SCR	SMB	ASR
385037	441037+442037+444037	EC	SCR	SMB	ASR
385038	441038+442038+444038	EC	SCR	SMB	ASR

385039	441039+442039+444039	EC	SCR	SMB	ASR
385040	441040+442040+444040	EC	SCR	SMB	ASR
385041	441041+442041+444041	EC	SCR	SMB	ASR
385042	441042+442042+444042	EC	SCR	SMB	ASR
385043	441043+442043+444043	EC	SCR	SMB	ASR
385044	441044+442044+444044	EC	SCR	SMB	ASR
385045	441045+442045+444045	EC	SCR	SMB	ASR
385046	441046+442046+444046	EC	SCR	SMB	ASR

Left: *The newest fleet of high-quality EMUs for use by ScotRail are the Class 385 (AT200) sets built by Hitachi. A total of 46 three-car and 24 four-car sets are in service, based at Edinburgh Craigentinny. Three-car No. 385032 is seen at Falkirk Grahamston with a Dunblane to Edinburgh Waverley service.* **Ian Lothian**

Class 385/1
AT200

Vehicle Length: 77ft 3in (23.57m)
Height: awaited 12ft 2in (3.7m)
Width: 9ft 2in (2.74m)
Horsepower: 1,341hp (1,000kW)
Seats (total/car): 20F/237S, 20F, 15S/80S/80S/62S

Number	*Formation* DMCO+PTSO+TSO+DMSO	*Depot*	*Livery*	*Owner*	*Operator*
385101	441101+442101+443101+444101	EC	SCR	SMB	ASR
385102	441102+442102+443102+444102	EC	SCR	SMB	ASR
385103	441103+442103+443103+444103	EC	SCR	SMB	ASR
385104	441104+442104+443104+444104	EC	SCR	SMB	ASR
385105	441105+442105+443105+444105	EC	SCR	SMB	ASR
385106	441106+442106+443106+444106	EC	SCR	SMB	ASR
385107	441107+442107+443107+444107	EC	SCR	SMB	ASR
385108	441108+442108+443108+444108	EC	SCR	SMB	ASR
385109	441109+442109+443109+444109	EC	SCR	SMB	ASR
385110	441110+442110+443110+444110	EC	SCR	SMB	ASR
385111	441111+442111+443111+444111	EC	SCR	SMB	ASR
385112	441112+442112+443112+444112	EC	SCR	SMB	ASR
385113	441113+442113+443113+444113	EC	SCR	SMB	ASR
385114	441114+442114+443114+444114	EC	SCR	SMB	ASR

Left: *The 24 four-car Class 385s have first class accommodation in one driving car and these sets usually operate on the high speed Edinburgh to Glasgow corridor, as well as other routes. With its first class seating end nearest the camera, set No. 385120 is seen near Linlithgow with an Edinburgh Waverley to Dunblane service.* **Ian Lothian**

385115	441115+442115+443115+444115	EC	SCR	SMB	ASR
385116	441116+442116+443116+444116	EC	SCR	SMB	ASR
385117	441117+442117+443117+444117	EC	SCR	SMB	ASR
385118	441118+442118+443118+444118	EC	SCR	SMB	ASR
385119	441119+442119+443119+444119	EC	SCR	SMB	ASR
385120	441120+442120+443120+444120	EC	SCR	SMB	ASR
385121	441121+442121+443121+444121	EC	SCR	SMB	ASR
385122	441122+442122+443121+444122	EC	SCR	SMB	ASR
385123	441123+442123+443123+444123	EC	SCR	SMB	ASR
385124	441124+442124+443124+444124	EC	SCR	SMB	ASR

Class 68 'UK Light'

Vehicle Length: 67ft 3in (20.5m)
Height: 12ft 6½in (3.82m)
Speed: 100mph (161km/h)
Engine: Caterpillar C175-16
Horsepower: 3,750hp (2,800kW)
Electrical Equipment: ABB

Number	*Depot*	*Pool*	*Livery*	*Owner*	*Operator*	*Name*
68006	CR	XHVE	SCR	BEA	DRS	***Daring***
68007	CR	XHVE	SCR	BEA	DRS	***Valiant***

Right: *To ease a shortage of multiple unit stock, ScotRail took on the lease of two Mk2 loco hauled passenger rakes and two DRS-operated Class 68s. These are still operating in 2020. The two Class 68s Nos. 68006 and 68007 carry full Scottish Railways blue and white livery, and while officially based at DRS Crewe, the pair receive maintenance at Polmadie. No. 68007 is shown with a ScotRail passenger set.*
Robin Ralston

Mk2 Hauled Stock

Vehicle Length: 66ft 0in (20.11m)
Height: 12ft 9½in (3.89m)
Width: 9ft 3in (2.81m)
Seats (total/car): 60S

AC2F - TSO *Seating 60S*

Number	*Depot*	*Livery*	*Op'r*
5945	ML	SCR	ASR
5955	ML	SCR	ASR
5971	ML	SCR	ASR
6001	ML	SCR	ASR
6008	ML	SCR	ASR
6027	ML	SCR	ASR
6064	ML	SCR	ASR
6117	ML	SCR	ASR
6173	ML	SCR	ASR

AE2F - BSO *Seating 32S*

Number	*Depot*	*Livery*	*Op'r*
9488	ML	SCR	ASR
9527	ML	SCR	ASR
9539	ML	SCR	ASR

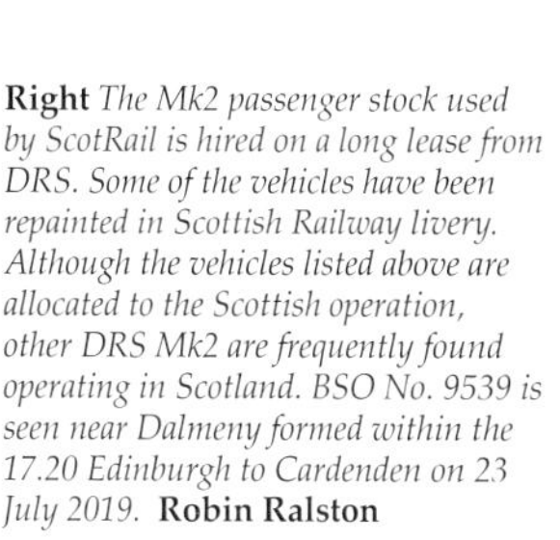

Right *The Mk2 passenger stock used by ScotRail is hired on a long lease from DRS. Some of the vehicles have been repainted in Scottish Railway livery. Although the vehicles listed above are allocated to the Scottish operation, other DRS Mk2 are frequently found operating in Scotland. BSO No. 9539 is seen near Dalmeny formed within the 17.20 Edinburgh to Cardenden on 23 July 2019.* **Robin Ralston**

Mk3 HST Stock

Vehicle Length: 75ft 0in (22.86m) Width: 8ft 11in (2.71m)
Height: 12ft 9in (3.88m) Bogie Type: BT10

A total of 121 Mk3 HST trailer vehicles, previously used on Great Western services are transferring to Scotland to operate the Inter7City services.

Vehicles allocated to ScotRail in January 2020, showing set numbers and formations. These will change.

Unrefurbished with slam doors and track deposit toilets

Set No.	*Formation*
HA01	41124 42255 42256 44029
HA02	41144 42295 42032 44039
HA03	41104 42206 42208 44066
HA04	41130 42267 42325 44032
HA05	41022 42030 42010 44010
HA06	41158 42200 42129 44086
HA07	41010 42069 42209 44004
HA10	41135 42279 42280 44035
HA11	41136 42207 42047 44015
HA31	41126 42344 42261 44030
HA32	46010 42012 42013 44023
HA33	41140 42287 42289 44037

Refurbished with sliding doors and retention toilets

Set No.	*Formation TFB+TS+TS+TS*
HA18	40624 (41116) 42265 42553 42293
HA19	40625 (41137) 42259 42578 42333
HA20	40616 (41142) 42291 42075 42177
HA21	40612 (41134) 42055 42576 42276
HA22	40608 (41122) 42275 42571 42019
HA23	40605 (41094) 42034 42184 42345
HA24	40604 (41024) 42183 42559 42343
HA25	40602 (41038) 42292 42562 42045
HA26	40601 (41032) 42004 42561 42046

TFB conversions

40601 (41032)
40602 (41038)
40603 (41052)
40604 (41024)
40605 (41094)
40606 (41104)
40607 (41136)
40608 (41122)
40609 (41020)
40610 (41103)
40611 (41130)
40612 (41134)
40613 (41135)
40614 (41010)
40615 (41022)
40616 (41142)
40617 (41144)
40618 (41016)
40619 (41124)
40620 (41158)
40621 (41146)
40622 (41006)
40623 (41180)
40624 (41116)
40625 (41137)
40626 (41012)

Above: *The recently introduced Inter7City ScotRail HSTs look attractive in their grey and blue livery with pictogram branding. The overhaul contract, being undertaken by Wabtec has been a protracted affair and deliveries of sets will continue through 2020. Led by power car 43182 with No. 43151 out of view on the rear, set HA21 forms a Stirling to Inverness service.* **Ian Lothian**

Left: *The extensive overhaul of the Inter7City passenger stock has seen the introduction of a new vehicle type a Trailer First Buffet, numbered in the 406xx series. These coaches have 32 first class seats and a good size buffet and catering outlet at the opposite end. These coaches are usually formed with the first class seating adjacent to the power car, with the buffet end coupled to the standard class seating. Car No. 40601, rebuilt from TF No. 41032.* **Ian Lothian**

Serco Caledonian Sleepers

Address: 1 Union Street, Inverness, IV1 1PP
enquiry@Sleeper.scot 0330 060 0500
www.sleeper.scot

Managing Director: Ryan Flaherty

Franchise Dates: 1 April 2015 - 1 April 2030

Principal Routes: Inverness, Aberdeen, Fort William, Edinburgh, Glasgow to London Euston

Depots: Edinburgh Craigentinny (EC), Inverness (IS), Polmadie (PO)

Parent Company: Serco

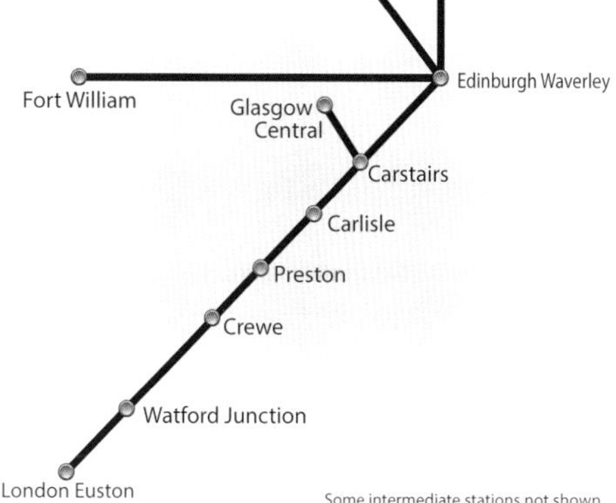

Class 73/9

Vehicle Length: 53ft 8in (16.35m)
Height: 12ft 5⁵⁄₁₆in (3.79m)
Width: 8ft 8in (2.64m)
Electrical Equipment: English Electric
Power: MTU 8V4000R43L
Horsepower: diesel - 1,550hp (1,119kW)
ETH index: 96

Number		Depot	Pool	Livery	Owner	Operator
73966	(73005)	EC	GBCS	SCS	GBR	SCS
73967	(73006)	EC	GBCS	SCS	GBR	SCS
73968	(73117)	EC	GBCS	SCS	GBR	SCS
73969	(73105)	EC	GBCS	SCS	GBR	SCS
73970	(73103)	EC	GBCS	SCS	GBR	SCS
73971	(73207/122)	EC	GBCS	SCS	GBR	SCS

Right: *GB Railfreight are the owners of six rebuilt Class 73/9s which are on long hire to Caledonian Sleepers to power the Scottish legs of London sleeping car trains, working between Edinburgh Waverley and Fort William, Inverness and Aberdeen, powering Mk5 CAF-built stock. To power Mk5s, the '73s' have been fitted with drop-head Dellner couplings and revised equipment. The locos sport Caledonian Sleepers teal green. No. 73970 is seen from its electrical end.* **CJM**

Class 92

Vehicle Length: 70ft 1in (21.34m) *Power Collection: 25kV ac overhead / 750V dc third rail*
Height: 13ft 0in (3.95m) *Horsepower: ac - 6,700hp (5,000kW) / dc - 5,360hp (4,000kW)*
Width: 8ft 8in (2.66m) *Electrical Equipment: Brush*

Number	Depot	Pool	Livery	Owner	Operator
92006	WN	GBSL	SCS	GBR	SCS
92010	WN	GBSL	SCS	GBR	SCS
92014	WN	GBSL	SCS	GBR	SCS
92018	WN	GBSL	SCS	GBR	SCS
92023	WN	GBSL	SCS	GBR	SCS
92028	WN	GBSL	SCS	GBR	SCS
92033	WN	GBSL	SCS	GBR	SCS
92038	WN	GBCT	SCS	GBR	SCS

Above: *GB Railfreight also supply the locomotives to operate the Caledonian Sleeper services between Scotland and London by way of the West Coast Main Line. For this a fleet of eight Class 92s are dedicated to the work and fitted with drop-head Dellner couplings and compatible jumpers for CAF Mk5 stock. No. 92010 is seen heading south with a Mk5 sleeper rake at Cheddington.* **David Ive**

Mk5 Hauled Stock

Mk5 Sleeper Seating Brake
31U, 32.5T

Number	Depot	Livery	Owner
15001	PO	CAS	LOM
15002	PO	CAS	LOM
15003	PO	CAS	LOM
15004	PO	CAS	LOM
15005	PO	CAS	LOM
15006	PO	CAS	LOM
15007	PO	CAS	LOM
15008	PO	CAS	LOM
15009	PO	CAS	LOM
15010	PO	CAS	LOM
15011	PO	CAS	LOM

Mk5 Sleeper Lounge
28U, 35.5T

Number	Depot	Livery	Owner
15101	PO	CAS	LOM
15102	PO	CAS	LOM
15103	PO	CAS	LOM
15104	PO	CAS	LOM
15105	PO	CAS	LOM
15106	PO	CAS	LOM
15107	PO	CAS	LOM
15108	PO	CAS	LOM
15109	PO	CAS	LOM
15110	PO	CAS	LOM

Mk5 Sleeper Accessible
4 Berths, 8 beds, 35.5T

Number	Depot	Livery	Owner
15201	PO	CAS	LOM
15202	PO	CAS	LOM
15203	PO	CAS	LOM
15204	PO	CAS	LOM
15205	PO	CAS	LOM
15206	PO	CAS	LOM
15207	PO	CAS	LOM
15208	PO	CAS	LOM
15209	PO	CAS	LOM
15210	PO	CAS	LOM
15211	PO	CAS	LOM
15212	PO	CAS	LOM
15213	PO	CAS	LOM
15214	PO	CAS	LOM

Mk5 Sleeper
10 berths, 38T

Number	Depot	Livery	Owner
15301	PO	CAS	LOM
15302	PO	CAS	LOM
15303	PO	CAS	LOM
15304	PO	CAS	LOM
15305	PO	CAS	LOM
15306	PO	CAS	LOM
15307	PO	CAS	LOM

15308	PO	CAS	LOM
15309	PO	CAS	LOM
15310	PO	CAS	LOM
15311	PO	CAS	LOM
15312	PO	CAS	LOM
15313	PO	CAS	LOM
15314	PO	CAS	LOM
15315	PO	CAS	LOM
15316	PO	CAS	LOM
15317	PO	CAS	LOM
15318	PO	CAS	LOM
15319	PO	CAS	LOM
15320	PO	CAS	LOM
15321	PO	CAS	LOM
15322	PO	CAS	LOM
15323	PO	CAS	LOM
15324	PO	CAS	LOM
15325	PO	CAS	LOM
15326	PO	CAS	LOM
15327	PO	CAS	LOM
15328	PO	CAS	LOM
15329	PO	CAS	LOM
15330	PO	CAS	LOM
15331	PO	CAS	LOM
15332	PO	CAS	LOM
15333	PO	CAS	LOM
15334	PO	CAS	LOM
15335	PO	CAS	LOM
15336	PO	CAS	LOM
15337	PO	CAS	LOM
15338	PO	CAS	LOM
15339	PO	CAS	LOM
15340	PO	CAS	LOM

Above: *While the Lowlander (Edinburgh/Glasgow Caledonian Sleeper services were taken over by Mk 5 stock in summer 2019, it was not until October that the Highlander services to Fort William, Inverness and Aberdeen went over to full Mk5 operation and the Mk2s and Mk3s could be withdrawn. Car No. 15334, a ten-berth sleeper vehicle is seen at Euston.* **Antony Christie**

Right Middle and Right Lower: *By 2020, all Mk5 sleeping vehicles were commissioned and introduced, enabling all Anglo-Scottish sleeper services to be operated by new stock. In the middle view, Sleeper Seating Brake No. 15004 is shown, while the image below shows Sleeper Lounge No. 15104. On the later vehicle, note the communications roof module at the far end.*
Both: **Antony Christie**

South Eastern

Address: ✉ Friars Bridge Court, 41-45 Blackfriars Road, London, SE1 8NZ
info@southeasternrailway.co.uk
✆ 08700 000 2222
ⓘ www.southeasternrailway.co.uk

Managing Director: David Stratham
Franchise Dates: 1 April 2006 - DfT extension to 04/20
Principal Routes: London to Kent and parts of East Sussex, domestic services on HS1
Depots: Slade Green (SG), Ramsgate (RM), Ashford* (AD) * Operated by Hitachi
Parent Company: Govia

Class 375/3
Electrostar

Vehicle Length: (Driving) 66ft 9in (20.3m)
(Inter) 65ft 6in (19.96m)
Height: 12ft 4in (3.75m)
Width: 9ft 2in (2.79m)
Horsepower: 1,341hp (1,000kW)
Seats (total/car): 16F-170S,60S/16F-50S/60S

Number	*Formation* DMSO+MCO+DMSO	*Depot*	*Livery*	*Owner*	*Operator*	*Name*
375301	67921+74351+67931	RM	SEB	EVL	SET	
375302	67922+74352+67932	RM	SEB	EVL	SET	
375303	67923+74353+67933	RM	SEB	EVL	SET	
375304	67924+74354+67934	RM	SEB	EVL	SET	
375305	67925+74355+67935	RM	SEB	EVL	SET	
375306	67926+74356+67936	RM	SEB	EVL	SET	
375307	67927+74357+67937	RM	SEB	EVL	SET	
375308	67928+74358+67938	RM	SEB	EVL	SET	
375309	67929+74359+67939	RM	SEB	EVL	SET	
375310	67930+74360+67940	RM	SEB	EVL	SET	

Class 375/6
Electrostar

Vehicle Length: (Driving) 66ft 9in (20.3m)
(Inter) 65ft 6in (19.96m)
Height: 12ft 4in (3.75m)
Width: 9ft 2in (2.79m)
Horsepower: 2,012hp (1,500kW)
Seats (total/car): 16F-226S, 60S/16F-50S/56S/60S

Number	*Formation* DMSO(A)+MCO+TSO+DMSO(B)	*Depot*	*Livery*	*Owner*	*Operator*	*Name*
375601	67801+74251+74201+67851	RM	SEB	EVL	SET	
375602	67802+74252+74202+67852	RM	SEB	EVL	SET	
375603	67803+74253+74203+67853	RM	SEB	EVL	SET	
375604	67804+74254+74204+67854	RM	SEB	EVL	SET	
375605	67805+74255+74205+67855	RM	SEB	EVL	SET	
375606	67806+74256+74206+67856	RM	SEB	EVL	SET	
375607	67807+74257+74207+67857	RM	SEB	EVL	SET	
375608	67808+74258+74208+67858	RM	SEB	EVL	SET	
375609	67809+74259+74209+67859	RM	SEB	EVL	SET	
375610	67810+74260+74210+67860	RM	SEB	EVL	SET	
375611	67811+74261+74211+67861	RM	SEB	EVL	SET	
375612	67812+74262+74212+67862	RM	SEB	EVL	SET	
375613	67813+74263+74213+67863	RM	SEB	EVL	SET	
375614	67814+74264+74214+67864	RM	SEB	EVL	SET	
375615	67815+74265+74215+67865	RM	SEB	EVL	SET	
375616	67816+74266+74216+67866	RM	SEB	EVL	SET	
375617	67817+74267+74217+67867	RM	SEB	EVL	SET	
375618	67818+74268+74218+67868	RM	SEB	EVL	SET	
375619	67819+74269+74219+67869	RM	SEB	EVL	SET	*Driver John Neve*

South Eastern

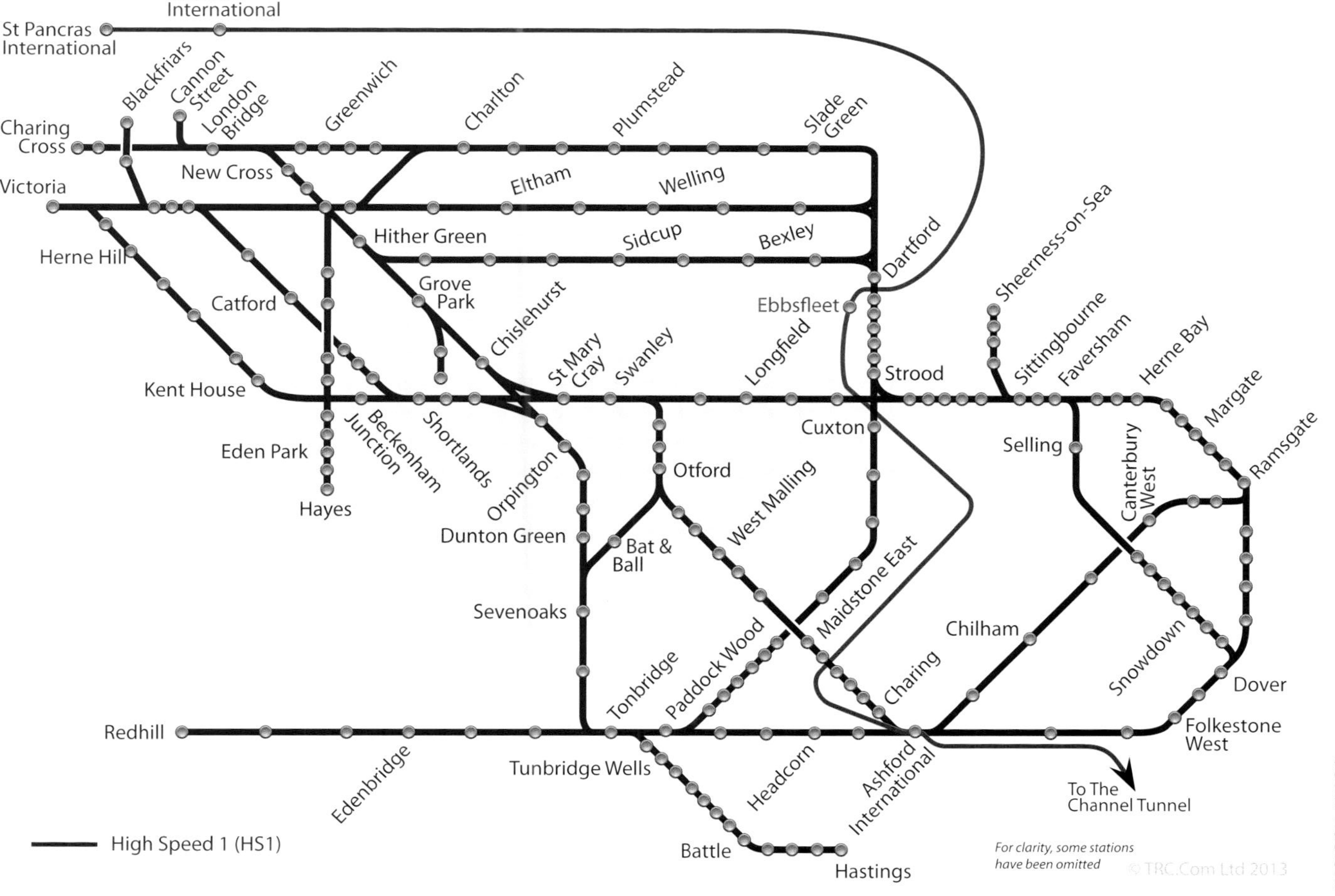

South Eastern

Number	Formation	Depot	Livery	Owner	Operator	Name
375620	67820+74270+74220+67870	RM	SEB	EVL	SET	
375621	67821+74271+74221+67871	RM	SEB	EVL	SET	
375622	67822+74272+74222+67872	RM	SEB	EVL	SET	
375623	67823+74273+74223+67873	RM	SEB	EVL	SET	*Hospice in the Weald*
375624	67824+74274+74224+67874	RM	SEB	EVL	SET	
375625	67825+74275+74225+67875	RM	SEB	EVL	SET	
375626	67826+74276+74226+67876	RM	SEB	EVL	SET	
375627	67827+74277+74227+67877	RM	SEB	EVL	SET	
375628	67828+74278+74228+67878	RM	SEB	EVL	SET	
375629	67829+74279+74229+67879	RM	SEB	EVL	SET	
375630	67830+74280+74230+67880	RM	SEB	EVL	SET	

Class 375/7
Electrostar

Vehicle Length: (Driving) 66ft 9in (20.3m)
(Inter) 65ft 6in (19.96m)
Height: 12ft 4in (3.75m)
Width: 9ft 2in (2.79m)
Horsepower: 2,012hp (1,500kW)
Seats (total/car): 16F-226S, 60S/16F-50S/56S/60S

Number	Formation DMSO(A)+MCO+TSO+DMSO(B)	Depot	Livery	Owner	Operator	Name
375701	67831+74281+74231+67881	RM	SEB	EVL	SET	*Kent Air Ambulance Explorer*
375702	67832+74282+74232+67882	RM	SEB	EVL	SET	
375703	67833+74283+74233+67883	RM	SEB	EVL	SET	
375704	67834+74284+74234+67884	RM	SEB	EVL	SET	
375705	67835+74285+74235+67885	RM	SEB	EVL	SET	
375706	67836+74286+74236+67886	RM	SEB	EVL	SET	
375707	67837+74287+74237+67887	RM	SEB	EVL	SET	
375708	67838+74288+74238+67888	RM	SEB	EVL	SET	
375709	67839+74289+74239+67889	RM	SEB	EVL	SET	
375710	67840+74290+74240+67890	RM	SEB	EVL	SET	*Rochester Castle*
375711	67841+74291+74241+67891	RM	SEB	EVL	SET	
375712	67842+74292+74242+67892	RM	SEB	EVL	SET	
375713	67843+74293+74243+67893	RM	SEB	EVL	SET	*Rochester Cathedral*
375714	67844+74294+74244+67894	RM	SEB	EVL	SET	
375715	67845+74295+74245+67895	RM	SEB	EVL	SET	

Class 375/8
Electrostar

Vehicle Length: (Driving) 66ft 9in (20.3m)
(Inter) 65ft 6in (19.96m)
Height: 12ft 4in (3.75m)
Width: 9ft 2in (2.79m)
Horsepower: 2,012hp (1,500kW)
Seats (total/car): 16F-226S, 60S/16F-50S/56S/60S

Number	Formation DMSO(A)+MCO+TSO+DMSO(B)	Depot	Livery	Owner	Operator	Name
375801	73301+79001+78201+73701	RM	SEB	EVL	SET	
375802	73302+79002+78202+73702	RM	SEB	EVL	SET	
375803	73303+79003+78203+73703	RM	SEB	EVL	SET	
375804	73304+79004+78204+73704	RM	SEB	EVL	SET	
375805	73305+79005+78205+73705	RM	SEB	EVL	SET	
375806	73306+79006+78206+73706	RM	SEB	EVL	SET	
375807	73307+79007+78207+73707	RM	SEB	EVL	SET	
375808	73308+79008+78208+73708	RM	SEB	EVL	SET	
375809	73309+79009+78209+73709	RM	SEB	EVL	SET	
375810	73310+79010+78210+73710	RM	SEB	EVL	SET	
375811	73311+79011+78211+73711	RM	SEB	EVL	SET	
375812	73312+79012+78212+73712	RM	SEB	EVL	SET	
375813	73313+79013+78213+73713	RM	SEB	EVL	SET	
375814	73314+79014+78214+73714	RM	SEB	EVL	SET	
375815	73315+79015+78215+73715	RM	SEB	EVL	SET	
375816	73316+79016+78216+73716	RM	SEB	EVL	SET	
375817	73317+79017+78217+73717	RM	SEB	EVL	SET	
375818	73318+79018+78218+73718	RM	SEB	EVL	SET	
375819	73319+79019+78219+73719	RM	SEB	EVL	SET	
375820	73320+79020+78220+73720	RM	SEB	EVL	SET	
375821	73321+79021+78221+73721	RM	SEB	EVL	SET	
375822	73322+79022+78222+73722	RM	SEB	EVL	SET	
375823	73323+79023+78223+73723	RM	SEB	EVL	SET	*Ashford Proudly served by rail for 175 years*
375824	73324+79024+78224+73724	RM	SEB	EVL	SET	
375825	73325+79025+78225+73725	RM	SEB	EVL	SET	

375826	73326+79026+78226+73726	RM	SEB	EVL	SET
375827	73327+79027+78227+73727	RM	SEB	EVL	SET
375828	73328+79028+78228+73728	RM	SEB	EVL	SET
375829	73329+79029+78229+73729	RM	SEB	EVL	SET
375830	73330+79030+78230+73730	RM	SEB	EVL	SET

Class 375/9
Electrostar

Vehicle Length: (Driving) 66ft 9in (20.3m)
(Inter) 65ft 6in (19.96m)
Height: 12ft 4in (3.75m)
Width: 9ft 2in (2.79m)
Horsepower: 2,012hp (1,500kW)
Seats (total/car): 16F-226S, 60S/16F-50S/56S/60S

Number	*Formation* DMSO(A)+MCO+TSO+DMSO(B)	*Depot*	*Livery*	*Owner*	*Operator*
375901	73331+79031+79061+73731	RM	SEB	EVL	SET
375902	73332+79032+79062+73732	RM	SEB	EVL	SET
375903	73333+79033+79063+73733	RM	SEB	EVL	SET
375904	73334+79034+79064+73734	RM	SEB	EVL	SET
375905	73335+79035+79065+73735	RM	SEB	EVL	SET
375906	73336+79036+79066+73736	RM	SEB	EVL	SET
375907	73337+79037+79067+73737	RM	SEB	EVL	SET
375908	73338+79038+79068+73738	RM	SEB	EVL	SET
375909	73339+79039+79069+73739	RM	SEB	EVL	SET
375910	73340+79040+79070+73740	RM	SEB	EVL	SET
375911	73341+79041+79071+73741	RM	SEB	EVL	SET
375912	73342+79042+79072+73742	RM	SEB	EVL	SET
375913	73343+79043+79073+73743	RM	SEB	EVL	SET
375914	73344+79044+79074+73744	RM	SEB	EVL	SET
375915	73345+79045+79075+73745	RM	SEB	EVL	SET
375916	73346+79046+79076+73746	RM	SEB	EVL	SET
375917	73347+79047+79077+73747	RM	SEB	EVL	SET
375918	73348+79048+79078+73748	RM	SEB	EVL	SET
375919	73349+79049+79079+73749	RM	SEB	EVL	SET
375920	73350+79050+79080+73750	RM	SEB	EVL	SET
375921	73351+79051+79081+73751	RM	SEB	EVL	SET
375922	73352+79052+79082+73752	RM	SEB	EVL	SET
375923	73353+79053+79083+73753	RM	SEB	EVL	SET
375924	73354+79054+79084+73754	RM	SEB	EVL	SET
375925	73355+79055+79085+73755	RM	SEB	EVL	SET
375926	73356+79056+79086+73756	RM	SEB	EVL	SET
375927	73357+79057+79087+73757	RM	SEB	EVL	SET

Right: *The rolling stock used on main line SouthEastern services are various fleets of Class 375 'Electrostar' units, formed into either three or four-car sets. Units are allocated to Ramsgate depot and carry SouthEastern blue livery, off-set by blue contrasting passenger doors. Each of the sub-classes have minor detail differences. Class 375/6 set No. 375614 is shown, note the red body panelling around the disabled access area and the yellow indicating the first class area.*
Howard Lewsey

Class 376
Electrostar

Vehicle Length: (Driving) 66ft 9in (20.3m)
(Inter) 65ft 6in (19.96m)
Height: 12ft 4in (3.75m)
Width: 9ft 2in (2.79m)
Horsepower: 2,682hp (2,000kW)
Seats (total/car): 216S, 36S/48S/48S/48S/36S + 116 perch

Number	*Formation* DMSO(A)+MSO+TSO+MSO+DMSO(B)	*Depot*	*Livery*	*Owner*	*Operator*	*Name*
376001	61101+63301+64301+63501+61601	SG	SET	EVL	SET	*Alan Doggett*
376002	61102+63302+64302+63502+61602	SG	SET	EVL	SET	
376003	61103+63303+64303+63503+61603	SG	SET	EVL	SET	
376004	61104+63304+64304+63504+61604	SG	SET	EVL	SET	
376005	61105+63305+64305+63505+61605	SG	SET	EVL	SET	

376006	61106+63306+64306+63506+61606	SG	SET	EVL	SET
376007	61107+63307+64307+63507+61607	SG	SET	EVL	SET
376008	61108+63308+64308+63508+61608	SG	SET	EVL	SET
376009	61109+63309+64309+63509+61609	SG	SET	EVL	SET
376010	61110+63310+64310+63510+61610	SG	SET	EVL	SET
376011	61111+63311+64311+63511+61611	SG	SET	EVL	SET
376012	61112+63312+64312+63512+61612	SG	SET	EVL	SET
376013	61113+63313+64313+63513+61613	SG	SET	EVL	SET
376014	61114+63314+64314+63514+61614	SG	SET	EVL	SET
376015	61115+63315+64315+63515+61615	SG	SET	EVL	SET
376016	61116+63316+64316+63516+61616	SG	SET	EVL	SET
376017	61117+63317+64317+63517+61617	SG	SET	EVL	SET
376018	61118+63318+64318+63518+61618	SG	SET	EVL	SET
376019	61119+63319+64319+63519+61619	SG	SET	EVL	SET
376020	61120+63320+64320+63520+61620	SG	SET	EVL	SET
376021	61121+63321+64321+63521+61621	SG	SET	EVL	SET
376022	61122+63322+64322+63522+61622	SG	SET	EVL	SET
376023	61123+63323+64323+63523+61623	SG	SET	EVL	SET
376024	61124+63324+64324+63524+61624	SG	SET	EVL	SET
376025	61125+63325+64325+63525+61625	SG	SET	EVL	SET
376026	61126+63326+64326+63526+61626	SG	SET	EVL	SET
376027	61127+63327+64327+63527+61627	SG	SET	EVL	SET
376028	61128+63328+64328+63528+61628	SG	SET	EVL	SET
376029	61129+63329+64329+63529+61629	SG	SET	EVL	SET
376030	61130+63330+64330+63530+61630	SG	SET	EVL	SET
376031	61131+63331+64331+63531+61631	SG	SET	EVL	SET
376032	61132+63332+64332+63532+61632	SG	SET	EVL	SET
376033	61133+63333+64333+63533+61633	SG	SET	EVL	SET
376034	61134+63334+64334+63534+61634	SG	SET	EVL	SET
376035	61135+63335+64335+63535+61635	SG	SET	EVL	SET
376036	61136+63336+64336+63536+61636	SG	SET	EVL	SET

Left: *Inner suburban or Metro services on the SouthEastern are operated by a fleet of 36 no frills five-car sets, with reduced seating and large standing areas, thus enabling large numbers of passengers to be transported. These sets mainly operate on the three routes to and from Dartford. The units carry SouthEastern white and beige livery with yellow passenger doors. Set No. 376027 is seen in this image leading a ten-car formation.* **Howard Lewsey**

Class 377/5
Electrostar

Vehicle Length: (Driving) 66ft 9in (20.40m)
(Inter) 65ft 6in (19.99m)
Height: 12ft 4in (3.77m)
Width: 9ft 2in (2.79m)
Horsepower: 2,012hp (1,500kW) (ac), dual-voltage sets
Seats (total/car): 20F-221S, 10F-48S/69S/56S/10F-48S

Number	*Formation* DMCO(A)+MSO+PTSO+DMCO(B)	*Depot*	*Livery*	*Owner*	*Operator*
377501	73501+75901+74901+73601	RM	SEB	PTR	SET
377502	73502+75902+74902+73602	RM	SEB	PTR	SET
377503	73503+75903+74903+73603	RM	SEB	PTR	SET
377504	73504+75904+74904+73604	RM	SEB	PTR	SET
377505	73505+75905+74905+73605	RM	SEB	PTR	SET
377506	73506+75906+74906+73606	RM	SEB	PTR	SET
377507	73507+75907+74907+73607	RM	SEB	PTR	SET
377508	73508+75908+74908+73608	RM	SEB	PTR	SET
377509	73509+75909+74909+73609	RM	SEB	PTR	SET

377510	73510+75910+74910+73610	RM	SEB	PTR	SET
377511	73511+75911+74911+73611	RM	SEB	PTR	SET
377512	73512+75912+74912+73612	RM	SEB	PTR	SET
377513	73513+75913+74913+73613	RM	SEB	PTR	SET
377514	73514+75914+74914+73614	RM	SEB	PTR	SET
377515	73515+75915+74915+73615	RM	SEB	PTR	SET
377516	73516+75916+74916+73616	RM	SEB	PTR	SET
377517	73517+75917+74917+73617	RM	SEB	PTR	SET
377518	73518+75918+74918+73618	RM	SEB	PTR	SET
377519	73519+75919+74919+73619	RM	SEB	PTR	SET
377520	73520+75920+74920+73620	RM	SEB	PTR	SET
377521	73521+75921+74921+73621	RM	SEB	PTR	SET
377522	73522+75922+74922+73622	RM	SEB	PTR	SET
377523	73523+75923+74923+73623	RM	SEB	PTR	SET

Right: *After operating for a period on Thameslink services, the 23 members of Class 377/5 are now operated on Southeastern, based at Ramsgate and operate alongside the Class 375 fleet. These sets retain their first class accommodation in the driving cars, directly behind the driver's cab. Set No. 377501 is illustrated.* **CJM**

Class 395
Javelin

Vehicle Length: (Driving) 67ft 7in (20.6m)
(Inter) 67ft 6in (20.5m)
Height: 12ft 6in (3.81m)
Width: 9ft 2in (2.79m)
Horsepower: 4,504hp (3,360kW)
Seats (total/car): 340S, 28S/66S/66S/66S/66S/48S

Number	*Formation* DMSO(A)+MSO(A)+MSO(B)+MSO(C)+MSO(D)+DMSO(B)	*Depot*	*Livery*	*Owner*	*Operator*	*Name*
395001	39011+39012+39013+39014+39015+39016	AD	HS1	EVL	SET	*Dame Kelly Holmes*
395002	39021+39022+39023+39024+39025+39026	AD	HS1	EVL	SET	*Sebastian Coe*
395003	39031+39032+39033+39034+39035+39036	AD	HS1	EVL	SET	*Sir Steve Redgrave*
395004	39041+39042+39043+39044+39045+39046	AD	HS1	EVL	SET	*Sir Chris Hoy*
395005	39051+39052+39053+39054+39055+39056	AD	HS1	EVL	SET	*Dame Tanni Grey-Thompson*
395006	39061+39062+39063+39064+39065+39066	AD	HS1	EVL	SET	*Daley Thompson*
395007	39071+39072+39073+39074+39075+39076	AD	HS1	EVL	SET	*Steve Backley*
395008	39081+39082+39083+39084+39085+39086	AD	HS1	EVL	SET	*Ben Ainslie*
395009	39091+39092+39093+39094+39095+39096	AD	HS1	EVL	SET	*Rebecca Adlington*
395010	39101+39102+39103+39104+39105+39106	AD	HS1	EVL	SET	*Duncan Goodhew*
395011	39111+39112+39113+39114+39115+39116	AD	HS1	EVL	SET	*Katherine Grainger*
395012	39121+39122+39123+39124+39125+39126	AD	HS1	EVL	SET	
395013	39131+39132+39133+39134+39135+39136	AD	HS1	EVL	SET	*Hornby Visitor Centre Margate Kent*
395014	39141+39142+39143+39144+39145+39146	AD	HS1	EVL	SET	*The Victoria Cross*
395015	39151+39152+39153+39154+39155+39156	AD	HS1	EVL	SET	
395016	39161+39162+39163+39164+39165+39166	AD	HS1	EVL	SET	*Passchendaele Javelin*
395017	39171+39172+39173+39174+39175+39176	AD	HS1	EVL	SET	
395018	39181+39182+39183+39184+39185+39186	AD	HS1	EVL	SET	*The Victory Javelin*
395019	39191+39192+39193+39194+39195+39196	AD	HS1	EVL	SET	*Jessica Ennis*
395020	39201+39202+39203+39204+39205+39206	AD	HS1	EVL	SET	*Jason Kenny*
395021	39211+39212+39213+39214+39215+39216	AD	HS1	EVL	SET	*Ed Clancy MBE*
395022	39221+39222+39223+39224+39225+39226	AD	HS1	EVL	SET	*Alistair Brownlee*
395023	39231+39232+39233+39234+39235+39236	AD	HS1	EVL	SET	*Ellie Simmonds*
395024	39241+39242+39243+39244+39245+39246	AD	HS1	EVL	SET	*Jonnie Peacock*
395025	39251+39252+39253+39254+39255+39256	AD	HS1	EVL	SET	*Victoria Pendleton*

South Eastern

395026	39261+39262+39263+39264+39265+39266	AD	HS1	EVL	SET	*Marc Woods*
395027	39271+39272+39273+39274+39275+39276	AD	HS1	EVL	SET	*Hannah Cockcroft*
395028	39281+39282+39283+39284+39285+39286	AD	HS1	EVL	SET	*Laura Trott*
395029	39291+39292+39293+39294+39295+39296	AD	HS1	EVL	SET	*David Weir*

Left: *SouthEastern High Speed domestic services, authorised to operate over High Speed 1 (HS1), are formed of a fleet of 29 Hitachi Japan built six car Class 395s. These sets are based at the Hitachi depot in Ashford, Kent. Sets are finished in SouthEastern blue, with sky blue passenger doors. The units operate under the 'Javelin' title. Set No. 395022 is shown in the domestic platforms at St Pancras International.* **Antony Christie**

Class 465/0
Networker

Vehicle Length: (Driving) 68ft 6½in (20.89m) (Inter) 65ft 9¾in (20.05m)
Height: 12ft 4½in (3.77m)
Width: 9ft 3in (2.81m)
Horsepower: 2,252hp (1,680kW)
Seats (total/car): 348S, 86S/90S/86S/86S

Number	*Formation* DMSO(A)+TSO+TSO+DMSO(B)	*Depot*	*Livery*	*Owner*	*Operator*
465001	64759+72028+72029+64809	SG	SET	EVL	SET
465002	64760+72030+72031+64810	SG	SET	EVL	SET
465003	64761+72032+72033+64811	SG	SET	EVL	SET
465004	64762+72034+72035+64812	SG	SET	EVL	SET
465005	64763+72036+72037+64813	SG	SET	EVL	SET
465006	64764+72038+72039+64814	SG	SET	EVL	SET
465007	64765+72040+72041+64815	SG	SET	EVL	SET
465008	64766+72042+72043+64816	SG	SET	EVL	SET
465009	64767+72044+72045+64817	SG	SET	EVL	SET
465010	64768+72046+72047+64818	SG	SET	EVL	SET
465011	64769+72048+72049+64819	SG	SET	EVL	SET
465012	64770+72050+72051+64820	SG	SET	EVL	SET
465013	64771+72052+72053+64821	SG	SET	EVL	SET
465014	64772+72054+72055+64822	SG	SET	EVL	SET
465015	64773+72056+72057+64823	SG	SET	EVL	SET
465016	64774+72058+72059+64824	SG	SET	EVL	SET
465017	64775+72060+72061+64825	SG	SET	EVL	SET
465018	64776+72062+72063+64826	SG	SET	EVL	SET
465019	64777+72064+72065+64827	SG	SET	EVL	SET
465020	64778+72066+72067+64828	SG	SET	EVL	SET
465021	64779+72068+72069+64829	SG	SET	EVL	SET
465022	64780+72070+72071+64830	SG	SET	EVL	SET
465023	64781+72072+72073+64831	SG	SET	EVL	SET
465024	64782+72074+72075+64832	SG	SET	EVL	SET
465025	64783+72076+72077+64833	SG	SET	EVL	SET
465026	64784+72078+72079+64834	SG	SET	EVL	SET
465027	64785+72080+72081+64835	SG	SET	EVL	SET
465028	64786+72082+72083+64836	SG	SET	EVL	SET
465029	64787+72084+72085+64837	SG	SET	EVL	SET
465030	64788+72086+72087+64838	SG	SET	EVL	SET
465031	64789+72088+72089+64839	SG	SET	EVL	SET
465032	64790+72090+72091+64840	SG	SET	EVL	SET
465033	64791+72092+72093+64841	SG	SET	EVL	SET
465034	64792+72094+72095+64842	SG	SET	EVL	SET
465035	64793+72096+72097+64843	SG	SET	EVL	SET
465036	64794+72098+72099+64844	SG	SET	EVL	SET
465037	64795+72100+72101+64845	SG	SET	EVL	SET
465038	64796+72102+72103+64846	SG	SET	EVL	SET
465039	64797+72104+72105+64847	SG	SET	EVL	SET

465040	64798+72106+72107+64848	SG	SET	EVL	SET
465041	64799+72108+72109+64849	SG	SET	EVL	SET
465042	64800+72110+72111+64850	SG	SET	EVL	SET
465043	64801+72112+72113+64851	SG	SET	EVL	SET
465044	64802+72114+72115+64852	SG	SET	EVL	SET
465045	64803+72116+72117+64853	SG	SET	EVL	SET
465046	64804+72118+72119+64854	SG	SET	EVL	SET
465047	64805+72120+72121+64855	SG	SET	EVL	SET
465048	64806+72122+72123+64856	SG	SET	EVL	SET
465049	64807+72124+72125+64857	SG	SET	EVL	SET
465050	64808+72126+72127+64858	SG	SET	EVL	SET

Right: *When Network SouthEast modernised the South East section, they invested in four-car 'Networker' sets built by ABB and Metro-Cammell. These sets, although heavily refurbished and modernised to meet latest standards, are still in front line service. The sets are based at Slade Green. Units display SouthEastern white and dark blue livery, off-set by sky blue passenger doors. ABB-built No. 465028 is shown at London Bridge.*
Nathan Williamson

Class 465/1
Networker

Vehicle Length: (Driving) 68ft 6½in (20.89m) (Inter) 65ft 9¾in (20.05m)
Height: 12ft 4½in (3.77m)
Width: 9ft 3in (2.81m)
Horsepower: 2,252hp (1,680kW)
Seats (total/car): 348S, 86S/90S/86S/86S

Number	*Formation* DMSO(A)+TSO+TSO+DMSO(B)	*Depot*	*Livery*	*Owner*	*Operator*
465151	65800+72900+72901+65847	SG	SET	EVL	SET
465152	65801+72902+72903+65848	SG	SET	EVL	SET
465153	65802+72904+72905+65849	SG	SET	EVL	SET
465154	65803+72906+72907+65850	SG	SET	EVL	SET
465155	65804+72908+72909+65851	SG	SET	EVL	SET
465156	65805+72910+72911+65852	SG	SET	EVL	SET
465157	65806+72912+72913+65853	SG	SET	EVL	SET
465158	65807+72914+72915+65854	SG	SET	EVL	SET
465159	65808+72916+72917+65855	SG	SET	EVL	SET
465160	65809+72918+72919+65856	SG	SET	EVL	SET
465161	65810+72920+72921+65857	SG	SET	EVL	SET
465162	65811+72922+72923+65858	SG	SET	EVL	SET
465163	65812+72924+72925+65859	SG	SET	EVL	SET
465164	65813+72926+72927+65860	SG	SET	EVL	SET
465165	65814+72928+72929+65861	SG	SET	EVL	SET
465166	65815+72930+72931+65862	SG	SET	EVL	SET
465167	65816+72932+72933+65863	SG	SET	EVL	SET
465168	65817+72934+72935+65864	SG	SET	EVL	SET
465169	65818+72936+72937+65865	SG	SET	EVL	SET
465170	65819+72938+72939+65866	SG	SET	EVL	SET
465171	65820+72940+72941+65867	SG	SET	EVL	SET
465172	65821+72942+72943+65868	SG	SET	EVL	SET
465173	65822+72944+72945+65869	SG	SET	EVL	SET
465174	65823+72946+72947+65870	SG	SET	EVL	SET
465175	65824+72948+72949+65871	SG	SET	EVL	SET
465176	65825+72950+72951+65872	SG	SET	EVL	SET
465177	65826+72952+72953+65873	SG	SET	EVL	SET
465178	65827+72954+72955+65874	SG	SET	EVL	SET
465179	65828+72956+72957+65875	SG	SET	EVL	SET
465180	65829+72958+72959+65876	SG	SET	EVL	SET
465181	65830+72960+72961+65877	SG	SET	EVL	SET

South Eastern

465182	65831+72962+72963+65878	SG	SET	EVL	SET
465183	65832+72964+72965+65879	SG	SET	EVL	SET
465184	65833+72966+72967+65880	SG	SET	EVL	SET
465185	65834+72968+72969+65881	SG	SET	EVL	SET
465186	65835+72970+72971+65882	SG	SET	EVL	SET
465187	65836+72972+72973+65883	SG	SET	EVL	SET
465188	65837+72974+72975+65884	SG	SET	EVL	SET
465189	65838+72976+72977+65885	SG	SET	EVL	SET
465190	65839+72978+72979+65886	SG	SET	EVL	SET
465191	65840+72980+72981+65887	SG	SET	EVL	SET
465192	65841+72982+72983+65888	SG	SET	EVL	SET
465193	65842+72984+72985+65889	SG	SET	EVL	SET
465194	65843+72986+72987+65890	SG	SET	EVL	SET
465195	65844+72988+72989+65891	SG	SET	EVL	SET
465196	65845+72990+72991+65892	SG	SET	EVL	SET
465197	65846+72992+72993+65893	SG	SET	EVL	SET

Above: *All the original ABB-built 'Networkers' have been re-equipped with Hitachi traction equipment, which has seen the between bogie skirts removed from driving cars, being retained on intermediate vehicles. The Alstom-built sets have so far retained their as-built traction package. Second phase ABB set No. 465190 is illustrated. Note the angled top above the front valance to stop train surfing.* **Nathan Williamson**

Class 465/2
Networker

Vehicle Length: (Driving) 68ft 6½in (20.89m) (Inter) 65ft 9¾in (20.05m)
Height: 12ft 4½in (3.77m)
Width: 9ft 3in (2.81m)
Horsepower: 2,252hp (1,680kW)
Seats (total/car): 348S, 86S/90S/86S/86S

Number	*Formation* DMSO(A)+TSO+TSO+DMSO(B)	*Depot*	*Livery*	*Owner*	*Operator*
465235	65734+72787+72788+65784	SG	SET	ANG	SET
465236	65735+72789+72790+65785	SG	SET	ANG	SET
465237	65736+72791+72792+65786	SG	SET	ANG	SET
465238	65737+72793+72794+65787	SG	SET	ANG	SET
465239	65738+72795+72796+65788	SG	SET	ANG	SET
465240	65739+72797+72798+65789	SG	SET	ANG	SET
465241	65740+72799+72800+65790	SG	SET	ANG	SET
465242	65741+72801+72802+65791	SG	SET	ANG	SET
465243	65742+72803+72804+65792	SG	SET	ANG	SET

465244	65743+72805+72806+65793	SG	SET	ANG	SET
465245	65744+72807+72808+65794	SG	SET	ANG	SET
465246	65745+72809+72810+65795	SG	SET	ANG	SET
465247	65746+72811+72812+65796	SG	SET	ANG	SET
465248	65747+72813+72814+65797	SG	SET	ANG	SET
465249	65748+72815+72816+65798	SG	SET	ANG	SET
465250	65749+72817+72818+65799	SG	SET	ANG	SET

Below: *The fleets of Class 465/0, 465/1 and 465/2 operate as a common pool and sets from any sub class can be found working any '465' service, sets from all sub-classes can be coupled together for multiple operation. Set No. 465239 is seen approaching Lewisham.* **CJM**

Class 465/9
Networker

Vehicle Length: (Driving) 68ft 6½in (20.89m)
(Inter) 65ft 9¾in (20.05m)
Height: 12ft 4½in (3.77m)
Width: 9ft 3in (2.81m)
Horsepower: 2,252hp (1,680kW)
Seats (total/car): 24F-302S, 12F-68S/76S/90S/12F-68S

Number	*Formation* DMCO(A)+TSO+TSO+DMCO(B)	*Depot*	*Livery*	*Owner*	*Operator*
465901 (465201)	65700+72719+72720+65750	SG	SET	ANG	SET
465902 (465202)	65701+72721+72722+65751	SG	SET	ANG	SET
465903 (465203)	65702+72723+72724+65752	SG	SET	ANG	SET
465904 (465204)	65703+72725+72726+65753	SG	SET	ANG	SET
465905 (465205)	65704+72727+72728+65754	SG	SET	ANG	SET
465906 (465206)	65705+72729+72730+65755	SG	SET	ANG	SET
465907 (465207)	65706+72731+72732+65756	SG	SET	ANG	SET
465908 (465208)	65707+72733+72734+65757	SG	SET	ANG	SET
465909 (465209)	65708+72735+72736+65758	SG	SET	ANG	SET
465910 (465210)	65709+72737+72738+65759	SG	SET	ANG	SET
465911 (465211)	65710+72739+72740+65760	SG	SET	ANG	SET
465912 (465212)	65711+72741+72742+65761	SG	SET	ANG	SET
465913 (465213)	65712+72743+72744+65762	SG	SET	ANG	SET
465914 (465214)	65713+72745+72746+65763	SG	SET	ANG	SET
465915 (465215)	65714+72747+72748+65764	SG	SET	ANG	SET
465916 (465216)	65715+72749+72750+65765	SG	SET	ANG	SET
465917 (465217)	65716+72751+72752+65766	SG	SET	ANG	SET
465918 (465218)	65717+72753+72754+65767	SG	SET	ANG	SET
465919 (465219)	65718+72755+72756+65768	SG	SET	ANG	SET
465920 (465220)	65719+72757+72758+65769	SG	SET	ANG	SET
465921 (465221)	65720+72759+72760+65770	SG	SET	ANG	SET
465922 (465222)	65721+72761+72762+65771	SG	SET	ANG	SET
465923 (465223)	65722+72763+72764+65772	SG	SET	ANG	SET
465924 (465224)	65723+72765+72766+65773	SG	SET	ANG	SET
465925 (465225)	65724+72767+72768+65774	SG	SET	ANG	SET
465926 (465226)	65725+72769+72770+65775	SG	SET	ANG	SET
465927 (465227)	65726+72771+72772+65776	SG	SET	ANG	SET
465928 (465228)	65727+72773+72774+65777	SG	SET	ANG	SET
465929 (465229)	65728+72775+72776+65778	SG	SET	ANG	SET
465930 (465230)	65729+72777+72778+65779	SG	SET	ANG	SET

South Eastern

465931 (465231)	65730+72779+72780+65780	SG	SET	ANG	SET
465932 (465232)	65731+72781+72782+65781	SG	SET	ANG	SET
465933 (465233)	65732+72783+72784+65782	SG	SET	ANG	SET
465934 (465234)	65733+72785+72786+65783	SG	SET	ANG	SET

Left: *A batch of 34 of the original Metro-Cammell Class 465/2 sets were rebuilt as Class 465/9 to operate longer distance outer-suburban services and were fitted with first class seating in both driving cars. These sets are thus identifiable by a yellow first class band behind the cabs. Set No. 465910 is captured approaching Tonbridge.* **Nathan Williamson**

Class 466
Networker

Vehicle Length: (Driving) 68ft 6½in (20.89m)
Height: 12ft 4½in (3.77m)
Width: 9ft 3in (2.81m)
Horsepower: 1,126hp (840kW)
Seats (total/car): 168S, 86S/82S

Number	*Formation DMSO+DTSO*	*Depot*	*Livery*	*Owner*	*Operator*
466001	64860+78312	SG	SET	ANG	SET
466002	64861+78313	SG	SET	ANG	SET
466003	64862+78314	SG	SET	ANG	SET
466004	64863+78315	SG	SET	ANG	SET
466005	64864+78316	SG	SET	ANG	SET
466006	64865+78317	SG	SET	ANG	SET
466007	64866+78318	SG	SET	ANG	SET
466008	64867+78319	SG	SET	ANG	SET
466009	64868+78320	SG	SET	ANG	SET
466010	64869+78321	SG	SET	ANG	SET
466011	64870+78322	SG	SET	ANG	SET
466012	64871+78323	SG	SET	ANG	SET
466013	64872+78324	SG	SET	ANG	SET
466014	64873+78325	SG	SET	ANG	SET
466015	64874+78326	SG	SET	ANG	SET
466016	64875+78327	SG	SET	ANG	SET
466017	64876+78328	SG	SET	ANG	SET
466018	64877+78329	SG	SET	ANG	SET
466019	64878+78330	SG	SET	ANG	SET
466020	64879+78331	SG	SET	ANG	SET
466021	64880+78332	SG	SET	ANG	SET
466022	64881+78333	SG	SET	ANG	SET
466023	64882+78334	SG	SET	ANG	SET
466024	64883+78335	SG	SET	ANG	SET
466025	64884+78336	SG	SET	ANG	SET
466026	64885+78337	SG	SET	ANG	SET
466027	64886+78338	SG	SET	ANG	SET
466028	64887+78339	SG	SET	ANG	SET
466029	64888+78340	SG	SET	ANG	SET
466030	64889+78341	SG	SET	ANG	SET
466031	64890+78342	SG	SET	ANG	SET
466032	64891+78343	SG	SET	ANG	SET
466033	64892+78344	SG	SET	ANG	SET
466034	64893+78345	SG	SET	ANG	SET
466035	64894+78346	SG	SET	ANG	SET
466036	64895+78347	SG	SET	ANG	SET
466037	64896+78348	SG	SET	ANG	SET
466038	64897+78349	SG	SET	ANG	SET
466039	64898+78350	SG	SET	ANG	SET
466040	64899+78351	SG	SET	ANG	SET
466041	64900+78352	SG	SET	ANG	SET
466042	64901+78353	SG	SET	ANG	SET
466043	64902+78354	SG	SET	ANG	SET

Below: *When the original fleet of Networker stock was ordered, a fleet of 43 two-car sets were built by Metro-Cammell, to enable trains to be formed of two, four, six, eight, ten or twelve-car formation. The sets seldom operate on their own. Strengthening a four-car to a six-car, set No. 466003 is seen attached to the rear of a Class 465.* **Nathan Williamson**

South Western Railway

Address: Friars Bridge Court, 41-45 Blackfriars Road, London, SE1 8NZ
customerrelations@swrailway.com
0345 6000 650 www.southwesternrailway.com

Managing Director: Mark Hopwood (intrim)

Franchise Dates: 20 August 2017 - August 2023

Principal Routes: London Waterloo - Weymouth, Exeter, Portsmouth and suburban services in Surrey, Berkshire, Hampshire

Depots: Wimbledon Park (WD), Bournemouth (BM), Clapham Junction (CJ) [Stabling point], Salisbury (SA), Northam (Siemens Transportation) (NT)

Parent Company: First Group (70%) / MTR (30%)

Class 158

Vehicle Length: 76ft 1¾in (23.21m)
Height: 12ft 6in (3.81m)
Width: 9ft 3¼in (2.82m)
Engine: 1 x Cummins NTA855R of 350hp per vehicle
Horsepower: 700hp (522kW)
Seats (total/car): 13F-114S, 13F-44S/70S

Number	*Formation* DMCL+DMSL	*Depot*	*Livery*	*Owner*	*Operator*
158880 (158737)	52737+57737	SA	SWN	PTR	SWR
158881 (158742)	52742+57742	SA	SWN	PTR	SWR
158882 (158743)	52743+57743	SA	SWM	PTR	SWR
158883 (158744)	52744+57744	SA	SWM	PTR	SWR
158884 (158772)	52772+57772	SA	SWM	PTR	SWR
158885 (158775)	52775+57775	SA	SWM	PTR	SWR
158886 (158779)	52779+57779	SA	SWM	PTR	SWR
158887 (158781)	52781+57781	SA	SWR	PTR	SWR
158888 (158802)	52802+57802	SA	SWR	PTR	SWR
158889 (158808)	52808+57808	NM	EMT	PTR	EMT (On loan to East Midlands Railway)
158890 (158814)	52814+57814	SA	SWR	PTR	SWR

Below: *South Western Railway has a fleet of 10 two-car Class 158s allocated to Salisbury depot for use on SWR non-electrified services such as the Salisbury to Romsey and Waterloo to Bristol routes. The fleet is also used to strengthen Waterloo to West of England services as required. The fleet is mid-way through a repaint to apply the latest livery. Showing SWR branded South West Trains white, orange and red colours, set No. 158880 is seen at Southampton with a Romsey service.* **CJM**

South Western Railway

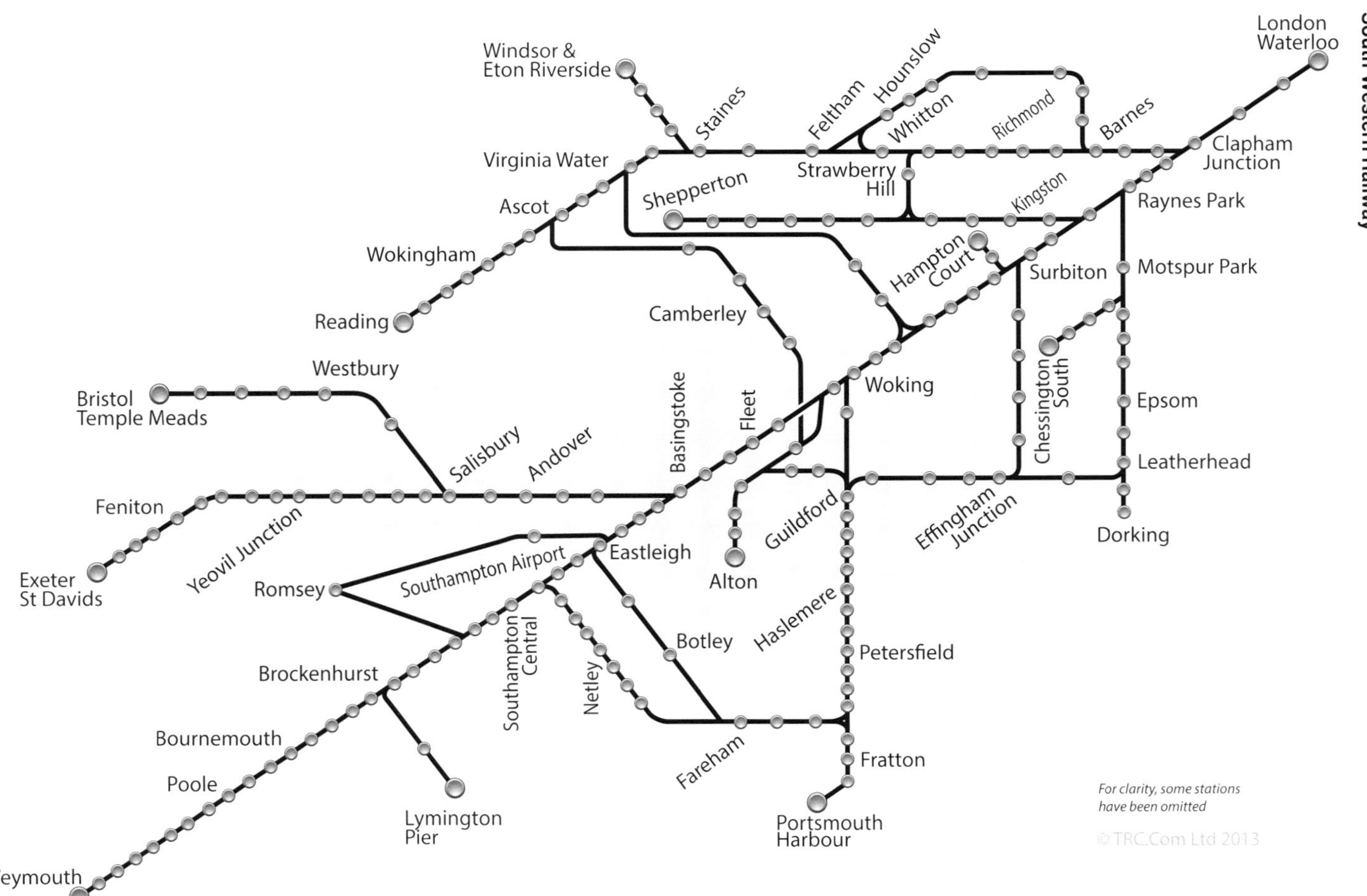

Class 159/0

Vehicle Length: 76ft 1¾in (23.21m)
Height: 12ft 6in (3.81m)
Width: 9ft 3¼in (2.82m)
Engine: 1 x Cummins NTA855R of 400hp per vehicle
Horsepower: 1,200hp (895kW)
Seats (total/car): 24F-172S, 24F-28S/72S/72S

Number	*Formation* DMCL+MSL+DMS	*Depot*	*Livery*	*Owner*	*Operator*
159001	52873+58718+57873	SA	SWR	PTR	SWR
159002	52874+58719+57874	SA	SWR	PTR	SWR
159003	52875+58720+57875	SA	SWR	PTR	SWR
159004	52876+58721+57876	SA	SWR	PTR	SWR
159005	52877+58722+57877	SA	SWR	PTR	SWR
159006	52878+58723+57878	SA	SWR	PTR	SWR
159007	52879+58724+57879	SA	SWR	PTR	SWR
159008	52880+58725+57880	SA	SWR	PTR	SWR
159009	52881+58726+57881	SA	SWR	PTR	SWR
159010	52882+58727+57882	SA	SWR	PTR	SWR
159011	52883+58728+57883	SA	SWR	PTR	SWR
159012	52884+58729+57884	SA	SWR	PTR	SWR
159013	52885+58730+57885	SA	SWR	PTR	SWR
159014	52886+58731+57886	SA	SWR	PTR	SWR
159015	52887+58732+57887	SA	SWR	PTR	SWR
159016	52888+58733+57888	SA	SWR	PTR	SWR
159017	52889+58734+57889	SA	SWR	PTR	SWR
159018	52890+58735+57890	SA	SWR	PTR	SWR
159019	52891+58736+57891	SA	SWR	PTR	SWR
159020	52892+58737+57892	SA	SWR	PTR	SWR
159021	52893+58738+57893	SA	SWR	PTR	SWR
159022	52894+58739+57894	SA	SWR	PTR	SWR

Above: *The 22 Class 159/0 and 8 Class 159/1 units operate on the Waterloo to Exeter via Salisbury route and are based at Salisbury depot. The sets have been repainted in the new SWR light grey and blue colours with opposite contrasting passenger doors. Front ends are lemon yellow. Set No. 159001 is seen at Salisbury, with Class 158 No. 158881 on the left.* **CJM**

Class 159/1

Vehicle Length: 76ft 1¾in (23.21m)
Height: 12ft 6in (3.81m)
Width: 9ft 3¼in (2.82m)
Engine: 1 x Cummins NTA855R of 350hp per vehicle
Horsepower: 1,050hp (782kW)
Seats (total/car): 24F-170S, 24F-28S/70S/72S

Number	*Formation* DMCL+MSL+DMSL	*Depot*	*Livery*	*Owner*	*Operator*
159101 (158800)	52800+58717+57800	SA	SWN	PTR	SWR
159102 (158803)	52803+58703+57803	SA	SWN	PTR	SWR
159103 (158804)	52804+58704+57804	SA	SWN	PTR	SWR
159104 (158805)	52805+58705+57805	SA	SWN	PTR	SWR
159105 (158807)	52807+58707+57807	SA	SWN	PTR	SWR
159106 (158809)	52809+58709+57809	SA	SWN	PTR	SWR
159107 (158811)	52811+58711+57811	SA	SWN	PTR	SWR
159108 (158801)	52801+58701+57801	SA	SWN	PTR	SWR

South Western Railway

Class 442

Vehicle Length: (Driving) 75ft 11½in (23.15m) (Inter) 75ft 5½in (22.99m)
Height: 12ft 4in (3.81m)
Width: 8ft 11½in (2.73m)
Horsepower: 1,608hp (1,200kW)
Seats (total/car): 24F-318S, 74S/76S/24F-28S/66S/74S
To be re-equiped with Kiepe ac traction equipment

Number	Formation DTSO(A)+TSO+MBC+TSO+DTSO(B)	Depot	Livery	Owner	Operator
442402	77383+71819+62938+71842+77407	BM	SWR	ANG	SWR
442403	77384+71820+62941+71843+77408	BM	SWR	ANG	SWR
442404	77385+71821+62939+71844+77409	BM	SWR	ANG	SWR
442406	77389+71823+62942+71846+77411	BM	SWR	ANG	SWR
442408	77387+71825+62945+71848+77413	BM	SWR	ANG	SWR
442409	77390+71826+62946+71849+77406	BM	SWR	ANG	SWR
442410	77391+71827+62948+71850+77415	BM	SWR	ANG	SWR
442411	77392+71828+62940+71851+77422	BM	SWR	ANG	SWR
442413	77394+71830+62949+71853+77418	BM	SWR	ANG	SWR
442414	77395+71831+62950+71854+77419	BM	SWR	ANG	SWR
442415	77396+71832+62951+71855+77420	BM	SWR	ANG	SWR
442416	77397+71833+62952+71856+77421	BM	SWR	ANG	SWR
442417	77398+71834+62953+71857+77416	BM	SWR	ANG	SWR
442418	77399+71835+62954+71852+77423	BM	SWR	ANG	SWR
442419§	77400+71836+62955+71859+77424	BM	SWR	ANG	SWR
442420	77401+71837+62956+71860+77425	BM	SWR	ANG	SWR
442422	77403+71839+62958+71862+77427	BM	SWR	ANG	SWR
442423	77404+71840+62959+71863+77428	BM	SWR	ANG	SWR

§ Kiepe Traction system

Left: *South Western Railway have now re-introduced a fleet of 18 Class 442 'Wessex Electric' sets for use on Waterloo Portsmouth services. The five-car sets have had a troubled return to service, delaying the launch of improved passenger services. Sets have been overhauled at Eastleigh and are currently receiving new Kiepe traction equipment. Set No. 442413 is seen at Waterloo.* **CJM**

Class 444
Desiro

Vehicle Length: 77ft 3in (23.57m)
Height: 12ft 1½in (3.7m)
Width: 9ft 2in (2.7m)
Horsepower: 2,682hp (2,000kW)
Seats (total/car): 35F-299S, 76S/76S/76S/47/35F-24S (refurbished 32F-327S, 76S/76S/76S/59S/32F-40S

Number	Formation DMSO+TSO+TSO+TSRMB(TSO)+DMCO	Depot	Livery	Owner	Operator	Name
444001	63801+67101+67151+67201+63851	NT	SWM	ANG	SWR	*Naomi House*
444002	63802+67102+67152+67202+63852	NT	SWM	ANG	SWR	
444003	63803+67103+67153+67203+63853	NT	SWM	ANG	SWR	
444004	63804+67104+67154+67204+63854	NT	SWM	ANG	SWR	
444005	63805+67105+67155+67205+63855	NT	SWM	ANG	SWR	
444006	63806+67106+67156+67206+63856	NT	SWR	ANG	SWR	
444007	63807+67107+67157+67207+63857	NT	SWR	ANG	SWR	
444008	63808+67108+67158+67208+63858	NT	SWM	ANG	SWR	
444009	63809+67109+67159+67209+63859	NT	SWM	ANG	SWR	
444010	63810+67110+67160+67210+63860	NT	SWM	ANG	SWR	
444011	63811+67111+67161+67211+63861	NT	SWM	ANG	SWR	
444012	63812+67112+67162+67212+63862	NT	SWR	ANG	SWR	*Destination Weymouth*
444013	63813+67113+67163+67213+63863	NT	SWM	ANG	SWR	
444014	63814+67114+67164+67214+63864	NT	SWM	ANG	SWR	
444015	63815+67115+67165+67215+63865	NT	SWR	ANG	SWR	
444016	63816+67116+67166+67216+63866	NT	SWM	ANG	SWR	
444017	63817+67117+67167+67217+63867	NT	SWM	ANG	SWR	

Number	Formation	Depot	Livery	Owner	Operator	Name
444018	63818+67118+67168+67218+63868	NT	SWM	ANG	SWR	*The FAB 444*
444019	63819+67119+67169+67219+63869	NT	SWM	ANG	SWR	
444020	63820+67120+67170+67220+63870	NT	SWM	ANG	SWR	
444021	63821+67121+67171+67221+63871	NT	SWM	ANG	SWR	
444022	63822+67122+67172+67222+63872	NT	SWM	ANG	SWR	
444023	63823+67123+67173+67223+63873	NT	SWM	ANG	SWR	
444024	63824+67124+67174+67224+63874	NT	SWM	ANG	SWR	
444025	63825+67125+67175+67225+63875	NT	SWM	ANG	SWR	
444026	63826+67126+67176+67226+63876	NT	SWM	ANG	SWR	
444027	63827+67127+67177+67227+63877	NT	SWM	ANG	SWR	
444028	63828+67128+67178+67228+63878	NT	SWM	ANG	SWR	
444029	63829+67129+67179+67229+63879	NT	SWM	ANG	SWR	
444030	63830+67130+67180+67230+63880	NT	SWM	ANG	SWR	
444031	63831+67131+67181+67231+63881	NT	SWM	ANG	SWR	
444032	63832+67132+67182+67232+63882	NT	SWM	ANG	SWR	
444033	63833+67133+67183+67233+63883	NT	SWM	ANG	SWR	
444034	63834+67134+67184+67234+63884	NT	SWM	ANG	SWR	
444035	63835+67135+67185+67235+63885	NT	SWM	ANG	SWR	
444036	63836+67136+67186+67236+63886	NT	SWM	ANG	SWR	
444037	63837+67137+67187+67237+63887	NT	SWM	ANG	SWR	
444038	63838+67138+67188+67238+63888	NT	SWM	ANG	SWR	*South Western Railway*
444039	63839+67139+67189+67239+63889	NT	SWM	ANG	SWR	
444040	63840+67140+67190+67240+63890	NT	SWR	ANG	SWR	*The D-Day Story Portsmouth*
444041	63841+67141+67191+67241+63891	NT	SWM	ANG	SWR	
444042	63842+67142+67192+67242+63892	NT	SWM	ANG	SWR	
444043	63843+67143+67193+67243+63893	NT	SWM	ANG	SWR	
444044	63844+67144+67194+67244+63894	NT	SWM	ANG	SWR	
444045	63845+67145+67195+67245+63895	NT	SWM	ANG	SWR	

Right: *A fleet of 45 five-car Siemens 'Desiro' main line sets are operated on the Waterloo to Bournemouth and Weymouth and Portsmouth routes. These low-density express sets have 2+2 seating with door positions at the end of each coach. Repainting into the new SWR livery has been slow. Showing the revised colours, No. 444040 is seen near Porchester on the Portsmouth route.* **Antony Christie**

Class 450/0
Desiro

Vehicle Length: 66ft 9in (20.4m)
Height: 12ft 1½in (3.7m)
Width: 9ft 2in (2.7m)
Horsepower: 2,682hp (2,000kW)
Seats (total/car): 16F/254S, 8F, 62S/69S/61S/8F,62S

Number	*Formation* DMCO+TSO+TSO+DMCO	*Depot*	*Livery*	*Owner*	*Operator*	*Name*
450001	63201+64201+68101+63601	NT	SWO	ANG	SWR	
450002	63202+64202+68102+63602	NT	SWO	ANG	SWR	
450003	63203+64203+68103+63603	NT	SWO	ANG	SWR	
450004	63204+64204+68104+63604	NT	SWO	ANG	SWR	
450005	63205+64205+68105+63605	NT	SWO	ANG	SWR	
450006	63206+64206+68106+63606	NT	SWO	ANG	SWR	
450007	63207+64207+68107+63607	NT	SWO	ANG	SWR	
450008	63208+64208+68108+63608	NT	SWO	ANG	SWR	

South Western Railway

450009		63209+64209+68109+63609	NT	SWO	ANG	SWR	
450010		63210+64210+68110+63610	NT	SWO	ANG	SWR	
450011		63211+64211+68111+63611	NT	SWO	ANG	SWR	
450012		63212+64212+68112+63612	NT	SWO	ANG	SWR	
450013		63213+64213+68113+63613	NT	SWO	ANG	SWR	
450014		63214+64214+68114+63614	NT	SWO	ANG	SWR	
450015		63215+64215+68115+63615	NT	SWO	ANG	SWR	*Desiro*
450016		63216+64216+68116+63616	NT	SWR	ANG	SWR	
450017		63217+64217+68117+63617	NT	SWO	ANG	SWR	
450018		63218+64218+68118+63618	NT	SWO	ANG	SWR	
450019		63219+64219+68119+63619	NT	SWO	ANG	SWR	
450020		63220+64220+68120+63620	NT	SWO	ANG	SWR	
450021		63221+64221+68121+63621	NT	SWR	ANG	SWR	
450022		63222+64222+68122+63622	NT	SWO	ANG	SWR	
450023		63223+64223+68123+63623	NT	SWR	ANG	SWR	
450024		63224+64224+68124+63624	NT	SWO	ANG	SWR	
450025		63225+64225+68125+63625	NT	SWO	ANG	SWR	
450026		63226+64226+68126+63626	NT	SWO	ANG	SWR	
450027		63227+64227+68127+63627	NT	SWO	ANG	SWR	
450028		63228+64228+68128+63628	NT	SWO	ANG	SWR	
450029		63229+64229+68129+63629	NT	SWO	ANG	SWR	
450030		63230+64230+68130+63630	NT	SWO	ANG	SWR	
450031		63231+64231+68131+63631	NT	SWO	ANG	SWR	
450032		63232+64232+68132+63632	NT	SWO	ANG	SWR	
450033		63233+64233+68133+63633	NT	SWO	ANG	SWR	*Treloar College*
450034		63234+64234+68134+63634	NT	SWO	ANG	SWR	
450035		63235+64235+68135+63635	NT	SWO	ANG	SWR	
450036		63236+64236+68136+63636	NT	SWR	ANG	SWR	
450037		63237+64237+68137+63637	NT	SWO	ANG	SWR	
450038		63238+64238+68138+63638	NT	SWO	ANG	SWR	
450039		63239+64239+68139+63639	NT	SWO	ANG	SWR	
450040		63240+64240+68140+63640	NT	SWO	ANG	SWR	
450041		63241+64241+68141+63641	NT	SWO	ANG	SWR	
450042		63242+64242+68142+63642	NT	SWO	ANG	SWR	
450043	(450543)	63243+64243+68143+63643	NT	SWO	ANG	SWR	
450044	(450544)	63244+64244+68144+63644	NT	SWO	ANG	SWR	
450045	(450545)	63245+64245+68145+63645	NT	SWO	ANG	SWR	
450046	(450546)	63246+64246+68146+63646	NT	SWO	ANG	SWR	
450047	(450547)	63247+64247+68147+63647	NT	SWR	ANG	SWR	
450048	(450548)	63248+64248+68148+63648	NT	SWO	ANG	SWR	
450049	(450549)	63249+64249+68149+63649	NT	SWO	ANG	SWR	
450050	(450550)	63250+64250+68150+63650	NT	SWO	ANG	SWR	
450051	(450551)	63251+64251+68151+63651	NT	SWR	ANG	SWR	
450052	(450552)	63252+64252+68152+63652	NT	SWO	ANG	SWR	
450053	(450553)	63253+64253+68153+63653	NT	SWO	ANG	SWR	
450054	(450554)	63254+64254+68154+63654	NT	SWO	ANG	SWR	
450055	(450555)	63255+64255+68155+63655	NT	SWO	ANG	SWR	
450056	(450556)	63256+64256+68156+63656	NT	SWR	ANG	SWR	
450057	(450557)	63257+64257+68157+63657	NT	SWO	ANG	SWR	
450058	(450558)	63258+64258+68158+63658	NT	SWO	ANG	SWR	
450059	(450559)	63259+64259+68159+63659	NT	SWO	ANG	SWR	
450060	(450560)	63260+64260+68160+63660	NT	SWO	ANG	SWR	
450061	(450561)	63261+64261+68161+63661	NT	SWO	ANG	SWR	
450062	(450562)	63262+64262+68162+63662	NT	SWO	ANG	SWR	
450063	(450563)	63263+64263+68163+63663	NT	SWO	ANG	SWR	
450064	(450564)	63264+64264+68164+63664	NT	SWO	ANG	SWR	
450065	(450565)	63265+64265+68165+63665	NT	SWO	ANG	SWR	
450066	(450566)	63266+64266+68166+63666	NT	SWO	ANG	SWR	
450067	(450567)	63267+64267+68167+63667	NT	SWO	ANG	SWR	
450068	(450568)	63268+64268+68168+63668	NT	SWO	ANG	SWR	
450069	(450569)	63269+64269+68169+63669	NT	SWO	ANG	SWR	
450070	(450570)	63270+64270+68170+63670	NT	SWO	ANG	SWR	
450071		63271+64271+68171+63671	NT	SWO	ANG	SWR	
450072		63272+64272+68172+63672	NT	SWO	ANG	SWR	

450073	63273+64273+68173+63673	NT	SWO	ANG	SWR	
450074	63274+64274+68174+63674	NT	SWO	ANG	SWR	
450075	63275+64275+68175+63675	NT	SWO	ANG	SWR	
450076	63276+64276+68176+63676	NT	SWO	ANG	SWR	
450077	63277+64277+68177+63677	NT	SWO	ANG	SWR	
450078	63278+64278+68178+63678	NT	SWO	ANG	SWR	
450079	63279+64279+68179+63679	NT	SWO	ANG	SWR	
450080	63280+64280+68180+63680	NT	SWO	ANG	SWR	
450081	63281+64281+68181+63681	NT	SWO	ANG	SWR	
450082	63282+64282+68182+63682	NT	SWO	ANG	SWR	
450083	63283+64283+68183+63683	NT	SWO	ANG	SWR	
450084	63284+64284+68184+63684	NT	SWO	ANG	SWR	
450085	63285+64285+68185+63685	NT	SWO	ANG	SWR	
450086	63286+64286+68186+63686	NT	SWO	ANG	SWR	
450087	63287+64287+68187+63687	NT	SWO	ANG	SWR	
450088	63288+64288+68188+63688	NT	SWO	ANG	SWR	
450089	63289+64289+68189+63689	NT	SWO	ANG	SWR	
450090	63290+64290+68190+63690	NT	SWO	ANG	SWR	
450091	63291+64291+68191+63691	NT	SWO	ANG	SWR	
450092	63292+64292+68192+63692	NT	SWO	ANG	SWR	
450093	63293+64293+68193+63693	NT	SWO	ANG	SWR	
450094	63294+64294+68194+63694	NT	SWO	ANG	SWR	
450095	63295+64295+68195+63695	NT	SWO	ANG	SWR	
450096	63296+64296+68196+63696	NT	SWO	ANG	SWR	
450097	63297+64297+68197+63697	NT	SWO	ANG	SWR	
450098	63298+64298+68198+63698	NT	SWO	ANG	SWR	
450099	63299+64299+68199+63699	NT	SWO	ANG	SWR	
450100	63300+64300+68200+63700	NT	SWO	ANG	SWR	
450101	63701+66851+66801+63751	NT	SWO	ANG	SWR	
450102	63702+66852+66802+63752	NT	SWO	ANG	SWR	
450103	63703+66853+66803+63753	NT	SWO	ANG	SWR	
450104	63704+66854+66804+63754	NT	SWO	ANG	SWR	
450105	63705+66855+66805+63755	NT	SWO	ANG	SWR	
450106	63706+66856+66806+63756	NT	SWO	ANG	SWR	
450107	63707+66857+66807+63757	NT	SWO	ANG	SWR	
450108	63708+66858+66808+63758	NT	SWO	ANG	SWR	
450109	63709+66859+66809+63759	NT	SWO	ANG	SWR	
450110	63710+66860+66810+63750	NT	SWO	ANG	SWR	
450111	63901+66921+66901+63921	NT	SWO	ANG	SWR	
450112	63902+66922+66902+63922	NT	SWO	ANG	SWR	
450113	63903+66923+66903+63923	NT	SWO	ANG	SWR	
450114	63904+66924+66904+63924	NT	SWO	ANG	SWR	*Fairbridge - investing in the Future*
450115	63905+66925+66905+63925	NT	SWO	ANG	SWR	
450116	63906+66926+66906+63926	NT	SWO	ANG	SWR	
450117	63907+66927+66907+63927	NT	SWO	ANG	SWR	

Above: *The bulk of outer suburban services operated by South Western Railway are in the hands of a fleet of Siemens 'Desiro four-car units. The majority of sets still carry SWT/Stagecoach blue livery with South West Railway branding. Two sets, with No. 450006 nearest the camera stand at Eastleigh.* **CJM**

450118	63908+66928+66908+63928	NT	SWO	ANG	SWR	
450119	63909+66929+66909+63929	NT	SWO	ANG	SWR	
450120	63910+66930+66910+63930	NT	SWO	ANG	SWR	
450121	63911+66931+66911+63931	NT	SWO	ANG	SWR	
450122	63912+66932+66912+63932	NT	SWO	ANG	SWR	
450123	63913+66933+66913+63933	NT	SWO	ANG	SWR	
450124	63914+66934+66914+63934	NT	SWO	ANG	SWR	
450125	63915+66935+66915+63935	NT	SWO	ANG	SWR	
450126	63916+66936+66916+63936	NT	SWO	ANG	SWR	
450127	63917+66937+66917+63937	NT	SWO	ANG	SWR	Dave Gunson

Above: *To create high capacity or HC sets, a fleet of 28 Class 450/0 units were modified with reduced seating and increased standing places by door pockets in an attempt to ease overcrowding on some busy routes. Originally the first class seating was removed and replaced by standard, but later the first class area was returned. The modified sets were re-classified as 450/5. Set 450568 approaches Eastleigh off the Portsmouth line. From late 2019, sets were being converted back to Class 450/0s.* **CJM**

Class 455/7

Vehicle Length: (Driving) 65ft 0½in (19.83m)
(Inter) 65ft 4½in (19.92m)
Height: 12ft 1½in (3.79m) [TSO- 11ft 6½in (3.58m)]
Width: 9ft 3¼in (2.82m)
Horsepower: 1,000hp (746kW)
Seats (total/car): 244S, 54S/68S/68S/54S

Number	Formation DMSO(A)+MSO+TSO+DTSO(B)	Depot	Livery	Owner	Operator	Note
(45)5701	77727+62783+71545+77728	WD	SWS	PTR	SWR	
(45)5702	77729+62784+71547+77730	WD	SWS	PTR	SWR	
(45)5703	77731+62785+71540+77732	WD	SWS	PTR	SWR	
(45)5704	77733+62786+71548+77734	WD	SWS	PTR	SWR	
(45)5705	77735+62787+71565+77736	WD	SWS	PTR	SWR	
(45)5706	77737+62788+71534+77738	WD	SWS	PTR	SWR	
(45)5707	77739+62789+71536+77740	WD	SWS	PTR	SWR	
(45)5708	77741+62790+71560+77742	WD	SWS	PTR	SWR	
(45)5709	77743+62791+71532+77744	WD	SWS	PTR	SWR	
(45)5710	77745+62792+71566+77746	WD	SWS	PTR	SWR	
(45)5711	77747+62793+71542+77748	WD	SWS	PTR	SWR	
(45)5712	77749+62794+71546+77750	WD	SWS	PTR	SWR	
(45)5713	77751+62795+71567+77752	WD	SWS	PTR	SWR	
(45)5714	77753+62796+71539+77754	WD	SWS	PTR	SWR	
(45)5715	77755+62797+71535+77756	WD	SWS	PTR	SWR	
(45)5716	77757+62798+71564+77758	WD	SWS	PTR	SWR	
(45)5717	77759+62799+71528+77760	WD	SWS	PTR	SWR	
(45)5718	77761+62800+71557+77762	WD	SWS	PTR	SWR	
(45)5719	77763+62801+71558+77764	WD	SWS	PTR	SWR	
(45)5720	77765+62802+71568+77766	WD	SWS	PTR	SWR	
(45)5721	77767+62803+71553+77768	WD	SWS	PTR	SWR	
(45)5722	77769+62804+71533+77770	WD	SWS	PTR	SWR	
(45)5723	77771+62805+71526+77772	WD	SWS	PTR	SWR	
(45)5724	77773+62806+71561+77774	WD	SWS	PTR	SWR	
(45)5725	77775+62807+71541+77776	WD	SWS	PTR	SWR	

(45)5726	77777+62608+71556+77778	WD	SWS	PTR	SWR	
(45)5727	77779+62809+71562+77780	WD	SWS	PTR	SWR	
(45)5728	77781+62810+71527+77782	WD	SWS	PTR	SWR	
(45)5729	77783+62811+71550+77784	WD	SWS	PTR	SWR	
(45)5730	77785+62812+71551+77786	WD	SWS	PTR	SWR	
(45)5731	77787+62813+71555+77788	WD	SWS	PTR	SWR	
(45)5732	77789+62814+71552+77790	WD	SWS	PTR	SWR	
(45)5733	77791+62815+71549+77792	WD	SWS	PTR	SWR	
(45)5734	77793+62816+71531+77794	WD	SWS	PTR	SWR	
(45)5735	77795+62817+71563+77796	WD	SWS	PTR	SWR	
(45)5736	77797+62818+71554+77798	WD	SWS	PTR	SWR	
(45)5737	77799+62819+71544+77800	WD	SWS	PTR	SWR	
(45)5738	77801+62820+71529+77802	WD	SWS	PTR	SWR	
(45)5739	77803+62821+71537+77804	WD	SWS	PTR	SWR	
(45)5740	77805+62822+71530+77806	WD	SWS	PTR	SWR	
(45)5741	77807+62823+71559+77808	WD	SWS	PTR	SWR	
(45)5742	77809+62824+71543+77810	WD	SWS	PTR	SWR	
(45)5750§	77811+62825+71538+77812	WD	SWS	PTR	SWR	§ Originally numbered (45)5743

Right: *Until the introduction of new Class 701 Bombardier 'Aventra' sets in 2020-2021, South Western Railway suburban services are in the hands of Class 455 stock. Three different breeds are in use. The Class 455/7s were built as three car sets and then incorporated a Trailer Standard removed from a Class 508 sets, thus these sets have one coach of a different design. Set No. 455736 (with its former 508 car third from front) is seen at Clapham Junction.* **Antony Christie**

Class 455/8

Vehicle Length: (Driving) 65ft 0½in (19.83m)
(Inter) 65ft 4½in (19.92m)
Height: 12ft 1½in (3.79m)
Width: 9ft 3¼in (2.82m)
Horsepower: 1,000hp (746kW)
Seats (total/car): 268S, 50S/84S/84S/50S

Number	*Formation* DMSO(A)+MSO+TSO+DTSO(B)	*Depot*	*Livery*	*Owner*	*Operator*
(45)5847	77671+62755+71683+77672	WD	SWS	PTR	SWR
(45)5848	77673+62756+71684+77674	WD	SWS	PTR	SWR
(45)5849	77675+62757+71685+77676	WD	SWS	PTR	SWR
(45)5850	77677+62758+71686+77678	WD	SWS	PTR	SWR
(45)5851	77679+62759+71687+77680	WD	SWS	PTR	SWR
(45)5852	77681+62760+71688+77682	WD	SWS	PTR	SWR
(45)5853	77683+62761+71689+77684	WD	SWS	PTR	SWR
(45)5854	77685+62762+71690+77686	WD	SWS	PTR	SWR
(45)5855	77687+62763+71691+77688	WD	SWS	PTR	SWR
(45)5856	77689+62764+71692+77690	WD	SWS	PTR	SWR
(45)5857	77691+62765+71693+77692	WD	SWS	PTR	SWR
(45)5858	77693+62766+71694+77694	WD	SWS	PTR	SWR
(45)5859	77695+62767+71695+77696	WD	SWS	PTR	SWR
(45)5860	77697+62768+71696+77698	WD	SWS	PTR	SWR
(45)5861	77699+62769+71697+77700	WD	SWS	PTR	SWR
(45)5862	77701+62770+71698+77702	WD	SWS	PTR	SWR
(45)5863	77703+62771+71699+77704	WD	SWS	PTR	SWR
(45)5864	77705+62772+71700+77706	WD	SWS	PTR	SWR
(45)5865	77707+62773+71701+77708	WD	SWS	PTR	SWR
(45)5866	77709+62774+71702+77710	WD	SWS	PTR	SWR
(45)5867	77711+62775+71703+77712	WD	SWS	PTR	SWR
(45)5868	77713+62776+71704+77714	WD	SWS	PTR	SWR
(45)5869	77715+62777+71705+77716	WD	SWS	PTR	SWR
(45)5870	77717+62778+71706+77718	WD	SWS	PTR	SWR
(45)5871	77719+62779+71707+77720	WD	SWS	PTR	SWR
(45)5872	77721+62780+71708+77722	WD	SWS	PTR	SWR
(45)5873	77723+62781+71709+77724	WD	SWS	PTR	SWR
(45)5874	77725+62782+71710+77726	WD	SWS	PTR	SWR

Left: *The original delivery of Class 455 stock, of Class 455/8, had a shaped cab roof incorporating the air horns. Displaying SWT red livery with South West Railway branding, No. 455852 formes the rear of an eight car train at Raynes Park.* **Nathan Williamson**

Class 455/9

Vehicle Length: (Driving) 65ft 0½in (19.83m) (Inter) 65ft 4½in (19.92m)
Height: 12ft 1½in (3.79m)
Width: 9ft 3¼in (2.82m)
Horsepower: 1,000hp (746kW)
Seats (total/car): 236S, 50S/68S/68S/50S

Number	Formation DMSO(A)+MSO+TSO+DTSO(B)	Depot	Livery	Owner	Operator
(45)5901	77813+62826+71714+77814	WD	SWS	PTR	SWR
(45)5902	77815+62827+71715+77816	WD	SWS	PTR	SWR
(45)5903	77817+62828+71716+77818	WD	SWS	PTR	SWR
(45)5904	77819+62829+71717+77820	WD	SWS	PTR	SWR
(45)5905	77821+62830+71725+77822	WD	SWS	PTR	SWR
(45)5906	77823+62831+71719+77824	WD	SWS	PTR	SWR
(45)5907	77825+62832+71720+77826	WD	SWS	PTR	SWR
(45)5908	77827+62833+71721+77828	WD	SWS	PTR	SWR
(45)5909	77829+62834+71722+77830	WD	SWS	PTR	SWR
(45)5910	77831+62835+71723+77832	WD	SWS	PTR	SWR
(45)5911	77833+62836+71724+77834	WD	SWS	PTR	SWR
(45)5912	77835+62837+67400+77836	WD	SWS	PTR	SWR
(45)5913	77837+62838+71726+77838	WD	SWS	PTR	SWR
(45)5914	77839+62839+71727+77840	WD	SWS	PTR	SWR
(45)5915	77841+62840+71728+77842	WD	SWS	PTR	SWR
(45)5916	77843+62841+71729+77844	WD	SWS	PTR	SWR
(45)5917	77845+62842+71730+77846	WD	SWS	PTR	SWR
(45)5918	77847+62843+71732+77848	WD	SWS	PTR	SWR
(45)5919	77849+62844+71718+77850	WD	SWS	PTR	SWR
(45)5920	77851+62845+71733+77852	WD	SWS	PTR	SWR

Left: *The final batch of Class 455s delivered were 20 Class 455/9s, these had revised heating and ventilation and therefore slightly different roof vents. Set No. 455917 approaches Raynes Park leading a ten car formation of two Class 455s and a Class 456.* **CJM**

Class 456

Vehicle Length: (Driving) 65ft 3¼in (19.89m)
Height: 12ft 4½in (3.77m)
Width: 9ft 3in (2.81m)
Horsepower: 500hp (370kW)
Seats (total/car): 152S, 79S/73S

Number	Formation DMSO+DTSO	Depot	Livery	Owner	Operator
456001	64735+78250	WD	SWS	PTR	SWR
456002	64736+78251	WD	SWS	PTR	SWR
456003	64737+78252	WD	SWS	PTR	SWR
456004	64738+78253	WD	SWS	PTR	SWR
456005	64739+78254	WD	SWS	PTR	SWR
456006	64740+78255	WD	SWS	PTR	SWR

456007	64741+78256	WD	SWS	PTR	SWR
456008	64742+78257	WD	SWS	PTR	SWR
456009	64743+78258	WD	SWS	PTR	SWR
456010	64744+78259	WD	SWS	PTR	SWR
456011	64745+78260	WD	SWS	PTR	SWR
456012	64746+78261	WD	SWS	PTR	SWR
456013	64747+78262	WD	SWS	PTR	SWR
456014	64748+78263	WD	SWS	PTR	SWR
456015	64749+78264	WD	SWS	PTR	SWR
456016	64750+78265	WD	SWS	PTR	SWR
456017	64751+78266	WD	SWS	PTR	SWR
456018	64752+78267	WD	SWS	PTR	SWR
456019	64753+78268	WD	SWS	PTR	SWR
456020	64754+78269	WD	SWS	PTR	SWR
456021	64755+78270	WD	SWS	PTR	SWR
456022	64756+78271	WD	SWS	PTR	SWR
456023	64757+78272	WD	SWS	PTR	SWR
456024	64758+78273	WD	SWS	PTR	SWR

Right: *A fleet of 24 two-car Class 456 sets are based at Wimbledon and operate alongside the Class 455 fleet to allow the formation of ten-coach trains. These sets have been refurbished in the same way as Class 455s and sport the old South West Trains red livery, now branded South Western Railway. These units were previously used on NSE central section and later Southern. No. 456005 is seen arriving at Wimbledon.* **CJM**

Class 458
Juniper

Vehicle Length: (Driving) 69ft 6in (21.16m) (Inter) 65ft 4in (19.91m)
Height: 12ft 3in (3.73m)
Width: 9ft 2in (2.79m)
Horsepower: 2,172hp (1,620kW)
Seats (total/car): 266S, 60S/52S/42S/52S/60S

Number	*Original Number*	*Formation DMSO(A)+TSO+TSO+MSO+DMSO(B)*	*Depot*	*Livery*	*Owner*	*Operator*
458501	(458001)	67601+74431+74001+74101+67701	WD	SWO	PTR	SWR
458502	(458002)	67602+74421+74002+74102+67702	WD	SWO	PTR	SWR
458503	(458003)	67603+74441+74003+74103+67703	WD	SWO	PTR	SWR
458504	(458004)	67604+74451+74004+74104+67704	WD	SWO	PTR	SWR
458505	(458005)	67605+74425+74005+74105+67705	WD	SWO	PTR	SWR
458506	(458006)	67606+74436+74006+74106+67706	WD	SWO	PTR	SWR
458507	(458007)	67607+74428+74007+74107+67707	WD	SWO	PTR	SWR
458508	(458008)	67608+74433+74008+74108+67708	WD	SWO	PTR	SWR
458509	(458009)	67609+74452+74009+74109+67709	WD	SWO	PTR	SWR
458510	(458010)	67610+74405+74010+74110+67710	WD	SWO	PTR	SWR
458511	(458011)	67611+74435+74011+74111+67711	WD	SWO	PTR	SWR
458512	(458012)	67612+74427+74012+74112+67712	WD	SWO	PTR	SWR
458513	(458013)	67613+74437+74013+74113+67713	WD	SWO	PTR	SWR
458514	(458014)	67614+74407+74014+74114+67714	WD	SWO	PTR	SWR
458515	(458015)	67615+74404+74015+74115+67715	WD	SWO	PTR	SWR
458516	(458016)	67616+74406+74016+74116+67716	WD	SWO	PTR	SWR
458517	(458017)	67617+74426+74017+74117+67717	WD	SWO	PTR	SWR
458518	(458018)	67618+74432+74018+74118+67718	WD	SWO	PTR	SWR
458519	(458019)	67619+74403+74019+74119+67719	WD	SWO	PTR	SWR
458520	(458020)	67620+74401+74020+74120+67720	WD	SWO	PTR	SWR
458521	(458021)	67621+74438+74021+74121+67721	WD	SWO	PTR	SWR
458522	(458022)	67622+74424+74022+74122+67722	WD	SWO	PTR	SWR
458523	(458023)	67623+74434+74023+74123+67723	WD	SWO	PTR	SWR
458524	(458024)	67624+74402+74024+74124+67724	WD	SWO	PTR	SWR
458525	(458025)	67625+74422+74025+74125+67725	WD	SWO	PTR	SWR
458526	(458026)	67626+74442+74026+74126+67726	WD	SWO	PTR	SWR
458527	(458027)	67627+74412+74027+74127+67727	WD	SWO	PTR	SWR
458528	(458028)	67628+74408+74028+74128+67728	WD	SWO	PTR	SWR
458529	(458029)	67629+74423+74029+74129+67729	WD	SWO	PTR	SWR
458530	(458030)	67630+74411+74030+74130+67730	WD	SWO	PTR	SWR
458531		67913+74418+74446+74458+67912	WD	SWO	PTR	SWR
458532		67904+74417+74447+74457+67905	WD	SWO	PTR	SWR
458533		67917+74413+74443+74453+67916	WD	SWO	PTR	SWR

South Western Railway

458534	67914+74414+74444+74454+67918	WD	SWO	PTR	SWR
458535	67915+74415+74445+74455+67911	WD	SWO	PTR	SWR
458536	67906+74416+74448+74456+67902	WD	SWO	PTR	SWR

Left: *Painted in outer-suburban blue livery are 36 five-car Class 458 sets. These started life as four-car Class 458/0s and were rebuilt by Wabtec as five-car sets incorporating a vehicle from a Class 460. Sufficient vehicles existed for six extra five-car sets to be converted. Vehicles and sets built from Class 460 stock have ribbon glazing. Set No. 458507 awaits departure from Clapham Junction bound for Waterloo.* **Nathan Williamson**

Class 701/0
Aventra

Vehicle Length: (Driving) 20m
(Inter) 20.16m
Height: awaited
Weight: awaited
Power output: 4,000kW
Seats (total/car): -556S

Number	*Formation* DM+PM+TL+M3+EM1+ EM2+M3+TL+PM+DM *(each set formed of two half trains)*	*Depot*	*Livery*	*O'ner*	*Op'r*
701001	480001+481001+482001+483001+484001+485001+486001+487001+488001+489001	WD	SWR	ROK	SWR
701002	480002+481002+482002+483002+484002+485002+486002+487002+488002+489002	WD	SWR	ROK	SWR
701003	480003+481003+482003+483003+484003+485003+486003+487003+488003+489003	WD	SWR	ROK	SWR
701004	480004+481004+482004+483004+484004+485004+486004+487004+488004+489004	WD	SWR	ROK	SWR
701005	480005+481005+482005+483005+484005+485005+486005+487005+488005+489005	WD	SWR	ROK	SWR
701006	480006+481006+482006+483006+484006+485006+486006+487006+488006+489006	WD	SWR	ROK	SWR
701007	480007+481007+482007+483007+484007+485007+486007+487007+488007+489007	WD	SWR	ROK	SWR
701008	480008+481008+482008+483008+484008+485008+486008+487008+488008+489008	WD	SWR	ROK	SWR
701009	480009+481009+482009+483009+484009+485009+486009+487009+488009+489009	WD	SWR	ROK	SWR
701010	480010+481010+482010+483010+484010+485010+486010+487010+488010+489010	WD	SWR	ROK	SWR
701011	480011+481011+482011+483011+484011+485011+486011+487011+488011+489011	WD	SWR	ROK	SWR
701012	480012+481012+482012+483012+484012+485012+486012+487012+488012+489012	WD	SWR	ROK	SWR
701013	480013+481013+482013+483013+484013+485013+486013+487013+488013+489013	WD	SWR	ROK	SWR
701014	480014+481014+482014+483014+484014+485014+486014+487014+488014+489014	WD	SWR	ROK	SWR
701015	480015+481015+482015+483015+484015+485015+486015+487015+488015+489015	WD	SWR	ROK	SWR
701016	480016+481016+482016+483016+484016+485016+486016+487016+488016+489016	WD	SWR	ROK	SWR
701017	480017+481017+482017+483017+484017+485017+486017+487017+488017+489017	WD	SWR	ROK	SWR
701018	480018+481018+482018+483018+484018+485018+486018+487018+488018+489018	WD	SWR	ROK	SWR
701019	480019+481019+482019+483019+484019+485019+486019+487019+488019+489019	WD	SWR	ROK	SWR
701020	480020+481020+482020+483020+484020+485020+486020+487020+488020+489020	WD	SWR	ROK	SWR
701021	480021+481021+482021+483021+484021+485021+486021+487021+488021+489021	WD	SWR	ROK	SWR
701022	480022+481022+482022+483022+484022+485022+486022+487022+488022+489022	WD	SWR	ROK	SWR
701023	480023+481023+482023+483023+484023+485023+486023+487023+488023+489023	WD	SWR	ROK	SWR
701024	480024+481024+482024+483024+484024+485024+486024+487024+488024+489024	WD	SWR	ROK	SWR
701025	480025+481025+482025+483025+484025+485025+486025+487025+488025+489025	WD	SWR	ROK	SWR
701026	480026+481026+482026+483026+484026+485026+486026+487026+488026+489026	WD	SWR	ROK	SWR
701027	480027+481027+482027+483027+484027+485027+486027+487027+488027+489027	WD	SWR	ROK	SWR
701028	480028+481028+482028+483028+484028+485028+486028+487028+488028+489028	WD	SWR	ROK	SWR
701029	480029+481029+482029+483029+484029+485029+486029+487029+488029+489029	WD	SWR	ROK	SWR
701030	480030+481030+482030+483030+484030+485030+486030+487030+488030+489030	WD	SWR	ROK	SWR
701031	480031+481031+482031+483031+484031+485031+486031+487031+488031+489031	WD	SWR	ROK	SWR
701032	480032+481032+482032+483032+484032+485032+486032+487032+488032+489032	WD	SWR	ROK	SWR
701033	480033+481033+482033+483033+484033+485033+486033+487033+488033+489033	WD	SWR	ROK	SWR
701034	480034+481034+482034+483034+484034+485034+486034+487034+488034+489034	WD	SWR	ROK	SWR
701035	480035+481035+482035+483035+484035+485035+486035+487035+488035+489035	WD	SWR	ROK	SWR
701036	480036+481036+482036+483036+484036+485036+486036+487036+488036+489036	WD	SWR	ROK	SWR
701037	480037+481037+482037+483037+484037+485037+486037+487037+488037+489037	WD	SWR	ROK	SWR
701038	480038+481038+482038+483038+484038+485038+486038+487038+488038+489038	WD	SWR	ROK	SWR
701039	480039+481039+482039+483039+484039+485039+486039+487039+488039+489039	WD	SWR	ROK	SWR

701040	480040+481040+482040+483040+484040+485040+486040+487040+488040+489040	WD	SWR	ROK	SWR
701041	480041+481041+482041+483041+484041+485041+486041+487041+488041+489041	WD	SWR	ROK	SWR
701042	480042+481042+482042+483042+484042+485042+486042+487042+488042+489042	WD	SWR	ROK	SWR
701043	480043+481043+482043+483043+484043+485043+486043+487043+488043+489043	WD	SWR	ROK	SWR
701044	480044+481044+482044+483044+484044+485044+486044+487044+488044+489044	WD	SWR	ROK	SWR
701045	480045+481045+482045+483045+484045+485045+486045+487045+488045+489045	WD	SWR	ROK	SWR
701046	480046+481046+482046+483046+484046+485046+486046+487046+488046+489046	WD	SWR	ROK	SWR
701047	480047+481047+482047+483047+484047+485047+486047+487047+488047+489047	WD	SWR	ROK	SWR
701048	480048+481048+482048+483048+484048+485048+486048+487048+488048+489048	WD	SWR	ROK	SWR
701049	480049+481049+482049+483049+484049+485049+486049+487049+488049+489049	WD	SWR	ROK	SWR
701050	480050+481050+482050+483050+484050+485050+486050+487050+488050+489050	WD	SWR	ROK	SWR
701051	480041+481051+482051+483051+484051+485051+486051+487051+488051+489051	WD	SWR	ROK	SWR
701052	480052+481052+482052+483052+484052+485052+486052+487052+488052+489052	WD	SWR	ROK	SWR
701053	480053+481053+482053+483053+484053+485053+486053+487053+488053+489053	WD	SWR	ROK	SWR
701054	480054+481054+482054+483054+484054+485054+486054+487054+488054+489054	WD	SWR	ROK	SWR
701055	480055+481055+482055+483055+484055+485055+486055+487055+488055+489055	WD	SWR	ROK	SWR
701056	480056+481056+482056+483056+484056+485056+486056+487056+488056+489056	WD	SWR	ROK	SWR
701057	480057+481057+482057+483057+484057+485057+486057+487057+488057+489057	WD	SWR	ROK	SWR
701058	480058+481058+482058+483058+484058+485058+486058+487058+488058+489058	WD	SWR	ROK	SWR
701059	480059+481059+482059+483059+484059+485059+486059+487059+488059+489059	WD	SWR	ROK	SWR
701060	480060+481060+482060+483060+484060+485060+486060+487060+488060+489060	WD	SWR	ROK	SWR

Class 701/1
Aventra

Vehicle Length: (Driving) 20m
(Inter) 20.16m
Height: awaited

Weight: awaited
Power output: 2,000kW
Seats (total/car): -274S

Number	*Formation* DM+M3+TL+PM+DM	*Depot*	*Livery*	*Owner*	*Operator*
701501	480101+481101+482101+483101+489101	WD	SWR	ROK	SWR
701502	480102+481102+482102+483102+489102	WD	SWR	ROK	SWR
701503	480103+481103+482103+483103+489103	WD	SWR	ROK	SWR
701504	480104+481104+482104+483104+489104	WD	SWR	ROK	SWR
701505	480105+481105+482105+483105+489105	WD	SWR	ROK	SWR
701506	480106+481106+482106+483106+489106	WD	SWR	ROK	SWR
701507	480107+481107+482107+483107+489107	WD	SWR	ROK	SWR
701508	480108+481108+482108+483108+489108	WD	SWR	ROK	SWR
701509	480109+481109+482109+483109+489109	WD	SWR	ROK	SWR
701510	480110+481110+482110+483110+489110	WD	SWR	ROK	SWR
701511	480111+481111+482111+483111+489111	WD	SWR	ROK	SWR
701512	480112+481112+482112+483112+489112	WD	SWR	ROK	SWR
701513	480113+481113+482113+483113+489113	WD	SWR	ROK	SWR
701514	480114+481114+482114+483114+489114	WD	SWR	ROK	SWR
701515	480115+481115+482115+483115+489115	WD	SWR	ROK	SWR
701516	480116+481116+482116+483116+489116	WD	SWR	ROK	SWR
701517	480117+481117+482117+483117+489117	WD	SWR	ROK	SWR
701518	480118+481118+482118+483118+489118	WD	SWR	ROK	SWR
701519	480119+481119+482119+483119+489119	WD	SWR	ROK	SWR

Right: *The first train of 60 ten-car and 30 five-car Class 701 'Aventra' sets for South Western Railway was completed at the end of 2019, in early 2020 several sets were under test in the UK and mainland Europe. One of the driving cars is seen in the test hall at Bombardier Derby, alongside a Class 345.* **Antony West**

701520	480120+481120+482120+483120+489120	WD	SWR	ROK	SWR
701521	480121+481121+482121+483121+489121	WD	SWR	ROK	SWR
701522	480122+481122+482122+483122+489122	WD	SWR	ROK	SWR
701523	480123+481123+482123+483123+489123	WD	SWR	ROK	SWR
701524	480124+481124+482124+483124+489124	WD	SWR	ROK	SWR
701525	480125+481125+482125+483125+489125	WD	SWR	ROK	SWR
701526	480126+481126+482126+483126+489126	WD	SWR	ROK	SWR
701527	480127+481127+482127+483127+489127	WD	SWR	ROK	SWR
701528	480128+481128+482128+483128+489128	WD	SWR	ROK	SWR
701529	480129+481129+482129+483129+489129	WD	SWR	ROK	SWR
701530	480130+481130+482130+483130+489130	WD	SWR	ROK	SWR

Class 707
Desiro City

Vehicle Length: (Driving) 20m
(Inter) 20.16m
Height: 3.73m

Weight: 160.3 tonnes
Power output: 1,073hp (800kW)
Seats (total/car): -271S, 46/64/53/62/46S

Number	Formation DMSO(A)+PTSO+TSO+TSO+DMSO(B)	Depot	Livery	Owner	Operator
707001	421001+422001+423001+424001+425001	WD	SWS	ANG	SWR
707002	421002+422002+423002+424002+425002	WD	SWS	ANG	SWR
707003	421003+422003+423003+424003+425003	WD	SWS	ANG	SWR
707004	421004+422004+423004+424004+425004	WD	SWS	ANG	SWR
707005	421005+422005+423005+424005+425005	WD	SWS	ANG	SWR
707006	421006+422006+423006+424006+425006	WD	SWS	ANG	SWR
707007	421007+422007+423007+424007+425007	WD	SWS	ANG	SWR
707008	421008+422008+423008+424008+425008	WD	SWS	ANG	SWR
707009	421009+422009+423009+424009+425009	WD	SWS	ANG	SWR
707010	421010+422010+423010+424010+425010	WD	SWS	ANG	SWR
707011	421011+422011+423011+424011+425011	WD	SWS	ANG	SWR
707012	421012+422012+423012+424012+425012	WD	SWS	ANG	SWR
707013	421013+422013+423013+424013+425013	WD	SWS	ANG	SWR
707014	421014+422014+423014+424014+425014	WD	SWS	ANG	SWR
707015	421015+422015+423015+424015+425015	WD	SWS	ANG	SWR
707016	421016+422016+423016+424016+425016	WD	SWS	ANG	SWR
707017	421017+422017+423017+424017+425017	WD	SWS	ANG	SWR
707018	421018+422018+423018+424018+425018	WD	SWS	ANG	SWR
707019	421019+422019+423019+424019+425019	WD	SWS	ANG	SWR
707020	421020+422020+423020+424020+425020	WD	SWS	ANG	SWR
707021	421021+422021+423021+424021+425021	WD	SWS	ANG	SWR
707022	421022+422022+423022+424022+425022	WD	SWS	ANG	SWR
707023	421023+422023+423023+424023+425023	WD	SWS	ANG	SWR
707024	421024+422024+423024+424024+425024	WD	SWS	ANG	SWR
707025	421025+422025+423025+424025+425025	WD	SWS	ANG	SWR
707026	421026+422026+423026+424026+425026	WD	SWS	ANG	SWR
707027	421027+422027+423027+424027+425027	WD	SWS	ANG	SWR
707028	421028+422028+423028+424028+425028	WD	SWS	ANG	SWR
707029	421029+422029+423029+424029+425029	WD	SWS	ANG	SWR
707030	421030+422030+423030+424030+425030	WD	SWS	ANG	SWR

Left: *The present fleet of 30 Siemens Desiro City sets of Class 707 will only have a short life with South Western Railway, as it has been announced that when all Class 701s are delivered, these new sets will be returned to lease owner Angel Trains. Presently the sets carry SWT red livery with South West Railway branding and are deployed on Waterloo Windsor route services. Set No. 707010 approaches Clapham Junction.*
Nathan Williamson

Transport for Wales Wales & Borders

Address: ✉ St Mary's House, 47 Penarth Road, Cardiff, CF10 5DJ
customer.relations@tfwrail.wales
✆ 03333 211202
ⓘ www.tfwrail.wales

Managing Director: Kevin Thomas
Franchise Dates: October 2018 - 14 October 2033
Principal Routes: Cardiff to Swansea and West Wales
Cardiff Valleys
Cardiff - Hereford - Shrewsbury - Crewe - Manchester Piccadilly
Cardiff - Hereford - Shrewsbury - Chester - Bangor - Holyhead
Manchester - Crewe - Bangor - Holyhead
Shrewsbury - Pwllheli / Aberystwyth
Swansea - Shrewsbury
Depots: Cardiff Canton (CV), Chester (CH), Holyhead* (HD)
Machynlleth (MN), Shrewsbury* (SX) * Stabling point
Parent Company: Transport for Wales / Keolis Amey

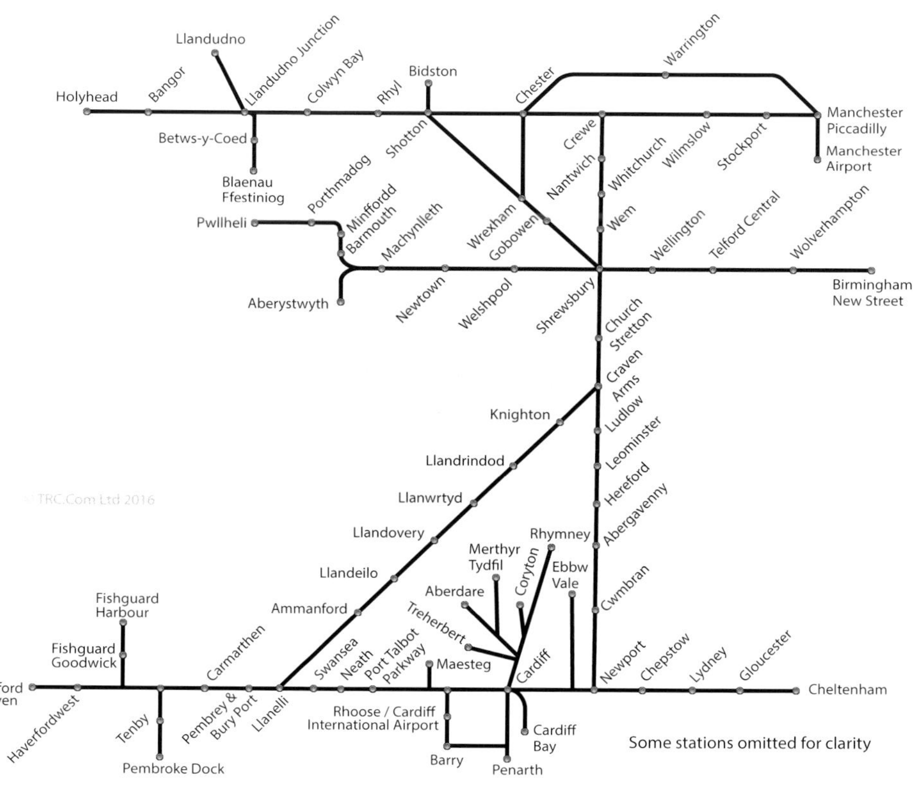

Transport for Wales

Class 67

Vehicle Length: 64ft 7in (19.68m)
Height: 12ft 9in (3.88m)
Width: 8ft 9in (2.66m)
Engine: EMD 12N-710G3B-EC
Horsepower: 2,980hp (2,223kW)
Electrical Equipment: EMD

Number	Depot	Pool	Livery	Owner	Operator
67008	CE	WACC	EWS	DBC	DBC/TFW
67017	CE	WACC	EWS	DBC	DBC/TFW
67025	CE	WACC	TFW	DBC	DBC/TFW

Left: *The Transport for Wales loco-hauled services are in the process of modernisation, with Mk4 stock replacing the Mk3s. A change of Class 67s is also taking place, with a small batch of locos repainted in TfW white and red. No. 67025 is seen in the new colours.* **Mark V. Pike**

Class 142
Pacer

Vehicle Length: 51ft 0½in (15.55m)
Height: 12ft 8in (3.86m)
Width: 9ft 2¼in (2.80m)
Engine: 1 x Cummins LTA10-R per vehicle
Horsepower: 460hp (343kW)
Seats (total/car): 90S, 46S/44S

Number	Formation DMS+DMSL	Depot	Livery	Owner	Operator
142002	55543+55593	CV	TOQ	ANG	TFW
142006	55547+55597	CV	TOQ	ANG	TFW
142010	55551+55601	CV	TOQ	ANG	TFW
142069	55719+55765	CV	TOQ	ANG	TFW
142072	55722+55768	CV	TOQ	ANG	TFW
142073(S)	55723+55769	CV	TOQ	ANG	-
142074	55724+55770	CV	TOQ	ANG	TFW
142075	55725+55771	CV	TOQ	ANG	TFW
142076	55726+55772	CV	TOQ	ANG	TFW
142077	55727+55773	CV	TOQ	ANG	TFW
142080	55730+55776	CV	TOQ	ANG	TFW
142081	55731+55777	CV	TOQ	ANG	TFW
142082	55732+55778	CV	TOQ	ANG	TFW
142083	55733+55779	CV	TOQ	ANG	TFW
142085	55735+55781	CV	TOQ	ANG	TFW

Name applied
142072 ***Myfanwy***

142012 55553+55603
142042 55583+55633
142049 55590+55640
142079 55729+55775
142086 55736+55782
Transferred from Northern and stored at Llandore, for spares

Left: *The Cardiff-allocated Class 142 'Pacer' sets are scheduled for a very early withdrawal and are likely to be out of service by the time this edition of ABC Rail guide 2020 is published. In 2019 bodyside branding was applied to the turquoise livery stating 'The start of a new journey', advising passengers that total fleet replacement was on its way. Carrying this branding, set No. 142074 is seen on a Penarth service.* **Antony Christie**

NEW TRAIN ORDERS
As part of the new Wales & Borders and South Wales Metro franchise operated by KeolisAmey and Transport for Wales, a fleet replacement project has been authorised. This consists of: 51 x two-car and 26 x three-car CAF-built 'Civity' sets, of Class 197/0 and 197/1. 11 x four-car Stadler 'Flirt' DMUs classified 231, 7 x three-car and 17 x four-car Stadler 'Flirt' tri-mode (diesel, battery and electric) sets classified as 756/0 and 756/1 and 36 three-car Stadler 'Citylink' TramTrains classified as 398. While this stock is under design, construction and delivery, 12 Mk4s displaced from LNER will be deployed on north-south services from spring/summer 2020. Five Class 230s and nine Class 769s will also be introduced.

Class 143
Pacer

Vehicle Length: 51ft 0½in (15.55m)
Height: 12ft 2¼in (3.73m)
Width: 8ft 10½in (2.70m)
Engine: 1 x Cummins LTA10-R per vehicle
Horsepower: 460hp (343kW)
Seats (total/car): 92S, 48S/44S

Number	Formation DMS+DMSL	Depot	Livery	Owner	Operator
143601	55642+55667	CV	ATT	BCC	TFW
143602	55651+55668	CV	ATT	PTR	TFW
143604	55645+55670	CV	ATT	PTR	TFW
143605	55646+55671	CV	ATT	PTR	TFW
143606	55647+55672	CV	ATT	PTR	TFW
143607	55648+55673	CV	ATT	PTR	TFW
143608	55649+55674	CV	ATT	PTR	TFW
143609	55650+55675	CV	TFW	CCC	TFW
143610	55643+55676	CV	TFW	BCC	TFW
143614	55655+55680	CV	TFW	BCC	TFW
143616	55657+55682	CV	ATT	PTR	TFW
143622	55663+55688	CV	ATT	PTR	TFW
143623	55664+55689	CV	ATT	PTR	TFW
143624	55665+55690	CV	ATT	PTR	TFW
143625	55666+55691	CV	TFI	PTR	TFW

Right: *The fleet of 15 Class 143 'Pacer' sets are all scheduled for rapid withdrawal, as soon as replacement stock is available. Originally the sets should have been taken out of service by the end of 2019, but this date has slightly slipped. A pair of '143s' Nos. 143622 and 143625 pass at Treforest on 27 August 2019.* **Antony Christie**

Class 150/2
Sprinter

Vehicle Length: 64ft 9¾in (19.74m)
Height: 12ft 4½in (3.77m)
Width: 9ft 3⅛in (2.82m)
Engine: 1 x NT855R5 of 285hp per vehicle
Horsepower: 570hp (425kW)
Seats (total/car): 128S, 60S/68S

Number	Formation DMSL+DMS	Depot	Livery	Owner	Operator
150208	52208+57208	CV	ATT	PTR	TFW
150213	52213+57213	CV	ATT	PTR	TFW
150217	52217+57217	CV	ATT	PTR	TFW
150227	52227+57227	CV	ATT	PTR	TFW
150229	52229+57229	CV	ATT	PTR	TFW
150230	52230+57230	CV	ATT	PTR	TFW
150231	52231+57231	CV	ATT	PTR	TFW
150235	52235+57235	CV	ATT	PTR	TFW
150236	52236+57236	CV	ATT	PTR	TFW
150237	52237+57237	CV	ATT	PTR	TFW
150240	52240+57240	CV	ATT	PTR	TFW
150241	52241+57241	CV	ATT	PTR	TFW
150242	52242+57242	CV	ATT	PTR	TFW
150245	52245+57245	CV	ATT	PTR	TFW
150250	52250+57250	CV	ATT	PTR	TFW
150251	52251+57251	CV	ATT	PTR	TFW
150252	52252+57252	CV	ATT	PTR	TFW
150253	52253+57253	CV	ATT	PTR	TFW
150254	52254+57254	CV	ATT	PTR	TFW
150255	52213+57255	CV	ATT	PTR	TFW
150256	52256+57256	CV	ATT	PTR	TFW
150257	52257+57257	CV	ATT	PTR	TFW
150258	52258+57258	CV	ATT	PTR	TFW
150259	52259+57259	CV	ATT	PTR	TFW
150260	52260+57260	CV	ATT	PTR	TFW
150262	52262+57262	CV	ATT	PTR	TFW

Right: *After new CAF-built 'Civity' sets are introduced by Transport for Wales, the Class 150 sets will be withdrawn. In 2020 a fleet of 22 units area based at Cardiff Canton and operated Valley and Cardiff area suburban and some north Wales duties. Currently no sets have emerged in TfW white and units still carry two-tone turquoise colours of the previous operator. Set No. 150231 is illustrated.* **Antony Christie**

Transport for Wales

150264	52264+57264	CV	ATT	PTR	TFW
150267	52267+57267	CV	ATT	PTR	TFW
150278	52278+57278	CV	ATT	PTR	TFW
150279	52279+57279	CV	ATT	PTR	TFW
150280	52280+57280	CV	ATT	PTR	TFW
150281	52281+57281	CV	ATT	PTR	TFW
150282	52282+57282	CV	ATT	PTR	TFW
150283	52283+57283	CV	ATT	PTR	TFW
150284	52284+57284	CV	ATT	PTR	TFW
150285	52285+57285	CV	ATT	PTR	TFW

Class 153

Vehicle Length: 76ft 5in (23.29m)
Height: 12ft 3⅛in (3.75m)
Width: 8ft 10in (2.70m)
Engine: 1 x NT855R5 of 285hp
Horsepower: 285hp (213kW)
Seats (total/car): 72S

Number	*Formation* DMSL	*Depot*	*Livery*	*Owner*	*Operator*
153303	52303	CV	ATT	ANG	TFW
153306	52306	CV	TFW	PTR	TFW
153309	52309	CV	TFW	PTR	TFW
155310	52310	CV	TFW	PTR	TFW
153312	52312	CV	ATT	ANG	TFW
155313	52313	CV	TFW	PTR	TFW
153314	52314	CV	AWT	PTR	TFW
153320	52320	CV	TFW	PTR	TFW
153321	52321	CV	TFW	PTR	TFW
153322	52322	CV	TFW	PTR	TFW
153323	52323	CV	TFW	PTR	TFW
153325	52325	CV	TFW	PTR	TFW
153326	52326	CV	TFW	PTR	TFW
153327	52327	CV	ATT	ANG	TFW
153329	52329	CV	TFW	ANG	TFW
153333	52333	CV	TFW	PTR	TFW
153335	52335	CV	TFW	PTR	TFW
153353	57353	CV	ATT	ANG	TFW
153361	57361	CV	TFW	ANG	TFW
153362	57362	CV	ATT	ANG	TFW
153367	57367	CV	TFW	PTR	TFW
153369	57369	CV	TFW	ANG	TFW

Left: *At the start of 2020, a fleet of 18 Class 153 'Bubble' cars were allocated to Cardiff for TfW use, deployed on Cardiff-Cardiff Bay shuttles and more lighter used services, frequently working in multiple. Additional vehicles were transferred in from Great Western and due to their external condition have been repainted in TfW white and red. turquoise liveried No. 153327 is seen from its small cab end.* **Nathan Williamson**

Class 158

Vehicle Length: 76ft 1¾in (23.21m)
Height: 12ft 6in (3.81m)
Width: 9ft 3¼in (2.82m)
Engine: 1 x Perkins 2006-TWH of 350hp per vehicle
Horsepower: 700hp (522kW)
Seats (total/car): 134S, 66S/68S

Number	*Formation* DMSL+DMSL	*Depot*	*Livery*	*Owner*	*Operator*
158818	52818+57818	MN	TFW	ANG	TFW
158819	52819+57819	MN	ATT	ANG	TFW
158820	52820+57820	MN	TFW	ANG	TFW
158821	52821+57821	MN	TFW	ANG	TFW
158822	52822+57822	MN	TFW	ANG	TFW
158823	52823+57823	MN	TFW	ANG	TFW
158824	52824+57824	MN	TFW	ANG	TFW
158825	52825+57825	MN	TFW	ANG	TFW
158826	52826+57826	MN	TFW	ANG	TFW
158827	52827+57827	MN	TFW	ANG	TFW
158828	52828+57828	MN	TFW	ANG	TFW
158829	52829+57829	MN	TFW	ANG	TFW
158830	52830+57830	MN	TFW	ANG	TFW
158831	52831+57831	MN	ATT	ANG	TFW
158832	52832+57832	MN	TFW	ANG	TFW
158833	52833+57833	MN	ATT	ANG	TFW
158834	52834+57834	MN	TFW	ANG	TFW
158835	52835+57835	MN	TFW	ANG	TFW

Left: *TfW longer distance services working over the Cambrian routes are in the hands of a fleet of 24 two-car Class 158s, allocated to Machynlleth. These sets are fitted with European Rail Traffic Management System (ERTMS) equipment, and have operated as a prototype for the equipment. Set No. 158829 is seen in TfW branded turquoise colours at Machynlleth.* **Nathan Williamson**

158836	52836+57836	MN	TFW	ANG	TFW	158839	52839+57839	MN	TFW	ANG	TFW
158837	52837+57837	MN	TFW	ANG	TFW	158840	52840+57840	MN	TFW	ANG	TFW
158838	52838+57838	MN	TFW	ANG	TFW	158841	52841+57841	MN	TFW	ANG	TFW

Class 170/2
Turbostar

Vehicle Length: 77ft 6in (23.62m)
Height: 12ft 4½in (3.77m)
Width: 8ft 10in (2.69m)
Engine: 1 x MTU 6R 183TD13H of 422hp per vehicle
Horsepower: 1,266hp (944kW)
Seats (total/car): 7F-173S 7F-39S/68S/66S

Number	*Formation* DMCL+MSL+DMSL	*Depot*	*Livery*	*Owner*	*Operator*
170201	50201+56201+79201	NC	TFW	PTR	TFW
170202	50202+56202+79202	NC	TFW	PTR	TFW
170203	50203+56203+79203	NC	TFW	PTR	TFW
170204	50204+56204+79204	NC	TFW	PTR	TFW
170205	50205+56205+79205	NC	TFW	PTR	TFW
170206	50206+56206+79206	NC	TFW	PTR	TFW
170207	50207+56207+79207	CV	TFW	PTR	TFW
170208	50208+56208+79208	NC	TFW	PTR	TFW

Vehicle Length: 77ft 6in (23.62m)
Height: 12ft 4½in (3.77m)
Width: 8ft 10in (2.69m)
Engine: 1 x MTU 6R 183TD13H of 422hp per vehicle
Horsepower: 844hp (629kW)
Seats (total/car): 9F-110S 57S/9F-53S

Number	*Formation* DMSL+DMCL	*Depot*	*Livery*	*Owner*	*Operator*
170270	50270+79270	CV	TFW	PTR	TFW
170271	50271+79271	CV	TFW	PTR	TFW
170272	50272+79272	CV	TFW	PTR	TFW
170273	50273+79273	CV	TFW	PTR	TFW

Right: *At the end of 2019, the Anglia-allocated Class 170s were replaced by Class 755 three and four car bi-mode sets, with the '170s' being transferred to Cardiff for Transport for Wales use. Before transfer, No. 170271 is seen displaying Greater Anglia livery at Norwich.* **Antony Christie**

Class 175/0
Coradia 1000

Vehicle Length: 75ft 7in (23.06m)
Height: 12ft 4in (3.75m)
Width: 9ft 2in (2.80m)
Engine: 1 x Cummins N14 of 450hp per vehicle
Horsepower: 900hp (671kW)
Seats (total/car): 118S, 54S/64S

Number	*Formation* DMSL+DMSL	*Depot*	*Livery*	*Owner*	*Operator*
175001	50701+79701	CH	TFW	ANG	TFW
175002	50702+79702	CH	TFW	ANG	TFW
175003	50703+79703	CH	TFW	ANG	TFW
175004	50704+79704	CH	ATW	ANG	TFW
175005	50705+79705	CH	ATW	ANG	TFW
175006	50706+79706	CH	TFW	ANG	TFW
175007	50707+79707	CH	ATW	ANG	TFW
175008	50708+79708	CH	ATW	ANG	TFW
175009	50709+79709	CH	TFW	ANG	TFW
175010	50710+79710	CH	TFW	ANG	TFW
175011	50711+79711	CH	TFW	ANG	TFW

Right: *A fleet of 11 two-car Class 170/0s are operated for Transport for Wales and work on longer-distance services. The sets are in the progress of being repainted into TfW white and red livery. Set No. 175003 is seen at Cardiff.* **Nathan Williamson**

Transport for Wales

Class 175/1
Coradia 1000

Vehicle Length: 75ft 7in (23.06m)
Height: 12ft 4in (3.75m)
Width: 9ft 2in (2.80m)
Engine: 1 x Cummins N14 of 450hp per vehicle
Horsepower: 1,350hp (1,007kW)
Seats (total/car): 186S, 54S/68S/64S

Number	Formation DMSL+MSL+DMSL	Depot	Livery	Owner	Op'r
175101	50751+56751+79751	CH	ATW	ANG	TFW
175102	50752+56752+79752	CH	ATW	ANG	TFW
175103	50753+56753+79753	CH	ATW	ANG	TFW
175104	50754+56754+79754	CH	ATW	ANG	TFW
175105	50755+56755+79755	CH	ATW	ANG	TFW
175106	50756+56756+79756	CH	ATW	ANG	TFW
175107	50757+56757+79757	CH	TFW	ANG	TFW
175108	50758+56758+79758	CH	ATW	ANG	TFW
175109	50759+56759+79759	CH	ATW	ANG	TFW
175110	50760+56760+79760	CH	ATW	ANG	TFW
175111	50761+56761+79761	CH	ATW	ANG	TFW
175112	50762+56762+79762	CH	ATW	ANG	TFW
175113	50763+56763+79763	CH	ATW	ANG	TFW
175114	50764+56764+79764	CH	ATW	ANG	TFW
175115	50765+56765+79765	CH	ATW	ANG	TFW
175116	50766+56766+79766	CH	ATW	ANG	TFW

Class 230
Vivarail D

Vehicle Length: (Driving) 60ft 3in (18.37m)
(Inter) 59ft 5in (18.12m)
Height: 11ft 11in (3.62m)
Width: 9ft 4in (2.85m)
Horsepower: awaited

Number	Formation	Depot	Livery	Owner	Operator
230006	300006 (7098)+300206 (17066)+300106 (7510)	--	TFW	TFW	TFW
230007	300007 (7103)+300207 (17063)+300107 (7529)	--	TFW	TFW	TFW
230008	300008 (7120)+300208 (17050)+300108 (7065)	--	TFW	TFW	TFW
230009	300009 (7055)+300209 (17084)+300109 (7523)	--	TFW	TFW	TFW
230010	300010 (7090)+300210 (17071)+300110 (7017)	--	TFW	TFW	TFW

Battery powered from charging points or from four gen-sets mounted below middle vehicle

Class 769
319 Flex

Vehicle Length: (Driving) 65ft 0¾in (19.83m)
(Inter) 65ft 4¼in (19.92m)
Height: 11ft 9in (3.58m)
Engine: MAN D2876
Width: 9ft 3in (2.82m)
Horsepower: electric 1,326hp (990kW)
Horsepower: diesel
Seats (total/car): 300S, 70S/78S/74S/78S

Number	Formation DMSL+MSL+DMSL	Depot	Livery	Owner	Operator
769002 (319002)	77293+62892+71773+77292	CV	TFW	PTR	TFW
769003 (319003)	77295+62893+71774+77294	CV	TFW	PTR	TFW
769006 (319006)	77301+62896+71777+77300	CV	TFW	PTR	TFW
769007 (319007)	77303+62897+71778+77302	CV	TFW	PTR	TFW
769008 (319008)	77305+62898+71779+77304	CV	TFW	PTR	TFW

Four further sets are on order

Hauled Stock
Class AJ1G / RFM

Vehicle Length: 75ft 0in (22.86m)
Height: 12ft 9in (3.88m)
Width: 8ft 11in (2.71m)
Bogie Type: BT10
Seats: 23F

Number	Type	Depot	Livery	Owner	Operator
10249 (10012)	RFM	CV	ATT	DBR	TFW
10259 (10025)	RFM	CV	ATT	ATW	TFW

Class AD1H / TSO

Vehicle Length: 75ft 0in (22.86m)
Height: 12ft 9in (3.88m)
Width: 8ft 11in (2.71m)
Bogie Type: BT10

Number	Type	Depot	Livery	Owner	Operator
12176 (11064)	TSO	CV	ATT	TFW	TFW
12177 (11065)	TSO	CV	ATT	TFW	TFW
12178 (11071)	TSO	CV	ATT	TFW	TFW
12179 (11083)	TSO	CV	ATT	TFW	TFW
12180 (11084)	TSO	CV	ATT	TFW	TFW
12181 (11086)	TSO	CV	ATT	TFW	TFW
12182 (11013)	TSO	CV	ATT	TFW	TFW
12183 (11027)	TSO	CV	ATT	TFW	TFW
12184 (11044)	TSO	CV	ATT	TFW	TFW
12185 (11089)	TSO	CV	ATT	TFW	TFW

Class NZAG / DVT

Length: 75ft 0in (22.86m)
Height: 12ft 9in (3.88m)
Width: 8ft 11in (2.71m)
Bogie Type: BT7

NZAG - DVT

Number	Depot	Livery	Owner	Operator
82306 (82144)	CV	ATT	TFW	TFW
82307 (82131)	CV	ATT	TFW	TFW
82308 (82108)	CV	ATT	DBR	TFW

Mk 4 Passenger formations. Stock to be introduced in spring-summer 2020.

Set No.	DVT+FO+RSB+TSO+TSOE+(loco)	Depot	Livery	Owner	Operator
001	82216+11325+10312+12446+12217	CF	TFW	EVL	TFW
HD02	82229+11324+10328+12447+12219	CF	TFW	EVL	TFW
003	82226+11323+10325+12454+12225	CF	TFW	EVL	TFW

West Midlands Railway

Address: 34 Edmund Street, Birmingham. B3 2ES
comments@westmidlandsrailway.co.uk
03333110039 www.westmidlandsrailway.co.uk

Managing Director: Julian Edwards

Franchise Dates: December 2017 - March 2026

Principal Routes: London Euston - Liverpool Lime Street, West Midlands routes to Stratford-upon-Avon, Worcester, Hereford, Shrewsbury, plus Bedford and St Albans Abbey branches

Depots: Northampton (NN)§, Soho (SI), Tyseley (TS), Stourbridge Junction (SJ) § Operated by Siemens

Parent Company: Abellio, East Japan Railway, Mitsui

36 x three-car 90mph and 45 five-car EMUs from Bombardier, plus 12 x two-car and 14 x four-car DMUs from CAF (funded by Corlink Rail Infrastructure) are on order. The London North Western trading name will be used for main-line services.

Class 08

Vehicle Length: 29ft 3in (8.91m)
Height: 12ft 8⅝in (3.87m)
Width: 8ft 6in (2.59m)
Engine: English Electric 6K
Horsepower: 400hp (298kW)
Electrical Equipment: English Electric

Number	*Depot*	*Pool*	*Livery*	*Owner*	*Operator*	*Name*
08616 (3783)	**TS**	**EJLO**	**LMI**	**WMT**	**WMT**	***Tyseley 100***
08805	**SI**	**EJLO**	**GRY**	**WMT**	**WMT**	***Robin Jones 40 Years Service***

Class 139

Vehicle Length: 28ft 6in (8.7m)
Width: 7ft 8in (2.4m)
Engine: 1 x MVH420 2.0ltr LPG, flywheel hybrid
Seats (total/car): 18S

Number	*Formation DMS*	*Depot*	*Livery*	*Owner*	*Operator*
139001	**39001**	**SJ**	**WMT**	**WMT**	**WMT§**
139002	**39002**	**SJ**	**WMT**	**WMT**	**WMT§**

§ By Pre-Metro Operations Ltd

Right: *A pair of Class 139 Parry People Mover vehicles are operated by Pre-Metro Operations Ltd on the West Midlands Stourbridge Junction to Stourbridge Junction 'shuttle' service. These dual-ended 18-seat vehicles are maintained in a small 'depot' at Stourbridge Junction. Both vehicles are finished in West Midlands mauve and gold livery. Set No. 139001 is illustrated.* **CJM**

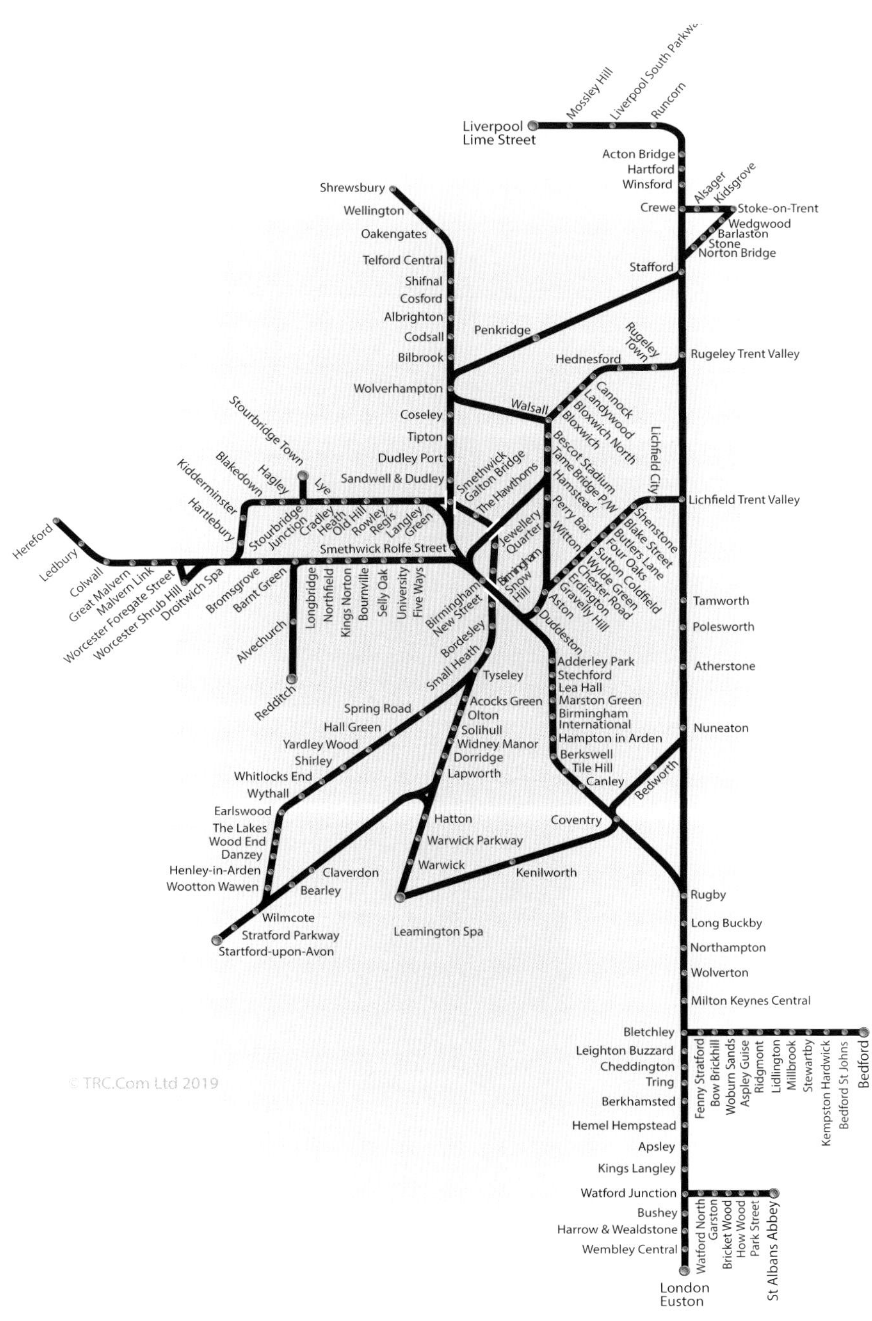
Liverpool Lime Street
Mossley Hill
Liverpool South Parkway
Runcorn
Acton Bridge
Hartford
Winsford
Crewe
Alsager
Kidsgrove
Stoke-on-Trent
Wedgwood
Barlaston
Stone
Norton Bridge
Stafford
Shrewsbury
Wellington
Oakengates
Telford Central
Shifnal
Cosford
Albrighton
Codsall
Bilbrook
Penkridge
Rugeley Town
Hednesford
Rugeley Trent Valley
Wolverhampton
Walsall
Cannock
Landywood
Bloxwich North
Bloxwich
Coseley
Tipton
Dudley Port
Sandwell & Dudley
Stourbridge Town
Blakedown
Hagley
Lye
Kidderminster
Hartlebury
Stourbridge Junction
Cradley Heath
Old Hill
Rowley Regis
Langley Green
Smethwick Galton Bridge
The Hawthorns
Jewellery Quarter
Bescot Stadium
Tame Bridge P/W
Hamstead
Perry Bar
Witton
Lichfield City
Lichfield Trent Valley
Shenstone
Blake Street
Butlers Lane
Four Oaks
Sutton Coldfield
Wylde Green
Chester Road
Erdington
Gravelly Hill
Aston
Duddeston
Hereford
Ledbury
Colwall
Great Malvern
Malvern Link
Worcester Foregate Street
Worcester Shrub Hill
Droitwich Spa
Bromsgrove
Barnt Green
Alvechurch
Redditch
Longbridge
Northfield
Kings Norton
Bournville
Selly Oak
University
Five Ways
Smethwick Rolfe Street
Birmingham New Street
Birmingham Snow Hill
Bordesley
Small Heath
Tyseley
Acocks Green
Olton
Solihull
Widney Manor
Dorridge
Lapworth
Spring Road
Hall Green
Yardley Wood
Shirley
Whitlocks End
Wythall
Earlswood
The Lakes
Wood End
Danzey
Henley-in-Arden
Wootton Wawen
Claverdon
Bearley
Wilmcote
Stratford Parkway
Startford-upon-Avon
Hatton
Warwick Parkway
Warwick
Leamington Spa
Kenilworth
Coventry
Adderley Park
Stechford
Lea Hall
Marston Green
Birmingham International
Hampton in Arden
Berkswell
Tile Hill
Canley
Bedworth
Tamworth
Polesworth
Atherstone
Nuneaton
Rugby
Long Buckby
Northampton
Wolverton
Milton Keynes Central
Bletchley
Leighton Buzzard
Cheddington
Tring
Berkhamsted
Hemel Hempstead
Apsley
Kings Langley
Watford Junction
Bushey
Harrow & Wealdstone
Wembley Central
London Euston
Fenny Stratford
Bow Brickhill
Woburn Sands
Aspley Guise
Ridgmont
Lidlington
Millbrook
Stewartby
Kempston Hardwick
Bedford St Johns
Bedford
Watford North
Garston
Bricket Wood
How Wood
Park Street
St Albans Abbey
© TRC.Com Ltd 2019

Class 153

Vehicle Length: 76ft 5in (23.29m)
Height: 12ft 3⅛in (3.75m)
Width: 8ft 10in (2.70m)
Engine: 1 x NT855R5 of 285hp
Horsepower: 285hp (213kW)
Seats (total/car): 72S

Number	Formation DMSL	Depot	Livery	Owner	Operator
153334	52334	TS	LMI	PTR	WMT
153354	57354	TS	LMI	PTR	WMT
153356	57356	TS	LMI	PTR	WMT
153364	57364	TS	LMI	PTR	WMT
153365	57365	TS	LMI	PTR	WMT
153366	57366	TS	LMI	PTR	WMT
153371	57371	TS	LMI	PTR	WMT
153375	57375	TS	LMI	PTR	WMT

Right: *Tyseley depot has an allocation of eight single car Class 153 'Bubble' vehicles for use on lightly used routes or to strengthen two or four car sets to three or five vehicles. Vehicles are decorated in the old London Midland green and grey livery with West Midlands Trains branding. No. 153366 is seen at Millbrook.* **CJM**

Class 170/5
Turbostar

Vehicle Length: 77ft 6in (23.62m)
Height: 12ft 4½in (3.77m)
Width: 8ft 10in (2.69m)
Engine: 1 x MTU 6R 183TD13H of 422hp per vehicle
Horsepower: 844hp (629kW)
Seats (total/car): 122S 55S/67S

Number	Formation DMSL+DMSL	Depot	Livery	Owner	Operator
170501	50501+79501	TS	WMT	PTR	WMT
170502	50502+79502	TS	WMT	PTR	WMT
170503	50503+79503	TS	WMT	PTR	WMT
170504	50504+79504	TS	WMT	PTR	WMT
170505	50505+79505	TS	WMT	PTR	WMT
170506	50506+79506	TS	WMT	PTR	WMT
170507	50507+79507	TS	WMT	PTR	WMT
170508	50508+79508	TS	WMT	PTR	WMT
170509	50509+79509	TS	WMT	PTR	WMT
170510	50510+79510	TS	WMT	PTR	WMT
170511	50511+79511	TS	WMT	PTR	WMT
170512	50512+79512	TS	WMT	PTR	WMT
170513	50513+79513	TS	WMT	PTR	WMT
170514	50514+79514	TS	WMT	PTR	WMT
170515	50515+79515	TS	WMT	PTR	WMT
170516	50516+79516	TS	WMT	PTR	WMT
170517	50517+79517	TS	WMT	PTR	WMT

Right: *Outer suburban diesel services are in the hands of Class 170 'Turbostar' stock with an allocation of 17 two-car sets to Tyseley depot. Units have now been rebranded in West Midlands grey, black and gold livery, as illustrated on set No. 170506 at Rugeley.* **CJM**

Class 170/6
Turbostar

Vehicle Length: 77ft 6in (23.62m)
Height: 12ft 4½in (3.77m)
Width: 8ft 10in (2.69m)
Engine: 1 x MTU 6R 183TD13H of 422hp per vehicle
Horsepower: 1,266hp (944kW)
Seats (total/car): 196S 55S/74S/67S

Number	Formation DMSL+MS+DMSL	Depot	Livery	Owner	Operator
170630	50630+56630+79630	TS	WMT	PTR	WMT

170631	50631+56631+79631	TS	WMT	PTR	WMT
170632	50632+56632+79632	TS	WMT	PTR	WMT
170633	50633+56633+79633	TS	WMT	PTR	WMT
170634	50634+56634+79634	TS	WMT	PTR	WMT
170635	50635+56635+79635	TS	WMT	PTR	WMT

Left: *Longer distance West Midlands outer-suburban routes are operated by a batch of five three-car Class 170/6s, these are based at Tyseley and all sport the grey, black and gold livery. No. 170635 is shown at Bromsgrove station forming a Worcester to Birmingham New Street service on 21 May 2019.* **CJM**

Class 172/0
Turbostar

Vehicle Length: 73ft 4in (22.37m)
Height: 12ft 4½in (3.77m)
Width: 8ft 8in (2.69m)
Engine: MTU 6H1800R83 of 360kW (483hp) per car
Horsepower: 966hp (720kW)
Seats (total/car): 124S, 60S/64S

Number	*Formation* DMS+DMS	*Depot*	*Livery*	*Owner*	*Operator*
172001	59311+59411	TS	LOG	ANG	WMT
172002	59312+59412	TS	LOG	ANG	WMT
172003	59313+59413	TS	LOG	ANG	WMT
172004	59314+59414	TS	LOG	ANG	WMT
172005	59315+59415	TS	LOG	ANG	WMT
172006	59316+59416	TS	LOG	ANG	WMT
172007	59317+59417	TS	LOG	ANG	WMT
172008	59318+59418	TS	LOG	ANG	WMT

Left: *2019 saw the introduction of eight Class 170/0 sets on West Midlands, these were previously used on London Overground. The sets have been refurbished, fitted with toilets and a disabled seating area and now sport West Midlands mauve, gold and black livery. The sets are used on the Leamington Spa-Nuneaton route and to supplement diesel services on the Birmingham Snow Hill routes. Set No. 172004 is seen at Kenilworth.* **CJM**

Class 172/2
Turbostar

Vehicle Length: 73ft 4in (22.37m)
Height: 12ft 4½in (3.77m)
Width: 8ft 8in (2.69m)
Engine: MTU 6H1800 of of 482hp (360kW) per vehicle
Horsepower: 964hp (720kW)
Seats (total/car): 121S, 53S/68S

Left: *The gangway fitted Class 172/2 and 172/3 sets were built for West Midlands use. A total of 12 two-car sets painted in mauve and gold livery are based at Tyseley and deployed on the Birmingham Snow Hill group of services. No. 172222 is recorded arriving at Worcester.* **Antony Christie**

Number	Formation DMS+DMS	Depot	Livery	Owner	Operator
172211	50211+79211	TS	LMI	PTR	WMT
172212	50212+79212	TS	LMI	PTR	WMT
172213	50213+79213	TS	LMI	PTR	WMT
172214	50214+79214	TS	LMI	PTR	WMT
172215	50215+79215	TS	LMI	PTR	WMT
172216	50216+79216	TS	LMI	PTR	WMT
172217	50217+79217	TS	LMI	PTR	WMT
172218	50218+79218	TS	LMI	PTR	WMT
172219	50219+79219	TS	LMI	PTR	WMT
172220	50220+79220	TS	LMI	PTR	WMT
172221	50221+79221	TS	LMI	PTR	WMT
172222	50222+79222	TS	LMI	PTR	WMT

Class 172/3
Turbostar

Vehicle Length: (Driving) 73ft 4in (22.37m)
(Inter): 76ft 7in (23.36m)
Height: 12ft 4½in (3.77m)
Width: 8ft 8in (2.69m)
Engine: MTU 6H1800 of 482hp (360kW) per vehicle
Horsepower: 1,446hp (1,080kW)
Seats (total/car): 193S, 53S/72S/68S

Number	Formation DMSO+MS+DMSO	Depot	Livery	Owner	Op'r
172331	50331+56331+79331	TS	WMT	PTR	WMT
172332	50332+56332+79332	TS	WMT	PTR	WMT
172333	50333+56333+79333	TS	WMT	PTR	WMT
172334	50334+56334+79334	TS	WMT	PTR	WMT
172335	50335+56335+79335	TS	WMT	PTR	WMT
172336	50336+56336+79336	TS	WMT	PTR	WMT
172337	50337+56337+79337	TS	WMT	PTR	WMT
172338	50338+56338+79338	TS	WMT	PTR	WMT
172339	50339+56339+79339	TS	WMT	PTR	WMT
172340	50340+56340+79340	TS	WMT	PTR	WMT
172341	50341+56341+79341	TS	WMT	PTR	WMT
172342	50342+56342+79342	TS	WMT	PTR	WMT
172343	50343+56343+79343	TS	WMT	PTR	WMT
172344	50344+56344+79344	TS	WMT	PTR	WMT
172345	50345+56345+79345	TS	WMT	PTR	WMT

Above: *A fleet of 15 three-car Class 172/3 sets are based at Tyseley, these are painted in mauve and gold West Midlands colours and operate in a common pool with the two-car sets. No. 172331 is seen departing from Stourbridge Junction.* **CJM**

Class 196
Civity

Vehicle Length: Driving - 24.03m
Inter - 23.35m
Height: 3.80m
Width: 2.55m
Engine: 1x | MTU 6H 1800 R85L
Horsepower: 523hp
Seats (total/car): 2-car awaited
3-car awaited

2-car sets

Number	Formation DMS+DMS	Depot	Livery	Owner	Operator
196001	*Details awaited*				
196002	*Details awaited*				
196003	*Details awaited*				
196004	*Details awaited*				
196005	*Details awaited*				
196006	*Details awaited*				
196007	*Details awaited*				
169008	*Details awaited*				
169009	*Details awaited*				
169010	*Details awaited*				
169011	*Details awaited*				
169012	*Details awaited*				

3-car sets

Number	Formation DMS+DMS	Depot	Livery	Owner	Operator
196101	*Details awaited*				
196102	*Details awaited*				
196103	*Details awaited*				
196104	*Details awaited*				
196105	*Details awaited*				
196106	*Details awaited*				
196107	*Details awaited*				
196108	*Details awaited*				
196109	*Details awaited*				
196110	*Details awaited*				
196111	*Details awaited*				
196112	*Details awaited*				
196113	*Details awaited*				
196114	*Details awaited*				

Left: *The first complete Class 196 three-car set for West Midlands, No. 196101 was completed at the CAF workshops in Spain during November 2019 and shipped, by rail, to the Velim test facility in the Czech Republic, before transfer to the UK for further testing, commissioning and staff training.* **West Midlands**

Class 230
Vivarail D

Vehicle Length: (Driving) 60ft 3in (18.37m) (Inter) 59ft 5in (18.12m)
Height: 11ft 11in (3.62m)
Width: 9ft 4in (2.85m)
Horsepower: 800hp (597kW)

Number	*Formation* DMSO+DMSO	*Depot*	*Livery*	*Owner*	*Operator*
230003	300003 (7069)+300103 (7127)	BY	WMT	WMT	WMT
230004	300004 (7100)+300104 (7500)	BY	WMT	WMT	WMT
230005	300005 (7066)+300105 (7128)	BY	WMT	WMT	WMT

Left: *In spring 2019, a fleet of three Class 230, converted ex London Underground 'D' stock sets entered service for London North Western, operating on the Marston Vale line between Bedford and Bletchley. Sets are painted in the NWR white and green livery and are route branded. The sets have experienced a number of power unit issues and it is hoped performance can be improved in 2020. No. 230004 calls at Millbrook.* **CJM**

Class 319

Vehicle Length: (Driving) 65ft 0¾in (19.83m) (Inter) 65ft 4¼in (19.92m)
Height: 11ft 9in (3.58m)
Width: 9ft 3in (2.82m)
Horsepower: 1,326hp (990kW)
Seats (total/car): 12F/277S, 12F-54S/77S/72S/74S

Number	*Formation* DTSO(A)+MSO+TSO+DTSO(B)	*Depot*	*Livery*	*Owner*	*Operator*
319005	77299+62895+71776+77298	NN	LMW	PTR	WMT
319012	77313+62902+71783+77312	NN	LMW	PTR	WMT
319013	77315+62903+71784+77314	NN	LMI	PTR	WMT
319214	77317+62904+71785+77316	NN	LMW	PTR	WMT
319215	77319+62905+71786+77318	NN	LMW	PTR	WMT

Left: *West Midlands Railway has a fleet of 15 four-car Class 319 units allocated to Northampton for use on Northwestern Railway services, operating peak hour services on the Euston-Northampton route, usually operating as twelve-car formations. Set No. 319216, displaying London Midland green livery with NWR branding, is seen at Euston.* **Antony Christie**

Number	Formation	Depot	Livery	Owner	Operator
319216	77321+62906+71787+77320	NN	LMW	PTR	WMT
319217	77323+62907+71788+77322	NN	WMT	PTR	WMT
319218	77325+62908+71789+77324	NN	WMT	PTR	WMT
319219	77327+62909+71790+77326	NN	WMT	PTR	WMT
319220	77329+62910+71791+77328	NN	TLK	PTR	WMT
319429	77347+62919+71800+77346	NN	LMI	PTR	WMT
319433	77355+62923+71804+77354	NN	LMI	PTR	WMT
319441	77371+62931+71812+77370	NN	LMW	PTR	WMT
319457	77451+62971+71876+77450	NN	LMW	PTR	WMT
319460	77457+62974+71879+77456	NN	LMI	PTR	WMT

Class 323

Vehicle Length: (Driving) 76ft 8¼in (23.37m)
(Inter) 76ft 10¾in (23.44m)
Height: 12ft 4¾in (3.78m)
Width: 9ft 2¼in (2.80m)
Horsepower: 1,565hp (1,168kW)
Seats (total/car): 284S, 98S/88S/98S

Number	*Formation* DMSO(A)+PTSO+DMSO(B)	*Depot*	*Livery*	*Owner*	*Operator*
323201	64001+72201+65001	SI	WMT	PTR	WMT
323202	64002+72202+65002	SI	WMT	PTR	WMT
323203	64003+72203+65003	SI	WMT	PTR	WMT
323204	64004+72204+65004	SI	WMT	PTR	WMT
323205	64005+72205+65005	SI	WMT	PTR	WMT
323206	64006+72206+65006	SI	WMT	PTR	WMT
323207	64007+72207+65007	SI	WMT	PTR	WMT
323208	64008+72208+65008	SI	WMT	PTR	WMT
323209	64009+72209+65009	SI	WMT	PTR	WMT
323210	64010+72210+65010	SI	WMT	PTR	WMT
323211	64011+72211+65011	SI	WMT	PTR	WMT
323212	64012+72212+65012	SI	WMT	PTR	WMT
323213	64013+72213+65013	SI	WMT	PTR	WMT
323214	64014+72214+65014	SI	WMT	PTR	WMT
323215	64015+72215+65015	SI	WMT	PTR	WMT
323216	64016+72216+65016	SI	WMT	PTR	WMT
323217	64017+72217+65017	SI	WMT	PTR	WMT
323218	64018+72218+65018	SI	WMT	PTR	WMT
323219	64019+72219+65019	SI	WMT	PTR	WMT
323220	64020+72220+65020	SI	WMT	PTR	WMT
323221	64021+72221+65021	SI	WMT	PTR	WMT
323222	64022+72222+65022	SI	WMT	PTR	WMT
323240	64040+72340+65040	SI	WMT	PTR	WMT
323241	64041+72341+65041	SI	WMT	PTR	WMT
323242	64042+72342+65042	SI	WMT	PTR	WMT
323243	64043+72343+65043	SI	WMT	PTR	WMT

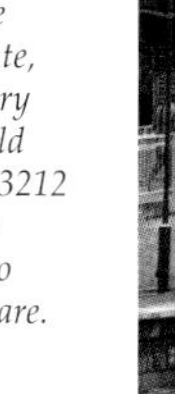

Right: *Until new stock is delivered, 26 three-car Class 323 sets operate on the Birmingham CrossCity route, based at Soho depot. The units carry West Midlands grey, black and gold livery, as illustrated on set No. 323212 at Longbridge. When displaced by new stock, 17 units will transfer to Northern and nine will become spare.* **CJM**

Class 350/1
Desiro

Vehicle Length: 66ft 9in (20.4m)
Height: 12ft 1½in (3.78m)
Width: 9ft 2in (2.7m)
Horsepower: 1,341hp (1,000kW)
Seats (total/car): 24F-209S, 60S/24F-32S/57S/60S
110mph max speed

Number	*Formation* DMSO(A)+TCO+PTSO+DMSO(B)	*Depot*	*Livery*	*Owner*	*Operator*
350101	63761+66811+66861+63711	NN	LMI	ANG	WMT
350102	63762+66812+66862+63712	NN	LMI	ANG	WMT
350103	63765+66813+66863+63713	NN	LMI	ANG	WMT

350104	63764+66814+66864+63714	NN	GRY	ANG	WMT
350105	63763+66815+66868+63715	NN	LMI	ANG	WMT
350106	63766+66816+66866+63716	NN	GRY	ANG	WMT
350107	63767+66817+66867+63717	NN	LMI	ANG	WMT
350108	63768+66818+66865+63718	NN	GRY	ANG	WMT
350109	63769+66819+66869+63719	NN	LMI	ANG	WMT
350110	63770+66820+66870+63720	NN	LMA	ANG	WMT
350111	63771+66821+66871+63721	NN	LMI	ANG	WMT
350112	63772+66822+66872+63722	NN	LMI	ANG	WMT
350113	63773+66823+66873+63723	NN	LMI	ANG	WMT
350114	63774+66824+66874+63724	NN	LMI	ANG	WMT
350115	63775+66825+66875+63725	NN	GRY	ANG	WMT
350116	63776+66826+66876+63726	NN	LMI	ANG	WMT
350117	63777+66827+66877+63727	NN	LMI	ANG	WMT
350118	63778+66828+66878+63728	NN	LMI	ANG	WMT
350119	63779+66829+66879+63729	NN	LMI	ANG	WMT
350120	63780+66830+66880+63730	NN	LMI	ANG	WMT
350121	63781+66831+66881+63731	NN	LMI	ANG	WMT
350122	63782+66832+66882+63732	NN	LMI	ANG	WMT
350123	63783+66833+66883+63733	NN	GRY	ANG	WMT
350124	63784+66834+66884+63734	NN	LMI	ANG	WMT
350125	63785+66835+66885+63735	NN	LMI	ANG	WMT
350126	63786+66836+66886+63736	NN	LMI	ANG	WMT
350127	63787+66837+66887+63737	NN	LMI	ANG	WMT
350128	63788+66838+66888+63738	NN	LMI	ANG	WMT
350129	63789+66839+66889+63739	NN	LMI	ANG	WMT
350130	63790+66840+66890+63740	NN	LMI	ANG	WMT

Left: *Outer suburban Northwestern services are operated by Class 350 Siemens 'Desiro' stock, based at Northampton. These four-car sets are formed into several sub-classes. There are 30 Class 350/1 sets, of which No. 350128 is seen passing South Kenton in north London.* **CJM**

Class 350/2
Desiro

Vehicle Length: 66ft 9in (20.4m)
Height: 12ft 1½in (3.78m)
Width: 9ft 2in (2.7m)
Horsepower: 1,341hp (1,000kW)
Seats (total/car): 24F-243S, 70S/24F-42S/61S/70S
100mph max speed

Number	*Formation* DMSO(A)+TCO+PTSO+DMSO(B)	*Depot*	*Livery*	*Owner*	*Operator*
350231	61431+65231+67531+61531	NN	LNW	PTR	WMT
350232	61432+65232+67532+61532	NN	LNW	PTR	WMT
350233	61433+65233+67533+61546	NN	LMI	PTR	WMT
350234	61434+65234+67534+61534	NN	LNW	PTR	WMT
350235	61435+65235+67535+61535	NN	LMI	PTR	WMT
350236	61436+65236+67536+61536	NN	LMI	PTR	WMT
350237	61437+65237+67537+61537	NN	LMI	PTR	WMT
350238	61438+65238+67538+61538	NN	LMI	PTR	WMT
350239	61439+65239+67539+61539	NN	LNW	PTR	WMT
350240	61440+65240+67540+61540	NN	LNW	PTR	WMT
350241	61441+65241+67541+61541	NN	LMI	PTR	WMT
350242	61442+65242+67542+61542	NN	LMI	PTR	WMT
350243	61443+65243+67543+61543	NN	LMI	PTR	WMT
350244	61444+65244+67544+61544	NN	LNW	PTR	WMT
350245	61445+65245+67545+61545	NN	LNW	PTR	WMT
350246§	61446+65246+67546+61533	NN	LMI	PTR	WMT
350247	61447+65247+67547+61547	NN	LMI	PTR	WMT
350248	61448+65248+67548+61548	NN	LMI	PTR	WMT

350249	61449+65249+67549+61549	NN	LMI	PTR	WMT
350250	61450+65250+67550+61550	NN	LMI	PTR	WMT
350251	61451+65251+67551+61551	NN	LMI	PTR	WMT
350252	61452+65252+67552+61552	NN	LNW	PTR	WMT
350253	61453+65253+67553+61553	NN	LNW	PTR	WMT
350254	61454+65254+67554+61554	NN	LNW	PTR	WMT
350255	61455+65255+67555+61555	NN	LMI	PTR	WMT
350256	61456+65256+67556+61556	NN	LMI	PTR	WMT
350257	61457+65257+67557+61557	NN	LNW	PTR	WMT
350258	61458+65258+67558+61558	NN	LNW	PTR	WMT
350259	61459+65259+67559+61559	NN	LNW	PTR	WMT
350260	61460+65260+67560+61560	NN	LMI	PTR	WMT
350261	61461+65261+67561+61561	NN	LMI	PTR	WMT
350262	61462+65262+67562+61562	NN	LNW	PTR	WMT
350263	61463+65263+67563+61563	NN	LNW	PTR	WMT
350264§	61464+65264+67564+61564	NN	LMI	PTR	WMT
350265	61465+65265+67565+61565	NN	LMI	PTR	WMT
350266	61466+65266+67566+61566	NN	LMI	PTR	WMT
350267	61467+65267+67567+61567	NN	LNW	PTR	WMT

■ In October 2018, Porterbrook unveiled a project to convert the Class 350/2 sets to battery/electric units after they are returned from WMT use, this would allow greater flexibility for the re-lease of the sets.

Right: *The 37 members of Class 350/2, owned by Porterbrook, are scheduled to go off lease with WMT trains. A project exists to convert these to bi-mode sets by installing underfloor mounted batteries. Painted in base Northwestern Railway livery, set No. 350252 formes a northbound Euston to Crewe stopping service at Rugeley.* **CJM**

Class 350/3
Desiro

Vehicle Length: 66ft 9in (20.4m)
Height: 12ft 1½in (3.78m)
Width: 9ft 2in (2.7m)

Horsepower: 1,341hp (1,000kW)
Seats (total/car): 24F-209S, 60S/24F-32S/57S/60S
110mph max speed

Number	*Formation* DMSO(A)+TCO+PTSO+DMSO(B)	*Depot*	*Livery*	*Owner*	*Operator*	*Name*
350368	60141+60511+60651+60151	NN	LNW	ANG	WMT	
350369	60142+60512+60652+60152	NN	LNW	ANG	WMT	
350370	60143+60513+60653+60153	NN	LNW	ANG	WMT	
350371	60144+60514+60654+60154	NN	LNW	ANG	WMT	
350372	60145+60515+60655+60155	NN	LNW	ANG	WMT	
350373	60146+60516+60656+60156	NN	LNW	ANG	WMT	
350374	60147+60517+60657+60157	NN	LNW	ANG	WMT	
350375	60148+60518+60658+60158	NN	LNW	ANG	WMT	*Vic Hall*
350376	60149+60519+60659+60159	NN	LNW	ANG	WMT	
350377	60150+60520+60660+60160	NN	LNW	ANG	WMT	*Graham Taylor OBE*

Class 350/4
Desiro

Vehicle Length: 66ft 9in (20.4m)
Height: 12ft 1½in (3.78m)
Width: 9ft 2in (2.7m)

Horsepower: 1,341hp (1,000kW)
Seats (total/car): 24F-209S, 60S/24F-32S/57S/60S
110mph max speed

Number	*Formation* DMSO(A)+TCO+PTSO+DMSO(B)	*Depot*	*Livery*	*Owner*	*Operator*
350401	60691+60901+60941+60671	NN	GRY	ANG	WMT
350402	60692+60902+60942+60672	NN	WMR	ANG	WMT
350403	60693+60903+60943+60673	NN	WMR	ANG	WMT
350404	60694+60904+60944+60674	NN	WMR	ANG	WMT
350405	60695+60905+60945+60675	NN	WMR	ANG	WMT
350406	60696+60906+60946+60676	NN	WMR	ANG	WMT
350407	60697+60907+60947+60677	NN	WMR	ANG	WMT
350408	60698+60908+60948+60678	NN	GRY	ANG	WMT
350409	60699+60909+60949+60679	NN	WMR	ANG	WMT
350410	60700+60910+60950+60680	NN	WMR	ANG	WMT

Colas Rail Freight

Address: ✉ Dacre House, 19 Dacre Street, London, SW1H 0DJ

enquiries@colasrail.co.uk, ✆ 0207 593 5353, ⓘ www.colasrail.co.uk

Managing Director: Debbie Francis

Depots: Washwood Heath (AW), Rugby (RU), Eastleigh Works (ZG), Nottingham Eastcroft (NM). Barrow Hill (BH)

Class 37

Vehicle Length: 61ft 6in (18.74m)
Height: 13ft 0¼in (3.96m)
Width: 8ft 11⅝in (2.73m)

Engine: English Electric 12CSVT
Horsepower: 1,750hp (1,304kW)
Electrical Equipment: English Electric

Number	*Depot*	*Pool*	*Livery*	*Owner*	*Operator*	*Name/Notes*
37025	NM	COTS	BLL	PRI	COL	***Inverness TMD***
37057 (D6757)	NM	COTS	GRN	COL	COL	
37099 (37324)	NM	COTS	COL	COL	COL	***Merl Evans 1947 - 2016***
37116	NM	COTS	COL	COL	COL	
37175	NM	COTS	COL	COL	COL	
37207(S)	-	-	-	-	-	*Sold to Europhoenix 01/19*
37219	NM	COTS	COL	COL	COL	
37240	NM	COTS	TRA	BOW	COL	
37254	NM	COTS	COL	COL	COL	***Cardiff Canton***
37418 (37271)	NM	COTS	BLL	PRI	COL	
37421 (37267)	NM	COTS	BLL	COL	COL	
37610 (37687)	BH	COTS	BLL	HNR	COL	

Above: *An operational fleet of 11 Class 37s from various sub classes are used by Colas Rail Freight to power engineering and Network Rail test trains. Some locos are owned by Colas, others are hired to the operator from the private sector. Colas owned No. 37219 is seen powering a test train through Crouch Hill on 28 May 2019.* **CJM**

Class 56

Vehicle Length: 63ft 6in (19.35m)
Height: 13ft 0in (3.96m)
Width: 9ft 2in (2.79m)

Engine: Ruston Paxman 16RK3CT
Horsepower: 3,250hp (2,420kW)
Electrical Equipment: Brush

Number	*Depot*	*Pool*	*Livery*	*Owner*	*Operator*	*Name*
56049	NM	COFS	COL	COL	COL	***Robin of Templecombe 1938-2013***
56051	NM	COLS	COL	COL	COL	***Survival***
56078	NM	COFS	COL	COL	COL	
56087	NM	COFS	COL	BEA	COL	
56090(S)	NM	COFS	COL	BEA	-	
56094	NM	COFS	COL	COL	COL	
56096	NM	COFS	COL	BEA	COL	
56105	NM	COFS	COL	BEA	COL	
56113	NM	COFS	COL	BEA	COL	
56302 (56124)	NM	COFS	COL	COL	COL	***Peco The Railway Modeller 2016 70 Years***

Right: *A fleet of heavy output Class 56s are on the books of Colas Rail Freight. Some locos are owned by Beacon Rail and leased to Colas, while others are owned directly by Colas. Beacon Rail No. 56113 and Colas No. 56094 pass through Ilkeston light engine.* **Antony Christie**

Class 66/8

Vehicle Length: 70ft 0½in (21.34m)
Height: 12ft 10in (3.91m)
Width: 8ft 8¼in (2.65m)
Engine: EMD 12N-710G3B-EC
Horsepower: 3,300hp (2,462kW)
Electrical Equipment: EMD

Number	Depot	Pool	Livery	Owner	Operator	Name
66846 (66573)	RU	COLO	COL	BEA	COL	
66847 (66574)	RU	COLO	COL	BEA	COL	*Terry Baker*
66848 (66575)	RU	COLO	COL	BEA	COL	
66849 (66576)	RU	COLO	COL	BEA	COL	*Wylam Dilly*
66850 (66577)	RU	COLO	COL	BEA	COL	*David Maidment OBE* *www.railwaychildren.org.uk*

Right: *A fleet of just five EMD Class 66s are operated by Colas Rail Freight, these are owned by Beacon Rail and carry Colas livery. The fleet is usually used to power infrastructure trains and can normally be found in the Westbury, Hoo Junction or Eastleigh areas. No. 66846 rests between duties at Eastleigh on 20 May 2019.* **Antony Christie**

Class 67

Vehicle Length: 64ft 7in (19.68m)
Height: 12ft 9in (3.88m)
Width: 8ft 9in (2.66m)
Engine: EMD 12N-710G3B-EC
Horsepower: 2,980hp (2,223kW)
Electrical Equipment: EMD

Number	Depot	Pool	Livery	Owner	Operator	Name
67023	RU	COTS	COL	BEA	COL	*Stella*
67027	RU	COTS	COL	BEA	COL	*Charlotte*

Right: *A pair of 100-125mph Class 67s are operated by Colas Rail Freight, but owned by Beacon Rail. The two locos usually operate 'top and tail' on one of the Network Rail monitoring trains. Once a year the pair stand-in for the New Measurement Train, when the HST based set is out of service for maintenance. The two locos are seen operating the temporary measurement train at Cockwood, Devon.* **CJM**

Colas Rail Freight

Class 70 - PH37ACmi

Vehicle Length: 71ft 2½in (21.71m)
Height: 12ft 10in (3.91m)
Width: 8ft 8in (2.64m)
Engine: GE V16-cylinder PowerHaul 616
Horsepower: 3,700hp (2,750kW)
Electrical Equipment: General Electric

Number	*Depot*	*Pool*	*Livery*	*Owner*	*Operator*
70801 (70099)	RU	COLO	COL	LOM	COL
70802	RU	COLO	COL	LOM	COL
70803	RU	COLO	COL	LOM	COL
70804	RU	COLO	COL	LOM	COL
70805	RU	COLO	COL	LOM	COL
70806	RU	COLO	COL	LOM	COL
70807	RU	COLO	COL	LOM	COL
70808	RU	COLO	COL	LOM	COL
70809	RU	COLO	COL	LOM	COL
70810	RU	COLO	COL	LOM	COL
70811	RU	COLO	COL	BEA	COL
70812	RU	COLO	COL	BEA	COL
70813	RU	COLO	COL	BEA	COL
70814	RU	COLO	COL	BEA	COL
70815	RU	COLO	COL	BEA	COL
70816	RU	COLO	COL	BEA	COL
70817	RU	COLO	COL	BEA	COL

No. 70099 was built as a demonstrator at the GE plant in Turkey, tested in mainland Europe then transferred to the UK, and sold to Colas Rail Freight.

Left: *Between 2013-2017, a fleet of 17 Class 70s were introduced by Colas. Today, the first 10 are financed by Lombard and the balance by Beacon Rail. The fleet can be found powering general freight or working infrastructure trains. The fleet carry standard Colas green and orange livery. The last of the build No. 70817 is seen at Clay Cross Junction.* **CJM**

Hauled Stock (NPCCS)

Mk1
Vehicle Length: 64ft 6in (19.65m)
Height: 12ft 9½in (3.89m)
Width: 9ft 3in (2.81m)

Barrier Vans

AW51

Number	*Depot*	*Livery*	*Owner*
6376 (ADB975973, 1021)	LE	BLU	PTR
6377 (ADB975975, 1042)	LE	BLU	PTR
6378 (ADB975971, 1054)	LE	ROG	PTR
6379 (ADB975972, 1039)	LE	ROG	PTR
6392 (81588/92183)	ZA	COL	COL
6397 (81600/92190)	ZA	COL	COL

Motorail Vans (Operated as brake force runners on Network Rail test trains)

96602 (96150)	RU	COL	NR
96603 (96155)	RU	COL	NR
96604 (96156)	RU	COL	NR
96605 (96157)	RU	COL	NR
96606 (96213)	RU	COL	NR
96607 (96215)	RU	COL	NR
96608 (96216)	RU	COL	NR
96609 (96217)	RU	COL	NR

Left: *Colas are the operator of the eight former Great Western side loading Motorail vans, which for a short time provided accommodation for cars between London Paddington and Penzance. The vehicles are now used as make up or brake runner carriages for Network Rail test trains and are painted in Network Rail yellow. No. 96604 is seen at Penzance.* **Antony Christie**

DB-Cargo

Address (UK): ✉ Lakeside Business Park, Caroline Way, Doncaster, DN4 5PN
info@uk.dbcargo.com, ✆ 0870 140 5000
ⓘ https://uk.dbcargo.com

Chief Executive: Hans-Georg Werner

Depots: Crewe Electric (CE), Toton (TO)

Class 58

For Class 58, please see Exported Locomotive section

Class 60

Vehicle Length: 70ft 0½in (21.34m)
Height: 12ft 10⅝in (3.92m)
Width: 8ft 8in (2.64m)
Engine: Mirrlees MB275T
Horsepower: 3,100hp (2,240kW)
Electrical Equipment: Brush

Number	*Depot*	*Pool*	*Livery*	*Owner*	*Operator*	*Name*
60001‡	**TO**	**WCAT**	**DBS**	**DBC**	**DBC**	
60003	**TO**	**WQCA**	**EWS**	**DBC**	**DBC**	***Freight Transport Association***
60005	**TO**	**WQCA**	**EWS**	**DBC**	-	
60007‡	**TO**	**WCBT**	**DBS**	**DBC**	-	***The Spirit of Tom Kendell***
60009(S)	**TO**	**WQCA**	**EWS**	**DBC**	-	
60010‡	**TO**	**WCBT**	**DBS**	**DBC**	**DBC**	
60011	**TO**	**WCAT**	**DBS**	**DBC**	**DBC**	
60012(S)	**TO**	**WQCA**	**EWS**	**DBC**	-	
60015‡	**TO**	**WCBT**	**DBS**	**DBC**	**DBC**	
60017‡	**TO**	**WCBT**	**DBS**	**DBC**	**DBC**	
60019‡	**TO**	**WCAT**	**DBS**	**DBC**	**DBC**	***Port of Grimsby & Immingham***
60020‡	**TO**	**WCBT**	**DBS**	**DBC**	**DBC**	***The Willows***
60022	**TO**	**WQCA**	**EWS**	**DBC**	-	
60024‡	**TO**	**WCAT**	**DBS**	**DBC**	**DBC**	***Clitheroe Castle***
60025	**TO**	**WQCA**	**EWS**	**DBC**	-	
60027	**TO**	**WQCA**	**EWS**	**DBC**	-	
60030	**TO**	**WQCA**	**EWS**	**DBC**	-	
60032	**TO**	**WQCA**	**EWS**	**DBC**	-	
60034(S)	**TO**	**WQCA**	**RFE**	**DBC**	-	***Carnedd Llewelyn***
60035	**TO**	**WCAT**	**EWS**	**DBC**	**DBC**	
60036(S)	**TO**	**WQCA**	**EWS**	**DBC**	-	***GEFCO***
60037	**TO**	**WQCA**	**EWS**	**DBC**	-	
60039‡	**TO**	**WCAT**	**DBS**	**DBC**	**DBC**	***Dove Holes***
60040‡	**TO**	**WCAT**	**DBS**	**DBC**	**DBC**	***The Territorial Army Centenary***
60043(S)	**TO**	**WQCA**	**EWS**	**DBC**	-	
60044‡	**TO**	**WCAT**	**DBS**	**DBC**	-	***Dowlow***
60045(S)	**TO**	**WQBA**	**EWS**	**DBC**	-	***The Permanent Way Institution***
60049	**TO**	**WQBA**	**EWS**	**DBC**	**DBC**	
60051	**TO**	**WQCA**	**EWS**	**DBC**	-	
60052	**TO**	**WQCA**	**EWS**	**DBC**	-	***Glofa Twr - The last deep mine in Wales - Tower Colliery***
60053(S)	**TO**	**WQCA**	**EWS**	**DBC**	-	
60054‡	**TO**	**WCBT**	**DBS**	**DBC**	**DBC**	
60057(S)	**TO**	**WQCA**	**RFE**	**DBC**	-	***Adam Smith***
60059‡	**TO**	**WCBT**	**DBS**	**DBC**	**DBC**	***Swinden Dalesman***
60062‡	**TO**	**WCAT**	**DBS**	**DBC**	**DBC**	***Stainless Pioneer***
60063‡	**TO**	**WCAT**	**DBS**	**DBC**	**DBC**	
60064■	**TO**	**WQCA**	**RFE**	**DBC**	-	***Back Tor***
60065	**TO**	**WCAT**	**EWS**	**DBC**	**DBC**	***Spirit of Jaguar***
60066‡	**TO**	**WCAT**	**ADV**	**DBC**	**DRC**	
60067(S)	**TO**	**WQCA**	**RFE**	**DBC**	-	
60069(S)	**TO**	**WQCA**	**EWS**	**DBC**	-	***Slioch***
60071(S)	**TO**	**WQBA**	**DBS**	**DBC**	-	***Ribblehead Viaduct***
60072(S)	**TO**	**WQCA**	**RFE**	**DBC**	-	***Cairn Toul***
60073(S)	**TO**	**WQCA**	**RFE**	**DBC**	-	***Cairn Gorm***
60074‡	**TO**	**WCAT**	**DBS**	**DBC**	**DBC**	
60077(S)	**TO**	**WQCA**	**RFE**	**DBC**	-	

DB-Cargo

60079‡	TO	WQAA	DBS	DBC	DBC	
60083(S)	TO	WQCA	EWS	DBC	-	
60084(S)	TO	WQCA	RFE	DBC	-	*Cross Fell*
60088(S)	TO	WQCA	MLG	DBC	-	
60090(S)	TO	WQCA	RFE	DBC	-	*Quinag*
60091‡	TO	WCBT	DBS	DBC	DBC	*Barry Needham*
60092‡	TO	WCBT	DBS	DBC	DBC	
60093(S)	TO	WQCA	EWS	DBC	-	
60094(S)	CD	WQCA	EWS	DBC	-	*Rugby Flyer*
60097(S)	TO	WQCA	EWS	DBC	-	
60099(S)	TO	WQCA	TAT	DBC	-	
60100‡	TO	WCAT	DBS	DBC	DBC	*Midland Railway - Butterley*
60500(S)*	TO	WQCA	EWS	DBC	-	

* Previously numbered 60016. ‡ Refurbished 'Super 60'. ADV = Drax biomass livery.
■ Offered for sale on December 2018, plus 60070/098

Left: *Of the 100-strong Class 60 fleet built by Brush for BR Railfreight, just a handful still operate daily for DB-Cargo. These are refurbished locos, which power the heaviest steel and fuel trains. A large number of locos are stored at Toton, while several have been sold to other companies and restored to main line operation. DB No. 60044 Dowlow is captured at Clay Cross, powering a northbound steel train on 3 June 2019.* **CJM**

Class 66

Vehicle Length: 70ft 0½in (21.34m)
Height: 12ft 10in (3.91m)
Width: 8ft 8¼in (2.65m)
Engine: EMD 12N-710G3B-EC
Horsepower: 3,300hp (2,462kW)
Electrical Equipment: EMD

Number	Depot	Pool	Livery	Owner	Operator
66001‡	TO	WBAE	DBS	DBC	DBC
66002‡	TO	WBAE	EWS	DBC	DBC
66003	TO	WBAE	EWS	DBC	DBC
66004	TO	WBAR	EWS	DBC	DBC
66005	TO	WBAE	MIM	DBC	DBC
66006	TO	WBAR	EWS	DBC	DBC
66007	TO	WBAR	EWS	DBC	DBC
66009	TO	WBAE	DBC	DBC	DBC
66010 ●	AZ	WBEN	EWS	DBC	DBC
66011	TO	WBAE	EWS	DBC	DBC
66012	TO	WBAE	EWS	DBC	DBC
66013 ●	TO	WBAE	EWS	DBC	DBC
66014	TO	WBAR	EWS	DBC	DBC
66015	TO	WBAR	EWS	DBC	DBC
66017	TO	WBAR	DBC	DBC	DBC
66018	TO	WBAE	DBC	DBC	DBC
66019	TO	WBAR	DBC	DBC	DBC
66020	TO	WBAE	DBC	DBC	DBC
66021	TO	WBAR	DBC	DBC	DBC
66022 ●	AZ	WBEN	EWS	DBC	DBC
66023	TO	WBAT	EWS	DBC	DBC
66024	TO	WBAE	EWS	DBC	DBC
66025	TO	WBAR	EWS	DBC	DBC
66026 ●	TO	WBEN	EWS	DBC	ECR
66027	TO	WBAE	DBC	DBC	DBC
66028 ●	AZ	WBEN	EWS	DBC	ECR
66029 ●	TO	WGEA	EWS	DBC	DBC
66030	TO	WBAR	EWS	DBC	DBC
66031 ●	DRS on loan				
66032 ●	AZ	WBES	EWS	DBC	ECR
66033 ●	AZ	WBEN	EWS	DBC	DBC
66034	TO	WBAE	DBC	DBC	DBC
66035	TO	WBAE	DBC	DBC	DBC
66036 ●	AZ	WBEN	EWS	DBC	ECR
66037	TO	WBAR	EWS	DBC	DBC
66038 ●	AZ	WBEN	EWS	DBC	ECR
66039	TO	WBAE	EWS	DBC	DBC
66040	TO	WBRT	EWS	DBC	DBC
66041	TO	WBAR	DBC	DBC	DBC
66042 ●	AZ	WFMS	EWS	DBC	ECR
66043	TO	WQAB	EWS	DBC	DBC
66044	TO	WBAE	DBC	DBC	DBC
66045 ●	AZ	WBEN	EWS	DBC	ECR
66047	TO	WBAE	MIM	DBC	DBC
66049 ●	AZ	WBEN	EWS	DBC	ECR
66050	TO	WBAE	EWS	DBC	DBC
66051	TO	WBAR	MIM	DBC	DBC
66052 ●	AZ	WFMS	EWS	DBC	ECR
66053	TO	WBAE	EWS	DBC	DBC
66054	TO	WBAR	EWS	DBC	DBC
66055	TO	WBAR	DBC	DBC	DBC
66056	TO	WBLE	EWS	DBC	DBC
66057	TO	WBLE	EWS	DBC	DBC
66059	TO	WBLE	EWS	DBC	DBC
66060	TO	WBAR	EWS	DBC	DBC

66061	TO	WBAE	EWS	DBC	DBC
66062 ●	AZ	WBEN	EWS	DBC	DBC
66063	TO	WBAE	EWS	DBC	DBC
66064 ●	AZ	WBEN	EWS	DBC	DBC
66065	TO	WBAR	DBC	DBC	DBC
66066	TO	WBAR	DBC	DBC	DBC
66067	TO	WBAR	EWS	DBC	DBC
66068	TO	WBAR	EWS	DBC	DBC
66069	TO	WBAR	EWS	DBC	DBC
66070	TO	WBAT	DBC	DBC	DBC
66071 ●	AZ	WBEN	EWS	DBC	DBC
66072 ●	AZ	WBEN	EWS	DBC	DBC
66073 ●	AZ	WBEN	EWS	DBC	ECR
66074	TO	WBAE	DBC	DBC	DBC
66075	TO	WBAE	EWS	DBC	DBC
66076	TO	WBAE	EWS	DBC	DBC
66077	TO	WBAR	DBC	DBC	DBC
66078	TO	WBAE	DBC	DBC	DBC
66079	TO	WBAR	EWS	DBC	DBC
66080	TO	WBAE	EWS	DBC	DBC
66082	TO	WBAE	DBC	DBC	DBC
66083	TO	WBAR	EWS	DBC	DBC
66084	TO	WBAR	EWS	DBC	DBC
66085	TO	WBAR	DBC	DBC	DBC
66086	TO	WBAE	EWS	DBC	DBC
66087	TO	WBAE	EWS	DBC	DBC
66088	TO	WBAE	EWS	DBC	DBC
66089	TO	WBAR	EWS	DBC	DBC
66090	TO	WBAE	MIM	DBC	DBC
66091	*With DRS*				
66092	TO	WBAE	EWS	DBC	DBC
66093	TO	WBAE	EWS	DBC	DBC
66094	TO	WBAE	DBC	DBC	DBC
66095	TO	WBAE	EWS	DBC	DBC
66096	TO	WBAR	EWS	DBC	DBC
66097	TO	WBAE	DBS	DBC	DBC
66098	TO	WBAE	EWS	DBC	DBC
66099	TO	WBBE	EWS	DBC	DBC
66100	TO	WBBE	DBC	DBC	DBC
66101	TO	WBBE	DBS	DBC	DBC
66102	TO	WBBE	EWS	DBC	DBC
66103	TO	WBBE	EWS	DBC	DBC
66104	TO	WBBT	DBC	DBC	DBC
66105	TO	WBAR	DBC	DBC	DBC
66106	TO	WBBE	EWS	DBC	DBC
66107	TO	WBBT	DBC	DBC	DBC
66108	*With DRS*				
66109	TO	WBAR	MIM	DBC	DBC
66110	TO	WBBE	EWS	DBC	DBC
66111	TO	WBAE	EWS	DBC	DBC
66112	TO	WBBE	EWS	DBC	DBC
66113	TO	WBBE	DBC	DBC	DBC
66114	TO	WBBT	DBS	DBC	DBC
66115	TO	WBAE	DBC	DBC	DBC
66116	TO	WBAE	EWS	DBC	DBC
66117	TO	WBAE	DBC	DBC	DBC
66118	TO	WBAE	DBC	DBC	DBC
66119	TO	WBAE	EWS	DBC	DBC
66120	TO	WBAE	EWS	DBC	DBC
66121	TO	WBAE	EWS	DBC	DBC
66122	*With DRS*				
66123 ●	AZ	WGEA	EWS	DBC	DBC
66124	TO	WBAR	DBC	DBC	DBC
66125	TO	WBAE	EWS	DBC	DBC
66126	*With DRS*				
66127	TO	WBAT	EWS	DBC	DBC
66128	TO	WBAE	DBC	DBC	DBC
66129	TO	WBAR	EWS	DBC	DBC
66130	TO	WBAR	DBC	DBC	DBC
66131	TO	WBAE	DBC	DBC	DBC
66133	TO	WBAE	EWS	DBC	DBC
66134	TO	WBAE	DBC	DBC	DBC
66135	TO	WBAE	DBC	DBC	DBC
66136	TO	WBAE	DBC	DBC	DBC
66137	TO	WBAE	DBC	DBC	DBC
66138	TO	WBAE	EWS	DBC	DBC
66139	TO	WBAE	EWS	DBC	DBC
66140	TO	WBAE	EWS	DBC	DBC
66142	TO	WBAR	MIM	DBC	DBC
66143	TO	WBAE	EWS	DBC	DBC
66144	TO	WBAR	EWS	DBC	DBC
66145	TO	WQAB	EWS	DBC	DBC
66146 P	PN	WBEP	EWS	DBC	DBC
66147	TO	WBAE	EWS	DBC	DBC
66148	TO	WBAE	MIM	DBC	DBC
66149	TO	WBAE	DBC	DBC	DBC
66150	TO	WBAE	DBC	DBC	DBC
66151	TO	WBAE	EWS	DBC	DBC
66152	TO	WBAE	DBS	DBC	DBC
66153 P	PN	WBEP	EWS	DBC	DBC
66154	TO	WBAE	EWS	DBC	DBC
66155	TO	WBAE	EWS	DBC	DBC
66156	TO	WBAE	EWS	DBC	DBC
66157 P	PN	WBEP	EWS	DBC	DBC
66158	TO	WBAE	EWS	DBC	DBC
66159 P	PN	WBEP	EWS	DBC	DBC
66160	TO	WBAR	EWS	DBC	DBC
66161	TO	WBAE	EWS	DBC	DBC
66162	TO	WBAR	MIM	DBC	DBC
66163 P	PN	WBEP	DBS	DBC	DBC
66164	TO	WBAE	EWS	DBC	DBC
66165	TO	WBAR	DBC	DBC	DBC
66166 P	PN	WBEP	EWS	DBC	DBC
66167	TO	WBAE	DBC	DBC	DBC
66168	TO	WBAR	EWS	DBC	DBC
66169	TO	WBAR	EWS	DBC	DBC
66170	TO	WBAE	EWS	DBC	DBC
66171	TO	WBAR	EWS	DBC	DBC
66172	TO	WBAE	EWS	DBC	DBC
66173 P	PN	WBEP	EWS	DBC	DBC
66174	TO	WBAE	EWS	DBC	DBC
66175	TO	WBAE	DBC	DBC	DBC
66176	TO	WBAR	EWS	DBC	DBC
66177	TO	WBAT	EWS	DBC	DBC
66178 P	PN	WBEP	EWS	DBC	DBC
66179 ●	TO	WBAK	EWS	DBC	ECR
66180 P	PN	WBEP	EWS	DBC	DBC
66181	TO	WBAR	EWS	DBC	DBC
66182	TO	WBAE	DBC	DBC	DBC
66183	TO	WBAE	EWS	DBC	DBC
66185	TO	WBAE	DBS	DBC	DBC
66186	TO	WBAR	EWS	DBC	DBC
66187	TO	WBAE	EWS	DBC	DBC
66188	TO	WBAR	EWS	DBC	DBC
66189 P	PN	WBEP	EWS	DBC	DBC
66190 ●	AZ	WBEN	EWS	DBC	ECR
66191 ●	AZ	WBEN	EWS	DBC	DBC
66192	TO	WBAR	DBC	DBC	DBC
66193 ●	AZ	WBEN	EWS	DBC	ECR
66194	TO	WBAR	EWS	DBC	DBC

DB-Cargo

66195 ●	TO	WBEN	EWS	DBC	ECR
66196 P	PN	WBEP	EWS	DBC	DBC
66197	TO	WBAE	EWS	DBC	DBC
66198	TO	WBAR	EWS	DBC	DBC
66199	TO	WBAE	EWS	DBC	DBC
66200	TO	WBAE	EWS	DBC	DBC
66201 ●	AZ	WBEN	EWS	DBC	ECR
66202 ●	AZ	WBEN	EWS	DBC	ECR
66203 ●	AZ	WBEN	EWS	DBC	ECR
66204 ●	AZ	WBEN	EWS	DBC	ECR
66205 ●	AZ	WBEN	EWS	DBC	ECR
66206	TO	WBAR	DBC	DBC	DBC
66207	TO	WBAE	EWS	DBC	DBC
66208 ●	AZ	WBEN	EWS	DBC	ECR
66209 ●	AZ	WBEN	EWS	DBC	ECR
66210 ●	AZ	WBEN	EWS	DBC	ECR
66211 ●	TO	WBEN	EWS	DBC	ECR
66212 ●	AZ	WBEN	EWS	DBC	ECR
66213 ●	AZ	WBEN	EWS	DBC	ECR
66214 ●	AZ	WBEN	EWS	DBC	ECR
66215 ●	AZ	WBEN	EWS	DBC	ECR
66216 ●	AZ	WBEN	EWS	DBC	ECR
66217 ●	AZ	WBEN	EWS	DBC	ECR
66218 ●	AZ	WGEA	EWS	DBC	ECR
66219 ●	AZ	WGEA	EWS	DBC	ECR
66220 P	PN	WBEP	DBC	DBC	DBC
66221	TO	WBAR	EWS	DBC	DBC
66222 ●	AZ	WBEN	EWS	DBC	ECR
66223 ●	AZ	WBEN	EWS	DBC	DBC
66224 ●	AZ	WBEN	EWS	DBC	ECR
66225 ●	AZ	WBEN	EWS	DBC	ECR
66226 ●	AZ	WBEN	EWS	DBC	ECR
66227 P	PN	WBEP	EWS	DBC	DBC
66228 ●	AZ	WBEN	EWS	DBC	ECR
66229 ●	AZ	WBEN	EWS	DBC	ECR
66230(S)	TO	WQAB	DBC	DBC	DBC
66231 ●	AZ	WBEN	EWS	DBC	ECR
66232 ●	AZ	WBEN	EWS	DBC	ECR
66233 ●	AZ	WBEN	EWS	DBC	ECR
66234 ●	AZ	WBEN	EWS	DBC	ECR
66235 ●	AZ	WBEN	EWS	DBC	ECR
66236 ●	AZ	WBEN	EWS	DBC	ECR
66237 P	PN	WBEP	EWS	DBC	DBC
66239 ●	AZ	WBEN	EWS	DBC	ECR
66240 ●	AZ	WBEN	EWS	DBC	ECR
66241 ●	AZ	WBEN	EWS	DBC	ECR
66242 ●	AZ	WGEA	EWS	DBC	ECR
66243 ●	TO	WBEN	EWS	DBC	ECR
66244 ●	AZ	WBEN	EWS	DBC	ECR
66245 ●	AZ	WBEN	EWS	DBC	DBC
66246 ●	AZ	WBEN	EWS	DBC	ECR
66247 ●	AZ	WBEN	EWS	DBC	ECR
66248 P	PN	WBEP	DBS	DBC	DBC
66249 ●	AZ	WBES	EWS	DBC	DBC

‡ Only fitted with standard drawgear

● Modified to operate with Euro Cargo Rail in mainland Europe.
P Locomotives operated by DB-Schenker in Poland. Only locos from the series 66146-250 can be modified for this contract.

Names applied

66002	*Lafarge Quorn*
66005	*Maritime Intermodal One*
66035	*Resourceful*
66047	*Maritime Intermodal Two*
66050	*EWS Energy*
66051	*Maritime Intermodal Four*
66055	*Alain Thauvette*
66066	*Geoff Spencer*
66077	*Benjamin Gimbert GC*
66079	*James Nightall GC*
66090	*Matitime Intermodal Six*
66100	*Armistice 100 1918 - 2018*
66109	*Teesport Express*
66142	*Maritime Intermodal Three*
66148	*Maritime Intermodal Seven*
66152	*Derek Holmes Railway Operator*
66162	*Maritime Intermodal Five*
66172	*Paul Melleney*
66185	*DP World London Gateway*

Left: *The core main line diesel fleet operated by DB-Cargo are Class 66s. Of the original fleet of 250, the UK fleet is now down to fewer than 160, with the balance operating in Europe. Originally painted in EWS maroon and gold, the fleet is currently being repainted in DB-Cargo red and grey, with a large DB badge on the bodyside. No. 66009 passes Blackhorse Road with an eastbound aggregate train.* **CJM**

Class 67

Vehicle Length: 64ft 7in (19.68m)
Height: 12ft 9in (3.88m)
Width: 8ft 9in (2.66m)
Engine: EMD 12N-710G3B-EC
Horsepower: 2,980hp (2,223kW)
Electrical Equipment: EMD

Number	Depot	Pool	Livery	Owner	Operator	Name
67001	CE	WAWC	ATW	DBC	DBC	
67002	CE	WAAC	ATW	DBC	DBC	
67003	CE	WQAA	ATW	DBC	DBC	
67004	CE	WABC	DBC	DBC	DBC	
67005	CE	WAAC	ROY	DBC	DBC	*Queen's Messenger*
67006	CE	WAAC	ROY	DBC	DBC	*Royal Sovereign*
67007	CE	WQAA	EWS	DBC	-	
67008	CE	WACC	EWS	DBC	DBC/TFW	
67009	CE	WABC	EWS	DBC	DBC	
67010	CE	WAAC	DBC	DBC	DBC	
67011	CE	WQBA	EWS	DBC	-	
67012	CE	WAAC	WSR	DBC	DBC	
67013	CE	WAAC	DBS	DBC	DBC	
67014	CE	WAWC	WSR	DBC	DBC	
67015	CE	WAAC	DBS	DBC	DBC	
67016	CE	WAAC	EWS	DBC	DBC	
67017	CE	WQAA	EWS	DBC	DBC/TFW	
67018	CE	WAAC	DBS	DBC	DBC	*Keith Heller*
67019	CE	WQAA	EWS	DBC	-	
67020	CE	WAWC	EWS	DBC	DBC	
67021	CE	WAAC	PUL	DBC	DBC	
67022	CE	WQAA	EWS	DBC	-	
67024	CE	WAAC	PUL	DBC	DBC	
67025	CE	WACC	TFW	DBC	DBC/TFW	
67026	CE	WQBA	ROJ	DBC	-	*Diamond Jubilee*
67028	CE	WAAC	DBC	DBC	DBC	
67029	CE	WACC	EWE	DBC	DBC	*Royal Diamond*
67030	CE	WQAA	EWS	DBC	-	

Right: *With DB-Cargo contracted to provide locos and staff to operate the Belmond British Pullman (VSOE), a pair of locos Nos. 67021 and 67024 have been repainted in full traditional Pullman livery of Umber and Cream. The two locos are usually deployed when ever possible on the VIP train and are seldom seen on freight workings. On 1 June 2019, the pair are seen approaching Dawlish with a Belmond special from Penzance to Bath.* **CJM**

Class 90

Vehicle Length: 61ft 6in (18.74m)
Height: 13ft 0¼in (3.96m)
Width: 9ft 0in (2.74m)
Power Collection: 25kV ac overhead
Horsepower: 7,860hp (5,860kW)
Electrical Equipment: GEC

Number		Depot	Pool	Livery	Owner	Operator	Name/Notes
90017		CE	WQBA	EWS	DBC	-	
90018		CE	WEAC	DBS	DBC	DBC	*The Pride of Bellshill*
90019		CE	WEDC	DBC	DBC	DBC	*Multimodal*
90020		CE	WEDC	EWS	DBC	DBC	*Collingwood*
90021(S)	(90221)	CE	WQAA	FGS	DBC	-	
90022(S)	(90222)	CE	WQBA	RFE	DBC	-	*Freightconnection*
90023(S)	(90223)	CE	WQBA	EWS	DBC	-	
90024(S)	(90224)	CE	WQAB	ADV±	DBC	-	
90025	(90225)	CE	WEAC	RFD	DBC	DBC	
90026		CE	WEDC	GTL	DBC	GTL	

DB-Cargo

Number		Depot	Pool	Livery	Owner	Operator	Name
90027(S)	(90227)	CE	WQBA	RFD	DBC	-	*Allerton T&RS Depot Quality Approved*
90028		CE	WEDC	DBC	DBC	DBC	*Sir William McAlpine*
90029		CE	WEDC	DBS	DBC	DBC	
90030(S)	(90130)	CE	WQBA	EWS	DBC	-	
90031(S)	(90131)	CE	WQBA	EWS	DBC	-	*The Railway Children Partnership - Working for Street Children Worldwide*
90032(S)	(90132)	CE	WQBA	EWS	DBC	-	
90033(S)	(90233)	CE	WQBA	RFI	DBC	DBC	
90034	(90134)	CE	WEDC	DRB	DBC	DBC	
90035	(90135)	CE	WEAC	DBC	DBC	DBC	
90036	(90136)	CE	WEDC	DBS	DBC	DBC	*Driver Jack Mills*
90037	(90137)	CE	WEDC	EWS	DBC	DBC	*Spirit of Dagenham*
90038(S)	(90238)	CE	WQBA	RFI	DBC	-	
90039	(90239)	CE	WEDC	EWS	DBC	DBC	
90040	(90140)	CE	WEAC	DBS	DBC	DBC	
90050(S)	(90150)	BA	DHLT	FLG	FLT	-	(Stored at Crewe Basford Hall, for scrap)

± Carries W H Malcolm livery

Left: *The EWS-owned Class 90s have little work, apart from a handful of container trains on the West Coast Main Line. Until late 2019 two locos were used each day on LNER passenger services, but this contract was lost after Class 800 and 801s entered service. In DB-Cargo red livery, No. 90036 is seen with an LNER Mk4 train at Doncaster.* **CJM**

Class 92

Vehicle Length: 70ft 1in (21.34m)
Height: 13ft 0in (3.95m)
Width: 8ft 8in (2.66m)
Power Collection: 25kV ac overhead / 750V dc third rail
Horsepower: ac - 6,700hp (5,000kW) / dc - 5,360hp (4,000kW)
Electrical Equipment: Brush

Number	*Depot*	*Pool*	*Livery*	*Owner*	*Operator*	*Name*
92001■	-	WGEE	DBS	HBS	*Sold to Locotech, Russia*● (91 53 0472 002-1)	*Mircea Eliade*
92002■	-	WGEE	DBS	DBC	*Sold to Locotech, Russia*● (91 53 0472 003-9)	
92003±	-	WGEE	RFE	DBC	*Exported Bulgaria* (91 53 0472 xxx-x)	*Beethoven*
92004(S)	CE	WQBA	RFE	DBC		*Jane Austen*
92005±		WGEE	DBS	DBC	*Sold to Locotech, Russia*● (91 53 0472 005-4)	*Emil Cioran*
92007(S)	CE	WQAA	RFE	DBC	-	*Schubert*
92008(S)	CE	WQAB	RFE	DBC	-	*Jules Verne*
92009§(S)	CE	WQBA	DBS	DBC	-	*Marco Polo*
92011	CE	WFBC	RFE	DBC	DBC	*Handel*
92012■	-	WGEE	DBS	HBS	*Sold to Locotech, Russia*● (91 53 0472 001-3)	*Mihai Eminescu*
92013(S)	CE	WQBA	RFE	DBC		*Puccini*
92015§	CE	WFBC	DBS	DBC	DBC	
92016(S)§	CE	WQBA	DBS	DBC	-	
92017(S)	CE	WQAA	STO	DBC	-	*Bart the Engine*
92019	CE	WFBC	RFE	DBC	DBC	*Wagner*
92022±	-	WGEE	RFE	DBC	*Exported Bulgaria* (91 52 1688 022-1)	*Charles Dickens*
92024■	-	WGEE	DBS	DBC	*Sold to Locotech, Russia*● (91 53 0472 004-7)	*Marin Preda*
92025±	-	WGEE	RFE	HBS	*Exported Bulgaria* (91 52 1688 025-1)	*Oscar Wilde*
92026±	-	WGEE	RFE	DBC	*Exported Romania* (91 53 0472 026-x)	*Britten*
92027±	-	WGEE	RFE	HBS	*Exported Bulgaria* (91 70 1688 027-1) OOU	*George Eliot*
92029±	CE	WQAB	RFE	DBC	-	*Dante*
92030±	-	WGEE	RFE	DBC	*Exported Bulgaria (91 52 1688 030-1)*	
92031§(S)	CE	WQBA	DBS	DBC	-	
92034±	-	WGEE	RFE	HBS	*Exported Bulgaria (91 52 1688 034-3). OOU*	*Kipling*
92035(S)	CE	WQBA	RFE	DBC	-	*Mendelssohn*
92036§	CE	WFBC	RFE	DBC	DBC	*Bertolt Brecht*
92037(S)	CE	WQBA	RFE	DBC	DBC	*Sullivan*
92039■	-	WGEE	DBS	DBC	*Sold to Locotech, Russia*● (91 53 0472 006-2)	*Eugen Ionescu*

92041	CE	WFBC	RFE	DBC	DBC	*Vaughan Williams*
92042§	CE	WFBC	DBS	DBC	DBC	

§ Fitted with equipment to allow operation over HS1, ± Exported to Bulgaria, ■ Exported to Romania
● Sold to Locotech, Russia, leased to Transagent Spediicija, Croatia

Right: *Only around seven Class 92s are still in regular operation by DB-Cargo, powering main line and international freight services through the Channel Tunnel. These are based at Crewe and equipped for both overhead and third rail power collection. No. 90042 is seen passing Otford with a clay train.* **Howard Lewsey**

Hauled Stock

AD1F - FO

Number	*Depot*	*Livery*	*Owner*
3279	TY	MAR	DBR

AC2B - TSO

Number	*Depot*	*Livery*	*Owner*
5482	TO	BLG	DBR

AE2D - BSO

Number	*Depot*	*Livery*	*Owner*
9494(S)	TY	MAR	DBR/SCR

AE2E - BSO

Number	*Depot*	*Livery*	*Location*
9506	ME	MAR	Brodie Eng

AE2F - BSO

Number	*Depot*	*Livery*	*Owner*
9529(S)	DN	MAR	DBR
9531(S)	DN	MAR	DBR

AJ1G - RFM

Number		*Depot*	*Livery*	*Owner*
10211	(40510)	TO	EWE	DBC
10237(S)	(10022)	BY	DRU	DBR
10242(S)	(10002)	LM	BLG	DBR

AU4G - SLEP

Number	*Depot*	*Livery*	*Owner*
10546	TO	EWE	DBC

AD1G - FO

Number	*Depot*	*Livery*	*Owner*
11019(S)	ZB	DRU	DBR
11028(S)	ZB	VIR	DBR
11030(S)	ZB	DRU	DBR

Right: *DB-Cargo operates a three vehicle and one DVT 'Business' train, used for transporting senior DB management and high-profile customers around the UK network and to private terminals. Mk3A No. 11039 is seen attached to a Class 67.* **CJM**

Mk2	*Height: 12ft 9½in (3.89m)*
Vehicle Length: 66ft 0in (20.11m)	*Width: 9ft 3in (2.81m)*

Mk 3	*Height: 12ft 9in (3.88m)*
Vehicle Length: 75ft 0in (22.86m)	*Width: 8ft 11in (2.71m)*

Mk 3 (DVT)	*Height: 12ft 9in (3.88m)*
Vehicle Length: 61ft 9in (18.83m)	*Width: 8ft 11in (2.71m)*

3A TSO

Number	*Depot*	*Livery*	*Owner*
11033(S)	LM	DRU	DBR
11039	TO	EWE	DBS
11046(S)	ZB	DRU	DBR
11054(S)	ZB	DRU	DBR

GK2G - TRSB

Number	*Depot*	*Livery*	*Owner*
40402(S) (40002)	LM	VIR	DBR
40403(S) (40003)	LM	VIR	DBR
40416(S) (40016)	LM	VIR	DBR
40434(S) (40234)	LM	VIR	DBR

Saloon

Number	*Depot*	*Livery*	*Owner*
45020(S)	TO	MAR	DBR

NZAG - DVT

Number	*Depot*	*Livery*	*Owner*
82138(S)	LM	VIR	DBR
82146	TO	DBE	DBC
82150(S)	LM	VIR	DBR

DB-Cargo

Euro Cargo Rail A part of DB-Cargo

Address: ✉ Immeuble la Palacio, 25-29 Place de la Madeleine, Paris, 75008

info@eurocargorail.com, ✆ +33 977 400000, ⓘ www.eurocargorail.com

Class 21

Vehicle Length: (21/5) 48ft 2in (14.70m), (21/6) 46ft 3in (14.13m)
Height: (21/5) 13ft 8in (4.16m), (21/6) 13ft 9in (4.19m)
Width: 8ft 8¼in (2.65m)
Engine: (21/5) Caterpillar 3512B DITA of 2,011hp
(21/6) MTU 8V 4000 R41L of 1,475hp
Hydraulic Equipment: Voith

Number	Depot	Pool	Livery	Owner	Operator
21544 (FB1544)	DM	WLAN	MAR	ANG	ECR
21545 (FB1545)	DM	WLAN	MAR	ANG	ECR
21546 (FB1546)	DM	WLAN	MAR	ANG	ECR
21547 (FB1547)	DM	WLAN	MAR	ANG	ECR
21610 (FB1610)	DM	WLAN	MAR	ANG	ECR
21611 (FB1611)	DM	WLAN	MAR	ANG	ECR

Royal Mail (operations contracted to DB-Cargo)

Address: ✉ 148 Old Street, London, EC1V 9HQ

press.office@royalmail.com

✆ 0207 250 2468 ⓘ www.royalmailgroup.com

Class 325

Vehicle Length: (Driving) 65ft 0¾in (19.82m)
(Inter) 65ft 4¼in (19.92m)
Height: 12ft 4¼in (3.76m)
Width: 9ft 2in (2.82m)
Horsepower: 1,278hp (990kW)
Seats (total/car): None - luggage space

Number	Formation DTPMV+MPMV+TPMV+DTPMV	Depot	Livery	Owner	Operator	Name
325001	68300+68340+68360+68301	CE	RMR	RML	DBC	
325002	68302+68341+68361+68303	CE	RMR	RML	DBC	
325003	68304+68342+68362+68305	CE	RMR	RML	DBC	
325004	68306+68343+68363+68307	CE	RMR	RML	DBC	
325005	68308+68344+68364+68309	CE	RMR	RML	DBC	
325006	68310+68345+68365+68311	CE	RMR	RML	DBC	
325007	68312+68346+68366+68313	CE	RMR	RML	DBC	*Peter Howarth C.B.E*
325008	68314+68347+68367+68315	CE	RMR	RML	DBC	
325009	68316+68348+68368+68317	CE	RMR	RML	DBC	
325011	68320+68350+68370+68321	CE	RMR	RML	DBC	
325012	68322+68351+68371+68323	CE	RMR	RML	DBC	
325013	68324+68352+68372+68325	CE	RMR	RML	DBC	
325014	68326+68353+68373+68327	CE	RMR	RML	DBC	
325015	68328+68354+68374+68329	CE	RMR	RML	DBC	
325016	68330+68355+68375+68331	CE	RMR	RML	DBC	

Above: *The Class 325 Royal Mail EMUs were introduced just before the rail industry lost the main by rail contract and today little work remains for the 15 fleet members. A couple of trains are operated each day by way of the West Coast Main Line, usually formed or two or three sets. No. 325009 leads a twelve-car formation northbound at South Kenton.* **Antony Christie**

Direct Rail Services

Address (UK): ✉ Kingmoor Depot, Etterby Road, Carlisle, Cumbria, CA3 9NZ
info@directrailservices.com ✆ 01228 406600
ⓘ www.directrailservices.com

Managing Director: Debbie Francis
Depots: Carlisle Kingmoor (KM), Crewe Gresty Bridge (CR)

Class 37/0

Vehicle Length: 61ft 6in (18.74m)
Height: 13ft $0\frac{1}{4}$in (3.96m)
Width: 8ft $11\frac{5}{8}$in (2.73m)
Class 37/4 - Electric Train Heat fitted
Engine: English Electric 12CSVT
Horsepower: 1,750hp (1,304kW)
Electrical Equipment: English Electric

Number	*Depot*	*Pool*	*Livery*	*Owner*	*Operator*
37038	KM	XHNC	DRC	DRS	DRS
37059	KM	XHNC	DRR	DRS	DRS
37069	KM	XHNC	DRR	DRS	DRS
37218	KM	XHNC	DRR	DRS	DBS
37259	KM	XHNC	DRU	DRS	DRS

Above: *Direct Rail Services operates a fleet of five standard Class 37/0 locos, numbered in the 370xx and 372xx range. These locos are used on general freight flows and carry DRS compass livery. No. 37069 is seen inside the loco bay at Arlington Fleet Services, Eastleigh, in October 2019.* **CJM**

Class 37/4

Number		*Depot*	*Pool*	*Livery*	*Owner*	*Operator*	*Name / Note*
37401	(37268)	KM	XHAC	BLL	DRS	DRS	*Mary Queen of Scots*
37402	(37274)	KM	XHAC	BLL	DRS	DRS	*Stephen Middlemore 23.12.1954 - 8.6.2013*
37403	(37307)	KM	XHAC	BLL	DRS	DRS	*Isle of Mull*
37405	(37282)	BH	XHAC	DRC	DRS	DRS	
37407	(37305)	KM	XHAC	BLL	DRS	DRS	*Blackpool Tower*
37409	(37270)	KM	XHAC	BLL	DRS	DRS	*Lord Hinton*
37419	(37291)	KM	XHAC	INC	DRS	DRS	*Carl Haviland 1954-2012*
37422(S)	(37266)	KM	XHSS	DRB	DRS	DRS	
37423	(37296)	KM	XHAC	BLL	DRS	DRS	*Spirit of the Lakes*
37424	(37279)	KM	XHAC	BLL	DRS	DRS	*Avro Vulcan XH558 (carries No. 37558)*
37425	(37292)	BH	XHAC	REG	DRS	DRS	*Sir Robert McAlpine / Concrete Bob*

Direct Rail Services

Left: *A fleet of 11 electric train supply-fitted Class 37/4s are operated by DRS. These have in the past operated passenger services for TOCs during multiple unit shortages. They also work charter services and one is available to power the Network Inspection saloon No. 975025, which has blue-star multiple controls to enable push-pull operation. No. 37402* Stephen Middlemore 23.12.1954 - 8.6.2013 *is seen passing Evesham propelling the saloon. The loco is painted in BR large-logo livery.* **CJM**

Class 37/6

Number		Depot	Pool	Livery	Owner	Operator
37602(S)	(37502)	KM	XHSS	DRC	DRS	-
37603(S)	(37504)	KM	XHSS	DRC	DRS	-
37604(S)	(37506)	KM	XHSS	DRC	DRS	-
37605(S)	(37507)	KM	XHSS	DRC	DRS	-
37606(S)	(37508)	KM	XHSS	DRS	DRS	-
37609(S)	(37514)	KM	XHSS	DRC	DRS	-

Class 37/7

Number		Hire No.	Depot	Pool	Livery	Owner	Operator
37703(S)	(37067)	L25	BH	XHSS	DRR	DRS	-
37716	(37094)	L23	KM	XHNC	DRC	DRS	DRS

Left: *A pair of Class 37/7 'heavyweight' locos are on the books of DRS. One loco is operational No. 37716, is illustrated at Norwich, the other, No. 37703 is stored. These two locos were exported by EWS to operate in Spain and after return to the UK were purchased by DRS.*
Nathan Williamson

Class 57/0

Vehicle Length: 63ft 6in (19.38m)
Height: 12ft 10⅛in (3.91m)
Width: 9ft 2in (2.79m)
Engine: EMD 645-12E3
Horsepower: 2,500hp (1,864kW)
Electrical Equipment: Brush

Number		Depot	Pool	Livery	Owner	Operator	Name
57002	(47322)	KM	XHCK	DRC	DRS	DRS	*Rail Express*
57003	(47317)	KM	XHCK	DRC	DRS	DRS	
57004(S)	(47347)	KM	XHSS	DRC	DRS	-	
57007(S)	(47332)	KM	XHSS	DRC	DRS	-	*John Scott 12.5.45 - 22.5.12*
57008(S)	(47060)	KM	XHSS	DRC	DRS	-	
57009(S)	(47079)	KM	XHSS	DRC	DRS	-	
57010(S)	(47231)	KM	XHSS	DRC	DRS	-	
57011(S)	(47329)	CR	XHSS	DRC	DRS	-	
57012(S)	(47204)	KM	XHSS	DRC	DRS	-	

Right: *Although nine ex-Freightliner Class 57/0s are owned by Direct Rail Services, at the start of 2020 only three were registered for main line use, the balance were stored. Looking immaculate, No. 57002 Rail Express is shown sporting the latest DRS livery with a red buffer-beam.* **Howard Lewsey**

Class 57/3

Vehicle Length: 63ft 6in (19.38m)
Height: 12ft 10$^{1}/_{8}$in (3.91m)
Width: 9ft 2in (2.79m)
Engine: EMD 645-12F3B
Horsepower: 2,750hp (2,051kW)
Electrical Equipment: Brush

Number		*Depot*	*Pool*	*Livery*	*Owner*	*Operator*	*Name*
57301	(47845)	KM	GROG	DRC	DRS	ROG	*Goliath*
57302(S)	(47827)	KM	XHSS	DRC	PTR	-	*Chad Varah*
57303	(47705)	KM	XHSS	DRC	DRS	-	*Pride of Carlisle*
57304	(47807)	KM	XHVT	DRC	PTR	DRS	*Pride of Cheshire*
57305	(47822)	LR	GROG	NBP	DRS	ROG	*Northern Princess*
57306	(47814)	KM	XHAC	DRC	DRS	DRS	*Her Majesty's Railway Inspectorate 175*
57307	(47225)	KM	XHVT	DRA	PTR	DRB	*Lady Penelope*
57308	(47846)	KM	XHVT	DRC	PTR	DRS	*Jamie Ferguson*
57309	(47806)	KM	XHVT	DRC	PTR	DRS	*Pride of Crewe*
57310	(47831)	KM	XHAC	DRS	DRS	DRS	*Pride of Cumbria*
57311(S)	(47817)	KM	XHSS	DRC	PTR	-	*Thunderbird*
57312	(47330)	LR	GROG	ROG	PTR	ROG	

Nos. 57301, 57303 and 57306 fitted with Tightlock couplings, Nos. 57310 and 57312 fitted with modified Dellner couplings.

Right: *DRS have a fleet of 12 Class 57/3 locos. These were transferred in from Virgin Trains and nine locos still retain their drop-head Dellner couplings and are made available to the West Coast operator if required to haul 'Pendolino' stock. Three have been fitted with 'Tightlock' couplings. Three locos are on lease to Rail Operations Group to power stock movements. With its coupling covered to avoid dirt ingress, No. 57303 is illustrated at Crewe.* **Cliff Beeton**

Class 66/3 & 66/4

Vehicle Length: 70ft 0$^{1}/_{2}$in (21.34m)
Height: 12ft 10in (3.91m)
Width: 8ft 8$^{1}/_{4}$in (2.65m)
Engine: EMD 12N-710G3B-EC
Horsepower: 3,300hp (2,462kW)
Electrical Equipment: EMD

Number	*Depot*	*Pool*	*Livery*	*Owner*	*Operator*
66301	KM	XHIM	DRC	BEA	DRS
66302	KM	XHIM	DRB	BEA	DRS
66303	KM	XHIM	DRC	BEA	DRS
66304	KM	XHIM	DRC	BEA	DRS
66305	KM	XHIM	DRB	BEA	DRS
66421	KM	XHIM	DRC	MAQ	DRS
66422	KM	XHIM	DRC	MAQ	DRS
66423	KM	XHIM	DRC	MAQ	DRS
66424	KM	XHIM	DRC	MAQ	DRS
66425	KM	XHIM	DRB	MAQ	DRS
66426	KM	XHIM	DRB	MAQ	DRS
66427	KM	XHIM	DRC	MAQ	DRS
66428	KM	XHIM	DRB	MAQ	DRS
66429	KM	XHIM	DRC	MAQ	DRS
66430	KM	XHIM	DRS	MAQ	DRS
66431	KM	XHIM	DRC	MAQ	DRS
66432	KM	XHIM	DRC	MAQ	DRS
66433	KM	XHIM	DRC	MAQ	DRS
66434	KM	XHIM	DRC	MAQ	DRS
66435 (66031)	KM	XHIM	XXX	DBC	DRS
66436 (66091)	KM	XHIM	XXX	DBC	DRS
66437 (66108)	KM	XHIM	XXX	DBC	DRS
66438 (66122)	KM	XHIM	XXX	DBC	DRS
66439 (66126)	KM	XHIM	XXX	DBC	DRS

66435-66439 leased from DBC for 10 years from October 2019 and scheduled to be renumbered

Direct Rail Services

Names applied

66301	***Kingmoor TMD***
66302	***Endeavour***
66421	***Gresty Bridge TMD***
66428	***Carlisle Eden Mind***

Left: *DRS maintains a fleet of 19 Class 66s, mainly to power container trains. The locos are based at Carlisle. Nos. 66301-305 are owned by Beacon Rail, with the 66/4s owned by Macquarie Group. No. 66429 is seen at Electro Motive, Stoke.* **Cliff Beeton**

Class 68 'UK Light'

Vehicle Length: 67ft 3in (20.5m)
Height: 12ft 6½in (3.82m)
Speed: 100mph (161km/h)
Engine: Caterpillar C175-16
Horsepower: 3,750hp (2,800kW)
Electrical Equipment: ABB

Number	*Depot*	*Pool*	*Livery*	*Owner*	*Operator*	*Name*
68001	CR	XHVE	DRS	BEA	DRS	***Evolution***
68002	CR	XHVE	DRS	BEA	DRS	***Intrepid***
68003	CR	XHVE	DRS	BEA	DRS	***Astute***
68004	CR	XHVE	DRS	BEA	DRS	***Rapid***
68005	CR	XHVE	DRS	BEA	DRS	***Defiant***
68006	CR	XHVE	SCR	BEA	DRS/SCR	***Daring***
68007	CR	XHVE	SCR	BEA	DRS/SCR	***Valiant***
68008§	CR	XHVE	DRS	BEA	DRS	***Avenger***
68009§	CR	XHVE	DRS	BEA	DRS	***Titan***
68010§	CR	XHCE	CRG	BEA	DRS/CRW	***Oxford Flyer***
68011§	CR	XHCE	CRG	BEA	DRS/CRW	
68012§	CR	XHCE	CRG	BEA	DRS/CRW	
68013§	CR	XHCE	CRG	BEA	DRS/CRW	
68014§	CR	XHCE	CRG	BEA	DRS/CRW	
68015§	CR	XHCE	CRG	BEA	DRS/CRW	
68016	CR	XHVE	BLU	BEA	DRS	***Fearless***
68017	CR	XHVE	BLU	BEA	DRS	***Hornet***
68018	CR	XHVE	DRS	BEA	DRS	***Vigilant***
68019	LG	XHTP	FTN	BEA	DRS/TPE	***Brutus***
68020	LG	XHTP	FTN	BEA	DRS/TPE	***Reliance***
68021	LG	XHTP	FTN	BEA	DRS/TPE	***Tireless***
68022	LG	XHTP	FTN	BEA	DRS/TPE	***Resolution***
68023	LG	XHTP	FTN	BEA	DRS/TPE	***Achilles***
68024	LG	XHTP	FTN	BEA	DRS/TPE	***Centaur***
68025	LG	XHTP	FTN	BEA	DRS/TPE	***Superb***
68026	LG	XHTP	FTN	BEA	DRS/TPE	***Enterprise***
68027	LG	XHTP	FTN	BEA	DRS/TPE	***Splendid***
68028	LG	XHTP	FTN	BEA	DRS/TPE	***Lord President***
68029	LG	XHTP	FTN	BEA	DRS/TPE	***Courageous***
68030	LG	XHTP	FTN	BEA	DRS/TPE	***Black Douglas***
68031	LG	XHTP	FTN	BEA	DRS/TPE	***Felix***
68032	LG	XHTP	FTN	BEA	DRS/TPE	***Destroyer***
68033	CR	XHVE	DRB	DRS	DRS	
68034	CR	XHVE	DRB	DRS	DRS	

§ Modified for operation with push-pull passenger stock, fitted with AAR controls. 68019-68032 modified to operate with Trans Pennine Express Mk5 stock

Left: *Although a fleet of 34 Class 68s are operated by DRS, only 12 are available for DRS operations, the others are on lease, to Abellio ScotRail (2), Chiltern Railways (6) and TransPennine Express (14). No. 68009 Titan is seen at Leamington Spa on hire to Chiltern.* **CJM**

Class 88 'Euro Dual'

Vehicle Length: 67ft 3in (20.5m)
Height: 12ft 6½in (3.82m)
Speed: 100mph (161km/h)
Electric train supply Index: 96
Engine: Caterpillar C27
Horsepower: Diesel - 940hp (700kW)
Electric - 5,360hp (4,000kW)
Electrical Equipment: ABB

Number	Depot	Pool	Livery	Owner	Operator	Name
88001	KM	XHVE	DRS	BEA	DRS	*Revolution*
88002	KM	XHVE	DRS	BEA	DRS	*Prometheus*
88003	KM	XHVE	DRS	BEA	DRS	*Genesis*
88004	KM	XHVE	DRS	BEA	DRS	*Pandora*
88005	KM	XHVE	DRS	BEA	DRS	*Minerva*
88006	KM	XHVE	DRS	BEA	DRS	*Juno*
88007	KM	XHVE	DRS	BEA	DRS	*Electra*
88008	KM	XHVE	DRS	BEA	DRS	*Ariadne*
88009	KM	XHVE	DRS	BEA	DRS	*Diana*
88010	KM	XHVE	DRS	BEA	DRS	*Aurora*

Below: *The 10 bi-mode Class 88s can be found operating freight, flask or engineers trains, using their overhead power capability, flask trains are often worked over the Cumbrian Coast route in pairs using the locos diesel engines. Working under the wire, No. 88001 passes York with an engineers train.* **CJM**

Coaching Stock

Mk2
Width: 9ft 3in (2.81m)
Vehicle Length: 66ft 0in (20.11m)
Height: 12ft 9½in (3.89m)

Mk 3
Height: 12ft 9in (3.88m)
Vehicle Length: 75ft 0in (22.86m)
Width: 8ft 11in (2.71m)

Number	Type	Depot	Livery	Operator
5787	AC2E/TSO	ML	DRC	ASR
5810	AC2E/TSO	ML	DRC	ASR
5919	AC2F/TSO	ML	DRC	ASR
5937	AC2F/TSO	ML	DRC	ASR
5945	AC2F/TSO	ML	SCR	ASR
5965	AC2F/TSO	BU	SCR	(S)
5971	AC2F/TSO	ML	DRC	DRS
5976	AC2F/TSO	BU	SCR	(S)
5995	AC25/TSO	ML	DRC	DRS
6001	AC2F/TSO	ML	DRC	DRS
6008	AC2F/TSO	ML	DRC	DRS
6046	AC2F/TSO	ML	DRC	DRS
6064	AC2F/TSO	ML	DRC	DRS
6117	AC2F/TSO	ML	DRC	DRS
6122	AC2F/TSO	ML	DRC	DRS
6173	AC2F/TSO	ML	DRS	DRS
6176	AC2F/TSO	BU	SCR	(S)
6177	AC2F/TSO	BU	SCR	(S)
6183	AC2F/TSO	BU	SCR	(S)
9419	AC2E/TSO	KM	DRC	DRS
9428	AE2E/BSO	KM	DRC	DRS
9488	AE2E/BSO	ML	SCR	DRS
9508	AE2E/BSO	ZA	BRC	DRS
9521	AE2E/BSO	KM	DRC	DRS
9525	AE2E/BSO	ML	DRC	ASR
9539	AE2E/BSO	KM	SCR	ASR
9704 (9512)	AF2F/DBSO	KM	DRC	DRS
9705 (9519) (S)	AF2F/DBSO	ZA	DRC	DRS
9707 (9511) (S)	AF2F/DBSO	BU	DRC	(S)
9709 (9515) (S)	AF2F/DBSO	BU	DRC	(S)
9710 (9518) (S)	AF2F/DBSO	KM	DRC	DRS
11006	AD1G/FO	BU	-	DRS
82101(S)	NZAK/DVT	ZA	VIR	DRS
82126	NZAK/DVT	KM	-	DRS

NX5G - NGV (Nightstar Generators)

Number	Depot	Livery	Owner
96372(S) (10564)	LM	EPS	DRS
96373(S) (10568)	LM	EPS	DRS
96375(S) (10587)	LM	EPS	DRS

GB Railfreight (GBRf)

Address: 15-25 Artillery Lane, London, E1 7HA

gbrfinfo@gbrailfreight.com © 0207 983 5177 ⓘ www.gbrailfreight.com

Managing Director: John Smith

Depots: Peterborough (PT), Willesden (WN), St Leonards (SE), Coquelles (CQ)

Parent Company: MG Prudential

Class 08 & 09

Vehicle Length: 29ft 3in (8.91m)
Height: 12ft $8^{5}/_{8}$in (3.87m)
Width: 8ft 6in (2.59m)
Engine: English Electric 6K
Horsepower: 400hp (298kW)
Electrical Equipment: English Electric

Number	*Depot*	*Pool*	*Livery*	*Owner*	*Operator*
08401	HH	GBWW	GRN	HEC	Hams Hall
08925	BH	GBWM	GRN	GBF	March
08934	BH	GBWM	GRN	GBF	BH
09002	BH	GBWM	GRN	GBF	GBR
09009	MR	GBWM	GRN	GBF	Dean Lane

Class 20

Vehicle Length: 46ft $9^{1}/_{4}$in (14.26m)
Height: 12ft $7^{5}/_{8}$in (3.84m)
Width: 8ft 9in (2.66m)
Engine: English Electric 8SVT Mk2
Horsepower: 1,000hp (745kW)
Electrical Equipment: English Electric

Number		*Depot*	*Pool*	*Livery*	*Owner*	*Operator*	*Name*
20096		PG	GBEE	BLU	PRI	GBR	
20107		PG	GBEE	BLU	PRI	GBR	
20118		PG	GBEE	GRY	PRI	GBR	
20132		PG	GBEE	GRY	PRI	GBR	*Barrow Hill Depot*
20901	(20101)	PG	GBEE	GBN	HNR	GBR	
20905	(20225)	PG	GBEE	GBN	HNR	GBR	*Dave Darwin*

Left: *For several years GB Railfreight have operated a small fleet of Class 20s, which were obtained to power Londn Underground stock moves between Bombardier Derby and the LU system, where they operated 'top and tail'. The locos also operated other services when available, such as the annual RHTT duties, on which No. 20905 is recorded powering at Tonbridge.* **Howard Lewsey**

Class 47/7

Vehicle Length: 63ft 6in (19.35m)
Height: 12ft $10^{3}/_{8}$in (3.91m)
Width: 9ft 2in (2.79m)
Electric Train Heat fitted
Engine: Sulzer 12LDA28C
Horsepower: 2,580hp (1,922kW)
Electrical Equipment: Brush
47739/749 fitted with Dellner couplings

Number		*Depot*	*Pool*	*Livery*	*Owner*	*Operator*	*Name*
47727	(47569)	LR	GBDF	SCS	GBR	GBR	*Edinburgh Castle / Caisteal Dhun Eideann*
47739	(47594)	LR	GBDF	GBB	GBR	GBR	
47749	(47625)	LR	GBDF	BLU	GBR	GBR	*City of Truro*

Left: *Three Class 47 are operated by GB Railfreight, being based at Leicester and operated by the companies Rail Services division, which looks after internal depot to depot and depot to works stock moves. Painted in BR Blue with GBRf branding, No. 47749 City of Truro is seen with No. 47727 painted in Caledonian Sleeper teal green passing Dawlish.* **CJM**

Class 50

Vehicle Length: 68ft 6in (20.88m)	Engine: English Electric 16CSVT
Height: 12ft 10¼ (3.92m)	Horsepower: 2700hp (2013kW)
Width: 9ft 1¼in (2.77m)	Electrical Equipment: English Electric

Number	Depot	Pool	Livery	Owner	Operator	Name
50007 (D407)	SV	-	GRN	C5A	GBR	*Hercules*
50049 (D449)	SV	-	GRN	C5A	GBR	*Defiance*

Right: *In early 2019, GB Railfreight took on the operation of two Class 50s, Nos. 50007 and 50049 owned by the Class 50 Alliance and based on the Severn Valley Railway. The two locos are operated on an 'as required' bases to power freight or charter passenger services. The two locos were repainted in full GBRf colours by Arlington Eastleigh. No. 50049 Defiance is illustrated at Crewe.* **Cliff Beeton**

Class 56

Vehicle Length: 63ft 6in (19.35m)	Engine: Ruston Paxman 16RK3CT
Height: 13ft 0in (3.96m)	Horsepower: 3,250hp (2,420kW)
Width: 9ft 2in (2.79m)	Electrical Equipment: Brush

In 2018, GBRf purchased a fleet of Class 56s for re-engineering, some will be fitted with new power units. The locos are allocated to pool GBGS. It is said that 10 are for re-engineering, three will be operated as standard Class 56s and three will be parts doners. Locos are officially allocated to PG, in Pool GBGS. Rebuilt locos will be Class 69 (001-010)

56007§	*56018§*	56032§	56038§	56065*	56077*	56098■	56106*	*56311§*
56009§	*56031§*	56037§	56060*	*56069§*	56081■	56104±	56128§	56312■

No. 56009 owned by EMD

* Stored at Leicester, § Conversion at EMD Longport, ± Stored at Castle Donnington, ■ In use at Peak Forest

Class 59/0

Vehicle Length: 70ft 0½in (21.34m)	Engine: EMD 16-645 E3C
Height: 12ft 10in (3.91m)	Horsepower: 3,000hp (2,462kW)
Width: 8ft 8¼in (2.65m)	Electrical Equipment: EMD

Number	Depot	Pool	Livery	Owner	Operator	Name
59003	PG	GBYH	GBN	GBR	GBR	*Yeoman Highlander*

Right: *One of the original Foster Yeoman Class 59s No. 59003, after working in Europe for a number of years, was returned to the UK and is now on the books of GBRf. It carries standard GBRf colours, but retains its original Yeoman Highlander name. The loco is used to power heavy general freight of infrastructure trains often in the Westbury/Eastleigh area. The loco is seen passing Swindon.*
Nathan Williamson

Class 60

Vehicle Length: 70ft 0½in (21.34m)	Engine: Mirrlees MB275T
Height: 12ft 10⅝in (3.92m)	Horsepower: 3,100hp (2,240kW)
Width: 8ft 8in (2.64m)	Electrical Equipment: Brush

Number	Depot	Pool	Livery	Owner	Operator	Name
60002	PG	GBTG	COL	BEA	GBR	
60004	-	-	EWS	GBR	-	
60008	-	-	EWS	GBR	-	

GBRf

60014	-	-	EWS	GBR	-	
60018	-	-	EWS	GBR	-	
60021	PG	GBTG	GBN	BEA	GBR	*Penyghent*
60026	PG	GBTG	GBB	BEA	GBR	*Helvellyn*
60047	PG	GBTG	COL	BEA	GBR	
60056	PG	GBTG	COL	BEA	GBR	
60076	PG	GBTG	COL	BEA	GBR	
60085	PG	GBTG	COL	BEA	GBR	
60087	PG	GBTG	COL	BEA	GBR	
60095	PG	GBTG	GBN	BEA	GBR	
60096	PG	GBTG	COL	BEA	GBR	

Left: *When DB placed a number of Class 60s on the market, Colas Rail Freight purchased a number for heavy freight operation. Later these 10 locos were transferred to GB Railfreight and are now owned by Beacon Rail and leased to GBRf. Gradually the locos are being repainted in GBRf colours at Arlington Eastleigh. Some are in standard GBRf colours while others carry special liveries, including No. 60026 carrying owner Beacon Rails blue colours. GBRf No. 66095 is shown, working on the Severn Valley Railway during the 2019 gala event.* **Nathan Williamson**

Class 66/7

Vehicle Length: 70ft 0½in (21.34m)
Height: 12ft 10in (3.91m)
Width: 8ft 8¼in (2.65m)
Engine: EMD 12N-710G3B-EC
Horsepower: 3,300hp (2,462kW)
Electrical Equipment: EMD

Number	Depot	Pool	Livery	Owner	Operator	Name
66701	PG	GBBT	GBR	EVL	GBR	
66702	PG	GBBT	GBN	EVL	GBR	*Blue Lightning*
66703	PG	GBBT	GBN	EVL	GBR	*Doncaster PSB 1981 - 2002*
66704	PG	GBBT	GBN	EVL	GBR	*Colchester Power Signalbox*
66705	PG	GBBT	GBR	EVL	GBR	*Golden Jubilee*
66706	PG	GBBT	GBN	EVL	GBR	*Nene Valley*
66707	PG	GBBT	GBN	EVL	GBR	*Sir Sam Fay / Great Central Railway*
66708	PG	GBBT	GBR	EVL	GBR	*Jayne*
66709	PG	GBBT	MSC	EVL	GBR	*Sorrento*
66710	PG	GBBT	GBN	EVL	GBR	*Phil Packer*
66711	PG	GBBT	AGI	EVL	GBR	*Sence*
66712	PG	GBBT	GBN	EVL	GBR	*Peterborough Power Signalbox*
66713	PG	GBBT	GBN	EVL	GBR	*Forest City*
66714	PG	GBBT	GBN	EVL	GBR	*Cromer Lifeboat*
66715	PG	GBBT	GBN	EVL	GBR	*Valour*
66716	PG	GBBT	GBN	EVL	GBR	*Locomotive & Carriage Institution Centenary 1911-2011*
66717	PG	GBBT	GBN	EVL	GBR	*Good Old Boy*
66718	PG	GBLT	SPL	EVL	GBR	*Sir Peter Hendy CBE*
66719	PG	GBLT	GBN	EVL	GBR	*Metro-Land*
66720	PG	GBLT	SPL	EVL	GBR	
66721	PG	GBLT	SPL	EVL	GBR	*Harry Beck*
66722	PG	GBLT	GBN	EVL	GBR	*Sir Edward Watkin*
66723 (ZA723)	PG	GBLT	GBN	EVL	GBR	*Chinook*
66724	PG	GBLT	GBN	EVL	GBR	*Drax Power Station*
66725	PG	GBLT	GBN	EVL	GBR	*Sunderland*
66726	PG	GBLT	GBN	EVL	GBR	*Sheffield Wednesday*
66727	PG	GBLT	ADV	EVL	GBR	*Maritime One*
66728	PG	GBLT	GBN	PTR	GBR	*Institution of Railway Operators*
66729	PG	GBLT	GBN	PTR	GBR	*Derby County*
66730	PG	GBLT	GBF	PTR	GBR	*Whitemoor*
66731	PG	GBLT	GBN	PTR	GBR	*interhubGB*

66732	PG	GBLT	GBN	PTR	GBR	*GBRf The First Decade 1999-2009 John Smith - MD*
66733 (66401)	PG	GBFM	BLU	PTR	GBR	*Cambridge PSB*
66735 (66403)	PG	GBBT	GBN	PTR	GBR	*Peterborough United*
66736 (66404)	PG	GBFM	GBN	PTR	GBR	*Wolverhampton Wanderers*
66737 (66405)	PG	GBFM	GBN	PTR	GBR	*Lesia*
66738 (66578)	PG	GBBT	GBN	GBR	GBR	*Huddersfield Town*
66739 (66579)	PG	GBFM	GBN	GBR	GBR	*Bluebell Railway*
66740 (66580)	PG	GBFM	GBN	GBR	GBR	*Sarah*
66741 (66581)	PG	GBBT	GBN	GBR	GBR	*Swanage Railway*
66742 (66406, 66841)	PG	GBBT	GBN	GBR	GBR	*Port of Immingham Centenary 1912 - 2012*
66743 (66407, 66842)	PG	GBFM	ROS	GBR	GBR	
66744 (66408, 66843)	PG	GBBT	GBN	GBR	GBR	*Crossrail*
66745 (66409, 66844)	PG	GBRT	GBN	GBR	GBR	*Modern Railways - The first 50 years*
66746 (66410, 66845)	PG	GBFM	ROS	GBR	GBR	
66747	PG	GBEB	ADV	GBR	GBR	*Made in Sheffield*
66748	PG	GBEB	GBN	GBR	GBR	*West Burton 50*
66749	PG	GBEB	GBN	GBR	GBR	*Christopher Hopcroft MBE 60 years Railway Service*
66750	PG	GBEB	GBN	GBN	GBR	*Bristol Panel Signal Box*
66751	PG	GBEB	GBN	BEA	GBR	*Inspiration Delivered Hitachi Rail Europe*
66752	PG	GBEL	GBN	GBR	GBR	*The Hoosier State*
66753	PG	GBEL	GBN	GBR	GBR	*EMD Roberts Road*
66754	PG	GBEL	GBN	GBR	GBR	*Northampton Saints*
66755	PG	GBEL	GBN	GBR	GBR	*Tony Berkley OBE RFG Chairman 1997-2018*
66756	PG	GBEL	GBN	GBR	GBR	*The Royal Corps Of Signals*
66757	PG	GBEL	GBN	GBR	GBR	*West Somerset Railway*
66758	PG	GBEL	GBN	GBR	GBR	*The Pavior*
66759	PG	GBEL	GBN	GBR	GBR	*Chippy*
66760	PG	GBEL	GBN	GBR	GBR	*David Gordon Harris*
66761	PG	GBEL	GBN	GBR	GBR	*Wensleydale Railway Association 25 Years 1990-2015*
66762	PG	GBEL	GBN	GBR	GBR	
66763	PG	GBEL	GBN	GBR	GBR	*Severn Valley Railway*
66764	PG	GBEL	GBN	GBR	GBR	
66765	PG	GBEL	GBN	GBR	GBR	
66766	PG	GBEL	GBN	GBR	GBR	
66767	PG	GBEL	GBN	GBR	GBR	
66768	PG	GBEL	GBN	GBR	GBR	
66769	PG	GBEL	GBN	GBR	GBR	
66770	PG	GBEL	GBN	GBR	GBR	
66771	PG	GBEL	GBN	GBR	GBR	*Amanda*
66772	PG	GBEL	GBN	GBR	GBR	*Maria*
66773	PG	GBNB	SPL	GBR	GBR	*Pride of GB Railfreight*
66774	PG	GBNB	GBN	GBR	GBR	
66775 (F231)	PG	GBNB	GBN	GBR	GBR	*HMS Argyll*
66776	PG	GBNB	GBN	GBR	GBR	*Joanne*
66777	PG	GBNB	GBN	GBR	GBR	*Annette*
66778	PG	GBNB	GBN	GBR	GBR	*Cambois Depot 25 Years*
66779	PG	GBEL	GRN	GBR	GBR	*Evening Star*
66780 (66008)	PG	GBOB	ADV	GBR	GBR	*The Cemex Express*
66781 (66016)	PG	GBOB	GBN	GBR	GBR	
66782 (66046)	PG	GBOB	SPL	GBR	GBR	
66783 (66058)	PG	GBOB	SPL	GBR	GBR	*The Flying Dustman*

Right: *GB Railfreight's largest fleet of locos are 91 Class 66. These were mainly built new for the company but some have been obtained from European operators. Most locos carry standard GBRf colours but some carry customer colours. Standard liveried No. 66712* Peterborough Signal Box *looking rather work stained is seen passing Doncaster.* **CJM**

GBRf

66784	(66081)	PG	GBOB	GBN	GBR	GBR	*Keighley & Worth Valley Railway 50th Anniversary 1968-2018*
66785	(66132)	PG	GBOB	GBN	GBR	GBR	
66786	(66141)	PG	GBOB	GBN	GBR	GBR	
66787	(66184)	PG	GBOB	GBN	GBR	GBR	
66788	(66238)	PG	GBOB	GBN	GBR	GBR	*Locomotion 15*
66789	(66250)	PG	GBOB	SPL	GBR	GBR	*British Rail 1948-1997*
66790	(T66 403)	PG	GBOB	GBN	GBR	GBR	
66791	(T66 404)	PG	GBOB	GBN	GBR	GBR	
66792	(T66 405)	PG	GBOB	GBN	GBR	GBR	

Class 69

Vehicle Length: 63ft 6in (19.35m)
Height: 13ft 0in (3.96m)
Width: 9ft 2in (2.79m)
Engine: EMD 12N-710G3B-T2
Horsepower: 3,300hp (2,462kW)
Electrical Equipment: EMD

Number	*Original No.*	*Depot*	*Pool*	*Livery*	*Owner*	*Operator*
69001	56311	PG	GBGS	SPL	PRO	GBR
69002	56031	PG	GBGS	GBN	PRO	GBR
69003	56018§	PG	GBGS	GBN	PRO	GBR
69004	56069§	PG	GBGS	GBN	PRO	GBR
69005	56128§	PG	GBGS	GBN	PRO	GBR
69006	56037§	PG	GBGS	GBN	PRO	GBR
69007	56007§	PG	GBGS	GBN	PRO	GBR
69008	56038§	PG	GBGS	GBN	PRO	GBR
69009	56065§	PG	GBGS	GBN	PRO	GBR
69010	56060§	PG	GBGS	GBN	PRO	GBR

§ Proposed renumbering order in January 2020, might change due to conversion issues.

Class 73/1, 73/2

Vehicle Length: 53ft 8in (16.35m)
Height: 12ft 5$\frac{5}{16}$in (3.79m)
Width: 8ft 8in (2.64m)
Power: 750V dc third rail or English Electric 6K
Horsepower: electric - 1,600hp (1,193kW)
Horsepower: diesel - 600hp (447kW)
Electrical Equipment: English Electric

Number		*Depot*	*Pool*	*Livery*	*Owner*	*Operator*	*Name/notes*
73101(S)		SE	GBSD	PUL	GBR	-	
73107		SE	GBED	GBN	GBR	GBR	*Tracy*
73109		SE	GBED	GBN	GBR	GBR	
73110		SE	GBSD	-	GBR	-	
73119		SE	GBED	GBN	GBR	GBR	
73128		SE	GBED	GBN	GBR	GBR	
73136		SE	GBED	GBU	GBR	GBR	*Mhairi*
73139(S)		SE	GBSD	NSE	GBR	-	
73141		SE	GBED	GBU	GBR	GBR	*Charlotte*
73201	(73142)	SE	GBED	BLU	GBR	GBR	*Broadlands*
73212	(73102)	SE	GBED	GBU	GBR	GBR	*Fiona*
73213	(73112)	SE	GBED	GBU	GBR	GBR	*Rhodalyn*

Class 73/9

Vehicle Length: 53ft 8in (16.35m)
Height: 12ft 5$\frac{5}{16}$in (3.79m)
Width: 8ft 8in (2.64m)
ETH Index 30 or 70 for sleeper locos
Power: 750V dc third rail or MTU 8V 4000 R43L
Horsepower: electric - 1,600hp (1,193kW)
Horsepower: diesel - 1,600hp (1,193kW)
Electrical Equipment: Brush

73961	(73209/120)	SE/TG	GBNR	GBB	GBR	GBR	*Alison*
73962	(73204/125)	SE/TG	GBNR	GBB	GBR	GBR	*Dick Mabbutt*

Left: *The five Class 73/9s operated on Network Rail trains carry standard GBRf livery. The locos retain their high-level multiple control and air pipes, buck-eye couplings, Pullman rubbing plates and adjustable buffers. Unnamed No. 73965 is shown with a Network Rail test train at Derby.* **Antony Christie**

73963	(73206/123)	SE/TG	GBNR	GBB	GBR	GBR	*Janice*
73964	(73205/124)	SE/TG	GBNR	GBB	GBR	GBR	*Jeanette*
73965	(73208/121)	SE/TG	GBNR	GBB	GBR	GBR	
73966	(73005)	EC	GBCS	SCS	GBR	SCS	
73967	(73006)	EC	GBCS	SCS	GBR	SCS	
73968	(73117)	EC	GBCS	SCS	GBR	SCS	
73969	(73105)	EC	GBCS	SCS	GBR	SCS	
73970	(73103)	EC	GBCS	SCS	GBR	SCS	
73971	(73207/122)	EC	GBCS	SCS	GBR	SCS	

Class 92

Vehicle Length: 70ft 1in (21.34m)
Height: 13ft 0in (3.95m)
Width: 8ft 8in (2.66m)
Power Collection: 25kV ac overhead / 750V dc third rail
Horsepower: ac - 6,700hp (5,000kW) / dc - 5,360hp (4,000kW)
Electrical Equipment: Brush

Number	*Depot*	*Pool*	*Livery*	*Owner*	*Operator*	*Name*
92006	WN	GBSL	SCS	GBR	GBR	
92010	WN	GBST	SCS	GBR	GBR	
92014	WN	GBSL	SCS	GBR	SCS	
92018	WN	GBST	SCS	GBR	SCS	
92020	WN	GBSL	GBN	GBR	GBR	
92021(S)	Brush	GBSD	EU2	GBR	-	*Purcell*
92023	CQ	GBSL	SCS	GBR	SCS	
92028	WN	GBST	GBN	GBR	SCS	
92032	CQ	GBST	GBN	GBR	GBR	*I Mech E Railway Division*
92033	WN	GBSL	SCS	GBR	SCS	
92038	WN	GBST	SCS	GBR	SCS	
92040(S)	Brush	GBSD	EU2	GBR	-	*Goethe*
92043	CQ	GBST	GBN	GBR	GBR	
92044	CQ	GBST	SCS	GBR	GBR	*Couperin*
92045(S)	Brush	GBSD	EU2	GBR	-	*Chaucer*
92046(S)	Brush	GBSD	EU2	GBR	-	*Sweelinck*

Right: *Over the years GB Railfreight have acquired a fleet of 16 Class 92s, not all are in service, with several stored, which could return to the main line in new work was obtained. A batch of eight locos sport Caledonian Sleeper teal livery, being used on the Edinburgh-London Euston leg of sleeper services. The Caledonian Sleeper locos have been modified with Dellner couplings and extra jumpers to attach to CAF built Mk5 sleeper stock. Caledonian liveried No. 92010 is seen with a Mk5 rake at Willesden.* **Antony Christie**

Class Di 8

Vehicle Length: 57ft 1in (17.38m)
Height: 13ft 3in (4.01m)
Width: 9ft 8in (2.95m)
Engine: Caterpillar 3516 DITA
Horsepower: 2,100hp (1,566kW)
Electrical Equipment: Siemens

GBRf purchased 12 former Cargo-Net, Norway, Class Di 8 locos for use within the SSI Lackenby Steelworks in Redcar. The 2,100hp (1,566kW) locos were built in 1996-97 by Mak in Kiel, Germany, as an order for 20 locos. In the UK the fleet is classified by the UIC as 308. With closure of the complex these locos have now been transferred to Scunthorpe to replace Class 20 operations.

8.701	8.703	8.708	8.712	8.717	8.719
8.702	8.704	8.711	8.716	8.718	8.720

Industrial 0-6-0DH

DH50-1 Works No. TH278V - 0-6-0DH 50-ton design, built 1978, fitted with a Cummins engine
DH50-2 Works No. TH246V - 0-6-0DH 50-ton design, built 1973

The above two industrial locos are operated by GBRf at the Celsa steel plant in Cardiff.

Freightliner

Address: 3rd Floor, 90 Whitfield Street, London. W1T 4EZ
pressoffice@freightliner.co.uk
0207 200 3900
www.freightliner.com

Chief Executive: Gary Long
Managing Director: Adam Cunliffe
Depots: Crewe Basford Hall (CB), Ipswich* (IP), Leeds Midland Road (LD), Southampton Maritime (SZ)
* Stabling point
Parent Company: Brookfield Infrastructure and GIC

Class 08/0

Vehicle Length: 29ft 3in (8.91m)
Height: 12ft 8⅝in (3.87m)
Width: 8ft 6in (2.59m)
Engine: English Electric 6K
Horsepower: 400hp (298kW)
Electrical Equipment: English Electric

Number	Depot	Pool	Livery	Owner	Operator
08530	TP	DFLS	FLR	PTR	FLR
08531	FEL	DFLS	FLP	PTR	FLR
08575	BU	DHLT	FLR	PTR	-
08585	SZ	DFLS	FLP	PTR	FLR
08591	FEL	DFLS	FLR	FLR	FLR
08624	LH	DFLS	FLP	PTR	FLR
08691	CB	DFLS	FLR	FLR	FLR
08785	LH	DFLS	FLR	PTR	FLR
08873	ZB	DFLS	FLR	PTR	FLR
08891	BU	DFLS	FLR	PTR	-

Names applied
08585 *Vicky*
08691 *Terri*
08624 *Rambo Paul Ramsey*

Left: *A number of standard Class 08 0-6-0 shunting locos are operated by Freightliner at their main terminals as well at Merehead and Whatley quarries. No. 08585 Vicky carries a version of Freightliner 'Powerhaul' livery when seen at Southampton Maritime terminal.* **Antony Christie**

Mendip Rail Locos

Number	Depot	Pool	Livery	Owner	Operator
08296	MD	MBDL	BLU	FOS	MRL
08643	MD	MBDL	GRN	FOS	MRL
08650	MD	MBDL	MRL	FOS	-
08652	MD	MBDL	HAN	HAN	MRL
08947	WH	MBDL	BLU	FOS	MRL

Class 47/4

Vehicle Length: 63ft 6in (19.35m)
Height: 12ft 10⅜in (3.91m)
Width: 9ft 2in (2.79m)
Electric Train Heat fitted
Engine: Sulzer 12LDA28C
Horsepower: 2,580hp (1,922kW)
Electrical Equipment: Brush

Number	Depot	Pool	Livery	Owner	Operator	Name
47830 (47649) D1645	CB	DFLH	GRN	FLR	FLR	*Beeching's Legacy*

Class 59/0 & 59/1

Vehicle Length: 70ft 0½in (21.34m)
Height: 12ft 10in (3.91m)
Width: 8ft 8¼in (2.65m)
Engine: EMD 16-645 E3C
Horsepower: 3,000hp (2,462kW)
Electrical Equipment: EMD

Number	Depot	Pool	Livery	Owner	Operator	Name
59001	MD	DFHG	AGI	FLR	FLR	*Yeoman Endeavour*
59002	MD	DFHG	AGI	FLR	FLR	*Alan J Day*
59004	MD	DFHG	AGI	FLR	FLR	*Paul A Hammond*
59005	MD	DFHG	AGI	FLR	FLR	*Kenneth J Painter*

59101	MD	DFHG	HAN	FLR	FLR	*Village of Whatley*
59102	MD	DFHG	HAN	FLR	FLR	*Village of Chantry*
59103	MD	DFHG	HAN	FLR	FLR	*Village of Mells*
59104	MD	DFHG	HAN	FLR	FLR	*Village of Great Elm*

Right: *As part of a new Freightliner contract to operate Mendip aggregate trains from the Westbury area, Freightliner took over the nine Class 59s operated by Aggregate Industries and Hanson from 2019, although the locos retain their previous business colours. Hanson-liveried No. 59102 is seen attached to a Class 92 at Crewe.* **Cliff Beeton**

Class 59/2

Vehicle Length: 70ft 0½in (21.34m)
Height: 12ft 10in (3.91m)
Width: 8ft 8¼in (2.65m)
Engine: EMD 16-645 E3C
Horsepower: 3,000hp (2,462kW)
Electrical Equipment: EMD

Number	*Depot*	*Pool*	*Livery*	*Owner*	*Operator*	*Name*
59201	MD	DFHG	RED	FLR	FLR	
59202	MD	DFHG	RED	FLR	FLR	*Alan Meddows Taylor MD, Mendip Rail Limited*
59203	MD	DFHG	RED	FLR	FLR	
59204	MD	DFHG	RED	FLR	FLR	
59205	MD	DFHG	RED	FLR	FLR	
59206	MD	DFHG	RED	FLR	FLR	*John F. Yeoman Rail Pioneer*

Right: *The six Class 59/2s, originally built for National Power and later sold to EWS for use on Mendip stone traffic from Merehead and Whatley quarries, were sold to Freightliner at the end of 2019 after DB lost the Mendip Rail aggregate flow. At the start of 2020, the six locos sport unbranded DB red/grey livery, No. 59204 is seen near Porchester.* **Antony Christie**

Class 66/4

Vehicle Length: 70ft 0½in (21.34m)
Height: 12ft 10in (3.91m)
Width: 8ft 8¼in (2.65m)
Engine: EMD 12N-710G3B-EC
Horsepower: 3,300hp (2,462kW)
Electrical Equipment: EMD

Number	*Depot*	*Pool*	*Livery*	*Owner*	*Operator*	*Name*
66411	*Exported, working in Poland for Freightliner Poland as 66013FPL*					
66412	*Exported, working in Poland for Freightliner Poland as 66015FPL*					
66413	LD	DFIN	GYF	CBR	FLR	*Lest we Forget*
66414	LD	DFIN	FLP	HAL	FLR	
66415	LD	DFIN	GYF	HAL	FLR	*You Are Never Alone*
66416	LD	DFIN	FLP	HAL	FLR	
66417	*Exported, working in Poland for Freightliner Poland as 66014FPL*					
66418	LD	DFIN	FLP	HAL	FLR	*Patriot - In Memory of Fallen Railway Employees*
66419	LD	DFIN	GYF	HAL	FLR	
66420	LD	DFIN	FLP	HAL	FLR	

Freightliner

Class 66/5

Vehicle Length: 70ft 0½in (21.34m)
Height: 12ft 10in (3.91m)
Width: 8ft 8¼in (2.65m)
Engine: EMD 12N-710G3B-EC
Horsepower: 3,300hp (2,462kW)
Electrical Equipment: EMD

Number	Depot	Pool	Livery	Owner	Operator	Name
66501	LD	DFIM	FLR	PTR	FLR	Japan 2001
66502	LD	DFIM	FLR	PTR	FLR	Basford Hall Centenary 2001
66503	LD	DFIM	GYF	PTR	FLR	The Railway Magazine
66504	LD	DFIM	FLP	PTR	FLR	
66505	LD	DFIM	FLR	PTR	FLR	
66506	LD	DFIM	FLR	EVL	FLR	Crewe Regeneration
66507	LD	DFIM	FLR	EVL	FLR	
66508	LD	DFIM	FLR	EVL	FLR	
66509	LD	DFIM	FLR	EVL	FLR	
66510	LD	DFIM	FLR	EVL	FLR	
66511	LD	DFIM	FLR	EVL	FLR	
66512	LD	DFIM	FLR	EVL	FLR	
66513	LD	DFIM	FLR	EVL	FLR	
66514	LD	DFIM	FLR	EVL	FLR	
66515	LD	DFIM	FLR	EVL	FLR	
66516	LD	DFIM	FLR	EVL	FLR	
66517	LD	DFIM	FLR	EVL	FLR	
66518	LD	DFIM	FLR	EVL	FLR	
66519	LD	DFIM	FLR	EVL	FLR	
66520	LD	DFIM	FLR	EVL	FLR	
66522	LD	DFIM	FLR	EVL	FLR	
66523	LD	DFIM	FLR	EVL	FLR	
66524	LD	DFIM	FLR	EVL	FLR	
66525	LD	DFIM	FLR	EVL	FLR	
66526	LD	DFIM	FLR	PTR	FLR	Driver Steve Dunn (George)
66527	Exported, working in Poland for Freightliner Poland					
66528	LD	DFIM	FLP	PTR	FLR	Madge Elliot MBE Borders Railway Opening 2015
66529	LD	DFIM	FLR	PTR	FLR	
66530	Exported, working in Poland for Freightliner Poland					
66531	LD	DFIM	FLR	PTR	FLR	
66532	LD	DFIM	FLR	PTR	FLR	P&O Nedlloyd Atlas
66533	LD	DFIM	FLR	PTR	FLR	Hanjin Express / Senator Express
66534	LD	DFIM	FLR	PTR	FLR	OOCL Express
66535	Exported, working in Poland for Freightliner Poland					
66536	LD	DFIM	FLR	PTR	FLR	
66537	LD	DFIM	FLR	PTR	FLR	
66538	LD	DFIM	FLR	EVL	FLR	
66539	LD	DFIM	FLR	EVL	FLR	
66540	LD	DFIM	FLR	EVL	FLR	Ruby
66541	LD	DFIM	FLR	EVL	FLR	
66542	LD	DFIM	FLR	EVL	FLR	
66543	LD	DFIM	FLR	EVL	FLR	
66544	LD	DFIM	FLR	PTR	FLR	
66545	LD	DFIM	FLR	PTR	FLR	
66546	LD	DFIM	FLR	PTR	FLR	
66547	LD	DFIM	FLR	PTR	FLR	
66548	LD	DFIM	FLR	PTR	FLR	
66549	LD	DFIM	FLR	PTR	FLR	
66550	LD	DFIM	FLR	PTR	FLR	
66551	LD	DFIM	FLR	PTR	FLR	
66552	LD	DFIM	FLR	PTR	FLR	Maltby Raider
66553	LD	DFIM	FLR	PTR	FLR	
66554	LD	DFIM	FLR	EVL	FLR	
66555	LD	DFIM	FLR	EVL	FLR	
66556	LD	DFIM	FLR	EVL	FLR	
66557	LD	DFIM	FLR	EVL	FLR	
66558	LD	DFIM	FLR	EVL	FLR	
66559	LD	DFIM	FLR	EVL	FLR	
66560	LD	DFIM	FLR	EVL	FLR	

Freightliner

Right: *At the start of 2020, a fleet of 81 Class 66/4 and 66/5 'standard' locos were in traffic with Freightliner to power their Intermodal and Heavyhaul services. The majority of locos still sport Freightliner green and yellow, but repainting has commenced to apply Genesee & Wyoming orange and black colours. No. 66513 is shown in green and yellow colours, powering just one Freightliner bogie wagon at Colton Junction.* **CJM**

66561	LD	DFIM	FLR	EVL	FLR	
66562	LD	DFIM	FLR	EVL	FLR	
66563	LD	DFIM	FLR	EVL	FLR	
66564	LD	DFIM	FLR	EVL	FLR	
66565	LD	DFIM	FLR	EVL	FLR	
66566	LD	DFIM	FLR	EVL	FLR	
66567	LD	DFIM	FLR	EVL	FLR	
66568	LD	DFIM	FLR	EVL	FLR	
66569	LD	DFIM	FLR	EVL	FLR	
66570	LD	DFIM	FLR	EVL	FLR	
66571	LD	DFIM	FLR	EVL	FLR	
66572	LD	DFIM	FLR	EVL	FLR	
66582	*Exported, working in Poland for Freightliner Poland as 66009FPL*					
66583	*Exported, working in Poland for Freightliner Poland as 66010FPL*					
66584	*Exported, working in Poland for Freightliner Poland as 66011FPL*					
66585	LD	DFIN	FLR	HAL	FLR	
66586	*Exported, working in Poland for Freightliner Poland as 66008FPL*					
66587	LD	DFIN	ONE	HAL	FLR	*As One, We Can*
66588	LD	DFIN	FLR	HAL	FLR	
66589	LD	DFIN	FLR	HAL	FLR	
66590	LD	DFIN	FLR	HAL	FLR	
66591	LD	DFIN	FLR	MAG	FLR	
66592	LD	DFIN	FLR	MAG	FLR	*Johnson Stevens Agencies*
66593	LD	DFIN	FLR	MAG	FLR	*3MG Mersey Multimodal Gateway*
66594	LD	DFIN	FLR	MAG	FLR	*NYK Spirit of Kyoto*
66595	*Exported, working in Poland for Freightliner Poland as 66595FPL*					
66596	LD	DFIN	FLR	BEA	FLR	
66597	LD	DFIN	FLR	BEA	FLR	*Viridor*
66598	LD	DFIN	FLR	BEA	FLR	
66599	LD	DFIN	FLR	BEA	FLR	

Right: *Before the introduction of the latest Genesee & Wyoming orange and black livery, a number of Class 66s were painted in Freightliner Powerhaul colours, as demonstrated on No. 66528* Madge Elliot MBE. **CJM**

Freightliner

Class 66/6

Number	Depot	Pool	Livery	Owner	Operator	Name
66601	LD	DFHH	FLR	PTR	FLR	The Hope Valley
66602	LD	DFHH	FLR	PTR	FLR	
66603	LD	DFHH	FLR	PTR	FLR	
66604	LD	DFHH	FLR	PTR	FLR	
66605	LD	DFHH	FLR	PTR	FLR	
66606	LD	DFHH	FLR	PTR	FLR	
66607	LD	DFHH	FLR	PTR	FLR	
66608	*Exported, working in Poland for Freightliner Poland as 66603FPL*					
66609	*Exported, working in Poland for Freightliner Poland as 66605FPL*					
66610	LD	DFHH	FLR	PTR	FLR	
66611	*Exported, working in Poland for Freightliner Poland as 66604FPL*					
66612	*Exported, working in Poland for Freightliner Poland as 66606FPL*					
66613	LD	DFHH	FLR	PTR	FLR	
66614	LD	DFHH	FLR	PTR	FLR	1916 Poppy 2016
66615	LD	DFHH	FLR	PTR	FLR	
66616	LD	DFHH	FLR	PTR	FLR	
66617	LD	DFHH	FLR	PTR	FLR	
66618	LD	DFHH	FLR	PTR	FLR	Railways Illustrated Annual Photographic Awards - Alan Barnes
66619	LD	DFHH	FLR	PTR	FLR	Derek W. Johnson MBE
66620	LD	DFHH	FLR	PTR	FLR	
66621	LD	DFHH	FLR	PTR	FLR	
66622	LD	DFHH	FLR	PTR	FLR	
66623	LD	DFHH	GYF	EVL	FLR	
66624	*Exported, working in Poland for Freightliner Poland as 66602FPL*					
66625	*Exported, working in Poland for Freightliner Poland as 66601FPL*					

Left: *The new Genesee & Wyoming orange and black colours look very smart on the Class 66s, with the Freightliner name being retained on the front end and within the Genesee & Wyoming bodyside emblem. High output Class 66/6 No. 66623 is shown, clearly displaying the livery application, especially to the roof, which is now painted mid-grey.* **Derek Holmes**

Class 66/9

Number	Depot	Pool	Livery	Owner	Operator	Name
66951	LD	DFIN	FLR	EVL	FLR	
66952	LD	DFIN	FLR	EVL	FLR	
66953	LD	DFIN	FLR	BEA	FLR	
66954	*Exported, working in Poland for Freightliner Poland as 66954FPL*					
66955	LD	DFIN	FLR	BEA	FLR	
66956	LD	DFIN	FLR	BEA	FLR	
66957	LD	DFIN	FLR	BEA	FLR	Stephenson Locomotive Society 1909-2009

Right: *A batch of seven locos numbered in the 669xx series are in use. These are basically Class 66/5s. However, the first two were development locos for reduced emissions and were fitted with extra equipment. Standard loco No. 66957 is shown passing Reading.* **CJM**

Class 70 - PH37ACmi

Vehicle Length: 71ft 2½in (21.71m)
Height: 12ft 10in (3.91m)
Width: 8ft 8in (2.64m)
Engine: GE V16-cylinder PowerHaul 616
Horsepower: 3,700hp (2,750kW)
Electrical Equipment: General Electric

Number	*Depot*	*Pool*	*Livery*	*Owner*	*Operator*	*Name*
70001	LD	DFGI	FLP	MAG	FLR	*PowerHaul*
70002	LD	DFGI	FLP	MAG	FLR	
70003(S)	LD	DFGI	FLP	MAG	-	
70004(S)	LD	DFGI	FLP	MAG	-	*The Coal Industry Society*
70005(S)	LD	DFGI	FLP	MAG	-	
70006(S)	LD	DFGI	FLP	MAG	-	
70007	LD	DFGI	FLP	MAG	FLR	
70008	LD	DFGI	FLP	MAG	FLR	
70009(S)	LD	DFGI	FLP	MAG	-	
70010	LD	DFGI	FLP	MAG	FLR	
70011	LD	DFGI	FLP	MAG	FLR	
70013(S)	LD	DFGI	FLP	MAG	-	
70014	LD	DFGI	FLP	MAG	FLR	
70015	LD	DFGI	FLP	MAG	FLR	
70016	LD	DFGI	FLP	MAG	FLR	
70017(S)	LD	DFGI	FLP	MAG	-	
70018(S)	LD	DFGI	FLP	MAG	-	
70019(S)	LD	DFGI	FLP	MAG	-	
70020	LD	DFGI	FLP	MAG	FLR	

Right: *Freightliner have a fleet of 19 General Electric Class 70s, based at Leeds Midland Road. In early 2020 not all were in service, with several long out of service awaiting parts. It is understood that a number are to be returned to front line service to operate the new Mendip aggregate traffic flows. No. 70008 is seen stabled at Crewe.* **Antony Christie**

Class 86/6

Vehicle Length: 58ft 6in (17.83m)
Height: 13ft 0⅝in (3.97m)
Width: 8ft 8¼in (2.64m)
Power Collection: 25kV ac overhead
Horsepower: 5,900hp (4,400kW)
Electrical Equipment: GEC

Number		*Depot*	*Pool*	*Livery*	*Owner*	*Operator*
86604	(86404)	CB	DFNC	FLR	FLR	FLR
86605	(86405)	CB	DFNC	FLR	FLR	FLR
86607	(86407)	CB	DFNC	FLR	FLR	FLR
86608	(86501/86408)	CB	DFNC	FLR	FLR	FLR
86609	(86409)	CB	DFNC	FLR	FLR	FLR
86610(S)	(86410)	CB	DFNC	FLR	FLR	-

Freightliner

86612	(86412)	CB	DFNC	FLR	FLR	FLR
86613	(86413)	CB	DFNC	FLR	FLR	FLR
86614	(86414)	CB	DFNC	FLR	FLR	FLR
86622	(86422)	CB	DFNC	FLP	FLR	FLR
86627	(86427)	CB	DFNC	FLR	FLR	FLR
86628	(86428)	CB	DFNC	FLR	FLR	FLR
86632	(86432)	CB	DFNC	FLR	FLR	FLR
86637	(86437)	CB	DFNC	FLP	FLR	FLR
86638	(86438)	CB	DFNC	FLR	FLR	FLR
86639	(86439)	CB	DFNC	FLR	FLR	FLR

Left: *The 16 Class 86/6s currently owned and operated by Freightliner are likely to be replaced by 13 Class 90s transferred from Greater Anglia in the course of 2020. Currently the Class 86s, often working in pairs, provide traction for Freightliner services from the North-west to London and Ipswich, by way of the North London Line. A mix of standard Freightliner and Powerhaul liveries can be found. In this view, standard-liveried No. 86628 and Powerhaul-coloured No. 86637 pass Camden Road.* **Antony Christie**

Class 90

Vehicle Length: 61ft 6in (18.74m)
Height: 13ft 0¼in (3.96m)
Width: 9ft 0in (2.74m)
Power Collection: 25kV ac overhead
Horsepower: 7,860hp (5,860kW)
Electrical Equipment: GEC

Number	*Depot*	*Pool*	*Livery*	*Owner*	*Operator*
90016	CB	DFLC	FLR	FLR	FLR
90041	CB	DFLC	FLR	FLR	FLR
90042	CB	DFLC	FLP	FLR	FLR
90043	CB	DFLC	FLP	FLR	FLR
90044	CB	DFLC	GYF	FLR	FLR
90045	CB	DFLC	FLP	FLR	FLR
90046	CB	DFLC	FLR	FLR	FLR
90047	CB	DFLC	FLY	FLR	FLR
90048	CB	DFLC	FLY	FLR	FLR
90049	CB	DFLC	FLP	FLR	FLR

Left: *In early 2020, 10 Class 90s were in traffic with Freightliner, but this number is scheduled to rise after 13 Greater Anglia locos Nos. 90003-90015 are transferred in following displacement from Liverpool Street-Norwich services. Powerhaul-liveried No. 90045 is seen passing Longport light engine.* **Cliff Beeton**

SW1001 'Switcher'

Vehicle Length: 40ft 6in (12.34m)
Height: 14ft 3in (4.34m)
Width: 10ft 0in (3.04m)
Engine: GM 8-645E
Horsepower: 1,000hp (746kW)
Electrical Equipment: EMD

Number	*Depot*	*Pool*	*Livery*	*Owner*	*Operator*	*Name*
44	MD	-	FOS	FOS	MRL	*Western Yeoman II*
120	WH	-	HAN	HAN	MRL	*Kenneth John Witcombe*

Locomotive Services Ltd, Crewe

Address: Crewe Diesel Depot, Crewe
alex@iconsofsteam.com www.iconsofsteam.com

Facilities: Steam and diesel locomotive owner/operator **Managing Director:** Jeremy Hosking

Class 08

Vehicle Length: 29ft 3in (8.91m)
Height: 12ft 8⅝in (3.87m)
Width: 8ft 6in (2.59m)
Engine: English Electric 6K
Horsepower: 400hp (298kW)
Electrical Equipment: English Electric

Number	Depot	Pool	Livery	Owner	Operator
08631	CL	LSLO		LSL	LSL*
08737	CL	LSLO	GRN	LSL	LSL
08780	CL	LSLO	GRN	LSL	LSL

* At Weardale

Named: 08780 *Zippy*

Class 37

Vehicle Length: 61ft 6in (18.74m)
Height: 13ft 0¼in (3.96m)
Width: 8ft 11⅝in (2.73m)
Engine: English Electric 12CSVT
Horsepower: 1,750hp (1,304kW)
Electrical Equipment: English Electric

Number	Depot	Pool	Livery	Owner	Operator
37190	CL	LSLO	-	LSL	LSL
37521 (37117)	CL	LSLO	GRN	LSL	LSL
37667 (D6851)	CL	LSLO	GRN	LSL	LSL
37688 (37205)	CL	LSLS	TLF	D05	LSL

Class 40

Vehicle Length: 69ft 6in (21.18m)
Height: 12ft 10⅝in (3.92m)
Width: 9ft (2.74m)
Engine: EE 16SVT Mk3
Horsepower: 2,000hp (1,491kW)
Electrical Equipment: EE

Number	Depot	Pool	Livery	Owner	Operator	Name
40013 (D213)	CL	LSLO	GRN	LSL	-	*Aureol*

Class 47

Vehicle Length: 63ft 6in (19.35m)
Height: 12ft 10⅜in (3.91m)
Width: 9ft 2in (2.79m)
Electric Train Heat fitted
Engine: Sulzer 12LDA28C
Horsepower: 2,580hp (1,922kW)
Electrical Equipment: Brush

Number			Depot	Pool	Livery	Owner	Operator	Name/Note
47501	D1944		CL	LSLO	GRN	LSL	LSL	*Craftsman*
47614	D1733	(47141/853)	CL	LSLO	BLU	LSL	LSL	
47712		(47505)	CL	-	SCR	LSL	LSL	(18 month loan from 12/18)
47593		(47272/790)	CL	LSLO	BLL	LSL	LSL	*Galloway Princess*
47805	D1935	(47257/650)	CL	LSLO	GRN	LSL	LSL	*Roger Hosking MA 1925-2013*
47810		(47247/655)	CL	LSLO	GRN	LSL	LSL	*Crewe Diesel Depot*
47811(S)		(47128/656)	CL	-	GRN	-	-	
47816(S)		(47066/661)	CL	-	GRN	-	-	(For spares)
47841		(47134/622)	CL	LSLS	ICS	LSL	at Margate	*The Institution of Mechanical Engineers*

Right: *Locomotive Services Ltd, based at Crewe, are a Train Operating Company who have a fleet of superbly restored locos sporting various liveries. One of their main locos is Class 47 No. 47593 Galloway Princess which displays Large Logo Blue livery. The immaculate loco is seen passing Dawlish from its No. 2 end on 13 May 2019.* **CJM**

Class 55

Vehicle Length: 69ft 6in (21.18m)
Height: 12ft 11in (3.94m)
Width: 8ft 9½in (2.69m)
Engine: 2x Napier D18.25
Horsepower: 3,300hp (2,461kW)
Electrical Equipment: EE

Number	Depot	Pool	Livery	Owner	Operator	Name
55016 (D9016)	MAR	LSLS	GRN	LSL	-	*Gordon Highlander*
55022 (D9000)	CL	LSLS	GRN	LSL	-	*Royal Scots Grey*

Loco Services Ltd

Class 60

Vehicle Length: 70ft 0½in (21.34m)
Height: 12ft 10⅝in (3.92m)
Width: 8ft 8in (2.64m)
Engine: Mirrlees MB275T
Horsepower: 3,100hp (2,240kW)
Electrical Equipment: Brush

Number	*Depot*	*Pool*	*Livery*	*Owner*	*Operator*	*Name*
60081	MAR	LSLS	GRN	LSL	-	***Isambard Kingdon Brunel***

Class 86

Vehicle Length: 58ft 6in (17.83m)
Height: 13ft 0⅝in (3.97m)
Width: 8ft 8¼in (2.64m)
Power Collection: 25kV ac overhead
Horsepower: 5,900hp (4,400kW)
Electrical Equipment: GEC

Number	*Depot*	*Pool*	*Livery*	*Owner*	*Operator*	*Name*
86101	CL	LSLS	SCS	LSL	LSL	***Sir William Stanier FRS***

Class 87

Vehicle Length: 58ft 6in (17.83m)
Height: 13ft 1¼in (3.99m)
Width: 8ft 8¼in (2.64m)
Power Collection: 25kV ac overhead
Horsepower: 7,860hp (5,680kW)
Electrical Equipment: GEC

Number	*Depot*	*Pool*	*Livery*	*Owner*	*Operator*	*Name*
87002	CL	LSLS	SCS	LSL	LSL	***Royal Sovereign***

Class 90

Vehicle Length: 61ft 6in (18.74m)
Height: 13ft 0¼in (3.96m)
Width: 9ft 0in (2.74m)
Power Collection: 25kV ac overhead
Horsepower: 7,860hp (5,860kW)
Electrical Equipment: GEC

Number	*Depot*	*Pool*	*Livery*	*Owner*	*Operator*	*Notes*
90001	CL	LSLO	GAR	LSL	LSL	*Awaiting delivery from Greater Anglia*
90002	CL	LSLO	GAR	LSL	LSL	*Awaiting delivery from Greater Anglia*

Coaching Stock

Mk1
Vehicle Length: 64ft 6in (19.65m)
Height: 12ft 9½in (3.89m)
Width: 9ft 3in (2.81m)

Mk2
Vehicle Length: 66ft 0in (20.11m)
Height: 12ft 9½in (3.89m)
Width: 9ft 3in (2.81m)

Number	*Type*	*Depot*	*Livery*	*Operator*
1211 (3305)	AJ1F/RFB	CL	CAR	LSL
1659 (16509)	AJ41/RBR	CL	CAR	LSL
3229	AD1E/FO	CL	CAR	LSL
3231	AD1E/FO	CL	CAR	LSL
3312	AD1E/FO	CL	CAR	LSL
3344	AD1F/FO	CL	CAR	LSL
3438	AD1F/FO	CL	CAR	LSL
5366	AC2A/TSO	CL	CAR	LSL
5912	AD2F/TSO	CL	CAR	LSL
5991	AD2F/TSO	CL	CCM	LSL
6708	AN1F/RLO	CL	PUL	LSL
17080	AO3/BCK	CL	CAR	LSL
17159	AB1D/BFK	CL	CCM	LSL
35511 (17130)	AB5C	CL	BRN	LSL
80044 (1659)	AJ41/RBR	CL	CCM	LSL
99993 (5067)	Mk1 TSO	CL	CAR	LSL

Names applied
6708 ***Mount Helicon***

Above: *Locomotive Services Ltd coaching stock is restored to a superb condition, with the majority sporting carmine and cream livery. Most overhaul work is undertaken at Arlington Fleet Services, Eastleigh. Mk 1 Club Car No. M99993, a rebuilt TSO No. 5067, is seen at Crewe.* **Antony Christie**

Rail Operations Group (ROG)

Address: ✉ ROG, Wyvern House, Railway Terrace, Derby. DE1 2RU
enquiries@railopsgroup.co.uk ⓘ www.railopsgroup.co.uk

Managing Director: K Watts

Class 37

Vehicle Length: 61ft 6in (18.74m)
Height: 13ft 0¼in (3.96m)
Width: 8ft 11⅝in (2.73m)
Engine: Ruston
Horsepower: 1,750hp (1,304kW)
Electrical Equipment: English Electric

Number	*Depot*	*Pool*	*Livery*	*Owner*	*Name*	*Operator/Notes*
37608 (37512)	**LR**	**GROG**	**EPX**	**EPX**	***Andromeda***	**ROG drophead Dellner fitted**
37611 (37690)	**LR**	**GROG**	**EPX**	**EPX**	***Pegasus***	**ROG**
37800 (37143)	**LR**	**GROG**	**EPX**	**EPX**		**ROG drophead Dellner fitted**
37884 (37183)	**LR**	**GROG**	**EPX**	**EPX**	***Cepheus***	**ROG drophead Tightlock fitted**

Class 47

Vehicle Length: 63ft 6in (19.35m)
Height: 12ft 10⅜in (3.91m)
Width: 9ft 2in (2.79m)
Electric Train Heat fitted
Engine: Sulzer 12LDA28C
Horsepower: 2,580hp (1,922kW)
Electrical Equipment: Brush

Number	*Depot*	*Pool*	*Livery*	*Owner*	*Operator*	*Name*
47769 (47491)	**CP**	**RTLO**	**VIR**	**ROG**	**ROG**	
47812 D1916 (47657)	**LR**	**GROG**	**ROG**	**ROG**	**ROG**	
47813 (47129/658)	**LR**	**GROG**	**ROG**	**ROG**	**ROG**	***Jack Frost***
47815 D1748 (47660)	**LR**	**GROG**	**ROG**	**ROG**	**ROG**	***Lost Boys 68-88***
47843 (47623)	**LR**	**SROG**	**ROG**	**ROG**	**-**	
47847 (47577)	**LR**	**SROG**	**ROG**	**ROG**	**-**	
47848 (47632)	**LR**	**GROG**	**ROG**	**ROG**	**ROG**	

Left: *Rail Operations Group core loco fleet are Class 47s, repainted in their house colours with a stylish ROG branding. No. 47815* Lost Boys 68-88 *is seen powering two barrier vans to Laira, passing Dawlish. These locos are air brake only and have fully operational electric train supply.* **CJM**

ROG also operate under lease three Class 57s from DRS, Nos. 57301, 57305 and 57312.

Class 91

Vehicle Length: 63ft 8in (19.40m)
Height: 12ft 4in (3.75m)
Width: 9ft 0in (2.74m)
Power Collection: 25kV ac overhead
Horsepower: 6,300hp (4,700kW)
Electrical Equipment: GEC

Number	*Depot*	*Pool*	*Livery*	*Owner*	*Operator*	*Name*
91122 (91022)	**LR**	**SROG**	**LNE**	**ROG**	**ROG**	
91128 (91028)	**LR**	**SROG**	**LNE**	**ROG**	**ROG**	

To be used to power a new overhead power collection test train for Data Acquisition Services.

Class 93

Railway Operations Group have a fleet of 10 tri-mode diesel, electric and Lithium Titanate Oxide (LTO) battery, locos, to be classified as 93 from Stadler Rail, funded by Beacon Rail on order. The fleet is a development of the Class 88 and uses a Caterpillar engine. The electric output will be 5438hp, weight will be 97 tonnes, with a top speed of 110mph. No. 93001 *Mercury* should be delivered in late 2020.

Class 319 Orion

Railway Operations Group have formed a light freight business called Orion, which plans to run small containerised freight between London Gateway and London Liverpool Street three times each day. The trains will be formed of converted Class 319 sets Nos. 319365 and 319366, rebuilt as Class 769 'Flex' sets. They will be fitted with roller shutter side doors and strengthening to handle light freight.

319365	**77467+63047+71933+77466**	**LM**	**-**	**PTR**	**ROG**
319366	**77469+63048+71934+77468**	**-**	**-**	**PTR**	**ROG**

Eurotunnel (GetLink)

Address (UK): ✉ The Channel Tunnel Group Ltd, Ashford Road, Folkestone, CT18 8XX
info@eurotunnel.com ✆ 01303 282222 ⓘ www.eurotunnel.com

Chairman & CEO: Jacques Gounon **Depot:** Coquelles, France (CO)

Shuttle

All locomotives are allocated to the Eurotunnel Maintenance Facility in Coquelles, France, but can be stabled and receive light repair at the Cheriton terminal in the UK.

Class 9/0

Vehicle Length: 72ft 2in (22m) | Height: 13ft 9in (4.20m) | Width: 9ft 9in (3.01m) | Power Collection: 25kV ac overhead | Horsepower: 7,720hp (5,760kW) | Electrical Equipment: Brush

Original loco order, many now rebuilt and upgraded to Class 9/8.

Left: *Cross Channel Eurotunnel (GetLink) services are in the hands of three sub-classes of Class 9 tri-bo locos, operating 'top and tail' on passenger or freight formations. Class 9/0 No. 9011* José Van Dam *is seen on the rear of a shuttle at the Cheriton terminal in Folkestone.* **Howard Lewsey**

9005	*Jessye Norman*	9018	*Wilhelmena Fernandez*	9033	*Montserrat Caballé*
9007	*Dame Joan Sutherland*	9022	*Dame Janet Baker*	9036	*Alain Fondary*
9011	*José Van Dam*	9024	*Gotthard 1882*	9037	*Gabriel Bacquier*
9013	*Maria Callas*	9026	*Furkatunnel 1982*		
9015	*Lötschberg 1913*	9029	*Thomas Allen*		

Class 9/7

Vehicle Length: 72ft 2in (22m) | Height: 13ft 9in (4.20m) | Width: 9ft 9in (3.01m) | Power Collection: 25kV ac overhead | Horsepower: 9,387hp (7,000kW) | Electrical Equipment: Brush

9701	9704	9707	9713 (9103)	9716 (9106)	9719 (9109)	9722 (9112)
9702	9705	9711 (9101)	9714 (9104)	9717 (9107)	9720 (9110)	9723 (9113)
9703	9706	9712 (9102)	9715 (9105)	9718 (9108)	9721 (9111)	

Class 9/8

Rebuilt from Class 9/0 locos; 800 added to original running number on conversion.

Vehicle Length: 72ft 2in (22m) | Height: 13ft 9in (4.20m) | Width: 9ft 9in (3.01m) | Power Collection: 25kV ac overhead | Horsepower: 9,387hp (7,000kW) | Electrical Equipment: Brush

9801	*Lesley Garrett*	9814	*Lucia Popp*	9828	*Dame Kiri Te Kanawa*
9802	*Stuart Burrows*	9816	*Willard White*	9831	
9803	*Benjamin Luxon*	9819	*Maria Ewing*	9832	*Renata Tebaldi*
9804		9820	*Nicolai Ghiaurov*	9834	*Mirella Freni*
9806	*Régine Crespin*	9821	*Teresa Berganza*	9835	*Nicolai Gedda*
9808	*Elisabeth Soderstrom*	9823	*Dame Elisabeth Legge-Schwarzkopf*	9838	*Hildegard Behrens*
9809	*François Pollet*			9840	
9810	*Jean-Philippe Courtis*	9825			
9812	*Luciano Pavarotti*	9827	*Barbara Hendricks*		

MaK DE1004

Vehicle Length: 54ft 2in (16.50m) | Horsepower: 1,260hp (939.5kW) | Diesel Engine: MTU 12V396tc | Electrical Equipment: BBC

0001 (21901)	0003 (21903)	0005 (21905)	0007 (21907) [6457]	0009 (21909) [6451]
0002 (21902)	0004 (21904)	0006 (21906) [6456]	0008 (21908) [6450]	0010 (21910) [6457]

Hunslet/Schöma

Diesel Engine: Deutz | Horsepower: 200hp (270kW) | Mechanical Equipment: Hunslet

0031	0032	0033	0034	0035	0036	0037	0038	0039	0040	0041	0042

In November 2018 Eurotunnel ordered a new fleet of 19 two-axle 40 ton locos from Socofer. They will be battery powered with a diesel engine used to charge the batteries if needed, usually charging will be from an external supply. Delivery is expected in 2021.

Network Rail

Address: 1 Eversholt Street, London NW1 2DN
ⓘ www.networkrail.co.uk
✆ Helpline: 08457 114141, Switchboard: 020 7557 8000

Chief Executive: Andrew Haines OBE

Depots: Heaton (HT), Barrow Hill (BH), Derby (DF), Rugby (RU), Eastleigh (ZG)

Class 08

Vehicle Length: 29ft 3in (8.91m)
Height: 12ft 8⅝in (3.87m)
Width: 8ft 6in (2.59m)
Engine: English Electric 6K
Horsepower: 400hp (298kW)
Electrical Equipment: English Electric

Number	*Depot*	*Pool*	*Livery*	*Owner*	*Operator*
08417	DF	QADD	NRL	NRL	NRL
08956§	DF	QADD	GRN	NRL	NRL

§ At Bombardier, Old Dalby test centre

Class 43

Vehicle Length: 58ft 5in (18.80m)
Height: 12ft 10in (3.90m)
Width: 8ft 11in (2.73m)
Engine: MTU 16V4000 R31R
Horsepower: 2,250hp (1,680kW)
Electrical Equipment: Brush

Number	*Depot*	*Pool*	*Livery*	*Owner*	*Operator*	*Name*
43013	ZA	QCAR	NRL	PTR	NRL	*Mark Carne CBE*
43014	ZA	QCAR	NRL	PTR	NRL	*The Railway Observer*
43062	ZA	QCAR	NRL	PTR	NRL	*John Armitt*

Right: *The so called 'New Measurement Train', operated by Network Rail and based at Derby is an HST set with various instrumentation vehicles marshalled between two power cars. These have received some attention and have MTU power units and forward facing cameras with a high-level marker light. The set is recorded passing Longport with Class 43 No. 43063* John Armitt *on the rear, this is the only one of the three PCs not to have buffers. Fleet maintained by Loram at Derby* **Cliff Beeton**

Class 73/1 & 73/9

Vehicle Length: 53ft 8in (16.35m)
Height: 12ft 5$\frac{5}{16}$in (3.79m)
Width: 8ft 8in (2.64m)
Power: 750V dc third rail or English Electric 6K
Horsepower: electric - 1,600hp (1,193kW)
diesel - 600hp (447kW)
Electrical Equipment: English Electric
Class 73/9 rebuilt with 2 x Cummins CSK19 755hp engines and revised electric equipment

Number	*Depot*	*Pool*	*Livery*	*Owner*	*Operator*	*Name*
73138(S)	DF	QADD	NRL	NRL	-	
73951 (73104)	DF	QADD	NRL	NRL	NRL	*Malcolm Brinded*
73952 (73211)	DF	QADD	NRL	NRL	NRL	*Janice King*

Right: *Three Class 73s are owned by Network Rail, one standard Class 73/1 No. 73138 which is currently stored and two modified Class 73/95s, each now has a pair of Cummins QS19 engines giving a total output of 1,510hp (1,111kW). The pair, based at Derby, usually 'top and tail' Network Rail test trains. The pair are seen passing Kidsgrove with a test special from the Liverpool area.* **Cliff Beeton**

Network Rail

Class 37 & 97/3

Vehicle Length: 61ft 6in (18.74m)
Height: 13ft 0¼in (3.96m)
Width: 8ft 11⅝in (2.73m)
Engine: English Electric 12CSVT
Horsepower: 1,750hp (1,304kW)
Electrical Equipment: English Electric

Number	*Depot*	*Pool*	*Livery*	*Owner*	*Operator*	*Name*
37198(S)	ZA	MBDL	NRL	NRL	-	***Chief Engineer*** *(spares doner)*
97301 (37100)§	ZA	QETS	NRL	NRL	NRL	
97302 (37170)±	ZA	QETS	NRL	NRL	NRL	***Rheilffyrdd Ffestiniog ac Eryri Ffestiniog & Welsh Highland Railways***
97303 (37178)±	ZA	QETS	NRL	NRL	NRL	
97304 (37217)±	ZA	QETS	NRL	NRL	NRL	***John Tiley***

§ Fitted with Hitachi ERTMS, ± Fitted with Ansaldo ERTMS

Left: *Four Class 97/3 locos, rebuilt from Class 37s are operated by Network Rail and were converted as test beds for European Rail Traffic Management System's on the Cambrian route. The four locos sport NR yellow livery and are used for engineering train and departmental train use. No. 97304* John Tiley *is shown from its No. 2 end.* **Howard Lewsey**

Class 313/1

Vehicle Length: (Driving) 64ft 11½in (19.80m)
(Inter) 65ft 4¼in (19.92m)
Height: 11ft 9in (3.58m)
Width: 9ft 3in (2.82m)
Horsepower: 880hp (656kW)

ERTMS development unit

Number	*Formation* DMSO+PTSO+BDMSO	*Depot*	*Livery*	*Owner*	*Operator*
313121(S)	62549+71233+61613	-	YEL	BEA	NRL (stored at Eastleigh)

Class 950

Vehicle Length: 64ft 9¾in (19.74m)
Height: 12ft 4½in (3.77m)
Width: 9ft 3⅛in (2.82m)
Engine: 1 x NT855R5 of 285hp per vehicle
Horsepower: 570hp (425kW)
Seats (total/car): 124S, 59S/65S

Number	*Formation*	*Depot*	*Livery*	*Owner*	*Operator*	*Note*
950001	999600+999601	ZA	NRL	NRL	NRL	Track assessment train (Class 150 outline)

Hauled Stock

Royal Train

Mk2
Vehicle Length: 66ft 0in (20.11m)
Height: 12ft 9½in (3.89m)
Width: 9ft 3in (2.81m)

Mk 3
Vehicle Length: 75ft 0in (22.86m)
Height: 12ft 9in (3.88m)
Width: 8ft 11in (2.71m)

Number	*Type*	*Depot*	*Livery*	*Operator*	*Use*
2903 (11001)	AT5G	ZN	ROY	NRL/DBC	HM The Queen's Saloon
2904 (12001)	AT5G	ZN	ROY	NRL/DBC	HRH The Duke of Edinburgh's Saloon
2915 (10735)	AT5G	ZN	ROY	NRL/DBC	Royal Household Sleeping Coach
2916 (40512)	AT5G	ZN	ROY	NRL/DBC	HRH The Prince of Wales's Dining Coach
2917 (40514)	AT5G	ZN	ROY	NRL/DBC	Kitchen Car and Royal Household Dining Coach
2918 (40515)	AT5G	ZN	ROY	NRL/DBC	Royal Household Coach
2919 (40518)	AT5G	ZN	ROY	NRL/DBC	Royal Household Coach
2920 (17109)	AT5B	ZN	ROY	NRL/DBC	Generator Coach and Household Sleeping Coach
2921 (17107)	AT5B	ZN	ROY	NRL/DBC	Brake, Coffin Carrier and Household Accommodation
2922	AT5G	ZN	ROY	NRL/DBC	HRH The Prince of Wales's Sleeping Coach
2923	AT5G	ZN	ROY	NRL/DBC	HRH The Prince of Wales's Saloon Coach

Right: *The UK Royal Train fleet of 11 vehicles, based at Wolverton is managed by Network Rail and operated on the main lines by DB-Cargo, using a pair of dedicated Class 67s Nos. 67005 and 67006. Here, HRH The Duke of Edinburgh's saloon No. 2904 is illustrated, this was a rebuild of prototype HST TS No. 12001.* **CJM**

Hauled Stock

Number	Type	Depot	Livery	Operator	Use
1256 (3296)	AJIF/RFO	ZA	NRL	NRL	PLPR3
5981	AC2F/TSO	ZA	NRL	NRL	PLPR2
6260 (92116)	AX51/GEN	ZA	NRL	NRL	Generator
6261 (92988)	AX51/GEN	ZA	NRL	NRL	Generator
6262 (92928)	AX51/GEN	ZA	NRL	NRL	Generator
6263 (92961)	AX51/GEN	ZA	NRL	NRL	Generator
6264 (92923)	AX51/GEN	ZA	NRL	NRL	Generator
9481	AE2D/BSO	ZA	NRL	NRL	Support vehicle
9516	AE2D/BSO	ZA	NRL	NRL	Brake force runner
9523	AE2D/BSO	ZA	NRL	NRL	Brake force runner
9701 (9528)	AF2F/DBSO	ZA	NRL	NRL	Remote driving car
9702 (9510)	AF2F/DBSO	ZA	NRL	NRL	Remote driving car
9703 (9517)	AF2F/DBSO	ZA	NRL	NRL	Remote driving car
9708 (9530)	AF2F/DBSO	ZA	NRL	NRL	Remote driving car
9713 (9535)	AF2F/DBSO	ZA	NRL	NRL	Remote driving car
9714 (9536)	AF2F/DBSO	ZA	NRL	NRL	Remote driving car
9801 (5760)	AN1F/BUO	ZA	CAS	NRL	Support vehicle
62287	MBS/CIG	ZA	NRL	NRL	Ultrasonic test car UTU2
62384	MBS/CIG	ZA	NRL	NRL	Ultrasonic test car UTU1
72612 (6156)	Mk2f/TSO	ZA	NRL	NRL	Brake force runner
72616 (6007)	Mk2f/TSO	ZA	NRL	NRL	Brake force runner
72630 (6094)	Mk2f/TSO	ZA	NRL	NRL	Structure Gauging Train 1
72631 (6096)	Mk2f/TSO	ZA	NRL	NRL	PLPR1
72639 (6070)	Mk2f/TSO	ZA	NRL	NRL	PLPR4
82111	MK3/DVT	CS	NRL	NRL	Driving Van Trailer
82115	MK3/DVT	ZA	VIR	NRL	Driving Van Trailer
82124	MK3/DVT	ZA	NRL	NRL	Driving Van Trailer
82129	MK3/DVT	CS	NRL	NRL	Driving Van Trailer
82145	MK3/DVT	CS	NRL	NRL	Driving Van Trailer
92114 (81443)	Mk1/BG	ZA	NRL	-	Special vehicle (stored)

Right: *Network Rail operates a sizeable fleet of ex revenue earning vehicles, which are now in departmental services performing a number of different tasks. The majority are painted in Network Rail yellow and often operate in semi-fixed formations depending on the type of test work being undertaken. Car No. 6264, a generator vehicle, converted from BG No. 92923 is shown, considerable modification to the body has been made from its revenue earning days.* **Antony Christie**

Network Rail

92939 (92039)	Mk1/BG	ZA	INT	NRL	Special vehicle
99666 (3250)	Mk2e/FO	ZA	NRL	NRL	Structure Gauging Train 1 (barrier)
971001 (94150)	Mk1/NKA	SP	NRL	NRL	Tool Van
971002 (94190)	Mk1/NKA	SP	NRL	NRL	Tool Van
971003 (94191)	Mk1/NKA	BS	NRL	NRL	Tool Van
971004 (94168)	Mk1/NKA	SP	NRL	NRL	Tool Van
975025 (60755)	6B Buffet	ZA	GRN	NRL	Control Inspection Saloon *Caroline*
975081 (35313)	Mk1/BSK	ZA	NRL	-	Former Structure Gauging Train (stored)
975087 (9)	MK1/BSK	SP	NRL	NRL	Recovery train support coach
975091 (34615)	Mk1/BSK	ZA	NRL	NRL	Overhead line test coach *Mentor*
975464 (35171)	Mk1/BSK	SP	NRL	NRL	Snowblower coach *Ptarmigan*
975477 (35108)	MK1/BSK	SP	NRL	NRL	Recovery train support coach
975486 (34100)	Mk1/BSK	SP	NRL	NRL	Snowblower coach *Polar Bear*
975814 (41000)	HST/TF	ZA	NRL	NRL	NMT Conference coach
975984 (40000)	HST/TRUB	ZA	NRL	NRL	NMT Lecture coach
977868 (5846)	Mk2e/TSO	ZA	NRL	NRL	Radio Survey coach
977869 (5858)	Mk2e/TSO	ZA	NRL	NRL	Radio Survey coach (stored)
977969 (14112)	Mk2/BFK	ZA	NRL	NRL	Staff coach (former Royal Saloon 2906)
977974 (5854)	Mk2e/TSO	ZA	NRL	NRL	Track Inspection coach (TIC 1)
977983 (72503)	Mk2f/FO	ZA	NRL	NRL	Overhead Line Inspection EMV (ex FO 3407)
977984 (40501)	HST/TRFK	ZA	NRL	NRL	NMT Staff coach
977985 (72715)	Mk2f/TSO	ZA	NRL	NRL	Structure Gauging Train (SGT2) (ex TSO 6019)
977986 (3189)	Mk2d/FO	ZA	NRL	NRL	Structure Gauging Train 2 (barrier)
977993 (44053)	HST/TGS	ZA	NRL	NRL	NMT Overhead Line Test coach
977994 (44087)	HST/TGS	ZA	NRL	NRL	NMT Recording coach
977995 (40719)	HST/TRFM	ZA	NRL	NRL	NMT Generator coach
977997 (72613)	Mk2f/TSO	ZA	NRL	NRL	Radio Survey Test Vehicle (originally TSO 6126)
999550	Mk2	ZA	NRL	NRL	Track Recording coach (purpose-built) HSTRC
999602 (62384)	Mk1/CIG	ZA	NRL	NRL	Ultrasonic Test coach - UTU3
999605 (62482)	Mk1/REP	ZA	NRL	NRL	Ultrasonic Test coach
999606 (62356)	Mk1/CIG	ZA	NRL	NRL	Ultrasonic Test coach - UTU4

Left Upper: *Track Inspection Coach 2, No. 977974, is a rebuild from Mk2e TSO No. 5854. This vehicle shows some recently applied graphics explaining what these vehicles do.* **Antony Christie**

Left Lower: *This former 'Hastings' line buffet and then the Southern Region General Managers saloon was upon privatisation transferred to Network Rail as an inspection saloon. It has been modified in recent years but retains its blue star push-pull controls, whereby the driving position in the saloon can control the propelling loco. The saloon is seen at Evesham.* **CJM**

Snowploughs

Independent Drift Ploughs – ZZA

Number	Allocation
ADB965203	Carlisle
ADB965206	York
ADB965208	Norwich
ADB965209	Motherwell
ADB965210	Tonbridge
ADB965211	Tonbridge
ADB965217	York
ADB965219	Norwich
ADB965223	Taunton
ADB965224	Inverness
ADB965230	Inverness
ADB965231	Motherwell
ADB965232	Peterborough
ADB965233	Crewe
ADB965234	Carlisle
ADB965235	Taunton
ADB965236	Tonbridge
ADB965237	Tonbridge
ADB965240	York
ADB965241	York
ADB965242	Carlisle
ADB965243	Slateford

Independent 'Drift' snowplough No. ADB965223 is seen at Taunton after refurbishment in April 2019. **Brian Garrett**

Beilhack Patrol Ploughs (ex-Class 40/45§ bogies) – ZZA

Number	Allocation
ADB965576	Doncaster
ADB965577	Doncaster
ADB965578	Carlisle
ADB965579	Carlisle
ADB965580	Wigan
ADB965581	Wigan
ADB966098§	Doncaster
ADB966099§	Doncaster

Left: *Four pairs of former 1Co loco bogies have been adapted as patrol snowploughs. Three pairs numbered in the 965xxx series are from Class 40 locos, while the two in the 966 number series are former Class 45 bogies. Ex Class 40 plough No. ADB965577 is seen in Doncaster West Yard in summer 2019.* **CJM**

Beilhack Snow Blowers – ZWA

Number	Allocation
ADB968500	Rutherglen
ADB968501	Rutherglen

Network Rail

Track Machines and Mechanical Plant

Left: *Painted in Balfour Beatty blue and white livery, Plasser & Theurer DTS-62-N Dynamic Stabiliser is shown on display at Long Marston in June 2019.* **CJM**

Number	Type	Operator
DR72211	Plasser & Theurer DTS-62-N – Dynamic Stabiliser	Balfour Beatty
DR72213	Plasser & Theurer DTS-62-N – Dynamic Stabiliser	Balfour Beatty
DR73108 *Tiger*	Plasser & Theurer 09-32-RT – Tamper/Liner	Colas
DR73109	Plasser & Theurer 09-3X – Tamper/Liner	SB Rail
DR73110 *Peter White*	Plasser & Theurer 09-3X – Tamper/Liner	SB Rail
DR73111	Plasser & Theurer 09-3X-D-RT – Tamper/Liner	Network Rail
DR73113 *Dai Evans*	Plasser & Theurer 09-3X-D-RT – Tamper/Liner	Network Rail
DR73114 *Ron Henderson*	Plasser & Theurer 09-3X-D-RT – Tamper/Liner	Network Rail
DR73115	Plasser & Theurer 09-3X-D-RT – Tamper/Liner	Network Rail
DR73116	Plasser & Theurer 09-3X-D-RT – Tamper/Liner	Network Rail
DR73117	Plasser & Theurer 09-3X-D-RT – Tamper/Liner	Network Rail
DR73118	Plasser & Theurer 09-3X-D-RT – Tamper/Liner	Network Rail
DR73120 (99 70 9123-120-6)	Plasser & Theurer 09-3x – Dynamic Tamper/Liner	Network Rail
DR73121 (99 70 9123 121-4)	Plasser & Theurer 09-3x – Dynamic Tamper/Liner	Network Rail
DR73122 (99 70 9123 122-2)	Plasser & Theurer 09-3x – Dynamic Tamper/Liner	Network Rail
DR73803 *Alexander Graham Bell*	Plasser & Theurer 08-32U RT – Plain Line Tamper	Babcock
DR73804 *James Watt*	Plasser & Theurer 08-16U RT – Plain Line Tamper	Babcock
DR73805	Plasser & Theurer 08-16(32)U RT – Plain Line Tamper	Colas
DR73806 *Karine*	Plasser & Theurer 08-16(32)U RT – Plain Line Tamper	Colas
DR73904 *Thomas Telford*	Plasser & Theurer 08-4x4/4S - RT – S&C Tamper	Babcock
DR73905	Plasser & Theurer 08-4x4/4S - RT – S&C Tamper	Colas
DR73906 *Panther*	Plasser & Theurer 08-4x4/4S - RT – S&C Tamper	Colas
DR73907	Plasser & Theurer 08-4x4/4S - RT – S&C Tamper	Colas
DR73908	Plasser & Theurer 08-4x4/4S - RT – S&C Tamper	Colas
DR73909 *Saturn*	Plasser & Theurer 08-4x4/4S - RT – S&C Tamper	Colas
DR73910 *Jupiter*	Plasser & Theurer 08-4x4/4S - RT – S&C Tamper	Colas
DR73911 *Puma*	Plasser & Theurer 08-16/4x4 C/RT – S&C Tamper	Colas
DR73912 *Lynx*	Plasser & Theurer 08-16/4x4 C/RT – S&C Tamper	Colas

DR73913	Plasser & Theurer 08-16/4x4 C/RT – S&C Tamper	Colas
DR73914	Plasser & Theurer 08-4x4S - RT – S&C Tamperr	Babcock
Robert McAlpine		
DR73915	Plasser & Theurer 08-16/4x4C - RT – S&C Tamper	Babcock
William Arrol		
DR73916	Plasser & Theurer 08-16/4x4C - RT – S&C Tamper	Babcock
First Engineering		
DR73917	Plasser & Theurer 08-4x4S - RT – S&C Tamper	Balfour Beatty
DR73918	Plasser & Theurer 08-4x4S - RT – S&C Tamper	Balfour Beatty
DR73919	Plasser & Theurer 08-16/4x4 C100 - RT – Tamper	Colas
DR73920	Plasser & Theurer 08-16/4x4C80 - RT – Tamper	Colas
DR73921	Plasser & Theurer 08-16/4x4C80 - RT – Tamper	Colas
DR73922	Plasser & Theurer 08-16/4x4C80 - RT – Tamper	Colas
John Snowdon		
DR73923	Plasser & Theurer 08-4x4S - RT – S&C Tamperr	Colas
Mercury		
DR73924	Plasser & Theurer 08-16/4x4 C100 - RT – Tamper	Colas
DR73925	Plasser & Theurer 08-16/4x4 C100 - RT – Tamper	Colas
Europa		
DR73926	Plasser & Theurer 08-16/4x4 C100 - RT – Tamper	Balfour Beatty
Stephen Keith Blanchard		
DR73927	Plasser & Theurer 08-16/4x4 C100 - RT – Tamper	Balfour Beatty
DR73928	Plasser & Theurer 08-16/4x4 C100 - RT – Tamper	Balfour Beatty
DR73929	Plasser & Theurer 08-4x4S - RT – S&C Tamperr	Colas
DR73930	Plasser & Theurer 08-4x4S - RT – S&C Tamperr	Colas
DR73931	Plasser & Theurer 08-16/4x4C100 - RT – Tamper	Colas
DR73932	Plasser & Theurer 08-4x4/4S - RT – S&C Tamper	Babcock
DR73933	Plasser & Theurer 08-16/4x4C100 - RT – Tamper	Babcock
DR73934	Plasser & Theurer 08-16/4x4C100 - RT – Tamper	Babcock
DR73935	Plasser & Theurer 08-4x4/4S - RT – S&C Tamper	Colas
DR73936	Plasser & Theurer 08-4x4/4S - RT – S&C Tamper	Colas
DR73937	Plasser & Theurer 08-16/4x4 C100 - RT – Tamper	Balfour Beatty
DR73938	Plasser & Theurer 08-16/4x4 C100 - RT – Tamper	Balfour Beatty
DR73939	Plasser & Theurer 08-16/4x4 C100 - RT – Tamper	Balfour Beatty
Pat Best		
DR73940	Plasser & Theurer 08-4x4/4S - RT – S&C Tamper	Babcock
DR73941	Plasser & Theurer 08-4x4/4S - RT – S&C Tamper	Babcock
DR73942	Plasser & Theurer 08-4x4/4S - RT – S&C Tamper	Colas
DR73943	Plasser & Theurer 08-16/4x4C100 - RT – Tamper	Balfour Beatty
DR73944	Plasser & Theurer 08-16/4x4C100 - RT – Tamper	Balfour Beatty
DR73945	Plasser & Theurer 08-16/4x4C100 - RT – Tamper	Balfour Beatty
DR73946	Plasser & Theurer Euromat 08-4x4/4S	VolkerRail
DR73947	Plasser & Theurer 08-4x4/4S - RT – S&C Tamper	Colas
DR73948	Plasser & Theurer 08-4x4/4S - RT – S&C Tamper	Colas
DR75301	Matisa B45 Tamper	VolkerRail
DR75302	Matisa B45 Tamper	VolkerRail
Gary Wright		
DR75303	Matisa B45 Tamper	VolkerRail
DR75401	Matisa B41UE Tamper	VolkerRail
DR75402	Matisa B41UE Tamper	VolkerRail
DR75404	Matisa B41UE Tamper	VolkerRail
DR75405	Matisa B41UE Tamper	VolkerRail

Right: *Plasser & Theurer 08-16/ 4x4C80 - RT – Tamper No. DR73922, owned and operated by Colas, carries the cast nameplate* John Snowdon. *The vehicle is seen stabled adjacent to Chester station.*
Antony Christie

Network Rail

Left: *Owned by Network Rail, No. DR73121 is a Plasser & Theurer 09-3x – Dynamic Tamper/Liner and is usually found working in the Western area, often from Reading depot. This vehicle also carries its international identity of 99 70 9123 121-4. It is seen at Westbury.* **Antony Christie**

DR75406 *Eric Machell*	Matisa B41UE Tamper	Colas
DR75407 *Gerry Taylor*	Matisa B41UE Tamper	Colas
DR75408	Matisa B41UE Tamper	Balfour Beatty
DR75409	Matisa B41UE Tamper	Balfour Beatty
DR75410	Matisa B41UE Tamper	Balfour Beatty
DR75411	Matisa B41UE Tamper	Balfour Beatty
DR75501	Matisa B66UC Tamper	Balfour Beatty
DR75502	Matisa B66UC Tamper	Balfour Beatty
DR76323	Plasser & Theurer RM95RT Ballast Cleaner	Network Rail
DR76324	Plasser & Theurer RM95RT Ballast Cleaner	Network Rail
DR76501 (HOBC-1)	Plasser & Theurer RM900RT Ballast Cleaner	Network Rail
DR76502 (HOBC-2)	Plasser & Theurer RM900RT Ballast Cleaner	Network Rail
DR76503 (HOBC-3)	Plasser & Theurer RM900RT Ballast Cleaner	Network Rail
DR76504 99 70 9314 504-0 (HOBC-4)	Plasser & Theurer RM900RT Ballast Cleaner	Network Rail
DR76701 (HOBC-3)	Plasser & Theurer VM80	Network Rail
DR76702 (HOBC-2)	Plasser & Theurer VM80	Network Rail
DR76703 (HOBC-1)	Plasser & Theurer VM80	Network Rail
DR76750 (HRTRT-2)	Matisa D75 Undercutter	Network Rail
DR76751 (HRTRT-1)	Matisa D75 Undercutter	Network Rail
DR76801 (HOBC-3)	Plasser & Theurer 09-16 CM NR	Network Rail
DR76802 99 70 9329 802-0 (HOBC-4)	Plasser & Theurer 09-16 CM NR	Network Rail
DR76901 (99 70 9131 001) *Brunel*	Windhoff MPV - High Output Plant System (GW electrification train)	Network Rail
DR76903 (99 70 9131 003)	Windhoff MPV - High Output Plant System (GW electrification train)	Network Rail
DR76905 (99 70 9131 005)	Windhoff MPV - High Output Plant System (GW electrification train)	Network Rail
DR76906 (99 70 9131 006)	Windhoff MPV - High Output Plant System (GW electrification train)	Network Rail
DR76910 (99 70 9131 010)	Windhoff MPV - High Output Plant System (GW electrification train)	Network Rail
DR76911 (99 70 9131 011)	Windhoff MPV - High Output Plant System (GW electrification train)	Network Rail
DR76913 (99 70 9131 013)	Windhoff MPV - High Output Plant System (GW electrification train)	Network Rail
DR76914 (99 70 9131 014)	Windhoff MPV - High Output Plant System (GW electrification train)	Network Rail
DR76915 (99 70 9131 015)	Windhoff MPV - High Output Plant System (GW electrification train)	Network Rail
DR76916 (99 70 9131 016)	Windhoff MPV - High Output Plant System (GW electrification train)	Network Rail
DR76920 (99 70 9131 020)	Windhoff MPV - High Output Plant System (GW electrification train)	Network Rail
DR76921 (99 70 9131 021)	Windhoff MPV - High Output Plant System (GW electrification train)	Network Rail
DR76922 (99 70 9131 022)	Windhoff MPV - High Output Plant System (GW electrification train)	Network Rail
DR76923 (99 70 9131 023) *Gavin Roberts*	Windhoff MPV - High Output Plant System (GW electrification train)	Network Rail

DR77001 Plasser & Theurer AFM 2000 RT – Finishing Machine Babcock
Anthony Lou Phillips
DR77002 Plasser & Theurer AFM 2000 RT – Finishing Machine Babcock
DR77010 Plasser & Theurer USP 6000 – Ballast Regulator Network Rail
99 70 9125 010-7
DR77315(S) Plasser & Theurer USP 5000C – Ballast Regulator Balfour Beatty
DR77316(S) Plasser & Theurer USP 5000C – Ballast Regulator Balfour Beatty
DR77322(S) Plasser & Theurer USP 5000C – Ballast Regulator Balfour Beatty
DR77327 Plasser & Theurer USP 5000C – Ballast Regulator Colas
DR77336(S) Plasser & Theurer USP 5000C – Ballast Regulator Balfour Beatty
DR77801 Matisa R24S – Ballast Regulator VolkerRail
DR77802 Matisa R24S – Ballast Regulator VolkerRail
DR77901 Plasser & Theurer USP 5000RT – Ballast Regulator Colas
DR77903 Plasser & Theurer USP 5000RT – Ballast Regulator Network Rail
DR77904 Plasser & Theurer USP 5000RT – Ballast Regulator Network Rail
DR77905 Plasser & Theurer USP 5000RT – Ballast Regulator Network Rail
DR77906 Plasser & Theurer USP 5000RT – Ballast Regulator Network Rail
DR77907 Plasser & Theurer USP 5000RT – Ballast Regulator Network Rail
DR77908 Plasser & Theurer USP 5000RT – Ballast Regulator Babcock
(Previously DR77902)
DR77909 Plasser & Theurer USP 5000RT – Ballast Regulator Network Rail
99 70 9125 909-0
DR78213 Plasser & Theurer Self-Propelled Twin Jib Crane VolkerRail
DR78215 Plasser & Theurer Self-Propelled Twin Jib Crane Babock
DR78216(S) Plasser & Theurer Self-Propelled Twin Jib Crane Balfour Beatty
DR78217(S) Plasser & Theurer Self-Propelled Twin Jib Crane Babock
DR78218(S) Plasser & Theurer Self-Propelled Twin Jib Crane Balfour Beatty
DR78219 Plasser & Theurer Self-Propelled Twin Jib Crane Babock
DR78221 Plasser & Theurer Self-Propelled Twin Jib Crane Balfour Beatty
DR78222 Plasser & Theurer Self-Propelled Twin Jib Crane Balfour Beatty
DR78223(S) Plasser & Theurer Self-Propelled Twin Jib Crane Balfour Beatty
DR78224(S) Plasser & Theurer Self-Propelled Twin Jib Crane Balfour Beatty
DR78226 Cowans Sheldon Self-Propelled Twin Jib Crane Colas
DR78229 Cowans Sheldon Self-Propelled Twin Jib Crane Network Rail
DR78231 Cowans Sheldon Self-Propelled Twin Jib Crane Network Rail
DR78234 Cowans Sheldon Self-Propelled Twin Jib Crane Network Rail
DR78235 Cowans Sheldon Self-Propelled Twin Jib Crane Colas
DR78237(S) Cowans Sheldon Self-Propelled Twin Jib Crane Network Rail
DR78701 Harsco Track Technologies NTC Power Wagon Balfour Beatty
DR78702 Harsco Track Technologies NTC Power Wagon Balfour Beatty
DR78801+DR78811+DR78821+DR78831 Matisa P95 Track Renewal Train Network Rail
DR78802+DR78812+DR78822+DR78832 Matisa P95 Track Renewal Train Network Rail
DR79101 Linsinger MG31UK – Rail Miller – ZWA CrossRail (TFL)
(99 70 9427 063-1)
DR79201 Loram SPML 17 Rail Grinder Network Rail
DR79221+DR79222+DR79223+DR79224+DR79225+DR79226 Speno RPS-32 Grinder Speno
DR79231+DR79232+DR79233+DR79234+DR79235+DR79236+DR79237 Loram C21 – Grinder Network Rail
Set 2101
DR79241+DR79242+DR79243+DR79244+DR79245+DR79246+DR79247 Loram C21 – Grinder Network Rail
Set 2102 *Roger Smith*

Right: *Plasser & Theurer built VM80, No. DR76701 and a part of High Output Ballast Cleaning train No. 3, is seen separated from its train in Fairwater Yard, Taunton. Fairwater Yard is the base for this train.*
Antony Christie

Network Rail

DR79251+DR79252+DR79253+DR79254+DR79255+DR79256+DR79257 Loram C21 – Grinder Network Rail
Set 2103 *Martin Elwood*

DR79261 + DR79271	Harsco RGH-20C S&C Rail Grinder	Network Rail
DR79262 + DR79272	Harsco RGH-20C S&C Rail Grinder	Network Rail
DR79263 + DR79273	Harsco RGH-20C S&C Rail Grinder	Network Rail
DR79265 + DR79264+DR79274	Harsco RGH-20C S&C Rail Grinder	Network Rail
DR79267 + DR79277	Harsco RGH-20C S&C Rail Grinder	Network Rail
DR79301+DR79302+DR79303+DR79304	Loram C44 Rail Grinder	Network Rail
99 70 9427 038 - 99 70 9427 041 Set C44-01		
DR79401+DR79402+DR79403+DR79404	Loram C44 Rail Grinder	Network Rail
99 70 9427 042 - 99 70 9427 045 Set C44-02		
DR79501+DR79502+DR79503+DR79504+DR79505+DR79506+DR79507	Loram C44 Grinder	Network Rail
99 70 9427 046 - 99 70 9427 052 Set C44-03		
DR80201	Pandrol Jackson – Stoneblower	Network Rail
DR80202	Pandrol Jackson – Stoneblower	Network Rail
DR80203	Pandrol Jackson – Stoneblower	Network Rail
DR80205	Pandrol Jackson – Stoneblower	Network Rail
DR80206	Pandrol Jackson – Stoneblower	Network Rail
DR80207	Pandrol Jackson – Stoneblower	NR (in Sweden)
DR80208	Pandrol Jackson – Stoneblower	Network Rail
DR80209	Pandrol Jackson – Stoneblower	Network Rail
DR80210	Pandrol Jackson – Stoneblower	Network Rail
DR80211	Pandrol Jackson – Stoneblower	Network Rail
DR80213	Harsco Track Technologies – Stoneblower	Network Rail
DR80214	Harsco Track Technologies – Stoneblower	Network Rail
DR80215	Harsco Track Technologies – Stoneblower	Network Rail
DR80216	Harsco Track Technologies – Stoneblower	Network Rail
DR80217	Harsco Track Technologies – Stoneblower	Network Rail
DR80301	Harsco Track Technologies – GP-Stoneblower	Network Rail
Stephen Cornish		
DR80302	Harsco Track Technologies – GP-Stoneblower	Network Rail
DR80303	Harsco Track Technologies – GP-Stoneblower	Network Rail
DR81505	Plasser & Theurer Diesel Hydraulic Crane	Balfour Beatty
DR81507(S)	Plasser & Theurer Diesel Hydraulic Crane	Balfour Beatty
DR81508	Plasser & Theurer Diesel Hydraulic Crane	Balfour Beatty
DR81511(S)	Plasser & Theurer Diesel Hydraulic Crane	Balfour Beatty
DR81513	Plasser & Theurer Diesel Hydraulic Crane	Balfour Beatty
DR81517	Plasser & Theurer Diesel Hydraulic Crane	Balfour Beatty
DR81519(S)	Plasser & Theurer Diesel Hydraulic Crane	Balfour Beatty
DR81522	Plasser & Theurer Diesel Hydraulic Crane	Balfour Beatty
DR81525	Plasser & Theurer Diesel Hydraulic Crane	Balfour Beatty
DR81532	Plasser & Theurer Diesel Hydraulic Crane	Balfour Beatty
DR81601	Kirow KRC810UK 100 tonne Diesel Hydraulic Crane	VolkerRail
Nigel Chester		
DRK81602	Kirow KRC810UK 100 tonne Diesel Hydraulic Crane	Balfour Beatty
DRK81611	Kirow KRC1200UK 125 tonne Diesel Hydraulic Crane	Balfour Beatty
Malcolm L Pearce		
DRK81612	Kirow KRC1200UK 125 tonne Diesel Hydraulic Crane	Colas
DRK81613	Kirow KRC1200UK 125 tonne Diesel Hydraulic Crane	VolkerRail
DRK81621	Kirow KRC250UK Diesel Hydraulic Crane	VolkerRail
DRK81622	Kirow KRC250UK Diesel Hydraulic Crane	VolkerRail

Left: *Displaying Colas yellow, orange and black livery, Matisa-built No. DR75407, a B41UE Tamper, is seen in the bay at Exeter St Davids. This two part machine carries the name* Gerry Taylor. **Antony Christie**

Right: *Owned and operated by Volker Rail, is Kirow crane No. DRK81622, a type KRC250UK Diesel Hydraulic engineering Crane.* **Antony Christie**

DRK81623	Kirow KRC250UK Diesel Hydraulic Crane	Babcock
DRK81624	Kirow KRC250UK Diesel Hydraulic Crane	Babcock
DRK81625	Kirow KRC250UK Diesel Hydraulic Crane	Babcock
DRK81626	Kirow KRC250UK Diesel Hydraulic Crane	Babcock
(99 70 9319 012-9)		
99 70 9319-013-7	Kirow KRC1200UK 125 tonne Diesel Hydraulic Crane	Network Rail
DR88101	Plasser & Theurer Loading Station	Network Rail
DR89005	Cowens Rail Train Power Machine	Network Rail
DR89007	Cowens Rail Train Power Machine	Network Rail
DR89008	Cowens Rail Train Power Machine	Network Rail
DR92201-DR92212	Starfer Single Line Spoil Handling System Train 12 vehicles	Network Rail
DR92213-DR92222	Skako Ballast Distribution Train 'Octopus' 10 vehicles	Network Rail
DR92223-DR92240	Plasser & Theurer NFS-D Ballast Train Hopper 18 vehicles	Network Rail
DR92241-DR92254	Plasser & Theurer MFS-D Ballast Train Hopper 14 vehicles	Network Rail
DR92259-DR92262	Plasser & Theurer MFS-SB Swivel Conveyer Wagon 4 vehicles	Network Rail
DR92263-DR92262	Plasser & Theurer MFS-PW/NB/PW Power Wagon 2 vehicles	Network Rail
DR92265-DR92279	Plasser & Theurer MFS-D Ballast Train Hopper 15 vehicles	Network Rail
DR92280-DR92281	Plasser & Theurer MFS-SB Swivel Conveyer Wagon 2 vehicles	Network Rail
DR92282-DR92283	Plasser & Theurer MFS-A Interfacer Wagon 2 vehicles	Network Rail
DR92285-DR92286	Plasser & Theurer PW-RT Power Wagon 2 vehicles	Network Rail
DR92287-DR92294	Plasser & Theurer MFS-SB Swivel Conveyer Wagon 8 vehicles	Network Rail
DR92295-DR92330	Plasser & Theurer MFS-D Ballast Train Hopper 36 vehicles	Network Rail
DR92331-DR92332	Plasser & Theurer PW-RT Power Wagon 2 vehicles	Network Rail
DR92333-DR93340	Plasser & Theurer MFS-SB Swivel Conveyer Wagon 8-vehicles	Network Rail
DR92341-DR92377	Plasser & Theurer MFS-D Ballast Train Hopper 37 vehicles	Network Rail
DR92400	Plasser & Theurer MFS-A Interfacer Wagon	Colas Rail
DR92431-DR92432	Plasser & Theurer PW-RT Power Wagon 2 vehicles	Network Rail
DR92433-DR92440	Plasser & Theurer MFS-SB Swivel Conveyer Wagon 8 vehicles	Network Rail
DR92441-DR92476	Plasser & Theurer MFS-D Ballast Train Hopper 36 vehicles	Network Rail
DR92477-DR92478	Plasser & Theurer PW-NPW Power Wagon 2 vehicles	Network Rail
99 70 9310 477-3 - 99 70 9310478-1)		
DR92510-DR92503 (S)	Sleeper Delivery Train – Generator Wagon 3 vehicles	Stored
DR92504-DR92512 (S)	Twin Jib Track Recovery Train 'Slinger' 9 vehicles	Stored
DR92513-DR92518 (S)	Single Jib Track Recovery Train 'Slinger' 6 vehocles	Stored
DR92519 (S)	Twin Jib Track Recovery Train 'Slinger'	Stored
DR92520-DR92525	Sleeper Delivery Train 'Slinger' Generator 6 vehicles	Stored
DR92526-DR92532	Sleeper Delivery Train 'Slinger' Twin-Jib 7 vehicles	Stored
DR92533-DR92534	Sleeper Delivery Train 'Slinger' Generator 2 vehicles	Stored
DR92535-DR92546	Sleeper Delivery Train 'Slinger' Twin-Jib 12 vehicles	Stored
DR92547-DR92549	Sleeper Delivery Train 'Slinger' Generator 3 vehicles	Stored
DR92550-DR92553	Sleeper Delivery Train 'Slinger' Twin-Jib 22 vehicles	Stored
DR92601-DR92665	WH Davis Sleeper Wagons 65 vehicles	Network Rail
DR92701-DR92706	WH Davis Workshop/Barrier 6 vehicles	Network Rail
3170 4629 001 - 3170 4629 050	International Sleeper Wagons 50 vehicles	Network Rail
DR969001-DR969050		
DR93325-DR93480	Sleeper Delivery Train - Manipulator 10 vehicles	Network Rail
DR93601-DR93609	Sleeper Delivery Train - Clamp 4 vehicles	Network Rail
ARDC96710 (S)	Cowans Sheldon 75 tonne Hydraulic Recovery Crane	Network Rail
ARDC96713 (S)	Cowans Sheldon 75 tonne Hydraulic Recovery Crane	Network Rail
ARDC96714 (S)	Cowans Sheldon 75 tonne Hydraulic Recovery Crane	Network Rail

Network Rail

Number	Description	Operator
ARDC96715 ¤	Cowans Sheldon 75 tonne Hydraulic Recovery Crane	Network Rail
DR97001	Eiv de Brieve DU94BA – TRAMM	High Speed 1 (HS1)
DU 94 B 001 URS		
DR97011	Windhoff Overhead Line – MPV	High Speed 1 (HS1)
DR97012	Windhoff Overhead Line – MPV	High Speed 1 (HS1)
Geoff Bell		
DR97013	Windhoff Overhead Line – MPV	High Speed 1 (HS1)
DR97014	Windhoff Overhead Line – MPV	High Speed 1 (HS1)
DR97501+DR97601+DR97801	Robel Self-Propelled Mobile Maintenance Train	Network Rail
DR97502+DR97602+DR97802	Robel Self-Propelled Mobile Maintenance Train	Network Rail
DR97503+DR97603+DR97803	Robel Self-Propelled Mobile Maintenance Train	Network Rail
DR97504+DR97604+DR97804	Robel Self-Propelled Mobile Maintenance Train	Network Rail
DR97505+DR97605+DR97805	Robel Self-Propelled Mobile Maintenance Train	Network Rail
DR97506+DR97606+DR97806	Robel Self-Propelled Mobile Maintenance Train	Network Rail
DR97507+DR97607+DR97807	Robel Self-Propelled Mobile Maintenance Train	Network Rail
DR97508+DR97608+DR97808	Robel Self-Propelled Mobile Maintenance Train	Network Rail
DR97509+DR97510+DR97511+DR97512	Robel Self-Propelled Maintenance Train	CrossRail (TFL)
DR98001	Windhoff Overhead Line – MPV	Network Rail
DR98002	Windhoff Overhead Line – MPV	Network Rail
DR98003	Windhoff Overhead Line – MPV – YXA	Network Rail
Anthony Wrighton 1944-2011		
DR98004	Windhoff Overhead Line – MPV – YXA	Network Rail
Philip Cattrell 1961-2011		
DR98005	Windhoff Overhead Line – MPV – YXA	Network Rail
DR98006	Windhoff Overhead Line – MPV – YXA	Network Rail
Jason McDonnell 1970-2016		
DR98007	Windhoff Overhead Line – MPV – YXA	Network Rail
DR98008	Windhoff MPV Track Monitoring single car	Network Rail
DR98009	Windhoff Overhead Line – MPV – YXA	Network Rail
Melvin Smith 1953-2011		
DR98010	Windhoff Overhead Line – MPV – YXA	Network Rail
Benjamin Gautrey 1992-2011		
DR98011	Windhoff Overhead Line – MPV – YXA	Network Rail
DR98012	Windhoff Overhead Line – MPV – YXA	Network Rail
Terence Hand 1962-2016		
DR98013	Windhoff Overhead Line – MPV – YXA	Network Rail
David Wood 1951-2015		
DR98014	Windhoff Overhead Line – MPV – YXA	Network Rail
Wayne Imlach 1955-2015		
DR98215 A+B	Plasser & Theurer General Purpose Machine (GP-TRAMM) – ZWA	Balfour Beatty
DR98216 A+B	Plasser & Theurer General Purpose Machine (GP-TRAMM) – ZWA	Balfour Beatty
DR98217 A+B	Plasser & Theurer General Purpose Machine (GP-TRAMM) – ZWA	Balfour Beatty
DR98218 A+B	Plasser & Theurer General Purpose Machine (GP-TRAMM) – ZWA	Balfour Beatty
DR98219 A+B	Plasser & Theurer General Purpose Machine (GP-TRAMM) – ZWA	Balfour Beatty
DR98220 A+B	Plasser & Theurer General Purpose Machine (GP-TRAMM) – ZWA	Balfour Beatty
DR98307 A+B	Geismar VMT860 PL/UM – ZWA	Colas
DR98308 A+B	Geismar VMT860 PL/UM – ZWA	Colas
DR98901 + DR98951	Windhoff Multi Purpose Vehicle (MPV) – YXA	Network Rail
DR98902 + DR98952	Windhoff Multi Purpose Vehicle (MPV) – YXA	Network Rail
DR98903 + DR98953	Windhoff Multi Purpose Vehicle (MPV) – YXA	Network Rail
DR98904 + DR98954	Windhoff Multi Purpose Vehicle (MPV) – YXA	Network Rail

Left: *Vehicle No. DR78831 is a part of the four vehicle Matisa P95 Track Renewal Train and is seen on a transit move at Taunton, Somerset. The train is owned by Network Rail.* **Antony Christie**

Right: *A fleet of ten of these Pandrol Jackson 'Stoneblower' machines are operated by Network Rail in all regions. The vehicle shown, No. DR80209 is based in the Nottingham area.* **Antony Christie**

Number	Vehicle	Operator
DR98905 + DR98955	Windhoff Multi Purpose Vehicle (MPV) – YXA	Network Rail
DR98906 + DR98956	Windhoff Multi Purpose Vehicle (MPV) – YXA	Network Rail
DR98907 + DR98957	Windhoff Multi Purpose Vehicle (MPV) – YXA	Network Rail
DR98908 + DR98958	Windhoff Multi Purpose Vehicle (MPV) – YXA	Network Rail
DR98909 + DR98959	Windhoff Multi Purpose Vehicle (MPV) – YXA	Network Rail
DR98910 + DR98960	Windhoff Multi Purpose Vehicle (MPV) – YXA	Network Rail
DR98911 + DR98961	Windhoff Multi Purpose Vehicle (MPV) – YXA	Network Rail
DR98912 + DR98962	Windhoff Multi Purpose Vehicle (MPV) – YXA	Network Rail
DR98913 + DR98963	Windhoff Multi Purpose Vehicle (MPV) – YXA	Network Rail
DR98914 + DR98964	Windhoff Multi Purpose Vehicle (MPV) – YXA	Network Rail
Dick Preston		
DR98915 + DR98965	Windhoff Multi Purpose Vehicle (MPV) – YXA	Network Rail
Nigel Cummins		
DR98916 + DR98966	Windhoff Multi Purpose Vehicle (MPV) – YXA	Network Rail
DR98917 + DR98967	Windhoff Multi Purpose Vehicle (MPV) – YXA	Network Rail
DR98918 + DR98968	Windhoff Multi Purpose Vehicle (MPV) – YXA	Network Rail
DR98919 + DR98969	Windhoff Multi Purpose Vehicle (MPV) – YXA	Network Rail
DR98920 + DR98970	Windhoff Multi Purpose Vehicle (MPV) – YXA	Network Rail
DR98921 + DR98971	Windhoff Multi Purpose Vehicle (MPV) – YXA	Network Rail
DR98922 + DR98972	Windhoff Multi Purpose Vehicle (MPV) – YXA	Network Rail
DR98923 + DR98973	Windhoff Multi Purpose Vehicle (MPV) – YXA	Network Rail
Chris Lemon		
DR98924 + DR98974	Windhoff Multi Purpose Vehicle (MPV) – YXA	Network Rail
DR98925 + DR98975	Windhoff Multi Purpose Vehicle (MPV) – YXA	Network Rail
DR98926 + DR98976	Windhoff Multi Purpose Vehicle (MPV) – YXA	Network Rail
John Denyer		
DR98927 + DR98977	Windhoff Multi Purpose Vehicle (MPV) – YXA	Network Rail
DR98928 + DR98978	Windhoff Multi Purpose Vehicle (MPV) – YXA	Network Rail
DR98929 + DR98979	Windhoff Multi Purpose Vehicle (MPV) – YXA	Network Rail
DR98930 + DR98980	Windhoff Multi Purpose Vehicle (MPV) – YXA	Network Rail
DR98931 + DR98981	Windhoff Multi Purpose Vehicle (MPV) – YXA	Network Rail
DR98932 + DR98982	Windhoff Multi Purpose Vehicle (MPV) – YXA	Network Rail
DR979001-DR979134	Rail Wagon 'Perch' - YEA 134-vehicles	Network Rail
DR979409-DR979415	Rail Clamping Wagon 'Perch' - YEA 3 vehicles	Network Rail
DR979505-DR979515	Rail Train End Wagon 'Porpoise' - YEA 7 vehicles	Network Rail
DR979500-DR979512	Rail Train Chute Wagon ' Porpoise' - YEA 8 vehicles	Network Rail
DR979604-DR979614	Rail Train Gantry Wagon 'Perch' - YEA 7 Wagons	Network Rail
DR999800-DR999801	(S) Plasser & Theurer EM-SAT RT900 Survey Vehicle 2 vehicles	Network Rail
642001-642050	Rail Head Treatment Train (RHTT) vehicles 50 vehicles	Network Rail
99 70 9128 001-3	Plasser & Theurer Unimat 09-4x4/45 Tamper	Babcock
99 70 9128 002-1	Plasser & Theurer Unimat 09-4x4/45 Tamper	Babcock
99 70 9515 001-4 (99709)	Railvac Machine, Railcare 16000-480UK	Railcare
99 70 9515 002-2	Railvac Machine, Railcare 16000-480UK	Railcare
99 70 9515 003-0	Railvac Machine, Railcare 16000-480UK	Railcare
99 70 9515 004-8	Railvac Machine, Railcare 16000-480UK	Railcare
99 70 9515 005-5	Railvac Machine, Railcare 16000-480UK	Railcare
99 70 9515 006-3	Railvac Machine, Railcare 16000-480UK	Railcare
99 70 9522 020-5	Railcare Ballast Feeder	Railcare
99 70 9594 014-1	Winter Snow Patrol Train 'Perch'	Network Rail - IS

Network Rail

DR 99 70 9231 001-7	Electrification Train - SVI RT250 Crane/platform vehicle	ABC Electrification
DR 99 70 9231 002-5	Electrification Train - SVI CTF28 Platform	ABC Electrification
DR 99 70 9231 003-3	Electrification Train - SVI Crane/drum	ABC Electrification
DR 99 70 9231 004-1	Electrification Train - SVI PT500 Wire/platform	ABC Electrification
DR 99 70 9231 005-8	Electrification Train - SVI RSM9 Platform	ABC Electrification
DR 99 70 9231 006-6	Electrification Train - SVI RSM9 Platform	ABC Electrification
DR 99 70 9231 007-4	Electrification Train - SVI APV250 Platform	ABC Electrification

Left Upper: *DR98008 is a unique twin-cab Windhoff MPV and is operated by Network Rail as a track monitoring vehicle and usually used on complex station or junction layouts, where its short length assists its operation. The vehicle is specially equipped with an Omni Inspector system.* **John Binch**

Left Middle: *To keep rail heads in a good condition a number of different rail grinding vehicles are in operation, some owned by Network Rail and others by the grinding companies. In this view at Plymouth, is one of the Network Rail owned two-vehicle formations, Nos. DR79263+DR79273, built by Harsco of type RGH-20C.* **Antony Christie**

Below: *A fleet of six 'Railvac' machines, of the 16000-480UK type are owned and operated by Railcare. They use high vacuum technology to perform excavations and collection of materials, which can be stored inside the machine for subsequent disposal. No. 99 70 9515 005-5 is illustrated at Toton.* **Antony Christie**

Infrastructure Companies - Network Rail

Alstom Transport

Address: PO Box 70, Newbold Road, Rugby, Warwickshire, CV21 2WR
info@transport.alstom.com 01788 577111 www.transport.alstom.com

Managing Director: Paul Robinson

Facilities: Following the assembly of the Virgin Trains Class 390 'Pendolino' stock, Alstom closed down its UK production facility at Washwood Heath, Birmingham. However, in 2017 a new purpose-built vehicle plant was opened at Widnes, where Class 390 stock is now overhauled. Any future 'new build' contracts would be built at this site.

Depots: Chester (CH), Liverpool - Edge Hill (LL), Wolverhampton - Oxley (OY), Wembley (WB)

Class 08

Vehicle Length: 29ft 3in (8.91m)
Height: 12ft 8⅝in (3.87m)
Width: 8ft 6in (2.59m)
Engine: English Electric 6K
Horsepower: 400hp (298kW)
Electrical Equipment: English Electric

Number	*Depot*	*Pool*	*Livery*	*Owner*	*Operator*
08451	**LO**	**ATLO**	**BLK**	**ALS**	**ALS**
08454	**WI**	**ATLO**	**BLU**	**ALS**	**ALS**
08611	**WB**	**ATLO**	**BLU**	**ALS**	**ALS**
08617	**EH**	**ATLO**	**BLU**	**ALS**	**ALS**
08696	**WB**	**ATLO**	**BLU**	**ALS**	**ALS**
08721	**AT**	**ATLO**	**BLU**	**ALS**	**ALS**
08790	**LL**	**ATLO**	**BLU**	**ALS**	**ALS**
08887	**PO**	**ATZZ**	**BLK**	**ALS**	**ALS**

Names applied
08451 ***Longsight TMD***
08617 ***Steve Purser***

Bombardier Transportation

Address: Litchurch Lane, Derby, DE24 8AD
info@bombardier.com 01332 344666 www.bombardier.com

Chief Country Representative: Paul Roberts **Works:** Derby (ZD), Crewe (ZC)

Facilities: Bombardier Transportation is one of the largest transport companies in the world, with offices and facilities in many countries. Its product range extends well beyond rail vehicles and includes aircraft, boats and leisure equipment. In terms of the UK, two main sites are located in Derby (Litchurch Lane) and Crewe. New-build work is undertaken at the Derby site.

Class 08

Vehicle Length: 29ft 3in (8.91m)
Height: 12ft 8⅝in (3.87m)
Width: 8ft 6in (2.59m)
Engine: English Electric 6K
Horsepower: 400hp (298kW)
Electrical Equipment: English Electric

Number	*Depot*	*Pool*	*Livery*	*Owner*	*Operator*	*Name*
08602 (004)	**ZD**	**KDSD**	**BLU**	**HNR**	**BOM**	
08682 (D3849)	**ZD**	**KDSD**	**SPL**	**HNR**	**BOM**	***Lionheart***

Progress Rail International Inc

Right: *Progress Rail has a sizeable plant in Longport, Stoke-on-Trent where Electro-Motive carry out repair and overhaul work to EMD products, such as Class 59 and 66 locos. The site has also been selected to perform the rebuilt of the GBRf Class 56s into new Class 69 locos fitted with EMD 710 power units. This major work will see the first loco No. 69001, rebuilt from 56311 emerge in summer 2020. This is a general view of the plant.* **Antony Christie**

Address: ✉ Progress Rail International Inc, 9301 West 55th Street, LaGrange, Illinois, USA, 60525
Progress Rail International Inc, Muncie, Indiana, USA
info@progressrail.com ✆ +1 (800) 255 5355, ⓘ www.progressrail.com

Facilities: Formerly part of General Motors, Progress Rail is one of the two largest loco builders in the world. Its main production facility is in Muncie, Indiana, USA. In terms of the UK, the JT42CWRM or Class 66 locomotives were originally built at the Canadian facility; however, the final order delivered in 2017 for GBRf saw production move to Muncie, Indiana. Progress Rail is part of the Caterpillar Group. In the UK Progress Rail International operates from premises at Longport, near Stoke-on-Trent, where the bodyshell of withdrawn Class 66 No. 66048 is stored.

In 2018 a contract was let between GB Railfreight and Progress Rail for the rebuilding of 10 former Class 56s with new General Motors prime movers to emerge as Class 69s in 2020.

General Electric (Wabtec)

Address: ✉ GE Transportation Rail, 2901 East Lake Road, Erie, Pennsylvania, USA, 16531
UK office: Inspira House, Martinfield, Welwyn Garden City, Herts, AL7 1GW
info@getransportation.com ✆ 01707 383700 ⓘ www.getransportation.com

Chief Executive Officer: Lorenzo Simonelli

Facilities: General Electric entered the UK loco arena in recent years, and built Class 70s for Freightliner and Colas Rail Freight. GE operates a construction facility in Erie, Pennsylvania, USA.

Hitachi Europe Ltd

Address: ✉ 16 Upper Woburn Place, London, WC1H 0AF
hirofumi.ojima@hitachi-eu.com ✆ 0207 970 2700, ⓘ www.hitachi-rail.com

Facilities: Hitachi's first UK contract was to design, build and introduce the Class 395 EMUs for domestic services on HS1. In 2009 it formed the construction arm of Agility Trains, awarded the IEP project to design, build and introduce new passenger trains in the UK. In 2015 the company opened construction facilities at Newton Aycliffe, County Durham. Soon other contracts were awarded.

At present the company is the process of designing and building Class 80x stock for First Open Access and East Midlands Trains and soon Aventi West Coast.

Hitachi also operate a major construction site in Pistoia, Italy, where the Class 802 stock for GWR, Hull Trains and Trans Pennine have been built.

Arlington Fleet Group

Address: ✉ Eastleigh Rail Works, Campbell Road, Eastleigh, Hampshire, SO50 5AD
info@Arlington-fleet.co.uk ✆ 02380 698789 ⓘ www.arlington-fleet.com

Managing Director: Barry Stephens

Facilities: Arlington Fleet Group offers high-quality rail engineering services to all vehicle owners. The company is based in the former loco/carriage works at Eastleigh.

Depots: Eastleigh (ZG), Shoeburyness (SN)

Class 07

Vehicle Length: 26ft 9½in (8.16m)
Height: 12ft 10in (3.91m)
Width: 8ft 6in (2.59m)
Engine: Paxman 6RPHL MkIII
Horsepower: 275hp (205kW)
Electrical Equipment: AEI

Number	*Depot*	*Pool*	*Livery*	*Owner*	*Operator*
07007 (D2991)	**ZG**	**MBDL**	**BLU**	**AFG**	**AFG**

Class 08

Vehicle Length: 29ft 3in (8.91m)
Height: 12ft 8⅝in (3.87m)
Width: 8ft 6in (2.59m)
Engine: English Electric 6K
Horsepower: 400hp (298kW)
Electrical Equipment: English Electric

Number	*Depot*	*Pool*	*Livery*	*Owner*	*Operator*
08567	**ZG**	**MBDL**	**EWS**	**AFG**	**AFG**

Class 47

Vehicle Length: 63ft 6in (19.35m)	Engine: Sulzer 12LDA28C
Height: 12ft 10⅜in (3.91m)	Horsepower: 2,580hp (1,922kW)
Width: 9ft 2in (2.79m)	Electrical Equipment: Brush
Electric Train Heat fitted	

Number	Depot	Pool	Livery	Owner	Operator
47818(S) (47240/663)	**ZG**	**MBDL**	**BLU**	**AFG**	**-**

Ex-DB (Germany) Class 323

Number	Depot	Pool	Livery	Owner	Operator
323-539-7	**ZG**	**-**	**GRN**	**NHR**	**AFG**
323-674-2	**ZG**	**-**	**GRN**	**NHR**	**-**

Former German shunting locos, built by Gmeinder and now owned by Northumbria Rail and used at Eastleigh Works by Arlington Fleet Group for pilotage.

Ex-Class 508 Barrier Vehicles

Former Class 508 driving cars now used as EMU barrier/translator vehicles, based at Eastleigh.

Number	Depot	Pool	Livery	Owner	Operator	Name
64664	**ZG**	**-**	**GRN**	**ANG**	**AFG**	***'Livet' Angel of Inventions***
64707	**ZG**	**-**	**GRN**	**ANG**	**AFG**	***'Labezerin' Angel of Success***

Barrier Vehicles

Former Class 489 DMBS de-icing vehicles rebuilt as barrier/translator vehicles, based at Eastleigh.

Number	Depot	Livery	Owner	Operator	Notes
68501	**LE**	**GRN**	**AFG**	**ROG**	Barrier vehicle modified from Class 489 DMBS
68504	**LE**	**GRN**	**AFG**	**ROG**	Barrier vehicle modified from Class 489 DMBS
68505(S)	**ZG**	**NRL**	**AFG**	**-**	Barrier vehicle modified from Class 489 DMBS

EMU barrier/translator vehicles, based at Eastleigh.

Number	Depot	Pool	Livery	Owner	Operator	Name
975974 (1030)	**ZG**	**-**	**GRN**	**ANG**	**AFG**	***Paschar***
975978 (1025)	**ZG**	**-**	**GRN**	**ANG**	**AFG**	***Perpetiel***

Right: *Originally a 2HAP DMBS, then a Gatwick Express GLV, No. 68501 is now a barrier/translator vehicle for multiple unit transit moves. Owned by Arlington Fleet Group, the vehicle is painted in green and usually operated by Rail Operations Group. It is seen at Leicester.* **Antony Christie**

CAF (Construcciones y Auxiliar de Ferrocarriles)

Address: C/ José Miguel Iturrioz, 26 20200 Beasain (Guipúzcoa), Spain
✆ +34 943 88 01 00 caf@caf.net ⓘ www.caf.net

Chairman: Andres Arizkorreta Garcia

Facilities: CAF currently operate a major construction plant at Irun, Spain and operate a new plant in Llanwern, South Wales. The company is fullfilling orders for Northern, TransPennine, West Midlands, Caledonian Sleepers and have also won a major order for Transport for Wales.

Arriva Train Care

Address: ✉ Arriva Train Care, PO Box 111, Crewe, Cheshire, CW1 2FB
allservicedeliverymanagers@lnwr.com ✆ 01270 508000 ⓘ www.lnwr.com

Managing Director: Mark Knowles

Facilities: ATC is a maintenance facility owned by Arriva Trains.

Depots: Crewe (CO), Bristol Barton Hill (BK), Eastleigh (EH), Cambridge (CA), Tyne (TY)

Class 08, 09

Vehicle Length: 29ft 3in (8.91m)
Height: 12ft 8⅝in (3.87m)
Width: 8ft 6in (2.59m)
Engine: English Electric 6K
Horsepower: 400hp (298kW)
Electrical Equipment: English Electric

Number	Depot	Pool	Livery	Owner	Operator	Name
08442	EH	MBDL	BRT	LNW	ATC	Richard J Wenham Eastleigh Depot December 1989 - July 1999
08511	EH	MBDL	RSS	RSS	GBR	
08516	BK	MBDL	LNW	LNW	ATC	
08735	EH	MBDL	ATB	LNW	ATC	Geoff Hobbs 42
08810	EH	MBDL	GRY	LNW	ATC	
08830	CO	MBDL	BLU	LNW	ATC	
09204	CO	MBDL	ATC	LNW	ATC	

Pullman Group (Colas Rail Freight)

Address: ✉ Train Maintenance Depot, Leckwith Road, Cardiff, CF11 8HP
sales@pullmans.net ✆ 029 2036 8850 ⓘ www.pullmans.net

Managing Director: Colin Robinson

Facilities: Maintenance facility based at Canton depot, Cardiff.

Class 08

Vehicle Length: 29ft 3in (8.91m)
Height: 12ft 8⅝in (3.87m)
Width: 8ft 6in (2.59m)
Engine: English Electric 6K
Horsepower: 400hp (298kW)
Electrical Equipment: English Electric

Number	Depot	Pool	Livery	Owner	Operator	Name
08499	CF	WSXX	BLU	DBS	PUL	Redlight

Gemini Rail Services

Address: ✉ Wolverton Works, Stratford Road, Wolverton, Milton Keynes, MK12 5NT
info@railcare.co.uk ✆ 08000 741122 ⓘ www.railcare.co.uk

Managing Director: Colin Love **Depots:** Wolverton (ZN)

Class 08

Vehicle Length: 29ft 3in (8.91m)
Height: 12ft 8⅝in (3.87m)
Width: 8ft 6in (2.59m)
Engine: English Electric 6K
Horsepower: 400hp (298kW)
Electrical Equipment: English Electric

Number	Depot	Pool	Livery	Owner	Operator	Name
08568	ZN	RCZH	GEM	GEM	GEM	
08629	ZN	RCZN	GEM	GEM	GEM	Wolverton
08649	ZN	RCZN	GEM	GEM	GEM	Bradwell
08730	ZN	RCZH	GEM	GEM	GEM	

Loram UK

Address: ✉ Vehicles Workshop, RTC Business Park, London Road, Derby, DE24 8UP
enquiries@rvel.co.uk ✆ 01332 331210 ⓘ www.rvel.co.uk

Managing Director: Richard Kelly **Depot:** Derby (DF)

Class 31/1 & 31/4

Vehicle Length: 56ft 9in (17.29m)
Height: 12ft 7in (3.91m)
Width: 8ft 9in (2.65m)
Class 31/4 - Electric Train Heat fitted
Engine: English Electric 12SVT
Horsepower: 1,470hp (1,097kW)
Electrical Equipment: Brush

Number		Depot	Pool	Livery	Owner	Operator
31106(S)		DF	RVLO	BLU	HJA	-
31468(S)	(31568, 31321)	DF	RVLS	BLK	LOR	-

Siemens Transportation

Address: ✉ Kings Heath Facility, Heathfield Way, Kings Heath, Northampton, NN5 7QP
enquiries@siemenstransportation.co.uk ✆ 01604 594500
ⓘ www.siemenstransportation.co.uk

✉ Ashby Park, Ashby de la Zouch, Leicestershire, LE65 1JD
uk.mobility@siemens.com ✆ 01530 258000 ⓘ www.siemens.co.uk/mobility

Managing Director UK: Vernon Baker
Depots: Ardwick, Manchester (AK), Kings Heath, Northampton (NN), Three Bridges, Hornsey (HE), Northam (NT), Glasgow Shields (GW)

Facilities: Siemens is a provider of UK EMU and DMU rolling stock with various derivatives of its 'Desiro' and 'Desiro City' product line. With facilities in the UK, and new-build undertakings in mainland Europe at its Krefeld/Uerdingen factory in Germany. Testing of vehicles is also performed in Germany at the world-famous test track at Wildenrath before delivery to customers. Siemens is to build a construction facility at Goole, to undertake the deep tube stock build contract.

Siemens operates lifetime maintenance contracts for its Class 185 stock at Ardwick, Manchester, Class 350 stock at Ardwick and Kings Heath, Northampton, Class 380 stock at Shields (Glasgow), Class 444 and 450 stock at Northam, Class 700 stock at Three Bridges and Hornsey, Class 717 stock at Hornsey. Wimbledon is the base for Class 707 sets used by South Western Railway.

Class 01.5

Number	*Depot*	*Pool*	*Livery*	*Owner*	*Operator*	*Name*
01551 (H016)	**AK**	**MBDL**	**WAB**	**WAB**	**SIE**	***Lancelot***

Talgo

Spanish train builder Talgo announced in late 2018 that they were to open a new train construction and testing site in the UK, located at the site of the long closed Longannet Power station. A 70,000m^2 facility will be built from early 2020, with the first trains constructed in 2022. Talgo are hopeful of winning new train orders, including HS2 rolling stock.

Vivarail

Address: ✉ Quinton Rail Technology Centre, Station Road, Long Marston, Stratford-upon-Avon, Warwickshire. CV37 8PL
info@vivarail.co.uk ✆ 07815 010373 ⓘ www.vivarail.co.uk

Chairman: Adrian Shooter

Vivarail, based at Southam, near Leamington Spa, has masterminded the re-use of redundant ex-London Transport 'D' stock, rebuilding vehicles to main-line standards, some as DMUs and others are battery powered. Vivarail owns around 150 motor cars and 300 trailer vehicles. Vivarail operates test facilities at Cambrian Transports facility in Barry, South Wales.

Vivarail is currently supplying Transport for Wales 5 x three-car and SWR Island Line 5 x two-car sets.

230001 DM(A) 300001 (7058), TS 300201 (17128), DM(B) 300101 (7511)
230002 BDM(A) 300002 (7122), BM 300202 (-), BDM(B) 300102 (7067) (Battery set)
7031 Battery test vehicle
7501 Battery and Steering Test Vehicle

Right: *Vivarail has its main workshops at Southam, near Leamington Spa, where the rebuilding of former LUL 'D' Stock into Class 230 sets is carried out. Testing and development of new technology is carried out at Barry, South Wales. In summer 2019, quick-charge battery vehicle No. 7031 is seen painted in Vivarail white and green livery. This driving vehicle is not certified for main line use and only operates within the confines of the Long Marston site.* **CJM**

Wabtec

Brush Traction, Loughborough

Address: ✉ PO Box 17, Loughborough, Leicestershire, LE11 1HS
sales@brushtraction.com ✆ 01509 617000 ⓘ www.brushtraction.com

Managing Director: Andy Derbyshire

Facilities: The world-famous name of Brush Traction, based in Loughborough, is now part of the Wabtec Group. In recent years the site has been responsible for the majority of UK loco building. The company has been synonymous with loco building for the UK and overseas markets for many years. Although recent main-line loco builds have been awarded overseas, the facilities at the Loughborough plant from which the Class 31, 47, 57, 60 and Eurotunnel Shuttle locos emerged are still available for new-build work. Wabtec also ownes L H Group Services. Wabtec purchased General Electric in 2017-2018.

Doncaster

Address: ✉ PO Box 400, Doncaster Works, Hexthorpe Road, Doncaster, DN1 1SL
wabtecrail@wabtec.com ✆ 01302 340700 ⓘ www.wabtecrail.co.uk

Managing Director: John Meehan **Depot:** Doncaster (ZB)

Class 08

Vehicle Length: 29ft 3in (8.91m)
Height: 12ft 8⁵⁄₈in (3.87m)
Width: 8ft 6in (2.59m)
Engine: English Electric 6K
Horsepower: 400hp (298kW)
Electrical Equipment: English Electric

Number	*Depot*	*Pool*	*Livery*	*Owner*	*Operator*	*Name*
08472	EC	HBSH	BLK	WAB	VEC	
08571	ZB	HBSH	WAB	WAB	VEC	
08596	EC	HBSH	WAB	WAB	VEC	
08615	LH	HBSH	WAB	WAB	TATA	*Uncle Dai*
08669	ZB	HBSH	WAB	WAB	LHG	*Bob Machin*
08724	ZB	HBSH	WAB	WAB	WAB	
08764	PO	MBDL	BLU	WAB	ALS	*Old Tom*
08853	ZB	HBSH	BLU	WAB	WAB	
08871	IL	MBDL	GRN	WAB	BOM	

Kilmarnock (previously Brush Barclay)

Address: ✉ Caledonia Works, West Langlands Street, Kilmarnock, Ayrshire, KA1 2QD
sales@brushtraction.com ✆ 01563 523573 ⓘ www.brushtraction.com

Managing Director: John Bidewell

Facilities: The Wabtec site in Scotland concentrates on vehicle overhaul and refurbishment, including EMU, DMU and loco-hauled vehicles as well as HST stock.

Artemis Engineering

Class 19

Vehicle Length: 61ft 9in (18.83m)
Height: 12ft 9in (3.88m)
Width: 8ft 11in (2.71m)
Engine: 2 x JCB
Horsepower: To be confirmed
Transmission: Hydrostatic

19001 (82113) Bo'ness

Left: *Former Mk3 West Coast Driving Van Trailer No. 82113 was obtained by a joint venture of Artemis Engineering and the Railway Safety and Standards Board as part of a development project for alternative traction systems. The vehicle was rebuilt as a demonstrator of the use of hydraulic pumps and motors to power a vehicle. The development coach is based at the Bo'ness and Kinneil Railway, Scotland.* **Gordon Kirkby**

Europhoenix Ltd

Address: 58A High Street, Stony Stratford, Milton Keynes, MK11 1AX
info@europhoenix.eu 01467 624366 www.europhoenix.eu

Facilities: Europhoenix has purchased redundant Class 56, 86, 87 amd 91 locos; these are offered to Continental European operators fully refurbished and modified to suit customer needs.

Class 37

Vehicle Length: 61ft 6in (18.74m)
Height: 13ft 0¼in (3.96m)
Width: 8ft 11⅝in (2.73m)
Engine: English Electric 12CSVT (37901-Mirrlees)
Horsepower: 1,750hp (1,304kW)
Electrical Equipment: English Electric

Number	*Depot*	*Pool*	*Livery*	*Owner*	*Name*	*Operator/Notes*
37510 (37112)	**LR**	**GROG**	**EPX**	**EPX**	***Orion***	**ROG drophead coupler**
37601 (37501)	**LR**	**GROG**	**EPX**	**EPX**	***Perseus***	**Spot hire**
37608 (37512)	**LR**	**GROG**	**EPX**	**EPX**	***Andromeda***	**ROG drophead Dellner fitted**
37611 (37690)	**LR**	**GROG**	**EPX**	**EPX**	***Pegasus***	**COL**
37800 (37143)	**LR**	**GROG**	**EPX**	**EPX**	***Cassiopeia***	**ROG drophead Dellner fitted**
37884 (37183)	**LR**	**GROG**	**EPX**	**EPX**	***Cepheus***	**ROG drophead Tightlock fitted**
37901 (37150)	**LR**	**EPUK**	**EPX**	**EPX**	***Mirrlees Pioneer***	**EPX**

Right: *Europhoenix operates a number of refurbished Class 37s and leases these to operators on short and long term hire contracts. One of their major customers is Rail Operations Group, who use a modified fleet fitted with drop-head Dellner or Tightlock couplings. No. 37601 is illustrated at Bristol powering a rake of new TPE Mk5 stock.* **Mark V. Pike**

Class 91

Vehicle Length: 63ft 8in (19.40m)
Height: 12ft 4in (3.75m)
Width: 9ft 0in (2.74m)
Power Collection: 25kV ac overhead
Horsepower: 6,300hp (4,700kW)
Electrical Equipment: GEC

91117 (91017)	**LR**	**EPUK**	**EPX**	**EPX**	**EPX**
91120 (91020)	**LR**	**EPUK**	**EPX**	**EPX**	**EPX**

Right: *In October 2019, Europhoenix obtained two off-lease LNER Class 91s for hire use. The two locos, Nos. 91117 and 91120 are seen on delivery from Bounds Green to Leicester depot.* **Jamie Squibbs**

For export to Eastern Europe to operate in pairs with No. 1 end facing outward. Re-geared by Voith for freight operation.

Coaching Stock

Mk 3
Vehicle Length: 75ft 0in (22.86m)
Height: 12ft 9in (3.88m)
Width: 8ft 11in (2.71m)

NX5G - NGV (Ex 'Nightstar' generator van)

Number	*Depot*	*Livery*	*Owner*	
96371(S) (10545)	**LR**	**EPS**	**EPX**	**(for scrap)**

Class 56

Vehicle Length: 63ft 6in (19.35m)
Height: 13ft 0in (3.96m)
Width: 9ft 2in (2.79m)
Engine: Ruston Paxman 16RK3CT
Horsepower: 3,250hp (2,420kW)
Electrical Equipment: Brush

Number	*Pool*	*Owner*	*Location*	*Livery*	*Operator*
56096	**COFS**	**EPX**	**WH**	**COL**	**COL**
56101 (92 55 0659 001-5)		**EPX**	**-**	**BLK**	**Hire to Floyd (Hungary)**
56115 (92 55 0659 002-3)		**EPX**	**-**	**BLK**	**Hire to Floyd (Hungary)**
56117 (92 55 0659 003-1)		**EPX**	**-**	**BLK**	**Hire to Floyd (Hungary)**
56301 (56045)	**UKRL**	**EPX**	**LR**	**FLF**	**-**

Class 86

Vehicle Length: 58ft 6in (17.83m)
Height: 13ft 0⅝in (3.97m)
Width: 8ft 8¼in (2.64m)
Power Collection: 25kV ac overhead
Horsepower: 5,900hp (4,400kW)
Electrical Equipment: GEC

Number	*Location*	*Hire to*
86215	EXP	Floyd (Hungary)
86217	EXP	Floyd (Hungary)
86218	EXP	Floyd (Hungary)
86228	EXP	Floyd (Hungary)
86233	EXP	Floyd (Hungary)
86234	LM	-
86242	EXP	Floyd (Hungary)
86248	EXP	Floyd (Hungary)
86250	EXP	Floyd (Hungary)
86251	CE	Freightliner *
86424	EXP	Floyd (Hungary) (for spares)

Class 87

Vehicle Length: 58ft 6in (17.83m)
Height: 13ft 1¼in (3.99m)
Width: 8ft 8¼in (2.64m)
Power Collection: 25kV ac overhead
Horsepower: 7,860hp (5,680kW)
Electrical Equipment: GEC

Number	*Owner*	*Status*	*Location*	*Livery*	*Name*
87009	EPX	Operational	EXP	BUL	
87017	EPX	Operational	EXP	EPX	*Iron Duke*
87023	EPX	Operational	EXP	EPX	*Velocity*
87025	EPX	Stored	EXP	VIR	

(Hire locomotives in Bulgaria working for short-line operator Bulmarket)

Porterbrook

Address: ✉ Burdett House, Becket Street, Derby, DE1 1JP
enquiries@porterbrook.co.uk ✆ 01332 262405 ⓘ www.porterbrook.co.uk

Chief Executive Officer: Mary Grant

Facilities: Porterbrook Leasing has made available the off-lease Class 87s to mainland European operators, with a significant number being exported to operate in Bulgaria.

Exported

Number	*Present operator*
87003	BZK Bulgaria
87004	BZK Bulgaria *Britannia*
87006	BZK Bulgaria
87007	BZK Bulgaria
87008	BZK Bulgaria
87010	BZK Bulgaria
87012	BZK Bulgaria
87013	BZK Bulgaria
87014	BZK Bulgaria
87019	BZK Bulgaria
87020	BZK Bulgaria
87022	BZK Bulgaria
87026	BZK Bulgaria
87028	BZK Bulgaria
87029	BZK Bulgaria
87033	BZK Bulgaria
87034	BZK Bulgaria

See Page 260 for numbering

A fleet of 17 Porterbrook Class 87s are currently in Bulgaria, where they should be deployed operating heavy freight services. However, reports from the country indicate that in late 2019, most locos were parked up and not working. NSE-liveried No. 87012 heads a line of five locos at Pirdop. **Howard Lewsey**

Angel Trains

Address: ✉ Portland House, Bressenden Place, London, SW1E 5BH
reception@angeltrains.co.uk ✆ 0207 592 0500 ⓘ www.angeltrains.co.uk
Chief Executive: David Jordan **Owned by:** Babcock Brown, AMP Capital and Deutsche Bank

British American Railway Services

Incorporating: RMS Locotec, RT Rail, Dartmoor Railway, Weardale Railway, Ealing Community Transport and Hanson Rail
Address: ✉ London Riverside, London, SE1 2AQ
President: Ed Ellis **Depots:** RMS Wakefield (ZS), Washwood Heath (WH)
UK operation is part of Iowa Pacific Holdings. BARS is also a Train Operating Company.

Class 08

Vehicle Length: 29ft 3in (8.91m)
Height: 12ft 8⅝in (3.87m)
Width: 8ft 6in (2.59m)
Engine: English Electric 6K
Horsepower: 400hp (298kW)
Electrical Equipment: English Electric

Number	Depot	Pool	Livery	Owner	Operator
08308	W	MRSO	RMS	ECT	Wear
08423	W	INDL	RMS	RMS	IND
08523	W	MRSO	RMS	RMS	Wear
08573	W	MRSO	BLK	ECT	Wear
08588	WH	MRSO	RMS	ECT	IND
08613	P	MOLO	BLU	RMS	IND
08622	KD	INDL	BLU	RMS	IND
08648	IS	INDL	GTO	BAR	FSR
08754	IS	MRSO	BLU	ECT	ASR
08756	MR	MRSO	GRY	ECT	GBR
08762	CD	MRSO	RMS	ECT	LNW
08870	W	MBDL	BLG	RMS	Wear
08874	ZB	MBDL	SIL	RMS	Wear
08885	ZS	INDL	GBR	RMS	GBR
08936	ZS	MBDL	BLU	RMS	IND

§ at Onllwyn, K - Ketton, P - P D Ports, Middlesbrough, W - Weardale

Class 31/1, 31/4

Vehicle Length: 56ft 9in (17.29m)
Height: 12ft 7in (3.91m)
Width: 8ft 9in (2.65m)
31/4 Electric Train Heat fitted
Engine: English Electric 12SVT
Horsepower: 1,470hp (1,097kW)
Electrical Equipment: Brush

Number		Depot	Pool	Livery	Owner	Location
31190		WH	HTLX	GRN	BAR	Weardale (stored)
31452	(31552, 31279)	-	HTLX	DCG	ECT	Dartmoor Rly (stored)
31454	(31554, 31228)	WH	HTLX	ICS	BAR	Weardale (Stored)

Cappaga Group (DC Rail)

Class 56

Vehicle Length: 63ft 6in (19.35m)
Height: 13ft 0in (3.96m)
Width: 9ft 2in (2.79m)
Engine: Ruston Paxman 16RK3CT
Horsepower: 3,250hp (2,420kW)
Electrical Equipment: Brush

Number		Depot	Pool	Livery	Owner	Operator	Name/Notes
56091		LR	HTLX	DCR	DCR	DCR	*Driver Wayne Gaskill 'The Godfather'*
56103		LR	HTLX	DCR	DCR	DCR	
56303(S)	(56125)	LR	HTLX	GRN	BAR	BAR	

Right: *Devon Cornwall Railway (DC Rail) operate two Class 56s on freight services. The pair, based at Leicester, sport mid grey livery with white DC Rail Freight branding. No. 56103 is seen heading south at Stenson Junction on 3 June 2019.* **CJM**

Class 60

Vehicle Length: 70ft 0½in (21.34m)
Height: 12ft 10⅝in (3.92m)
Width: 8ft 8in (2.64m)
Engine: Mirrlees MB275T
Horsepower: 3,100hp (2,240kW)
Electrical Equipment: Brush

Number	*Depot*	*Pool*	*Livery*	*Owner*	*Operator*	*Name*
60028	TO	HTLX	BLU	CAP	DCR	
60029	TO	HTLX	GRY	CAP	DCR	
60046	TO	HTLX	GRY	CAP	DCR	*William Wilberforce*
60055	TO	HTLX	GRY	CAP	DCR	*Thomas Barnardo*

Above: *Devon Cornwall Railway (now trading as DC Rail Freight and owned by Cappaga Group) have four Class 60s on their roster for heavy freight work. The locos have received heavy refurbishment by DB at Toton. Sporting grey livery with white DC Rail Freight branding. No. 60055* Thomas Barnardo *is illustrated at Salisbury.* **Mark V. Pike**

UK Rail Leasing

Address: ✉ Leicester Depot, Leicester.

CEO: Mark Winter **Depot:** Leicester (LR)

Purchaser and restorer of ex-BR locomotives for hire to the UK and overseas rail industries

Class 37/9

Vehicle Length: 61ft 6in (18.74m)
Height: 13ft 0¼in (3.96m)
Width: 8ft 11⅝in (2.73m)
Engine: Ruston RK270T
Horsepower: 1,800hp (1,342kW)
Electrical Equipment: English Electric

Number	*Depot*	*Pool*	*Livery*	*Owner*	*Operator*
37905 (D6836, 37136)	LR	UKRS	GRN	URL	URL
37906 (37206)	LR	UKRS	RFD	URL	at Battlefield Line

Class 56

Vehicle Length: 63ft 6in (19.35m)
Height: 13ft 0in (3.96m)
Width: 9ft 2in (2.79m)
Engine: Ruston Paxman 16RK3CT
Horsepower: 3,250hp (2,420kW)
Electrical Equipment: Brush

Number	*Depot*	*Pool*	*Livery*	*Owner*	*Operator*
56006	LR	UKRS	BLU	URL	ELR
58025	LR	UKRS	BLU	P	-

Class 58

Vehicle Length: 62ft 9½in (19.13m)
Height: 12ft 10in (3.91m)
Width: 9ft 1in (2.72m)
Engine: Ruston Paxman 12RK3ACT
Horsepower: 3,300hp (2,460kW)
Electrical Equipment: Brush

Number	*Depot*	*Pool*	*Livery*	*Owner*	*Operator*
58016	LR	UKRS	GRY	C58LG	-

Eversholt Rail Group

Address: ✉ PO Box 29499, 1 Eversholt Street, London, NW1 2ZF

info@eversholtrail.co.uk ✆ 0207 380 5040 ⓘ www.eversholtrail.co.uk

Chief Operating Officer: Mary Kenny
Owned by C K Investments
One of the three main rolling stock lease companies in the UK, responsible for the ownership and hire of rolling stock of all types to the train operating companies.

Harry Needle Railroad Company

Address: ✉ Harry Needle Railway Shed, Barrow Hill Roundhouse, Campbell Drive, Chesterfield, Derbyshire, S43 2PR
Managing Director: Harry Needle
Depot: Barrow Hill (BH), Worksop Wagon Depot

Class 01.5

Number	Depot	Pool	Livery	Owner	Operator	Note
01552 (TH167V)	BH	HNRL	IND	HNR	IND	
01564 (12088)	-	HNRL	BLK	HNR	IND	Preserved at Aln Valley Railway

Class 08 and 09

Vehicle Length: 29ft 3in (8.91m)
Height: 12ft 8⅝in (3.87m)
Width: 8ft 6in (2.59m)
Engine: English Electric 6K
Horsepower: 400hp (298kW)
Electrical Equipment: English Electric

Number	Depot	Pool	Livery	Owner	Operator
08389	CEL	HNRL	EWS	HNR	Celsa
08500	BU	HNRL	EWS	HNR	-
08527	BH	HNRL	JAR	HNR	Attero
08578	BH	HNRL	EWS	HNR	QRT
08630	BH	HNRL	COL	HNR	-
08653	BH	HNRL	EWS	HNR	QRT
08676	-	HNRL	EWS	HNR	EKR
08685	BH	HNRL	EWS	HNR	EKR
08700	BH	HNRL	BLU	HNR	BOM
08701	BH	HNRL	-	HNR	QRT
08714	BH	HNRL	DBS	HNR	Hope
08765	BH	HNRL	ORG	HNR	HNR
08786	BH	HNRL	BRD	HNR	HNR
08798	BH	HNRL	EWS	HNR	HNR
08802	BH	HNRL	-	HNR	-
08818	BH	HNRL	GBR	HNR	GBR
08824	BH	HNRL	BLK	HNR	-
08834	AN	HNRL	HNR	HNR	NOR
08865	CZ	HNRL	EWS	HNR	BOM
08868	CP	HNRL	ATC	HNR	LNW
08877	BH	HNRL	BRD	HNR	Celsa
08879	BH	HNRL	HNR	HNR	HOPE
08892	HE	HNRL	DRS	HNR	HNR
08904	BH	HNRL	EWS	HNR	Worksop
08905	BH	HNRL	EWS	HNR	IND
08918	BH	HNRL	EWS	HNR	-
08924	BH	HNRL	GBR	HNR	GBR
08929(S)	LM	HNRS	BLK	HNR	-
08943	BH	MBDL	HNR	HNR	-
08954	LL	HNRS	BLU	HNR	ALS
09006§	BH	HNRL	EWS	HNR	-
09014§	BU	HNRS	ORG	HNR	-
09018	BU	HNRS	HNR	HNR	LAF
09106	BH	HNRS	HNR	HNR	Celsa
09201	BH	HNRL	BRD	HNR	LAF

Name applied
08630 ***Celsa Endeavour***

Class 20

Vehicle Length: 46ft 9¼in (14.26m)
Height: 12ft 7⅝in (3.84m)
Width: 8ft 9in (2.66m)
Engine: English Electric 8SVT Mk2
Horsepower: 1,000hp (745kW)
Electrical Equipment: English Electric

Number	Depot	Pool	Livery	Owner	Operator
20016(S) §	BH	HNRS	BLU	HNR	-
20056	BH	HNRL	COR	HNR	TAT
20066	BH	HNRL	TAT	HNR	HCM*
20081(S) §	LM	HNRS	BLU	HNR	-
20088(S) §	LM	HNRS	RFG	HNR	-
20096	BH	GBEE	BLU	HNR	HNR
20107‡	BH	GBEE	ORG	HNR	HNR
20110§	BH	HNRL	GRN	HNR	-
20118	BH	GBEE	RFG	HNR	HNR
20121(S)§	WEN	HNRS	ORG	HNR	-
20132‡	BH	GBEE	RFG	HNR	HNR
20138(S)	LM	HNRS	RFT	HNR	-
20166	WEN	HNRS	ORG	HNR	HNR
20168	BH	HNRL	WHT	HNR	Hope

‡ Main line certified
* HCM Hope Construction Materials
§ For sale

Number		Depot	Pool	Livery	Owner	Operator	Note
20311	(20102)	BH	GBEE	ORG	HNR	HNR	
20314	(20117)	BH	GBEE	ORG	HNR	HNR	Allocated number 92 70 0020314-5
20903(S)§	(20083)	LM	HNRS	DRS	HNR	-	

20904(S)§ (20041)	LM	HNRS	DRS	HNR	-
20906 (20219)	BH	HNRL	WHT	HNR	HNR

20056 carries Tata Steel No. 81. 20066 carries Tata Steel No. 82.

Names applied

20096	*Ian Goddard 1938-2016*
20118	*Saltburn-by-the-Sea*
20132	*Barrow Hill Depot*
20168	*Sir George Earle*
20906	*Dave Darwin*

Class 31

Vehicle Length: 56ft 9in (17.29m)
Height: 12ft 7in (3.91m)
Width: 8ft 9in (2.65m)
Engine: English Electric 12SVT
Horsepower: 1,470hp (1,097kW)
Electrical Equipment: Brush

Number	*Depot*	*Pool*	*Livery*	*Owner*	*Operator*
31235	BH	-	-	HNR	-
31285	BH	-	NRL	HNR	-
31459	BH	-	BLU	HNR	-
31465	BH	-	NRL	HNR	At Weardale

Class 37

Vehicle Length: 61ft 6in (18.74m)
Height: 13ft 0¼in (3.96m)
Width: 8ft 11⅝in (2.73m)
Engine: English Electric 12CSVT
Horsepower: 1,750hp (1,304kW)
Electrical Equipment: English Electric

Number	*Depot*	*Pool*	*Livery*	*Owner*	*Operator/Note*
37029	BH	HNRS	GRN	HNR	HNR (at Epping & Ongar Railway)
37607 (37511)	BH	COTS	BLU	HNR	COL
37610 (37687)	BH	HNRL	BLU	HNR	HNR
37612 (37691)	BH	COTS	BLU	HNR	COL

Above: *A large number of locos have been handled by Harry Needle Railroad Company over the years, many ending up preserved. HNRC also operates a quality fleet of hire locos, No. 37610 being one. This was a former Eurostar UK loco and later a DRS machine. It is now restored to Rail Blue with wrap around yellow ends and a small BR logo. It is usually hired to Colas to power Network Rail test trains. The loco is approaching Filton Abbey Wood.* **Mark V. Pike**

Class 47

Vehicle Length: 63ft 6in (19.35m)
Height: 12ft 10⅜in (3.91m)
Width: 9ft 2in (2.79m)
Electric Train Heat fitted
Engine: Sulzer 12LDA28C
Horsepower: 2,580hp (1,922kW)
Electrical Equipment: Brush

Number	*Depot*	*Pool*	*Livery*	*Owner*	*Operator*	*Notes/Name*
47703 (47514)	Wab	HNRL	-	HNR	heating	
47714 (47511)	OD	HNRL	ANG	HNR	SEC	At RIDC (Old Dalby test track)
47715 (47502)	WK	HNRL	NSE	HNR	Worksop	*Haymarket*
47769 (47491)	BH	HNRL	RES	HNR	ROG	

RIDC - Rail Innovation and Development Centre, Old Dalby

Beacon Rail

Address: ✉ Beacon Rail Leasing, 111 Buckingham Palace Road, London, SW1W 0SR

rail@beaconrail.com.com ✆ 0207 015 00001 ⓘ www.beaconrail.com

UK and international loco, multiple unit and wagon hire company.

Managing Director (UK): Neil Bennett **Parent Company:** J P Morgan

Nemesis Rail

Address: ✉ Nemesis Rail Ltd, Burton Depot, Burton-on-Trent, DE14 1RS

enquiries@nemesisrail.com ✆ 01246 472331 ⓘ www.nemesisrail.com

Formed from the demise of FM Rail

Depot: Burton (BU)

Class 31/1

Vehicle Length: 56ft 9in (17.29m)
Height: 12ft 7in (3.91m)
Width: 8ft 9in (2.65m)
Engine: English Electric 12SVT
Horsepower: 1,470hp (1,097kW)
Electrical Equipment: Brush

Number	*Depot*	*Pool*	*Livery*	*Owner*	*Operator*	*Name*
31128	BU	NRLO	BLU	NEM	WCR	***Charybdis***

Right: *Nemesis Rail, based at Burton, operate Class 31/1 No. 31128 Charybdis. The loco is restored to 1970s BR Rail Blue with full yellow warning ends and three section snowploughs. It is available for hire to either passenger, freight or charter operators and usually based at Burton. It is seen passing Kidsgrove on 10 June 2019.* **Cliff Beeton**

Class 33/1

Vehicle Length: 50ft 9in (15.47m)
Height: 12ft 8in (3.86m)
Width: 9ft 3in (2.81m)
Engine: Sulzer 8LDA28A
Horsepower: 1,550hp (1,156kW)
Electrical Equipment: Crompton Parkinson

Number	*Depot*	*Pool*	*Livery*	*Owner*	*Operator*	*Name*
33103	BU	MBDL	BLU	NEM	-	***Swordfish***

Class 45/1

Vehicle Length: 67ft 11in (20.70m)
Height: 12ft 10½in (3.91m)
Width: 9ft 1½in (2.78m)
Engine: Sulzer 12LDA28B
Horsepower: 2,500hp (1,862kW)
Electrical Equipment: Crompton Parkinson

Number	*Depot*	*Pool*	*Livery*	*Owner*	*Operator*	*Name*
45112	BU	MBDL	BLU	NEM	NEM	***Royal Army Ordnance Corps***

Class 47

Vehicle Length: 63ft 6in (19.35m)
Height: 12ft 10⅜in (3.91m)
Width: 9ft 2in (2.79m)
Class 47/4 and 47/7 - Electric Train Heat fitted
Engine: Sulzer 12LDA28C
Horsepower: 2,580hp (1,922kW)
Electrical Equipment: Brush

Number	*Depot*	*Pool*	*Livery*	*Owner*	*Operator*
47488	BU	MBDL	MAR	CRS	NEM
47701	BU	MBDL	BLK	NEM	NEM
47744	BU	MBDL	EWS	NEM	NEM

Nos. 47488/701/744 also destined for export to Hungary for Continental Railway Solutions

Porterbrook

Address: ✉ Ivatt House, The Point, Pinnacle Way, Pride Park, Derby, DE24 8ZS
enquiries@porterbrook.co.uk ✆ 01332 285050 ⓘ www.porterbrook.co.uk

Chief Executive Officer: Mary Grant

Owned by: Deutsche Bank

Porterbrook Leasing Company is one of the three major ROSCOs in the United Kingdom. Created in 1994 as part of the privatisation of British Rail, it specialises in the leasing of railway rolling stock and associated equipment to Freight and Passenger Train Operating Companies.

The company is one of leading lights in rail innovation, with a number of projects ongoing to develop the use of different fuel and power systems, including hydrogen. Another major project is the rebuilding of off-lease Class 319 electric mutliple units as bi-mode stock, by installing a diesel raft below the driving cars, enabling sets to operate from either the overhead or third rail electrification or from an on-board diesel alternator set. These sets are marketed under the Class 769 banner and will be used by Northern, Transport for Wales and Great Western.

Above and Left: *In summer 2019, Porterbrook unveiled their prototype 'Hydro-Flex' hydrogen powered Class 799 development train. As a alternative method of providing traction power, the set has had hydrogen fuel cells placed inside the original motor car, this fuel cell mixes hydrogen with oxygen to produce electric power. Rebuilt from Class 319 set No. 319001, the set is likely to undertake main line testing in 2020. Production trains will have the fuel cells and hydrogen tanks mounted on the underframe. The image left shows the modified Motor Standard Open vehicle. Both:* **CJM**

Transmart Trains

Address: ✉ Green Farm House, Falfield, Wootton-under-Edge, Gloucestershire, GL12 8DL
Managing Director: Oliver Buxton
Depots: Cambrian Transport

Class 73/1

Vehicle Length: 53ft 8in (16.35m)
Height: 12ft 5⁵⁄₁₆in (3.79m)
Width: 8ft 8in (2.64m)

Power: 750V dc third rail or English Electric 6K
Horsepower: electric - 1,600hp (1,193kW)
diesel - 600hp (447kW)
Electrical Equipment: English Electric

‡ *At Barry Railway*
• *Not main-line certified*

Number	*Depot*	*Pool*	*Livery*	*Owner*	*Operator*
73118•	‡	-	GRY	TTS	TTS
73133•	EH	-	GRN	TTS	-

■ Former 'Gatwick Express' Class 488 vehicles Nos. 72505, 72620, 72621, 72629, 72710 from sets 488206 and 488311 are also owned by Transmart Trains.

Above: *Class 73 No. 73133, with modified cab ends sporting light clusters, was for a long time used at Bournemouth depot by South West Trains. It is currently at Arlington Eastleigh, where it is occasionally used for pilotage operations.* **Mark V. Pike**

Class 20 Loco Ltd

Class 20

Vehicle Length: 46ft 9¼in (14.26m)
Height: 12ft 7⅝in (3.84m)
Width: 8ft 9in (2.66m)

Engine: English Electric 8SVT Mk2
Horsepower: 1,000hp (745kW)
Electrical Equipment: English Electric

Number	*Depot*	*Pool*	*Livery*	*Owner*	*Operator*
20205	SK	MOLO	BLU	C2L	Spot hire
20227	SK	MOLO	LUL	C2L	GBR

Right: *Class 20 Locomotives Ltd operate a pair of superbly restored Class 20s, fully certificated for main line operations. No. 20205 is seen at Crewe in summer 2019, sporting 1970s BR Rail Blue.* **Antony Christie**

Listings provide details of locomotives and stock authorised for operation on the UK National Rail network and that can be seen operating special and charter services.
Preserved locomotives authorised for main-line operation are found in the preserved section.

Bo'ness & Kinneil Railway

Number	Type	Depot	Livery	Operator	Use
464	AO3/BCK	BT	CAL	BOK	Charter train use
1375 (99803)	AO2/TK	BT	CAL	BOK	Charter train use
3096 (99827)	AD11/FO	BT	MAR	BOK	Charter train use
3115	AD11/FO	BT	MAR	BOK	Charter train use
3150	AD11/FO	BT	MAR	BOK	Charter train use
4831 (99824)	AC21/TSO	BT	MAR	BOK	Charter train use
4832 (99823)	AC21/TSO	BT	MAR	BOK	Charter train use
4836 (99831)	AC21/TSO	BT	MAR	BOK	Charter train use
4856 (99829)	AC21/TSO	BT	MAR	BOK	Charter train use
5028 (99830)	AC21/TSO	BT	MAR	BOK	Charter train use
13229 (99826)	AA11/FK	BT	MAR	BOK	Charter train use
13230 (99828)	AA11/FK	BT	MAR	BOK	Charter train use

Royal Scotsman

Great Scottish & Western Railway Co

Number	Type	Depot	Livery	Operator	Notes
99337 (337)	AO11/PSK	CS	RSM	GSW	State Spa Car
99960 (321)	AO11/PFK	CS	RSM	GSW	Dining Car 2
99961 (324)	AO11/PFP	CS	RSM	GSW	State Car No. 1
99962 (329)	AO11/PFP	CS	RSM	GSW	State Car No. 2
99963 (331)	AO11/PFP	CS	RSM	GSW	State Car No. 3
99964 (313)	AO11/PFK	CS	RSM	GSW	State Car No. 4
99965 (319)	AO11/PFK	CS	RSM	GSW	Observation Car
99967 (317)	AO11/PFK	CS	RSM	GSW	Dining Car 1
99968 (10541)	AO4G/SSV	CS	RSM	GSW	State Car No. 5
99969 (10556)	AO4G/SSV	CS	RSM	GSW	Service Car

Left: *The Royal Scotsman luxury Land Cruise train is a very impressive formation of former BR Pullman vehicles and ex Mk3 stock. It is painted in deep maroon with gold branding and usually operates in Scotland, making one or two trips to England and Wales each year. State Car No. 2, 99962, rebuilt from Pullman 329 is illustrated.* CJM

Above: *Two former BR Mk3 sleeper cars operate as part of the Royal Scotsman train, one No. 99968 (10541) as State Car No. 5 and the other 99969 (10556) as a staff and service vehicle. State Car No. 5 is shown, illustrating the major nature of the rebuild, including windows with opening quarter lights.* CJM

Hastings Diesels Limited

The following vehicles are owned by Hastings Diesels Ltd and kept at St Leonards. Usually a six-car train is formed, which is fitted with central door locking and is main-line certified (original class numbers shown in brackets).
60000 (201), 60019 (202), 60116 (202), 60118 (202), 60501 (201), 60528 (202), 60529 (202), 69337 (422 EMU), 70262 (411 EMU).
Set **1001** is formed of **60116+60529+70262+69337+60501+60118**

Mid-Hants Railway

Number	*Type*	*Depot*	*Livery*	*Operator*
1105	**AJ41/RG**	**RL**	**GRN**	**MHR**
21252	**AB31/BCK**	**RL**	**GRN**	**MHR**

North Yorkshire Moors Railway

Class 08

Vehicle Length: 29ft 3in (8.91m)
Height: 12ft 8⅝in (3.87m)
Width: 8ft 6in (2.59m)
Engine: English Electric 6K
Horsepower: 400hp (298kW)
Electrical Equipment: English Electric

Number	*Depot*	*Pool*	*Livery*	*Owner*	*Operator*	*Note*
08850	**NY**	**MBDL**	**BLU**	**NYM**	**NYM**	Restricted main-line use

Class 25

Vehicle Length: 50ft 6in (15.39m)
Height: 12ft 8in (3.86m)
Width: 9ft 1in (2.76m)
Engine: Sulzer 6LDA28B
Horsepower: 1,250hp (932kW)
Electrical Equipment: Brush

Number	*Depot*	*Pool*	*Livery*	*Owner*	*Operator*	*Name*	*Note*
25278	**NY**	**MBDL**	**GRN**	**NYM**	**NYM**	***Sybilia***	Restricted main-line use

Coaching Stock

Number	*Type*	*Depot*	*Livery*	*Operator*
1823	**AN21/RMB**	**NY**	**MAR**	**NYM**
3860	**AC21/TSO**	**NY**	**MAR**	**NYM**
3872	**AC21/TSO**	**NY**	**MAR**	**NYM**
3948	**AC2I/TSO**	**NY**	**CAR**	**NYM**
4198	**AC21/TSO**	**NY**	**CAR**	**NYM**
4252	**AC21/TSO**	**NY**	**CAR**	**NYM**
4290	**AC21/TSO**	**NY**	**MAR**	**NYM**
4455	**AC21/TSO**	**NY**	**CAR**	**NYM**
4786	**AC21/TSO**	**HQ**	**MAR**	**NYM**
4817	**AC21/TSO**	**NY**	**CHC**	**NYM**
5000	**AC21/TSO**	**NY**	**MAR**	**NYM**
5029	**AC21/TSO**	**NY**	**MAR**	**NYM**
9267	**AE21/BSO**	**NY**	**CHC**	**NYM**
9274	**AE21/BSO**	**NY**	**CHC**	**NYM**
16156 (7156)	**AA31/CK**	**NY**	**MAR**	**NYM**
21100	**AB31/BCK**	**NY**	**CHC**	**NYM**
35089	**AB2I/BSK**	**NY**	**MAR**	**NYM**

Railfilms Limited/Statesman Rail

Number	*Type*	*Depot*	*Livery*	*Operator*	*Name*
84 (99884)	**Mk1 Pantry**	**CS**	**PUL**	**RAF**	
310 (99107)	**AO11/PFL**	**BO**	**PUL**	**RAF**	***Pegasus / Trianon Bar***
3188	**AD1D/FO**	**CL**	**PUL**	**RAF**	
4362	**AC21/SO**	**BU**	**-**	**RAF**	
9005	**GWR**	**SDR**	**GWR**	**RAF**	
13508	**AA1B/FK**	**BU**	**MAR**	**RAF**	

Ridings Railtours

Number	*Type*	*Depot*	*Livery*	*Operator*
5520 (S)	**AC2C/TSO**	**SV**	**PUL**	**RRS**
13581 (S)	**AA1D/FK**	**SV**	**ICS**	**RRS**
13583 (S)	**AA1D/FK**	**SV**	**ICS**	**RRS**

Riviera Trains

Class 08

Vehicle Length: 29ft 3in (8.91m)
Height: 12ft 8⅝in (3.87m)
Width: 8ft 6in (2.59m)
Engine: English Electric 6K
Horsepower: 400hp (298kW)
Electrical Equipment: English Electric

Number	*Depot*	*Pool*	*Livery*	*Owner*	*Operator*
08507	**EH**	**RTLO**	**RIV**	**RIV**	**AFS**

Riviera

Coaching Stock

Number	Type	Depot	Livery	Operator	Name
1200 (6459)	AJ1F/RFO	EH	BLG	RIV	
1203 (3291)	AJ1F/RFO	PO	CCM	RIV	
1212 (6453)	AJ1F/RFO	PO	BLG	RIV	
1651	AJ41/RBR	EH	chc	RIV	
1657	AJ41/RBR	BU	BLG	RIV	
1671	AJ41/RBR	ZG	CHC	RIV	
1683	AJ41/RBR	BO	BLU	RIV	*Carol*
1691	AJ41/RBR	BU	BLG	RIV	
1813	AN21/RMB	ZG	CHC	RIV	
1832	AN21/RMB	EH	CCM	RIV	
1863	AN21/RMB	CL	CHC	RIV	
3066 (99566)	AD11/FO	ZG	CCM	RIV	
3068 (99568)	AD11/FO	ZG	CCM	RIV	
3069 (99540)	AD11/FO	EH	CCM	RIV	
3097	AD11/FO	EH	CCM	RIV	
3098	AD11/FO	ZG	CHC	RIV	
3100	AD11/FO	CL	CHC	RIV	
3110 (99124)	AD11/FO	ZG	CHC	RIV	
3112 (99357)	AD11/FO	ZG	CHC	RIV	
3119	AD11/FO	ZG	CCM	RIV	
3120	AD11/FO	ZG	CHC	RIV	
3121	AD11/FO	EH	CHC	RIV	
3122	AD11/FO	CL	CHC	RIV	
3123	AD11/FO	EH	CHC	RIV	
3125	AD11/FO	CL	CCM	RIV	
3141 (3608)	AD11/FO	ZG	CHC	RIV	
3144 (3602)	AD11/FO	BQ	MRN	RIV	
3146	AD11/FO	ZG	CHC	RIV	
3147 (3604)	AD11/FO	EH	LNE	RIV	
3148	AD11/FO	CL	CHC	RIV	
3149	AD11/FO	EH	CHC	RIV	
3181 (S)	AD1D/FO	EH	RIV	RIV	*Topaz*
3223 (S)	AD1E/FO	CL	RIV	RIV	*Diamond*
3227	AD1E/FO	EH	RIV	RIV	
3240	AD1E/FO	CL	RIV	RIV	*Sapphire*
3278	AD1F/FO	EH	BLG	RIV	
3304	AD1F/FO	EH	BLG	RIV	
3314	AD1F/FO	BO	BLG	RIV	
3325	AD1F/FO	ZG	VIR	RIV	
3330	AD1F/FO	CL	CCM	RIV	
3333	AD1F/FO	EH	BLG	RIV	
3340	AD1F/FO	EH	BLG	RIV	
3345	ADIF/FO	EH	BLG	RIV	
3356	AD1F/FO	EH	BLG	RIV	
3364	AD1F/FO	EH	BLG	RIV	
3384	AD1F/FO	CL	PUL	RIV	*Pen-y-Ghent*
3386	AD1F/FO	EH	BLG	RIV	
3390	AD1F/FO	EH	BLG	RIV	
3397	AD1F/FO	EH	BLG	RIV	
3426	AD1F/FO	CL	PUL	RIV	*Ben Nevis*
4927	AC21/TSO	ZG	CHC	RIV	
4946	AC21/TSO	ZG	CHC	RIV	
4949	AC21/TSO	ZG	CHC	RIV	
4959	AC21/TSO	ZA	CHC	RIV	
4991	AC21/TSO	EH	CHC	RIV	
4998	AC21/TSO	EH	CHC	RIV	
5007	AC21/TSO	WH	CHC	RIV	
5009	AC21/TSO	ZG	CHC	RIV	
5292	AC2A/TSO	EH	CHC	RIV	
5309 (S)	AC2A/TSO	EH	CHC	RIV	
5494 (S)	AC2B/TSO	SV	NSE	RIV	
5647 (S)	AC2D/TSO	EH	RIV	RIV	
5910	AC2F/TSO	BU	BLG	RIV	

5921	AC2F/TSO	EH	ANG	RIV	
5929	AC2F/TSO	EH	BLG	RIV	
5937	AC2F/TSO	KM	DRS	RIV	
5950	AC2F/TSO	EH	RIV	RIV	
5961	AC2F/TSO	CF	BLG	RIV	
5964	AC2F/TSO	EH	ANG	RIV	
5985	AC2F/TSO	EH	ANG	RIV	
5998	AC2F/TSO	CF	BLG	TFW	
6006	AC2F/TSO	BU	ANG	RIV	
6024	AC2F/TSO	CF	BLG	TFW	
6042	AC2F/TSO	CF	ANG	TFW	
6051	AC2F/TSO	EH	BLG	RIV	
6054	AC2F/TSO	CF	BLG	RIV	
6059	AC2F/TSO	EH	BLG	RIV	
6067	AC2F/TSO	CF	BLG	TFW	
6141	AC2F/TSO	BU	RIV	RIV	
6158	AC2F/TSO	CF	BLG	RIV	
6310 (81448)	AX51/GEN	ZG	CHC	RIV	
6320	AZ5Z/SAL	SK	MRN	RIV	
9504	AC2E/BSO	BU	BLG	RIV	
9507	AC2E/BSO	CF	BLG	TFW	
9509	AE2E/BSO	BO	ATW	RIV	
9520	AE2F/BSO	CF	RIV	RIV	
9526	AC2F/BSO	CF	RIV	TFW	
9527	AC2F/BSO	ML	SCR	SCR	
9537	AE2F/BSO	BU	ADV	RIV	
17056 (14056)	AB1A/BFK	ZG	CCM	RIV	
17105 (2905)	AX5B/BFK	EH	BLG	RIV	
21224	AB31/BCK	EH	MAR	RIV	
21245 (99356)	AB31/BCK	ZG	MAR	RIV	
21269	AB31/BCK	EH	CCM	RIV	
21272 (99129)	AB31/BCK	ZG	CHC	RIV	Directors Saloon
35469 (99763)	AB21/BSK	EH	CHC	RIV	
80041 (1690)	AK51/RK	EH	MAR	RIV	
80042 (1646)	AJ41/RK	ZG	CHC	RIV	

§ Stored East Dereham

Right: *One of the largest suppliers of coaching stock to charter operators and TOCs is Riviera Trains who have a large fleet of Mk1 and Mk2 vehicles. No. 35469, a BSK is seen from its brake end, which now houses a generator.* **Antony Christie**

Below: *Former Mk2f First Open No. 3426, is now finished as a Pullman car with the name* Ben Nevis. *The vehicle is seen at Crewe in mid 2019.* **Antony Christie**

Scottish Railway Preservation Society

Number	Type	Depot	Livery	Operator
1859 (99822)	AN21/RMB	BT	MAR	SRP
21241	AB31/BCK	BT	MAR	SRP
35185	AB21/BSK	BT	MAR	SRP

Stratford Class 47 Group

Class 47

Vehicle Length: 63ft 6in (19.35m)
Height: 12ft 10$^{3}/_{8}$in (3.91m)
Width: 9ft 2in (2.79m)
Electric Train Heat fitted
Engine: Sulzer 12LDA28C
Horsepower: 2,580hp (1,922kW)
Electrical Equipment: Brush

Number	Depot	Pool	Livery	Owner	Operator	Name
47580 (S) (47167/732)	MNR	MBDL	LLB	S4G	S4G	*County of Essex*

Belmond British Pullman (VSOE)

Number	Name	Type	Depot	Livery	Operator
213 (99535)	*Minerva*	AO40/PFP	SL	PUL	VSO
239 (S)	*Agatha*	AO40/PFP	SL	PUL	VSO
243 (99541)	*Lucille*	AO40/PFP	SL	PUL	VSO
245 (99534)	*Ibis*	AO40/PFK	SL	PUL	VSO
254 (99536)	*Zena*	AO40/PFP	SL	PUL	VSO
255 (99539)	*Ione*	AO40/PFK	SL	PUL	VSO
261 (S)	Car No. 83	AO40/PTP	SL	PUL	VSO
264 (S)	*Ruth*	AO40/PCK	SL	PUL	VSO
280 (99537)	*Audrey*	AO40/PFK	SL	PUL	VSO
281 (99546)	*Gwen*	AO40/PFK	SL	PUL	VSO
283 (S)	*Mona*	AO40/PFK	SL	PUL	VSO
284 (99543)	*Vera*	AO40/PFK	SL	PUL	VSO
285 (S)	Car No. 85	AO40/PTP	SL	PUL	VSO
286 (S)	Car No. 86	AO40/PTP	SL	PUL	VSO
288 (S)	Car No. 88	AO40/PTB	SL	PUL	VSO
292 (S)	Car No. 92	AO40/PTB	SL	PUL	VSO
293 (S)	Car No. 93	AO40/PTB	SL	PUL	VSO
301 (99530)	*Perseus*	AO41/PFP	SL	PUL	VSO
302 (99531)	*Phoenix*	AO41/PFP	SL	PUL	VSO
307 (S)	*Carina*	AO41/PFK	SL	PUL	VSO
308 (99532)	*Cygnus*	AO41/PFP	SL	PUL	VSO
6313 (92167)		AX51/GEN	SL	PUL	VSO
9502		AE2E/BSO	SL	PUL	VSO
35466 (99545)		AB21/BSK	SL	PUL	VSO

Left: *One of the most prestigious trains to operate in the UK is the Belmond British Pullman, previously identified as the VSOE. The train, mainly formed of historic Pullman Car Company vehicles, is fully restored and when not in use kept at Stewarts Lane. Pullman Car* Lucille *No. 243, with Network Rail No. 99541 allocated, was built in 1928 and originally operated on the LNER. It transferred to the Southern, where it worked for many years in the Bournemouth Belle.* **Antony Christie**

Vintage Trains

Class 47

Vehicle Length: 63ft 6in (19.35m)
Height: 12ft 10⅜in (3.91m)
Width: 9ft 2in (2.79m)
Electric Train Heat fitted
Engine: Sulzer 12LDA28C
Horsepower: 2,580hp (1,922kW)
Electrical Equipment: Brush

Number	Depot	Pool	Livery	Owner	Operator
47773 (47541)	TM	MBDL	GRN	VTN	VTN

Coaching Stock

Number	Type	Depot	Livery	Owner	Operator
335 (99361)	AO11/PSK	TM	PUL	VTN	VTN
349 (99349)	AO11/PSP	TM	PUL	VTN	VTN
353 (99353)	AO11/PSP	TM	PUL	VTN	VTN
5157	AC2Z/TSO	TM	CHC	VTN	VTN
5177	AC2Z/TSO	TM	CHC	VTN	VTN
5191	AC2Z/TSO	TM	CHC	VTN	VTN
5198	AC2Z/TSO	TM	CHC	VTN	VTN
5212	AC2Z/TSO	TM	CHC	VTN	VTN
9101 (9398)	AH2Z/BSOT	TM	CHC	VTN	VTN
17018 (99108)	AB11/BFK	TM	CHC	VTN	VTN
17090	AB1A/BFK	TM	CHC	VTN	VTN
96100 (86374)	GUV	TM	BRN	VTN	VTN

Boden Rail Engineering Ltd

Class 50

Vehicle Length: 68ft 6in (20.88m)
Height: 12ft 10¼ (3.92m)
Width: 9ft 1¼in (2.77m)
Engine: English Electric 16CSVT
Horsepower: 2700hp (2013kW)
Electrical Equipment: English Electric

Number	Depot	Pool	Livery	Owner	Operator	Name
50008 (D408)	NM	HTLX	BLU	BRE	BRE	*Thunderer*
50050 (D400)	NM	MBDL	BLU	BRE	BRE	*Fearless*

West Coast Railway Company

Class 03

Vehicle Length: 26ft 3in (7.92m)
Height: 12ft 7⁷⁄₁₆in (3.72m)
Width: 8ft 6in (2.59m)
Engine: Gardner 8L3
Horsepower: 204hp (149kW)
Mechanical Equipment: Wilson-Drewry

Number	Depot	Pool	Livery	Owner	Operator	Name
03196(S)	CS	MBDL	GRN	WCR	WCR	*Joyce*
D2381(S)	CS	MBDL	BLK	WCR	WCR	

Class 08

Vehicle Length: 29ft 3in (8.91m)
Height: 12ft 8⅝in (3.87m)
Width: 8ft 6in (2.59m)
Engine: English Electric 6K
Horsepower: 400hp (298kW)
Electrical Equipment: English Electric

Number	Depot	Pool	Livery	Owner	Operator
08418	CS	MBDL	EWS	WCR	WCR
08485	CS	MBDL	BLU	WCR	WCR
08678	CS	AWCX	WCR	WCR	WCR

Class 33

Vehicle Length: 50ft 9in (15.47m)
Height: 12ft 8in (3.86m)
Width: 33/0, 9ft 3in (2.81m),
33/2, 8ft 8in (2.64m)
Engine: Sulzer 8LDA28A
Horsepower: 1,550hp (1,156kW)
Electrical Equipment: Crompton Parkinson

Number	Depot	Pool	Livery	Owner	Operator	Name
33025	CS	AWCA	WCR	WCR	WCR	
33029	CS	AWCA	WCR	WCR	WCR	
33207	CS	AWCA	WCR	WCR	WCR	*Jim Martin*

WCRC

Left: *Three of the ever popular Class 33s are on the roster of West Coast Railway. All sport company deep maroon livery, with a small yellow warning panel front end. The fleet consists of two Class 33/0 standard locos and one 33/2 'Hastings' profile loco. No. 33025 is seen from its No. 2 end.* **Howard Lewsey**

Class 37

Vehicle Length: 61ft 6in (18.74m)
Height: 13ft 0¼in (3.96m)
Width: 8ft 11⅝in (2.73m)
Engine: English Electric 12CSVT
Horsepower: 1,750hp (1,304kW)
Electrical Equipment: English Electric

Number	*Depot*	*Pool*	*Livery*	*Owner*	*Operator*	*Name*
37516 (37086)	CS	AWCA	WCR	WCR	WCR	*Loch Laidon*
37517 (S) (37018)	CS	MBDL	LHL	WCR	-	
37518 (37076)	CS	AWCA	WCR	WCR	WCR	
37668 (37257)	CS	AWCA	WCR	WCR	WCR	
37669 (37129)	CS	AWCA	WCR	WCR	WCR	
37676 (37126)	CS	AWCA	WCR	WCR	WCR	*Loch Rannoch*
37685 (37234)	CS	AWCA	WCR	WCR	WCR	*Loch Arkaig*
37706 (37016)	CS	AWCA	WCR	WCR	WCR	
37710 (S) (37044)	CS	MBDL	LHL	WCR	-	
37712 (37102)	CS	AWCX	WCR	WCR	WCR	

Nos. 37668 and 37669 fitted with Hitachi ETRMS for Cambrian Line duties

Left: *Eight operational Class 37s are in the West Coast Carnforth-based fleet, these are examples of Classes 37/5 and 37/7s. Two other '37s' are owned by the company but stored. No. 37668 is seen at Crewe. The loco carries standard WCRC maroon livery with a small yellow warning end. This loco is fitted with Cambrian Coast Hitachi ERTMS equipment.* **Antony Christie**

Class 47

Vehicle Length: 63ft 6in (19.35m)
Height: 12ft 10⅜in (3.91m)
Width: 9ft 2in (2.79m)
Class 47/4, 47/7 and 47/8 Electric Train Heat fitted
Engine: Sulzer 12LDA28C
Horsepower: 2,580hp (1,922kW)
Electrical Equipment: Brush

Number	*Depot*	*Pool*	*Livery*	*Owner*	*Operator*	*Name*
47194 (S)	CS	AWCX	TLF	WCR	-	
47237	CS	AWCA	WCR	WCR	WCR	
47245	CS	AWCA	WCR	WCR	WCR	
47270	CS	AWCA	BLU	WCR	WCR	*Swift*
47355 (S)	CS	AWCX	BLK	WCR	-	
47492	CS	AWCX	RES	WCR	WCR	
47746 (47605)	CS	AWCA	WCR	WCR	WCR	*Chris Fudge 29.7.70-22.6.10*
47760 (47562)	CS	AWCA	WCR	WCR	WCR	
47768 (47490)	CS	AWCX	EWS	WCR	WCR	
47772 (47537)	CS	AWCA	WCR	WCR	WCR	*Carnforth TMD*
47776 (S) (47578)	CS	AWCX	RES	WCR	-	

47786 (47821)	CS	AWCA	WCR	WCR	WCR	*Roy Castle OBE*
47787 (47823)	CS	AWCX	WCR	WCR	WCR	
47802 (47552)	CS	AWCA	WCR	WCR	WCR	
47804 (47792)	CS	AWCA	WCR	WCR	WCR	
47826 (47637)	CS	AWCA	WCR	WCR	WCR	
47828 (47629)	CS	AWCA	ICS	PLG	WCR	
47832 (47560)	CS	AWCA	WCR	WCR	WCR	
47851 (47639)	CS	AWCA	WCR	WCR	WCR	
47854 (47674)	CS	AWCA	WCR	WCR	WCR	*Diamond Jubilee*

Right: *A sizeable fleet of Class 47s from various sub-classes operate for West Coast Railway. These are the prime power for charter services and can frequently be found operating in the 'top and tail' mode. No. 47802 is seen running light through Totnes in conjunction with a steam charter service operating in the area.* **Nathan Williamson**

Class 57

Vehicle Length: 63ft 6in (19.38m)
Height: 12ft 10⅛in (3.91m)
Width: 9ft 2in (2.79m)
Engine: EMD 645-12E3
Horsepower: 2,500hp (1,860kW)
Electrical Equipment: Brush

Number	*Depot*	*Pool*	*Livery*	*Owner*	*Operator*	*Name*
57001 (47356)	CS	AWCA	WCR	WCR	WCR	
57005 (47350)(S)	CS	AWCX	WCR	WCR	-	
57006 (47187)(S)	CS	AWCX	WCR	WCR	-	
57313 (47371)	CS	AWCA	PUL	WCR	WCR	
57314 (47372)	CS	AWCA	WCR	WCR	WCR	
57315 (47234)	CS	AWCA	WCR	WCR	WCR	
57316 (47290)	CS	AWCA	WCR	WCR	WCR	
57601 (47165/590/825)	CS	AWCA	PUL	WCR	WCR	*Windsor Castle*

Right: *The four Class 57/3 and one Class 57/6 are the most popular WCRC locos to be used on passenger services, again, often operating in the 'top and tail' style. The unique No. 57601* Windsor Castle, *originally built as an ETH-fitted demonstrator, is now painted in full Pullman livery with an Umber body and cream upper panel to match Pullman stock. The loco is seen at Bristol Temple Meads.* **Mark V. Pike**

Coaching Stock

Number	*Name*	*Type*	*Depot*	*Livery*	*Operator*	*Notes*
159 (99980)		AO10/SAL	CS	MAR	WCR*	LNWR saloon (ex-'Q of Scots')
326 (S) (99402)	*Emerald*	AO11/PFP	CS	PUL	WCR	
347 (99347)	Car No. 347	AO11/PSO	CS	WCR	WCR	

WCRC

348 (99348)	*Topaz*	AO11/PSP	CS	WCR	WCR	
350 (99350)	Car No. 350	AO11/PSP	CS	WCR	WCR	
351 (99351)	*Sapphire*	AO11/PSP	CS	WCR	WCR	
352 (99352)	*Amethyst*	AO11/PSP	CS	PUL	WCR	
354 (99354)	*The Hadrian Bar*	AO11/PSP	CS	PUL	WCR	
504 (99678)	*Ullswater*	AP1Z/PFK	CS	PUL	WCR	
506 (99679)	*Windermere*	AP1Z/PFK	CS	PUL	WCR	
546 (S) (99670)	*City of Manchester*	AQ1Z/PFP	CS	PUL	WCR	
548 (99671)	*Grasmere*	AQ1Z/PFP	CS	PUL	WCR	
549 (99672)	*Bassenthwaite*	AQ1Z/PFP	CS	PUL	WCR	
550 (99673)	*Rydal Water*	AQ1Z/PFP	CS	PUL	WCR	
551 (99674)	*Buttermere*	AQ1Z/PFP	CS	PUL	WCR	
552 (99675)	*Ennerdale Water*	AQ1Z/PFP	CS	PUL	WCR	
553 (99676)	*Crummock Water*	AQ1Z/PFP	CS	PUL	WCR	
586 (99677)	*Derwentwater*	AR1Z/PFB	CS	PUL	WCR	
807 (99881)		AO10/SAL	CS	SPL	WCR*	GNR Saloon (ex-Q of Scots)
1644 (S)		AJ41/RBR	CS	ICS	WCR	
1650 (S)		AJ41/RBR	CS	ICS	WCR	
1652 (S)		AJ41/RBR	CS	ICS	WCR	
1655 (S)		AJ41/RBR	CS	ICS	WCR	
1663 (S)		AJ41/RBR	CS	ICS	WCR	
1666		AJ41/RBR	CS	WCR	WCR	
1670 (S)		AJ41/RBR	CS	ICS	WCR	
1730		AJ41/RBR	CS	WCR	WCR	
1840		AN21/RMB	CS	WCR	WCR	
1860		AN21/RMB	CS	WCR	WCR	
1861 (99132)		AN21/RMB	CS	WCR	WCR	
1882 (99311)		AN21/RMB	CS	WCR	WCR	
1961		AJ41/RBR	CS	WCR	WCR	
2127 (S)		AO11/SLF	CS	MAR	WCR	
3058	*Florence*	AD11/FO	CS	WCR	WCR	
3093 (977594)	*Florence*	AD11/FO	CS	WCR	WCR	
3105 (99121)	*Julia*	AD11/FO	CS	WCR	WCR	
3106 (99122)	*Alexandra*	AD11/FO	CS	WCR	WCR	
3113 (99125)	*Jessica*	AD11/FO	CS	WCR	WCR	
3117 (99127)	*Christina*	AD11/FO	CS	WCR	WCR	
3128 (99371)	*Victoria*	AD11/FO	CS	WCR	WCR	
3130 (99128)	*Pamela*	AD11/FO	CS	WCR	WCR	
3136 (3605)	*Diana*	AD11/FO	CS	WCR	WCR	
3143 (3609)	*Patricia*	AD11/FO	CS	WCR	WCR	
3313		AD1F/FO	CS	WCR	WCR	
3326		AD1F/FO	CS	WCR	WCR	
3348		AD1F/FO	CS	PUL	WCR	
3350		AD1F/FO	CS	WCR	WCR	
3352		AD1F/FO	CS	WCR	WCR	
3359		AD1F/FO	CS	WCR	WCR	
3360		AD1F/FO	CS	ICS	WCR	
3362		AD1F/FO	CS	PUL	WCR	
3395		AD1F/FO	CS	WCR	WCR	
3431		AD1F/FO	CS	WCR	WCR	
4854		AD1F/FO	CS	WCR	WCR	
4860 (S) (99193)		AC21/TSO	CS	MAR	WCR	
4905		AC21/TSO	CS	WCR	WCR	
4912 (99318)		AC21/TSO	CS	WCR	WCR	
4931 (99329)		AC21/TSO	CS	WCR	WCR	
4932 (S)		AC21/TSO	CS	BLG	WCR	
4940		AC21/TSO	CS	WCR	WCR	
4951		AC21/TSO	CS	WCR	WCR	
4954 (99326)		AC21/TSO	CS	WCR	WCR	
4958		AC21/TSO	CS	WCR	WCR	
4960		AC21/TSO	CS	WCR	WCR	
4973		AC21/TSO	CS	WCR	WCR	
4984		AC21/TSO	CS	WCR	WCR	
4994		AC21/TSO	CS	WCR	WCR	
4997 (S)		AC21/TSO	CS	BLG	WCR	
5032 (99194)		AC21/TSO	CS	WCR	WCR	
5033 (99328)		AC21/TSO	CS	WCR	WCR	
5035 (99195)		AC21/TSO	CS	WCR	WCR	
5044 (99327)		AC21/TSO	CS	WCR	WCR	

5125 (S)		AC2Z/TSO	BH	GRN	WCR	
5171		AC2Z/TSO	CS	MAR	WCR	
5200		AC2Z/TSO	CS	GRN	WCR	
5216		AC2Z/TSO	CS	MAR	WCR	
5222		AC2Z/TSO	CS	MAR	WCR	
5229	*The Green Knight*	AC2Z/SO	CS	MAR	WTN	
5236		AC2Z/SO	CS	MAR	WCR	
5237		AD2Z/SO	CS	MAR	WCR	
5239	*The Red Knight*	AD2Z/SO	CS	MAR	WTN	
5249		AD2Z/SO	CS	MAR	WCR	
5278	*Melisande*	AC2A/TSO	CS	CHC	WTN	
5419		AC2A/TSO	CS	WCR	WTN	
5487		AC2C/TSO	CS	WCR	WCR	
5756 (S)		AC2E/TSO	CS	WCR	WCR	
6000		AC2F/TSO	CS	WCR	WCR	
6012		AC2F/TSO	CS	WCR	WCR	
6014 (S)		AC2F/TSO	CS	ICS	WCR	
6021		AC3F/TSO	CS	WCR	WCR	
6022		AC2F/TSO	CS	WCR	WCR	
6103		AC2F/TSO	CS	WCR	WCR	
6115		AC2F/TSO	CS	WCR	WCR	
6135 (S)		AC2F/TSO	CS	ICS	WCR	
6312 (92925)		AX51/GEN	CS	WCR	WCR	
6528 (5592)		AG2C/TSOT	CS	WCR	WCR	
6723		AN1D/RMBF	CS	WCR	WCR	
6724		AN1D/RMBF	CS	WCR	WCR	
9104 (S) (9401)		AH2Z/BSOT	CS	WCR	WCR	
9391	*Pendragon*	AE2Z/BSO	CS	PUL	WTN	
9392		AE2Z/BSO	CS	WCR	WCR	
9448 (S)		AE2C/BSO	CS	WCR	WCR	
9493		AE2D/BSO	CS	WCR	CWR	
10688		AS4G/SLE	CS	SRB	WCR	
13227		AA11/FK	CD	WCR	WCR	
13306	*Joanna*	AA11/FK	CS	WCR	WCR	
13320	*Anna*	AA11/FO	CS	WCR	WCR	
13321 (99316)		AA11/FK/RBR	CS	WCR	WCR	
13440 (S)		AA1A/FK	CS	GRN	WCR	
17102 (99680)		AB1A/BFK	CS	WCR	WCR	
17168 (S) (99319)		AB1D/BFK	CS	WCR	WCR	
18756 (25756)		AA21/SK	SH	MAR	WCR	
18806 (99722)		AA21/SK	CS	WCR	WCR	
18893 (99712)		Kitchen	CS	WCR	WCR	
19208 (99884)	Car No. 84	AA21/SK	CS	WCR	WCR	
21256 (99304)		AB31/BCK	CS	WCR	WCR	
21266		AB31/BCK	CS	WCR	WCR	
34525 (S) (99966)		AR51/GEN	CS	WCR	WCR	
35407 (99886)		AB21/BSK	CS	MAR	WCR	LNWR livery ('Q of Scots')
45018 (99052)		AO10/SAL	CS	QOS	WCR	
45026 (S)		SAL	CS	MAR	WCR	LMS Inspection Saloon
80043 (1680)		AJ41/RBR	CS	PUL	WCR	
96175		GUV	CS	MAR	WCR	Water carrier
99723 (35459)		AB21/BSK	CS	WCR	WCR	

WCR* - Owned by Scottish Highland Railway Co

Right: *A large fleet of quality Mk1 and Mk2 passenger stock is operated by West Coast Railway and used for many charter services throughout the country. Many carry West Coast maroon livery, while others sport Pullman, green, or blue/grey livery. No. 99677 is one of the original Manchester Pullman Mk2 vehicles, Pullman First Brake No. 586. It is now painted in Pullman Umber and Cream and carries the name* Derwentwater. **Antony Christie**

WCRC

Above: *Displaying standard West Coast Railway lined maroon, with West Coast Railway branding at the near end, Mk2 BFK No. 17102, now numbered 99680 is seen from its brake end.* **Antony Christie**

Northern Belle

Number	*Name*	*Type*	*Depot*	*Livery*	*Operator*
325 (2907)	***Durat***	**AJ11/RFO**	**CS**	**PUL**	**WCR**
1207 (6422)		**AJ11/RFO**	**CS**	**-**	**WCR**
1221 (3371)		**AJ11/RFO**	**CS**	**PUL**	**WCR**
1566	***Caerdydd***	**AK51/RKB**	**CS**	**PUL**	**WCR**
1953		**AJ41/RBR**	**CS**	**PUL**	**WCR**
3174	***Glamis***	**AD1D/FO**	**CS**	**PUL**	**WCR**
3182	***Warwick***	**AD1D/FO**	**CS**	**PUL**	**WCR**
3232		**AD1E/FO**	**CS**	**PUL**	**WCR**
3247	***Chatsworth***	**AD1E/FO**	**CS**	**PUL**	**WCR**
3267	***Belvoir***	**AD1E/FO**	**CS**	**PUL**	**WCR**
3273	***Alnwick***	**AD1E/FO**	**CS**	**PUL**	**WCR**
3275	***Harlech***	**AD1E/FO**	**CS**	**PUL**	**WCR**
10569 (S)	***Leviathan***	**AU4G/SLEP**	**CS**	**PUL**	**WCR**
10729	***Crewe***	**AS4G/SLE**	**CS**	**PUL**	**VSO**
10734 (2914)	***Balmoral***	**AS4G/SLE**	**CS**	**PUL**	**WCR**
17167 (14167)	***Mow Cop***	**AB1D/BFK**	**CS**	**PUL**	**WCR**
92904		**NBA**	**CS**	**PUL**	**VSO**

Left: *The Northern Belle luxury land cruise train is operated by West Coast Railway. Vehicle No. 10734* Balmoral *is a 12-berth sleeping car used for staff accommodation. This vehicle was previously used as staff accommodation on the Royal Train, when it was numbered 2914.* **Antony Christie**

Most preserved locomotives authorised for main-line operation, either steam or diesel, operate with a support coach conveying owners' representatives, engineering staff and light maintenance equipment. Support coaches can be allocated to a specific locomotive or operate with a pool of locos.

Number	*Type*	*Depot*	*Livery*	*Support Coach for*
14007 (99782) *Mercator*	AB11/BSK	NY	MAR	61264 / 60163
14060 (17060)	AB11/BSK	TM	MAR	45596
17019 (14019)	AB11/BFK	CS	MAR	61994
17025 (14025)	AB11/BFK	CS	MAR	45690
17096	AB1B/BFK	SL	CHC	35028
21096 (99080)	AB31/BCK	NY	MAR	60007
21232 (99040)	AB31/BCK	SK	MAR	46201
21236 (99120)	AB31/BCK	ZG	GRN	30828
21249	AB21/BCK	SL	CCM	60163
35317	AD21/BSK	CL	GRN	46100 / 70000
35322 (99035)	AB21/BSK	CS	MAR	70000 and WCRC traction
35329	AB21/BSK	RL	GRN	Mid-Hants fleet
35451	AB21/BSK	CL	GRN	34046
35461 (99720)	AB21/BSK	CL	CHC	5029
35463 (99312)	AB21/BSK	CS	WCR	WCR fleet
35464	AB21/BSK	PR	MAR	Swanage Railway
35465 (99991)	AB21/BSK	CL	CCM	LSL / 70000
35468 (99953)	AB21/BSK	YK	MAR	National Railway Museum, 60103
35470	AB21/BSK	TM	CHC	Vintage Trains fleet
35476 (99041)	AB21/BSK	SK	MAR	6233
35479	AB21/BSK	SH	MAR	61306
35486 (99405)	AB21/BSK	--	MAR	60009 / 61994
35508	AB1C/BSK	BQ	MAR	45212 / 44871 / 45407
35517 (17088)	ABIK/BSK	BQ	MAR	45212 / 44871 / 45407
35518 (17097)	AB11/BFK	SH	GRN	34067
80204 (35297)	NNX	TN	MAR	61994
80217 (35299)	NNX	CS	MAR	WCRC fleet
80220 (35276)	NNX	NY	MAR	62005

Below: *With the operation of privately owned steam and diesel locos over Network Rail tracks generates a requirement for loco support coaches. These are generally ex passenger/brake vehicles which provide riding space for loco support crew members and an area for carrying small maintenance items in case of on-the-road problems. Generally the support coach is coupled between the loco and train. Carrying LMS maroon livery support coach No. 99041 is a rebuild of Mk1 BSK No. 35476 and provides a travelling companion for 'Duchess' No. 6233.* **Antony Christie**

Off-Lease Rolling Stock

Introduction of large numbers of new vehicles, has seen a sizeable amount of vehicles with a reasonable life expectancy taken out of service and stored. Many will find new uses, but it is expected that a significant number will end up in scrap yards. The tables below show the position at the start of 2020.

Power Cars

Number	Owner	Loc'n
43017	ANG	EL
43018	ANG	HA
43020	ANG	EL
43024	ANG	EL
43025	ANG	EL
43053	PTR	LM
43056	PTR	LM
43061	PTR	TYN
43069	PTR	LM
43070	PTR	LM
43071	PTR	LM
43075	PTR	TYN
43078	PTR	LM
43079	PTR	LM
43087	PTR	LM
43091	PTR	LM
43159	PTR	LM
43165	ANG	EL
43174	ANG	EL
43185	ANG	HA
43190	ANG	EL
43191	ANG	EL
43193	PTR	LM
43195	FGP	LA
43196	ANG	LM
43197	PTR	LM
43206	ANG	EL
43208§	ANG	EH
43239§	ANG	EH
43296	ANG	EL
43300	ANG	NL
43309	ANG	EL
43311	ANG	EL
43313	ANG	BN
43315	ANG	EL
43320	ANG	EL
43367	ANG	EL

§ For CrossCountry

Electric Multiple Units

Class 317/6

Vehicle Length: (Driving) 65ft 0¾in (19.83m) (Inter) 65ft 4¼in (19.92m) Height: 12ft 1½in (3.58m) Width: 9ft 3in (2.82m) Horsepower: 1,000hp (746kW) Seats (total/car): 24F/244S, 64S/70S/62S/24F-48S

Number	Former Number	Formation DTSO+MSO+TSO+DTCO	Owner	Location
317663	(317363)	77214+62860+71748+77234	ANG	EL
317669(S)	(317369)	77280+62886+71762+77284	ANG	EL

Class 319

Vehicle Length: (Driving) 65ft 0¾in (19.83m) (Inter) 65ft 4¼in (19.92m) Height: 11ft 9in (3.58m) Width: 9ft 3in (2.82m) Horsepower: 1,326hp (990kW)

Number	Formation DTSO(A)+MSO+TSO+DTSO(B)	Owner	Location
319009	77307+62899+71780+77306	PTR	LM
319010	77309+62900+71781+77308	PTR	LM
319011	77311+62901+71782+77310	PTR	LM
319362	77461+63044+71930+77460	PTR	LM
319364	77465+63046+71932+77464	PTR	LM
319371	77479+63053+71939+77478	PTR	LM
319373	77483+63055+71941+77482	PTR	LM
319376	77489+63058+71944+77488	PTR	LM
319377	77491+63059+71945+77490	PTR	LM
319380	77497+63062+71948+77496	PTR	LM
319382	77975+63094+71980+77976	PTR	LM
319384	77979+63096+71982+77980	PTR	LM
319421	77331+62911+71792+77330	PTR	LM
319426	77431+62916+71797+77430	PTR	LM
319444	77377+62934+71815+77376	PTR	LM
319451	77439+62965+71870+77438	PTR	LM
319453	77443+62967+71872+77442	PTR	LM
319454	77445+62968+71873+77444	PTR	LM

Class 365

Vehicle Length: (Driving) 68ft 6½in (20.89m) (Inter) 65ft 9¾in (20.89m) Height: 12ft 4½in (3.77m) Width: 9ft 2½in (2.81m) Horsepower: 1,684hp (1,256kW)

Number	Formation DMCO(A)+TSO+PTSO+DMCO(B)	Owner	Loc'n
365501	65894+72241+72240+65935	DFT	Crewe
365503	65896+72245+72244+65937	DFT	Crewe
365505	65898+72249+72248+65939	DFT	Crewe
365507	65900+72253+72252+65941	DFT	Crewe
365509	65902+72257+72256+65943	DFT	Crewe
365513	65906+72265+72264+65947	DFT	Crewe
365515	65908+72269+72268+65949	DFT	Crewe
365517	65910+72273+72272+65951	DFT	Crewe
365519	65912+72277+72276+65953	DFT	Crewe
365521	65914+72281+72280+65955	DFT	Crewe
365523	65916+72285+72284+65957	DFT	Crewe
365525	65918+72289+72288+65959	DFT	Crewe
365527	65920+72293+72292+65961	DFT	Crewe
365529	65922+72297+72296+65963	DFT	Crewe
365531	65924+72301+72300+65965	DFT	Crewe
365533	65926+72305+72304+65967	DFT	Crewe
365535	65928+72309+72308+65969	DFT	Crewe
365537	65930+72313+72312+65971	DFT	Crewe
365541	65934+72321+72320+65975	DFT	Crewe

Class 442

Vehicle Length: (Driving) 75ft 11½in (23.15m) (Inter) 75ft 5½in (22.99m) Width: 8ft 11½in (2.73m) Height: 12ft 4in (3.81m) Horsepower: 1,608hp (1,200kW)

Number	Formation DTSO(A)+TSO+MBC+TSO+DTSO(B)	Owner	Location
442401	77382+71818+62937+71842+77414	ANG	EL
442405	77386+71822+62944+71845+77410	ANG	ZG (for scrap)
442407	77388+71824+62943+71847+77412	ANG	EL
442412	77393+71829+62947+71858+77417	ANG	EL
442421	77402+71838+62957+71861+77426	ANG	EL
442424	77405+71841+62960+71864+77429	ANG	ZG (for scrap)

Class 314 PTSO vehicles 71452, 71454, 71463 and 71464 stored at Long Marston

Coaching Stock - Passenger

Number	*Type*	*Owner*	*Location*
1209 (6457)	RFO	EVL	ZH
1219 (3418)	RFO	EVL	KT
5636	TSO	EVL	PM
5888	TSO	EVL	CS
6121	TSO	EVL	KT
6160	TSO	EVL	LM
6164	TSO	EVL	KT
10204 (40502)	RFM	PTR	3M
10212	RFB	PTR	LG
10231 (10016)	RFM	PTR	§
10241 (10009)	RFM	PTR	IL
10256 (10028)	RFM	PTR	YO¶
10260 (10001)	RFM	PTR	YO¶
11018	FO	PTR	LG
11048	FO	PTR	LG
12078	TSO	PTR	LG
12122	TSO	PTR	LG
12133	TSO	PTR	LG
12138	TSO	PTR	LG

¶ Instruction vehicle - Yoker
§ Fire Training School

10547	SLE	PTR	IS
10661	Concept vehicle at Wolverton		
10667	SLE	-	LM
10698	SLE	-	LM
10733	SLE	-	MM

Coaching Stock - HST

Number	*Type*	*Owner*	*Location*
40102 (42223)	TSRB	PTR	LM
40103 (42316)	TSRB	PTR	LM
40104 (42254)	TSRB	PTR	LM
40105 (42084)	TSRB	PTR	LM
40106 (42162)	TSRB	PTR	LM
40107 (42334)	TSRB	PTR	LM
40108 (42314)	TSRB	PTR	LM
40109 (42262)	TSRB	PTR	LM
40110 (42187)	TSRB	PTR	LM
40111 (42248)	TSRB	PTR	LM
40112 (42336)	TSRB	PTR	LM
40114 (42086)	TSRB	PTR	LM
40117 (42249)	TSRB	PTR	LM
40118 (42338)	TRSB	PTR	LM
40210	TRS	ANG	EL
40231	TRS	ANG	EL
40402 (40002)	TRSB	DBR	ZR
40417 (40017)	TRSB	DBR	ZK
40424 (40024)	TRSB	ANG	DY
40425 (40025)	TRSB	DBR	ZK
40426 (40026)	TRSB	ANG	EL
40433 (40033)	TRSB	ANG	EL
40703	TRFB	QNG	EL
40704	TRFB	ANG	TYNE
40707	TRFB	ANG	EL
40710	TRFB	ANG	EL
40713	TRFB	ANG	EL
40715	TRFB	ANG	EL
40716	TRFB	ANG	EL
40718	TRFB	ANG	EL
40720	TRFB	ANG	EL
40721	TRFB	ANG	EL
40722	TRFB	ANG	EL
40727	TRFB	ANG	EL
40733	TRFB	ANG	EL
40734	TRFB	ANG	EL
40739	TRFB	ANG	EL
40742	TRFB	ANG	EL
40743	TRFB	ANG	EL
40752	TRFB	ANG	EL
40755	TRFB	ANG	EL
40757	TRFB	ANG	EL
40801	TRFB	PTR	LM
40802	TRFB	PTR	LM
40803	TRFB	PTR	LM
40804	TRFB	PTR	LM
40806	TRFB	PTR	LM
40808	TRFB	PTR	LM
40809	TRFB	PTR	LM
40901 (40436)	TFB	PTR	LM
40903 (40437)	TFB	PTR	LM
41006	TF	ANG	EL
41012	TF	ANG	EL
41016	TF	ANG	EL
41018	TF	ANG	EL
41020	TF	ANG	EL
41028	TF	ANG	EL
41030	TF	ANG	EL
41034	TF	ANG	EL
41052	TF	ANG	EL
41056	TF	ANG	EL
41059	TF	FGP	LM
41066	TF	ANG	EL
41089	TF	ANG	EL
41091	TF	ANG	TYNE
41092	TF	ANG	TYNE
41102	TF	ANG	EL
41103	TF	ANG	EL
41106	TF	ANG	EL
41108	TF	PTR	LM
41110	TF	ANG	EL
41118	TF	ANG	EL
41128	TF	ANG	EL
41130	TF	ANG	EL
41132	TF	ANG	EL
41137	TF	ANG	EL
41138	TF	ANG	EL
41149	TF	PTR	LM
41161	TF	PTR	LM
41162	TF	PTR	LM
41164	TF	PTR	LM
41166	TF	PTR	LM
41167	TF	PTR	LM
41169	TF	PTR	LM
41170	TF	ANG	EL
41176	TF	PTR	LM
41180	TF	ANG	EL
41182	TF	PTR	LM
41183	TF	PTR	LM
41187	TF	PTR	LM
41189	TF	PTR	LM
41192	TF	PTR	LM
42005	TS	PTR	-
42006	TS	ANG	EL
42009	TS	ANG	EL
42012	TS	ANG	EL
42014	TS	ANG	EL
42015	TS	ANG	-
42016	TS	ANG	-
42021	TS	ANG	EL
42024	TS	ANG	EL
42025	TS	ANG	EL
42026	TS	ANG	EL
42028	TS	ANG	EL
42029	TS	ANG	EL
42031	TS	ANG	EL
42039	TS	ANG	EL
42040	TS	ANG	EL
42041	TS	ANG	EL
42043	TS	ANG	EL
42048	TS	ANG	EL
42049	TS	ANG	EL
42050	TS	ANG	EL
42056	TS	ANG	EL
42060	TS	ANG	EL
42061	TS	ANG	EL
42062	TS	ANG	EL
42066	TS	ANG	EL
42067	TS	ANG	EL
42068	TS	ANG	EL
42070	TS	ANG	EL
42071	TS	ANG	EL
42072	TS	ANG	EL
42074	TS	ANG	EL
42077	TS	ANG	EL
42078	TS	ANG	EL
42079	TS	ANG	EL
42080	TS	ANG	EL
42081	TS	ANG	EL
42083	TS	ANG	EL
42089	TS	ANG	EL
42092	TS	PTR	LM
42094	TS	PTR	LM
42095	TS	PTR	LM
42096	TS	ANG	EL
42098	TS	ANG	EL
42099	TS	ANG	EL
42103	TS	PTR	LM
42105	TS	PTR	LM
42106	TS	ANG	TYNE
42115	TS	PTR	LM
42116	TS	ANG	EL
42123	TS	ANG	EL
42126	TS	ANG	EL
42134	TS	ANG	EL
42158	TS	ANG	EL
42166	TS	PTR	LM
42167	TS	PTR	LM
42169	TS	PTR	LM
42173	TS	PTR	LM
42176	TS	PTR	LM
42178	TS	PTR	LM
42179	TS	ANG	TYNE
42180	TS	ANG	TYNE
42185	TS	ANG	EL
42187	TS	ANG	TYNE
42188	TS	SNG	TYNE
42195	TS	PTR	LM
42196	TS	ANG	EL
42197	TS	ANG	EL
42209	TS	ANG	EL
42213	TS	ANG	EL
42216	TS	ANG	EL

Number	Type	Owner	Location
42217	TS	PTR	LM
42221	TS	ANG	EL
42231	TS	PTR	LM
42233	TS	PTR	LM
42236	TS	ANG	EL
42241	TS	ANG	EL
42242	TS	ANG	EL
42243	TS	ANG	EL
42244	TS	ANG	EL
42245	TS	ANG	EL
42247	TS	PTR	LM
42250	TS	ANG	EL
42252	TS	ANG	EL
42253	TS	ANG	EL
42257	TS	ANG	EL
42260	TS	ANG	EL
42261	TS	ANG	EL
42263	TS	ANG	EL
42267	TS	ANG	EL
42268	TS	ANG	EL
42272	TS	ANG	EL
42277	TS	ANG	EL
42281	TS	ANG	EL
42283	TS	ANG	EL
42284	TS	ANG	EL
42294	TS	PTR	LM
42296	TS	ANG	EL
42297	TS	ANG	EL
42302	TS	PTR	LM
42303	TS	PTR	LM
42304	TS	PTR	LM
42305	TS	PTR	LM
42308	TS	PTR	LM
42310	TS	PTR	LM
42319	TS	PTR	LM
42323	TS	ANG	EL
42325	TS	ANG	EL
42332	TS	ANG	EL
42340	TS	ANG	EL
42346	TS	ANG	EL
42347	TS	ANG	EL
42348	TS	ANG	EL
42350	TS	ANG	EL
42351	TS	ANG	EL
42353	TS	PTR	LM
42355 (41172)	TS	ANG	EL
42356	TS	ANG	EL
42357 (41174)	TS	ANG	EL
42360	TS	ANG	EL
42362	TS	ANG	EL
42363	TS	ANG	EL
42364	TS	PTR	LM
42381 (41058)	TS	PTR	LM
42382 (12128)	TS	PTR	LM
42383 (12172)	TS	PTR	LM
42501 (40744)	TS	ANG	EL
42502 (40731)	TS	ANG	EL
42503 (40712)	TS	ANG	EL
42504 (40714)	TS	ANG	EL
42505 (40228)	TS	ANG	EL
42506 (40724)	TS	ANG	EL
42507 (40209)	TS	ANG	EL
42508 (40725)	TS	ANG	EL
42509 (40736)	TS	ANG	EL
42510 (40717)	TS	ANG	EL
42512 (40208)	TS	ANG	EL
42513 (40738)	TS	ANG	EL
42514 (40726)	TS	ANG	EL
42515 (40747)	TS	ANG	EL
42516 (40723)	TS	ANG	EL
42517 (40745)	TS	ANG	EL
42518 (40403)	TS	PTR	LM
42519 (40416)	TS	PTR	LM
42551 (41013)	TS	ANG	EL
42552 (41007)	TS	ANG	EL
42555 (41015)	TS	ANG	EL
42556 (41017)	TS	ANG	EL
42557 (41019)	TS	ANG	EL
42560 (410270	TS	ANG	EL
42563 (41045)	TS	PTR	LM
42564 (41051)	TS	ANG	EL
42568 (41101)	TS	ANG	EL
42569 (41105)	TS	ANG	EL
42572 (41123)	TS	ANG	EL
42573 (41127)	TS	ANG	EL
42575 (41131)	TS	ANG	EL
42582 (41163)	TS	PTR	LM
44001	TGS	ANG	EL
44002	TGS	ANG	EL
44005	TGS	ANG	-
44007	TGS	ANG	EL
44009	TGS	ANG	EL
44016	TGS	ANG	EL
44018	TGS	ANG	EL
44020	TGS	ANG	EL
44022	TGS	ANG	EL
44024	TGS	ANG	EL
44025	TGS	ANG	EL
44026	TGS	ANG	EL
44028	TGS	ANG	EL
44031	TGS	ANG	EL
44034	TGS	ANG	EL
44038	TGS	ANG	EL
44042	TGS	PTR	LM
44043	TGS	ANG	EL
44049	TGS	ANG	EL
44058	TGS	ANG	TYNE
44059	TGS	ANG	EL
44060	TGS	PTR	LM
44068	TGS	PTR	LM
44069	TGS	PTR	LM
44074	TGS	PTR	LM
44076	TGS	PTR	LM
44078	TGS	PTR	LM
44081	TGS	PTR	LM
44089	TGS	AUT	LM
44093	TGS	ANG	EL
44098	THS	ANG	EL
46001 (41005)	TC	ANG	EL
46002 (41029)	TC	ANG	EL
46003 (41033)	TC	ANG	EL
46004 (41055)	TC	ANG	EL
46005 (41065)	TC	ANG	EL
46008 (41109)	TC	PTR	LM
46011 (41139)	TC	ANG	EL
46012 (41147)	TC	PTR	LM
46014 (41168)	TC	PTR	LM
46015 (41179)	TC	ANG	EL
46016 (41181)	TC	PTR	LM
46018 (411910	TC	PTR	LM

Coaching Stock - Mk4

Number	Type	Owner	Location
10310	RSB	EVL	BN
10311	RSB	EVL	WK
10317	RSB	EVL	WK
10319	RSB	EVL	WN§
10321	RSB	EVL	WK
10329	RSB	EVL	WK
11295 (12475)	FO	EVL	WK
11326 (11206)	FOD	EVL	WK
11327 (11236)	FO	EVL	WN§
11328 (11274)	FO	EVL	WK
11329 (11243)	FO	EVL	WK
11330 (11249)	FOD	EVL	WK
11420 (11242	FOD	EVL	WK
11426 (11252)	FO	EVL	WK
11430 (11248)	FO	EVL	WK
11998 (10314)	FO	EVL	WK
11999 (10316)	FO	EVL	WK
12204	TSOE	EVL	WK
12216	TSOE	EVL	WK
12217	TSOE	EVL	WK
12218	TSOE	EVL	WK
12220	TSOE	EVL	WK
12224	TSOE	EVL	WK
12227	TSOE	EVL	WN§
12317	TSOD	EVL	WK
12318	TSOD	EVL	WK
12319	TSOD	EVL	WK
12320	TSOD	EVL	WK
12321	TSOD	EVL	WN§
12322	TSOD	EVL	WK
12325	TSOD	EVL	WK
12326	TSOD	EVL	WK
12331	TSOE	EVL	WK
12438	TSO	EVL	WK
12439	TSO	EVL	WK
12440	TSO	EVL	WK
12449	TSO	EVL	WK
12458	TSO	EVL	WK
12462	TSO	EVL	WK
12463	TSO	EVL	WK
12465	TSO	EVL	WK
12471	TSO	EVL	WN§
12472	TSO	EVL	WK
12474	TSO	EVL	WK
12477	TSO	EVL	WK
12533	TSO	EVL	WK
12534	TSO	EVL	WK
82203	DVT	EVL	WK
82216	DVT	EVL	WK
82217	DVT	EVL	WK
82200	DVT	EVL	WK
82223	DVT	EVL	WK
82228	DVT	EVL	WN§
82231	DVT	EVL	WK

§ Vehicles scheduled to move to Alliance Rail for Euston-Blackpool use.

Coaching Stock - NPCCS

Number	Type	Owner	Location
82109	DVT	PTR	ZB
82149	DVT	PTR	FC
92159 (81534)	BG	EVL	KT
92901 (92001)	BG	EVL	WB
92931 (92031)	BG	EVL	PY
96139 (93751)	GUV	EVL	WB
96181 (93875)	GUV	EVL	LM

Over the years a number of former BR locomotives have, after withdrawal from normal duties, been taken up for use by industrial operators. The list below represents those that are understood to be still in existence in early 2020. Some locos operated at preservation sites are deemed to be 'industrial' but these are grouped in the preserved section.

Class 08/09

08220	Traditional Traction, at Nottingham Heritage Centre, Ruddington
08375	Port of Boston
08411	RSS Rye Farm, Wishaw
08441	RSS Rye Farm, Wishaw
08445	Daventry International Railfreight Terminal (DIRFT) – at LH Group, Burton
08447	John G. Russell Transit, Hillington, Glasgow
08460	GBRf Eastleigh
08480	RSS Norwich Crown Point
08484	Hitachi, Newton Aycliffe
08502	East Kent Railway
08535	Corus, Shotton Works
08536	RSS, Wishaw, Sutton Coldfield
08580	LNER Bounds Green
08593	RSS Rye Farm, Wishaw
08598	RSS Rye Farm, Wishaw
08600	LH Group Services, Barton-under-Needwood
08623	Hope Cement Works
08632	GBRf Bescot
08663	RSS at GBRf, Dagenham
08670	GBRf Bescot
08683	RSS Norwich Crown Point
08704	Ecclesbourne Valley Railway
08709	Traditional Traction, Colne Valley Railway
08728	St Modwen Storage, Long Marston
08731	Aggregate Industries, Merehead
08738	Arriva, Eastleigh
08743 *Bryan Turner*	LH Group Services, Barton-under-Needwood
08752	RSS at Gemini Rail Group, Wolverton
08757	GBRf, Dagenham
08774 *Arthur Vernon Dawson*	AV Dawson, Middlesbrough
08782	HNRC, Barrow Hill
08787	Hanson Aggregates, Whatley
08788	PD Ports, Grangemouth
08807	AV Dawson, Middlesbrough
08809	Ketton Cement Works
08823 (D3991) *Kelva*	Tata Steel, Shotton
08846	RSS, at Neville Hill
08847	PD Ports, Teesport
08872	HNRC, European Metal Reprocessing, Attercliffe
08903 *John W. Antill*	SembCorp Utilities Teesside, Wilton
08912	AV Dawson, Middlesbrough
08915	Stephenson Railway Museum
08921	RSS Rye Farm, Wishaw
08922	EMD, Longport
08927	LNER Bounds Green
08933	Aggregate Industries, Merehead
08939	Freightliner Felizstowe
09022	Boston Docks Co
09023	European Metal Reprocessing, Attercliffe

Class 11

12088	Butterwell

Class 14

D9529 (14029)	Aggregate Industries, Bardon Quarry

UK Exported Motive Power

These lists give details of former UK diesel and electric locos exported for further use overseas and understood to be still operational.

Class 03/04

D2019 Italy
D2032 Italy
D2033 Italy
D2036 Italy
D2098 Italy
D2153 Italy
D2156 Italy
D2157 Italy
D2164 Italy
D2216 Italy
D2232 Italy
D2295 Italy

Class 06

D2432 Italy

Class 07

07009 Italy

Class 08

D3047 Lamco Liberia as 101
D3092 Lamco Liberia as 102
D3094 Lamco Liberia as 103
D3098 Lamco Liberia as 104
D3100 Lamco Liberia as 105

Class 14

D9534 Bruges

Class 47

47375 CRS, Hungary
92 70 0047-375-5

Class 56

56101 Floyd, Hungary as 92 55 0659-001-5
56115 Floyd, Hungary as 92 55 0659-002-3
56117 Floyd, Hungary as 92 55 0659-003-1

Class 58

58001 ETF France
58004 TSO France
58005 ETF France
58006 ETF France
58007 TSO France
58009 TSO France
58010 TSO France
58011 TSO France
58013 ETF France
58015 Transfesa, Spain
58018 TSO France
58020 Transfesa, Spain
58021 TSO France
58024 Transfesa, Spain
58025 Cont'l Rail, Spain
58026 TSO France
58027 Continental Rail, Spain
58029 Transfesa, Spain
58030 Transfesa, Spain
58031 Transfesa, Spain
58032 ETF France
58033 TSO France
58034 TSO France
58035 TSO France
58036 ETF France
58038 ETF France
58039 ETF France
58040 TSO France
58041 Transfesa, Spain
58042 TSO France
58043 Transfesa, Spain
58044 ETF France
58046 TSO France
58047 Transfesa, Spain
58049 ETF France
58050 Continental Rail, Spain

Class 66

66010 ECR, France
66022 ECR, France
66026 ECR, France
66028 ECR, France
66029 ECR, France
66032 ECR, France
66033 ECR, France
66036 ECR, France
66038 ECR, France
66042 ECR, France
66045 ECR, France
66049 ECR, France
66052 ECR, France
66062 ECR, France
66064 ECR, France
66071 ECR, France
66072 ECR, France
66073 ECR, France
66123 ECR, France
66146 ECR, Poland
66153 ECR, Poland
66157 ECR, Poland
66159 ECR, Poland
66163 ECR, Poland
66166 ECR, Poland
66173 ECR, Poland
66178 ECR, Poland
66179 ECR, France
66180 ECR, Poland
66189 ECR, Poland
66190 ECR, France
66191 ECR, France
66193 ECR, France
66195 ECR, France

66196	ECR, Poland
66201	ECR, France
66202	ECR, France
66203	ECR, France
66204	ECR, France
66205	ECR, France
66208	ECR, France
66209	ECR, France
66210	ECR, France
66211	ECR, France
66212	ECR, France
66213	ECR, France
66214	ECR, France
66215	ECR, France
66216	ECR, France
66217	ECR, France
66218	ECR, France
66219	ECR, France
66220	ECR, Poland
66222	ECR, France
66223	ECR, France
66224	ECR, France
66225	ECR, France
66226	ECR, France
66227	ECR, Poland
66228	ECR, France
66229	ECR, France
66231	ECR, France
66233	ECR, France
66234	ECR, France
66235	ECR, France
66236	ECR, France
66237	ECR, Poland
66239	ECR, France
66240	ECR, France
66241	ECR, France
66242	ECR, France
66243	ECR, France
66244	ECR, France
66245	ECR, France
66246	ECR, France
66247	ECR, France
66248	ECR, Poland
66249	ECR, France
66411	Freightliner PL, as 66013FPL
66412	Freightliner PL, as 66015FPL
66417	Freightliner PL, as 66014FPL
66527	Freightliner PL, as 66016FPL
66530	Freightliner PL, as 66017FPL
66535	Freightliner PL, as 66018FPL
66582	Freightliner PL, as 66009FPL
66583	Freightliner PL, as 66010FPL
66584	Freightliner PL, as 66011FPL
66586	Freightliner PL, as 66008FPL
66595	Freightliner PL, as 66595FPL
66608	Freightliner PL, as 66603FPL
66609	Freightliner PL, as 66605FPL
66611	Freightliner PL, as 66604FPL
66612	Freightliner PL, as 66606FPL
66624	Freightliner PL, as 66602FPL
66625	Freightliner PL, as 66601FPL
66954	Freightliner PL, as 66954FPL

Below: *DB-Cargo Class 66/0 No. 66010 operating on hire to ECR in France is recorded at Marseille Blancarde on 4 September 2019 with a loaded Bauxite train.* **Howard Lewsey**

Class 86

86213	Bulmarket, Bulgaria as 91 52 00 85003-9
86215	Floyd, Hungary as 91 55 0450-005-8
86217	Floyd, Hungary as 91 55 0450-006-6
86218	Floyd, Hungary as 91 55 0450-004-1
86228	Floyd, Hungary as 91 55 0450-007-4
86231	Bulmarket, Bulgaria as 91 52 00 85005-4
86232	Floyd, Hungary as 91 55 0450-003-3
86233	Bulmarket, Bulgaria (spares)
86234	Bulmarket, Bulgaria as 91 52 00 85006-2
86235	Bulmarket, Bulgaria as 91 52 00 87704-0
86242	Floyd, Hungary as 91 55 0450-008-2
86248	Floyd, Hungary as 91 55 0450-001-7
86250	Floyd, Hungary as 91 55 0450-002-5
86424	Floyd, Hungary as 91 55 0450-009 spares loco
86701	Bulmarket, Bulgaria as 91 52 00 85001-3
86702	Bulmarket, Bulgaria as 91 52 00 85002-1

Class 87

87003	BZK Bulgaria, as 91 52 00 87003-0
87004	BZK Bulgaria, as 91 52 00 87004-8
87006	BZK Bulgaria, as 91 52 00 87006-3
87007	BZK Bulgaria, as 91 52 00 87007-1
87008	BZK Bulgaria, as 91 52 00 87008-9
87009	Bulmarket, Bulgaria as 91 52 00 87009-4
87010	BZK Bulgaria, as 91 52 00 87010-5
87012	BZK Bulgaria, as 91 52 00 87012-1
87013	BZK Bulgaria, as 91 52 00 87013-9
87014	BZK Bulgaria, as 91 52 00 87014-7
87017	Bulmarket, Bulgaria as 91 52 00 87017-7
87019	BZK Bulgaria, as 91 52 00 87019-6
87020	BZK Bulgaria, as 91 52 00 87020-4
87022	BZK Bulgaria, as 91 52 00 87022-0
87023	Bulmarket, Bulgaria as 91 52 00 87023-5
87025	Bulmarkt, Bulgaria as 91 52 00 87025-0
87026	BZK Bulgaria, as 91 52 00 87026-1
87028	BZK Bulgaria, as 91 52 00 87028-8
87029	BZK Bulgaria, as 91 52 00 87029-2
87033	BZK Bulgaria, as 91 52 00 87033-7
87034	BZK Bulgaria, as 91 52 00 87034-5

Left: *Now working for Floyd in Hungary, former Class 86/2 No. 86215 is seen in Floyd black and pink livery as No. 450 005.* **Gavin Lake**

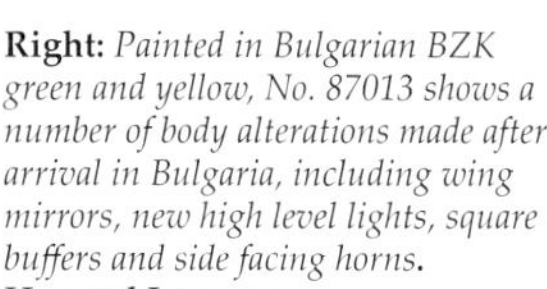
Right: *Painted in Bulgarian BZK green and yellow, No. 87013 shows a number of body alterations made after arrival in Bulgaria, including wing mirrors, new high level lights, square buffers and side facing horns.* **Howard Lewsey**

Class 92

92001	LocoTech, Russia, Lease to Transagent, Rijeka, Croatia, as 91 53 0472-002-1
92002	LocoTech, Russia, Lease to Transagent, Rijeka, Croatia, as 91 53 0472-003-9
92003	DBS Romania, as 91 53 0472 xxx-x
92005	LocoTech, Russia, Lease to Transagent, Rijeka, Croatia, as 91 53 0472-005-4
92012	LocoTech, Russia, Lease to Transagent, Rijeka, Croatia, as 91 53 0472-001-3
92022	DBS Bulgaria, as 91 52 1688 022-1
92024	LocoTech, Russia, Lease to Transagent, Rijeka, Croatia, as 91 53 0472-004-7
92025	DBS Bulgaria, as 91 52 1688 025-1
92026	DBS Romania, as 91 53 0472-026-x
92027	DBS Bulgaria, as 91 70 1688 027-1
92030	DBS Bulgaria, as 91 52 1688 030-1
92034	DBS Bulgaria, as 91 52 1688 034-3
92039	DBS Romania, as 91 53 0472-006-2

Above: *Working in Croatia as 91 53 0472005-4, the former UK Class 92 No. 92005 is seen in full Transagent Rail shaded black livery with blue and red branding. Note that the cast BR double arrow logo and Channel Tunnel segments have been left applied, but painted over in black.* **Toma Bacic**

Right: *Carrying much the same livery as it did in the UK, No. 92034 has its international number applied on the front end and sports Euro style two-section ploughs. The original stick-on name* Kipling *is still carried as is the BR double arrow and Channel Tunnel segments.* **Howard Lewsey**

Northern Ireland Railways (NIR)

Class 3000

Three-car sets for use in the Belfast area. Built by CAF, with seating for 200 standard class passengers. Each vehicle powered by one MAN D2876 LUH03 of 453hp (338kW). Max speed 90mph (145km/h). Introduced in 2004-05.

3001	3005	3009	3013	3017	3021
3002	3006	3010	3014	3018	3022
3003	3007	3011	3015	3019	3023
3004	3008	3012	3016	3020	

Sets 3001-3006 are fitted with CAWS and Irish Rail safety equipment to allow cross-border operation if needed.

These sets cannot operate in multiple with 40xx sets in passenger traffic.

Left: *All Northern Ireland passenger services are formed of CAF-built Class 3000 or 4000 DMUs. 3000 class No. 3007 is seen at Lisburn. The front end livery of the two designs is different, so recognition of the fleets is easy.* **CJM**

Class 4000

Three-car suburban sets for use in the Belfast area. Built by CAF, with seating for 212 standard class passengers. Each vehicle powered by one MTU 6H1800 R84 of 520hp (390kW). Max speed 90mph (145km/h). Introduced in 2010-12.

4001	4005	4009	4013	4017
4002	4006	4010	4014	4018
4003	4007	4011	4015	4019
4004	4008	4012	4016	4020

These sets cannot operate in multiple with 30xx sets in passenger traffic.

In December 2018, 21 extra intermediate vehicles were ordered for delivery in 2021-2022, to form seven, six-car sets.

Above: *Showing its revised front end style, compared to the earlier Class 3000 design, set No. 4012 is seen with a Belfast bound train at Lisburn in August 2019.* **CJM**

Class 111

These three locomotives are the same as the Irish Rail Class 071s and were built by General Motors in the late 1970s. The 57ft (17.37m)-long double-cab design is mounted on a Co-Co wheel configuration and carries an EMD 12-645-E3C prime mover. They have a top speed of 90mph (145km/h). Today the NIR fleet operates in departmental service.

8111	*Great Northern*	8112	*Northern Counties*	8113	*Belfast & County Down*

Class 201

Two locomotives of the 34-strong Class 201 fleet are owned by NIR for use on the Belfast-Dublin 'Enterprise' services. Built by General Motors EMD in Canada in 1994-95, these 3200hp (2400kW) locos are classified as JT42HCW, and have a top speed of 102mph (164km/h). They are fitted with retractable buffers, auto couplers, event recorders and NIR cab controls.

8208 *River Lagan*

8209 *(River Foyle)*

Right: *Just two of the Class 201 General Motors locos are officially owned by Northern Ireland Railways, Nos. 208 and 209, which carry the identities of 8208 and 8209. The pair, painted in Enterprise livery, can usually be found on the Enterprise route between Belfast and Dublin. No. 8209 is seen at Dublin Connolly station.* **CJM**

Service Stock

Five former Class 80 DMU vehicles and one Class 450 DMU set are retained by NIR for autumn sandite and rail cleaning, and are usually to be found at York Road depot, Belfast. These vehicles are likely to be replaced by on-track plant in the near future.

Class 80

8069 (DMBSO)
8094 (DMBSO)
8097 (DMBSO)
8749 (DTSO)
8752 (DTSO)

Class 450

Set 5 8455+8795+8785 *Galgorm Castle*
Stored at Ballymena

Irish Railways (IR)

Class 071

A fleet of 18 Irish Rail Class 071s was built by General Motors, Canada, in the late 1970s. The 57ft (17.37m)-long double-cab design is mounted on a Co-Co wheel configuration and has a EMD 12-645-E3C prime mover. They have a top speed of 90mph (145km/h). These locos are currently going through an overhaul project.

071
072
073
074
075
076
077
078
079
080
081
082 *Cumann Na nInnealtoiri / The Institution Of Engineers Of Ireland*
083
084
085
086
087
088

Right: *Irish Rail, which today runs very little freight traffic, operates a fleet of 18 General Motors-built Class 071s. These carry a 645 series prime mover. The fleet is painted in IR grey, with one loco sporting CIE orange colours. No. 078 is seen powering a log train at Kildare on 22 August 2019.* **CJM**

Class 201

IR has a fleet of 32 Class 201 main-line diesel-electric locos. Built by General Motors EMD in Canada in 1994-95, these 3200hp (2400kW) locos are classified as JT42HCW and have a top speed of 102mph (164km/h). Several different variants exist within the current fleet. Locos Nos. 201-207/210-214 have fixed buffers and use shackle couplings. Nos. 215-226/229/232/234 have push-pull control, retractable buffers, electronic fuel systems and both knuckle and shackle couplings. Nos. 206-207/228/230/231/233 are similar to the 215 batch but have event recorders and cab equipment to allow operation on the NIR network.
** Loco No. 216 dedicated to Belmond Pullman Train and painted in Belmond blue livery.*

No.	Irish name	English name
201(S)	*Abhainn na Sionnainne*	*River Shannon*
202(S)	*Abhainn na Laoi*	*River Lee*
203(S)	*Abhainn na Coiribe*	*River Corrib*
204(S)	*Abhainn na Bearu*	*River Barrow*
205(S)	*Abhainn na Feoire*	*River Nore*
206	*(Abhainn na Life)*	*River Liffey*
207	*Abhainn na Bóinne*	*River Boyne*
210(S)	*Abhainn na hEirne*	*River Erne*
211(S)	*Abhainn na Suca*	*River Suck*
212(S)	*Abhainn na Slaine*	*River Slaney*
213(S)	*Abhainn na Muaidhe*	*River Moy*
214(S)	*Abhainn na Broshai*	*River Brosna*
215	*An Abhainn Mhor*	*River Avonmore*
216*	*Abhainn na Dothra*	*River Dodder*
217	*Abhainn na Fleisce*	*River Flesk*
218	*Abhainn na Garbhoige*	*River Garavogue*
219	*(Abhainn na Tulchann)*	*River Tolka*
220	*An Abhainn Dhubh*	*River Blackwater*
221	*Abhainn na Feilge*	*River Fealge*
222	*(Abhainn na Dargaile)*	*River Dargle*
223	*Abhainn na hAinnire*	*River Anner*
224	*Abhainn na Féile*	*(River Feale)*
225(S)	*Abhainn na Daoile*	*River Deel*
226	*Abhainn na Siuire*	*(River Suir)*
227	*(Abhainn na Leamhna)*	*River Laune*
228	*An Abhainn Bhui*	*(River Owenboy)*
229	*Abhainn na Mainge*	*River Maine*
230	*Abhainn na Bandan*	*(River Bandon)*
231	*Abhainn na Maighe*	*(River Maigue)*
232	*(Abhainn na Chaomaraigh)*	*River Cummeragh*
233	*Abhainn na Chlair*	*River Clare*
234	*(Abhainn na hEatharlai)*	*River Aherlow*

Names in brackets are reported missing.

Above Left: *Irish Rail 201 class No. 233 on Intercity duty between Cork and Dublin is seen at Kildare painted in silver and black livery.* **CJM**

Above Right: *Loco No. 216 is dedicated to the Belmond 'Grand Hibernian' land cruise train and is painted in dark blue to match the train. No. 216 is seen light engine at Portarlington.* **CJM**

Below: *Class 201s which operate the loco-hauled InterCity service between Dublin and Cork, are mainly painted in InterCity silver and green, with InterCity bodyside branding. When not required for passenger use, the locos can be operated on freight duties, as is the case with No. 234 passing Kildare with a Dublin bound container train on 22 August 2019.* **CJM**

Class 2600

A fleet of 17 Class 2601 vehicles was introduced in 1993-94, built by Tokyu Car in Japan. Each two-car set seats 130 standard class passengers. The top speed is 70mph (110km/h). Today the remaining 16 vehicles operate in eight pairs allocated to Cork, usually working on the Mallow, Midleton and Cobh routes, occasionally being seen in the Limerick area.

2601 + 2602	2605 + 2616	2607 + 2608	2611 + 2612
2603 + 2604	2606 + 2615	2610 + 2613	2614 + 2617

Right: *Eight pairs of gangway fitted Class 2600 sets are found in the Cork area. Nos. 2601 and 2602 are seen shunting at Cork.* **CJM**

Class 2800

A fleet of 10 Class 2801 vehicles was introduced in 2000, built by Tokyu Car in Japan. Each two-car set seats 85 standard class passengers. The top speed is 75mph (120km/h). Today the sets are allocated to Limerick, working local services.

2801 + 2802	2805 + 2806	2809 + 2810	2813 + 2814	2817 + 2818
2803 + 2804	2807 + 2808	2811 + 2812	2815 + 2816	2819 + 2820

Right: *Many of the branch line services operating from Limerick depot are serviced by a fleet of 10 two-vehicle Class 2800s, which have had their original gangway connections removed. Displaying standard Irish Rail silver and green livery, Nos. 2802 and 2801 approach Manulla Junction with the shuttle service from Ballina.* **CJM**

Class 22000

As part of the modernisation of the IR passenger system a total of 234 22000 class vehicles are now in service operating commuter and Intercity services. The sets are presently formed into three-, four- and five-car sets. The stock was built by the partnership of Mitsui of Japan and Rotem of South Korea. Sets have a top speed of 100mph (160km/h) and each vehicle is powered by an underfloor MTU 6H 1800 R83 engine of 483hp (327kW).

Three-car Intercity/commuter sets able to operate into Northern Ireland

22001	22002	22003	22004	22005	22006

Three-car Intercity/commuter sets

22007	22008	22009	22010

The last two digits of numbers represent the set number.

Right: *The most common class of DMU operating on Irish Rail are the Class 22000 design, built by Mitsui and Rotem. This Intercity set, led by car No. 22202, calls at Tullamore with a service bound for Galway.* **CJM**

Four-car Intercity/commuter sets

22011	22014	22017	22020	22023	22026	22029
22012	22015	22018	22021	22024	22027	22030
22013	22016	22019	22022	22025	22028	

Five-car Intercity sets with premier seating (first class)

22031	22033	22035	22037	22039
22032	22034	22036	22038	22040

Four-car Intercity/commuter high-capacity sets

22041	22042	22043	22044	22045

Three-car Intercity/commuter sets

22046	22048	22050	22052	22054	22056	22058	22060	22062
22047	22049	22051	22053	22055	22057	22059	22061	22063

Left: *One of the three-car Intercity or commuter sets, with vehicle No. 22249 (set 49) departs from Kildare with a service from Portlaoise to Dublin Heuston.* **CJM**

In late 2019, 41 additional intermediate vehicles were ordered from Hyundai-Rotem, for delivery in 2021-22, this will enable the fleet to be reformed as 21 x three-car, 20 x four-car and 22 x six-car.

Class 29000

Introduced between 2002 and 2005, a fleet of 29 four-car CAF-built sets is allocated to the Dublin area for commuter work. Each set seats 185 standard class passengers and each vehicle is powered by an underfloor MAN D2876 LUH01 engine developing 400hp (298kW).

29001	29009	29017	29025
29002	29010	29018	29026
29003	29011	29019	29027
29004	29012	29020	29028
29005	29013	29021	29029
29006	29014	29022	
29007	29015	29023	
29008	29016	29024	

Sets are formed with 290xx vehicles at one end and 294xx vehicles at the other, with the same last two digits.

Left: *A fleet of 29 four-car CAF sets operate in the Dublin area, painted in wither green or green and blue colours. No. 29412 departs from Gormanston bound for Dublin* **CJM**

Hauled Stock

'Enterprise' stock used on Belfast-Dublin route, built 1997 by De Dietrich Ferroviaire

Driving Trailer Brake First (DTBF)

9001	9003
9002	9004

Left: *The service between Belfast and Dublin is branded 'Enterprise' and is formed of Class 201 locos, hauled stock and a Driving Trailer Brake at the Dublin end. Driving Trailer No. 9002 leads a train away from Dundalk.* **CJM**

9101	9102	9103	9104

Trailer Standard (TS)

9201	9205	9209	9213
9202	9206	9210	9214
9203	9207	9211	9215
9204	9208	9212	9216

Above: *The 'Enterprise' stock was built in 1997 by De Dietrich and shares some common equipment styles with the Class 373 Eurostar stock. Above left is Trailer Standard (TS) No. 9205, while above right is Trailer Cafe (TC) No. 9403 which provides an at seat first class and buffet service for standard class. Both:* **CJM**

Trailer Cafe (TC)

9401	9402	9403	9404

Generator Car (GEN)

9602	9605	9613
9604	9608	

Odd-numbered sets are owned by Irish Rail, even-numbered sets are owned by Northern Ireland Railways.

Right: *The Class 201s powering the 'Enterprise' service do not provide hotel power for the train, this comes from a Generator Car, housing two Cummins diesel/alternator groups, coupled between the loco and train. No. 9602 is seen at Drogheda.* **CJM**

Mk4 Inter-City stock built by CAF in 2006. Operated on Dublic to Cork route

Driving Van Trailer (DVT)

4001	4002	4003	4004	4005	4006	4007	4008

Right: *A fleet of CAF-built Mk4 loco-hauled vehicles operate on the Dublin-Cork route. These are powered by a Class 201 loco coupled at the Cork end of trains, with a Driving Van Trailer (DVT) at the Dublin end. These DVTs house twin MAN 2846 LE 202 (320 kW) / Letag engine and generator sets. Vehicle No. 4001 is seen at Limerick Junction.* **CJM**

Open Standard (*End) (OS)

4101	4107	4113	4119	4125*	4131	4137	4143
4102	4108	4114	4120*	4126	4132	4138	
4103	4109	4115*	4121	4127	4133	4139	
4104	4110*	4116	4122	4128	4134	4140*	
4105*	4111	4117	4123	4129	4135*	4141	
4106	4112	4118	4124	4130*	4136	4142	

Above Left: *A fleet of 43 Open Standard vehicles were built for the Intercity operation, eight are dedicated end vehicles with no gangway connection at one end. No. 4111 is illustrated. These vehicles seat 69 in the 2+2 style.* **CJM**

Above Right: *Catering facilities on the Intercity services between Dublin and Cork are provided by a fleet of eight Restaurant Buffet Standard vehicles, seating 28. The other side of the vehicle has four windows plated. No. 4405 is seen from the open side.* **CJM**

Open First (OF)

4201	4202	4203	4204	4205	4206	4207	4208

Restaurant Buffet Standard (RBS)

4401	4402	4403	4404	4405	4406	4407	4408

Belmond Pullman 'Grand Hibernian'

In 2016 luxury train operator Belmond launched an Irish high-quality land cruise train. Formed of 10 former CIE Mk3s first introduced in 1980-85 and withdrawn in 2009, the coaches have been totally rebuilt by Brodie Engineering in Kilmarnock, Scotland, and fitted out at Mivan Engineering in Ireland. The train is usually powered by IR Class 201 No. 216 which carries the Belmond blue livery.

Sleeping Cabin Cars

7116 (55 60 76 87001-8)	Fermanagh
7129 (55 60 76 87003-4)	Waterford
7137 (55 60 76 87005-0)	Kerry
7149 (55 60 76 87004-2)	Down
7158 (55 60 76 87002-6)	Leitrim

Dining Cars

7169 (55 60 88 87102-0)	Wexford
7171 (55 60 88 87101-2)	Sligo

Observation/Bar Car

7104 (55 60 89 87103-7)	Kildare

Crew Car

7130 (55 60 89 87110-2)	Donegal

Generator Car

7601 (55 60 99 87104-3)	Carlow

Vehicle No. 7122 is also owned by Belmond and stored unrefurbished in Dublin.

Left: *The Belmond-operated 'Grand Hibernian' luxury land cruise train is formed of converted Mk3 stock. The coaches have been totally rebuilt and now sport a dark blue livery, with Grand Hibernian cast branding. Vehicle No. 7171, a dining car carrying the name* Sligo *is shown.* **CJM**

Dublin DART

The Dublin Area Rapid Transit (DART) is a local network around Dublin, opened in 1983. It is electrified at 1500V dc overhead. The original stock supplied by GEC / Linke Hofmall Busch has been supplemented by stock from Tokyu Car. All sets are maintained at Fairview, Dublin. Trains are formed as four-car sets with driving trailers at the outer end and driving motor cars in the middle.

Class 8100

Original two-car sets built by GEC / LHB - 8100 series

8101+8301	8108+8308	8115+8315	8122+8322	8129+8329	8137+8337
8102+8302	8109+8309	8116+8316	8123+8323	8130+8330	8138+8338
8103+8303	8110+8310	8117+8317	8124+8324	8131+8331	8139+8339
8104+8304	8111+8311	8118+8318	8125+8325	8132+8332	8140+8340
8105+8305	8112+8312	8119+8319	8126+8326	8133+8333	
8106+8306	8113+8313	8120+8320	8127+8327	8134+8334	
8107+8307	8114+8314	8121+8321	8128+8328	8135+8335	

Right: *The Dublin Area Rapid Transit or DART system operates a fleet of two and four-car sets, which usually run in four, six or eight-car formations. Two-car set 8309+8109 is illustrated at Dublin Connolly. All sets sport two-tone green livery.* **CJM**

Class 8500

2000-built four-car sets by Tokyu Car - 8500 series

8601+8501+8502+8602	8603+8503+8504+8604	8605+8505+8506+8606	8607+8507+8508+8608

Class 8510

2001-built four-car sets by Tokyu Car - 8510 series

8611+8511+8512+8612	8613+8513+8514+8614	8615+8515+8516+8616

Right: *In 2001 four additional four-car sets were built by Tokyu Car, with seating for 160 using high-back seats. These sets have a two section front windscreen and carry the standard DART two-tone green livery. No. 8615 is illustrated at Dun Laoghaire.* **CJM**

Class 8520

2003-04-built four-car sets by Tokyu Car - 8520 series

8621+8521+8522+8622	8627+8527+8528+8628	8633+8533+8534+8634	8639+8539+8540+8640
8623+8523+8524+8624	8629+8529+8530+8630	8635+8535+8536+8636	
8625+8525+8526+8626	8631+8531+8532+8632	8637+8537+8538+8638	

Transport for London London Underground

Address: ✉ Floor 11, Windsor House, 50 Victoria Street, London, SW1H 0TL
pressoffice@tfl.gov.uk
✆ 0845 604 4141
ⓘ www.tfl.gov.uk

Managing Director: Andy Lord

Operations: The London Underground system, now operated by Transport for London (TfL), operates services on 10 lines in and around the capital and uses a mix of surface and tunnel stock.

Bakerloo Line

Tube Line. Operates between Elephant & Castle and Harrow & Wealdstone.
Rolling Stock: 1972 Mk2, livery - red, white and blue, allocated to Stonebridge Park. Scheduled for replacement in 2018-19.

Central Line

Tube Line. Operates services between West Ruislip/Ealing and Epping.
Rolling Stock: 1992, livery - red, white and blue, allocated to Hainault.

Circle Line

Sub-Surface Line. Operates circle network in Central London and the branch from Edgware Road to Hammersmith.
Rolling Stock: 'S' stock, introduced 2013-14, livery - red, white and blue, allocated to Hammersmith.

District Line

Sub-Surface Line. Operates services between Wimbledon, Richmond, Ealing, Edgware Road, Kensington Olympia and Upminster.
Rolling Stock: 'S' stock, livery - red, white and blue, allocated to Ealing Common and Upminster.

Jubilee Line

Tube Line. Operates services between Stanmore and Stratford.
Rolling Stock: 1996, livery - red, white and blue, allocated to Wembley Park.

Metropolitan Line

Sub-Surface Line. Operates services from Amersham, Chesham, Watford and Uxbridge to Aldgate.
Rolling Stock: 'S', livery - red, white and blue, allocated to Wembley Park.

Northern Line

Tube Line. Operates services between Morden and Edgware, Mill Hill East and High Barnet.
Rolling Stock: 1995 stock, livery - red, white and blue, allocated to Morden.

Piccadilly Line

Tube Line. Operates between Heathrow Airport/Uxbridge and Cockfosters.
Rolling Stock: 1973 stock, livery - red, white and blue, allocated to Northfields and Cockfosters.

Victoria Line

Tube Line. Operates services between Brixton and Walthamstow Central.
Rolling Stock: 2009 stock, livery - red, white and blue, allocated to Northumberland Park.

Waterloo & City Line

Tube Line. Operates services between Waterloo and Bank.
Rolling Stock: 1992 stock, livery - red, white and blue, allocated to Waterloo.

Hammersmith & City

Sub-Surface Line. Operates between Hammersmith and Barking.
Rolling Stock: 'S', livery - red, white and blue

New Tube Stock for London Underground

It was announced in mid-2018, that Siemens Mobility had been awarded the contract, valued at around £1.5bn to design and build 94 new generation tube trains, based on the 'Inspiro' platform, that will transform the experience of millions of London Underground passengers, with those on the Piccadilly line the first to benefit.

More than 700,000 passengers use the Piccadilly line every day. However, a combination of limited fleet size and old infrastructure has restricted TfL's ability to increase capacity across the line for many decades. This long-term investment will support London's growing population, which is set to increase to 10.8 million by 2041.

A number of UK suppliers are to work with Siemens Mobility on the project. Some of the trains will be built at a new Siemens factory in Goole, East Yorkshire, where dynamic commissioning facilities will also be built. The trains will then be delivered to London Underground by rail. The new Siemens plant will employ around 700 people.

The Siemens order, the first under the LUL Deep Tube Upgrade Programme, will mean the replacement of the entire 1970s built Piccadilly line fleet. From 2023, 94 new trains will be delivered, enabling up to 27 trains-per-hour to operate at peak times by the end of 2026.

Originally, the Deep Tube Upgrade Programme aimed to replace the life-expired rolling stock, signalling and control systems across all the four deep level lines by 2035, but in 2019 new trains for the Northern, Central and Waterloo & City lines were placed on the back burner.

The Siemens 'Inspiro' trains will be six metres longer than existing Piccadilly stock. They will include walk-through, fully air conditioned carriages, and will be designed to optimise the space constraints in the narrow tube tunnels. The stock will also be fitted with a full and advanced passenger information system.

Although the initial confirmed order for 94 trains is for the Piccadilly Line, it can be expected that when funding and authorisation for upgrading other deep tube lines is available, the same design of train will be ordered.

This will allow TfL to maximise cost savings through greater standardisation, including staff training, equipment, spares and maintenance. ■

Above: *Artist's impression on how the new deep tube stock will look. The first line to see the new 'standard' deep tube trains will be the Piccadilly Line.* **LUL**

BAKERLOO LINE

1972 Tube Stock

Builder: Metro-Cammell
Years built: 1972-1974
Formation: DM+T+T+MM+UNDM+T+DM
Construction: Steel underframe, aluminium body
Max speed: 45mph (72km/h)
Length: Cab - 52ft 8in (16.09m),
Intermediate - 52ft 4in (15.98m)
Width: 8ft 6in (2.64m)

Height: 9ft 4in (2.87m)
Gangway: Emergency end doors
Seating: Total 268
DM-40, T-36, MM-40, UNDM-40
Doors: Sliding bi-parting
Traction equipment: 4 x Brush LT115 of 71hp (53kW) on each power car

4-car single-ended sets (formed at south end of train)

Formation: (South end) DM+T+T+MM

3231+4231+4331+3331
3232+4232+4332+3332
3233+4233+4333+3333
3234+4234+4334+3334
3235+4235+4335+3335
3236+4236+4336+3336
3237+4237+4337+3337
3238+4238+4338+3338
3239+4239+4339+3339
3240+4240+4340+3340
3241+4241+4341+3341
3242+4242+4342+3342
3243+4243+4343+3343
3244+4244+4344+3344
3245+4245+4345+3345
3246+4246+4346+3346
3247+4247+4347+3347
3248+4248+4348+3348
3250+4250+4350+3350
3251+4251+4351+3351
3252+4252+4352+3352
3253+4253+4353+3353
3254+4254+4354+3354
3255+4255+4355+3355
3256+4256+4356+3356
3258+4258+4358+3358
3259+4259+4359+3359
3260+4260+4360+3360
3261+4261+4361+3361
3262+4262+4362+3362
3263+4263+4363+3363
3264+4264+4364+3364
3265+4265+4365+3365
3266+4266+4366+3366
3267+4267+4367+3367
3299+4299+4399+3399*

3-car single-ended sets (formed at north end of train)

Formation: UNDM+T+DM (North end)

3431+4531+3531
3432+4532+3532
3433+4533+3533
3434+4534+3534
3435+4535+3535
3436+4536+3536
3437+4537+3537
3438+4538+3538
3440+4540+3540
3441+4541+3541
3442+4542+3542
3443+4543+3543
3444+4544+3544
3445+4545+3545
3446+4546+3546
3447+4547+3547
3448+4548+3548
3449+4549+3549
3450+4550+3550
3451+4551+3551
3452+4552+3552
3453+4553+3553
3454+4554+3554
3455+4555+3555
3456+4556+3556
3457+4557+3557
3458+4558+3558
3459+4559+3559
3460+4560+3560
3461+4561+3561
3462+4562+3562
3463+4563+3563
3464+4564+3564
3465+4565+3565
3466+4566+3566
3467+4567+3567

Notes: Nos. 4352-4363 fittted with de-icing equipment.
* UNDM vehicle

Left: *A 1972 Bakerloo Line set, led by Driving Motor No. 3248 approaches Stonebridge Park with a service from Harrow & Wealdstone bound for Elephant & Castle.* **CJM**

WATERLOO & CITY LINE

1992 Tube Stock

Builder: ADtranz
Years built: 1993
Formation: DM+M+M+DM
Construction: Aluminium
Max speed: 53mph (85km/h)
Length: 53ft 3in (16.25m)
Width: 8ft 5½in (2.62m)
Height: 9ft 4in (2.87m)
Gangway: Emergency end doors
Seating: Total 136
DM-34, M-34
Doors: Sliding bi-parting
Traction equipment: 4 x Brush LT118 of 65hp (49kW) on each power car

2-car sets - east

Formation: DM+M

65501+67501	**65505+67505**	**65509+67509**
65503+67503	**65507+67507**	

2-car sets - west

Formation: M+DM

67502+65502	**67506+65506**	**67510+65510**
67504+65504	**67508+65508**	

Right Above: *The former BR line linking Waterloo with Bank is now operated by London Underground, using stock introduced under Network SouthEast and thus it carries their numbering system. Five four-car trains operate the system based at Waterloo. Led by Driving Motor 65502, a train awaits departure from Waterloo to Bank.* **Antony Christie**

Right Below: *In 2019 some of the Waterloo & City vehicles emerged in all-over advertising livery, which partly blocked the passenger windows. Car No. 67504 is seen at Waterloo with advertising for software company Freshworks.* **Antony Christie**

CENTRAL LINE

1992 Tube Stock

Builder: ADtranz
Years built: 1991-1994
Formation: DM+M+M+M+M+M+M+DM
Construction: Aluminium
Max speed: 53mph (85km/h)
Length: 53ft 3in (16.25m)
Width: 8ft 5½in (2.62m)
Height: 9ft 4in (2.87m)
Gangway: Emergency end doors
Seating: Total 272
DM-34, NDM-34
Doors: Sliding bi-parting
Traction equipment: 4 x Brush LT118 of 65hp (49kW) on each power car

2-car single-ended sets

Formation: A+B - DM+NDM

91001+92001	91071+92071	91141+92141	91211+92211	91281+92281
91003+92003	91073+92073	91143+92143	91213+92213	91283+92283
91005+92005	91075+92075	91145+92145	91215+92215	91285+92285
91007+92007	91077+92077	91147+92147	91217+92217	91287+92287
91009+92009	91079+92079	91149+92149	91219+92219	91289+92289
91011+92011	91081+92081	91151+92151	91221+92221	91291+92291
91013+92013	91083+92083	91153+92153	91223+92223	91293+92293
91015+92015	91085+92085	91155+92155	91225+92225	91295+92295
91017+92017	91087+92087	91157+92157	91227+92227	91297+92297
91019+92019	91089+92089	91159+92159	91229+92229	91299+92299
91021+92021	91091+92091	91161+92161	91231+92231	91301+92301
91023+92023	91093+92093	91163+92163	91233+92233	91303+92303
91025+92025	91095+92095	91165+92165	91235+92235	91305+92305
91027+92027	91097+92097	91167+92167	91237+92237	91307+92307
91029+92029	91099+92099	91169+92169	91239+92239	91309+92309
91031+92031	91101+92101	91171+92171	91241+92241	91311+92311
91033+92033	91103+92103	91173+92173	91243+92243	91313+92313
91035+92035	91105+92105	91175+92175	91245+92245	91315+92315
91037+92037	91107+92107	91177+92177	91247+92247	91317+92317
91039+92039	91109+92109	91179+92179	91249+92249	91319+92319
91041+92041	91111+92111	91181+92181	91251+92251	91321+92321
91043+92043	91113+92113	91183+92183	91253+92253	91323+92323
91045+92045	91115+92115	91185+92185	91255+92255	91325+92325
91047+92047	91117+92117	91187+92187	91257+92257	91327+92327
91049+92049	91119+92119	91189+92189	91259+92259	91329+92329
91051+92051	91121+92121	91191+92191	91261+92261	91331+92331
91053+92053	91123+92123	91193+92193	91263+92263	91333+92333
91055+92055	91125+92125	91195+92195	91265+92265	91335+92335
91057+92057	91127+92127	91197+92197	91267+92267	91337+92337
91059+92059	91129+92129	91199+92199	91269+92269	91339+92339
91061+92061	91131+92131	91201+92201	91271+92271	91341+92341
91063+92063	91133+92133	91203+92203	91273+92273	91343+92343
91065+92065	91135+92135	91205+92205	91275+92275	91345+92345
91067+92067	91137+92137	91207+92207	91277+92277	91347+92347
91069+92069	91139+92139	91209+92209	91279+92279	91349+92349

2-car non-driving sets

Formation: B+C - NDM+NDM

92002+93002	92026+93026	92050+93050	92074+93074	92098+93098
92004+93004	92028+93028	92052+93052	92076+93076	92100+93100
92006+93006	92030+93030	92054+93054	92078+93078	92102+93102
92008+93008	92032+93032	92056+93056	92080+93080	92104+93104
92010+93010	92034+93034	92058+93058	92082+93082	92106+93106
92012+93012	92036+93036	92060+93060	92084+93084	92108+93108
92014+93014	92038+93038	92062+93062	92086+93086	92110+93110
92016+93016	92040+93040	92064+93064	92088+93088	92112+93112
92018+93018	92042+93042	92066+93066	92090+93090	92114+93114
92020+93020	92044+93044	92068+93068	92092+93092	92116+93116
92022+93022	92046+93046	92070+93070	92094+93094	92118+93118
92024+93024	92048+93048	92072+93072	92096+93096	92120+93120

92122+93122
92124+93124
92126+93126
92128+93128
92130+93130
92132+93132
92134+93134
92136+93136
92138+93138
92140+93140
92142+93142
92144+93144
92146+93146
92148+93148
92150+93150
92152+93152
92154+93154
92156+93156
92158+93158
92160+93160
92162+93162
92164+93164
92166+93166
92168+93168
92170+93170
92172+93172
92174+93174
92176+93176
92178+93178
92180+93180
92182+93182
92184+93184
92186+93186
92188+93188
92190+93190
92192+93192
92194+93194
92196+93196
92198+93198
92200+93200
92202+93202
92204+93204
92206+93206
92208+93208
92210+93210
92212+93212
92214+93214
92216+93216
92218+93218
92220+93220
92222+93222
92224+93224
92226+93226
92228+93228
92230+93230
92232+93232
92234+93234
92236+93236
92238+93238
92240+93240
92242+93242
92244+93244
92246+93246
92248+93248
92250+93250
92252+93252
92254+93254
92256+93256
92258+93258
92260+93260
92262+93262
92264+93264
92266+93266

2-car non-driving sets

Formation: B+D - NDM+NDM

92402+93402
92404+93404
92406+93406
92408+93408
92410+93410
92412+93412
92414+93414
92416+93416
92418+93418
92420+93420
92422+93422
92424+93424
92426+93426
92428+93428
92430+93430
92432+93432
92434+93434
92436+93436
92438+93438
92440+93440
92442+93442
92444+93444
92446+93446
92448+93448
92450+93450
92452+93452
92454+93454
92456+93456
92458+93458
92460+93460
92462+93462
92464+93464

Right: *The Central Line is operated by a large fleet of Adtranz-built 1992 stock, formed into eight-car sets. DM No. 91043 is recorded at Leytonstone with a train bound for West Ruislip.* **CJM**

Below: *Led by DM No. 91123, a Central Line service slows for the station stop at Woodford with a service bound for Epping on 3 October 2019.* **CJM**

PICCADILLY LINE

1973 Tube Stock

Builder: Metro Cammell
Years built: 1974-1977
Formation: DM+T+UNDM+UNDM+T+DM or
DM+T+UNDM+DM+T+DM
Construction: Steel underframe, aluminium body
Max speed: 45mph (72km/h)
Length: Cab - 57ft 3in (17.47m)
Intermediate - 58ft 0in (17.68m)

Width: 8ft 5¾in (2.63m)
Height: 9ft 4in (2.88m)
Gangway: Emergency end doors
Seating: Total 228
DM-38, T-38, UNDM-38
Doors: Sliding bi-parting
Traction equipment: 4 x Brush LT118 of 65hp (49kW) on each power car

3-car single-ended sets

Formation: DM+T+UNDM

100+500+300
101+501+301
102+502+302
103+503+303
104+504+304
105+505+305
106+506+306
107+507+307
108+508+308
109+509+309
110+510+310
111+511+311
112+512+312
113+513+313
115+515+315
116+516+316
117+517+317
118+518+318
119+519+319
120+520+320
121+521+321
122+522+322
123+523+323
124+524+324
125+525+325
126+526+326
127+527+327
128+528+328
129+529+329
130+530+330
131+531+331
132+532+332
133+533+333
134+534+334
135+535+335
136+536+336
137+537+337
138+538+338
139+539+339
140+540+340
141+541+341
142+542+342
143+543+343
144+544+344
145+545+345
146+546+346
147+547+347
148+548+348
149+549+349
150+550+350
151+551+351
152+552+352
153+553+353
154+554+354
155+555+355
156+556+356
157+557+357
158+558+358
159+559+359
160+560+360
161+561+361
162+562+362
163+563+363
164+564+364
165+565+365
166+566+366
(Stored bomb dam)
167+567+367
168+568+368
169+569+369
170+570+370
171+571+371
172+572+372
173+573+373
174+574+374
175+575+375
176+576+376
177+577+377
178+578+378
179+579+379
180+580+380
181+581+381
182+582+382
183+583+383
184+584+384
185+585+385
186+586+386
187+587+387
188+588+388
189+589+389
190+590+390
191+591+391
192+592+392
193+593+393
194+594+394
195+595+395
196+596+396
197+597+397
198+598+398
199+599+399
200+600+400
201+601+401
202+602+402
203+603+403
205+605+405
206+606+406
207+607+407
208+608+408
209+609+409
210+610+410
211+611+411
212+612+412
213+613+413
214+614+414
215+615+415
216+616+416
217+617+417
218+618+418
219+619+419
220+620+420
221+621+421
222+622+422
223+623+423
224+624+424
225+625+425
226+626+426
227+627+427
228+628+428
229+629+429
230+630+430
231+631+431
232+632+432
233+633+433
234+634+434
235+635+435
236+636+436
237+637+437
238+638+438
239+639+439
240+640+440
241+641+441
242+642+442
243+643+443
244+644+444
245+645+445
246+646+446
247+647+447
248+648+448
249+649+449
250+650+450
251+651+451
252+652+452
253+653+453

3-car double-ended sets

Formation: DM+T+DM

854+654+855
856+656+857
858+658+859
860+660+861
862+662+863
864+664+865
866+666+867
868+668+869§
870+670+871
872+672+873
874+674+875
876+676+877
878+678+879
880+680+881
882+682+883
884+684+885
886+686+887
890+690+891§
892+692+893
894+694+895
896+696+897

§ Sandite fitted

Left: *Pulling out the turnback siding at Rayners Lane on the Uxbridge branch of the Piccadilly Line, DM No. 149 leads a six car set in to the platform to form a service to Central London and Cockfosters.* **Antony Christie**

JUBILEE LINE

1996 Tube Stock

Builder: GEC Alstom, CAF Spain§
Years built: 1996-1998, 2005§
Formation: DM+T+T+UNDM+UNDM+T+DM
Construction: Aluminium
Max speed: 62mph (100km/h)
Length: 58ft 2in (17.77m)
Width: 8ft 5¾in (2.63m)

Height: 9ft 4in (2.87m)
Gangway: Emergency end doors
Seating: Total 238
DM-32, T-34, UNDM-34
Doors: Sliding bi-parting
Traction equipment: 4 x GEC LT200 of 120hp (90kW) on each power car

4-car single-ended sets. Formation: DM+T+T§+UNDM

96001+96201+96601+96401
96003+96203+96603+96403
96005+96205+96605+96405
96007+96207+96607+96407
96009+96209+96609+96409
96011+96211+96611+96411
96013+96213+96613+96413
96015+96215+96615+96415
96017+96217+96617+96417
96019+96219+96619+96419
96021+96221+96621+96421
96023+96223+96623+96423
96025+96225+96625+96425
96027+96227+96627+96427
96029+96229+96629+96429
96031+96231+96631+96431
96033+96233+96633+96433
96035+96235+96635+96435
96037+96237+96637+96437
96039+96239+96639+96439
96041+96241+96641+96441
96043+96243+96643+96443
96045+96245+96645+96445
96047+96247+96647+96447
96049+96249+96649+96449
96051+96251+96651+96451
96053+96253+96653+96453
96055+96255+96655+96455
96057+96257+96657+96457
96059+96259+96659+96459
96061+96261+96661+96461
96063+96263+96663+96463
96065+96265+96665+96465
96067+96267+96667+96467
96069+96269+96669+96469
96071+96271+96671+96471
96073+96273+96673+96473
96075+96275+96675+96475
96077+96277+96677+96477
96079+96279+96679+96479
96081+96281+96681+96481
96083+96283+96683+96483
96085+96285+96685+96485
96087+96287+96687+96487
96089+96289+96689+96489
96091+96291+96691+96491
96093+96293+96693+96493
96095+96295+96695+96495
96097+96297+96697+96497
96099+96299+96699+96499
96101+96301+96701+96501
96103+96303+96703+96503
96105+96305+96705+96505
96107+96307+96707+96507
96109+96309+96709+96509
96111+96311+96711+96511
96113+96313+96713+96513
96115+96315+96715+96515
96117+96317+96717+96517
§96119+96319+96719+96519
§96121+96321+96721+96521
§96123+96323+96723+96523
§96125+96325+96725+96525

3-car single-ended sets. Formation: DM+T+UNDM

96402+96202+96002
96404+96204+96004
96406+96206+96006
96408+96208+96008
96410+96210+96010
96412+96212+96012
96414+96214+96014
96416+96216+96016
96418+96218+96018
96420+96220+96020
96422+96222+96022
96424+96224+96024
96426+96226+96026
96428+96228+96028
96430+96230+96030
96432+96232+96032
96434+96234+96034
96436+96236+96036
96438+96238+96038
96440+96240+96040
96442+96242+96042
96444+96244+96044
96446+96246+96046
96448+96248+96048
96450+96250+96050
96452+96252+96052
96454+96254+96054
96456+96256+96056
96458+96258+96058
96460+96260+96060
96462+96262+96062
96464+96264+96064
96466+96266+96066
96468+96268+96068
96470+96270+96070
96472+96272+96072
96474+96274+96074
96476+96276+96076
96478+96278+96078
96480+96280+96080
96482+96282+96082
96484+96284+96084
96486+96286+96086
96488+96288+96088
96490+96290+96090
96492+96292+96092
96494+96294+96094
96496+96296+96096
96498+96298+96098
96500+96300+96100
96502+96302+96102
96504+96304+96104
96506+96306+96106
96508+96308+96108
96510+96310+96110
96512+96312+96112
96514+96314+96114
96516+96316+96116
96518+96318+96118
§96520+96320+96120
§96522+96322+96122
§96524+96324+96124
§96526+96326+96126

Right: *Seven-car trains of 1996 stock operate on the Jubilee Line. These were built by GEC-Alstom/CAF. With DM No. 96073 nearest the camera, a set is seen at Stratford station in East London.* **Antony Christie**

NORTHERN LINE

1995 Tube Stock

Builder: GEC Alstom
Years built: 1996-2000
Formation: DM+T+UNDM+UNDM+T+DM
Construction: Aluminium
Max speed: 45mph (72km/h)
Length: 58ft 2in (17.77m)
Width: 8ft 5¾in (2.63m)
Height: 9ft 4in (2.87m)
Gangway: Emergency end doors
Seating: Total 200
DM-32, T-38, T-34, UNDM-34
Doors: Sliding bi-parting
Traction equipment: 4 x GEC G355AZ of 114hp (85kW) on each power car

6-car double-ended sets

Formation: DM+T+UNDM+UNDM+T+DM

51501+52501+53501+53701+52701+51701§
51502+52502+53502+53503+52503+51503
51504+52504+53504+53505+52505+51505
51506+52506+53506+53507+52507+51507
51508+52508+53508+53702+52702+51702§
51509+52509+53509+53510+52510+51510
51511+52511+53511+53512+52512+51512
51513+52513+53513+53514+52514+51514
51515+52515+53515+53703+52703+51703§
51516+52516+53516+53517+52517+51517
51518+52518+53518+53519+52519+51519
51520+52520+53520+53704+52704+51704§
51521+52521+53521+53522+52522+51522
51523+52523+53523+53524+52524+51524
51525+52525+53525+53705+52705+51705§
51526+52526+53526+53527+52527+51527
51528+52528+53528+53529+52529+51529
51530+52530+53530+53531+52531+51531
51532+52532+53532+53706+52706+51706§
51533+52533+53533+53534+52534+51534
51535+52535+53535+53536+52536+51536
51537+52537+53537+53538+52538+51538
51539+52539+53539+53707+52707+51707§
51540+52540+53540+53541+52541+51541
51542+52542+53542+53543+52543+51543
51544+52544+53544+53545+52545+51545
51546+52546+53546+53708+52708+51708§
51547+52547+53547+53548+52548+51548
51549+52549+53549+53550+52550+51550
51551+52551+53551+53711+52711+51711§
51553+52553+53553+53709+52709+51709
51554+52554+53554+53555+52555+51555
51556+52556+53556+53557+52557+51557
51558+52558+53558+53559+52559+51559
51560+52560+53560+53710+52710+51710§
51561+52561+53561+53562+52562+51562
51563+52563+53563+53564+52564+51564
51565+52565+53565+53566+52566+51566
51567+52567+53567+53552+52552+51552
51568+52568+53568+53569+52569+51569
51570+52570+53570+53571+52571+51571
51572+52572+53572+53573+52573+51573
51574+52574+53574+53712+52712+51712§
51575+52575+53575+53576+52576+51576
51577+52577+53577+53578+52578+51578
51579+52579+53579+53580+52580+51580
51581+52581+53581+53713+52713+51713§
51582+52582+53582+53583+52583+51583
51584+52584+53584+53585+52585+51585
51586+52586+53586+53587+52587+51587
51588+52588+53588+53714+52714+51714§
51589+52589+53589+53590+52590+51590
51591+52591+53591+53592+52592+51592
51593+52593+53593+53594+52594+51594
51595+52595+53595+53715+52715+51715§
51596+52596+53596+53597+52597+51597
51598+52598+53598+53599+52599+51599
51600+52600+53600+53601+52601+51601
51602+52602+53602+53716+52716+51716§
51603+52603+53603+53604+52604+51604
51605+52605+53605+53606+52606+51606
51607+52607+53607+53608+52608+51608
51609+52609+53609+53717+52717+51717§
51610+52610+53610+53611+52611+51611
51612+52612+53612+53613+52613+51613
51614+52614+53614+53615+52615+51615
51616+52616+53616+53718+52718+51718§
51617+52617+53617+53618+52618+51618
51619+52619+53619+53620+52620+51620
51621+52621+53621+53622+52622+51622
51623+52623+53623+53719+52719+51719§
51624+52624+53624+53625+52625+51625
51626+52626+53626+53627+52627+51627
51628+52628+53628+53629+52629+51629
51630+52630+53630+53720+52720+51720§
51631+52631+53631+53632+52632+51632
51633+52633+53633+53634+52634+51634
51635+52635+53635+53636+52636+51636
51637+52637+53637+53721+52721+51721§
51638+52638+53638+53639+52639+51639
51640+52640+53640+53641+52641+51641
51642+52642+53642+53643+52643+51643
51644+52644+53644+53722+52722+51722§
51645+52645+53645+53646+52646+51646
51647+52647+53647+53648+52648+51648
51649+52649+53649+53650+52650+51650
51651+52651+53651+53723+52723+51723§
51652+52652+53652+53653+52653+51653
51654+52654+53654+53655+52655+51655
51656+52656+53656+53657+52657+51657
51658+52658+53658+53724+52724+51724§
51659+52659+53659+53660+52660+51660
51661+52661+53661+53662+52662+51662
51663+52663+53663+53664+52664+51664
51665+52665+53665+53725+52725+51725§
51666+52666+53666+53667+52667+51667
51668+52668+53668+53669+52669+51669
51670+52670+53670+53671+52671+51671
51672+52672+53672+53726+52726+51726§
51673+52673+53673+53674+52674+51674
51675+52675+53675+53676+52676+51676
51677+52677+53677+53678+52678+51678

51679+52679+53679+53680+52680+51680
51681+52681+53681+53682+52682+51682
51683+52683+53683+53684+52684+51684
51685+52685+53685+53686+52686+51686

§ Fitted with Sandite equipment

Above: *A fleet of six-car double-ended GEC Alstom 1995 sets operate on the Northern Line. With DM No. 51543 nearest the camera, a set is seen under the overall roof at Edgware on 3 October 2019.* **CJM**

Right Middle: *Car No. 51626 leads a train into Burnt Oak station with a service bound for Morden.* **CJM**

Right Below: *Interior of Northern 1995 stock, showing the typical London Underground longitudinal seating, with large stand-back areas in doorways and fold down seats to enable wheelchairs to be parked.* **CJM**

VICTORIA LINE

2009 Tube Stock

Builder: Bombardier, Derby
Years built: 2009-2011
Formation: DM+T+NDM+UNDM+UNDM+NDM+T+DM
Construction: Aluminium
Max speed: 50mph (80.5km/h)
Length: Driving - 54ft 4in (16.60m)
Intermediate - 53ft 6in (16.35m)
Width: 8ft 5½in (2.61m)
Height: 9ft 4⅜in (2.88m)
Gangway: Emergency end doors
Seating: Total 252
DM-32, T-32, NDM-32, UNDM-30
Doors: Sliding bi-parting
Traction equipment: 4 x Bombardier Mitrac of 100hp (75kW) on each power car

8-car double-ended sets

Formation: DM (south)+T+NDM+UNDM+UNDM+NDM+T+DM (north)

11001+12001+13001+14001+14002+13002+12002+11002
11003+12003+13003+14003+14004+13004+12004+11004
11005+12005+13005+14005+14006+13006+12006+11006
11007+12007+13007+14007+14008+13008+12008+11008
11009+12009+13009+14009+14010+13010+12010+11010
11011+12011+13011+14011+14012+13012+12012+11012
11013+12013+13013+14013+14014+13014+12014+11014
11015+12015+13015+14015+14016+13016+12016+11016
11017+12017+13017+14017+14018+13018+12018+11018
11019+12019+13019+14019+14020+13020+12020+11020
11021+12021+13021+14021+14022+13022+12022+11022
11023+12023+13023+14023+14024+13024+12024+11024
11025+12025+13025+14025+14026+13026+12026+11026
11027+12027+13027+14027+14028+13028+12028+11028
11029+12029+13029+14029+14030+13030+12030+11030
11031+12031+13031+14031+14032+13032+12032+11032
11033+12033+13033+14033+14034+13034+12034+11034
11035+12035+13035+14035+14036+13036+12036+11036
11037+12037+13037+14037+14038+13038+12038+11038
11039+12039+13039+14039+14040+13040+12040+11040
11041+12041+13041+14041+14042+13042+12042+11042
11043+12043+13043+14043+14044+13044+12044+11044
11045+12045+13045+14045+14046+13046+12046+11046
11047+12047+13047+14047+14048+13048+12048+11048
11049+12049+13049+14049+14050+13050+12050+11050
11051+12051+13051+14051+14052+13052+12052+11052
11053+12053+13053+14053+14054+13054+12054+11054
11055+12055+13055+14055+14056+13056+12056+11056
11057+12057+13057+14057+14058+13058+12058+11058
11059+12059+13059+14059+14060+13060+12060+11060
11061+12061+13061+14061+14062+13062+12062+11062
11063+12063+13063+14063+14064+13064+12064+11064
11065+12065+13065+14065+14066+13066+12066+11066
11067+12067+13067+14067+14068+13068+12068+11068
11069+12069+13069+14069+14070+13070+12070+11070
11071+12071+13071+14071+14072+13072+12072+11072
11073+12073+13073+14073+14074+13074+12074+11074
11075+12075+13075+14075+14076+13076+12076+11076
11077+12077+13077+14077+14078+13078+12078+11078
11079+12079+13079+14079+14080+13080+12080+11080
11081+12081+13081+14081+14082+13082+12082+11082
11083+12083+13083+14083+14084+13084+12084+11084
11085+12085+13085+14085+14086+13086+12086+11086
11087+12087+13087+14087+14088+13088+12088+11088
11089+12089+13089+14089+14090+13090+12090+11090
11091+12091+13091+14091+14092+13092+12092+11092
11093+12093+13093+14093+14094+13094+12094+11094

Below: *The Victoria Line, running between Brixton in the south and Walthamstow Central in the north via central London, is operated by a fleet of eight car 2009 sets, constructed by Bombardier. With DM No. 11012 leading, a train is seen arriving at Walthamstow Central.* **CJM**

DISTRICT LINE

HAMMERSMITH & CITY LINE

S7 Sub-Surface Stock

Builder: Bombardier, Derby
Years built: 2011-2015
Formation: DM+M1+MS+MS+M2+M1+DM
Construction: Aluminium
Max speed: 62mph (100km/h)
Length: Driving - 57ft 2in (17.44m)
Intermediate - 50ft 6in (15.43m)
Width: 9ft 5in (2.92m)
Height: 12ft 0in (3.68m)
Gangway: Emergency end doors
Seating: Total 212
DM-32, M1-30, M2-30, MS-29
Doors: Sliding bi-parting
Traction equipment: 4 x Bombardier MJB20093 of 87hp (65kW) on each power car

7-car double-ended sets

Formation: DM+M1+MS+MS+M2+M1+DM

21301+22301+24301+24302+25302+22302+21302
21303+22303+24303+24304+25304+22304+21304
21305+22305+24305+24306+25306+22306+21306
21307+22307+24307+24308+25308+22308+21308
21309+22309+24309+24310+25310+22310+21310
21311+22311+24311+24312+25312+22312+21312
21313+22313+24313+24314+25314+22314+21314
21315+22315+24315+24316+25316+22316+21316
21317+22317+24317+24318+25318+22318+21318
21319+22319+24319+24320+25320+22320+21320
21321+22321+24321+24322+25322+22322+21322
21325+22325+24325+24326+25326+22326+21326
21327+22327+24327+24328+25328+22328+21328
21329+22329+24329+24330+25330+22330+21330
21331+22331+24331+24332+25332+22332+21332
21333+22333+24333+24334+25334+22334+21334
21335+22335+24335+24336+25336+22336+21336
21337+22337+24337+24338+25338+22338+21338
21339+22339+24339+24340+25340+22340+21340
21341+22341+24341+24342+25342+22342+21342
21343+22343+24343+24344+25344+22344+21344
21345+22345+24345+24346+25346+22346+21346
21347+22347+24347+24348+25348+22348+21348
21349+22349+24349+24350+25350+22350+21350
21351+22351+24351+24352+25352+22352+21352
21353+22353+24353+24354+25354+22354+21354
21355+22355+24355+24356+25356+22356+21356
21357+22357+24357+24358+25358+22358+21358
21359+22359+24359+24360+25360+22360+21360
21361+22361+24361+24362+25362+22362+21362
21363+22363+24363+24364+25364+22364+21364
21365+22365+24365+24366+25366+22366+21366
21367+22367+24367+24368+25368+22368+21368
21369+22369+24369+24370+25370+22370+21370
21371+22371+24371+24372+25372+22372+21372
21373+22373+24373+24374+25374+22374+21374
21375+22375+24375+24376+25376+22376+21376
21377+22377+24377+24378+25378+22378+21378
21379+22379+24379+24380+25380+22380+21380
21381+22381+24381+24382+25382+22382+21382
21383+22383+24383+24384+25384+22384+21384
21385+22385+24385+24386+23386+22386+21386
21387+22387+24387+24388+23388+22388+21388
21389+22389+24389+24390+23390+22390+21390
21391+22391+24391+24392+23392+22392+21392
21393+22393+24393+24394+23394+22394+21394
21395+22395+24395+24396+23396+22396+21396
21397+22397+24397+24398+23398+22398+21398
21399+22399+24399+24400+23400+22400+21400
21401+22401+24401+24402+23402+22402+21402
21403+22403+24403+24404+23404+22404+21404
21405+22405+24405+24406+23406+22406+21406
21407+22407+24407+24408+23408+22408+21408
21409+22409+24409+24410+23410+22410+21410
21411+22411+24411+24412+23412+22412+21412
21413+22413+24413+24414+23414+22414+21414
21415+22415+24415+24416+23416+22416+21416
21417+22417+24417+24418+23418+22418+21418
21419+22419+24419+24420+23420+22420+21420
21421+22421+24421+24422+23422+22422+21422
21423+22423+24423+24424+23424+22424+21424
21425+22425+24425+24426+23426+22426+21426
21427+22427+24427+24428+23428+22428+21428
21429+22429+24429+24430+23430+22430+21430
21431+22431+24431+24432+23432+22432+21432
21433+22433+24433+24434+23434+22434+21434
21435+22435+24435+24436+23436+22436+21436
21437+22437+24437+24438+23438+22438+21438
21439+22439+24439+24440+23440+22440+21440
21441+22441+24441+24442+23442+22442+21442
21443+22443+24443+24444+23444+22444+21444
21445+22445+24445+24446+23446+22446+21446
21447+22447+24447+24448+23448+22448+21448
21449+22449+24449+24450+23450+22450+21450
21451+22451+24451+24452+23452+22452+21452
21453+22453+24453+24454+23454+22454+21454
21455+22455+24455+24456+23456+22456+21456
21457+22457+24457+24458+23458+22458+21458
21459+22459+24459+24460+23460+22460+21460
21461+22461+24461+24462+23462+22462+21462
21463+22463+24463+24464+23464+22464+21464
21465+22465+24465+24466+23466+22466+21466
21467+22467+24467+24468+23468+22468+21468
21469+22469+24469+24470+23470+22470+21470
21471+22471+24471+24472+23472+22472+21472
21473+22473+24473+24474+23474+22474+21474
21475+22475+24475+24476+23476+22476+21476
21477+22477+24477+24478+23478+22478+21478
21479+22479+24479+24480+23480+22480+21480
21481+22481+24481+24482+23482+22482+21482
21483+22483+24483+24484+23484+22484+21484
21485+22485+24485+24486+23486+22486+21486
21487+22487+24487+24488+23488+22488+21488
21489+22489+24489+24490+23490+22490+21490
21491+22491+24491+24492+23492+22492+21492
21493+22493+24493+24494+23494+22494+21494

21495+22495+24495+24496+23496+22496+21496
21497+22497+24497+24498+23498+22498+21498
21499+22499+24499+24500+23500+22500+21500
21501+22501+24501+24502+23502+22502+21502
21503+22503+24503+24504+23504+22504+21504
21505+22505+24505+24506+23506+22506+21506
21507+22507+24507+24508+23508+22508+21508
21509+22509+24509+24510+23510+22510+21510
21511+22511+24511+24512+23512+22512+21512
21513+22513+24513+24514+23514+22514+21514
21515+22515+24515+24516+23516+22516+21516
21517+22517+24517+24518+23518+22518+21518
21519+22519+24519+24520+23520+22520+21520
21521+22521+24521+24522+23522+22522+21522
21523+22523+24523+24524+23524+22524+21524
21525+22525+24525+24526+23526+22526+21526
21527+22527+24527+24528+23528+22528+21528
21529+22529+24529+24530+23530+22530+21530
21531+22531+24531+24532+23532+22532+21532
21533+22533+24533+24534+23534+22534+21534
21535+22535+24535+24536+23536+22536+21536
21537+22537+24537+24538+23538+22538+21538
21539+22539+24539+24540+23540+22540+21540
21541+22541+24541+24542+23542+22542+21542
21543+22543+24543+24544+23544+22544+21544
21545+22545+24545+24546+23546+22546+21546
21547+22547+24547+24548+23548+22548+21548
21549+22549+24549+24550+23550+22550+21550
21551+22551+24551+24552+23552+22552+21552
21553+22553+24553+24554+23554+22554+21554
21555+22555+24555+24556+23556+22556+21556
21557+22557+24557+24558+23558+22558+21558
21559+22559+24559+24560+23560+22560+21560
21561+22561+24561+24562+23562+22562+21562
21563+22563+24563+24564+23564+22564+21564
21565+22565+24565+24566+23566+22566+21566
21567+22567+24567+24568+23568+22568+21568

S7+1 Sub-Surface Stock

8-car double-ended sets

Formation: DM+M1+M2+MS+MS+M2+M1+DM

21323+22323+25384+24323+24324+25324+22324+21324

Note
25xxx vehicles classified as M2D and fitted with de-icing equipment

Below: *The Sub-Surface stock operating on London Underground is now all of the Bombardier-built 'S' type, formed into either seven or eight car trains. The Circle, District and Hammersmith and City lines are operated by a common pool of seven-car sets, fitted with longitudinal seating. DM No. 21468 on the rear of a seven-car set is seen at Liverpool Street, forming a Circle Line service.* **Antony Christie**

METROPOLITAN LINE

S8 Sub-Surface Stock

Builder: Bombardier, Derby
Years built: 2008-2012
Formation: DM+M1+M2+MS+MS+M2+M1+DM
Construction: Aluminium
Max speed: 62mph (100km/h)
Length: Driving - 57ft 2in (17.44m)
Intermediate - 50ft 6in (15.43m)
Width: 9ft 5in (2.92m)
Height: 12ft 0in (3.68m)
Gangway: Emergency end doors
Seating: Total 264
DM-34, M1-34, M2-34, MS-23
Doors: Sliding bi-parting
Traction equipment: 4 x Bombardier MJB20093 of 87hp (65kW) on each power car

8-car double-ended sets

Formation: DM+M1+M2+MS+MS+M2+M1+DM

21001+22001+23001+24001+24002+25002+22002+21002
21003+22003+23003+24003+24004+25004+22004+21004
21005+22005+23005+24005+24006+25006+22006+21006
21007+22007+23007+24007+24008+25008+22008+21008
21009+22009+23009+24009+24010+25010+22010+21010
21011+22011+23011+24011+24012+25012+22012+21012
21013+22013+23013+24013+24014+25014+22014+21014
21015+22015+23015+24015+24016+25016+22016+21016
21017+22017+23017+24017+24018+25018+22018+21018
21019+22019+23019+24019+24020+25020+22020+21020
21021+22021+23021+24021+24022+25022+22022+21022
21023+22023+23023+24023+24024+25024+22024+21024
21025+22025+23025+24025+24026+25026+22026+21026
21027+22027+23027+24027+24028+25028+22028+21028
21029+22029+23029+24029+24030+25030+22030+21030
21031+22031+23031+24031+24032+25032+22032+21032
21033+22033+23033+24033+24034+25034+22034+21034
21035+22035+23035+24035+24036+25036+22036+21036
21037+22037+23037+24037+24038+25038+22038+21038
21039+22039+23039+24039+24040+25040+22040+21040
21041+22041+23041+24041+24042+25042+22042+21042
21043+22043+23043+24043+24044+25044+22044+21044
21045+22045+23045+24045+24046+25046+22046+21046
21047+22047+23047+24047+24048+25048+22048+21048
21049+22049+23049+24049+24050+25050+22050+21050
21051+22051+23051+24051+24052+25052+22052+21052
21053+22053+23053+24053+24054+25054+22054+21054
21055+22055+23055+24055+24056+25056+22056+21056
21057+22057+23057+24057+24058+23058+22058+21058
21059+22059+23059+24059+24060+23060+22060+21060
21061+22061+23061+24061+24062+23062+22062+21062
21063+22063+23063+24063+24064+23064+22064+21064
21065+22065+23065+24065+24066+23066+22066+21066
21067+22067+23067+24067+24068+23068+22068+21068
21069+22069+23069+24069+24070+23070+22070+21070
21071+22071+23071+24071+24072+23072+22072+21072
21073+22073+23073+24073+24074+23074+22074+21074
21075+22075+23075+24075+24076+23076+22076+21076
21077+22077+23077+24077+24078+23078+22078+21078
21079+22079+23079+24079+24080+23080+22080+21080
21081+22081+23081+24081+24082+23082+22082+21082
21083+22083+23083+24083+24084+23084+22084+21084
21085+22085+23085+24085+24086+23086+22086+21086
21087+22087+23087+24087+24088+23088+22088+21088
21089+22089+23089+24089+24090+23090+22090+21090
21091+22091+23091+24091+24092+23092+22092+21092
21093+22093+23093+24093+24094+23094+22094+21094
21095+22095+23095+24095+24096+23096+22096+21096
21097+22097+23097+24097+24098+23098+22098+21098
21099+22099+23099+24099+24100+23100+22100+21100
21101+22101+23101+24101+24102+23102+22102+21102
21103+22103+23103+24103+24104+23104+22104+21104
21105+22105+23105+24105+24106+23106+22106+21106
21107+22107+23107+24107+24108+23108+22108+21108
21109+22109+23109+24109+24110+23110+22110+21110
21111+22111+23111+24111+24112+23112+22112+21112
21113+22113+23113+24113+24114+23114+22114+21114
21115+22115+23115+24115+24116+23116+22116+21116

Vehicle named
21100 ***Tim O'Toole CBE***

Notes
25xxx vehicles classified as M2D and fitted with de-icing equipment

Left: *The S8 stock is operated on the Metropolitan Line and has a mix of longitudinal and facing seats. With DM No. 21036 on the rear, a train is seen departing from Chorleywood with a southbound service.* **CJM**

SERVICE STOCK

Former Passenger Stock

Rail Adhesion Train (RAT)

D78 stock
7010+8123+17010+8010+7123
7040+8107+17040+8040+7107

Above: *Good rail adhesion is important not only on the Network Rail system, but also London Underground and light rail systems, and during the autumn leaf-fall season adhesion improvement trains have to operate. Two former D78 four-car sets are in operation on the sub-surface lines. With car No. 7107 nearest the camera, an adhesion improvement train is seen passing North Harrow.* **CJM**

Track Recording Train

1960, 1967, 1972 and 1973 Tube stock
L132 (3901)+TRC666 (514)+L133 (3905)

3213+4213+3178 - For conversion into new inspection train
3079+4313+3313 - For conversion into new inspection train

Rail Adhesion (Sandite) and Pilot Stock

1956 and 1962 Stock
1406+2682+9125+1681+1682+9577+2406+1407 - Ued for Sandite and adhesion operations
1570+9691+2440+9441+1441 - Used for Sandite and adhesion operations

Filming Train

(at Aldwych)

1972 Stock
3229+4229+4329+3329

Locomotives
Schoma/Clayton

1	Diesel Hydraulic	Britta Lotta	8	Battery/Electric	Emma
2	Battery/Electric	Nikki	9	Diesel Hydraulic	Debora
3	Diesel Hydraulic	Claire	10	Battery/Electric	Clementine
4	Battery/Electric	Pam	11	Battery/Electric	Joan
5	Battery/Electric	Sophie	12	Diesel Hydraulic	Melanie
6	Battery/Electric	Denise	13	Battery/Electric	Michele
7	Battery/Electric	Annemarie	14	Battery/Electric	Carol

Track Machines

C623	7.5t crane
C624	7.5t crane
C625	7.5t crane
C626	7.5t crane
TRM627	Track relaying crane
TRM628	Track relaying crane
TMM771	Plasser 07-16 Universal
TMM772	Plasser 07-16 Universal
TMM773	Plasser 07-16 Universal - *Alan Jenkins*
TMM774	Plasser 08-275
TMM775	Matisa B45UE (99 70 9128 003-9)
TMM776	Matisa B45UE (99 70 9128 004-7)

Battery / Electric

L15	69015, 97015, 97715
L16§	69016, 97016 - Seltrac equipped
L17§	69017, 97017 - Seltrac equipped
L18§	69018. 97018 - Seltrac equipped
L19§	69019, 97019 - Seltrac equipped
L20	69020, 97020, 97720 - Seltrac equipped
L21	64021, 97021 - Seltrac equipped
L22§	64022, 97022, 97722
L23§	64023, 97023
L24§	64024, 97024
L25§	64025, 97025
L26§	64026, 97026
L27§	64027, 97027 - Victoria line ATP equipped
L28§	64028, 97028 - Victoria line ATP equipped
L29§	64029, 97029 - Victoria line ATP equipped
L30§	64030, 97030 - Victoria line ATP equipped
L31§	64031, 97031 - Victoria line ATP equipped
L32§	64032, 97032, 97732 - Victoria line ATP equipped
L44§	73044, 97044 - Seltrac equipped
L45§	73045, 97045 - Seltrac equipped
L46§	73046, 97046 - Seltrac equipped
L47	73047, 97047 - Seltrac equipped
L48	73048, 97048 - Seltrac equipped
L49§	73049, 97049 - Seltrac equipped
L50§	73050, 97050, 97750 - Seltrac equipped
L51§	73051, 97051, 97751 - Seltrac equipped
L52	73052, 97052, 97752 - Seltrac equipped
L53§	73053, 97053, 97753 - Seltrac equipped
L54	73054, 97054 - Seltrac equipped

§ - Refurbished

Above: *To provide motive power for engineering trains a fleet of tube size battery-electric locos are in use, with various locos fitted with different signalling to all power to be available for all lines. No. 51 is seen in the deep tube section of the Northern Line southern extension from Kennington to Battersea via Nine Elms.* **LUL**

Transport for London Docklands Light Railway

Operated by KeolisAmey Docklands for Transport for London under contract until 2021.

Class B90 (twin)

Train Length: 94ft 5in (28.80m)
Width: 8ft 7in (2.65m)
Power Supply: 750V dc third rail
Seating: 52 + 4 tip-up
Horsepower: 375hp (280kW)
Electrical Equipment: Brush

22 24 26 28 30 32 34 36 38 40 42 44
23 25 27 29 31 33 35 37 39 41 43

Left: *The current Docklands Light Rail (DLR) system operates four different fleets of two-vehicle trains. A fleet of 23 B90 sets are in use. No. 24 is illustrated at Poplar.* **Antony Christie**

Class B92 (twin)

Train Length: 94ft 5in (28.80m)
Width: 8ft 7in (2.65m)
Power Supply: 750V dc third rail
Seating: 54 + 4 tip-up
Horsepower: 375hp (280kW)
Electrical Equipment: Brush

45 49 53 57 61 65 69 73 77 81 85 89
46 50 54 58 62 66 70 74 78 82 86 90
47 51 55 59 63 67 71 75 79 83 87 91
48 52 56 60 64 68 72 76 80 84 88

Left: *In 1992 a batch of 47 B92 twin sets were built by BN Construction in Belgium. These sets seat 54 passengers with vast amounts of space for standees. Painted in standard DLR red livery with grey contrasting doors, set No. 60 is seen at Poplar.* **CJM**

Class B2K (twin)

Train Length: 94ft 5in (28.80m)
Width: 8ft 7in (2.65m)
Power Supply: 750V dc third rail
Seating: 52 + 4 tip-up
Horsepower: 375hp (280kW)
Electrical Equipment: Brush

01 03 05 07 09 11 13 15 92 94 96 98
02 04 06 08 10 12 14 16 93 95 97 99

Right: *In 2000 further stock was delivered to the DLR system, identified as B2K, these were again twin sets with seating for 52. These sets were numbered 92 onwards, but after No. 99, the numbering reverted to 01-16 for the remainder of the fleet of 24 sets. No. 04 is illustrated.* **CJM**

Class B07 (twin)

Train Length: 94ft 5in (28.80m)
Width: 8ft 7in (2.65m)
Power Supply: 750V dc third rail
Seating: 52 + 4 tip-up
Horsepower: 375hp (280kW)
Electrical Equipment: Bombardier

101	106	111	116	121	126	131	136	141	146	151
102	107	112	117	122	127	132	137	142	147	152
103	108	113	118	123	128	133	138	143	148	153
104	109	114	119	124	129	134	139	144	149	154
105	110	115	120	125	130	135	140	145	150	155

Right: *In 2007 a batch of slightly different design twin sets were introduced, built by Bombardier. Set No. 143 is seen at Stratford.* **CJM**

■ CAF have been awarded a contract to design and build a new fleet of 43 Docklands trains. These will be five-car sets and enter service from 2023.

Emirates Air Line
(Thames Cable Car) Transport for London

The Emirates Air Line or Thames Cable Car is a connection over the River Thames from Greenwich to the Royal Docks. The 1km line is operated by a fleet of 34 10-seat 'gondolas', and the end-to-end journey takes between 5 and 10 minutes depending on the speed of the service.

01	10	19	28
02	11	20	29
03	12	21	30
04	13	22	31
05	14	23	32
06	15	24	33
07	16	25	34
08	17	26	
09	18	27	

Right: *The Thames Cable Car or Emirates Air Line. Gondola No. 25 is shown, each can accommodate up to 10 passengers.* **Antony Christie**

Transport for London Croydon Tramlink

Contact details as London Underground.

Bombardier *Flexity Swift* CR4000

Train Length: 98ft 9in (30.1m)
Width: 8ft 7in (2.65m)
Power Supply: 750V dc overhead
Seating: 70
Horsepower: 643hp (480kW)
Electrical Equipment: Bombardier

2530	2533	2536	2539	2542	2545	2548	2551§	§ Stored
2531	2534	2537	2540	2543	2546	2549	2552	
2532	2535	2538	2541	2544	2547	2550	2553	

Name applied: **2535** ***Stephen Parascandolo 1980-2007***

Left: *The Croydon Tramlink operates from Wimbledon to Beckingham Junction, Elmers End and New Addington via Croydon. Originally the route was worked by a fleet of 24 Bombardier 'Flexity Swift' three section cars, this was later supplemented by Stadler stock. Set No. 2550 is seen at Merton Park bound for Croydon.* **CJM**

Stadler *Variobahn*

Train Length: 106ft 2½in (32.37m)
Width: 8ft 7in (2.65m)
Power Supply: 750V dc overhead
Seating: 70
Horsepower: 650hp (483kW)
Electrical Equipment: Stadler

2554	2556	2558	2560	2562	2564
2555	2557	2559	2561	2563	2565

Below: *Between 2011-2016 a fleet of five-section Stadler 'Variobahn' sets were introduced, with seating for 70 and increased standing space. The sets operate in a common pool with the earlier Bombardier vehicles. Set No. 2556 calls at Mitcham Junction, with a service bound for Wimbledon. All Croydon trams have doors on both sides.* **CJM**

Edinburgh Tramway

Address: ✉ 55 Annandale Street, Edinburgh, EH7 4AZ

customer@edinburghtrams.com ✆ 0131 475 0177 ⓘhttp://edinburghtrams.com

CAF 7-section *Urbos 3*

Train Length: 140ft 5in (42.8m)
Width: 8ft 7in (2.65m)
Power Supply: 750V dc overhead
Seating: 78 + 170 standing
Horsepower: 1,287hp (960kW)
Electrical Equipment: CAF

251	255	259	263	267	271	275
252	256	260	264	268	272	276
253	257	261	265	269	273	277
254	258	262	266	270	274	

Right: *A fleet of 27 CAF-built Urbos 3 seven-section trams operate the Edinburgh tram system, operating from Edinburgh Airport to the city centre. Permission has been granted to extend the system by 2.8 miles to Newhaven, which should open in 2023. Vehicle No. 265 is seen at Edinburgh Airport.* **CJM**

Below: *At the city end of the Edinburgh tram system, vehicles operate along the middle of Princes Street, sharing space with cars and buses. Tram No. 259 heads along Princes Street heading for the airport.* **CJM**

Blackpool Trams

Address: ✉ Blackpool Transport, Rigby Road, Blackpool, FY1 5DD
jean.cox@blackpooltransport.com
✆ 01253 473001 ⓘ www.blackpooltrams.info

Blackpool Tramway is operated by Blackpool Transport.

Flexity 2

Train Length: 105ft 9in (32.23m)
Width: 8ft 8in (2.65m)
Power Supply: 600V dc overhead
Seating: 74 + 148 standing
Horsepower: 4 x 160hp (120kW) three phase TMs
Electrical Equipment: Bombardier

001	003	005	007	009	011	013	015	017
002	004	006	008	010	012	014	016	018

Names applied

002 ***Alderman E E Wynne***
007 ***Alan Whitbread***

Right: *Blackpool Tramway, which runs 11 miles between Starr Gate and Fleetwood Ferry via Blackpool sea front and Tower, is now operated by a fleet of 18 five-section Bombardier Flexity 2 trams. The sets are based at Starr Gate depot. Set No. 007 is seen close to Blackpool Tower on 25 June 2019.* **CJM**

Below: *Most trams carry some form of advertising, with some carrying full body wrap colours. Set No. 006 is seen at Fleetwood turning on the passenger loop heading back to Blackpool. This section of the route has street running, although some sections are segregated.* **CJM**

Heritage Fleet

40	Fleetwood Box	648	Centenary	717	Balloon
66	Bolton Tram	680	Railcoach	718	Balloon
147	Standard	700	Balloon	719	Balloon
600	Boat	701	Balloon	723	Balloon
621	Brush	711	Balloon	733+734	Twin
631	Brush	713	Balloon	736	Illuminated (Frigate)
642	Centenary	715	Balloon	737	Illuminated (Boat)

Above: *Blackpool Transport still operate a sizeable fleet of 'Heritage' trams of the 'BC' fleet as it is known locally. These vehicles, operate during the summer months in the central Blackpool area and take part in gala events. No. 680 is seen near Central Pier. This vehicle built in 1935 and rebuilt several times, is owned by the Manchester Tramway Museum Society and is on loan to Blackpool trams.* **CJM**

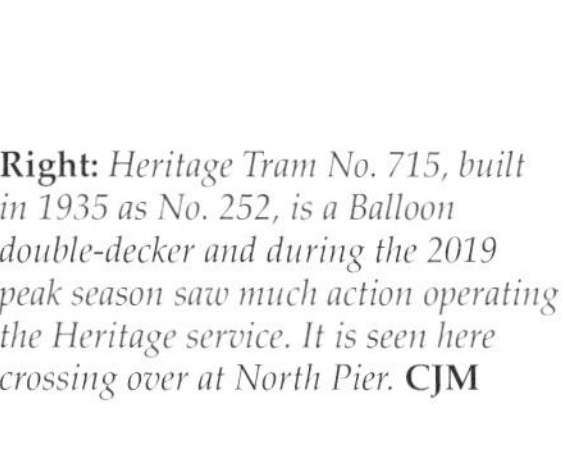
Right: *Heritage Tram No. 715, built in 1935 as No. 252, is a Balloon double-decker and during the 2019 peak season saw much action operating the Heritage service. It is seen here crossing over at North Pier.* **CJM**

Glasgow Subway

Address: ✉ SPT, Consort House, 12 West George Street, Glasgow, G2 1HN
enquiry@spt.co.uk ✆ 0141 332 6811 ⓘ www.spt.co.uk

Glasgow Subway is operated by Strathclyde Partnership for Transport (SPT).
Gauge: 4ft (1219mm)

Single Power Cars

Length: 42ft 2in (12.81m)
Width: 7ft 7in (2.34m)
Power Supply: 600V dc third rail
Seating: 36S
Horsepower: 190hp (142.4kW)
Electrical Equipment: GEC

101	104	107	110	113	116	119	122(S)	125	128	131
102	105	108	111	114	117	120	123	126	129	132
103	106	109	112	115	118	121	124	127	130	133

Trailer Cars

Length: 41ft 6in (12.70m)
Width: 7ft 7in (2.34m)
Seating: 40S

201	202	203	204	205	206	207	208

Left: *The Glasgow Underground, or 'Clockwork Orange' as it is often called, operates an inner and outer circular route below Glasgow. The line is in the process of considerable modernisation. Car No. 130, painted in grey livery, is illustrated on the outer Circle line at Partick.* **Antony Christie**

Stadler Metro Sets

Train Length: 128ft 9in (39.24m)
Width: 7ft 7in (2.34m)
Height: 8ft 8in (2.65m)
Seating: 104S + 6 folding, standing for 199S

New four-car articulated sets under construction by Stadler in Altenrhein, Switzerland. Eventually to operate under Automatic Train Operation following total route modernisation.

301	303	305	307	309	311	313	315	317
302	304	306	308	310	312	314	316	

Left: *New four-vehicle Stadler trains are currently under construction and delivery to the Glasgow Underground and should go into service from late 2020-early 2021. The sets are a major change from the existing stock and when fully commissioned will feature automatic driverless train operation. The first set to be delivered, No. 301, is seen stabled next to a 1977 Metro-Cammell set at Broomloan depot.* **SPT**

Manchester Metrolink

Address: ✉ Greater Manchester PTE, 2 Piccadilly Gardens, Manchester, M1 3BG
RATP Metrolink, Metrolink House, Queens Road, Manchester, M8 ORY
customerservices@metrolink.co.uk ✆ 0161 205 2000 ⓘ www.metrolink.co.uk

Metrolink is operated for GMPTE by Keolis Amey.

M5000 stock

Train Length: 93ft 1in (28.4m)
Width: 8ft 7in (2.65m)
Power Supply: 750V dc overhead
Seating: 52 + 8 tip-up
Horsepower: 643hp (480kW)
Electrical Equipment: Bombardier

3001	3015	3029	3043	3057	3071	3085	3099	3113	3127	3141
3002	3016	3030	3044	3058	3072	3086	3100	3114	3128	3142
3003	3017	3031	3045	3059	3073	3087	3101	3115	3129	3143
3004	3018	3032	3046	3060	3074	3088	3102	3116	3130	3144
3005	3019	3033	3047	3061	3075	3089	3103	3117	3131	3145
3006	3020	3034	3048	3062	3076	3090	3104	3118	3132	3136
3007	3021	3035	3049	3063	3077	3091	3105	3119	3133	3147
3008	3022	3036	3050	3064	3078	3092	3106	3120	3134	
3009	3023	3037	3051	3065	3079	3093	3107	3121	3135	
3010	3024	3038	3052	3066	3080	3094	3108	3122	3136	
3011	3025	3039	3053	3067	3081	3095	3109	3123	3137	
3012	3026	3040	3054	3068	3082	3096	3110	3124	3138	
3013	3027	3041	3055	3069	3083	3097	3111	3125	3139	
3014	3028	3042	3056	3070	3084	3098	3112	3126	3140	

Names applied

3009	***50th Anniversary of Coronation Street 1960-2010***
3020	***Lancashire Fusilier***
3022	***Spirit of MCR***
3098	***Gracie Fields***

Trams 3121-3147 on order

Right: *The large Manchester Metrolink system is operated by a fleet of 147 two-section M5000 Bombardier 'Flexity Swift' sets. These are painted silver and yellow. No. 3068 is seen departing from the Broadway stop on the Eccles line heading into Manchester City Centre.* **CJM**

Left: *Several sections of the Manchester Metrolink system, which now extends to 59 miles with eight lines, has street running, where trams, people and road vehicles have common access. One of these is in Manchester City Centre around Piccadilly Gardens. No. 3070 is seen passing through the main shopping area on 27 June 2019. Trams either operate as a single two-car or double four-car formation.* **CJM**

West Midlands Metro

Address: ✉ Travel West Midlands, PO Box 3565, Birmingham, B1 3JR
info@travelmetro.co.uk ✆ 0121 254 7272 ⓘ www.travelmetro.co.uk

Urbos 3

Train Length: 108ft 3in (29m)
Width: 8ft 8in (2.65m)
Power Supply: 750V dc overhead
Seating: 54 + 156 standing
Horsepower: 1,320hp (960kW)
Builder: CAF

17§	
18§	
19§	
20§	
21§	
22§	
23§	
24§	
25§	
26	
27§	
28§	*Jasper Carrott*
29§	
30§	
31§	*Cyrille Regis MBE 1958-2018*
32§	
33§	
34§	
35§	
36§	
37§	*Ozzy Osbourne*

§ Fitted with traction batteries

21 additional CAF Urbos trams were ordered in October 2019, with an option on a further 29.

Above: *The West Midlands Metro running from the middle of Birmingham City Centre to Wolverhampton is currently operated by 21 CAF Urbos 3 five-section trams. At the start of 2020 the fleet was under conversion to bi-mode vehicles, able to operate from overhead power collection or battery. Bi-mode, West Midlands Metro blue-liveried No. 28* Jasper Carrott *is shown.* **CJM**

Left: *A number of the West Midlands Trams now carry advertising liveries, No. 27 advertising the Indian-based OLA Cab company. When photographed in November 2019, this set was still electric only and not fitted with traction batteries.* **CJM**

Nottingham Express Transit

Address: ✉ Transdev Tram UK Ltd, Garrick House, 74 Chiswick High Road, London, W4 1SY
Nottingham City Transport Ltd, Lower Parliament Street, Nottingham, NG1 1GG
info@thetram.net ✆ 0115 942 7777 ⓘ www.thetram.net

Incentro AT6/5

Train Length: 108ft 3in (29m)
Width: 7ft 9in (2.4m)
Power Supply: 750V dc overhead
Seating: 54 + 4 tip-up
Horsepower: 697hp (520kW)
Electrical Equipment: Bombardier

201	*Torvill and Dean*	206	*Angela Alcock*	211	*Robin Hood*
202	*DH Lawrence*	207	*Mavis Worthington*	212	*William Booth*
203	*Bendigo Thompson*	208	*Dinah Minton*	213	*Mary Potter*
204	*Erica Beardsmore*	209	*Sidney Standard*	214	*Dennis McCarthy MBE*
205	*Lord Byron*	210	*Sir Jesse Boot*	215	*Brian Clough OBE*

Citadis 302

Train Length: 104ft 11¾in (32m)
Width: 7ft 9in (2.4m)
Power Supply: 750V dc overhead
Seating: 58 + 6 tip-up
Horsepower: 644hp (480kW)
Builder: Alstom

216	*Dame Laura Knight*	224	*Vicky McClure*	232	*William Ivory*
217	*Carl Froch MBE*	225	*Doug Scott CBE*	233	*Ada Lovelace*
218	*Jim Taylor*	226	*Jimmy Sirrel & Jack Wheeler*	234	*George Africanus*
219	*Alan Sillitoe*	227	*Sir Peter Mansfield*	235	*David Clarke*
220	*Sophie Robson*	228	*Local Armed Forces Heroes*	236	*Sat Bains*
221	*Stephen Lowe*	229	*Viv Anderson MBE*	237	*Stuart Broad MBE*
222	*David S Stewart OBE*	230	*George Green*		
223	*Colin Slater MBE*	231	*Rebecca Adlington OBE*		

Right: *Nottingham Express Transit operates two fleets of trams. The original fleet consisted of 15 five-section Bombardier Incentro sets. A number of sets now carry advertising liveries. Tram No. 211* Robin Hood *illustrated near Nottingham railway station carries green and mauve advertising livery of Deliveroo.* **Antony Christie**

Left: *As the Nottingham system developed, extra trams were needed and these came in the form of 22 Alstom five-section Citadis 302 sets. Originally all were painted in mid green and silver-grey, as seen on No. 222* David S Stewart OBE. *These sets have 58 seats with large standing areas.* **Antony Christie**

South Yorkshire SuperTram

Address: ✉ Stagecoach SuperTram, Nunnery Depot, Woodburn Road, Sheffield, S9 3LS
enquiries@supertram.com ✆ 0114 272 8282 ⓘ www.supertram.com

Six-axle Stock

Train Length: 113ft 6in (34.75m)	*Seating: 88 + 6 tip-up*
Width: 8ft 7in (2.65m)	*Horsepower: 800hp (596kW)*
Power Supply: 750V dc overhead	*Electrical Equipment: Siemens*

101	103	105	107	109	111	113	115	117	119	121	123	125
102	104	106	108	110	112	114	116	118	120	122	124	

Name applied
123 ***Pete McKee***

Left: *The 22 mile long South Yorkshire Supertram system is operated by 25 three-section Siemens vehicles, built in 1993-1994. Today the system is operated by Stagecoach. Painted in standard livery, No. 106 is departing from Halfway heading to the city centre.* **CJM**

Below: *Some of the trams carry full vehicle advertising wraps. This is shown on No. 116 displaying Doncaster/Sheffield airport colours. The tram is seen at the Cathedral stop, the main interchange point in the city centre.* **CJM**

Class 399
CityLink

Train Length: 122ft 0¾in (37.2m)
Width: 8ft 8½in (2.65m)
Power supply: 750V dc overhead (equipped for 25kV ac operation)
Power equipment: 6 x 145kW VEM traction motors
Seats (total/car): 88S, 22S/44S/22S

Number	*Formation* DMOSW+MOS+DMOSW	*Depot*	*Livery*	*Owner*	*Operator*	*Name*
399201 (201)*	**999001+999101+999201**	§	**SST**	**SST**	**SST**	
399202 (202)*	**999002+999102+999202**	§	**SST**	**SST**	**SST**	*Theo The Childrens Hospital Charity*
399203 (203)*	**999003+999103+999203**	§	**SST**	**SST**	**SST**	
399204 (204)*	**999004+999104+999204**	§	**SST**	**SST**	**SST**	
399205 (205)	**999005+999105+999205**	§	**SST**	**SST**	**SST**	
399206 (206)*	**999006+999106+999206**	§	**SST**	**SST**	**SST**	
399207 (207)	**999007+999107+999207**	§	**SST**	**SST**	**SST**	

* Authorised for TramTrain operation. § - Sheffield Nunnery SST - Sheffield Super Tram

Above: *In 2018 the long awaited opening of the UKs first 'Tramtrain' line operated running from Sheffield Cathedral to Rotherham Parkgate. To operate the system a fleet of seven three-section Vossloh sets were ordered which are maintained at the Supertram depot at Nunnery. The Tramtrain operates along the tram system to near Meadowhall, where it branches off onto the Network Rail operated line via Rotherham Central to Parkgate. Set No. 399201 passes through the high level Network Rail platforms at Rotherham Central.* **CJM**

Right: *Set No. 399202 arrives at the Parkgate station in Rotherham, where low level tram platforms are provided. The Class 399s are painted in Stagecoach blue swirl livery.* **CJM**

Tyne & Wear Metro

Address: ✉ Tyne & Wear Passenger Transport Executive (NEXUS), Nexus House, 33 St James Boulevard, Newcastle upon Tyne, NE1 4AX

enquiries@nexus.co.uk

✆ 0191 203 3333 ⓘ www.nexus.org.uk

Tyne & Wear Metro stock is allocated TOPS classification 994 for operation over Network Rail metals between Pelaw and South Hylton.

Six-axle Stock

Train Length: 91ft 3in (27.80m)
Width: 8ft 7in (2.65m)
Power Supply: 1500V dc overhead
Seating: 68 §64
Horsepower: 500hp (374kW)
Electrical Equipment: Siemens

4001§	4013	4025	4037	4049	4061	4073	4085
4002§	4014	4026	4038	4050	4062	4074	4086
4003	4015	4027	4039	4051	4063	4075	4087
4004	4016	4028	4040	4052	4064	4076	4088
4005	4017	4029	4041	4053	4065	4077	4089
4006	4018	4030	4042	4054	4066	4078	4090
4007	4019	4031	4043	4055	4067	4079	
4008	4020	4032	4044	4056	4068	4080	
4009	4021	4033	4045	4057	4069	4081	
4010	4022	4034	4046	4058	4070	4082	
4011	4023	4035	4047	4059	4071	4083	
4012	4024	4036	4048	4060	4072	4084	

Name applied (inside)
4041 ***Harry Cowans***

Tyne and Wear Metro sets are based at Gosforth depot. In 2019 a new depot will open at Howdon, to provide extra cover while Gosforth depot is modernised to cope with new stock. Howdon will also be a delivery point for new trains.

Below: *The 90 two-section trams which operate the Tyne & Wear Metro are set to be replaced in the next few years. Introduced between 1978-1981, seating is for 64 and sets currently carry black and yellow livery. It is usual for trains to operate formed of two sets. No. 4028 arrives at Bank Foot station with a service from Newcastle Airport to South Hylton. The entire network is 48 miles with 60 stations.* **Antony Christie**

■ Tyne & Wear Metro also operates three battery-electric shunting locomotives at South Gosforth, BL1-BL3, these are registered National Fleet numbers 97901, 97902 and 97903.

■ In 2020 a fleet of 42 new-design five-car sets were ordered from Stadler Rail to replace the present fleet. This £362 contract will see new units delivered from late 2021.

Great Orme Tramway

Address: ✉ Victoria Station, Church Walks, Llandudno, North Wales. LL30 2NB.
tramwayenquiries@conwy.gov.uk
✆ 01492 577 877 ⓘ www.greatormetramway.co.uk

The Great Orme Tramway operates between Victoria station in Llandudno and the summit of the Great Orme. The line is operated in two sections: Llandudno to Halfway and Halfway to Summit.

Single Bogie Cars

Built By: Hurst Nelson, Motherwell
Introduced: 1902
Power: Cable
Seating: 48
Speed: 5mph (8km/h)
Gauge: 3ft 6in (1067mm)

Lower section
4 *St Tudno*
5 *St Silio*

Upper section
6 *St Seiriol*
7 *St Trillo*

Right: *The Great Orme Tramway which runs between Llandudno and the top of the Great Orme operates in two sections, between Llandudno and Halfway and between Halfway and summit, with two dedicated pairs of trains working each section. Lower section tram No. 4* St Silio *is seen soon after departing from the town terminal.* **CJM**

Hythe Pier Tramway

Address: ✉ The Pier, Prospect Place, Hythe, Southampton. SO45 6AU.
ticketoffice@hytheferry.co.uk ✆ 023 8084 0722 ⓘ http://hytheferry.co.uk

The Hythe Pier Tramway operates along the pier in Hythe near Southampton and takes ferry boat passengers from the end of the pier on a 700 yard (640m) journey to the town. The line is electrified using the third rail system at 250V dc. Operated by Blue Funnel Ferries Ltd.

4-wheel locos

Built By: Brush
Introduced: 1917 as battery, now electric
Power: 250V dc third rail
Seating: Nil
Speed: 10mph (16km/h)
Gauge: 2ft (610mm)

1 **Works No. 16302**
2 **Works No. 16307**

Rolling stock
Four bogie passenger carriages, two fitted with remote driving controls
One four-wheel freight platform wagon, one oil carrying tank car

Right: *One of the most unusual trams in the UK is the Hythe Pier Tramway near Southampton which trundles up and down the 700 yard pier taking passengers from and to the ferry to Southampton. Each train is formed of one electric loco at the Hythe end and three carriages with a luggage flat on the pier end. The passenger coach at the pier end has a small driving compartment.* **CJM**

Southend Pier Tramway

Address: ✉ Western Esplanade, Southend-on-Sea SS1 2EL
council@southend.gov.uk
✆ 01702 611214 ⓘ www.southend.gov.uk

Southend Pier Railway operates as a tourist attraction between the Shore Station and the Pier Head, a distance of 1.25 miles (2.01km). It is operated by two diesel-hydraulic locos and 12 passenger cars

Seven-vehicle sets

Built By: Severn Lamb Engineering
Introduced: 1986
Power: Diesel
Seating: Train - 200
Speed: 10mph (16km/h)
Gauge: 3ft (914mm)

A	*Sir John Betjeman*
B	*Sir William Heygate*

Left: *The 1¼ mile long Southend Pier has transport for those who don't wish to walk, with the provision of the Southend Pier Railway. Each of two trains is formed of one loco, at the pier head end, and six trailers, the shore-end trailer housing a driving compartment. Tram 'A'* Sir John Betjeman *heads along the pier to the shore station.* **CJM**

■ Two new electric train sets ordered in 2019 from Seven Lamb Engineering for delivery in early 2021.

Volks Electric Railway

Address: ✉ Madeira Drive, Brighton and Hove BN2, UK
contact via website
✆ 01273 292718 ⓘ www.volkselectricrailway.co.uk

Volks Electric Railway operates along the sea front at Brighton between Aquarium to Black Rock, a distance of 1.02 miles (1.64km). It is electrified at 110V dc and currently has a fleet of seven electric passenger cars.

3	**40 seat open of 1892**
4	**40 seat open of 1892**
6	**40 seat open of 1901**
7	**40 seat open of 1901**
8	**40 seat open of 1901**
9	**40 seat open of 1910**
10	**40 seat open of 1926**

Left: *The oldest electric railway in the UK, is the Volks Electric Railway, running along the sea front in Brighton between Aquarium and Black Rock a distance of just 1.02 miles. Car No. 9, a 40 seat vehicle built in 1910, is shown at Black Rock.* **CJM**

Seaton Tramway

Address: ✉ Seaton Tramway, Harbour Road, Seaton, Devon. EX12 2NQ.
info@tram.co.uk ✆ 01297 20375 ⓘ www.tram.co.uk

The Seaton Tramway operates between Seaton and Colyton along the bank of the River Axe with one intermediate station at Colyford. It is a 2ft 9in (838 mm) narrow gauge electric tramway, 3 miles (4.8 km) in length. It operates over part of the former Seaton Branch line of the L&SWR (SR), which closed in March 1966. The tramway was established in 1970, and previously operated in Eastbourne between 1954 and 1969.

02	1952	Works vehicle
2	1964	Based on London Metropolitan Tramways Type A vehicle No. 14
4	1961	Based on Blackpool 'Open Boat' design
6	1954	Based on Bournemouth open topper design. Originally single decker in Llandudno
7	1958	Based on Bournemouth open topper design
8	1968	Based on Bournemouth open topper design, displays Bristol blue livery
9	2004	Hybrid design based on Plymouth and Blackburn trams
10	2006	Hybrid design based on Plymouth and Blackburn trams
11	2007	Based on Bournemouth open topper design, displays 'pink' charity livery
12	1966	Based on London 'Feltham' design
14	1904	Oldest tram built as Metropolitan Tramways Type A car No. 94 (originally standard gauge)
15	1988	Enclosed saloon, based on Isle of Man design and in Isle of Man livery
16	1921	Originally Bournemouth open top car No. 106
19	1909	Originally Exeter Tramways vehicle

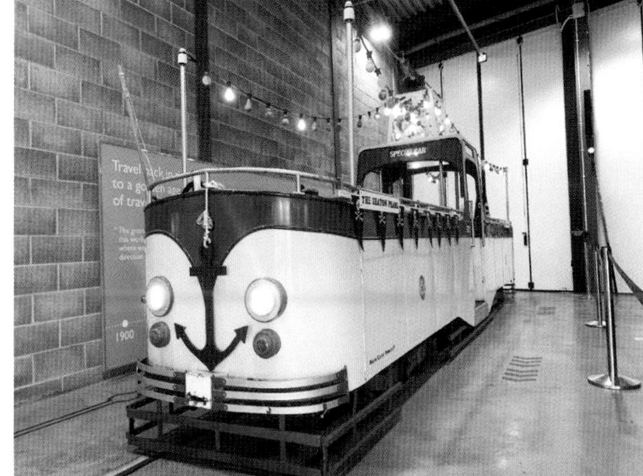

Right Upper: *Although not a tramway or light railway in the same way as other lines, the Seaton Tramway is a unique operation using purpose built miniature trams, replicas of main system types. It operates over the former main railway line track bed from Seaton to Colyton with a gauge of 2ft 9in. A stunning collection of trams are operated. Here, No. 4, a replica of a Blackpool 'Open Boat Car' is seen inside the new covered station at Seaton.* **Thomas Walters**

Right Lower: *Seaton Tramway No. 8, built in 1968, is based on a Bournemouth open topper design and carries Bristol blue livery. The vehicle is seen here in the change end siding at Colyton.* **CJM**

Dublin 'Luas' Trams

Trams returned to the streets of Dublin in 2004, and currently two lines operate with three batches of Alstom Citadis trams. Overhead power is provided at 750V dc. Seating on trams is for 70-72, with standing room for three times that number.

Alstom Citadis TGA301 five-section vehicles introduced 2002-03

3001	3005	3009	3013	3017	3021	3025
3002	3006	3010	3014	3018	3022	3026
3003	3007	3011	3015	3019	3023	
3004	3008	3012	3016	3020	3024	

Left Upper: *Dublin, Ireland has an excellent tram system, radiating from the city centre on two lines, the red and green. Three fleets of Alstom Citadis vehicles operate the services. They are of similar design but with detail differences. The first sets introduced were a fleet of 26 TGA301 vehicles, which are now operated as five-section sets. These operate on the red line. No. 3002 is seen in the city centre where the route crosses over the green line on a flat crossing.* **CJM**

Left Lower: *The interior of the Luas trams is spacious, with seating in the 2+2 style, with good standing room and disabled space. The interior shown is from red line 3000 series vehicle No. 3025.* **CJM**

Alstom Citadis TGA401 five-section vehicles introduced 2002-03

4001	4003	4005	4007	4009	4011	4013
4002	4004	4006	4008	4010	4012	4014

Right: *A fleet of 14 Alstom Citadis TGA401 five-section vehicles were introduced in 2002-2003 and are very similar to the earlier 3000 series sets. No. 4011 is seen departing from the Dublin Museum stop bound for The Point on 19 August 2019.* **CJM**

Alstom Citadis TGA402 seven-section, vehicles introduced 2008-2010

5001	5005	5009	5013	5017	5021§	5025
5002	5006	5010	5014	5018	5022	5026
5003	5007	5011	5015	5019	5023	
5004	5008	5012	5016	5020	5024	

§ Extended to nine section vehicles

Right: *In 2008-2010 a fleet of 26 longer and slightly different style Citadis TGA402 trams with seven sections entered service. These were for use on the green line, which radiates north and south from the city centre. No. 5005 is seen at Windy Arbour.* **CJM**

Below: *A batch of seven nine-section Citadis TGA402 vehicles entered service from 2017. These very long sets are confined to sections of the green line. No. 5027 is seen in the heart of the city in August 2019.* **CJM**

Alstom Citadis TGA402 nine-section vehicles introduced 2017-2018

5027	5028	5029	5030	5031	5032	5033

Eight more nine-section trams on order.

Isle of Man Railways

Manx Electric Railway

The Manx Electric Railway is a 3ft (914mm)-gauge twin-track line which operates from Douglas Derby Castle to Ramsey, a distance of 17 miles (27.4km). It is energised at 550V dc using the overhead power collection system. The main car shops are located at Derby Castle. At Laxey a passenger interchange with the Snaefell Mountain Railway is provided. Trains usually operate only between March and October.

Power Cars

Number	Type	Builder	Year
1	Un-vestibuled saloon	G F Milnes	1893
2	Un-vestibuled saloon	G F Milnes	1893
5	Vestibuled 'Tunnel car'	G F Milnes	1894
6	Vestibuled 'Tunnel car'	G F Milnes	1894
7	Vestibuled 'Tunnel car'	G F Milnes	1894
9	Vestibuled 'Tunnel car'	G F Milnes	1894
14	Cross-bench open saloon	G F Milnes	1898
15 (S)	Cross-bench open saloon	G F Milnes	1898
16	Cross-bench open saloon	G F Milnes	1898
17 (S)	Cross-bench open saloon	G F Milnes	1898
18 (S)	Cross-bench open saloon	G F Milnes	1898
19	Winter saloon	G F Milnes	1899
20	Winter saloon	G F Milnes	1899
21	Winter saloon	G F Milnes	1899
22	Winter saloon	McArds/MER	1992*
23 (S)	Locomotive	MER Co	1900
25 (S)	Cross-bench open	G F Milnes	1893
26 (S)	Cross-bench open	G F Milnes	1893
27 (S)	Cross-bench open	G F Milnes	1893
28 (S)	Cross-bench open	ER&T Ltd	1904
29 (S)	Cross-bench open	ER&T Ltd	1904
30 (S)	Cross-bench open	ER&T Ltd	1904
31 (S)	Cross-bench open	ER&T Ltd	1904
32	Cross-bench 'Toastrack'	United Car	1906
33	Cross-bench 'Toastrack'	United Car	1906
34	Locomotive	IOM	1996

* rebuilt following fire damage - new body on old frame

Left: *Built in 1906 by United Car, Crossbench 'Toastrack' No. 33 is one of the historic vehicles used on the Manx Electric on special events and services. It is shown departing from Derby Castle bound for Laxey on 27 July 2019.* **CJM**

Below: *Vestibuled 'Tunnel Car' No. 7, of 1894, painted in Douglas & Laxey Electric Tramway blue and white livery, approaches Ballameanagh, hauling trailer No. 59 on 1 August 2019 with a service from Derby Castle to Ramsey.* **CJM**

Above: *What looks to be an early tram, Winter Saloon No. 22 was built in 1992 following serious fire damage to the original vehicle. It is seen with trailer No. 37 near Ballagawne on 1 August 2019.* **CJM**

Right: *United Car 'Toastrack' No. 33 painted in Manx Electric Railway red livery is seen arriving at Laxey on 27 July 2019.* **CJM**

Below: *One of the oldest vehicles on the Manx Electric, an un-vestibuled saloon of 1893 vintage No. 2 is seen with Royal Saloon 59 at Ramsey.* **CJM**

Above: *1898-built cross-bench open saloon No. 14, recently restored, poses next to trailer No. 37 at Laxey on 27 July 2019.* **CJM**

Left: *No. 6, an 1894 'Tunnel Car' passes Bellevue with a service from Ramsey to Derby Castle on 31 July 2019.* **CJM**

Below: *Built in 1996 as a loco for the Snaefell Mountain Railway as a replica to No. 7. No. 34 was re-gauged and is now with the Manx Electric Railway, it is seen in the horse tram shed at Derby Castle during the period of track relaying on the Douglas Horse Tramway in 2019.* **CJM**

Trailer Cars

Number	Type	Builder	Year
36 (S)	Cross-bench	G F Milnes	1894
37	Cross-bench	G F Milnes	1894
40	Cross-bench	English Electric	1930
41	Cross-bench	English Electric	1930
42	Cross-bench	G F Milnes	1903
43	Cross-bench	G F Milnes	1903
44	Cross-bench	English Electric	1930
46	Cross-bench	G F Milnes	1899
47	Cross-bench	G F Milnes	1899
48	Cross-bench	G F Milnes	1899
49 (S)	Cross-bench	G F Milnes	1893
50 (S)	Cross-bench	G F Milnes	1893
51	Cross-bench	G F Milnes	1893
53 (S)	Cross-bench	G F Milnes	1893
54 (S)	Cross-bench	G F Milnes	1893
55 (S)	Cross-bench	ER&T Ltd	1904
56	Disabled persons	ER&T Ltd	1904*
57	Enclosed saloon	ER&T Ltd	1904
58	Enclosed saloon	ER&T Ltd	1904
59	Special/Directors saloon	G F Milnes	1895
60	Cross-bench	G F Milnes	1896
61	Cross-bench	United Electric	1906
62	Cross-bench	United Electric	1906

* Modified by MER 1995

Right Upper: *In the peak season, most trains on the Manx Electric Railway operate with a power car and a trailer. Many of these are open vehicles and some have roller shutters which can be lowered in the case of rain. No. 37, a cross-bench vehicle, built by G F Milnes in 1894 is seen with power car No. 22.* **CJM**

Right Middle: *Another G F Milnes trailer is No. 60, introduced in 1896 and is currently painted in red and white Manx Electric Railway livery. The vehicle is seen at Derby Castle.* **CJM**

Right Lower: *The oldest operational trailer on the Manx Electric Railway is No. 51, originally built in 1893. This very open vehicle offers no protection in poor weather and is usually only used during enthusiast events or when the weather is kind. It is seen with 'Tunnel' motor car No. 5 passing Ballaragh on 31 July 2019.* **CJM**

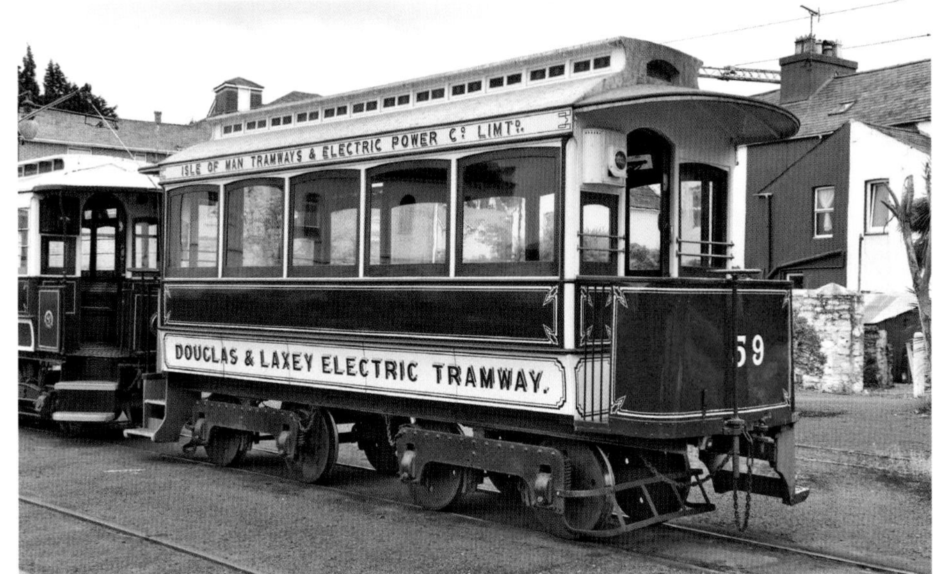

Above: *One of the masterpieces of restoration on the Manx Electric is trailer 59. Built in 1895 as a director's saloon, it became the Royal Saloon on 25 August 1902 when it carried King Edward VII and Queen Alexandra from Derby Castle to Walpole Drive, Ramsey. After many years out of service it was restored in 2018 and is now in regular use. It is seen attached to power car No. 2 at Ramsey. This vehicle was originally a four-wheeler, converted to bogie stock.* **CJM**

Freight and Service Vehicles

Number	Type	Builder	Year
1	Tower wagon	G F Milnes	1894
3	Van	G F Milnes	1894
4	Travelling Post Office van	G F Milnes	1894
8	Open wagon	G F Milnes	1897
10	Open wagon	G F Milnes	1897
11	Van 6-ton	G F Milnes	1898
12	Van 6-ton	G F Milnes	1899
13	Van 5-ton	G F Milnes	1903
14	Van 5-ton	G F Milnes	1904
16	Mail van	MER	1908
21	Flat wagon	MER	1926
26	Freight trailer	G F Milnes	1918*
45	Flat wagon	G F Milnes	1899§
52	Flat wagon with work lift	G F Milnes	1893±
RF308	Tipper wagon	Hudson	1993■
13/24-4(S)	Tipper wagon	W G Allan	1997
13/24-5(S)	Tipper wagon	W G Allan	1997
13/24-6(S)	Tipper wagon	W G Allan	1997
7442/2	Trailer	Wickham	2014

* Rebuilt from frame of power car 10
§ Rebuilt from trailer passenger car 45 in 2004
± Rebuilt from passenger trailer 52 in 1947, lift fitted 2008
■ Former Channel Tunnel vehicle

Locomotive

Number/Name	Type	Builder	Year
LM344 *Pig*	60SL 4-wheel	Simplex	1980

Works No. 60SL751, ex-Bord na Mona Peat Railway, Ireland as No. LM344.

Left: *Now officially owned by Isle of Man construction company Auldyn, this loco was on the books of the railway for many years as 'Pig'. It is seen on 27 July 2019 in the siding at Laxey with an engineers' train. Later this loco was involved with the reconstruction of the Douglas Bay horse tramway track on Douglas promenade.* **CJM**

Snaefell Mountain Railway

The Snaefell Mountain Railway is a 3ft 6in (1067mm)-gauge twin-track line which operates from Laxey to Snaefell Summit, a distance of 5 miles (8km). It is energised at 550V dc using the overhead power collection system. The line climbs the Snaefell Mountain and reaches 2,034ft (620m) above sea level. The depot is located at Laxey, where there is a passenger interchange with the Manx Electric Railway. Trains operate only between April and September.

Power Cars

Number	Type	Builder	Year
1	Vestibuled saloon	G F Milnes	1895
2	Vestibuled saloon	G F Milnes	1895
4	Vestibuled saloon	G F Milnes	1895
5§	Vestibuled saloon	H D Kinnin	1971
6 (S)	Vestibuled saloon	G F Milnes	1895

§ Original Car No. 5 destroyed by fire in August 1970

Right Upper: *Currently four motor cars provide the service on the Snaefell Mountain Railway, Nos. 1, 2 and 4 date from 1895, while No. 5 is a 1971 rebuilt to the original design. Painted in Snaefell mountain Railway blue and white livery, No. 1 departs from Laxey for the mountain on 27 July 2019. During the period of the 2018-2019 closed season, following serious brake issues, magnetic track brakes have now been installed and can be 'dropped' by the motorman if a problem arises.* **CJM**

Right Lower: *With wood panelling and a green and white lower panel, No. 4 stands at Laxey. Due to the high winds experienced on the Snaefell Mountain, these vehicles retain bow power collectors rather than have poles.* **CJM**

Freight and Service Vehicles

Number	Type	Builder	Year
-	Flat wagon	MER	1981
-	Flat wagon	P Keefe	?
-	Flat / tipper	Allens	1940
-	Tower wagon	MER	1998
4	Wickham (11730)	Wickham	1991

Left: *A new freight car was assembled in 2018-2019 for use on the Snaefell Mountain Railway, not that much if any freight is carried. The unnumbered wagon is seen at Bungalow. Note it is fitted with a Fell brake.* **CJM**

Douglas Bay Horse Tramway

One of the only remaining commercial horse-drawn tramways in the world, the Douglas Horse Tramway operates during the summer months between Douglas Sea Terminal and Derby Castle. The 1.6-mile (2.6km) 3ft (914mm)-gauge line is twin track and operates between 09.00 and 18.00. The horses are stabled near to Derby Castle and the welfare of the animals is uppermost in the operation, with each horse working only two or three return trips before returning to 'depot'.

Horses (2019-season)

Alec *Bobby* *Douglas* *Keith* *Mary+* *Rocky* *Zeba+*
Amby *Charles* *Ginger+* *Kewin* *Philip* *Torin*
Andrew *Chloe* *Harry* *Nelson* *Robin* *William*

Above: *1892-built single deck saloon No. 29 has recently been restored and is seen in the sidings at Derby Castle.* **CJM**

Below Left: *Powered by* William, *Toastrack saloon No. 45 awaits departure from Derby Castle.* **CJM**

Below: *Open 'Toastrack' saloon No. 42, built in 1905, is another that has recently been restored. It is seen stabled at Derby Castle.* **CJM**

Passenger Trailer Cars

Number	Type	Builder	Year
1	Single-ended saloon	Milnes Voss	1913
11(S§)	Toastrack saloon	Starbuck	1886
12	Toastrack saloon	G F Milnes	1888
14±	Double-deck car	Metro C&W	1883
18	Double-deck car	Metro C&W	1883
21	Toastrack saloon	G F Milnes	1890
22 (S§)	Toastrack saloon	G F Milnes	1890
27	Single-deck saloon	G F Milnes	1892
29	Single-deck saloon	G F Milnes	1892
32	Toastrack saloon	G F Milnes	1896
35■	Toastrack saloon	G F Milnes	1896
36	Toastrack saloon	G F Milnes	1896
38	Toastrack saloon	G F Milnes	1902
42	Toastrack saloon	G F Milnes	1905
43	Toastrack saloon	United Elec	1907
44	Toastrack saloon	United Elec	1907*
45	Toastrack saloon	Milnes Voss	1908
47(S§)	Toastrack saloon	Milnes Voss	1911

* Royal Car
S§ Stored/displayed at Jurby Transport Museum
± Preserved by National Railway Museum at Manx Museum, Douglas
■ Located at Home of Rest for Old Horses, Douglas

Isle of Man Steam Railway

The Isle of Man Steam Railway is a 3ft - (914mm) gauge line operating from Douglas to Port Erin, a distance of 15.3 miles (24.6km). The main depot and workshop is located at Douglas and much of the railway is single line with passing places at most stations. The railway usually operates four round trips each day. The line is mainly operated by steam traction, but a diesel is available and sometimes operates the line's popular dining train.

Locomotives

Steam

Number	Name	Builder	Wheel Arrangement	Year built	Notes
1(S)	*Sutherland*	Beyer Peacock	2-4-0T	1873	To move to Port Erin Museum in 2020
4	***Loch***	**Beyer Peacock**	**2-4-0T**	**1874**	
5(S)	*Mona*	Beyer Peacock	2-4-0T	1874	
6	*Peveril*	Beyer Peacock	2-4-0T	1875	In Museum at Port Erin
8	*Fenella*	Beyer Peacock	2-4-0T	1894	
9(S)	*Douglas*	Beyer Peacock	2-4-0T	1896	
10	*G. H. Wood*	Beyer Peacock	2-4-0T	1905	
11	*Maitland*	Beyer Peacock	2-4-0T	1905	Due back in service in 2020
12	*Hutchinson*	Beyer Peacock	2-4-0T	1908	
13	***Kissack***	**Beyer Peacock**	**2-4-0T**	**1910**	
4 (15)	***Caledonia***	**Dubs & Co**	**0-6-0T**	**1885**	
16§	*Mannin*	Beyer Peacock	2-4-0T	1926	In Museum at Port Erin

§ May return to service, due to move to Douglas for detailed inspection

Diesel

Number	Name	Builder	Wheel Arrangement	Year built	Notes
17(S)	*Viking*	Schoema	0-4-0	1958	Diesel-hydraulic - out of use
18	*Ailsa*	Hunslet	0-4-0	1994	Diesel pilot loco
21	**-**	**Motive Power**	**Bo-Bo**	**2013**	**MP550-B1 diesel-electric**
22	-	D Wickham	4-wheel P	1956	Ex Lochaber Railway
23	-	D Wickham	4-wheel P	1961	Ex Lochaber Railway
24	-	Motorail	4-wheel DM	1959	Ex B & S Massey, Openshaw
25	-	Motorail	4-wheel DM	1966	Ex NCB Kilnhurst

Locos shown in **Bold**, should form the core fleet for the 2020 season

Right Upper: *The Isle of Man Steam Railway locomotives and stock are housed in depot facilities at Douglas, with one train 'overnighting' at Port Erin during the operating season. No. 13* Kissack*, built in 1910 by Beyer Peacock of Manchester, carries green livery and is seen at Castletown with a service bound for Douglas on 2 August 2019.* **CJM**

Right Lower: *Withdrawn from service at the end of the 2019 season, as its 'ticket' had expired, No. 8* Fenella*, built in 1894 by Beyer Peacock, will now have to receive major attention and possibly a new boiler before returning to service. On 27 July 2019, the loco pulls off shed at Douglas.* **CJM**

Above: *One of the most popular locos operating on the Isle of Man Steam Railway is Manx Northern Railway-liveried No. 4 (Isle of Man Railway No. 15)* Caledonia, *built by Dubs & Co in 1885. The 0-6-0T operated throughout the 2019 season and should work again in 2020. The stunning looking loco is seen with a train bound for Port Erin at Castletown on 2 August 2019.* **CJM**

Railcars

Number	Builder	Year built	Notes
19(S)	Walker	1949	Ex-County Donegal Railway - out of use
20(S)	Walker	1950	Ex-County Donegal Railway - out of use

Passenger Coaches

Number	Builder	Style	Year built
F9	Brown Marshalls	Bogie	1881
F10	Brown Marshalls	Bogie	1881
F11	Brown Marshalls	Bogie	1881
F15	Brown Marshalls	Bogie	1894
F18	Brown Marshalls	Bogie	1894
F21(S)	Metropolitan C&W	Bogie	1896
F25(S)	Metropolitan C&W	Bogie	1896
F26	Metropolitan C&W	Bogie	1896
F27	Metropolitan C&W	Bogie	1897 *
F28(S)	Metropolitan C&W	Bogie	1897 *
F29	Metropolitan C&W	Bogie	1905
F30	Metropolitan C&W	Bogie	1905
F31	Metropolitan C&W	Bogie	1905
F32	Metropolitan C&W	Bogie	1905
F35	Metropolitan C&W	Bogie	1905
F36§	Metropolitan C&W	Bogie	1905
F39	Oldbury C & W	Bogie	1887
F43	Metropolitan C&W	Bogie	1908
F45	Metropolitan C&W	Bogie	1913
F46	Metropolitan C&W	Bogie	1913
F47	Metropolitan C&W	Bogie	1923
F48	Metropolitan C&W	Bogie	1923
F49	Metropolitan C&W	Bogie	1926
F54	Metropolitan C&W	Bogie	1923
F63(S)	Metropolitan C&W	Bogie	1920
F66(S)	Metropolitan C&W	Bogie	1920
F67(S)	Metropolitan C&W	Bogie	1920
F74(S)	Metropolitan C&W	Bogie	1921
F75§	Metropolitan C&W	Bogie	1926

* Luggage/Kitchen
§ On display at Port Erin, Museum

Left: *One of the more modern coaches used on the Isle of Man Steam Railway is bogie coach No. F48, constructed by Metropolitan C&W in 1923. The six-bay vehicle is seen at Castletown.* **CJM**

Freight & Service Vehicles

Number	Type	Builder	Year
G1	Van 6-ton	Metropolitan C&W	1873
W2	Well	IOM	1998
WW111	Well	IOM	2014
Gr12	Van 6-ton	Swansea Wagon	1879
G19§	Van 6-ton	IOM	1921
F23	Flat	Metropolitan C&W	1896
F33	Flat	Metropolitan C&W	1905-25
F40	Flat	Metropolitan C&W	1905-25
F41	Flat	Metropolitan C&W	1905-25
F44	Flat	Metropolitan C&W	1905-25
F50	Flat	Metropolitan C&W	1911-25
F57	Flat	Metropolitan C&W	1919
F65	Hopper	Metropolitan C&W	1910 *
F70	Hopper	Metropolitan C&W	1922 *
F71	Flat	Metropolitan C&W	1911-25
F73	Flat	Metropolitan C&W	1920
M69§	2-plank wagon	Metropolitan C&W	1926
M78§	2-plank wagon	Metropolitan C&W	1926
F430	Flat	Hudson	c1980
RF274	Flat	Hudson	c1980

* Coach chassis
§ On display at Port Erin Museum

Right Upper: *Although the Isle of Man Steam Railway does not operate a freight service, several wagons form the rolling stock fleet, used for engineering trains or at the depot to move equipment. This purpose-built well wagon is used to transport heavy items of equipment and machinery within the depot and station area at Douglas.* **CJM**

Right Middle Upper: *Originally passenger coach No. F57 built in 1919, its body was removed and broken up in 1995 with the frame now acting as a yard flat at Douglas.* **CJM**

Right Middle: *Built by the Isle of Man Steam Railway in 1998 is 4-wheel Well Wagon No. WW2, which is used within the depot at Douglas for moving materials, including entire steam loco boilers. The boiler from No. 10 is illustrated stored on the vehicle.* **CJM**

Right Below: *Built in 1920 by Metropolitan Carriage and Wagon in Saltley, this was once a bogie composite coach. After its body was broken up it became a depot 'runner' for materials movement. It is seen loaded with sleepers and track equipment at Douglas.* **CJM**

Below: *A number of items of rolling stock and locos can be found in the museum at Port Erin, adjacent to the station. One of the exhibits is 1926-built 4-wheel two-plank wagon No. M78.* **CJM**

UK Heritage Railways

Avon Valley Railway
Bitton Station, Bath Rd, Bristol, South Gloucestershire, BS30 6HD

Battlefield Line
Shackerstone Railway Society Ltd, Shackerstone Station, Shackerstone, Leicestershire, CV13 6NW

Bluebell Railway
The Bluebell Railway, Sheffield Park Station, East Sussex. TN22 3QL

Bodmin & Wenford Railway
Bodmin & Wenford Railway, Bodmin General Station, Bodmin, Cornwall, PL31 1AQ

Bo'ness & Kinneil Railway
Bo'ness & Kinneil Railway, Bo'ness Station, Union St, Bo'ness, EH51 9AQ

Bristol Harbour Railway
Bristol Harbour Railway, Wapping Road, Bristol, BS1 4RN

Buckinghamshire Railway Centre
Quainton Road Station, Station Road, Quainton, Aylesbury, HP22 4BY

Caledonian Railway
Caledonian Railway, The Station, Park Road, Brechin, Angus, DD9 7AF

Chasewater Railway
Chasewater Country Park, Brownhills West Station, Pool Lane, Burntwood, Staffordshire, WS8 7NL

Chinnor & Princes Risborough Railway
Chinnor & Princes Risborough Railway, Station Road, Chinnor, Oxfordshire, OX39 4ER

Cholsey & Wallingford Railway
Cholsey & Wallingford Railway, Wallingford Station, 5 Hithercroft Road, Wallingford, Oxfordshire, OX10 9GQ

Churnet Valley Railway
Churnet Valley Railway, Consall Station, Consall, Leek, Staffordshire, ST13 7EE

Colne Valley Railway
Colne Valley Railway, Castle Hedingham, Halstead, CO9 3DZ

Dartmoor Railway
Dartmoor Railway, Okehampton Railway Station, Station Road, Okehampton, EX20 1EJ

Dean Forest Railway
Dean Forest Railway, Forest Road, Lydney, Gloucestershire, GL15 4ET

Derwent Valley Light Railway
Derwent Valley Light Railway, Murton Park, Murton Lane, Murton, York, YO19 5UF

East Kent Railway
East Kent Railway, Station Road, Shepherdswell, Dover, CT15 7PD

East Lancashire Railway
East Lancashire Railway, Bury Bolton Street Station, Bolton Street, Bury, Lancashire, BL9 0EY

East Somerset Railway
East Somerset Railway, Cranmore Railway Station, Cranmore, Shepton Mallet, Somerset, BA4 4QP

Ecclesbourne Valley Railway
Ecclesbourne Valley Railway, Wirksworth Station, Coldwell Street, Wirksworth, Derbyshire, DE4 4FB

Eden Valley Railway
Eden Valley Railway, Warcop Station, Warcop, Appleby, Cumbria, CA16 6PR

Elsecar Heritage Railway
Elsecar Heritage Railway, The Railway Office, Wath Road, Elsecar, Barnsley, S74 8HJ

Embsay and Bolton Abbey Steam Railway
Embsay Railway, Embsay Station, Embsay, Skipton, North Yorkshire, BD23 6QX

Epping Ongar Railway
Epping Ongar Railway, Ongar Station, Station Approach, Ongar, Essex, CM5 9BN

Foxfield Railway
Foxfield Railway, Foxfield Station, Caverswall Road, Blythe Bridge, Stoke-on-Trent, ST11 9BG

Gloucestershire Warwickshire Railway
Gloucestershire Warwickshire Railway, Railway Station, Toddington, Gloucestershire, GL54 5DT

Great Central Railway
Great Central Railway PLC, Loughborough Central Station, Great Central Road, Loughborough, Leicestershire, LE11 1RW

Great Central Railway (Nottingham)
Great Central Railway - Nottingham, Mere Way, Ruddington, Nottinghamshire, NG11 6JS

Gwili Railway
Gwili Railway, Bronwydd Arms Station, Carmarthen, SA33 6HT

Helston Railway
Helston Railway, Trevarno Farm, Prospidnick, Helston, TR13 0RY

Isle of Wight Steam Railway
Isle of Wight Steam Railway, The Railway Station, Havenstreet, Isle of Wight, PO33 4DS

Kent & East Sussex Steam Railway
Kent & East Sussex Railway, Tenterden Town Station, Station Road, Tenterden, Kent, TN30 6HE

Keith & Dufftown Railway
Keith & Dufftown Railway, Dufftown Station, Dufftown, Banffshire, AB55 4BA

Keighley & Worth Valley Railway
Keighley & Worth Valley Railway, The Railway Station, Haworth, West Yorkshire, BD22 8NJ

Llangollen Railway
Llangollen Railway, The Station, Abbey Road, Llangollen, Denbighshire, LL20 8SN

Llanelli & Mynydd Mawr Railway
Llanelli & Mynydd Mawr Railway, Cynheidre, Llanelli, Carmarthenshire, SA15 5YF

Lavender Line
Lavender Line, Isfield Station, Isfield, Near Uckfield, East Sussex, TN22 5XB

Lakeside & Haverthwaite Railway
Lakeside & Haverthwaite Railway, Haverthwaite Station, Near Ulverston, Cumbria, LA12 8AL

Lincolnshire Wolds Railway
Lincolnshire Wolds Railway, Ludborough Station, Station Road, Ludborough, Lincolnshire, DN36 5SQ

Middleton Railway
Middleton Railway Trust Ltd, The Station, Moor Road, Hunslet, Leeds, LS10 2JQ

Midland Railway Centre
Midland Railway, Butterley Station, Ripley, Derbyshire, DE5 3QZ

Mid Hants Railway
Mid Hants Railway, The Railway Station, Alresford, Hampshire, SO24 9JG

Mid-Norfolk Railway
Mid-Norfolk Railway, Dereham Station, Station Road, Norfolk, NR19 1DF

Mid Suffolk Light Railway
Mid Suffolk Light Railway, Brockford Station, Wetheringsett, Stowmarket, Suffolk, IP14 5PW

Nene Valley Railway
Nene Valley Railway, Wansford Station, Stibbington, Peterborough, PE8 6LR

North Norfolk Railway
North Norfolk Railway, Sheringham Station, Station Approach, Sheringham, Norfolk, NR26 8RA

North Tyneside Steam Railway
Stephenson Railway Museum, Middle Engine Lane, North Shields, Tyne and Wear, NE29 8DX

North Yorkshire Moors Railway
North Yorkshire Moors Railway, Pickering Station, Pickering, North Yorkshire, YO18 7AJ

Northampton & Lamport Railway
Northampton & Lamport Railway, Pitsford & Brampton Station, Pitsford Road, Chapel Brampton, NN6 8BA

Dartmouth Steam Railway
Dartmouth Steam Railway, Queens Park Station, Torbay Road, Paignton, Devon, TQ4 6AF

Peak Rail
Peak Rail, Matlock Station, Matlock, Derbyshire, DE4 3NA

Plym Valley Railway
Plym Valley Railway, Coypool Road, Plympton, Plymouth, PL7 4NW

Pontypool & Blaenavon Railway
Pontypool & Blaenavon Railway, Railway Station, Furnace sidings, Garn Yr Erw, Blaenavon, NP4 9SF

Ribble Steam Railway
Ribble Steam Railway, Chain Caul Road, Preston, Lancashire, PR2 2PD

Royal Deeside Railway
The Royal Deeside Railway, Milton of Crathes, Banchory, Aberdeenshire, AB31 5QH

Severn Valley Railway
Severn Valley Railway, Kidderminster Station, Kidderminster, DY10 1QR

Somerset & Dorset Railway
Somerset & Dorset Railway Heritage Trust, Midsomer Norton Station, Silver Street, Midsomer Norton, BA3 2EY

South Devon Railway
South Devon Railway, Buckfastleigh Station, Dartbridge Road, Buckfastleigh, Devon, TQ11 0DZ

Spa Valley Railway
Spa Valley Railway, Tunbridge Wells West Station, Royal Tunbridge Wells, Kent, TN2 5QY

Strathspey Railway
Strathspey Railway, Aviemore Station, Dalfaber Road, Aviemore, Invernessshire, PH22 1PY

Swanage Railway
Swanage Railway, Station House, Swanage, Dorset, BH19 1HB

Swindon & Cricklade Railway
Swindon & Cricklade Railway, Blunsdon Station, Tadpole Lane, Swindon, SN25 2DA

Tanfield Railway
Tanfield Railway, Marley Hill, Engine Shed, Old Marley Hill, Gateshead, NE16 5ET

Weardale Railway
Weardale Railway, Stanhope Station, County Durham, DL13 2YS

Wensleydale Railway
Wensleydale Railway, Leases Road, Leeming Bar, North Yorkshire, DL7 9AR

West Somerset Railway
West Somerset Railway, The Railway Station, Minehead, Somerset, TA24 5BG

Railway Centres and Museums

Appleby Frodingham Railway
Appleby Frodingham Railway, British Steel, Gate E, Brigg Road, Scunthorpe, Lincolnshire, DN16 1XA

Barrow Hill Roundhouse
Barrow Hill Roundhouse, Campbell Drive, Barrow Hill, Chesterfield, Derbyshire, S43 2PR

Beamish Museum & Railway Centre
Beamish Museum, Beamish, County Durham, DH9 0RG

Bideford Railway Heritage Centre
Bideford Railway Centre, Bideford Station, Bideford, Devon, EX39 4BB

Bressingham Steam & Gardens
Bressingham Steam & Gardens, Low Road, Bressingham, Diss, Norfolk, IP22 2AA

Crewe Heritage Centre (The Railway Age)
The Railway Age, Vernon Way, Crewe, CW1 2DB

Didcot Railway Centre
Didcot Parkway railway station, Didcot, Oxfordshire, OX11 7NJ

East Anglian Railway Museum
East Anglian Railway Museum, Chappel Station, Colchester, Essex, CO6 2DS

Glasgow Museum of Transport (Riverside Museum)
Riverside Museum, Pointhouse Place, Glasgow, G3 8RS

Head of Steam, Darlington
Head of Steam - Darlington Railway Museum, Station Road, Darlington, DL3 6ST

Locomotion, Shildon (National Railway Museum)
Locomotion - National Railway Museum, Dale Road Industrial Estate, Dale Road, Shildon, County Durham, DL4 2RE

London Transport Museum
Covent Garden Piazza, London, WC2E 7BB

London Transport Museum Depot
118-120 Gunnersbury Lane, Acton Town, London, W3 9BQ

Mangapps Railway Museum
Mangapps Railway Museum, Southminster Road, Burnham-on-Crouch, Essex, CM0 8QG

Monkwearmouth Station Museum
Monkwearmouth Station Museum , North Bridge Street, Sunderland, SR5 1AP

National Railway Museum
National Railway Museum, Leeman Road, York, YO26 4XJ

Rocks by Rail (Rutland Railway Museum)
Rocks by Rail, Ashwell Road, Cottesmore, Oakham, Leicestershire, LE15 7FF

Rushden Transport Museum
Rushden Transport Museum, Rushden Station, Station Approach, Rushden, Northamptonshire, NN10 0AW

Stainmore Railway
Stainmore Railway, Station Road, Kirkby Stephen, Cumbria, CA17 4LA

Steam – Museum of the Great Western Railway
Steam, Fire Fly Avenue, Swindon, SN2 2EY

Telford Steam Railway
Telford Steam Railway, The Old Loco Shed, Bridge Road, Horsehay, Telford, Shropshire, TF4 3UH

Tyseley Railway Centre
Vintage Trains, 670 Warwick Road, Tyseley, Birmingham, B11 2HL

Vale of Berkeley Railway Museum
Vale of Berkeley Railway, The Old Engine House, Dock Road, Sharpness, Gloucestershire, GL13 9UD

Yeovil Railway Centre
Yeovil Railway Centre, Yeovil Junction Station, Stoford, Yeovil, Somerset, BA22 9UU

Above: *In October 2019, HST power car No. 43002 arrived at the National Railway Museum, York. It is now part of the National Collection and it is hoped that it will stay on display for visitors to see.* **CJM**

Preserved Modern Traction - Locomotives

Class 01

D2953	(11503)	Peak Rail, Heritage Shunters Trust
D2956	(11506)	East Lancashire Railway

Class 02

(D2853)	02003	Barrow Hill Roundhouse
D2854		Peak Rail, Heritage Shunters Trust
D2858		Midland Railway Centre
D2860		National Railway Museum
D2866		Peak Rail, Heritage Shunters Trust
D2867		Battlefield Railway
D2868		Barrow Hill

Class 03

(03018)	(D2018)	Mangapps Farm - as 11205
(03020)	(D2020)	Sonic Rail Services, Burnham - 11207
(03022)	D2022	Swindon & Cricklade Railway
(D2023)		Kent & East Sussex Railway - 11210
(D2024)		Kent & East Sussex Railway - 11211
03027	D2027	Peak Rail, Heritage Shunters Trust
03037	D2037	Royal Deeside Railway
D2041		Colne Valley Railway
D2046		Plym Valley Railway
D2051		North Norfolk Railway
03059	D2059	Isle of Wight Steam Railway
03062	D2062	East Lancashire Railway
03063	D2063	North Norfolk Railway
03066	D2066	Barrow Hill Roundhouse
03069	D2069	Dean Forest Railway
03072	D2072	Lakeside & Haverthwaite Railway
03073	D2073	Railway Age, Crewe
03078	D2078	North Tyneside Steam Railway
03079	D2079	Derwent Valley Light Railway
03081	D2081	Mangapps Farm Railway Museum
03084	D2084	East Lancashire Railway
03089	D2089	Mangapps Farm Railway Museum
03090	D2090	National Railway Museum, Shildon
03094	D2094	Royal Deeside Railway
03099	D2099	Peak Rail, Heritage Shunters Trust
03112	D2112	Rother Valley Railway
03113	D2113	Peak Rail, Heritage Shunters Trust
D2117		Lakeside & Haverthwaite Rly - No. 8
D2118		Great Central Railway, Nottingham
03119	D2119	Epping & Ongar Railway
03120	D2120	Fawley Hill Railway
03128	D2128	S&D Midsomer Norton as 03901
D2133		West Somerset Railway
03134	D2134	Royal Deeside Railway
D2138		Midland Railway Centre, Butterley
D2139		Peak Rail, Heritage Shunters Trust
03141	D2141	Pontypool & Blaenavon Railway
03144	D2144	Wensleydale Railway
03145	D2145	Moreton Park Rly, Moreton-on-Lugg
D2148		Ribble Steam Railway
03152	D2152	Swindon & Cricklade Railway
03158	D2158	Mangapps Farm
03162	D2162	Llangollen Railway
03170	D2170	Epping and Ongar Railway
D2178		Gwili Railway
03179	D2179	Rushden Transport Museum
03180	D2180	Peak Rail, Rowsley
D2182		Gloucester Warwickshire Railway
D2184		Colne Valley Railway
03189	D2189	Ribble Steam Railway
D2192		Dartmouth Steam Railway
D2196		WCRC Carnforth
03197	D2197	Mangapps Farm
D2199		Peak Rail, Heritage Shunters Trust
03371	D2371	Dartmouth Steam Railway
03399	D2399	Mangapps Farm Railway

Class 04

D2203	11103	Embsay & Bolton Abbey Railway
D2205		Peak Rail, Heritage Shunters Trust
D2207	11108	North Yorkshire Moors Railway
D2229	11135	Peak Rail, Heritage Shunters Trust
D2245	11215	Derwent Valley Light Railway
D2246		South Devon Railway
D2271		South Devon Railway
D2272		Peak Rail, Heritage Shunters Trust
D2279		East Anglian Railway
D2280		North Norfolk Railway
D2284		Peak Rail, Heritage Shunters Trust
D2289		Peak Rail, Heritage Shunters Trust
D2298		Buckinghamshire Railway Centre
D2302		Moreton Park Rly, Moreton-on-Lugg
D2310		Battlefield Railway, Shackerstone
D2324		Peak Rail, Heritage Shunters Trust
D2325		Mangapps Farm Railway
D2334		Mid Norfolk Railway
D2337		Peak Rail, Heritage Shunters Trust

Class 05

05001	D2554	Isle of Wight Steam Railway
D2578		Moreton Park Rly, Moreton-on-Lugg
D2587		Peak Rail, Heritage Shunters Trust
D2595		Ribble Steam Railway

Class 06

06003	D2420	Peak Rail, Heritage Shunters Trust

Class 07

07001	D2985	Peak Rail, Heritage Shunters Trust
07005	D2989	Great Central Railway
07010	D2994	Avon Valley Railway
07011	D2995	St. Leonards Railway Engineering
07012	D2996	Barrow Hill Roundhouse
07013	D2997	East Lancashire Railway

Classes 08, 09 and 10

D3000		Peak Rail
D3002	13002	Plym Valley Railway
D3014		Dartmouth Steam Railway
08011	D3018	Chinnor & Princes Risborough Rly
08012	D3019	Cambrian Heritage Railways
08015	D3022	Severn Valley Railway - as 13022
08016	D3023	Peak Rail, HST - as 13023
08021	D3029	Tyseley Locomotive Works - as 13029
08022	D3030	Cholsey & Wallingford Rly - as 13030
08032	D3044	Mid Hants Railway - as 13044
08046	D3059	Caledonian Rly, Brechin - as 13059
08054	D3067	Embsay & Bolton Abbey Railway
08060	D3074	Cholsey & Wallingford Rly - as 13074
08064	D3079	National Railway Museum - as 13079
D3101	13101	Great Central Rly, Loughborough
08102	D3167	Lincolnshire Wolds Railway
08108	D3174	Kent & East Sussex Railway - as 13174
08114	D3180	Great Central Rly, Nottingham

08123	D3190	Cholsey & Wallingford Railway
08133	D3201	Severn Valley Railway - as 13201
08164	D3232	East Lancashire Railway - as 13232
08168	D3236	Nemesis Rail, Burton-on-Trent
D3261		Swindon & Cricklade Rly - as 13261
08195	D3265	Llangollen Railway - as 13265
08202	D3272	Avon Valley Railway
08220	D3290	GCR, Nottingham
08238	D3308	Dean Forest Railway - as 13308
08266	D3336	Keighley & Worth Valley Railway
08288	D3358	Mid Hants Railway
08331	D3401	Midland Railway Centre, Butterley
08359	D3429	Telford Steam Railway
08377	D3462	Mid Hants Railway
08436	D3551	Swanage Railway
08443	D3558	Bo'ness & Kinneil Railway
08444	D3559	Bodmin & Wenford Railway
08471	D3586	Severn Valley Railway
08473	D3588	Dean Forest Railway (parts only)
08476	D3591	Swanage Railway
08479	D3594	East Lancashire Railway
08490	D3605	Strathspey Railway
08495	D3610	North Yorkshire Moors Railway
08503	D3658	Barry Island Railway
08507	D3662	LNWR, Crewe
08528	D3690	Great Central Railway, Loughborough
08556	D3723	North Yorkshire Moors Railway
08590	D3757	Midland Railway Centre
08604	D3771	Didcot Railway Centre
08605	D3772	Ecclesbourne Valley Railway
08631	D3798	LNWR, Crewe
08633	D3800	Churnet Valley Railway
08635	D3802	Severn Valley Railway
08663	D3830	RSS at GBRf, Dagenham
08685	D3852	East Kent Railway
08694	D3861	Great Central Railway, Loughborough
08700	D3867	HNRC at Bombardier Ilford
08704	D3871	Ecclesbourne Valley Railway
08737	D3905	LNWR, Crewe
08742	D3910	Barrow Hill
08757	D3925	Telford Steam Railway
08767	D3935	North Norfolk Railway
08769	D3937	Dean Forest Railway
08772	D3940	North Norfolk Railway
08773	D3941	Embsay & Bolton Abbey Railway
08780	D3948	LNW Crewe
08784	D3952	Great Central Railway, Nottingham
08795	D3963	Llanelli & Mynydd Mawr Railway
08825	D3993	Chinnor & Princes Risborough Rly
08830	D3998	Peak Rail, Rowsley
08850	D4018	North Yorkshire Moors Railway
08881	D4095	S&D Midsomer Norton
08888	D4118	Kent & East Sussex Railway Stored
08896	D4126	Severn Valley Railway
08907	D4137	Great Central Railway, Loughborough
08911	D4141	National Railway Museum
08915	D4145	North Tyneside Steam Railway
08937	D4167	Dartmoor Railway
08944	D4174	East Lancashire Railway
08993	D3759	Keighley & Worth Valley Railway
09001	D3665	Peak Rail, Rowsley
09004	D3668	Swindon & Cricklade Railway
09010	D3721	South Devon Railway
09012	D4100	Severn Valley Railway
09015	D4103	Avon Valley Railway
09017	D4105	National Railway Museum
09018	D4106	Bluebell Railway
09019	D4107	West Somerset Railway
09024	D4112	East Lancashire Railway
09025	D4113	Lavender Line
09026	D4114	Spa Valley Railway
09107	D4013	Severn Valley Railway
D3452		Bodmin & Wenford Railway
D3489		Spa Valley Railway
D4067		Great Central Rly, Loughborough
D4092		Barrow Hill Roundhouse
Class 11		
12052		Caledonian Railway
12077		Midland Railway Centre, Butterley
12082		Mid Hants Railway
12083		Battlefield Railway
12088		Aln Valley Railway
12093		Caledonian Railway
12099		Severn Valley Railway
12131		North Norfolk Railway
12139		North Yorkshire Moors Railway
Class 12		
15224		Spa Valley Line
Class 14		
D9500		Peak Rail, Rowsley
D9502		East Lancs Railway
D9504		Kent and East Sussex Railway
D9513		Embsay and Bolton Abbey Railway
D9516		Didcot Railway Centre
D9518		West Somerset Railway
D9520		Nene Valley Railway
D9521		Dean Forest Railway
D9523		Leaming Bar
D9524		Churnet Valley Railway
D9525		Peak Rail, Heritage Shunters Trust
D9526		West Somerset Railway
D9529		Nene Valley Railway
D9531		East Lancs Railway
D9537		East Lancs Railway
D9539		Ribble Steam Railway
D9551		Severn Valley Railway (89151)
D9553		Allelys, Wishaw
D9555		Dean Forest Railway
Class 15		
D8233		East Lancs Railway
Class 17		
D8568		Chinnor & Princes Risborough Rly
Class 20		
20050	D8000	National Railway Museum
20001	D8001	Epping & Ongar Railway
20007§	D8007	Nottingham Transport Centre
20020	D8020	Bo'ness & Kinneil Railway SRPS
20031	D8031	Keighley & Worth Valley Railway
20048	D8048	Midland Railway Centre
20057	D8057	Churnet Valley Railway
20059	D8059	Mid Hants Railway
20063	D8063	Battlefield Railway, Shackerstone
20069	D8069	Mid Norfolk Railway
20087	D8087	East Lancashire Railway
20098	D8098	Great Central Railway
20105	D8105	Barrow Hill Roundhouse

20110	D8110	East Lancashire Railway HNRC
20228	D8128	Barry Rail Centre
20137	D8137	Gloucester Warwickshire Railway
20154	D8154	Great Central Railway, Nottingham
20166	D8166	Wensleydale Railway HNRC
20177	D8177	Severn Valley Railway
20188	D8188	Midland Railway Centre
20205	D8305	Midland Railway Centre
20214	D8314	Lakeside & Haverthwaite Railway
20227	D8327	North Norfolk Railway

Class 24

24032	D5032	North Yorkshire Moors Railway
24054	D5054	East Lancashire Railway
24061	D5061	North Yorkshire Moors Railway
24081	D5081	Gloucestershire Warwickshire Rly

Class 25

25035	D5185	Great Central Railway
25057	D5207	HNRC Worksop, for main line use
25059	D5209	Keighley & Worth Valley Railway
25067	D5217	Nemesis Rail, Burton-on-Trent
25072	D5222	Caledonian Railway, Brechin
25083	D5233	Caledonian Railway, Brechin
25173	D7523	Battlefield Line, Shackerstone
25185	D7535	South Devon Railway
25191	D7541	South Devon Railway
25235	D7585	Bo'ness & Kinneil Railway
25244	D7594	Kent & East Sussex Railway
25901	D7612	South Devon Railway
25265	D7615	Nemesis Rail, Burton-on-Trent
25278	D7628	North Yorkshire Moors Railway
25279	D7629	Great Central Railway, Nottingham
25904	D7633	HNRC
25309	D7659	Peak Rail
25313	D7663	HNRC for main line use
25321	D7671	Midland Railway Centre
25322	D7672	Churnet Valley Railway

Class 26 and 27

26007	D5300	Barrow Hill Roundhouse
26001	D5301	Caledonian Railway
26002	D5302	Strathspey Railway
26004	D5304	Nemesis Rail, Burton-on-Trent
26010	D5310	Llangollen Railway
26011	D5311	Nemesis Rail, Burton-on-Trent
26014	D5314	Caledonian Railway, Brechin
26024	D5324	Bo'ness & Kinneil Railway
26025	D5325	Strathspey Railway
26035	D5335	Caledonian Railway, Brechin
26038	D5338	Bo'ness & Kinneil Railway
26040	D5340	Whitrope Heritage Centre
26043	D5343	Gloucestershire Warwickshire Rly
27001	D5347	Bo'ness & Kinneil Railway
27005	D5351	Bo'ness & Kinneil Railway
27007	D5353	Goodman's Yard, Wishaw
27024	D5370	Caledonian Railway, Brechin
27066	D5386	Barrow Hill Roundhouse
27050	D5394	Strathspey Railway
27056	D5401	Great Central Railway
27059	D5410	UKRL Leicester

Class 28

D5705		East Lancashire Railway

Class 31

31018	D5500	National Railway Museum
31101	D5518	Avon Valley Railway
31105	D5523	Mangapps Farm
31418	D5522	Midland Railway Centre
31108	D5526	Midland Railway Centre
31466	D5533	Dean Forest Railway
31119	D5537	Embsay & Bolton Abbey Railway
31128	D5546	Nemesis Rail, Burton-on-Trent
31461	D5547	Nemesis Rail, Burton-on-Trent
31130	D5548	Avon Valley Railway
31438	D5557	Epping and Ongar Railway
31162	D5580	Great Central Railway, Nottingham
31163	D5581	Chinnor & Princes Ris Rly (as 97205)
31435	D5600	Embsay & Bolton Abbey Railway
31190	D5613	Weardale Railway
31203	D5627	Pontypool & Blaenavon Railway
31206	D5630	Ecclesbourne Valley Railway
31207	D5631	North Norfolk Railway
31210	D5634	Dean Forest Railway
31233	D5660	Mangapps Farm
31235	D5662	Dean Forest Railway
31255	D5683	Mid Norfolk Railway
31430	D5695	Spa Valley Railway
31270	D5800	Peak Rail, Rowsley
31271	D5801	Llangollen Railway
31452	D5809	Dartmoor Railway
31514/414	D5814	Midland Railway Centre
31285	D5817	Dartmoor Railway
31289	D5821	Northampton & Lamport Railway
31297	D5830	Great Central Rly, Loughborough
31327	D5862	Strathspey Railway
31601	D5609	Ecclesbourne Valley Railway

Class 33

33002	D6501	South Devon Railway
33008	D6508	Battlefield Railway
33102	D6513	Churnet Valley Railway
33103	D6514	Ecclesbourne Valley Railway
33012	D6515	Swanage Railway
33108	D6521	Severn Valley Railway
33109	D6525	East Lancashire Railway
33110	D6527	Bodmin & Wenford Railway
33111	D6528	Swanage Railway
33018	D6530	Midland Railway, Butterley
33115	D6533	St. Leonards Railway Engineering
33019	D6534	Battlefield Railway
33116	D6535	Great Central Railway, Nottingham
33117	D6536	East Lancashire Railway
33021	D6539	Churnet Valley Railway
33035	D6553	Wensleydale Railway
33046	D6564	East Lancashire Railway
33048	D6566	West Somerset Railway
33052	D6570	Kent & East Sussex Railway
33053	D6571	Leicester
33057	D6575	West Somerset Railway
33063	D6583	Spa Valley Railway
33065	D6585	Spa Valley Railway
33201	D6586	Spa Valley Railway
33202	D6587	Mid Norfolk Railway
33208	D6593	Battlefield Railway

Class 35

D7017		West Somerset Railway
D7018		West Somerset Railway
D7029		Severn Valley Railway
D7076		East Lancashire Railway

Class 37

37308	D6608	Dean Forest Railway
37119	D6700	National Railway Museum

37003	D6703	Leicester Depot
37009	D6709	Great Central Railway, Nottingham
37503	D6717	Wensleydale Railway
37023	D6723	Pontypool & Blaenavon Railway
37714	D6724	Great Central Rly, Loughborough
37029	D6729	Epping and Ongar Railway
37032	D6732	North Norfolk Railway
37037	D6737	South Devon Railway
37042	D6742	Eden Valley Railway, Warcop
37075	D6775	Keighley & Worth Valley Railway
37097	D6797	Caledonian Railway, Brechin
37108	D6808	Crewe Heritage Centre
37109	D6809	East Lancashire Railway
37521	D6817	Loco Services Ltd
37679	D6823	East Lancashire Railway
37142	D6842	Bodmin & Wenford Railway
37146	D6846	Wensleydale Railway (for scrap)
37901	D6850	Mid Hants Railway
37152	D6852	Peak Rail, Rowsley, as 37310
37159	D6859	Barrow Hill Roundhouse
37674	D6869	Wensleydale Railway
37188	D6888	Barrow Hill
37688	D6905	Severn Valley Railway
37215	D6915	Gloucester & Warwickshire Railway
37216	D6916	Pontypool & Blaenavon Railway
37227	D6927	Chinnor & Princes Risborough Rly
37240	D6940	Bowden Rail, Nottinghm for main line
37248	D6948	Gloucester & Warwickshire Railway
37250	D6950	Wensleydale Railway
37255	D6955	Nemesis Rail, Burton-on-Trent
37261	D6961	Bo'ness & Kinneil Railway
37263	D6963	Telford Steam Railway
37264	D6964	North Yorkshire Moors Railway
37418	D6971	Barrow Hill Roundhouse
37275	D6975	Paignton & Dartmouth Railway
37294	D6994	Embsay & Bolton Abbey Railway

Class 40

40122	D200	National Railway Museum
40012	D212	Barrow Hill Roundhouse
40013§	D213	Loco Services Crewe
40106	D306	East Lancashire Railway
40118	D318	Tyseley Locomotive Works
40135	D335	East Lancashire Railway
40145§	D345	East Lancashire Railway

Class 41

43000	41001	National Railway Museum, Shildon

Class 42

D821		Severn Valley Railway
D832		East Lancashire Railway

Class 43

43002		National Railway Museum, York

Class 44

44004	D4	Midland Railway Centre, Butterley
44008	D8	Peak Rail, Rowsley

Class 45

45015	D14	Battlefield, Railway
45060	D100	Barrow Hill Roundhouse
45108	D120	East Lancashire Railway
45125	D123	Great Central Rly, Loughborough
45149	D135	Gloucester & Warwickshire Railway
45132	D22	Epping & Ongar Railway
45133	D40	Midland Railway Centre, Butterley
45041	D53	Nene Valley Railway
45112	D61	Nemesis Rail, Burton-on-Trent
45118	D67	LSL at Barrow Hill Roundhouse
45105	D86	Barrow Hill Roundhouse
45135	D99	East Lancashire Railway

Class 46

46010	D147	Great Central Railway, Nottingham
46035	D172	Crewe Heritage Centre
46045	D182	Midland Railway Centre

Class 47

47401	D1500	Midland Railway Centre
47402	D1501	East Lancashire Railway
47417	D1516	Midland Railway Centre
47004	D1524	Embsay & Bolton Abbey Railway
47449	D1566	Llangollen Railway
47635	D1606	Epping & Ongar Railway
47761	D1619	Midland Railway Centre
47765	D1643	East Lancashire Railway
47799	D1654	Eden Valley Railway
47798	D1656	National Railway Museum
47077	D1661	West Somerset Railway
47484	D1662	Rye Farm, Wishaw (Pioneer DG)
47105	D1693	Gloucester Warwickshire Railway
47117	D1705	Great Central Rly, Loughborough
47488	D1713	Nemesis Rail, Burton-on-Trent
47773	D1755	Tyseley Locomotive Works
47580	D1762	Stratford 47 Group
47579	D1778	Mid Hants Railway
47306	D1787	Bodmin Steam Railway
47192	D1842	Weardale Railway
47205	D1855	Northampton & Lamport Railway
47367	D1886	Mid Norfolk Railway
47376	D1895	Gloucester Warwickshire Railway
47785	D1909	Stainmore Railway
47640	D1921	Battlefield Railway, Shackerstone
47744	D1927	Nemesis Rail, Burton-on-Trent
47701	D1932	Nemesis Rail, Burton-on-Trent
47596	D1933	Mid-Norfolk Railway
47712	D1948	Crewe Heritage Centre (For main line)
47503	D1946	Colne Valley Railway
47714	D1955	Great Central R1y, Loughborough
47643	D1970	Bo'ness & Kinneil Railway
47292	D1994	Great Central Railway, Nottingham
47828§	D1966	Pioneer Diesel Group, with WCR

Class 50

50002	D402	South Devon Railway
50007§	D407	Boden Engineering, Eastcroft
50008	D408	Boden Engineering, Eastcroft
50015	D415	East Lancashire Railway
50017	D417	Private on Great Central Railway
50019	D419	Mid Norfolk Railway
50021	D421	Arlington Fleet Services, Eastleigh
50026	D426	Arlington Fleet Services, Eastleigh
50027	D427	Mid Hants Railway
50029	D429	Peak Rail, Rowsley
50030	D430	Peak Rail, Rowsley
50031	D431	Severn Valley Railway
50033	D433	Vintage Trains, at Eastleigh
50035	D435	Severn Valley Railway
50042	D442	Bodmin & Wenford Railway
50044	D444	Severn Valley Railway
50049§	D449	Severn Valley Railway
50050	D400	Boden Engineering, Eastcroft

Class 52

D1010		West Somerset Railway
D1013		Severn Valley Railway
D1015§		Severn Valley Railway
D1023		National Railway Museum
D1041		East Lancashire Railway
D1048		Midland Railway Centre, Butterley
D1062		Severn Valley Railway

Class 55

55002	D9002	National Railway Museum
55009	D9009	Barrow Hill Roundhouse
55015	D9015	Barrow Hill Roundhouse
55016	D9016	Loco Services, Margate
55019§	D9019	Barrow Hill Roundhouse
55022§	D9000	Loco Services, Crewe

Class 56

56003		Nene Valley Railway
56006		East Lancashire Railway
56097		Great Central Railway, Nottingham

Class 58

58012		Battlefield Line
58016		UK Rail Leasing, Leicester
58022		Peak Rail
58023		With UKRL, Leicester
58048		Battlefield Line

Class 60

60050		Weardale Railway, Leaming Bar
60086		Weardale Railway, Leaming Bar

Class 71

71001	E5001	Barrow Hill Roundhouse

Class 73

73001	E6001	Loco Services Ltd, Crewe
73002	E6002	Loco Services Ltd, Eastleigh
73003	E6003	(Under restoration at Eastleigh)
73110	E6016	Great Central Railway, Nottingham
73114	E6020	Battlefield Railway, Shackerstone
73118	E6024	Barry Railway
73129	E6036	Gloucester Warwickshire Railway
73130	E6037	Barry Railway
73140	E6047	Spa Valley Railway
73210	E6022	Ecclesbourne Valley Railway

Class 76

76020	26020	National Railway Museum

Class 77

E27000		Midland Railway Centre
E27001		Museum of Science & Ind, Manchester
E27003		Workgroup 1501 Rotterdam

Class 81

81002	E3003	Barrow Hill Roundhouse

Class 82

82008	E3054	Barrow Hill Roundhouse

Class 83

83012	E3035	Barrow Hill Roundhouse

Class 84

84001	E3036	NRM, at Barrow Hill Roundhouse

Class 85

85101	E3061	Barrow Hill Roundhouse

Class 86

86259§	E3137	Willesden Depot
86101§	E3191	Willesden Depot
86401§	E3199	Willesden Depot

Class 87

87001		National Railway Museum
87002§		Willesden Depot
87035		Crewe Heritage Centre

Class 89

89001		Barrow Hill Roundhouse

Class 97

97650	PWM650	Lincolnshire Wolds Railway
97651	PWM651	Swindon & Cricklade Railway
97654	PWM654	Peak Rail, Heritage Shunter Trust

Unclassified locos

18000		Didcot Railway Centre
D0226		Keighley & Worth Valley Railway
D2511		Keighley & Worth Valley Railway
D2767		Bo'ness & Kinneil Railway
D2774		Strathspey Railway
D2959		Telford Steam Railway
D2971		Telford Steam Railway
Deltic	DP1	National Railway Museum

§ Certified for main line operation

Left: *Class 25 No. 25322 (D7672) is preserved at the Churnet Valley Railway, where it carries a BR Rail Blue body and wrap around yellow ends, as it did in its final years of service. It also carries the Tamworth Castle name, applied in sticky backed letters.* **Cliff Beeton**

Preserved Modern Traction - Diesel Multiple Unit Stock

APT-E	National Railway Museum
LEV1	National Railway Museum at Wensleydale
LEV2	Connecticut Trolley Museum, USA
LEV3	Downpatrick & County Down Railway
RB002	Riverstone Old Corn Railway, USA
RB004	Waverley Route Heritage Centre
GWR 4	National Railway Museum
GWR 20	Kent & East Sussex Railway
GWR 22	Didcot Railway Centre
50015	Midland Railway Centre
50019	Midland Railway Centre
50160	North Yorkshire Moors Railway
50164	North Yorkshire Moors Railway
50170	Ecclesbourne Valley Railway
50193	Great Central Railway
50203	Great Central Railway
50204	North Yorkshire Moors Railway
50222	Barry Island Railway
50253	Ecclesbourne Valley Railway
50256	Wensleydale Railway
50266	Great Centrtal Railway
50321	Great Central Railway
50338	Barry Island Railway
50413	Helston Railway
50416	Llangollen Railway
50437	Llangollen Railway
50447	Llangollen Railway
50454	Llangollen Railway
50455	East Lancashire Railway
50479	Telford Steam Railway
50494	East Lancashire Railway
50517	East Lancashire Railway
50528	Llangollen Railway
50531	Telford Steam Railway
50556	East Lancashire Railway /
50599	Ecclesbourne Valley Railway
50619	Dean Forest Railway
50628	Keith & Dufftown Railway
50632	Pontypool & Blaenavon Railway
50645	Great Central Railway North
50746	Wensleydale Railway
50926	Great Central Railway North
50928	Keighley & Worth Valley Railway
50933	Severn Valley Railway
50971	Kent & East Sussex Railway
50980	Weardale Railway
51017	Bo'ness & Kinneil Railway
51043	Bo'ness & Kinneil Railway
51073	Ecclesbourne Valley Railway
51074	Swindon & Cricklade Railway
51104	Swindon & Cricklade Railway
51118	Midland Railway Centre
51131	Battlefield Line
51138	Great Central Railway North
51151	Great Central Railway North
51187	Cambrian Railway
51188	NRM at Ecclesbourne Valley Railway
51189	Keighley & Worth Valley Railway
51192	National Railway Museum at NNR
51205	Cambrian Railway
51210	Wensleydale Railway
51213	East Anglian Railway Museum
51226	Mid Norfolk Railway
51228	Mid Norfolk Railway
51317	Arlington Eastleigh
51321	Battlefield Line
51339	East Lancashire Railway
51342	Epping & Ongar Railway
51347	Gwili Railway
51351	Pontypool & Blaenavon Railway
51352	Long Marston
51353	Wensleydale Railway
51354	West Somerset Railway
51356	Swanage Railway
51360	Gloucestershire Warwickshire Railway
51363	Gloucestershire Warwickshire Railway
51365	Plym Valley Railway
51367	Strathspey Railway
51370	Whitwell & Reepham Railway
51371	North Somerset Rly at Eastleigh
51372	Gloucestershire Warwickshire Railway
51375	Chinnor and Princes Risborough Rly
51376	Long Marston
51381	Mangapps Farm Museum
51382	East Lancashire Railway
51384	Epping and Ongar Railway
51388	Swanage Railway
51392	Swanage Railway
51396	Peak Rail
51397	Pontypool & Blaenavon Railway
51400	Wensleydale Railway
51401	Gwili Railway
51402	Strathspey Railway
51405	Gloucestershire Warwickshire Railway
51407	Plym Valley Railway
51412	Whitwell & Reepham Stn, Suffolk
51413	North Somerset Rly at Eastleigh
51427	Great Central Railway
51434	Mid Norfolk Railway
51485	East Lancashire Railway
51499	Mid Norfolk Railway
51503	Mid Norfolk Railway
51505	Ecclesbourne Valley Railway
51511	North Yokshire Moors Railway
51512	Cambrian Railway
51562	National Railway Museum
51565	Keighley & Worth Valley Railway
51566	Dean Forest Railway
51567	Ecclesbourne Valley Railway
51568	Keith & Dufftown Railway
51571	Kent & East Sussex Railway
51572	Wensleydale Railway
51591	Midland Railway Centre
51610	Midland Railway Centre
51616	Helston Railway
51618	Llangollen Railway
51622	Helston Railway
51625	Midland Railway Centre
51655	Rosyth Dockyard
51663	West Somerset Railway (frame only)
51669	Midland Railway, Butterley
51803	Keighley & Worth Valley Railway
51813	East Lancashire Railway
51842	East Lancashire Railway
51849	Midland Railway, Butterley
51859	West Somerset Railway
51880	West Somerset Railway
51886	Birmingham Railway Museum
51887	West Somerset Railway
51899	Buckingham Railway Centre
51907	Llangollen Railway

51909 East Somerset Railway
51914 Dean Forest Railway
51919 Garw Valley Railway
51922 National Railway Museum
51933 Swanage Railway
51937 Poulton & Wyre Railway
51941 Severn Valley Railway
51942 Mid Norfolk Railway
51947 Bodmin & Wenford Railway (for disposal)
51950 Telford Steam Railway
51990 Strathspey Railway
51993 Tanat Valley Railway
52005 Tanat Valley Railway
52006 Avon Valley Railway
52008 Strathspey Railway
52012 Tanat Valley Railway
52025 Avon Valley Railway
52029 Gloucestershire Warwickshire Railway
52030 Strathspey Railway
52031 Tanat Valley Railway
52044 Pontypool & Blaenavon Railway
52048 Garw Valley Railway
52053 Keith & Dufftown Railway
52054 Weardale Railway
52062 Telford Steam Railway
52064 Severn Valley Railway
52071 Lakeside & Haverthwaite Railway
52077 Lakeside & Haverthwaite Railway
54223 Llangollen Railway
54270 Mid Norfolk Railway
54504 Swanage Railway
55000 South Devon Railway
55001 East Lancashire Railway
55003 Gloucestershire Warwickshire Railway
55005 Battlefield Line
55006 Ecclesbourne Valley Railway
55009 Mid Norfolk Railway
55012 Weardale Railway
55019 Llanelli & Mynydd Mawr Railway
55020 Bodmin & Wenford Railway
55023 Chinnor & Princes Risborough Railway
55024 Chinnor & Princes Risborough Railway
55025 Long Marston (for sale)
55027 Ecclesbourne Valley Railway
55028 Swanage Railway
55029 Rushden Transport Museum
55031 Eccclesbourne Valley Railway
55032 Wensleydale Railway
55033 Colne Valley Railway
55034 Locomotive Services, Crewe
56006 Midland Railway Centre
56015 Midland Railway Centre
56055 Cambrian Railway
56057 Strathspey Railway
56062 North Norfolk Railway
56097 Midland Railway Centre
56121 East Lancashire Railway
56160 Bodfari, Denbigh (private)
56169 Helston Railway
56171 Llangollen Railway
56182 North Norfolk Railway
56207 BSC Scunthorpe
56208 Severn Valley Railway
56224 Keith & Dufftown Railway
56271 East Somerset Railway
56274 Wensleydale Railway
56279 Lavendar Line
56287 Epping & Ongar Railway
56289 East Lancashire Railway
56301 Mid Norfolk Railway (main line)
56342 Great Central Railway
56343 Wensleydale Railway
56347 Mid Norfolk Railway
56352 NRM at Ecclesbourne Valley Railway
56356 Barry Island Railway
56358 East Anglian Railway Museum
56408 Spa Valley Railway
56456 Llangollen Railway
56484 Poulton & Wyre Railway
56490 Llangollen Railway
56491 Keith & Dufftown Railway
56492 Dean Forest Railway
56495 Kirklees Light Railway
56505 Swanage Railway
59003 Dartmouth Steam Railway
59004 Dartmouth Steam Railway
59117 Mid Norfolk Railway
59137 East Lancashire Railway
59228 Telford Steam Railway
59245 BSC Scunthorpe
59250 Severn Valley Railway
59276 Great Central Railway
59303 Ecclesbourne Valley Railway
59387 Dean Forest Railway
59404 Bo'ness & Kinneil Railway
59444 Chasewater Railway
59486 Swanage Railway
59488 Dartmouth Steam Railway
59492 Swanage Railway
59493 South Devon Railway
59494 Dartmouth Steam Railway
59500 Wensleydale Railway (static)
59501 Great Central Railway North
59503 Dartmouth Steam Railway
59505 Gloucestershire Warwickshire Railway
59506 Peak Rail
59507 Dartmouth Steam Railway
59508 Gwili Railway
59509 Wensleydale Railway
59510 Gloucestershire Warwickshire Railway
59511 Strathspey Railway
59513 Dartmouth Steam Railway
59514 Swindon & Cricklade Railway
59515 Yeovil Railway Centre
59517 Dartmouth Steam Railway
59520 Dartmoor Railway
59521 Helston Railway
59522 Nottingham Transport Heritage Trust
59539 North Yorkshire Moors Railway
59575 Great Central Railway
59603 Chasewater Railway
59609 Midland Railway Centre
59659 Midland Railway Centre
59664 Midsomer Norton Railway
59678 West Somerset Railway
59701 East Lancs Railway
59719 Mid Hants Railway
59740 South Devon Railway
59761 Buckinghamshire Railway Centre
59791 Tanat Valley Railway
79018 Ecclesbourne Valley Railway
79443 Bo'ness & Kinneil Railway
79612 Ecclesbourne Valley Railway
79900 Ecclesbourne Valley Railway
79960 Ribble Steam Railway
79962 Keighley & Worth Valley Railway

79963	East Anglian Railway
79964	Keighley & Worth Valley Railway
79976	Nemesis Rail, Burton
79978	Swindon & Cricklade Railway
998900	Middleton Railway
999507	Lavender Line

Second Generation

140001	Keith & Dufftown
141108	Loco Services, Margate
141113	Midland Railway Centre
142001	National Railway Museum, Shildon
142017	East Kent Railway
142019	Waverley Route Her Ctr, Whiterope
142020	Waverley Route Her Ctr, Whiterope
142027	Chasewater Railway (spares)
142029	Chasewater Railway
142030	Chasewater Railway
142033	South Wales Police Development, Bridgend
142084	Rushden, Higham & Wellingborough Rly
142091	Rushden, Higham & Wellingborough Rly
144003	Great Central Railway (N) (planned)
144004	Aln Valley Railway (planned)
143603	Swindon & Cricklade (planned)

Southern Region DEMU Stock

Class 201, 202, 203 (6S, 6L, 6B)

60000	1001	BR/SR	DMBS	Hastings Diesels Ltd
60001	1001	BR/SR	DMBS	Hastings Diesels Ltd
60016	1012	BR/SR	DMBS	Hastings Diesels Ltd (as 60116)
60018	1013	BR/SR	DMBS	Hastings Diesels Ltd (as 60118)
60019	1013	BR/SR	DMBS	Hastings Diesels Ltd
60500	1001	BR/SR	TS	Hastings Diesels Ltd
60501	1001	BR/SR	TS	Hastings Diesels Ltd
60502	1001	BR/SR	TS	Hastings Diesels Ltd
60527	1013	BR/SR	TS	Hastings Diesels Ltd
60528	1013	BR/SR	TS	Hastings Diesels Ltd
60529	1013	BR/SR	TS	Hastings Diesels Ltd
60700	1001	BR/SR	TF	Hastings Diesels Ltd
60708	1012	BR/SR	TF	Hastings Diesels Ltd
60709	1013	BR/SR	TF	Hastings Diesels Ltd
60750	1032	BR/SR	TBUF	Hastings Diesels Ltd (ex Departmental)

Class 205 (2H, 3H)

60108	1109	BR/SR	DMBSO	Eden Valley Railway
60110	1111	BR/SR	DMBSO	Epping & Ongar Railway
60117	1118	BR/SR	DMBSO	Lavender Line
60122	1123	BR/SR	DMBSO	Lavender Line
60124	1125	BR/SR	DMBSO	Mid Hants Railway
60146	1128	BR/SR	DMBSO	Dartmoor Railway
60150	1132	BR/SR	DMBSO	Dartmoor Railway
60151	1133	BR/SR	DMBSO	Lavender Line
60154	1101	BR/SR	DMBSO	East Kent Railway
60658	1109	BR/SR	TSO	Eden Valley Railway
60669	1120	BR/SR	TSO	Swindon & Cricklade Railway
60673	1128	BR/SR	TSO	Dartmoor Railway
60677	1132	BR/SR	TSO	Dartmoor Railway
60678	1133	BR/SR	TSO	Lavender Line
60800	1101	BR/SR	DTC	East Kent Railway
60808	1109	BR/SR	DTC	Eden Valley Railway
60810	1111	BR/SR	DTS	Epping & Ongar Railway
60820	1121	BR/SR	DTC	Lavender Line
60822	1123	BR/SR	DTC	Swindon & Cricklade Railway
60824	1125	BR/SR	DTC	Mid Hants Railway
60827	1128	BR/SR	DTC	Dartmoor Railway
60828	1118	BR/SR	DTC	Lavender Line
60830	1131	BR/SR	DTC	Lavender Line
60831	1132	BR/SR	DTC	Dartmoor Railway
60832	1133	BR/SR	DTC	Lavender Line

Class 207 (3D)

60127	1302	BR/SR	DMBS	Swindon & Cricklade Railway
60130	1305	BR/SR	DMBS	East Lancs Railway
60142	1317	BR/SR	DMBS	Spa Valley Railway
60616	1317	BR/SR	TC	Spa Valley Railway
60904	1305	BR/SR	DTS	East Lancs Railway
60916	1317	BR/SR	DTS	Spa Valley Railway

Preserved Modern Traction - Electric Multiple Unit Stock

Unclassified				
3267		LNER	DMBL	Percy Main (National Railway Museum owned)
8143		LNWR	DMBS	National Railway Museum York
117 and 121		MSJ&AR	T	Midland Railway Centre
79998	-	BR/ScR	DMBS	Milton of Crathes (Battery set)
79999	-	BR/ScR	DTC	Milton of Crathes (Battery set)
5BEL				
279	3051	SR	TFK	5-BEL Trust
281	3053	SR	TFK	VSOE Stewarts Lane
280	3052	SR	TFK	VSOE Stewarts Lane
282	3051	SR	TFK	5-BEL Trust
283	3053	SR	TFK	VSOE Stewarts Lane
284	3052	SR	TFK	VSOE Stewarts Lane
285	3053	SR	TPT	5-BEL Trust
286	3051	SR	TPT	VSOE Stewarts Lane
287	3052	SR	TPT	5-BEL Trust
288	3051	SR	DMBPT	5-BEL Trust
289	3051	SR	DMBPT	Little Mill Inn, Rowarth, Derbyshire
291	3052	SR	DMBPT	5-BEL Trust
292	3053	SR	DMBPT	VSOE Stewarts Lane
293	3053	SR	DMBPT	VSOE Stewarts Lane
6PUL				
264	3012	SR	TKC	VSOE Stewarts Lane
278	3017	SR	TKC	VSOE Stewarts Lane
2BIL (Class 401)				
10656	2090	SR	DMBS	National Railway Museum Shildon
12123	2090	SR	DTC	National Railway Museum Shildon
4COR (Class 404)				
10096	3142	SR	TSK	East Kent Railway
11161	3142	SR	DMBS	Sellinge
11179	3131	SR	DMBS	National Railway Museum York
11187	3135	SR	DMBS	East Kent Railway
11201	3142	SR	DMBS	Sellinge
11825	3142	SR	TC	Sellinge
4DD				
13003	4002	SR	DMBT	Sellinge
13004	4002	SR	DMBT	Northampton Ironstone Railway
AM2 (Class 302)				
75033	302201	BR/ER	DTSO	Mangapps Farm
75250	302277	BR/ER	DTSO	Mangapps Farm
AM3 (Class 303)				
61503	303023	BR/ScR	MBS	Bo'ness & Kinneil Railway
75597	303032	BR/ScR	DTSO	Bo'ness & Kinneil Railway
75632	303032	BR/ScR	BDTSO	Bo'ness & Kinneil Railway
AM6 (Class 306)				
65217	306017	BR/ER	DMSO	National Railway Museum, Shildon
65417	306017	BR/ER	TBC	National Railway Museum, Shildon
65617	306017	BR/ER	DTSO	National Railway Museum, Shildon
AM7 (Class 307)				
75023	307123	BR/ER	DTBSO	Coulsdon Historic Vehicles, Finmere
AM8 (Class 308)				
75881	308136	BR/ER	DTCO	Coulsdon Historic Vehicles, Finmere
AM9 (Class 309)				
61928	309624	BR/ER	MBSO	Lavender Line
61937	309616	BR/ER	MBSO	Tanat Valley Railway

75642	309616	BR/ER	BDTC	Tanat Valley Railway
75965	309624	BR/ER	BDTC	Lavender Line
75972	309624	BR/ER	DTSO	Lavender Line
75981	309616	BR/ER	DTSO	Tanat Valley Railway

AM11 (Class 311)

62174	311103	BR/ScR	MBSO	Summerlee
76433	311103	BR/ScR	DTSO	Summerlee

AM12 (Class 312)

71205	312792	BR/ER	TS	Colne Valley Railway
78037	312792	BR/ER	DTS	Colne Valley Railway

Class 373 (Eurostar)

3101		Eurostar	DM (only)	Training vehicle at Doncaster Academy
3102		Eurostar	DM (only)	Training vehicle at Birmingham Training Academy
3106		Eurostar	DM, plus car 9	Train World, Brussels
3304		Eurostar	DM+R1	RTC Derby (for LSL Margate)
3308		Eurostar	DM (only)	National Railway Museum, York
3314		Eurostar	DM	Temple Mills depot - plinthed

4 SUB (Class 405)

8143	4308	SR	DMBS	National Railway Museum, York
10239	4732	BR/SR	TS	Loco Storage Ltd, Margate
12354	4732	BR/SR	TSO	Loco Storage Ltd, Margate
12795	4732	BR/SR	DMBS	Loco Storage Ltd, Margate
12796	4732	BR/SR	DMBS	Loco Storage Ltd, Margate

4CEP/BEP (Class 411/412)

61229	1537	BR/SR	DMBSO	Eastleigh Works
61230	1537	BR/SR	DMBSO	Eastleigh Works
61736	1198	BR/SR	DMBSO	Chinnor & Princess Risborough Railway
61737	1198	BR/SR	DMBSO	Chinnor & Princess Risborough Railway
61742	1589	BR/SR	DMBSO	Dartmoor Railway
61743	1589	BR/SR	DMBSO	Dartmoor Railway
61798	2315	BR/SR	DMBSO	Eden Valley Railway
61799	2315	BR/SR	DMBSO	Eden Valley Railway
61804	2311	BR/SR	DMBSO	Eden Valley Railway
61805	2311	BR/SR	DMBSO	Eden Valley Railway
69013	7012	BR/SR	TBS	Epping and Ongar Railway
70229	2315	BR/SR	TSO	Eden Valley Railway
70235	7107	BR/SR	TBCK	Epping and Ongar Railway
70262	1524	BR/SR	TSO	Hastings Diesels Ltd
70284	1520	BR/SR	TSO	Northampton Ironstone Railway
70292	1554	BR/SR	TSO	Speyside Railway, Grantown
70296	1559	BR/SR	TSO	Northampton Ironstone Railway
70300	1698	BR/SR	TSO	Fighting Cocks Pub, Middleton St George
70345	1500	BR/SR	TBCK	Hydraulic House, Sutton Bridge, Cambridgeshire
70354	2315	BR/SR	TBCK	Eden Valley Railway
70510	1597	BR/SR	TSO	Northampton Ironstone Railway
70527	1589	BR/SR	TSO	Great Central Railway
70531	1610	BR/SR	TSO	Speyside Railway, Grantown
70539	2311	BR/SR	TBCK	Eden Valley Railway
70547	1569	BR/SR	TSO	Private in Hungerford
70549	1567	BR/SR	TSO	East Lancs Railway
70573	1198	BR/SR	TBCK	Chinnor & Princess Risborough Railway
70576	1589	BR/SR	TBCK	Great Central Railway
70607	2311	BR/SR	TSO	Eden Valley Railway

2HAP (Class 414)

61275	4308	BR/SR	DMBS	National Railway Museum, Shildon
61287	4311	BR/SR	DMBS	AB Loco, Peak Rail, Darley Dale
75395	4308	BR/SR	DTC	National Railway Museum, Shildon
75407	4311	BR/SR	DTS	AB Loco, Peak Rail, Darley Dale

4EPB (Class 415)

14351	5176	BR/SR	DMBSO	Northampton Ironstone Railway

14352	5176	BR/SR	DMBSO	Loco Storage Ltd, Margate
15354	5176	BR/SR	TSO	Northampton Ironstone Railway
15396	5176	BR/SR	TSO	Northampton Ironstone Railway

2EPB (Class 416)

14573	6307	BR/SR	DMBS	Hope Farm, Sellindge
16117	6307	BR/SR	DTS	Hope Farm, Sellindge
65321	5791	BR/SR	DMBS	Peak Rail, Darley Dale
65373	5759	BR/SR	DMBS	Southall
77112	5793	BR/SR	DTS	Peak Rail, Darley Dale
77558	5759	BR/SR	DTS	Southall

MLV (Class 419)

68001	9001	BR/SR	DMBL	Southall
68002	9002	BR/SR	DMBL	Southall
68003	9003	BR/SR	DMBL	Eden Valley Railway
68004	9004	BR/SR	DMBL	Mid-Norfolk Railway
68005	9005	BR/SR	DMBL	Eden Valley Railway
68008	9008	BR/SR	DMBL	Southall
68009	9009	BR/SR	DMBL	Southall
68010	9010	BR/SR	DMBL	Eden Valley Railway

4CIG (Class 421)

62043	1753	BR/SR	MBSO	Nemesis Rail, Burton-on-Trent
62287	1303	BR/SR	MBSO	Lincolnshire Wolds Railway
62385	1399	BR/SR	MBSO	East Kent Railway
62402	1497	BR/SR	MBSO	Spa Valley Railway
70721	1753	BR/SR	TSO	Nemesis Rail, Burton-on-Trent
71041	1306	BR/SR	TSO	Private in Hever
71080	1881	BR/SR	TSO	Dean Forest Railway
71085	1884	BR/SR	TSO	Private in Kent
76048	1753	BR/SR	DTC	Nemesis Rail, Burton-on-Trent
76102	1753	BR/SR	DTC	Nemesis Rail, Burton-on-Trent
76740	1392	BR/SR	DTC	Southall
76747	1399	BR/SR	DTC	Dartmoor Railway
76764	1497	BR/SR	DTC	Spa Valley Railway
76835	1497	BR/SR	DTC	Spa Valley Railway

4BIG (Class 422)

69302	2251	BR/SR	TRSB	Abbey View Centre, Neath
69304	2260	BR/SR	TRSB	Northampton Ironstone Railway
69306	2254	BR/SR	TRSB	Spa Valley Railway
69310	2255	BR/SR	TRSB	Dartmoor Railway
69316	2258	BR/SR	TRSB	Waverley Heritage Centre
69318	2259	BR/SR	TRSB	Colne Valley Railway
69332	2257	BR/SR	TRSB	Dartmoor Railway
69333	2262	BR/SR	TRSB	Lavender Line
69335	2209	BR/SR	TRSB	Wensleydale Railway
69337	2210	BR/SR	TRSB	Hastings Diesels Ltd
69339	2205	BR/SR	TRSB	Nemesis Rail, Burton-on-Trent

4VEP/VOP (Class 423)

62236	3417	BR/SR	MBSO	Bluebell Railway
70797	3417	BR/SR	TSO	Bluebell Railway
70904	3905	BR/SR	TSO	East Kent Railway
76262	3417	BR/SR	DTCO	Bluebell Railway
76263	3417	BR/SR	DTCO	Bluebell Railway
76397	3905	BR/SR	DTC	East Kent Railway
76398	3905	BR/SR	DTC	East Kent Railway
76875	3545	BR/SR	DTC	East Kent Railway
76887	3568	BR/SR	DTC	Woking Miniature Railway

TC (Class 438)

70823	428	BR/SR	TBSK	London Transport set
70824	413	BR/SR	TBSK	Swanage Railway
70826	415	BR/SR	TBSK	Sandford & Barnwell Station
70855	412	BR/SR	TFK	Swanage Railway
70859	416	BR/SR	TFK	Stravithie Station

70860	417	BR/SR	TFK	Cambridge North Road
71163	428	BR/SR	TFK	London Transport set
76275	404	BR/SR	DTSO	Swanage Railway
76277	405	BR/SR	DTSO	Dartmoor Railway
76297	428	BR/SR	DTSO	London Transport set
76298	415	BR/SR	DTSO	Swanage Railway
76301	417	BR/SR	DTSO	Bellingham, Northumberland
76302	417	BR/SR	DTSO	Bellingham, Northumberland
76322	427	BR/SR	DTSO	Swanage Railway (Barrow Hill)
76324	428	BR/SR	DTSO	London Transport set

Class 457

67300	7001	BR/WR	DMSO	East Kent Railway

1940 Waterloo & City (Class 487)

61		SR	DMSO	LT Museum, Acton

GLV (Class 489)

68500	9101	BR/IC	DMBL	Ecclesbourne Valley Railway
68503	9104	BR/IC	DMBL	Spa Valley Railway
68506	9106	BR/IC	DMBL	Ecclesbourne Valley Railway
68507	9108	BR/IC	DMBL	Great Central Railway
68509	9110	BR/IC	DMBL	Vale of Glamorgan Railway

Class 501

61183	501183	BR/LM	DMBS	Coulsdon Historic Vehicles, Finmere
75186	501183	BR/LM	DTBS	Coulsdon Historic Vehicles, Finmere

Class 502

28361		LMS	DMBS	Burscough
29896		LMS	DTC	Burscough

Class 503

28690		LMS	DMBS	Loco Services, Margate
29282		LMS	DTS	Loco Services, Margate
29720		LMS	TCO	Loco Services, Margate

Class 504

65451	-	BR/LM	DMBSO	East Lancs Railway
77172	-	BR/LM	DTBSO	East Lancs Railway

Class 370 (APT)

48103		BR	DTSOL	Crewe Heritage Centre
48106		BR	DTSOL	Crewe Heritage Centre
48602		BR	TBFOL	Crewe Heritage Centre
48603		BR	TBFOL	Crewe Heritage Centre
48404		BR	TSRBL	Crewe Heritage Centre
49002		BR	M	Crewe Heritage Centre
49006	-	BR	M	Crewe Heritage Centre

Right: *When large numbers of first generation DMMU middle cars were offered for sale, several light railways purchased these to act as hauled stock. They were vacuum braked and usually offered a high seating capacity. One railway to use such vehicles was, and still is, the Dartmouth Steam Railway. Former Class 117 TCL No. 59513 is seen restored to Great Western colours and named* Heidi *at Kingswear.* **CJM**

Left: *Based on the Spa Valley Railway, the remains of the Tunbridge Wells-Eridge line, Class 33/0 No. 33063 is restored to immediately pre-privatisation Mainline freight grey with blue and gold company branding.* **Howard Lewsey**

Right: *Displaying a non-authentic black livery with Lion on Wheel badge and cast number plates, Class 14 No. D9537 is based on the East Lancs Railway, but seen on the Ecclesbourne Valley Railway. The livery shows what might have been if the locos had been introduced in the mid-1950s.* **Antony Christie**

Below: *Preserved main line certified Class 20s Nos. 20007 and 20142 pass Wendover station on 25 August 2019 with 1Z34, the 12.25 Quainton Road to Watford (Metropolitan) leg of UK Railtours' Metroland & Quainton Railtour. Swanage-based Class 33 No. 33012 is on the rear of the London Transport 4TC set.* **David Ive**

Above: *Class 03 No. 03371 is currently operating on the Dartmouth Steam Railway as a pilot loco. It is restored to 1970s BR Rail Blue and seen 'on shed' at Paignton.* **CJM**

Right Middle: *The body shell of Class 58 No. 58022 has been purchased as part of 'Project Icon' to built a replica of LMS prototype No. 10000. The Class 58 is at Rowsley on Peak Rail. It will be dismantled, with its frame used as the basis for a reconstruction of No. 10000. Bogies and a power unit have already been obtained.* **Antony Christie**

Right Below: *Owned by the National Railway Museum, the surviving prototype HST power car No. 41001 (43000) is preserved for the nation and kept at the NRM Shildon. Restored to its original condition and livery, the vehicle is certified for movement over Network Rail tracks. It is seen working at the Keighley & Worth Valley Railway gala on 4 May 2019, on the straight between Keighley and Ingrow working the 10.50 from Keighley to Oxenhope.* **Peter Marsh**

Preserved Steam Locomotives

Great Western and constitute companies

No.	Name	Class	Wheel Arrangement	Location
426			0-6-2T	Keighley & Worth Valley Rly
450			0-6-2T	NRM at Gwili Railway
813			0-6-0ST	Severn Valley Railway
1338			0-6-0ST	Didcot Railway Centre
1340	*Trojan*		0-6-0ST	Didcot Railway Centre
1363		1361	0-6-0ST	Didcot Railway Centre
1369		1366	0-6-0PT	South Devon Railway
1420		1400	0-4-2T	South Devon Railway
1442		1400	0-4-2T	Tiverton Museum
1450		1400	0-4-2T	Severn Valley Railway
1466		1400	0-4-2T	Dean Forest Railway
1501		1500	0-6-0PT	Severn Valley Railway
1638		1600	0-6-0PT	Kent & East Sussex Railway
2516		Dean Goods	0-6-0	Swindon Museum, Swindon
2807		2800	2-8-0	Gloucestershire Warwickshire Railway
2818		2800	2-8-0	Steam, Swindon
2857		2800	2-8-0	Severn Valley Railway
2859		2800	2-8-0	Private in Congleton
2861		2800	2-8-0	Barry
2873		2800	2-8-0	South Devon Railway (parts for 3803)
2874		2800	2-8-0	Gloucestershire Warwickshire Railway
2885		2800	2-8-0	Tyseley
2999	*Lady of Legend*	2900	4-6-0	Didcot Railway Centre
3205		2251	0-6-0	South Devon Railway
3440	*City of Truro*	City	4-4-0	Steam Museum, Swindon
3650		5700	0-6-0PT	Didcot Railway Centre
3738		5700	0-6-0PT	Didcot Railway Centre
3802		2800	2-8-0	Llangollen Railway
3803		2800	2-8-0	South Devon Railway
3814		2800	2-8-0	Llangollen Railway
3822		2800	2-8-0	Gloucestershire Warwickshire Railway
3845		2800	2-8-0	West Somerset Railway
3850		2800	2-8-0	Gloucestershire Warwickshire Railway
3855		2800	2-8-0	East Lancs Railway
3862		2800	2-8-0	Northampton & Lamport
4003	*Lode Star*	Star	4-6-0	National Railway Museum York
4073	*Caerphilly Castle*	Castle	4-6-0	Steam Museum, Swindon
4079	*Pendennis Castle*	Castle	4-6-0	Didcot Railway Centre
4110		5101	2-6-2T	East Somerset Railway
4115		5101	2-6-2T	Didcot Railway Centre
4121		5101	2-6-2T	Tyseley Museum
4141		5101	2-6-2T	Epping and Ongar Railway
4144		5101	2-6-2T	Didcot Railway Centre
4150		5101	2-6-2T	Severn Valley Railway
4160		5101	2-6-2T	Llangollen Railway
4247		4200	2-8-0T	Bodmin & Wenford
4248		4200	2-8-0T	Steam Museum, Swindon
4253		4200	2-8-0T	Kent & East Sussex Railway
4270		4200	2-8-0T	Gloucestershire Warwickshire Railway
4277		4200	2-8-0T	Dartmouth Steam Railway
4555	*Warrior*	4500	2-6-2T	Dartmouth Steam Railway
4561		4500	2-6-2T	West Somerset Railway
4566		4500	2-6-2T	Severn Valley Railway
4588		4500	2-6-2T	Tyseley Museum
4612		5700	0-6-0PT	Bodmin & Wenford Railway
4920	*Dumbleton Hall*	Hall	4-6-0	South Devon Railway
4930	*Hagley Hall*	Hall	4-6-0	Severn Valley Railway
4936	*Kinlet Hall*	Hall	4-6-0	Tyseley Museum
4953	*Pitchford Hall*	Hall	4-6-0	Epping and Ongar Railway

4965	*Rood Ashton Hall*	Hall	4-6-0	Tyseley Museum
4979	*Wootton Hall*	Hall	4-6-0	Ribble Steam Railway
5029	*Nunney Castle*	Castle	4-6-0	Didcot Railway Centre
5043	*Earl of Mt Edgecumbe*	Castle	4-6-0	Tyseley Museum
5051	*Earl Bathurst*	Castle	4-6-0	Didcot Railway Centre
5080	*Defiant*	Castle	4-6-0	Tyseley Museum
5164		5101	2-6-2T	Barrow Hill
5193		5101	2-6-2T	West Somerset Rly (rebuilt as Mogul 9351)
5199		5101	2-6-2T	Llangollen Railway
5224		5205	2-8-0T	West Somerset Railway
5227		5205	2-8-0T	Barry
5239	*Goliath*	5205	2-8-0T	Dartmouth Steam Railway
5322		4300	2-8-0T	Didcot Railway Centre
5521		4500	2-6-2T	Avon Valley Railway
5526		4500	2-6-2T	South Devon Railway
5532		4500	2-6-2T	Llangollen Railway
5538		4500	2-6-2T	Flower Mill
5539		4500	2-6-2T	Barry Railway
5541		4500	2-6-2T	Dean Forest Railway
5542		4500	2-6-2T	South Devon Railway
5552		4500	2-6-2T	Bodmin & Wenford Railway
5553		4500	2-6-2T	Peak Rail
5572		4500	2-6-2T	Didcot Railway Centre
5619		5600	0-6-2T	Midland Railway Centre
5637		5600	0-6-2T	Swindon & Cricklade Railway
5643		5600	0-6-2T	Embsay and Bolton Abbey
5668		5600	0-6-2T	Kent & East Sussex Railway
5764		5700	0-6-0PT	Severn Valley Railway
5775		5700	0-6-0PT	Keighley & Worth Valley Railway
5786		5700	0-6-0PT	South Devon Railway as L92
5900	*Hinderton Hall*	Hall	4-6-0	Didcot Railway Centre
5952	*Cogan Hall*	Hall	4-6-0	Llangollen Railway
5967	*Bickmarsh Hall*	Hall	4-6-0	Northampton & Lamport
5972	*Olton Hall*	Hall	4-6-0	Carnforth
6000	*King George V*	King	4-6-0	Swindon Museum, Swindon
6023	*King Edward II*	King	4-6-0	Didcot Railway Centre
6024	*King Edward I*	King	4-6-0	West Somerset Railway (GWS)
6106		6100	2-6-2T	Didcot Railway Centre
6412		6400	0-6-0PT	South Devon Railway
6430		6400	0-6-0PT	Llangollen Railway
6435		6400	0-6-0PT	Bodmin & Wenford
6619		5600	0-6-2T	Kent & East Sussex Railway
6634		5600	0-6-2T	Peak Rail
6686		5600	0-6-2T	Barry
6695		5600	0-6-2T	Swindon & Cricklade Railway
6697		5600	0-6-2T	Didcot Railway Centre
6960	*RaveninghamHall*	Mod Hall	4-6-0	Severn Valley Railway
6984	*Owsden Hall*	Mod Hall	4-6-0	Buckingham Railway Centre
6989	*Wightwick Hall*	Mod Hall	4-6-0	Quainton Road
6990	*Witherslack Hall*	Mod Hall	4-6-0	Great Central Railway
6998	*Burton Agnes Hall*	Mod Hall	4-6-0	Didcot Railway Centre
7027	*Thornbury Castle*	Castle	4-6-0	Private at Great Central Railway
7029	*Clun Castle*	Castle	4-6-0	Tyseley Museum
7200		7200	2-8-2T	Quainton Road
7202		7200	2-8-2T	Didcot Railway Centre
7229		7200	2-8-2T	East Lancs Railway
7325		4300	2-6-0	Severn Valley Railway
7714		5700	0-6-0PT	Severn Valley Railway
7715		5700	0-6-0PT	Quainton Road as L99
7752		5700	0-6-0PT	Tyseley Museum
7754		5700	0-6-0PT	Llangollen Railway
7760		5700	0-6-0PT	Tyseley Museum
7802	*Bradley Manor*	Manor	4-6-0	Severn Valley Railway
7808	*Cookham Manor*	Manor	4-6-0	Didcot Railway Centre
7812	*Erlestoke Manor*	Manor	4-6-0	Tyseley Museum
7819	*Hinton Manor*	Manor	4-6-0	Severn Valley Railway
7820	*Dinmore Manor*	Manor	4-6-0	GWR

7821	*Ditcheat Manor*	Manor	4-6-0	Retail Park, Swindon
7822	*Foxcote Manor*	Manor	4-6-0	Steam Museum, Swindon
7827	*Lydham Manor*	Manor	4-6-0	Dartmouth Steam Railway
7828	*Odney Manor*	Manor	4-6-0	West Somerset Railway
7903	*Foremarke Hall*	Mod Hall	4-6-0	GWR
7927	*Willington Hall*	Mod Hall	4-6-0	Llangollen Railway
9017	*Earl of Berkeley*	Dukedog	4-4-0	Bluebell Railway
9351		(rebuild)	2-6-0	West Somerset Railway
9400		9400	0-6-0PT	Steam Museum, Swindon
9466		9400	0-6-0PT	Gloucestershire Warwickshire Railway
9600		5700	0-6-0PT	Tyseley Museum
9629		5700	0-6-0PT	Pontypool & Blaenavon
9642		5700	0-6-0PT	GWR
9681		5700	0-6-0PT	Dean Forest Railway
9682		5700	0-6-0PT	Dean Forest Railway

Southern and constitute companies

No.	Name	Class	Wheel Arrangement	Location
W24	*Calbourne*	O2	0-4-4T	IoW Steam Railway
30053		M7	0-4-4T	Swanage Railway
30064		USA	0-6-0T	Bluebell Railway
30065		USA	0-6-0T	Kent & East Sussex Railway
30070 (DS238)		USA	0-6-0T	Kent & East Sussex Railway
30072		USA	0-6-0T	Keighley & Worth Valley Railway
30075		USA	0-6-0T	Mid-Hants Railway (Yugoslav loco)
30076		USA	0-6-0T	Mid-Hants Railway (Yugoslav loco)
30096	*Normandy*	B4	0-4-0T	Bluebell Railway
30102	*Granville*	B4	0-4-0T	Bressingham
30120		T9	4-4-0	Swanage Railway
30245		M7	0-4-4T	National Railway Museum
30499		S15	4-6-0	Mid Hants Railway
30506		S15	4-6-0	Mid-Hants Railway
30541		Q	0-6-0	Bluebell Railway
30583		0415	4-4-2T	Bluebell Railway
30585		0298	2-4-0WT	Quainton
30587		0298	2-4-0WT	National Railway Museum Shildon
30777	*Sir Lamiel*	N15	4-6-0	Great Central Railway
30825		S15	4-6-0	North Yorkshire Moors Railway
30828		S15	4-6-0	Mid-Hants Railway
30830		S15	4-6-0	North Yorkshire Moors Railway
30847		S15	4-6-0	Bluebell Railway
30850	*Lord Nelson*	LN	4-6-0	Mid-Hants Railway
30925	*Cheltenham*	V	4-4-0	Mid-Hants Railway
30926	*Repton*	V	4-4-0	North Yorkshire Moors Railway
30928	*Stowe*	V	4-4-0	Bluebell Railway
31027		P	0-6-0T	Bluebell Railway
31065 (65)		O1	0-6-0	Bluebell Railway
31178		P1	0-6-0T	Bluebell Railway
31263		H	0-4-4T	Bluebell Railway
31323 (323)		P	0-6-0T	Bluebell Railway
31556		P	0-6-0T	Kent & East Sussex Railway
31592		C	0-6-0	Bluebell Railway
31618		U	2-6-0	Bluebell Railway
31625		U	2-6-0	Swanage Railway
31638		U	2-6-0	Bluebell Railway
31737		D	4-4-0	National Railway Museum York
31806		U	2-6-0	Swanage Railway
31874		N	2-6-0	Swanage Railway
32110	*Cannock Wood*	E1	0-6-0T	IoW Railway
32473	*Birch Grove*	E4	0-6-2T	Bluebell Railway
32636	*Fenchurch*	A1X	0-6-0T	Bluebell Railway
32640 W11	*Newport*	A1X	0-6-0T	IoW Steam Railway
32646	*Freshwater*	A1X	0-6-0T	IoW Steam Railway
32650	*Whitechapel*	A1X	0-6-0T	Spa Valley Railway

32654	*Waddon*	A1X	0-6-0T	Canadian Railway Museum
32655	*Stepney*	A1X	0-6-0T	Bluebell Railway
32662	*Martello*	A1X	0-6-0T	Bressingham
32670	*Poplar*	A1X	0-6-0T	Kent & East Sussex Railway
32672	*Fenchurch*	A1X	0-6-0T	Bluebell Railway
32678	*Knowle*	A1X	0-6-0T	Kent & East Sussex Railway
32682	*Boxhill*	A1X	0-6-0T	National Railway Museum
33001		Q1	0-6-0	National Railway Museum
34007	*Wadebridge*	WC	4-6-2	Mid-Hants Railway
34010	*Sidmouth*	WC	4-6-2	Swanage Railway
34016	*Bodmin*	WC	4-6-2	WCRC Carnforth
34023	*Blackmore Vale*	WC	4-6-2	Bluebell Railway
34027	*Taw Valley*	WC	4-6-2	Severn Valley Railway
34028	*Eddystone*	WC	4-6-2	Swanage Railway
34039	*Boscastle*	WC	4-6-2	Great Central Railway
34046	*Braunton*	WC	4-6-2	Southall
34051	*Winston Churchill*	BB	4-6-2	National Railway Museum York
34053	*Sir Keith Park*	BB	4-6-2	Swanage Railway
34058	*Sir Frederick Pile*	BB	4-6-2	Midland Railway Centre
34059	*Sir Archibald Sinclair*	BB	4-6-2	Bluebell Railway
34067	*Tangmere*	BB	4-6-2	WCRC Carnforth
34070	*Manston*	BB	4-6-2	Swanage Railway
34072	*257 Squadron*	BB	4-6-2	Swanage Railway
34073	*249 Squadron*	BB	4-6-2	East Lancs Railway
34081	*92 Squadron*	BB	4-6-2	North Norfolk Railway
34092	*City of Wells*	WC	4-6-2	East Lancs Railway
34101	*Hartland*	WC	4-6-2	North Yorkshire Moors Railway
34105	*Swanage*	WC	4-6-2	Mid-Hants Railway
35005	*Canadian Pacific*	MN	4-6-2	Mid-Hants Railway
35006	*Peninsular & Oriental S. N Co*	MN	4-6-2	Gloucestershire Warwickshire Railway
35009	*Shaw Savill*	MN	4-6-2	Riley & Son, Heywood
35010	*Blue Star*	MN	4-6-2	Colne Valley Railway
35011	*General Steam Navigation*	MN	4-6-2	Sellinge (restoration)
35018	*British India Line*	MN	4-6-2	WCRC Carnforth
35022	*Holland America Line*	MN	4-6-2	Private at Bury
35025	*Brocklebamk Line*	MN	4-6-2	Private at Sellindge
35027	*Port Line*	MN	4-6-2	Private in Bury
35028	*Clan Line*	MN	4-6-2	Stewarts Lane
35029	*Ellerman Lines*	MN	4-6-2	National Railway Museum York
B110		E1	0-6-0T	East Somerset Railway
214	*Gladstone*	B	0-4-0	National Railway Museum York
563		T3	4-4-0	Flower Mill/Swanage

London Midland Scottish and constitute companies

No.	Name	Class	Wheel Arrangement	Location
790	*Hardwicke*	LNWR	2-4-0	National Railway Museum York
1000		MC	4-4-0	NRM at Barrow Hill
1719	*Lady Nan*		0-4-0ST	East Somerset Railway
3020	*Cornwall*	LNWR	2-2-2	NRM at Buckingham Railway
16379		GSWR	0-6-0T	Glasgow Museum
41241		Class 2	2-6-2T	Keighley & Worth Valley Railway
41298		Class 2	2-6-2T	Isle of Wight Railway
41312		Class 2	2-6-2T	Mid-Hants Railway
41313		Class 2	2-6-2T	Isle of Wight Railway
41708		1F	0-6-0T	Barrow Hill
41966	*Thundersley*		4-4-2T	Bressingham
42073			2-6-4T	Lakeside and Haverthwaite Railway
42085			2-6-4T	Lakeside and Haverthwaite Railway
42500			2-6-4T	National Railway Museum York
42700		Crab	2-6-0	National Railway Museum York
42765		Crab	2-6-0	East Lancs Railway
42859		Crab	2-6-0	RAF Binbrook

42968		Crab	2-6-0	Severn Valley Railway
43106		4MT	2-6-0	Severn Valley Railway
43924		4F	0-6-0	Keighley & Worth Valley Railway
44027		4F	0-6-0	Vale of Berkley Railway
44123		4F	0-6-0	Avon Valley Railway
44422		4F	0-6-0	Churnet ValleyRailway
44767	*George Stephenson*	Black 5	4-6-0	WCRC Carnforth
44806	*Kenneth Aldcroft*	Black 5	4-6-0	North Yorkshire Moors Railway
44871	*Sovereign*	Black 5	4-6-0	East Lancs Railway
44901		Black 5	4-6-0	Vale of Berkeley Railway
44932		Black 5	4-6-0	Carnforth
45000		Black 5	4-6-0	National Railway Museum, Shildon
45025		Black 5	4-6-0	Strathspey Railway
45110	*RAF Biggin Hill*	Black 5	4-6-0	Severn Valley Railway
45163		Black 5	4-6-0	Churnet Valley Railway
45212		Black 5	4-6-0	Keighley & Worth Valley Railway
45231	*The Sherwood Forester*	Black 5	4-6-0	Crewe
45293		Black 5	4-6-0	Churnet Valley Railway
45305		Black 5	4-6-0	Great Central Railway
45337		Black 5	4-6-0	Llangollen Railway
45379		Black 5	4-6-0	Loco Storage, Margate
45407	*Lancashire Fusilier*	Black 5	4-6-0	East Lancs Railway
45428	*Eric Treacy*	Black 5	4-6-0	North Yorkshire Moors Railway
45491		Black 5	4-6-0	Great Central Railway
45593	*Kolhapur*	Jubilee	4-6-0	Tyseley Museum
45596	*Bahamas*	Jubilee	4-6-0	Tyseley Museum
45690	*Leander*	Jubilee	4-6-0	WCRC Carnforth
45699	*Galatea*	Jubilee	4-6-0	WCRC Carnforth
46100	*Royal Scot*	Royal Scot	4-6-0	Southall
46115	*Scots Guardsman*	Royal Scot	4-6-0	Carnforth
46201	*Princess Elizabeth*	Princess	4-6-2	Carnforth
46203	*Princess Margaret Rose*	Princess	4-6-2	Midland Railway Centre
46229	*Duchess of Hamilton*	Coronation	4-6-2	National Railway Museum
46233	*Duchess of Sutherland*	Coronation	4-6-2	Midland Railway Centre
46235	*City of Birmingham*	Coronation	4-6-2	Millenium Point, Birmingham
46428		2MT	2-6-0	East Lancs Railway
46441		2MT	2-6-0	Lakeside & Haverthwaite Railway
46443		2MT	2-6-0	Severn Valley Railway
46447		2MT	2-6-0	East Somerset Railway
46464		2MT	2-6-0	Bridge of Dun
46512		2MT	2-6-0	Strathspey Railway
46521		2MT	2-6-0	Great Central Railway
47279		Jinty	0-6-0T	Keighley & Worth Valley Railway
47298		Jinty	0-6-0T	Bury
47324		Jinty	0-6-0T	East Lancs Railway
47327		Jinty	0-6-0T	Midland Railway Centre
47357		Jinty	0-6-0T	Midland Railway Centre
47383		Jinty	0-6-0T	Severn Valley Railway
47406		Jinty	0-6-0T	Ecclesbourne Valley Railway
47445		Jinty	0-6-0T	Midland Railway Centre
47493		Jinty	0-6-0T	Spa Valley Railway
47564		Jinty	0-6-0T	Midland Railway Centre
48151		8F	2-8-0	Carnforth
48173		8F	2-8-0	Churnet Valley Railway
48274		8F	2-8-0	Great Central Railway-N (Ex-Turkey)
48305		8F	2-8-0	Great Central Railway
48431		8F	2-8-0	Keighley & Worth Valley Railway
48624		8F	2-8-0	Great Central Railway
48773		8F	2-8-0	Severn Valley Railway
49395		7F	0-8-0	National Railway Museum
50621		LYR	2-4-2T	National Railway Museum
51218		LYR	0-4-0ST	Keighley & Worth Valley Railway
52044		LYR	0-6-0	Keighley & Worth Valley Railway
52322		LYR	0-6-0	East Lancs Railway
53808 (88)		7F	2-8-0	West Somerset Railway
53809		7F	2-8-0	Midland Railway, Butterley

55189			0-4-4T	Scottish Railway Pres Society
57566			0-6-0	Strathspey Railway
58850			0-6-0T	Barrow Hill
58926			0-6-2T	Keighley & Worth Valley Railway
11243			0-4-0ST	Ribble Steam Railway
11456		752	0-6-0ST	Keighley & Worth Valley Railway
123			4-2-2	Riverside Museum, Glasgow
103			4-6-0	Riverside Museum, Glasgow
158A			2-4-0	Midland Railway Centre
419			0-4-4T	Bo'ness and Kinneil
673		Spinner	4-2-2	National Railway Museum
828		812	0-6-0	Strathspey Railway
2271 (NSR 2)			0-6-2T	National Railway Museum at Foxfield
1439			0-4-0ST	NRM at Ribble Steam Railway
49	*Columbine*		2-2-2	Science Museum
3	*Coppernob*	FR	0-4-0	National Railway Museum
FR20			0-4-0	Ribble Valley Steam Railway
FR25			0-4-0ST	Ribble Valley Railway
57	*Lion*	L&M	0-4-2	Liverpool Museum
5	*Cecil Raikes*		0-6-4T	Liverpool Museum

London North Eastern and constitute companies

No.	Name	Class	Wheel Arrangement	Location
GNR 1		Stirling	4-2-2	National Railway Museum
66	*Aerolite*	X1	2-2-4T	National Railway Museum
251		C1	4-4-2	National Railway Museum
910	*Fletcher*		2-4-0	NRM at Kirkby Stephen East
990	*Henry Oakley*	C2	4-4-2	National Railway Museum
1275		1001	0-6-0	National Railway Museum
1310		Y7	0-4-0T	Middleton Railway
1463	*Tennant*	E5	2-4-0	NRM at Darlington
1621		D17	4-4-0	National Railway Museum
60007	*Sir Nigel Gresley*	A4	4-6-2	North Yorkshire Moors Railway
60008	*Dwight D Eisenhower*	A4	4-6-2	Green Bay, Wisconsin, USA
60009	*Union of South Africa*	A4	4-6-2	Severn Valley Railway
60010	*Dominion of Canada*	A4	4-6-2	Canadian Railway Museum
60019	*Bittern*	A4	4-6-2	Loco Storage, Margate
60022	*Mallard*	A4	4-6-2	National Railway Museum
60103	*Flying Scotsman*	A3	4-6-2	National Railway Museum
60532	*Blue Peter*	A2	4-6-2	LNWR Crewe
60800	*Green Arrow*	V2	2-6-2	National Railway Museum
61264		B1	4-6-0	North Yorkshire Moors Railway
61306	*Mayflower*	B1	4-6-0	WCRC Southall
61572		B12	4-6-0	North Norfolk Railway
61994	*Great Marquess*	K4	2-6-0	Severn Valley Railway
62005		K1	2-6-0	North Yorkshire Moors Railway
62277	*Gordon Highlander*	D40	4-4-0	Glasgow Transport Museum
62469	*Glen Douglas*	D34	4-4-0	Scottish Railway Pres Society
62660	*Butler Henderson*	D11	4-4-0	NRM at Great Central Railway
62712	*Morayshire*	D49	4-4-0	Scottish Railway Pres Society
62785		E4	2-4-0	Bressingham
63395		Q6	0-8-0	North Yorkshire Moors Railway
63460		Q7	0-8-0	NRM at Darlington Museum
63601		O4	2-8-0	Great Central Railway
65033		J21	0-6-0	Loco Services, Loughborough
65243	*Maude*	J36	0-6-0	Scottish Railway Pres Society
65462		J15	0-6-0	North Norfolk Railway
65567		J17	0-6-0	NRM at Barrow Hill
65894		J27	0-6-0	North Yorkshire Moors Railway
68011		J94	0-6-0ST	In Belgium
68030		J94	0-6-0ST	Churnet Valley Railway
68077		J94	0-6-0ST	Spa Valley Railway
68088		Y7	0-4-0T	Great Central Railway
68095		Y9	0-4-0ST	Scottish Railway Pres Society

68153	Y1/2	4w	Middleton Railway
68633	J69	0-6-0T	National Railway Museum
68846	J52	0-6-0ST	NRM at Great Central Railway
69023	J72	0-6-0T	Wensleydale Railway
69523	N2	0-6-2T	North Norfolk Railway
69621	N7	0-6-2T	EAR

British Railways

No.	Name	Class	Wheel Arrangement	Location
70000	*Britannia*	Britannia	4-6-2	Crewe
70013	*Oliver Cromwell*	Britannia	4-6-2	Great Central Railway
71000	*Duke of Gloucester*		4-6-2	Tyseley Museum
73050	*City of Peterborough*	Class 5	4-6-0	Nene Valley Railway
73082	*Camelot*	Class 5	4-6-0	Bluebell Railway
73096	*Merlin*	Class 5	4-6-0	Mid-Hants Railway
73129		Class 5	4-6-0	Midland Railway Centre
73156		Class 5	4-6-0	Great Central Railway
75014		Class 4	4-6-0	Dartmouth Steam Railway
75027		Class 4	4-6-0	Bluebell Railway
75029	*The Green Knight*	Class 4	4-6-0	North Yorkshire Moors Railway
75069		Class 4	4-6-0	Severn Valley Railway
75078		Class 4	4-6-0	Keighley & Worth Valley Railway
75079		Class 4	4-6-0	Mid-Hants Railway
76017		Class 4	2-6-0	Mid-Hants Railway
76077		Class 4	2-6-0	Gloucestershire Warwickshire Railway
76079		Class 4	2-6-0	North Yorkshire Moors Railway
76084		Class 4	2-6-0	North Norfolk Railway
78018		Class 2	2-6-0	Great Central Railway
78019		Class 2	2-6-0	Great Central Railway
78022		Class 2	2-6-0	Keighley & Worth Valley Railway
80002		Class 4	2-6-4T	Keighley & Worth Valley Railway
80064		Class 4	2-6-4T	Bluebell Railway
80072		Class 4	2-6-4T	Llangollen Railway
80078		Class 4	2-6-4T	Mangapps Farm
80079		Class 4	2-6-4T	Severn Valley Railway
80080		Class 4	2-6-4T	Midland Railway Centre
80097		Class 4	2-6-4T	East Lancs Railway
80098		Class 4	2-6-4T	Midland Railway Centre
80100		Class 4	2-6-4T	Bluebell Railway
80104		Class 4	2-6-4T	Swanage Railway
80105		Class 4	2-6-4T	Scottish Railway Pres Society
80135		Class 4	2-6-4T	North Yorkshire Moors Railway
80136		Class 4	2-6-4T	North Yorkshire Moors Railway
80150		Class 4	2-6-4T	Mid-Hants Railway
80151		Class 4	2-6-4T	Bluebell Railway
90733		WD	2-10-0	Keighley & Worth Valley Railway
90775		WD	2-10-0	North Norfolk Railway (Ex Greece)
600	*Gordon*	WD	2-10-0	Severn Valley Railway
92134		9F	2-10-0	North Yorkshire Moors Railway
92203	*Black Prince*	9F	2-10-0	North Norfolk Railway
92207		9F	2-10-0	Shillingstone Station
92212		9F	2-10-0	Mid-Hants Railway
92214	*Lieicester City*	9F	2-10-0	Great Central Railway
92219		9F	2-10-0	Wensleydale Railway
92220	*Evening Star*	9F	2-10-0	National Railway Museum
92240		9F	2-10-0	Bluebell Railway
92245		9F	2-10-0	Barry Island Railway

Above: *The Isle of Wight Steam Railway operates some superbly restored locos and stock. Here, Class 02 0-4-4T No. W24* Calbourne *arrives at Haven Street.* **Antony Christie**

Right: *Preserved BR 'Standard' 9F No. 92203* Black Prince *is based at the North Norfolk Railway, where the loco is seen at Sheringham.*
Antony Christie

Below: *Recently restored to main line standard, is Bulleid Merchant Navy Class No. 35018* British India Line*, seen operating on the main line at Southampton in July 2019.*
Mark V. Pike

Left Above: *Built at the Baldwin Loco Works in the USA in 1945 for war use, No. 6046 later spent time working in France and Hungary before being preserved in the UK. In recent years the loco has visited a number of light railways and is shown at Kingswear on the Dartmouth Steam Railway in summer 2019.* **CJM**

Left Middle: *Ivatt Class 2 No. 41298 was built after nationalisation at Crewe Works in 1951, emerging in BR black livery. It is currently preserved in operational condition on the Isle of Wight Steam Railway, where this view of the loco was recorded in summer 2019.* **Antony Christie**

Far Right: *A number of preserved steam locos are authorised to operate over Network Rail tracks, having main-line certification. One such loco is LNER/BR B1 No. 61306* Mayflower, *captured passing Nine Elms with a Waterloo to Windsor & Eton Riverside charter.* **Mark V. Pike**

Below: *One of the prime exhibits at the Steam Museum, Swindon is restored GWR 'Castle' No. 4073* Caerphilly Castle, *which is cosmetically restored and positioned in the main display area so that visitors can walk below the loco in an inspection pit. This museum houses a number of GW artifacts and is an interesting place to visit.* **CJM**

Several preserved steam locomotives have been allocated five-digit TOPS numbers to allow their operation over the National Network. The numbers allocated are shown below; not all locos may currently be authorised for use over Network Rail metals.

TOPS No.	Railway No.	Type	Name
98150	1450	GWR 14xx	
98166	1466	GWR 14xx	
98186	686	0-6-0T	*Lady Armaghdale*
98212	41312	LMS 2MT	
98219	55189	CR 0-4-4T	
98221	46521	LMS 2MT	
98238	1638	GWR 16xx	
98240	3440	GWR 34xx	*City of Truro*
98241	46441	LMS 2MT	
98243	46443	LMS 2MT	
98253	30053	SR M7	
98254	58926	LNWR 2F	
98273	65243	NBR J36	*Maude*
98315	7715	GWR 57xx	
98321	69621	GER N7	*A. J. Hill*
98372	30072	SR USA	
98400	41000	LMS 4P	
98406	43106	LMS 4MT	
98414	75014	BR 4MT	
98425	7325	GWR 7321	
98426	31625	SR U	
98427	44027	LMS 4F	
98435	80135	BR 4MT	
98455	4555	GWR 45xx	
98457	9600	GWR 8750	
98460	7760	GWR 57xx	
98466	9466	GWR 94xx	
98469	75069	BR 4MT	
98472	5572	GWR 4575	
98476	76079	BR 4MT	
98478	68078	WD 4F	
98479	80079	BR 4MT	
98480	80080	BR 4MT	
98482	3882	0-6-0ST	*Barbara*
98484	76084	BR 4MT	
98488	4588	GWR 4575	
98494	65894	LNER J27	
98498	80098	BR 4MT	
98500	45000	LMS 5MT	
98502	7802	GWR 78xx	*Bradley Manor*
98505	45305	LMS 5MT	*Alderman A E Draper*
98507	45407	LMS 5MT	*Lancashire Fusilier*
98510	45110	LMS 5MT	
98512	7812	GWR 78xx	*Erlestoke Manor*
98519	7819	GWR 78xx	*Hinton Manor*
98525	45025	LMS 5MT	
98526	30925	SR V	*Cheltenham*
98529	73129	BR 5MT	
98530	4930	GWR 49xx	*Hagley Hall*
98531	45231	LMS 5MT	*Sherwood Forester*
98532	44932	LMS 5MT	
98536	4936	GWR 49xx	*Kinlet Hall*
98549	4965	GWR 49xx	*Rood Ashton Hall*
98553	4953	GWR 49xx	*Pitchford Hall*
98560	6960	GWR 6959	*Raveningham Hall*
98564	61264	LNER B1	
98565	42765	LMS 5MT	
98567	44767	LMS 5MT	*George Stephenson*
98568	42968	LMS 5MT	
98571	44871	LMS 5MT	
98572	5972	GWR 49xx	*Olton Hall*
98577	30777	SR N15	*Sir Lamiel*
98596	73096	BR 5MT	
98598	6998	GWR 6959	*Burton Agnes Hall*
98605	62005	LNER K1	
98628	30828	SR S15	
98641	30841	SR S15	
98642	61994	LNER K4	*The Great Marquess*
98690	45690	LMS 6P5F	*Leander*
98693	45593	LMS 6P5F	*Kolhapur*
98696	45596	LMS 6P5F	*Bahamas*
98699	45699	LMS 6P5F	*Galatea*
98700	70000	BR 7P	*Britannia*
98701	34101	SR WC	*Hartland*
98709	53809	SDJR 7F	
98713	70013	BR 7P	*Oliver Cromwell*
98715	46115	LMS 7P	*Scots Guardsman*
98716	34016	SR WC	*Bodmin*
98727	34027	SR WC	*Taw Valley*
98728	5029	GWR 4073	*Nunney Castle*
98729	7029	BR 4073	*Clun Castle*
98746	34046	SR WC	*Braunton*
98750	30850	SR LN	*Lord Nelson*
98751	5051	GWR 4073	*Earl Bathurst*
98767	34067	SR BB	*Tangmere*
98771	60800	LNER V2	*Green Arrow*
98772	34072	SR BB	*257 Squadron*
98780	5080	GWR 4073	*Defiant*
98792	34092	SR WC	*City of Wells*
98800	6000	GWR 60xx	*King George V*
98801	46201	LMS 8P	*Princess Elizabeth*
98802	71000	BR 8P	*Duke of Gloucester*
98803	46203	LMS 8P	*Princess Margaret Rose*
98805	35005	SR MN	*Canadian Pacific*
98809	60009	LNER A4	*Union of South Africa*
98824	6024	GWR 60xx	*King Edward I*
98828	35028	BR MN	*Clan Line*
98829	46229	LMS 8P	*Duchess of Hamilton*
98832	60532	LNER A2	*Blue Peter*
98834	46233	LMS 8P	*Duchess of Sutherland*
98851	48151	LMS 8F	
98857	2857	GWR 28xx	
98863	60163	LNER A1	*Tornado*
98868	60022	LNER A4	*Mallard*
98872	60103	LNER A3	*Flying Scotsman*
98873	48773	LMS 8F	
98898	60007	LNER A4	*Sir Nigel Gresley*
98920	92220	BR 9F	*Evening Star*

Class 89 No.	BR TOPS No.	Type	Name
89100	20050	Class 20	-
89101	20001	Class 20	-
89127	20227	Class 20	-
89151	D9551	Class 14	-
89188	20188	Class 20	-
89200	31018	Class 31	-
89204	26004	Class 26	-
89210	27059	Class 27	-
89212	LT 12	LT	*Sarah Siddons*
89218	D5910	Class 23	-
89223	25173	Class 25	-
89233	25283	Class 25	-
89247	27001	Class 27	-
89254	24054	Class 24	-
89259	25309	Class 25	-
89261	24061	Class 24	-
89262	25262	Class 25	-
89280	31162	Class 31	-
89317	D7017	Class 35	-
89376	D7076	Class 35	-
89400	E27000	Class 77	*Electra*
89401	47401	Class 47	*North Eastern*
89402	50002	Class 50	*Superb*
89403	71001	Class 71	-
89404	44004	Class 44	*Great Gable*
89405	47117	Class 47	-
89412	40012	Class 40	*Aureol*
89413	D1013	Class 52	*Western Ranger*
89415	50015	Class 50	*Valiant*
89416	D1015	Class 52	*Western Champion*
89417	50017	Class 50	*Royal Oak*
89420	45108	Class 45	-
89421	D821	Class 42	*Greyhound*
89422	50021	Class 50	*Rodney*
89423	45125	Class 45	-
89424	D1023	Class 52	*Western Fusilier*
89427	50027	Class 50	*Lion*
89431	50031	Class 50	*Hood*
89432	D832	Class 42	*Onslaught*
89435	40135	Class 40	-
89440	45133	Class 45	-
89441	D1041	Class 52	*Western Prince*
89442	47192	Class 47	-
89443	50042	Class 50	*Triumph*
89444	50044	Class 50	*Exeter*
89445	40145	Class 40	-
89448	D1048	Class 52	*Western Lady*
89449	50049	Class 50	*Defiance*
89453	45041	Class 45	*Royal Tank Regiment*
89460	45060	Class 45	*Sherwood Forester*
89462	D1062	Class 52	*Western Courier*
89466	47449	Class 47	-
89472	46035	Class 46	*Ixion*
89500	55022	Class 55	*Royal Scots Grey*
89502	55002	Class 55	*The King's Own Yorkshire Light Infantry*
89503	81002	Class 81	-
89509	55009	Class 55	*Alycidon*
89515	55015	Class 55	*Tulyar*
89516	55016	Class 55	*Gordon Highlander*
89519	55019	Class 55	*Royal Highland Fusilier*
89523	DP1	Proto	*Deltic*
89535	83012	Class 83	-
89561	85101	Class 85	-

Below: *London Transport electric loco No. 12* Sarah Siddons *is authorised to operate over Network Rail and several years ago actually operated on Southern Region electrified lines under its own power. The loco is shown, with the LU 4-TC set, passing Chalfont and Latimer during a gala on the Metropolitan line in summer 2019.* **Antony Christie**

With the introduction of modern traction from the 1950s a number of different methods of multiple operation were introduced, covering the different control principles of locomotives, for example those using electro-pneumatic or electro-magnetic systems.

Six main systems are in operation today:

Blue Star ★ using the electro-pneumatic system and fitted to Classes 20, 25, 31, 33, 37, 40 and 73.

Green Spot ● a unique system installed on some Class 47s operated by the freight sector.

Orange Square ■ an English Electric system used only on the Class 50s.

Red Diamond ♦ a 1970s system developed for the modern freight locos of Classes 56 and 58.

In addition to the above coded systems, the American-developed main-line locos of Classes 59, 66, 67 and 70 use the US standard AAR (Association of American Railroads) system. Direct Rail Services (DRS) has also developed a unique system, which is installed on some of the company's Class 20, 37, 47 and 57 locos.

A number of locomotives have either been built with or modified to incorporate Time Division Multiplex (TDM) remote operation equipment, which uses coach lighting-type Railway Clearing House (RCH) nose-end jumper cables.

Some of the surviving first generation DMMU sets carry a **Blue Square** ■ multiple operation system.

Details of the main coupling systems in operation in the UK are included in the accompanying illustrations.

Above: *Class 59 and 66 front-end layout (non-DB-S operated). 1-Coupling hook, 2-Coupling shackle, 3-Air brake pipe (red), 4-Main reservoir pipe (yellow), 5-Buffer, 6-Association of American Railroads (AAR) jumper socket. No. 66726 is illustrated.* **CJM**

Above: *Standard coupling arrangement to be found on many classes of UK loco. 1-Electric Train Supply (ETS) jumper socket, 2-Main reservoir air pipe (yellow), 3-Vacuum brake pipe, 4-Coupling hook and shackle, 5-Air brake pipe (red), 6-Electric Train Supply (ETS) jumper cable. No. 47580 is illustrated.* **CJM**

Above: *The unique front-end layout of the Royal Mail Class 325. 1-Brake pipe (red), 2-Main reservoir pipe (yellow), 3-Electric Train Supply (ETS) socket, 4-Time Division Multiplex (TDM) jumper socket, 5-Drophead buckeye coupling, 6-Electric Train Supply (ETS) cable.* **CJM**

Couplings

Coupling Codes & Couplings

Dropheaded Dellner Coupling

Above: *Following the introduction of Virgin Trains 'Voyager' and 'Pendolino' stock, a fleet of 16 Class 57/3s was introduced with drophead Dellner couplers and cabling to provide 'hotel power'. The coupling is seen in this illustration in the raised position. 1-Electric Train Supply (ETS) jumper socket, 2-Main reservoir pipe (yellow), 3-Air brake pipe (red), 4-Coupling hook, 5-Dellner coupling face, 6-Electric Train Supply (ETS) jumper cable.* **CJM**

BSI Coupling

Above: *With the birth of modern multiple unit trains came the Bergische Stahl Industrie (BSI) automatic coupling, first seen in the UK on the Tyne & Wear Metro vehicles in 1978. The modern generation of UK DMUs now concentrates on the Compact BSI coupler with a CK2 coupling interface. The couplers are engaged by the compression of the two coupling faces, which completes a physical connection and also opens a watertight cover to an electrical connection box. The full train air connection is made during the coupling compression process. The coupling is completed by the driver pressing a 'couple' button in the driving cab. 1-Emergency air connection, 2-Coupling face, 3-Electric connection (behind plate), 4-Air connection. The coupling shown is on a Class 166.* **CJM**

Tightlock with Drum Connection

Above: *The Tightlock coupler is a derivative of the Association of American Railroads (AAR) Type H coupler, later under the control of the American Public Transportation Association (APTA). A modified Type H coupler was introduced in the UK from the early 1970s and has become a standard fitting on many of the later BR and several post-privatisation EMUs. The UK Tightlock design can be supplied with or without an electrical connection box and with or without a pneumatic connection. This view shows a fully automated version as fitted to the 'Networker' fleet. Attachment is achieved by driving the two vehicles together, which physically connects them, while a 'roll-cover' box opens to connect electric and pneumatic services. 1-Emergency air connector, 2-Manual release handle, 3-Semi-rotary electric/pneumatic cover, 4-Physical coupler.* **CJM**

Tightlock with Nose End Connections

Above: *The BR Southern Region-designed Class 455 and 456 units have a semi-automatic Tightlock used for physical connections, while air and electrical connections are made by waist-height flexible pipes. 1-Main reservoir pipe (yellow), 2-Control jumper, 3-Tightlock coupler, 4-Couple/Uncouple drum switch, 5-Manual release handle, 6-Control jumper receptacle.* **CJM**

Dellner Coupling with Drum Connector

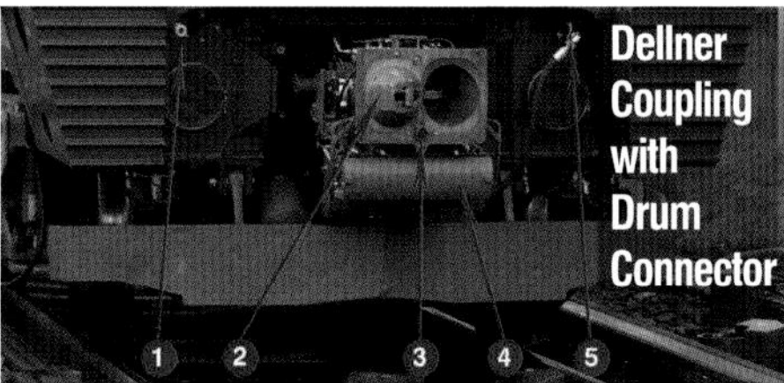

Above: *Dellner couplers have become the standard in the UK and much of Europe; these are fully automatic and come in various forms. 1-Emergency air supply, 2-Dellner coupling plate, 3-Pneumatic connection, 4-Roll-cover to electrical connections, 5-Air supply. Coupling of a Class 360 is illustrated.* **CJM**

Above: *A large number of different designs of Dellner couplers exist on UK rolling stock. Some feature full automatic operation including pneumatic and electrical connections, while others only provide physical coupling. This view shows a pair of 'Voyager' units coupled together with Dellner couplers. The electrical connection box is above the physical coupler. After trains are 'pushed' together the driver operates a 'couple' button in the cab to complete the attachment. Uncoupling is achieved by the driver pressing an 'uncouple' button and driving the trains apart.* **CJM**

Right: *The Virgin Trains 'Pendolino' stock uses Dellner couplers with a rotary covered electrical connector plate above. These couplers are supplemented by electric train supply connections on either side to provide 'hotel power' to Class 390 sets from attached Class 57 locos. 1-Electric Train Supply (ETS) socket, 2-Emergency air connector, 3-Electrical connector plate under semi-rotary cover, 4-Dellner physical coupler, 5-Pneumatic connections. In normal use the Dellner coupler on 'Pendolino' stock is covered by a front fairing.* **CJM**

Above: *Under the front-end fairing of the Eurostar Class 373 stock a standard Scharfenberg coupler is located for assistance purposes and shunting. No electrical provision is made and the couplers are seldom used. 1-Scharfenberg coupling face, 2-Pneumatic connections, 3-Manual uncoupling handle.* **CJM**

Above: *In as-installed condition and having never been coupled to another set, a Class 380 Scharfenberg coupler is viewed, showing the auto opening electrical connection box above. 1-Electrical connection box, 2-Coupling face plate, 3-Pneumatic connection.* **CJM**

Emergency HST Bar Coupling

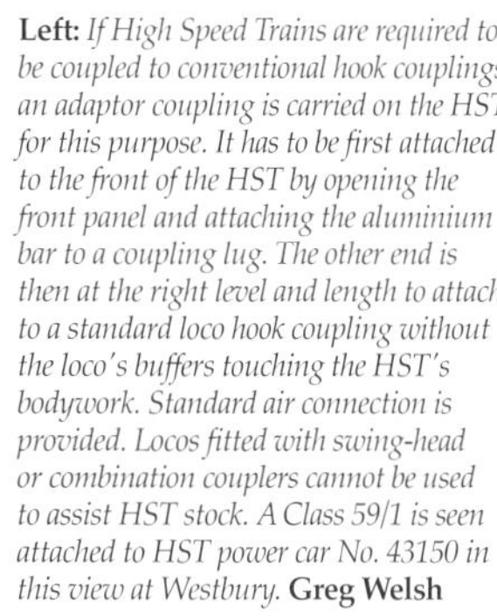

Left: *If High Speed Trains are required to be coupled to conventional hook couplings an adaptor coupling is carried on the HST for this purpose. It has to be first attached to the front of the HST by opening the front panel and attaching the aluminium bar to a coupling lug. The other end is then at the right level and length to attach to a standard loco hook coupling without the loco's buffers touching the HST's bodywork. Standard air connection is provided. Locos fitted with swing-head or combination couplers cannot be used to assist HST stock. A Class 59/1 is seen attached to HST power car No. 43150 in this view at Westbury.* **Greg Welsh**

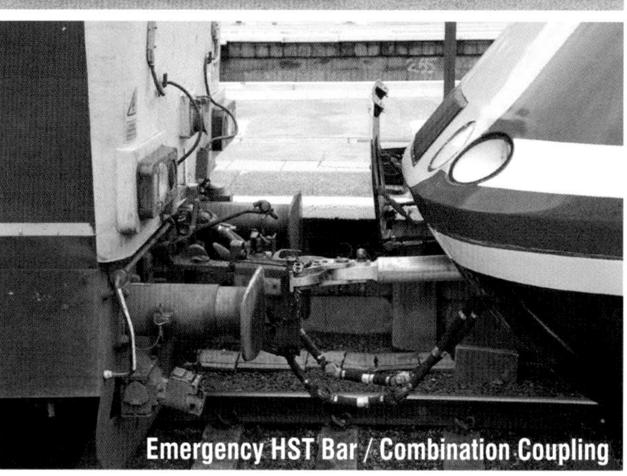

Emergency HST Bar / Combination Coupling

Left: *With the introduction of combination couplings on Class 66s and 67s and the deployment of Class 67s as East Coast 'Thunderbirds' came the need to develop a revised HST bar coupling, which could attach to the extended jaw of the auto coupler. To use this coupling method, a pair of short extension air hoses are required to bridge the increased space between the HST and Class 67 hoses. The Class 67 to HST coupling using the auto coupler and extension hoses is shown with the attachment of No. 67030 and East Coast power car No. 43315.* **Antony Christie**

DBS Combination Coupler

Left Below: *All DBS Class 66s (except Nos. 66001/002) and all Class 67s are fitted with swing-head combination couplers allowing attachment to other like-fitted locos or rolling stock using a knuckle coupling. Two Class 66s are seen here attached using the swing-head coupler. Note that the buffers do not touch and that all traction and braking forces are transmitted through the coupler. Standard buffer-beam air connections are provided on one main reservoir and one brake pipe. The auto coupler can be disconnected by using the white uncoupling handle seen on the left.* **Antony Christie**

Right: *Front end equipment positions for the latest 'state-of-the-art Class 88 electro-diesel locomotives now in service with DRS. 1: Air warning horns located behind grille panel, 2: High level marker light, 3: Multiple control jumper connections (cable for use is carried in engine compartment). 4: Light cluster (headlight, marker and tail light), 5: Lamp bracket, 6: Electric Train Supply (ETS) jumper cable, 7: Main reservoir pipe (yellow), 8: Air brake pipe (red), 9: Coupling shackle and hook, 10: Electric Train Supply jumper socket, 11: Adjustable height obstacle deflector plate.* **CJM**

Right: *Class 800, 801 and 802 Dellner coupling, showing bi-parting doors in open position. Above the physical 'cup and cone' coupling is the electrical connection box, at the base of the coupling plate is a main reservoir pipe connection. A shore electrical connection socket (orange) is on the far side.* **CJM**

Livery Codes

Code	Description
AGI	Aggregate Industries - green, silver and green
AIN	Aggregate Industries - blue
ALS	Alstom Transportation
ANG	Anglia - mid blue
ANN	Anglia - turquoise/white with Greater Anglia branding
ATE	Arriva Trains Executive - turquoise/cream with branding
ATT	Arriva Trains Wales - Welsh Government
ATW	Arriva Trains Wales - turquoise/cream
AVC	Avanti West Coast
AWT	Abellio - white Greater Anglia
AWW	Avanti West Coast white
AXC	Arriva Cross Country - brown, silver, pink
AZU	LNER 'Azuma' red and white
BBR	Balfour Beatty Rail - blue/white
BLG	Blue and grey
BLK	Black
BLL	BR Rail Blue with large logo
BLU	Blue
BLW	Carillion Rail - blue/white
BOM	Bombardier Transportation
BPM	Blue Pullman - Nankin blue and white
BRD	BR Departmental mid-grey
BRT	BR Trainload two-tone grey
C2C	c2c - blue/pink
CAL	Caledonian Railway
CAS	Caledonian Sleepers
CAR	Carmine and cream
CEN	Central Trains - blue and two-tone green
CHC	Chocolate and cream
CIV	BR Civil Engineers - grey and yellow
COL	Colas - orange, lime green and black
CON	Continental Rail - light/mid-blue
COR	Corus Steel - light blue or yellow
COX	Connex - white and yellow
CRG	Chiltern Railways - grey
CRO	CrossRail
CRR	Chitern Railways local revised
CRW	Chiltern Railways - white/blue
CTL	Central Trains - blue, green with yellow doors
CWR	Cotswold Rail - silver with branding
DBB	DB-Schenker - light blue
DBM	DB-Schenker - maroon
DBS	DB-Schenker - red
DCG	Devon & Cornwall Railways - green
DCN	Devon & Cornwall Railways - grey
DRB	Direct Rail Services - blue
DRC	Direct Rail Services - blue 'Compass' branding
DRO	Direct Rail Services - Ocean Liner blue
DRS	Direct Rail Services - blue
DRU	Direct Rail Services - unbranded blue
ECG	East Coast - grey
ECR	European Cargo Rail - grey
ECS	East Coast - silver
ECW	East Coast - white
ECT	East Coast - branded National Express livery
EMT	East Midlands Trains - white, blue, swirl cab ends
EPR	Europhoenix - red/silver with ROG brand
EPS	European Passenger Services
EPX	Europhoenix - red/silver
ETF	ETF Rail - yellow with green band
EUB	Eurostar new style - blue/grey
EUS	Eurostar - white, yellow and blue
EWE	DBS Executive
EWS	English Welsh & Scottish - red with gold band
FER	Fertis - grey with branding
FGB	First Great Western - blue
FGF	First Group - GBRf (Barbie)
FGL	First Great Western - local lines
FGS	First Group ScotRail with EWS branding
FGW	First Great Western - as FST with FGW branding
FHT	First Hull Trains - as FST with Hull Trains branding
FLG	Freightliner - green unbranded
FLP	Freightliner - green/yellow - PowerHaul
FLR	Freightliner - green/yellow - original
FLU	Freightliner - green/yellow - unbranded
FLY	Freightliner - grey
FNA	First livery with National Express East Anglia branding
FSN	Northern branded First Group
FST	First Group - dark blue, pink and white swirl
FSW	First Group - green and white with gold branding
FTN	First TransPennine - silver, blue and mauve
FTP	First TransPennine - as FST with FTP branding
GAR	Greater Anglia Railways
GAZ	Greater Anglia Railways - Renatus
GBE	GB Railfreight - Europorte branding
GBF	GB Railfreight - swirl
GBN	GB Railfreight/Eurotunnel new livery
GBR	GB Railfreight - blue
GBU	GB Railfreight - swirl (no First branding)
GEM	Gemini Rail Services
GLX	Glaxochem - grey, blue and black
GRN	Green
GRY	Grey
GSW	Great Scottish & Western Railway - maroon
GTO	Grand Central Railway - black with orange
GWG	Great Western - green
GWR	Great Western Railway - green
GYF	Genesee & Wyoming / Freightliner - orange
HAN	Hanson
HEC	Heathrow Connect - grey, orange
HEL	Heathrow Connect - Terminal 4 'Link'
HEX	Heathrow Express - silver, grey
HNR	Harry Needle Railroad - yellow/grey
HS1	High Speed 1 - blue with powder blue doors
HUN	Hunslet
ICS	InterCity Swallow
IND	Industrial colours of operator

INT InterCity - two-tone grey offset with red and white body band
JAR Jarvis - maroon
KBR Knorr Bremse Rail - blue, white, green
LAF Lafarge Aggregates - green/white
LHL Loadhaul Freight - black and orange
LLB Large Logo Blue
LMI London Midland - grey, green and black
LNE LNER white/red
LNR LNER Red (ex Virgin)
LNW West Midlands Trains LNW branding
LOG London Overground - white and blue/orange
LON London Overground - New style
LUL London Underground - red
MAI MainTrain - blue with branding
MAL Malcolm Rail
MAR Maroon
MER Merseyrail - silver and yellow
MIM DB/Maritime Intermodal blue
MLF Mainline Freight - aircraft blue
MLG Mainline Freight - branded double grey
MML Midland Main Line - turquoise/white
MRS Mutares Rail Services
MSC Mediterranean Shipping Company
NBP Northern Belle Pullman - cream/umber
NE2 National Express with c2c branding
NGE First Great Eastern - grey/blue with cab end swirl, branded National Express
NRE Northern Rail - Electric
NNR New Northern Rail - blue/white
NOM Northern Rail - blue Metro branded
NOR Northern Rail - blue, purple, grey
NOU Northern Rail - unbranded
NRL Network Rail - yellow with branding
NSE Network SouthEast - red, white and blue
NUB Northern Rail blue - unbranded ScotRail
NWT North West Trains - dark blue
GAR National Express East Anglia (now Abellio)
NXU National Express unbranded white/grey
ONE One Anglia - mid-blue (now Abellio)
ORA One Railway with Greater Anglia branding
ORG HNRC - orange
PTR Porterbrook
PUL Pullman - umber/cream
QOS Queen of Scots Pullman
RFD Railfreight Distribution
RFE Railfreight - grey with EWS branding
RFG Railfreight - grey
RFI Railfreight International
RFP Railfreight with Petroleum branding
RFT BR Railfreight - grey, red and yellow, with large logo and numbers
RIV Riviera Trains - maroon
RML Royal Mail Limited - red
ROG Rail Operations Group - branding
ROZ Rail Operations Group - blue with flash
ROY Royal Train - claret
RTB Railtrack - blue
RTK Railtrack - grey/brown
SCC Strathclyde - carmine and cream (some with turquoise band)
SCE Stagecoach - white with East Midlands branding original
SCF Stagecoach - white with East Midlands branding modified
SCI ScotRail Intercity
SCR Scottish Railways - blue with Saltire
SCS Serco Caledonian Sleepers
SCT ScotRail Caledonian Sleepers - mauve/white
SCQ Scottish Railways - White
SEB South Eastern Trains - blue
SEC Serco
SET South Eastern Trains - white with branding
SGK Southern Gatwick Express - blue, white and red with swirl ends
SIL Silver
SKL Silverlink London Overground, SLK with London Overground branding
SLF Silverlink, with First Great Western branding
SLK Silverlink - mauve, green and white
SNF Railfreight grey with SNCF branding
SNT SNCF domestic on Eurostar - silver, white and yellow
SOU Southern - white, black and green
SPL Special livery
SRB Scotrail blue
STN Stansted Express
SWM South West Trains - main-line white and blue
SWN South West Trains - main-line white (modified)
SWO South West Trains - outer-suburban blue
SWR South Western Railway
SWS South West Trains - suburban red
SWT South West Trains - blue, red, grey
TAT Tata Steel - blue
TES Tesco
TEX TransPennine Express - as FST with TPE brand
TFI Transport for Wales - ATW with TfW branding
TFW Transport for Wales white/red
TGG Transrail - grey with 'T' branding
THM Thameslink - blue, white, yellow
TLF Trainload Freight - grey
TLK Thameslink new
TLL Trainload - grey with Loadhaul branding
TOQ Turquoise, former Arriva Trains Wales
TSO Travaux du Sud Ouest - yellow
TTG Two-tone grey
VIR Virgin - red/grey
VSN VSOE Northern
VWC Virgin West Coast - silver, red, white and black
VWN Virgin West Coast - revised
WAB Wabtec Rail - black
WAG West Anglia Great Northern - purple
WCR West Coast Railway - maroon
WES Wessex Trains - maroon
WET Wessex Trains - silver, maroon/pink doors
WEX Wessex Rail Engineering
WHT White
WMT West Midlands Trains - mauve
YEL Yellow

Operational Pool Codes

Code	Description
ATLO	West Coast Traincare - Locomotives
AWCX	West Coast Railway - Stored locos
COFS	Colas Rail - Class 56
COLO	Colas Rail - Operational locomotives
COLS	Colas Rail - Stored locomotives
COTS	Colas Rail - For refurbishment
DFFT	Freightliner - Restricted duties
DFGC	Freightliner - Class 86/5 trials locomotive
DFGH	Freightliner - Heavy Haul Class 70
DFGI	Freightliner - Class 70
DFHH	Freightliner - Heavy Haul Class 66/6
DFIM	Freightliner - Class 66/5
DFIN	Freightliner - Class 66/5 low emission
DFLC	Freightliner - Class 90
DFLH	Freightliner - Class 47
DFLS	Freightliner - Class 08
DFNC	Freightliner - Class 86/6
DFRT	Freightliner - Class 66 Infrastructure contracts
DFTZ	Freightliner - Stored Class 66
DHLT	Freightliner - Awaiting repairs
EFOO	First Great Western - Class 57
EFPC	First Great Western - HST power cars
EFSH	First Great Western - Class 08
EHPC	CrossCountry Trains - HST power cars
EJLO	London Midland - Class 08
EMPC	East Midlands Trains - HST power cars
EMSL	East Midlands Trains - Class 08
EPXX	Europhoenix - Class 86
GBBR	GBRf - Class 73/9
GBBT	GBRf - Class 66 large fuel tanks
GBCD	GBRf - Class 92 Channel Tunnel
GBCM	GBRf - Class 66 commercial contracts
GBDR	GBRf - Class 66 new ex-DB
GBEB	GBRf - Class 66 Euro large tanks
GBED	GBRf - Class 73/1, 73/2
GBEL	GBRf - Class 66 Euro small tanks
GBET	GBRf - Class 92
GBFM	GBRf - Class 66 modified with RETB
GBHN	GBRf - HNRC locos on loan
GBLT	GBRf - Class 66 small fuel tanks
GBMU	GBRf - Class 66 modified for MU
GBNL	GBRf - Class 66 new ex-NL
GBOB	GBRf - Class 66 ex DB-Cargo
GBRT	GBRf - Class 66 Infrastructure
GBSL	GBRf - Class 92 Caledonian Sleepers
GBST	GBRf - Class 92 Sleeper & C Tunn
GBTG	GBRf - Class 60
GBWM	GBRf - Class 08
GBZZ	GBRf - Stored locomotives
GCHP	Grand Central - HST power cars
GPSS	Eurostar UK - Class 08
GROG	Rail Operations Group - operational locos
HNRL	Harry Needle Railroad - Class 08, 20 hire locos
HNRS	Harry Needle Railroad - Stored locomotives
HTCX	Hanson Traction - Class 56
IANA	Abellio East Anglia - Class 90
IECA	LNER - Class 91
IECP	LNER - HST power cars
LSLO	Loco Services - operational
LSLS	Loco Services - stored
MBDL	Private operators - Diesel traction
PTXX	Eurotunnel - Europorte2 Class 92
QCAR	Network Rail - HST power cars
QETS	Network Rail - Class 97/3
RFSH	Wabtec Rail Doncaster - Class 08
RVLO	Rail Vehicle Engineering Derby - Locos
RVLS	Rail Vehicle Engineering Derby - Stored locos
SROG	Rail Operations Group - stored locos
TTLS	Traditional Traction - Locomotives
WAAC	DB-Cargo - Class 67
WABC	DB-Cargo - Class 67 RETB fitted
WACC	DB-Cargo - Class 67 hire to TfW
WAWC	DB-Cargo - Class 67 hire to TfW
WBAE	DB-Cargo - Class 66 stop/start fitted
WBAR	DB-Cargo - Class 66 RHTT
WBAT	DB-Cargo - Class 66 general
WBBE	DB-Cargo - Class 66 stop/start fitted, RETB
WBBT	DB-Cargo - Class 66 RETB fitted
WBLE	DB-Cargo - Class 66 Lickey banker stop/start
WBLT	DB-Cargo - Class 66 Lickey banker
WBRT	DB-Cargo - Class 66 RHTT general
WBSN	DB-Cargo - Class 66 RHTT general
WCAT	DB-Cargo - Class 60 standard fuel capacity
WCBT	DB-Cargo - Class 60 extended fuel capacity
WDAM	DB-Cargo - Class 59/2
WEAC	DB-Cargo - Class 90 general
WEDC	DB-Cargo - Class 90 hire Virgin
WFMS	DB-Cargo - Class 60 Fleet Management
WGEA	DB-Cargo - Class 66 for Export
WLAN	DB-Cargo - Euro Cargo Rail Class 21
WNTS	DB-Cargo - Stored locos, serviceable
WNXX	DB-Cargo - Stored locos, unserviceable
WNYX	DB-Cargo - Stored locos, parts recovery
WNZX	DB-Cargo - Awaiting disposal
WFAC	DB-Cargo - Class 92 general
WFBC	DB-Cargo - Class 92 HS1 equipped
WFCC	DB-Cargo - Class 92 HS1 equipped DRS
WFDC	DB-Cargo - Class 92 Hire DRS
XHAC	Direct Rail Services - Class 47
XHCE	Direct Rail Services - Class 68 Chiltern
XHCK	Direct Rail Services - Class 57
XHNB	Direct Rail Services - Northern Belle
XHND	Direct Rail Services - Class 37 Network Rail
XHHP	Direct Rail Services - Holding Pool
XHIM	Direct Rail Services - Class 66, Intermodal
XHNC	Direct Rail Services - Nuclear Traffic
XHSS	Direct Rail Services - Stored
XHTP	Direct Rail Services - Class 68 Trans Pennine
XHVE	Direct Rail Services - Class 68
XHVT	Direct Rail Services - Class 57 Thunderbird

■ Pools are given only for locomotive groups which are included in this book. Pool codes for multiple units are not included.

Operator Codes

Code	Operator
AFG	Arlington Fleet Group
ALL	Allelys Heavy Haul
ALS	Alstom
AMS	Amec Spie Rail
ASR	Abellio Scottish Railways
ATW	Arriva Trains Wales
AXC	Arriva Cross Country
AXI	Axiom Rail
BAR	British American Railway
BBR	Balfour Beatty
BHE	Barrow Hill Roundhouse
BOK	Bo'ness & Kinneil
BOM	Bombardier
BRM	Birmingham Railway Mus
BTL	Brush Traction Limited
C2C	c2c Rail
CAR	Carillion
CHS	Crewe Heritage Centre
COL	Colas Rail
CON	Continental Rail (Spain)
COR	Corus Steel
CRW	Chiltern Railways
DBA	DB Arriva
DBR	DB Regio
DBS	DB-Schenker West
DRS	Direct Rail Services
ECR	Euro Cargo Rail (DBS)
ELR	East Lancashire Railway
EMT	East Midlands Trains
ERS	Eastern Rail Services
ETF	ETF Freight (France)
ETL	Electric Traction Ltd
EUR	Eurotunnel
EUS	Eurostar
FDH	Felixstowe Dock & Hbr
FHN	First Hull Trains (new)
FIL	First Island Line
FLR	Freightliner
FSL	Flying Scotsman Railways
FTP	First TransPennine
GBR	GB Railfreight
GEM	Gemini Rail Services
GRP	Grant Rail Plant
GTL	Grand Central Railway
GTR	Govia Thameslink Rly
GWR	Great Western Railway
GWS	Great Western Society
HEC	Heathrow Connect
HEX	Heathrow Express
HIT	Hitachi
HNR	Harry Needle Railroad
IND	Industrial operator
IRY	Ian Riley
JHS	Jeremy Hosking
KBR	Knorr Bremse Rail
KRS	Knights Rail Services
LAF	Lafarge Aggregates
LNW	L&NWR Railway Co
LOG	London Overground
LOR	Loram UK
LUL	London Underground Ltd
MAQ	Macquarie Group
MER	Merseyrail
MHR	Mid-Hants Railway
MoD	Ministry of Defence
MRC	Midland Railway Centre
MRL	Mendip Rail Ltd
NDZ	NedTrains
NOR	Northern Rail
NOT	Northumbria Rail
NRL	Network Rail
NRM	National Railway Mus'm
NVR	Nene Valley Railway
NYM	North Yorkshire Moors Rly
OLD	Old Dalby Test Track
POB	Port of Boston
PUL	Pullman Group
RAF	Railfilms Ltd
RCL	Railcare Ltd
RIV	Riviera Trains
RRS	Ridings Railtours
S4G	Stratford 47 Group
SCR	Scottish Railways
SET	SouthEastern Trains
SIE	Siemens
SLR	St Leonards Rail Eng'g
SNB	Société Nationale des Chemins de fer Belges
SNF	Société Nationale des Chemins de fer Français
SOU	Southern
SRP	Scottish Railway Pres Soc
SVR	Severn Valley Railway
SWR	South West Railway
TfL	Transport for London
TfW	Transport for Wales
TRN	Transfesa
TSO	Travaux du Sud Ouest
TTS	Transmart Trains
VSO	Venice Simplon Orient Exp
VTN	Vintage Trains
VEC	Virgin East Coast
VWC	Virgin West Coast
WAB	Wabtec
WCR	West Coast Railway Co
WMR	West Midlands Trains

DMU and EMU Vehicle Codes

Code	Vehicle
BDMSO	Battery Driving Motor Standard Open
DM	Driving Motor
DMBO	Driving Motor Brake Open
DMBS	Driving Motor Brake Standard
DMCL	Driving Motor Composite Lavatory
DMCO	Driving Motor Composite Open
DMF	Driving Motor First
DMFLO	Driving Motor First Luggage Open
DMRFO	Driving Motor Restaurant First Open
DMS	Driving Motor Standard
DMSL	Driving Motor Standard Lavatory
DMSO	Driving Motor Standard Open
DTCO	Driving Trailer Composite Open
DTPMV	Driving Trailer Parcels Mail Van
DTSO	Driving Trailer Standard Open
MBC	Motor Brake Composite
MBSO	Motor Brake Standard Open
MC	Motor Composite
MFL	Motor First Lavatory
MPMV	Motor Parcels Mail Van
MS	Motor Standard
MSL	Motor Standard Lavatory
MSLRB	Motor Standard Lavatory Restaurant Buffet
MSO	Motor Standard Open
MSRMB	Motor Standard Restaurant Micro Buffet
PTSO	Pantograph Trailer Standard Open
RB	Restaurant Buffet
TBFO	Trailer Brake First Open
TCO	Trailer Composite Open
TFO	Trailer First Open
TPMV	Trailer Parcels Mail Van
TSO	Trailer Standard Open
TSRMB	Trailer Standard Restaurant Micro Buffet

(A) - A Car
(B) - B Car

Depot Codes

Code	Facility	Name	Operator
AB	SD	Aberdeen Guild Street	DBS
AC	CSD	Aberdeen Clayhills	LNE
AD	EMUD	Ashford Hitachi	HIT/SET
AF	T&RSMD	Ashford Chart Leacon	BOM
AH	MoD	Ashchurch	MoD
AK	DMUD	Ardwick	SIE/FTP
AL	DMUD	Aylesbury	CRW
AN	TMD/WRD	Allerton, Liverpool	NOR
AP	TMD	Ashford Rail Plant	BBR
AS	Store	Allelys	ALL
AT	TMD	Various sites	ALS
AZ	TMD	Ashford	BBR
AZ	TMD	Alizay (France)	ECR (DBS)
BA	TMD	Crewe Basford Hall	FLR
BC	MoD	Bicester	MoD
BD	T&RSMD	Birkenhead North	MER
BF	EMUD	Bedford Cauldwell Walk	GTR
BG	SD	Hull Botanic Gardens	NOR
BH	Eng	Barrow Hill Roundhouse	BHE
BI	EMUD	Brighton	GTR
BK	T&RSMD	Barton Hill	LNW
BL	T&RSMD	Crewe Basford Hall	FLR
BM	T&RSMD	Bournemouth	SWR
BN	T&RSMD	Bounds Green	LNE
BO	T&RSMD	Burton	Nemesis
BP	SD	Blackpool CS	NOR
BQ	TMD	Bury	ELR
BR	SD	Bristol Kingsland Road	NRL
BS	TMD	Bescot	DBS
BT	TMD	Bo'ness	BOK
BW	SD	Barrow-in-Furness	NOR
BZ	T&RSMD	St Blazey	DBS
CA	SD	Cambridge Coldhams Ln	AXI
CB	STORE	Crewe Brook Sidings	DBS
CC	T&RSMD	Clacton	GAR
CD	SD	Crewe Diesel	LSL
CE	IEMD	Crewe Electric	DBS
CF	DMUD	Cardiff Canton	PUL
CG	TMD	Crewe Gresty Bridge	DRS
CH	DMUD	Chester	ALS, TFW
CJ	SD	Clapham Junction	SWR
CK	DMUD	Corkerhill	SCR
CL	TMD	Crewe Loco Services	LSL
CO	IEMD	Coquelles (France)	EUR
CP	CARMD	Crewe Carriage Shed	LNW
CQ	T&RSMD	Crewe Railway Age	CHC
CR	SD	Colchester	GAR
CS	T&RSMD	Carnforth	WCR
CT	SD	Cleethorpes	FTP
CV	TMD	Cardiff Canton	TFW
CW	MoD	Caerwent	MoD
CX	Store	Cardiff Tidal	DBS
CY	Store	Crewe Coal/South Yards	DRS/RIV
CZ	TMD	Central Rivers	BOM
DD	SD	Doncaster Wood Yard	DBS
DF	T&RSMD	Rail Vehicle Engineering	RVE
DI	Pres	Didcot Railway Centre	GWS
DM	TMD	Dollands Moor	DBS
DR	TMD	Doncaster Carr IET	HIT
DT	SD	Didcot Triangle	DBS
DV	SD	Dover	SET
DW	SD	Doncaster West Yard	NRL, WAB
DY	T&RSMD	Derby Etches Park	EMR
EA	SD	Earles Sidings	DBS
EC	T&RSMD	Craigentinny (Edinburgh)	LNE
ED	DMUD	Eastfield	SCR
EF	MPVD	Effingham Junction	AMS
EH	SD	Eastleigh	DBS
EM	EMUD	East Ham	c2c
EN	CARMD	Euston Downside	NRL
EU	SD	Euston Station Sidings	FWC
EZ	DMUD	Exeter	FGW
FB	Store	Ferrybridge	DBS
FC*		Fire College (Moreton-in-Marsh)	
FD	Mobile	Diesel loco	FLR
FE	Mobile	Electric loco	FLR
FF	TRSMD	Forest, Brussels	SNCB, NMBS, EUS
FH	TRACK	Frodingham	GRP
FN	Hire	France	ECR
FP	CSD	Ferme Park	VEC
FR	EMUD	Fratton	SWR
FS	Mobile	Diesel Shunter	FLR
FW	SD	Fort William	DBS
FX	TMD	Felixstowe	FDH
GI	EMUD	Gillingham	SET
GP	SD	Grove Park	SET
GW	EMUD	Glasgow Shields	SCR
HA	TMD	Haymarket	SCR
HD	SD	Holyhead	TFW
HE	EMUD	Hornsey	GTR
HF	SD	Hereford	DBS
HG	Store	Hither Green	DBS
HI	TM	Hitchin	BBR
HJ	SD	Hoo Junction	DBS
HM	SD/WRD	Healey Mills	DBS
HT	T&RSMD	Heaton	NOR, GTL
HY	SD	Oxford Hinksey Yard	NRL
IL	T&RSMD	Ilford	GAR
IM	SD	Immingham	DBS
IP	SD	Ipswich	FLR
IS	TMD	Inverness	SCR
KC	Store	Carlisle Currock WRD	DBS
KD	SD	Kingmoor Yard	DRS
KK	EMUD	Kirkdale	MER
KM	TMD	Carlisle Kingmoor	DRS
KR	T&RSMD	Kidderminster	SVR
KT	MoD	Kineton	MoD
KY	SD/WRD	Knottingley	DBS
LA	T&RSMD	Laira	FGW
LB	Eng	Loughborough	BTL
LD	TMD	Leeds Midland Road	FLR
LE	T&RSMD	Landore	FGW
LG	T&RSMD	Longsight Electric	ALT
LH	Eng	LH Group	LHG
LL	CSD	Liverpool Edge Hill	ALS
LM	Store	Long Marston	-
LO	T&RSMD	Longsight Diesel	NOR/TPE
LP*	Eng	EMD Longport	EMD
LR	Eng	Leicester	UKR
LU	MoD	Ludgershall	MoD

LW	MoD	Longtown	MoD
LY	T&RSMD	Le Landy (Paris)	SNCF, EUS
MA	CARMD	Manchester International	ALS/FTP
MD	TMD	Merehead	MRL
MG	TMD	Margam	DBS
MH	SD	Millerhill	DBS
ML	SD	Motherwell	DRS
MM	Store	Moreton-in-Marsh	-
MN	DMUD	Machynlleth	TFW
MQ	Store	Meldon Quarry	BAR
MR	SD	March	GBR
MW	MoD	Marchwood Military Port	MoD
MY	SD/Store	Mossend Yard	DBS, FLR
NA	Eng	Newton Aycliffe	HIT
NB	SD	New Brighton	MER
NC	T&RSMD	Norwich Crown Point	GAR
ND	Works	NedTrans, Tilburg	NDZ
NG	T&RSMD	New Cross Gate	LOL
NH	DMUD	Newton Heath	NOR
NL	T&RSMD	Neville Hill (Leeds)	EMR, LNE
NM	SD	Nottingham Eastcroft	EMR
NN	EMUD	Northampton, Kings Heath	SIE, WMR
NT	EMUD	Northam	SIE, SWR
NY	T&RSMD	Grosmont	NYM
OC	T&RSMD	Old Oak Common	CRO
OD	Eng	Old Dalby	ALS
OH	EMUD	Old Oak Common Electric	SIE
ON	SD	Orpington	SET
OX	CSD	Oxford Carriage Sidings	FGW
OY	CARMD	Oxley	ALS
PB	SD	Peterborough	DBS
PC	TRSMD	Polmadie	ALS
PE	SD	Peterborough Nene	GTR
PF	SD	Peak Forest	DBS
PH	SD	Perth	SCR
PM	TRSMD	St Philip's Marsh (Bristol)	FGW
PN	SD	Preston Station	NOR
PN	TMD	Poznan (Poland)	ECR (DBS)
PQ	SD	Harwich Parkeston Quay	DBS
PT	SD	Peterborough	GBR
PY	MoD	Shoeburyness (Pigs Bay)	MoD
PZ	TRSMD	Penzance (Long Rock)	FGW
RE	EMUD	Ramsgate	SET
RG	DMUD	Reading	FGW
RH	SD	Redhill	DBS
RL	TRSMD	Ropley	MHR
RO	SD	Rotherham Steel	DBS
RU	TMD	Rugby Rail Plant	GRP
RY	EMUD	Ryde	SWR
SA	DMUD	Salisbury	SWR
SB	TMD	Shrewsbury	NOR
SE	TRSMD	St Leonards	SLR
SG	EMUD	Slade Green	SET
SH	CARMD	Southall Railway Centre	WCR
SI	EMUD	Soho	WMT
SJ	TRSMD	Stourbridge Junction	WMT
SK	TRSMD	Swanwick	MRC
SL	TRSMD	Stewarts Lane	DBS, VSO, GTR
SM	SP	Sheringham	NOR
SN	SD	Shoeburyness	c2c
SP	CRDC	Springs Branch	DBS
SQ	SD	Stockport	NOR
ST	SD	Southport	MER
SU	TRSMD	Selhurst	GTR
SX	SD	Shrewsbury	TFW
SZ	TMD	Southampton Maritime	FLR
TB	TMD	Three Bridges	GTR
TE	TMD	Thornaby/Tees Yard	TLK
TF	SD	Orient Way	GAR
TG	SD	Tonbridge	GBR
TI	TRSMD	Temple Mills	EUS
TJ	TMD	Tavistock Junction	COL
TM	SD	Tyseley Loco Works	BRM
TN	SD	Taunton Fairwater	NRL
TO	TMD	Toton	DBS
TS	DMUD	Tyseley	WMR
TT	Store	Toton Training Compound	DBS
TY	Store	Tyne Yard	DBS
VI	SD	Victoria	SET
VR	SD	Aberystwyth	TFW
VZ	EMUD	Strawberry Hill	SIE, SWR
WA	SD	Warrington Arpley	DBS
WB	TRSMD	Wembley	ALS
WD	EMUD	East Wimbledon	SWR
WE	SD	Willesden Brent	DBS
WF	SD	Wansford	NVR
WH	Eng	Whatley	MRL
WK	SD	West Kirby	MER
WN	EMUD	Willesden	BOM
WO	TMD	Wolsingham	WER
WP	SD	Worksop	DBS
WS	SD	Worcester	WMR
WS	Store	Worksop	HNR
WW	SD	West Worthing	GTR
WY	SD/CSD	Westbury Yard	DBS
WZ*	TRSMD	Washwood Heath	HAN
XW	TMD	Crofton	BOM
XX	-	Exported	-
YK	DMUD	Siemens York	SIE, FTP
YL	TMD	York Leeman Road	JAR, FLF
YM	Store	National Railway Museum	NRM
YN	SD	York North Yard	DBS
YO	SD	Yoker	SCR
ZA	Eng	RTC Derby	SER, NRL
ZB	Eng	Doncaster	WAB
ZC	Eng	Crewe	BOM
ZD	Eng	Derby Litchurch Lane	BOM
ZE	Eng	Washwood Heath	COL
ZG	Eng	Eastleigh Works	KRS
ZI	Eng	Ilford	BOM
ZK	Eng	Kilmarnock	BTL
ZL	Eng	Cardiff Canton	PUL
ZN	Eng	Wolverton	GRS
ZE	Eng	York	NRL
ZS	Eng	Locotech Wakefield	BAR
ZW	Eng	Stoke-on-Trent (Marcroft)	AXI
WZ		Warsaw (Poland)	DBS
3M*		3M Industries, Bracknell	

* Unofficial code

Owner Codes

Code	Owner
201	20189 Ltd (Michael Owen)
3RL	345 Rail Leasing
AEA	AEA Rail Technology
ALS	Alstom
ANG	Angel Trains
ATW	Arriva Trains Wales
AUT	Arriva UK Trains
BAA	British Airports Authority
BCC	Bridgend County Council
BEA	Beacon Rail
BOM	Bombardier
BOT	Bank of Tokyo (Mitsubishi)
BRO	Brodie Engineering
BTM	BTMU Capital Corp
C20	Class 20 Locomotive Ltd
CBR	CB Rail
CCC	Cardiff County Council
COL	Colas Rail
CRW	Chiltern Railways
CWR	Cotswold Rail
DBR	DB Regio
DBS	DB-Schenker West
DBS/T	DB-Schenker/Transfesa
DRS	Direct Rail Service
ECR	Euro Cargo Rail (DBS)
ECT	ECT Main Line Rail
EMT	East Midlands Trains
ETL	Electric Traction Ltd
EU2	Eurotunnel Europorte2
EUR	Eurotunnel
EUS	Eurostar
EVL	Eversholt Leasing
FGP	First Group
FLF	Fastline Freight
FLR	Freightliner
FOS	Foster Yeoman
GBR	GB Railfreight
GEM	Gemini Rail Services
GTL	Grand Central Railway Ltd
HAN	Hanson Traction
HEC	Hunslet Engine Co
HBS	Halifax-Bank of Scotland
HJA	Howard Johnson Assoc's
HNR	Harry Needle Railroad
IRY	Ian Riley
JAR	Jarvis
KBR	Knorr Bremse Rail
KRS	Knights Rail Services
LOM	Lombard Finance
LOR	Loram UK
MAG	Macquarie Euro Rail
NRL	Network Rail
NYM	North Yorkshire Moors Rly
PTR	Porterbrook
QWR	QW Rail Leasing
RCL	Railcare Limited
RIV	Riviera Trains
RML	Royal Mail
RMS	RMS Locotech
RTR	RT Rail
S4G	Stratford Class 47 Group
SCS	Serco Caledonian Sleepers
SEC	Serco
SIE	Siemens
SNF	Société Nationale des Chemins de fer Français
SOU	Southern (Govia)
SWT	South Western Railway
TTS	Transmart Trains
UKG	UK Government
URL	UK Rail Leasing
VTN	Vintage Trains
WAB	Wabtec
WCR	West Coast Railway Co
WMT	West Midlands Trains
WYP	West Yorkshire PTE

Preserved site codes

Code	Site
ACL	AC Locomotive Group
ALY	Allelys, Studley
APF	Appleby-Frodingham RPS
AVR	Avon Valley Railway
BAT	Battlefield Line
BEL	5BEL Trust Barrow Hill
BHR	Barrow Hill Roundhouse
BIR	Barry Island Railway
BKR	Bo'ness & Kinneil Rail'y
BLU	Bluebell Railway
BRC	Buckinghamshire Railway
BRM	Birmingham Rly Mus
BVR	Bridgend Valleys Railway
BWR	Bodmin & Wenford Rly
CAN	Canton (Pullman Rail)
CHS	Chasewater Railway
COL	Colne Valley Railway
C4P	Class 40 Preservation Soc
CPR	Chinnor & Princes Risborough Railway
CRB	Caledonian Railway
CRT	Cambrian Railway Trust
CVR	Churnet Valley Railway
CWR	Cholsey & Wallingford Rly
DAR	Dartmoor Railway
DEE	Royal Deeside Railway
DER	Derwent Valley Railway
DFR	Dean Forest Railway
DID	Didcot Railway Centre
EAR	East Anglian Rly Mus
ECC	Ecclesbourne Valley Rly
EDR	Eden Valley Railway
EHC	Elsecar Heritage Centre
EHD	Eastleigh DBS Depot
EKR	East Kent Railway
ELR	East Lancashire Railway
EMB	Embsay Steam Railway
EPO	Epping and Ongar Rly
FHL	Fawley Hall (private)
FIN	Finmere Station
GCN	Great Central Railway (N)
GCR	Great Central Railway
GKR	Graham Kirk Rail
GWI	Gwili Railway
GWR	Glouces Warwick Rly
HAD	Hastings Diesels
IOW	Isle of Wight Railway
IVT	Ivatt Diesel Preservation
KEI	Keith & Dufftown Rly
KES	Kent & East Sussex Rly
KIN	MoD Kineton
KWV	Keighley & Worth Valley
LAN	Llangollen Railway
LDL	Lavender Line
LHG	LH Group Services
LHR	Lakeside & Haverthwaite
LNW	London & North Western
LWR	Lincolnshire Wolds Rly
MET	Methill (Private)
MFM	Mangapps Farm Railway
MHR	Mid Hants Railway
MID	Middleton Railway
MLM	Motorail, Long Marston
MNF	Mid-Norfolk Railway
MOR	Moreton-on-Lugg
MRC	Middleton Railway
MSM	Mus of Science & Indu'y
MSR	Midsomer Norton
NHD	Newton Heath Depot
NIR	Northamptonshire Ironstone Railway
NLR	Northampton & Lamport Rly
NNR	North Norfolk Railway
NRM	National Railway Mus
NYM	North Yorkshire Moors Rly
PBR	Pontypool & Blaenavon Rly
PDR	Paignton & Dartmouth Rly
PRL	Peak Rail
PVR	Plym Valley Railway
RAC	Railway Age, Crewe
RAM	Rampart, Derby
RHW	Rushden, Higham & Wellingborough Rly
RIB	Ribble Steam Railway
RIP	Rippingdale Station
ROW	Rowley Mill
RST	Rushden Station
SEL	St Leonards Railway Eng
SLN	Stewarts Lane Depot
SPV	Spa Valley Railway
SRC	Stainmore Railway Co
STR	Strathspey Railway
SVR	Severn Valley Railway
SWI	Swindon & Cricklade Railway
SWN	Swanage Railway
TEB	Friends of 502 Group, Tebay
TEL	Telford Horsehay Steam Trust
THK	Throckmorton Airfield
TLW	Tyseley Locomotive Works
TIT	Titley Junction
TSR	Telford Steam Railway
TYN	North Tyneside Railway
VBR	Vale of Berkeley Railway
VOG	Vale of Glamorgan Railway
WAS	Washwood Heath
WCR	West Coast Railway Co
WED	Weardale Railway
WEN	Wensleydale Railway
WPH	Walthamstow Pump House
WST	West Somerset Railway
XXX	Private unspecified site
YEO	Yeovil Railway Centre

Cross Number Check List

This cross number checklist indicates in which section of the *abc Rail Guide 2020* full details of rolling stock can be found.

Number Cross-Link Codes

Code	Operator
3MP	3M Productions
AFG	Arlington Fleet Group
ALS	Alstom
ASR	Abellio ScotRail
ATC	Arriva Train Care
AXC	Arriva CrossCountry
BAR	British American Railway
BOK	Bo'ness & Kinneil Railway
BOM	Bombardier Transportation
C2C	c2c Railway
COL	Colas
CRW	Chiltern Railways
DBC	DB Cargo
DBR	DB Regio
DRS	Direct Rail Services
ECR	Euro Cargo Rail
EMR	East Midlands Railway
EPX	Europhoenix Ltd
ETL	Electric Traction Ltd
EUR	Eurotunnel / Europorte 2
EUS	Eurostar UK
EXP	Exported
FHT	First Hull Trains
FLR	Freightliner
FSL	Flying Scotsman Railway Ltd
FTP	First TransPennine
GAR	Abellio Greater Anglia
GBR	GB Railfreight
GRS	Gemini Rail Services
GSW	Great Scottish & Western Rly
GTL	Grand Central Railway
GTR	Govia Thameslink Railway
GWR	Great Western Railway
HAN	Hanson Traction
HEX	Heathrow Express
HNR	Harry Needle Railroad Co
IND	Industrial
JHS	Jeremy Hosking
LNE	London North Eastern
LOG	London Overground
LSL	Loco Services Ltd
MER	Merseyrail
MHR	Mid-Hants Railway
NEM	Nemesis Rail
NOR	Northern Railways
NRL	Network Rail Limited
NYM	North Yorkshire Moors Railway
OLS	Off Lease
PUL	Pullman Rail
RAF	Railfilms
RIV	Riviera Trains
RRS	Ridings Railtours
RVE	Rail Vehicle Engineering
S4L	Stratford Class 47 Group
SET	South Eastern Trains
SCS	Serco Caledonian Sleepers
SIE	Siemens
SNF	SNCF (French Railways)
SRP	Scottish Railway Preservation Soc
SUP	Support Coaches
SWR	South Western Railway
TFW	Transport for Wales
TTS	Transmart Trains
URL	UK Rail Leasing
VSO	Venice Simplon Orient Express
VTN	Vintage Trains
VWC	Virgin West Coast
WAB	Wabtec
WCR	West Coast Railway
WMR	West Midlands Railway

Locomotives – Diesel & Electric

Number	Code
❑ 44	FLR
❑ 120	FLR
❑ 9005	EUR
❑ 9007	EUR
❑ 9011	EUR
❑ 9013	EUR
❑ 9015	EUR
❑ 9018	EUR
❑ 9022	EUR
❑ 9024	EUR
❑ 9026	EUR
❑ 9029	EUR
❑ 9033	EUR
❑ 9036	EUR
❑ 9037	EUR
❑ 9701	EUR
❑ 9702	EUR
❑ 9703	EUR
❑ 9704	EUR
❑ 9705	EUR
❑ 9706	EUR
❑ 9707	EUR
❑ 9711	EUR
❑ 9712	EUR
❑ 9713	EUR
❑ 9714	EUR
❑ 9715	EUR
❑ 9716	EUR
❑ 9717	EUR
❑ 9718	EUR
❑ 9719	EUR
❑ 9720	EUR
❑ 9721	EUR
❑ 9722	EUR
❑ 9723	EUR
❑ 9801	EUR
❑ 9802	EUR
❑ 9803	EUR
❑ 9804	EUR
❑ 9806	EUR
❑ 9808	EUR
❑ 9809	EUR
❑ 9810	EUR
❑ 9812	EUR
❑ 9814	EUR
❑ 9816	EUR
❑ 9819	EUR
❑ 9820	EUR
❑ 9821	EUR
❑ 9823	EUR
❑ 9825	EUR
❑ 9827	EUR
❑ 9828	EUR
❑ 9831	EUR
❑ 9832	EUR
❑ 9834	EUR
❑ 9835	EUR
❑ 9838	EUR
❑ 9840	EUR
❑ 01509	CRW
❑ 01551	SIE
❑ 01552	HNR
❑ 01564	HNR
❑ D2019	EXP
❑ D2032	EXP
❑ D2033	EXP
❑ D2036	EXP
❑ D2098	EXP
❑ D2153	EXP
❑ D2156	EXP
❑ D2157	EXP
❑ D2164	EXP
❑ D2216	EXP
❑ D2232	EXP
❑ D2295	EXP
❑ D2432	EXP
❑ D3047	EXP
❑ D3092	EXP
❑ D3094	EXP
❑ D3098	EXP
❑ D3100	EXP
❑ D9534	EXP
❑ 03196	WCR
❑ 03381	WCR
❑ 07007	AFG
❑ 08220	IND
❑ 08296	FLR
❑ 08308	BAR
❑ 08375	IND
❑ 08389	HNR
❑ 08401	GBR
❑ 08405	EMR
❑ 08410	GWR
❑ 08411	IND
❑ 08417	NRL
❑ 08418	WCR
❑ 08423	BAR
❑ 08441	IND
❑ 08442	ATC
❑ 08445	IND
❑ 08447	IND
❑ 08451	ALS
❑ 08454	ALS
❑ 08460	IND
❑ 08472	WAB
❑ 08480	IND
❑ 08483	GWR
❑ 08484	IND
❑ 08485	WCR
❑ 08499	PUL
❑ 08500	HNR
❑ 08502	IND
❑ 08507	RIV
❑ 08511	ATC
❑ 08516	ATC
❑ 08523	BAR
❑ 08525	EMR
❑ 08527	HNR
❑ 08530	FLR
❑ 08531	FLR
❑ 08535	IND
❑ 08536	IND
❑ 08567	AFG
❑ 08568	GRS
❑ 08571	WAB
❑ 08573	BAR
❑ 08575	FLR
❑ 08578	HNR
❑ 08580	IND
❑ 08585	FLR
❑ 08588	BAR
❑ 08591	FLR
❑ 08593	IND
❑ 08596	WAB
❑ 08598	IND
❑ 08600	IND
❑ 08602	BOM
❑ 08611	ALS
❑ 08613	BAR
❑ 08615	WAB

08616	WMR
08617	ALS
08622	BAR
08623	IND
08624	FLR
08629	GRS
08630	HNR
08631	LSL
08632	IND
08641	GWR
08643	FLR
08644	GWR
08645	GWR
08648	BAR
08649	GRS
08650	FLR
08652	FLR
08653	HNR
08663	IND
08669	WAB
08670	IND
08676	HNR
08678	WCR
08682	BOM
08683	IND
08685	HNR
08690	EMR
08691	FLR
08696	ALS
08700	HNR
08701	HNR
08704	IND
08709	IND
08714	HNR
08721	ALS
08724	WAB
08728	IND
08730	GRS
08731	IND
08735	ATC
08737	LSL
08738	IND
08743	IND
08752	IND
08754	BAR
08756	BAR
08757	IND
08762	BAR
08764	WAB
08765	HNR
08774	IND
08780	LSL
08782	IND
08785	FLR
08786	HNR
08787	IND
08788	IND
08790	ALS
08798	HNR
08802	HNR
08805	WMR
08807	IND
08809	IND
08810	ATC
08818	HNR
08822	GWR
08823	IND
08824	HNR
08830	ATC
08834	HNR
08836	GWR
08846	IND
08847	IND
08850	NYM
08853	WAB
08865	HNR
08868	HNR
08870	BAR
08871	WAB
08872	IND
08873	FLR
08874	BAR
08877	HNR
08879	HNR
08885	BAR
08887	ALS
08891	FLR
08892	HNR
08899	EMR
08903	IND
08904	HNR
08905	HNR
08908	EMR
08912	IND
08915	IND
08918	HNR
08921	IND
08922	IND
08924	HNR
08925	GBR
08927	IND
08929	HNR
08933	IND
08934	GBR
08936	BAR
08939	IND
08943	HNR
08947	FLR
08948	EUS
08950	EMR
08954	HNR
08956	NRL
09002	GBR
09006	HNR
09007	LOG
09009	GBR
09014	HNR
09018	HNR
09022	IND
09023	IND
09106	HNR
09201	HNR
09204	ATC
12088	IND
14029	IND
19001	ATE
20016	HNR
20056	HNR
20066	HNR
20081	HNR
20088	HNR
20096	HNR
20107	HNR
20110	HNR
20118	HNR
20121	HNR
20132	HNR
20138	HNR
20142	GBR
20166	HNR
20168	HNR
20189	GBR
20205	C2L
20227	GBR
20311	HNR
20314	HNR
20901	GBR
20903	HNR
20904	HNR
20905	GBR
20906	HNR
21544	ECR
21545	ECR
21546	ECR
21547	ECR
21610	ECR
21611	ECR
25278	NYM
31106	LOR
31128	NEM
31190	BAR
31235	HNR
31285	HNR
31452	BAR
31454	BAR
31459	HNR
31465	HNR
31468	LOR
33025	WCR
33029	WCR
33103	NEM
33207	WCR
37025	COL
37029	HNR
37038	DRS
37057	COL
37059	DRS
37069	DRS
37099	COL
37116	COL
37175	COL
37190	LSL
37198	NRL
37207	COL
37218	DRS
37219	COL
37254	COL
37259	DRS
37401	DRS
37402	DRS
37403	DRS
37405	DRS
37407	DRS
37409	DRS
37418	COL
37419	DRS
37421	COL
37422	DRS
37423	DRS
37424	DRS
37425	DRS
37510	EPX
37516	WCR
37517	WCR
37518	WCR
37601	EPX
37602	DRS
37603	DRS
37604	DRS
37605	DRS
37606	DRS
37607	HNR
37608	ROG
37609	DRS
37610	COL
37611	ROG
37612	HNR
37667	LSL
37668	WCR
37669	WCR
37676	WCR
37685	WCR
37703	DRS
37706	WCR
37710	WCR
37712	WCR
37716	DRS
37800	ROG
37884	ROG
37901	EPX
37905	URL
37906	URL
43003	ASR
43004	GWR
43005	GWR
43009	-
43010	-
43012	ASR
43013	NRL
43014	NRL
43015	ASR
43016	GWR
43017	OLS
43018	ASR
43020	-
43021	ASR
43022	-
43023	-
43024	OLS
43025	OLS
43026	ASR
43027	-
43028	ASR
43029	-
43030	ASR
43031	ASR
43032	ASR
43033	ASR
43034	ASR
43035	ASR
43036	ASR
43037	ASR
43040	GWR
43041	GWR
43042	GWR
43043	EMR
43044	EMR
43045	EMR
43046	EMR
43047	EMR
43048	EMR
43049	EMR
43050	EMR
43052	EMR
43053	OLS
43054	EMR
43055	EMR
43056	OLS
43058	EMR
43059	EMR
43060	EMR
43061	EMR
43062	NRL
43063	GWR
43064	EMR
43066	EMR
43069	OLS
43070	OLS
43071	GWR
43073	EMR
43075	EMR
43076	EMR
43078	OLS
43079	GWR
43081	EMR
43082	EMR
43083	EMR
43086	GWR
43087	OLS
43088	-
43089	EMR
43091	OLS
43092	GWR
43093	GWR

Number	Operator
43094	GWR
43097	GWR
43098	GWR
43122	GWR
43124	ASR
43125	ASR
43126	ASR
43127	ASR
43128	ASR
43129	ASR
43130	ASR
43131	ASR
43132	ASR
43133	ASR
43134	ASR
43135	ASR
43136	ASR
43137	ASR
43138	ASR
43139	ASR
43140	ASR
43141	ASR
43142	ASR
43143	ASR
43144	ASR
43145	ASR
43146	ASR
43147	ASR
43148	ASR
43149	ASR
43150	ASR
43151	ASR
43152	ASR
43153	GWR
43154	GWR
43155	GWR
43156	-
43158	GWR
43159	OLS
43160	-
43161	GWR
43162	-
43163	ASR
43164	ASR
43165	-
43168	ASR
43169	ASR
43170	GWR
43171	-
43172	-
43174	OLS
43175	ASR
43176	ASR
43177	ASR
43179	ASR
43180	-
43181	ASR
43182	ASR
43183	ASR
43185	OLS
43186	GWR
43187	GWR
43188	-
43189	GWR
43190	-
43191	-
43192	-
43193	OLS
43194	GWR
43195	OLS
43196	-
43197	OLS
43198	GWR
43206	LNE
43207	AXC
43208	LNE
43238	LNE
43239	LNE
43251	LNE
43257	LNE
43272	LNE
43274	LNE
43277	LNE
43285	AXC
43290	LNE
43295	LNE
43296	LNE
43299	LNE
43300	LNE
43301	AXC
43302	LNE
43303	AXC
43304	AXC
43305	LNE
43306	LNE
43307	LNE
43308	LNE
43309	LNE
43310	LNE
43311	LNE
43312	LNE
43313	LNE
43314	LNE
43315	LNE
43316	LNE
43317	LNE
43318	LNE
43319	LNE
43320	LNE
43321	AXC
43357	AXC
43366	AXC
43367	LNE
43378	AXC
43384	AXC
43423	EMR
43465	EMR
43467	EMR
43468	EMR
43480	EMR
43484	EMR
45112	NEM
47194	WCR
47237	WCR
47245	WCR
47270	WCR
47355	WCR
47375	EXP
47488	NEM
47492	WCR
47501	LSL
47580	S4G
47593	LSL
47614	LSL
47701	NEM
47703	HNR
47712	LSL
47714	HNR
47715	HNR
47727	GBR
47739	GBR
47744	NEM
47746	WCR
47749	GBR
47760	WCR
47768	WCR
47769	ROG
47772	WCR
47773	VTN
47776	WCR
47786	WCR
47787	WCR
47802	WCR
47804	WCR
47805	LSL
47810	LSL
47811	LSL
47812	ROG
47813	ROG
47815	ROG
47816	LSL
47818	AFG
47826	WCR
47830	FLR
47832	WCR
47841	LSL
47843	ROG
47847	ROG
47848	ROG
47851	WCR
47854	WCR
50007	GBR
50008	BRE
50049	GBR
50050	BRE
56006	URL
56007	GBR
56009	GBR
56018	GBR
56031	GBR
56032	GBR
56037	GBR
56038	GBR
56049	COL
56051	COL
56060	GBR
56065	GBR
56069	GBR
56077	GBR
56078	COL
56081	GBR
56087	COL
56091	BAR
56090	COL
56094	COL
56096	COL
56098	GBR
56101	EXP
56103	BAR
56104	GBR
56105	COL
56106	GBR
56113	COL
56115	EXP
56117	EXP
56128	GBR
56301	EPX
56302	COL
56303	BAR
56311	GBR
56312	GBR
57001	WCR
57002	DRS
57003	DRS
57004	DRS
57005	WCR
57006	WCR
57007	DRS
57008	DRS
57009	DRS
57010	DRS
57011	DRS
57012	DRS
57301	DRS
57302	DRS
57303	DRS
57304	DRS
57305	DRS
57306	DRS
57307	DRS
57308	DRS
57309	DRS
57310	DRS
57311	DRS
57312	DRS
57313	WCR
57314	WCR
57315	WCR
57316	WCR
57601	WCR
57602	GWR
57603	GWR
57604	GWR
57605	GWR
58001	DBC
58004	DBC
58005	DBC
58006	DBC
58007	DBC
58009	DBC
58010	DBC
58011	DBC
58013	DBC
58015	DBC
58016	URL
58017	DBC
58018	DBC
58020	DBC
58021	DBC
58024	DBC
58025	DBC
58026	DBC
58027	DBC
58029	DBC
58030	DBC
58031	DBC
58032	DBC
58033	DBC
58034	DBC
58035	DBC
58036	DBC
58038	DBC
58039	DBC
58040	DBC
58041	DBC
58042	DBC
58043	DBC
58044	DBC
58046	DBC
58047	DBC
58048	URL
58049	DBC
58050	DBC
59001	FLR
59002	FLR
59003	GBR
59004	FLR
59005	FLR
59101	FLR
59102	FLR
59103	FLR
59104	FLR
59201	DBC
59202	DBC
59203	DBC
59204	DBC
59205	DBC
59206	DBC
60001	DBC
60002	GBR
60003	DBC
60004	GBR
60005	DBC
60007	DBC
60008	GBR

Number	Operator
❑ 60009	DBC
❑ 60010	DBC
❑ 60011	DBC
❑ 60012	DBC
❑ 60014	GBR
❑ 60015	DBC
❑ 60017	DBC
❑ 60018	GBR
❑ 60019	DBC
❑ 60020	DBC
❑ 60021	GBR
❑ 60022	DBC
❑ 60024	DBC
❑ 60025	DBC
❑ 60026	GBR
❑ 60027	DBC
❑ 60028	GBR
❑ 60029	DCR
❑ 60030	DBC
❑ 60032	DBC
❑ 60034	DBC
❑ 60035	DBC
❑ 60036	DBC
❑ 60037	DBC
❑ 60038	DBC
❑ 60039	DBC
❑ 60040	DBC
❑ 60043	DBC
❑ 60044	DBC
❑ 60045	DBC
❑ 60046	DCR
❑ 60047	GBR
❑ 60049	DBC
❑ 60051	DBC
❑ 60052	DBC
❑ 60053	DBC
❑ 60054	DBC
❑ 60055	DCR
❑ 60056	GBR
❑ 60057	DBC
❑ 60059	DBC
❑ 60060	DBC
❑ 60062	DBC
❑ 60063	DBC
❑ 60064	DBC
❑ 60065	DBC
❑ 60066	DBC
❑ 60067	DBC
❑ 60069	DBC
❑ 60071	DBC
❑ 60072	DBC
❑ 60073	DBC
❑ 60074	DBC
❑ 60076	GBR
❑ 60077	DBC
❑ 60079	DBC
❑ 60083	DBC
❑ 60084	DBC
❑ 60085	GBR
❑ 60086	DBC
❑ 60087	GBR
❑ 60088	DBC
❑ 60090	DBC
❑ 60091	DBC
❑ 60092	DBC
❑ 60093	DBC
❑ 60094	DBC
❑ 60095	GBR
❑ 60096	GBR
❑ 60097	DBC
❑ 60099	DBC
❑ 60100	DBC
❑ 60500	DBC
❑ 66001	DBC
❑ 66002	DBC
❑ 66003	DBC
❑ 66004	DBC
❑ 66005	DBC
❑ 66006	DBC
❑ 66007	DBC
❑ 66009	DBC
❑ 66010	EXP
❑ 66011	DBC
❑ 66012	DBC
❑ 66013	DBC
❑ 66014	DBC
❑ 66015	DBC
❑ 66017	DBC
❑ 66018	DBC
❑ 66019	DBC
❑ 66020	DBC
❑ 66021	DBC
❑ 66022	EXP
❑ 66023	DBC
❑ 66024	DBC
❑ 66025	DBC
❑ 66026	EXP
❑ 66027	DBC
❑ 66028	EXP
❑ 66029	EXP
❑ 66030	DBC
❑ 66031	DBC
❑ 66032	EXP
❑ 66033	EXP
❑ 66034	DBC
❑ 66035	DBC
❑ 66036	EXP
❑ 66037	DBC
❑ 66038	EXP
❑ 66039	DBC
❑ 66040	DBC
❑ 66042	EXP
❑ 66043	DBC
❑ 66044	DBC
❑ 66045	EXP
❑ 66047	DBC
❑ 66049	EXP
❑ 66050	DBC
❑ 66051	DBC
❑ 66052	EXP
❑ 66053	DBC
❑ 66054	DBC
❑ 66055	DBC
❑ 66056	DBC
❑ 66057	DBC
❑ 66059	DBC
❑ 66060	DBC
❑ 66061	DBC
❑ 66062	EXP
❑ 66063	DBC
❑ 66064	EXP
❑ 66065	DBC
❑ 66066	DBC
❑ 66067	DBC
❑ 66068	DBC
❑ 66069	DBC
❑ 66070	DBC
❑ 66071	EXP
❑ 66072	EXP
❑ 66073	EXP
❑ 66074	DBC
❑ 66075	DBC
❑ 66076	DBC
❑ 66077	DBC
❑ 66078	DBC
❑ 66079	DBC
❑ 66080	DBC
❑ 66082	DBC
❑ 66083	DBC
❑ 66084	DBC
❑ 66085	DBC
❑ 66086	DBC
❑ 66087	DBC
❑ 66088	DBC
❑ 66089	DBC
❑ 66090	DBC
❑ 66092	DBC
❑ 66093	DBC
❑ 66094	DBC
❑ 66095	DBC
❑ 66096	DBC
❑ 66097	DBC
❑ 66098	DBC
❑ 66099	DBC
❑ 66100	DBC
❑ 66101	DBC
❑ 66102	DBC
❑ 66103	DBC
❑ 66104	DBC
❑ 66105	DBC
❑ 66106	DBC
❑ 66107	DBC
❑ 66109	DBC
❑ 66110	DBC
❑ 66111	DBC
❑ 66112	DBC
❑ 66113	DBC
❑ 66114	DBC
❑ 66115	DBC
❑ 66116	DBC
❑ 66117	DBC
❑ 66118	DBC
❑ 66119	DBC
❑ 66120	DBC
❑ 66121	DBC
❑ 66123	EXP
❑ 66124	DBC
❑ 66125	DBC
❑ 66127	DBC
❑ 66128	DBC
❑ 66129	DBC
❑ 66130	DBC
❑ 66131	DBC
❑ 66133	DBC
❑ 66134	DBC
❑ 66135	DBC
❑ 66136	DBC
❑ 66137	DBC
❑ 66138	DBC
❑ 66139	DBC
❑ 66140	DBC
❑ 66142	DBC
❑ 66143	DBC
❑ 66144	DBC
❑ 66145	DBC
❑ 66146	EXP
❑ 66147	DBC
❑ 66148	DBC
❑ 66149	DBC
❑ 66150	DBC
❑ 66151	DBC
❑ 66152	DBC
❑ 66153	EXP
❑ 66154	DBC
❑ 66155	DBC
❑ 66156	DBC
❑ 66157	EXP
❑ 66158	DBC
❑ 66159	EXP
❑ 66160	DBC
❑ 66161	DBC
❑ 66162	DBC
❑ 66163	EXP
❑ 66164	DBC
❑ 66165	DBC
❑ 66166	EXP
❑ 66167	DBC
❑ 66168	DBC
❑ 66169	DBC
❑ 66170	DBC
❑ 66171	DBC
❑ 66172	DBC
❑ 66173	EXP
❑ 66174	DBC
❑ 66175	DBC
❑ 66176	DBC
❑ 66177	DBC
❑ 66178	EXP
❑ 66179	EXP
❑ 66180	EXP
❑ 66181	DBC
❑ 66182	DBC
❑ 66183	DBC
❑ 66185	DBC
❑ 66186	DBC
❑ 66187	DBC
❑ 66188	DBC
❑ 66189	EXP
❑ 66190	EXP
❑ 66191	EXP
❑ 66192	DBC
❑ 66193	EXP
❑ 66194	DBC
❑ 66195	EXP
❑ 66196	EXP
❑ 66197	DBC
❑ 66198	DBC
❑ 66199	DBC
❑ 66200	DBC
❑ 66201	EXP
❑ 66202	EXP
❑ 66203	EXP
❑ 66204	EXP
❑ 66205	EXP
❑ 66206	DBC
❑ 66207	DBC
❑ 66208	EXP
❑ 66209	EXP
❑ 66210	EXP
❑ 66211	EXP
❑ 66212	EXP
❑ 66213	EXP
❑ 66214	EXP
❑ 66215	EXP
❑ 66216	EXP
❑ 66217	EXP
❑ 66218	EXP
❑ 66219	EXP
❑ 66220	DBC
❑ 66221	DBC
❑ 66222	EXP
❑ 66223	EXP
❑ 66224	EXP
❑ 66225	EXP
❑ 66226	EXP
❑ 66227	EXP
❑ 66228	EXP
❑ 66229	EXP
❑ 66230	EXP
❑ 66231	EXP
❑ 66232	EXP
❑ 66233	EXP
❑ 66234	EXP
❑ 66235	EXP
❑ 66236	EXP
❑ 66237	EXP
❑ 66239	EXP
❑ 66240	EXP
❑ 66241	EXP
❑ 66242	EXP
❑ 66243	EXP
❑ 66244	EXP
❑ 66245	EXP
❑ 66246	EXP
❑ 66247	EXP
❑ 66248	EXP
❑ 66249	EXP
❑ 66301	DRS
❑ 66302	DRS
❑ 66303	DRS
❑ 66304	DRS

Number	Operator
❑ 66305	DRS
❑ 66411	EXP
❑ 66412	EXP
❑ 66413	FLR
❑ 66414	FLR
❑ 66415	FLR
❑ 66416	FLR
❑ 66417	EXP
❑ 66418	FLR
❑ 66419	FLR
❑ 66420	FLR
❑ 66421	DRS
❑ 66422	DRS
❑ 66423	DRS
❑ 66424	DRS
❑ 66425	DRS
❑ 66426	DRS
❑ 66427	DRS
❑ 66428	DRS
❑ 66429	DRS
❑ 66430	DRS
❑ 66431	DRS
❑ 66432	DRS
❑ 66433	DRS
❑ 66434	DRS
❑ 66435	DRS
❑ 66436	DRS
❑ 66437	DRS
❑ 66438	DRS
❑ 66439	DRS
❑ 66501	FLR
❑ 66502	FLR
❑ 66503	FLR
❑ 66504	FLR
❑ 66505	FLR
❑ 66506	FLR
❑ 66507	FLR
❑ 66508	FLR
❑ 66509	FLR
❑ 66510	FLR
❑ 66511	FLR
❑ 66512	FLR
❑ 66513	FLR
❑ 66514	FLR
❑ 66515	FLR
❑ 66516	FLR
❑ 66517	FLR
❑ 66518	FLR
❑ 66519	FLR
❑ 66520	FLR
❑ 66522	FLR
❑ 66523	FLR
❑ 66524	FLR
❑ 66525	FLR
❑ 66526	FLR
❑ 66527	EXP
❑ 66528	FLR
❑ 66529	FLR
❑ 66530	EXP
❑ 66531	FLR
❑ 66532	FLR
❑ 66533	FLR
❑ 66534	FLR
❑ 66535	EXP
❑ 66536	FLR
❑ 66537	FLR
❑ 66538	FLR
❑ 66539	FLR
❑ 66540	FLR
❑ 66541	FLR
❑ 66542	FLR
❑ 66543	FLR
❑ 66544	FLR
❑ 66545	FLR
❑ 66546	FLR
❑ 66547	FLR
❑ 66548	FLR
❑ 66549	FLR
❑ 66550	FLR
❑ 66551	FLR
❑ 66552	FLR
❑ 66553	FLR
❑ 66554	FLR
❑ 66555	FLR
❑ 66556	FLR
❑ 66557	FLR
❑ 66558	FLR
❑ 66559	FLR
❑ 66560	FLR
❑ 66561	FLR
❑ 66562	FLR
❑ 66563	FLR
❑ 66564	FLR
❑ 66565	FLR
❑ 66566	FLR
❑ 66567	FLR
❑ 66568	FLR
❑ 66569	FLR
❑ 66570	FLR
❑ 66571	FLR
❑ 66572	FLR
❑ 66582	EXP
❑ 66583	EXP
❑ 66584	EXP
❑ 66585	FLR
❑ 66586	EXP
❑ 66587	FLR
❑ 66588	FLR
❑ 66589	FLR
❑ 66590	FLR
❑ 66591	FLR
❑ 66592	FLR
❑ 66593	FLR
❑ 66594	FLR
❑ 66595	EXP
❑ 66596	FLR
❑ 66597	FLR
❑ 66598	FLR
❑ 66599	FLR
❑ 66601	FLR
❑ 66602	FLR
❑ 66603	FLR
❑ 66604	FLR
❑ 66605	FLR
❑ 66606	FLR
❑ 66607	FLR
❑ 66608	EXP
❑ 66609	EXP
❑ 66610	FLR
❑ 66611	EXP
❑ 66612	EXP
❑ 66613	FLR
❑ 66614	FLR
❑ 66615	FLR
❑ 66616	FLR
❑ 66617	FLR
❑ 66618	FLR
❑ 66619	FLR
❑ 66620	FLR
❑ 66621	FLR
❑ 66622	FLR
❑ 66623	FLR
❑ 66624	EXP
❑ 66625	EXP
❑ 66701	GBR
❑ 66702	GBR
❑ 66703	GBR
❑ 66704	GBR
❑ 66705	GBR
❑ 66706	GBR
❑ 66707	GBR
❑ 66708	GBR
❑ 66709	GBR
❑ 66710	GBR
❑ 66711	GBR
❑ 66712	GBR
❑ 66713	GBR
❑ 66714	GBR
❑ 66715	GBR
❑ 66716	GBR
❑ 66717	GBR
❑ 66718	GBR
❑ 66719	GBR
❑ 66720	GBR
❑ 66721	GBR
❑ 66722	GBR
❑ 66723	GBR
❑ 66724	GBR
❑ 66725	GBR
❑ 66726	GBR
❑ 66727	GBR
❑ 66728	GBR
❑ 66729	GBR
❑ 66730	GBR
❑ 66731	GBR
❑ 66732	GBR
❑ 66733	GBR
❑ 66735	GBR
❑ 66736	GBR
❑ 66737	GBR
❑ 66738	GBR
❑ 66739	GBR
❑ 66740	GBR
❑ 66741	GBR
❑ 66742	GBR
❑ 66743	GBR
❑ 66744	GBR
❑ 66745	GBR
❑ 66746	GBR
❑ 66747	GBR
❑ 66748	GBR
❑ 66749	GBR
❑ 66750	GBR
❑ 66751	GBR
❑ 66752	GBR
❑ 66753	GBR
❑ 66754	GBR
❑ 66755	GBR
❑ 66756	GBR
❑ 66757	GBR
❑ 66758	GBR
❑ 66759	GBR
❑ 66760	GBR
❑ 66761	GBR
❑ 66762	GBR
❑ 66763	GBR
❑ 66764	GBR
❑ 66765	GBR
❑ 66766	GBR
❑ 66767	GBR
❑ 66768	GBR
❑ 66769	GBR
❑ 66770	GBR
❑ 66771	GBR
❑ 66772	GBR
❑ 66773	GBR
❑ 66774	GBR
❑ 66775	GBR
❑ 66776	GBR
❑ 66777	GBR
❑ 66778	GBR
❑ 66779	GBR
❑ 66780	GBR
❑ 66781	GBR
❑ 66782	GBR
❑ 66783	GBR
❑ 66784	GBR
❑ 66785	GBR
❑ 66786	GBR
❑ 66787	GBR
❑ 66788	GBR
❑ 66789	GBR
❑ 66790	GBR
❑ 66791	GBR
❑ 66792	GBR
❑ 66846	COL
❑ 66847	COL
❑ 66848	COL
❑ 66849	COL
❑ 66850	COL
❑ 66951	FLR
❑ 66952	FLR
❑ 66953	FLR
❑ 66954	EXP
❑ 66955	FLR
❑ 66956	FLR
❑ 66957	FLR
❑ 67001	DBC
❑ 67002	DBC
❑ 67003	DBC
❑ 67004	DBC
❑ 67005	DBC
❑ 67006	DBC
❑ 67007	DBC
❑ 67008	DBC
❑ 67009	DBC
❑ 67010	DBC
❑ 67011	DBC
❑ 67012	DBC
❑ 67013	DBC
❑ 67014	DBC
❑ 67015	DBC
❑ 67016	DBC
❑ 67017	DBC
❑ 67018	DBC
❑ 67019	DBC
❑ 67020	DBC
❑ 67021	DBC
❑ 67022	DBC
❑ 67023	COL
❑ 67024	DBC
❑ 67025	DBC
❑ 67026	DBC
❑ 67027	COL
❑ 67028	DBC
❑ 67029	DBC
❑ 67030	DBC
❑ 68001	DRS
❑ 68002	DRS
❑ 68003	DRS
❑ 68004	DRS
❑ 68005	DRS
❑ 68006	ASR
❑ 68007	ASR
❑ 68008	DRS
❑ 68009	DRS
❑ 68010	CRW
❑ 68011	CRW
❑ 68012	CRW
❑ 68013	CRW
❑ 68014	CRW
❑ 68015	CRW
❑ 68016	DRS
❑ 68017	DRS
❑ 68018	DRS
❑ 68019	TPE
❑ 68020	TPE
❑ 68021	TPE
❑ 68022	TPE
❑ 68023	TPE
❑ 68024	TPE
❑ 68025	TPE
❑ 68026	TPE
❑ 68027	TPE
❑ 68028	TPE
❑ 68029	TPE
❑ 68030	TPE

❑ 68031 TPE
❑ 68032 TPE
❑ 68033 DRS
❑ 68034 DRS

❑ 70001 FLR
❑ 70002 FLR
❑ 70003 FLR
❑ 70004 FLR
❑ 70005 FLR
❑ 70006 FLR
❑ 70007 FLR
❑ 70008 FLR
❑ 70009 FLR
❑ 70010 FLR
❑ 70011 FLR
❑ 70013 FLR
❑ 70014 FLR
❑ 70015 FLR
❑ 70016 FLR
❑ 70017 FLR
❑ 70018 FLR
❑ 70019 FLR
❑ 70020 FLR

❑ 70801 COL
❑ 70802 COL
❑ 70803 COL
❑ 70804 COL
❑ 70805 COL
❑ 70806 COL
❑ 70807 COL
❑ 70808 COL
❑ 70809 COL
❑ 70810 COL
❑ 70811 COL
❑ 70812 COL
❑ 70813 COL
❑ 70814 COL
❑ 70815 COL
❑ 70816 COL
❑ 70817 COL

❑ 73101 GBR
❑ 73107 GBR
❑ 73109 GBR
❑ 73110 GBR
❑ 73118 TTS
❑ 73119 GBR
❑ 73128 GBR
❑ 73133 TTS
❑ 73136 GBR
❑ 73138 NRL
❑ 73139 GBR
❑ 73141 GBR
❑ 73201 GBR
❑ 73202 GTR
❑ 73212 GBR
❑ 73213 GBR
❑ 73235 SWR

❑ 73951 NRL
❑ 73952 NRL
❑ 73961 GBR
❑ 73962 GBR
❑ 73963 GBR
❑ 73964 GBR
❑ 73965 GBR
❑ 73966 SCS
❑ 73967 SCS
❑ 73968 SCS
❑ 73969 SCS
❑ 73970 SCS
❑ 73971 SCS

❑ 86101 LSL
❑ 86213 EXP
❑ 86215 EXP
❑ 86217 EXP
❑ 86218 EXP
❑ 86228 EXP
❑ 86231 EXP
❑ 86232 EXP
❑ 86233 EXP
❑ 86234 EPX
❑ 86235 EXP
❑ 86242 EXP
❑ 86248 EXP
❑ 86250 EXP
❑ 86251 EPX
❑ 86401 PRE
❑ 86424 EXP
❑ 86604 FLR
❑ 86605 FLR
❑ 86607 FLR
❑ 86608 FLR
❑ 86609 FLR
❑ 86610 FLR
❑ 86612 FLR
❑ 86613 FLR
❑ 86614 FLR
❑ 86622 FLR
❑ 86627 FLR
❑ 86628 FLR
❑ 86632 FLR
❑ 86637 FLR
❑ 86638 FLR
❑ 86639 FLR
❑ 86701 EXP
❑ 86702 EXP

❑ 87002 LSL
❑ 87003 EXP
❑ 87004 EXP
❑ 87006 EXP
❑ 87007 EXP
❑ 87008 EXP
❑ 87009 EXP
❑ 87010 EXP
❑ 87012 EXP
❑ 87013 EXP
❑ 87014 EXP
❑ 87017 EXP
❑ 87019 EXP
❑ 87020 EXP
❑ 87022 EXP
❑ 87023 EXP
❑ 87025 EXP
❑ 87026 EXP
❑ 87028 EXP
❑ 87029 EXP
❑ 87033 EXP
❑ 87034 EXP

❑ 88001 DRS
❑ 88002 DRS
❑ 88003 DRS
❑ 88004 DRS
❑ 88005 DRS
❑ 88006 DRS
❑ 88007 DRS
❑ 88008 DRS
❑ 88009 DRS
❑ 88010 DRS

❑ 90001 GAR
❑ 90002 GAR
❑ 90003 GAR
❑ 90004 GAR
❑ 90005 GAR
❑ 90006 GAR
❑ 90007 GAR
❑ 90008 GAR
❑ 90009 GAR
❑ 90010 GAR
❑ 90011 GAR
❑ 90012 GAR
❑ 90013 GAR
❑ 90014 GAR
❑ 90015 GAR
❑ 90016 FLR
❑ 90017 DBC
❑ 90018 DBC
❑ 90019 DBC
❑ 90020 DBC
❑ 90021 DBC
❑ 90022 DBC
❑ 90023 DBC
❑ 90024 DBC
❑ 90025 DBC
❑ 90026 DBC
❑ 90027 DBC
❑ 90028 DBC
❑ 90029 DBC
❑ 90030 DBC
❑ 90031 DBC
❑ 90032 DBC
❑ 90033 DBC
❑ 90034 DBC
❑ 90035 DBC
❑ 90036 DBC
❑ 90037 DBC
❑ 90038 DBC
❑ 90039 DBC
❑ 90040 DBC
❑ 90041 FLR
❑ 90042 FLR
❑ 90043 FLR
❑ 90044 FLR
❑ 90045 FLR
❑ 90046 FLR
❑ 90047 FLR
❑ 90048 FLR
❑ 90049 FLR
❑ 90050 FLR

❑ 91101 LNE
❑ 91102 LNE
❑ 91103 OLS
❑ 91104 LNE
❑ 91105 LNE
❑ 91106 LNE
❑ 91107 LNE
❑ 91108 OLS
❑ 91109 LNE
❑ 91110 LNE
❑ 91111 LNE
❑ 91112 LNE
❑ 91113 LNE
❑ 91114 LNE
❑ 91115 LNE
❑ 91116 LNE
❑ 91117 EPX
❑ 91118 LNE
❑ 91119 LNE
❑ 91120 EPX
❑ 91121 LNE
❑ 91122 ROG
❑ 91124 LNE
❑ 91125 LNE
❑ 91126 LNE
❑ 91127 LNE
❑ 91128 ROG
❑ 91129 LNE
❑ 91130 LNE
❑ 91131 LNE
❑ 91132 LNE

❑ 92001 EXP
❑ 92002 EXP
❑ 92003 EXP
❑ 92004 DBC
❑ 92005 EXP
❑ 92006 SCS
❑ 92007 DBC
❑ 92008 DBC
❑ 92009 DBC
❑ 92010 SCS
❑ 92011 DBC
❑ 92012 EXP
❑ 92013 DBC
❑ 92014 SCS
❑ 92015 DBC
❑ 92016 DBC
❑ 92017 DBC
❑ 92018 SCS
❑ 92019 DBC
❑ 92020 GBR
❑ 92021 GBR
❑ 92022 EXP
❑ 92023 SCS
❑ 92024 EXP
❑ 92025 EXP
❑ 92026 EXP
❑ 92027 EXP
❑ 92028 SCS
❑ 92029 DBC
❑ 92030 EXP
❑ 92031 DBC
❑ 92032 GBR
❑ 92033 SCS
❑ 92034 EXP
❑ 92035 DBC
❑ 92036 DBC
❑ 92037 DBC
❑ 92038 SCS
❑ 92039 EXP
❑ 92040 GBR
❑ 92041 DBC
❑ 92042 DBC
❑ 92043 GBR
❑ 92044 GBR
❑ 92045 GBR
❑ 92046 GBR

❑ 97301 NRL
❑ 97302 NRL
❑ 97303 NRL
❑ 97304 NRL

❑ 323 539-7 AFG
❑ 323 674-2 AFG

❑ DH50-1 GBR
❑ DH50-2 GBR
❑ 8.701 GBR
❑ 8.702 GBR
❑ 8.703 GBR
❑ 8.704 GBR
❑ 8.708 GBR
❑ 8.711 GBR
❑ 8.712 GBR
❑ 8.716 GBR
❑ 8.717 GBR
❑ 8.718 GBR
❑ 8.719 GBR
❑ 8.720 GBR

Diesel Multiple Units

❑ 60000 HDL
❑ 60019 HDL
❑ 60116 HDL
❑ 60118 HDL
❑ 60501 HDL
❑ 60528 HDL
❑ 60529 HDL

❑ 69337 HDL

❑ 70262 HDL

❑ 139001 WMR
❑ 139002 WMR

❑ 142002 TFW
❑ 142006 TFW
❑ 142010 TFW
❑ 142069 TFW
❑ 142072 TFW
❑ 142073 TFW
❑ 142074 TFW
❑ 142075 TFW
❑ 142076 TFW
❑ 142077 TFW
❑ 142080 TFW
❑ 142081 TFW
❑ 142082 TFW
❑ 142083 TFW
❑ 142085 TFW

❑ 143601 TFW
❑ 143602 TFW
❑ 143603 GWR
❑ 143604 TFW
❑ 143605 TFW
❑ 143606 TFW
❑ 143607 TFW
❑ 143608 TFW
❑ 143609 TFW
❑ 143610 TFW
❑ 143611 GWR
❑ 143612 GWR
❑ 143614 TFW
❑ 143616 TFW
❑ 143617 GWR
❑ 143618 GWR
❑ 143619 GWR
❑ 143620 GWR
❑ 143621 GWR
❑ 143622 TFW
❑ 143623 TFW
❑ 143624 TFW
❑ 143625 TFW

❑ 144001 NOR
❑ 144002 NOR
❑ 144003 NOR
❑ 144004 NOR
❑ 144005 NOR
❑ 144006 NOR
❑ 144007 NOR
❑ 144008 NOR
❑ 144009 NOR
❑ 144010 NOR
❑ 144011 NOR
❑ 144012 NOR
❑ 144013 NOR
❑ 144014 NOR
❑ 144015 NOR
❑ 144016 NOR
❑ 144017 NOR
❑ 144018 NOR
❑ 144019 NOR
❑ 144020 NOR
❑ 144021 NOR
❑ 144022 NOR
❑ 144023 NOR

❑ 150001 GWR
❑ 150002 GWR

❑ 150101 NOR
❑ 150102 NOR
❑ 150103 NOR
❑ 150104 NOR
❑ 150105 NOR
❑ 150106 NOR
❑ 150107 NOR
❑ 150108 NOR
❑ 150109 NOR
❑ 150110 NOR
❑ 150111 NOR
❑ 150112 NOR
❑ 150113 NOR
❑ 150114 NOR
❑ 150115 NOR
❑ 150116 NOR
❑ 150117 NOR
❑ 150118 NOR
❑ 150119 NOR
❑ 150120 NOR
❑ 150121 NOR
❑ 150122 NOR
❑ 150123 NOR
❑ 150124 NOR
❑ 150125 NOR
❑ 150126 NOR
❑ 150127 NOR
❑ 150128 NOR
❑ 150129 NOR
❑ 150130 NOR
❑ 150131 NOR
❑ 150132 NOR
❑ 150133 NOR
❑ 150134 NOR
❑ 150135 NOR
❑ 150136 NOR
❑ 150137 NOR
❑ 150138 NOR
❑ 150139 NOR
❑ 150140 NOR
❑ 150141 NOR
❑ 150142 NOR
❑ 150143 NOR
❑ 150144 NOR
❑ 150145 NOR
❑ 150146 NOR
❑ 150147 NOR
❑ 150148 NOR
❑ 150149 NOR
❑ 150150 NOR

❑ 150201 NOR
❑ 150202 GWR
❑ 150203 NOR
❑ 150204 NOR
❑ 150205 NOR
❑ 150206 NOR
❑ 150207 GWR
❑ 150208 TFW
❑ 150209 NOR
❑ 150210 NOR
❑ 150211 NOR
❑ 150213 TFW
❑ 150214 NOR
❑ 150215 NOR
❑ 150216 GWR
❑ 150217 TFW
❑ 150218 NOR
❑ 150219 GWR
❑ 150220 NOR
❑ 150221 GWR
❑ 150222 NOR
❑ 150223 NOR
❑ 150224 NOR
❑ 150225 NOR
❑ 150226 NOR
❑ 150227 TFW
❑ 150228 NOR
❑ 150229 TFW
❑ 150230 TFW
❑ 150231 TFW
❑ 150232 GWR
❑ 150233 GWR
❑ 150234 GWR
❑ 150235 TFW
❑ 150236 TFW
❑ 150237 TFW
❑ 150238 GWR
❑ 150239 GWR
❑ 150240 TFW
❑ 150241 TFW
❑ 150242 TFW
❑ 150243 GWR
❑ 150244 GWR
❑ 150245 TFW
❑ 150246 GWR
❑ 150247 GWR
❑ 150248 GWR
❑ 150249 GWR
❑ 150250 TFW
❑ 150251 TFW
❑ 150252 TFW
❑ 150253 TFW
❑ 150254 TFW
❑ 150255 TFW
❑ 150256 TFW
❑ 150257 TFW
❑ 150258 TFW
❑ 150259 TFW
❑ 150260 TFW
❑ 150261 GWR
❑ 150262 TFW
❑ 150263 GWR
❑ 150264 TFW
❑ 150265 GWR
❑ 150266 GWR
❑ 150267 TFW
❑ 150268 NOR
❑ 150269 NOR
❑ 150270 NOR
❑ 150271 NOR
❑ 150272 NOR
❑ 150273 NOR
❑ 150274 NOR
❑ 150275 NOR
❑ 150276 NOR
❑ 150277 NOR
❑ 150278 TFW
❑ 150279 TFW
❑ 150280 TFW
❑ 150281 TFW
❑ 150282 TFW
❑ 150283 TFW
❑ 150284 TFW
❑ 150285 TFW

❑ 153301 NOR
❑ 153302 EMR
❑ 153303 TFW
❑ 153304 NOR
❑ 153305 ASR
❑ 153306 TFW
❑ 153307 NOR
❑ 153308 EMR
❑ 153309 TFW
❑ 153310 TFW
❑ 153311 EMR
❑ 153312 TFW
❑ 153313 TFW
❑ 153314 TFW
❑ 153315 NOR
❑ 153316 NOR
❑ 153317 NOR
❑ 153318 EMR
❑ 153319 EMR
❑ 153320 TFW
❑ 153321 TFW
❑ 153322 TFW
❑ 153323 TFW
❑ 153324 NOR
❑ 153325 TFW
❑ 153326 TFW
❑ 153327 TFW
❑ 153328 NOR
❑ 153329 TFW
❑ 153330 NOR
❑ 153331 NOR
❑ 153332 NOR
❑ 153333 TFW
❑ 153334 WMR
❑ 153335 TFW

❑ 153351 NOR
❑ 153352 NOR
❑ 153353 TFW
❑ 153354 WMR
❑ 153355 EMR
❑ 153356 WMR
❑ 153357 EMR
❑ 153358 NOR
❑ 153359 NOR
❑ 153360 NOR
❑ 153361 TFW
❑ 153362 TFW
❑ 153363 NOR
❑ 153364 WMR
❑ 153365 WMR
❑ 153366 WMR
❑ 153367 TFW
❑ 153368 EMR
❑ 153369 TFW
❑ 153370 ASR
❑ 153371 WMR
❑ 153372 EMR
❑ 153373 NOR
❑ 153374 EMR
❑ 153375 WMR
❑ 153376 EMR
❑ 153377 ASR
❑ 153378 NOR
❑ 153379 EMR
❑ 153380 NOR
❑ 153381 EMR
❑ 153382 EMR
❑ 153383 EMR
❑ 153384 EMR
❑ 153385 EMR

❑ 155341 NOR
❑ 155342 NOR
❑ 155343 NOR
❑ 155344 NOR
❑ 155345 NOR
❑ 155346 NOR
❑ 155347 NOR

❑ 156401 EMR
❑ 156902 EMR
❑ 156403 EMR
❑ 156404 EMR
❑ 156405 EMR
❑ 156406 EMR
❑ 156907 EMR
❑ 156408 EMR
❑ 156909 EMR
❑ 156410 EMR
❑ 156411 EMR
❑ 156912 EMR
❑ 156413 EMR
❑ 156414 EMR
❑ 156415 EMR
❑ 156916 EMR
❑ 156917 EMR
❑ 156918 EMR
❑ 156919 EMR
❑ 156420 NOR
❑ 156421 NOR
❑ 156922 EMR
❑ 156423 NOR
❑ 156424 NOR
❑ 156425 NOR
❑ 156426 NOR
❑ 156427 NOR
❑ 156428 NOR
❑ 156429 NOR
❑ 156430 ASR
❑ 156431 ASR
❑ 156432 ASR
❑ 156433 ASR

❑ 156434 ASR
❑ 156435 ASR
❑ 156436 ASR
❑ 156437 ASR
❑ 156438 NOR
❑ 156439 ASR
❑ 156440 NOR
❑ 156441 NOR
❑ 156442 ASR
❑ 156443 NOR
❑ 156444 NOR
❑ 156445 ASR
❑ 156446 ASR
❑ 156447 NOR
❑ 156448 NOR
❑ 156449 NOR
❑ 156450 ASR
❑ 156451 NOR
❑ 156452 NOR
❑ 156453 ASR
❑ 156454 NOR
❑ 156455 NOR
❑ 156456 ASR
❑ 156457 ASR
❑ 156458 ASR
❑ 156459 NOR
❑ 156460 NOR
❑ 156461 NOR
❑ 156462 ASR
❑ 156463 NOR
❑ 156464 NOR
❑ 156465 NOR
❑ 156466 NOR
❑ 156467 ASR
❑ 156468 NOR
❑ 156469 NOR
❑ 156470 EMR
❑ 156471 NOR
❑ 156472 NOR
❑ 156473 EMR
❑ 156474 ASR
❑ 156475 NOR
❑ 156476 ASR
❑ 156477 ASR
❑ 156478 ASR
❑ 156479 NOR
❑ 156480 NOR
❑ 156481 NOR
❑ 156482 NOR
❑ 156483 NOR
❑ 156484 NOR
❑ 156485 NOR
❑ 156486 NOR
❑ 156487 NOR
❑ 156488 NOR
❑ 156489 NOR
❑ 156490 NOR
❑ 156491 NOR
❑ 156492 ASR
❑ 156493 ASR
❑ 156494 ASR
❑ 156495 ASR
❑ 156496 NOR
❑ 156497 EMR
❑ 156498 EMR
❑ 156499 ASR
❑ 156500 ASR
❑ 156501 ASR
❑ 156502 ASR
❑ 156503 ASR
❑ 156504 ASR
❑ 156505 ASR
❑ 156506 ASR
❑ 156507 ASR
❑ 156508 ASR
❑ 156509 ASR
❑ 156510 ASR
❑ 156511 ASR
❑ 156512 ASR
❑ 156513 ASR
❑ 156514 ASR

❑ 158701 ASR
❑ 158702 ASR
❑ 158703 ASR
❑ 158704 ASR
❑ 158705 ASR
❑ 158706 ASR
❑ 158707 ASR
❑ 158708 ASR
❑ 158709 ASR
❑ 158710 ASR
❑ 158711 ASR
❑ 158712 ASR
❑ 158713 ASR
❑ 158714 ASR
❑ 158715 ASR
❑ 158716 ASR
❑ 158717 ASR
❑ 158718 ASR
❑ 158719 ASR
❑ 158720 ASR
❑ 158721 ASR
❑ 158722 ASR
❑ 158723 ASR
❑ 158724 ASR
❑ 158725 ASR
❑ 158726 ASR
❑ 158727 ASR
❑ 158728 ASR
❑ 158729 ASR
❑ 158730 ASR
❑ 158731 ASR
❑ 158732 ASR
❑ 158733 ASR
❑ 158734 ASR
❑ 158735 ASR
❑ 158736 ASR
❑ 158737 ASR
❑ 158738 ASR
❑ 158739 ASR
❑ 158740 ASR
❑ 158741 ASR
❑ 158745 GWR
❑ 158747 GWR
❑ 158749 GWR
❑ 158751 GWR
❑ 158752 NOR
❑ 158753 NOR
❑ 158754 NOR
❑ 158755 NOR
❑ 158756 NOR
❑ 158757 NOR
❑ 158758 NOR
❑ 158759 NOR
❑ 158760 GWR
❑ 158761 GWR
❑ 158762 GWR
❑ 158763 GWR
❑ 158764 GWR
❑ 158765 GWR
❑ 158766 GWR
❑ 158767 GWR
❑ 158769 GWR
❑ 158770 EMR
❑ 158773 EMR
❑ 158774 EMR
❑ 158777 EMR
❑ 158780 EMR
❑ 158782 NOR
❑ 158783 EMR
❑ 158784 NOR
❑ 158785 EMR
❑ 158786 NOR
❑ 158787 NOR
❑ 158788 EMR
❑ 158789 NOR
❑ 158790 NOR
❑ 158791 NOR
❑ 158792 NOR
❑ 158793 NOR
❑ 158794 NOR
❑ 158795 NOR
❑ 158796 NOR
❑ 158797 NOR
❑ 158798 GWR
❑ 158799 EMR

❑ 158806 EMR
❑ 158810 EMR
❑ 158812 EMR
❑ 158813 EMR
❑ 158815 NOR
❑ 158816 NOR
❑ 158817 NOR
❑ 158818 TFW
❑ 158819 TFW
❑ 158820 TFW
❑ 158821 TFW
❑ 158822 TFW
❑ 158823 TFW
❑ 158824 TFW
❑ 158825 TFW
❑ 158826 TFW
❑ 158827 TFW
❑ 158828 TFW
❑ 158829 TFW
❑ 158830 TFW
❑ 158831 TFW
❑ 158832 TFW
❑ 158833 TFW
❑ 158834 TFW
❑ 158835 TFW
❑ 158836 TFW
❑ 158837 TFW
❑ 158838 TFW
❑ 158839 TFW
❑ 158840 TFW
❑ 158841 TFW
❑ 158842 NOR
❑ 158843 NOR
❑ 158844 NOR
❑ 158845 NOR
❑ 158846 EMR
❑ 158847 EMR
❑ 158848 NOR
❑ 158849 NOR
❑ 158850 NOR
❑ 158851 NOR
❑ 158852 EMR
❑ 158853 NOR
❑ 158854 EMR
❑ 158855 NOR
❑ 158856 EMR
❑ 158857 EMR
❑ 158858 EMR
❑ 158859 NOR
❑ 158860 NOR
❑ 158861 NOR
❑ 158862 EMR
❑ 158863 EMR
❑ 158864 EMR
❑ 158865 EMR
❑ 158866 EMR
❑ 158867 NOR
❑ 158868 NOR
❑ 158869 NOR
❑ 158870 NOR
❑ 158871 NOR
❑ 158872 NOR
❑ 158880 SWR
❑ 158881 SWR
❑ 158882 SWR
❑ 158883 SWR
❑ 158884 SWR
❑ 158885 SWR
❑ 158886 SWR
❑ 158887 SWR
❑ 158888 SWR
❑ 158889 EMR
❑ 158890 SWR

❑ 158901 NOR
❑ 158902 NOR
❑ 158903 NOR
❑ 158904 NOR
❑ 158905 NOR
❑ 158906 NOR
❑ 158907 NOR
❑ 158908 NOR
❑ 158909 NOR
❑ 158910 NOR
❑ 158956 GWR
❑ 158957 GWR
❑ 158958 GWR
❑ 158959 GWR

❑ 159001 SWR
❑ 159002 SWR
❑ 159003 SWR
❑ 159004 SWR
❑ 159005 SWR
❑ 159006 SWR
❑ 159007 SWR
❑ 159008 SWR
❑ 159009 SWR
❑ 159010 SWR
❑ 159011 SWR
❑ 159012 SWR
❑ 159013 SWR
❑ 159014 SWR
❑ 159015 SWR
❑ 159016 SWR
❑ 159017 SWR
❑ 159018 SWR
❑ 159019 SWR
❑ 159020 SWR
❑ 159021 SWR
❑ 159022 SWR

❑ 159101 SWR
❑ 159102 SWR
❑ 159103 SWR
❑ 159104 SWR
❑ 159105 SWR
❑ 159106 SWR
❑ 159107 SWR
❑ 159108 SWR

❑ 165001 CRW
❑ 165002 CRW
❑ 165003 CRW
❑ 165004 CRW
❑ 165005 CRW
❑ 165006 CRW
❑ 165007 CRW
❑ 165008 CRW
❑ 165009 CRW
❑ 165010 CRW
❑ 165011 CRW
❑ 165012 CRW
❑ 165013 CRW
❑ 165014 CRW
❑ 165015 CRW
❑ 165016 CRW
❑ 165017 CRW
❑ 165018 CRW
❑ 165019 CRW
❑ 165020 CRW
❑ 165021 CRW
❑ 165022 CRW
❑ 165023 CRW
❑ 165024 CRW
❑ 165025 CRW
❑ 165026 CRW

❑ 165027 CRW
❑ 165028 CRW
❑ 165029 CRW
❑ 165030 CRW
❑ 165031 CRW
❑ 165032 CRW
❑ 165033 CRW
❑ 165034 CRW
❑ 165035 CRW
❑ 165036 CRW
❑ 165037 CRW
❑ 165038 CRW
❑ 165039 CRW

❑ 165101 GWR
❑ 165102 GWR
❑ 165103 GWR
❑ 165104 GWR
❑ 165105 GWR
❑ 165106 GWR
❑ 165107 GWR
❑ 165108 GWR
❑ 165109 GWR
❑ 165110 GWR
❑ 165111 GWR
❑ 165112 GWR
❑ 165113 GWR
❑ 165114 GWR
❑ 165116 GWR
❑ 165117 GWR
❑ 165118 GWR
❑ 165119 GWR
❑ 165120 GWR
❑ 165121 GWR
❑ 165122 GWR
❑ 165123 GWR
❑ 165124 GWR
❑ 165125 GWR
❑ 165126 GWR
❑ 165127 GWR
❑ 165128 GWR
❑ 165129 GWR
❑ 165130 GWR
❑ 165131 GWR
❑ 165132 GWR
❑ 165133 GWR
❑ 165134 GWR
❑ 165135 GWR
❑ 165136 GWR
❑ 165137 GWR

❑ 166201 GWR
❑ 166202 GWR
❑ 166203 GWR
❑ 166204 GWR
❑ 166205 GWR
❑ 166206 GWR
❑ 166207 GWR
❑ 166208 GWR
❑ 166209 GWR
❑ 166210 GWR
❑ 166211 GWR
❑ 166212 GWR
❑ 166213 GWR
❑ 166214 GWR
❑ 166215 GWR
❑ 166216 GWR
❑ 166217 GWR
❑ 166218 GWR
❑ 166219 GWR
❑ 166220 GWR
❑ 166221 GWR

❑ 168001 CRW
❑ 168002 CRW
❑ 168003 CRW
❑ 168004 CRW
❑ 168005 CRW

❑ 168106 CRW
❑ 168107 CRW
❑ 168108 CRW
❑ 168109 CRW
❑ 168110 CRW
❑ 168111 CRW
❑ 168112 CRW
❑ 168113 CRW

❑ 168214 CRW
❑ 168215 CRW
❑ 168216 CRW
❑ 168217 CRW
❑ 168218 CRW
❑ 168219 CRW

❑ 168321 CRW
❑ 168322 CRW
❑ 168323 CRW
❑ 168324 CRW
❑ 168325 CRW
❑ 168326 CRW
❑ 168327 CRW
❑ 168328 CRW
❑ 168329 CRW

❑ 170101 AXC
❑ 170102 AXC
❑ 170103 AXC
❑ 170104 AXC
❑ 170105 AXC
❑ 170106 AXC
❑ 170107 AXC
❑ 170108 AXC
❑ 170109 AXC
❑ 170110 AXC
❑ 170111 AXC
❑ 170112 AXC
❑ 170113 AXC
❑ 170114 AXC
❑ 170115 AXC
❑ 170116 AXC
❑ 170117 AXC

❑ 170201 TFW
❑ 170202 TFW
❑ 170203 TFW
❑ 170204 TFW
❑ 170205 TFW
❑ 170206 TFW
❑ 170207 TFW
❑ 170208 TFW
❑ 170270 TFW
❑ 170271 TFW
❑ 170272 TFW
❑ 170273 TFW

❑ 170393 ASR
❑ 170394 ASR
❑ 170395 ASR
❑ 170396 ASR
❑ 170397 AXC
❑ 170398 AXC

❑ 170401 ASR
❑ 170402 ASR
❑ 170403 ASR
❑ 170404 ASR
❑ 170405 ASR
❑ 170406 ASR
❑ 170407 ASR
❑ 170408 ASR
❑ 170409 ASR
❑ 170410 ASR
❑ 170411 ASR
❑ 170412 ASR
❑ 170413 ASR
❑ 170414 ASR
❑ 170415 ASR
❑ 170416 ASR
❑ 170417 ASR
❑ 170418 ASR
❑ 170419 ASR
❑ 170420 ASR
❑ 170425 ASR
❑ 170426 ASR
❑ 170427 ASR
❑ 170428 ASR
❑ 170429 ASR
❑ 170430 ASR
❑ 170431 ASR
❑ 170432 ASR
❑ 170433 ASR
❑ 170434 ASR
❑ 170450 ASR
❑ 170451 ASR
❑ 170452 ASR
❑ 170453 NOR
❑ 170454 NOR
❑ 170455 NOR
❑ 170456 NOR
❑ 170457 NOR
❑ 170458 NOR
❑ 170459 NOR
❑ 170460 NOR
❑ 170461 NOR
❑ 170470 NOR
❑ 170471 NOR
❑ 170472 NOR
❑ 170473 NOR
❑ 170474 NOR
❑ 170475 NOR
❑ 170476 NOR
❑ 170477 NOR
❑ 170478 NOR

❑ 170501 WMR
❑ 170502 WMR
❑ 170503 WMR
❑ 170504 WMR
❑ 170505 WMR
❑ 170506 WMR
❑ 170507 WMR
❑ 170508 WMR
❑ 170509 WMR
❑ 170510 WMR
❑ 170511 WMR
❑ 170512 WMR
❑ 170513 WMR
❑ 170514 WMR
❑ 170515 WMR
❑ 170516 WMR
❑ 170517 WMR
❑ 170518 AXC
❑ 170519 AXC
❑ 170520 AXC
❑ 170521 AXC
❑ 170522 AXC
❑ 170523 AXC

❑ 170630 WMR
❑ 170631 WMR
❑ 170632 WMR
❑ 170633 WMR
❑ 170634 WMR
❑ 170635 WMR
❑ 170636 AXC
❑ 170637 AXC
❑ 170638 AXC
❑ 170639 AXC

❑ 171201 GTR
❑ 171202 GTR

❑ 171401 GTR
❑ 171402 GTR

❑ 171721 GTR
❑ 171722 GTR
❑ 171723 GTR
❑ 171724 GTR
❑ 171725 GTR
❑ 171726 GTR
❑ 171727 GTR
❑ 171728 GTR
❑ 171729 GTR
❑ 171730 GTR

❑ 171801 GTR
❑ 171802 GTR
❑ 171803 GTR
❑ 171804 GTR
❑ 171805 GTR
❑ 171806 GTR

❑ 172001 WMR
❑ 172002 WMR
❑ 172003 WMR
❑ 172004 WMR
❑ 172005 WMR
❑ 172006 WMR
❑ 172007 WMR
❑ 172008 WMR

❑ 172101 CRW
❑ 172102 CRW
❑ 172103 CRW
❑ 172104 CRW

❑ 172211 WMR
❑ 172212 WMR
❑ 172213 WMR
❑ 172214 WMR
❑ 172215 WMR
❑ 172216 WMR
❑ 172217 WMR
❑ 172218 WMR
❑ 172219 WMR
❑ 172220 WMR
❑ 172221 WMR
❑ 172222 WMR

❑ 172331 WMR
❑ 172332 WMR
❑ 172333 WMR
❑ 172334 WMR
❑ 172335 WMR
❑ 172336 WMR
❑ 172337 WMR
❑ 172338 WMR
❑ 172339 WMR
❑ 172340 WMR
❑ 172341 WMR
❑ 172342 WMR
❑ 172343 WMR
❑ 172344 WMR
❑ 172345 WMR

❑ 175001 TFW
❑ 175002 TFW
❑ 175003 TFW
❑ 175004 TFW
❑ 175005 TFW
❑ 175006 TFW
❑ 175007 TFW
❑ 175008 TFW
❑ 175009 TFW
❑ 175010 TFW
❑ 175011 TFW

❑ 175101 TFW
❑ 175102 TFW
❑ 175103 TFW
❑ 175104 TFW
❑ 175105 TFW
❑ 175106 TFW

❑ 175107 TFW
❑ 175108 TFW
❑ 175109 TFW
❑ 175110 TFW
❑ 175111 TFW
❑ 175112 TFW
❑ 175113 TFW
❑ 175114 TFW
❑ 175115 TFW
❑ 175116 TFW

❑ 180101 GTL
❑ 180102 GTL
❑ 180103 GTL
❑ 180104 GTL
❑ 180105 GTL
❑ 180106 GTL
❑ 180107 GTL
❑ 180108 GTL
❑ 180109 EMR
❑ 180110 EMR
❑ 180111 EMR
❑ 180112 GTL
❑ 180113 EMR
❑ 180114 GTL

❑ 185101 FTP
❑ 185102 FTP
❑ 185103 FTP
❑ 185104 FTP
❑ 185105 FTP
❑ 185106 FTP
❑ 185107 FTP
❑ 185108 FTP
❑ 185109 FTP
❑ 185110 FTP
❑ 185111 FTP
❑ 185112 FTP
❑ 185113 FTP
❑ 185114 FTP
❑ 185115 FTP
❑ 185116 FTP
❑ 185117 FTP
❑ 185118 FTP
❑ 185119 FTP
❑ 185120 FTP
❑ 185121 FTP
❑ 185122 FTP
❑ 185123 FTP
❑ 185124 FTP
❑ 185125 FTP
❑ 185126 FTP
❑ 185127 FTP
❑ 185128 FTP
❑ 185129 FTP
❑ 185130 FTP
❑ 185131 FTP
❑ 185132 FTP
❑ 185133 FTP
❑ 185134 FTP
❑ 185135 FTP
❑ 185136 FTP
❑ 185137 FTP
❑ 185138 FTP
❑ 185139 FTP
❑ 185140 FTP
❑ 185141 FTP
❑ 185142 FTP
❑ 185143 FTP
❑ 185144 FTP
❑ 185145 FTP
❑ 185146 FTP
❑ 185147 FTP
❑ 185148 FTP
❑ 185149 FTP
❑ 185150 FTP
❑ 185151 FTP

❑ 195001 NOR
❑ 195002 NOR
❑ 195003 NOR
❑ 195004 NOR
❑ 195005 NOR
❑ 195006 NOR
❑ 195007 NOR
❑ 195008 NOR
❑ 195009 NOR
❑ 195010 NOR
❑ 195011 NOR
❑ 195012 NOR
❑ 195013 NOR
❑ 195014 NOR
❑ 195015 NOR
❑ 195016 NOR
❑ 195017 NOR
❑ 195018 NOR
❑ 195019 NOR
❑ 195020 NOR
❑ 195021 NOR
❑ 195022 NOR
❑ 195023 NOR
❑ 195024 NOR
❑ 195025 NOR

❑ 195101 NOR
❑ 195102 NOR
❑ 195103 NOR
❑ 195104 NOR
❑ 195105 NOR
❑ 195106 NOR
❑ 195107 NOR
❑ 195108 NOR
❑ 195109 NOR
❑ 195110 NOR
❑ 195111 NOR
❑ 195112 NOR
❑ 195113 NOR
❑ 195114 NOR
❑ 195115 NOR
❑ 195116 NOR
❑ 195117 NOR
❑ 195118 NOR
❑ 195119 NOR
❑ 195120 NOR
❑ 195121 NOR
❑ 195122 NOR
❑ 195123 NOR
❑ 195124 NOR
❑ 195125 NOR
❑ 195126 NOR
❑ 195127 NOR
❑ 195128 NOR
❑ 195129 NOR
❑ 195130 NOR
❑ 195131 NOR
❑ 195132 NOR
❑ 195133 NOR

❑ 220001 AXC
❑ 220002 AXC
❑ 220003 AXC
❑ 220004 AXC
❑ 220005 AXC
❑ 220006 AXC
❑ 220007 AXC
❑ 220008 AXC
❑ 220009 AXC
❑ 220010 AXC
❑ 220011 AXC
❑ 220012 AXC
❑ 220013 AXC
❑ 220014 AXC
❑ 220015 AXC
❑ 220016 AXC
❑ 220017 AXC
❑ 220018 AXC
❑ 220019 AXC
❑ 220020 AXC
❑ 220021 AXC
❑ 220022 AXC
❑ 220023 AXC
❑ 220024 AXC
❑ 220025 AXC
❑ 220026 AXC
❑ 220027 AXC
❑ 220028 AXC
❑ 220029 AXC
❑ 220030 AXC
❑ 220031 AXC
❑ 220032 AXC
❑ 220033 AXC
❑ 220034 AXC

❑ 221101 AWC
❑ 221102 AWC
❑ 221103 AWC
❑ 221104 AWC
❑ 221105 AWC
❑ 221106 AWC
❑ 221107 AWC
❑ 221108 AWC
❑ 221109 AWC
❑ 221110 AWC
❑ 221111 AWC
❑ 221112 AWC
❑ 221113 AWC
❑ 221114 AWC
❑ 221115 AWC
❑ 221116 AWC
❑ 221117 AWC
❑ 221118 AWC
❑ 221119 AXC
❑ 221120 AXC
❑ 221121 AXC
❑ 221122 AXC
❑ 221123 AXC
❑ 221124 AXC
❑ 221125 AXC
❑ 221126 AXC
❑ 221127 AXC
❑ 221128 AXC
❑ 221129 AXC
❑ 221130 AXC
❑ 221131 AXC
❑ 221132 AXC
❑ 221133 AXC
❑ 221134 AXC
❑ 221135 AXC
❑ 221136 AXC
❑ 221137 AXC
❑ 221138 AXC
❑ 221139 AXC
❑ 221140 AXC
❑ 221141 AXC
❑ 221142 AWC
❑ 221143 AWC
❑ 221144 AXC

❑ 222001 EMR
❑ 222002 EMR
❑ 222003 EMR
❑ 222004 EMR
❑ 222005 EMR
❑ 222006 EMR
❑ 222007 EMR
❑ 222008 EMR
❑ 222009 EMR
❑ 222010 EMR
❑ 222011 EMR
❑ 222012 EMR
❑ 222013 EMR
❑ 222014 EMR
❑ 222015 EMR
❑ 222016 EMR
❑ 222017 EMR
❑ 222018 EMR
❑ 222019 EMR
❑ 222020 EMR
❑ 222021 EMR
❑ 222022 EMR
❑ 222023 EMR

❑ 222101 EMR
❑ 222102 EMR
❑ 222103 EMR
❑ 222104 EMR

❑ 230001 VIV
❑ 230002 VIV
❑ 230003 WMR
❑ 230004 WMR
❑ 230005 WMR
❑ 230006 TFW
❑ 230007 TFW
❑ 230008 TFW
❑ 230009 TFW
❑ 230010 TFW

Electric Multiple Units

❑ 62384 NRL

❑ 313121 NRL

❑ 313201 GTR
❑ 313202 GTR
❑ 313203 GTR
❑ 313204 GTR
❑ 313205 GTR
❑ 313206 GTR
❑ 313207 GTR
❑ 313208 GTR
❑ 313209 GTR
❑ 313210 GTR
❑ 313211 GTR
❑ 313212 GTR
❑ 313213 GTR
❑ 313214 GTR
❑ 313215 GTR
❑ 313216 GTR
❑ 313217 GTR
❑ 313219 GTR
❑ 313220 GTR

❑ 315801 LOG
❑ 315802 LOG
❑ 315803 LOG
❑ 315804 LOG
❑ 315805 LOG
❑ 315806 LOG
❑ 315807 LOG
❑ 315808 LOG
❑ 315809 LOG
❑ 315810 LOG
❑ 315811 LOG
❑ 315812 LOG
❑ 315815 LOG
❑ 315816 LOG
❑ 315817 LOG
❑ 315818 CRO
❑ 315819 CRO
❑ 315820 CRO
❑ 315824 CRO
❑ 315826 CRO
❑ 315827 CRO
❑ 315829 CRO
❑ 315830 CRO
❑ 315833 CRO
❑ 315834 CRO
❑ 315836 CRO
❑ 315837 CRO
❑ 315838 CRO
❑ 315839 CRO
❑ 315843 CRO

❑ 315844 CRO
❑ 315847 CRO
❑ 315848 CRO
❑ 315849 CRO
❑ 315851 CRO
❑ 315852 CRO
❑ 315853 CRO
❑ 315854 CRO
❑ 315856 CRO
❑ 315857 CRO

❑ 317337 GAR
❑ 317338 GAR
❑ 317339 GAR
❑ 317340 GAR
❑ 317341 GAR
❑ 317342 GAR
❑ 317343 GAR
❑ 317344 GAR
❑ 317345 GAR
❑ 317346 GAR
❑ 317347 GAR
❑ 317348 GAR

❑ 317501 GAR
❑ 317502 GAR
❑ 317503 GAR
❑ 317504 GAR
❑ 317505 GAR
❑ 317506 GAR
❑ 317507 GAR
❑ 317508 GAR
❑ 317509 GAR
❑ 317510 GAR
❑ 317511 GAR
❑ 317512 GAR
❑ 317513 GAR
❑ 317514 GAR
❑ 317515 GAR

❑ 317649 GAR
❑ 317650 GAR
❑ 317651 GAR
❑ 317652 GAR
❑ 317653 GAR
❑ 317654 GAR
❑ 317655 GAR
❑ 317656 GAR
❑ 317657 GAR
❑ 317658 GAR
❑ 317659 GAR
❑ 317660 GAR
❑ 317661 GAR
❑ 317662 GAR
❑ 317663 OLS
❑ 317664 GAR
❑ 317665 GAR
❑ 317666 GAR
❑ 317667 GAR
❑ 317668 GAR
❑ 317669 OLS
❑ 317670 GAR
❑ 317671 GAR
❑ 317672 GAR

❑ 317708 LOG
❑ 317709 LOG
❑ 317710 LOG
❑ 317714 LOG
❑ 317719 LOG
❑ 317723 LOG
❑ 317729 LOG
❑ 317732 LOG

❑ 317881 GAR
❑ 317882 GAR
❑ 317883 GAR
❑ 317884 GAR
❑ 317885 GAR
❑ 317886 GAR
❑ 317887 LOG
❑ 317888 LOG
❑ 317889 LOG
❑ 317890 LOG
❑ 317891 LOG
❑ 317892 LOG

❑ 318250 ASR
❑ 318251 ASR
❑ 318252 ASR
❑ 318253 ASR
❑ 318254 ASR
❑ 318255 ASR
❑ 318256 ASR
❑ 318257 ASR
❑ 318258 ASR
❑ 318259 ASR
❑ 318260 ASR
❑ 318261 ASR
❑ 318262 ASR
❑ 318263 ASR
❑ 318264 ASR
❑ 318265 ASR
❑ 318266 ASR
❑ 318267 ASR
❑ 318268 ASR
❑ 318269 ASR
❑ 318270 ASR

❑ 319001 PTR
❑ 319005 WMR
❑ 319009 OLS
❑ 319010 OLS
❑ 319011 OLS
❑ 319012 WMR
❑ 319013 WMR

❑ 319214 WMR
❑ 319215 WMR
❑ 319216 WMR
❑ 319217 WMR
❑ 319218 WMR
❑ 319219 WMR
❑ 319220 WMR
❑ 319361 NOR
❑ 319362 NOR
❑ 319363 NOR
❑ 319364 NOR
❑ 319365 NOR
❑ 319366 NOR
❑ 319367 NOR
❑ 319368 NOR
❑ 319369 NOR
❑ 319370 NOR
❑ 319371 NOR
❑ 319372 NOR
❑ 319373 NOR
❑ 319374 NOR
❑ 319375 NOR
❑ 319376 ROG
❑ 319377 ROG
❑ 319378 NOR
❑ 319379 NOR
❑ 319380 NOR
❑ 319381 NOR
❑ 319382 OLS
❑ 319383 NOR
❑ 319384 OLS
❑ 319385 NOR
❑ 319386 NOR

❑ 319421 OLS
❑ 319426 OLS
❑ 319429 WMR
❑ 319433 WMR
❑ 319441 WMR
❑ 319444 OLS
❑ 319446 NOR
❑ 319451 OLS
❑ 319453 OLS
❑ 319454 OLS
❑ 319455 WMR
❑ 319457 WMR
❑ 319460 WMR

❑ 320301 ASR
❑ 320302 ASR
❑ 320303 ASR
❑ 320304 ASR
❑ 320305 ASR
❑ 320306 ASR
❑ 320307 ASR
❑ 320308 ASR
❑ 320309 ASR
❑ 320310 ASR
❑ 320311 ASR
❑ 320312 ASR
❑ 320313 ASR
❑ 320314 ASR
❑ 320315 ASR
❑ 320316 ASR
❑ 320317 ASR
❑ 320318 ASR
❑ 320319 ASR
❑ 320320 ASR
❑ 320321 ASR
❑ 320322 ASR
❑ 320401 ASR
❑ 320402 ASR
❑ 320404 ASR
❑ 320411 ASR
❑ 320412 ASR
❑ 320413 ASR
❑ 320414 ASR
❑ 320415 ASR
❑ 320416 ASR
❑ 320417 ASR
❑ 320418 ASR
❑ 320420 ASR

❑ 321301 GAR
❑ 321302 GAR
❑ 321303 GAR
❑ 321304 GAR
❑ 321305 GAR
❑ 321306 GAR
❑ 321307 GAR
❑ 321308 GAR
❑ 321309 GAR
❑ 321310 GAR
❑ 321311 GAR
❑ 321312 GAR
❑ 321313 GAR
❑ 321314 GAR
❑ 321315 GAR
❑ 321316 GAR
❑ 321317 GAR
❑ 321318 GAR
❑ 321319 GAR
❑ 321320 GAR
❑ 321321 GAR
❑ 321322 GAR
❑ 321323 GAR
❑ 321324 GAR
❑ 321325 GAR
❑ 321326 GAR
❑ 321327 GAR
❑ 321328 GAR
❑ 321329 GAR
❑ 321330 GAR
❑ 321331 GAR
❑ 321332 GAR
❑ 321333 GAR
❑ 321334 GAR
❑ 321335 GAR
❑ 321336 GAR
❑ 321337 GAR
❑ 321338 GAR
❑ 321339 GAR
❑ 321340 GAR
❑ 321341 GAR
❑ 321342 GAR
❑ 321343 GAR
❑ 321344 GAR
❑ 321345 GAR
❑ 321346 GAR
❑ 321347 GAR
❑ 321348 GAR
❑ 321349 GAR
❑ 321350 GAR
❑ 321351 GAR
❑ 321352 GAR
❑ 321353 GAR
❑ 321354 GAR
❑ 321355 GAR
❑ 321356 GAR
❑ 321357 GAR
❑ 321358 GAR
❑ 321359 GAR
❑ 321360 GAR
❑ 321361 GAR
❑ 321362 GAR
❑ 321363 GAR
❑ 321364 GAR
❑ 321365 GAR
❑ 321366 GAR

❑ 321403 GAR
❑ 321405 GAR
❑ 321406 GAR
❑ 321407 GAR
❑ 321408 GAR
❑ 321409 GAR
❑ 321410 GAR
❑ 321419 GAR
❑ 321421 GAR
❑ 321422 GAR
❑ 321423 GAR
❑ 321424 GAR
❑ 321425 GAR
❑ 321426 GAR
❑ 321427 GAR
❑ 321428 GAR
❑ 321429 GAR
❑ 321430 GAR
❑ 321431 GAR
❑ 321432 GAR
❑ 321433 GAR
❑ 321434 GAR
❑ 321435 GAR
❑ 321436 GAR
❑ 321437 GAR
❑ 321438 GAR
❑ 321439 GAR
❑ 321440 GAR
❑ 321441 GAR
❑ 321442 GAR
❑ 321443 GAR
❑ 321444 GAR
❑ 321445 GAR
❑ 321446 GAR
❑ 321447 GAR
❑ 321448 GAR

❑ 321901 NOR
❑ 321902 NOR
❑ 321903 NOR

❑ 322481 NOR
❑ 322482 NOR
❑ 322483 NOR
❑ 322484 NOR
❑ 322485 NOR

❑ 323201 WMR

❑ 323202 WMR
❑ 323203 WMR
❑ 323204 WMR
❑ 323205 WMR
❑ 323206 WMR
❑ 323207 WMR
❑ 323208 WMR
❑ 323209 WMR
❑ 323210 WMR
❑ 323211 WMR
❑ 323212 WMR
❑ 323213 WMR
❑ 323214 WMR
❑ 323215 WMR
❑ 323216 WMR
❑ 323217 WMR
❑ 323218 WMR
❑ 323219 WMR
❑ 323220 WMR
❑ 323221 WMR
❑ 323222 WMR
❑ 323223 NOR
❑ 323224 NOR
❑ 323225 NOR
❑ 323226 NOR
❑ 323227 NOR
❑ 323228 NOR
❑ 323229 NOR
❑ 323230 NOR
❑ 323231 NOR
❑ 323232 NOR
❑ 323233 NOR
❑ 323234 NOR
❑ 323235 NOR
❑ 323236 NOR
❑ 323237 NOR
❑ 323238 NOR
❑ 323239 NOR
❑ 323240 WMR
❑ 323241 WMR
❑ 323242 WMR
❑ 323243 WMR

❑ 325001 DBC
❑ 325002 DBC
❑ 325003 DBC
❑ 325004 DBC
❑ 325005 DBC
❑ 325006 DBC
❑ 325007 DBC
❑ 325008 DBC
❑ 325009 DBC
❑ 325011 DBC
❑ 325012 DBC
❑ 325013 DBC
❑ 325014 DBC
❑ 325015 DBC
❑ 325016 DBC

❑ 331001 NOR
❑ 331002 NOR
❑ 331003 NOR
❑ 331004 NOR
❑ 331005 NOR
❑ 331006 NOR
❑ 331007 NOR
❑ 331008 NOR
❑ 331009 NOR
❑ 331010 NOR
❑ 331011 NOR
❑ 331012 NOR
❑ 331013 NOR
❑ 331014 NOR
❑ 331015 NOR
❑ 331016 NOR
❑ 331017 NOR
❑ 331018 NOR
❑ 331019 NOR
❑ 331020 NOR
❑ 331021 NOR
❑ 331022 NOR
❑ 331023 NOR
❑ 331024 NOR
❑ 331025 NOR
❑ 331026 NOR
❑ 331027 NOR
❑ 331028 NOR
❑ 331029 NOR
❑ 331030 NOR
❑ 331031 NOR

❑ 331101 NOR
❑ 331102 NOR
❑ 331103 NOR
❑ 331104 NOR
❑ 331105 NOR
❑ 331106 NOR
❑ 331107 NOR
❑ 331108 NOR
❑ 331109 NOR
❑ 331110 NOR
❑ 331111 NOR
❑ 331112 NOR

❑ 333001 NOR
❑ 333002 NOR
❑ 333003 NOR
❑ 333004 NOR
❑ 333005 NOR
❑ 333006 NOR
❑ 333007 NOR
❑ 333008 NOR
❑ 333009 NOR
❑ 333010 NOR
❑ 333011 NOR
❑ 333012 NOR
❑ 333013 NOR
❑ 333014 NOR
❑ 333015 NOR
❑ 333016 NOR

❑ 334001 ASR
❑ 334002 ASR
❑ 334003 ASR
❑ 334004 ASR
❑ 334005 ASR
❑ 334006 ASR
❑ 334007 ASR
❑ 334008 ASR
❑ 334009 ASR
❑ 334010 ASR
❑ 334011 ASR
❑ 334012 ASR
❑ 334013 ASR
❑ 334014 ASR
❑ 334015 ASR
❑ 334016 ASR
❑ 334017 ASR
❑ 334018 ASR
❑ 334019 ASR
❑ 334020 ASR
❑ 334021 ASR
❑ 334022 ASR
❑ 334023 ASR
❑ 334024 ASR
❑ 334025 ASR
❑ 334026 ASR
❑ 334027 ASR
❑ 334028 ASR
❑ 334029 ASR
❑ 334030 ASR
❑ 334031 ASR
❑ 334032 ASR
❑ 334033 ASR
❑ 334034 ASR
❑ 334035 ASR
❑ 334036 ASR
❑ 334037 ASR
❑ 334038 ASR
❑ 334039 ASR
❑ 334040 ASR

❑ 345001 CRO
❑ 345002 CRO
❑ 345003 CRO
❑ 345004 CRO
❑ 345005 CRO
❑ 345006 CRO
❑ 345007 CRO
❑ 345008 CRO
❑ 345009 CRO
❑ 345010 CRO
❑ 345011 CRO
❑ 345012 CRO
❑ 345013 CRO
❑ 345014 CRO
❑ 345015 CRO
❑ 345016 CRO
❑ 345017 CRO
❑ 345018 CRO
❑ 345019 CRO
❑ 345020 CRO
❑ 345021 CRO
❑ 345022 CRO
❑ 345023 CRO
❑ 345024 CRO
❑ 345025 CRO
❑ 345026 CRO
❑ 345027 CRO
❑ 345028 CRO
❑ 345029 CRO
❑ 345030 CRO
❑ 345031 CRO
❑ 345032 CRO
❑ 345033 CRO
❑ 345034 CRO
❑ 345035 CRO
❑ 345036 CRO
❑ 345037 CRO
❑ 345038 CRO
❑ 345039 CRO
❑ 345040 CRO
❑ 345041 CRO
❑ 345042 CRO
❑ 345043 CRO
❑ 345044 CRO
❑ 345045 CRO
❑ 345046 CRO
❑ 345047 CRO
❑ 345048 CRO
❑ 345049 CRO
❑ 345050 CRO
❑ 345051 CRO
❑ 345052 CRO
❑ 345053 CRO
❑ 345054 CRO
❑ 345055 CRO
❑ 345056 CRO
❑ 345057 CRO
❑ 345058 CRO
❑ 345059 CRO
❑ 345060 CRO
❑ 345061 CRO
❑ 345062 CRO
❑ 345063 CRO
❑ 345064 CRO
❑ 345065 CRO
❑ 345066 CRO
❑ 345067 CRO
❑ 345068 CRO
❑ 345069 CRO
❑ 345070 CRO

❑ 350101 WMR
❑ 350102 WMR
❑ 350103 WMR
❑ 350104 WMR
❑ 350105 WMR
❑ 350106 WMR
❑ 350107 WMR
❑ 350108 WMR
❑ 350109 WMR
❑ 350110 WMR
❑ 350111 WMR
❑ 350112 WMR
❑ 350113 WMR
❑ 350114 WMR
❑ 350115 WMR
❑ 350116 WMR
❑ 350117 WMR
❑ 350118 WMR
❑ 350119 WMR
❑ 350120 WMR
❑ 350121 WMR
❑ 350122 WMR
❑ 350123 WMR
❑ 350124 WMR
❑ 350125 WMR
❑ 350126 WMR
❑ 350127 WMR
❑ 350128 WMR
❑ 350129 WMR
❑ 350130 WMR

❑ 350231 WMR
❑ 350232 WMR
❑ 350233 WMR
❑ 350234 WMR
❑ 350235 WMR
❑ 350236 WMR
❑ 350237 WMR
❑ 350238 WMR
❑ 350239 WMR
❑ 350240 WMR
❑ 350241 WMR
❑ 350242 WMR
❑ 350243 WMR
❑ 350244 WMR
❑ 350245 WMR
❑ 350246 WMR
❑ 350247 WMR
❑ 350248 WMR
❑ 350249 WMR
❑ 350250 WMR
❑ 350251 WMR
❑ 350252 WMR
❑ 350253 WMR
❑ 350254 WMR
❑ 350255 WMR
❑ 350256 WMR
❑ 350257 WMR
❑ 350258 WMR
❑ 350259 WMR
❑ 350260 WMR
❑ 350261 WMR
❑ 350262 WMR
❑ 350263 WMR
❑ 350264 WMR
❑ 350265 WMR
❑ 350266 WMR
❑ 350267 WMR

❑ 350368 WMR
❑ 350369 WMR
❑ 350370 WMR
❑ 350371 WMR
❑ 350372 WMR
❑ 350373 WMR
❑ 350374 WMR
❑ 350375 WMR
❑ 350376 WMR
❑ 350377 WMR

❑ 350401 WMR
❑ 350402 WMR

❑ 350403 WMR
❑ 350404 WMR
❑ 350405 WMR
❑ 350406 WMR
❑ 350407 WMR
❑ 350408 WMR
❑ 350409 WMR
❑ 350410 WMR

❑ 357001 C2C
❑ 357002 C2C
❑ 357003 C2C
❑ 357004 C2C
❑ 357005 C2C
❑ 357006 C2C
❑ 357007 C2C
❑ 357008 C2C
❑ 357009 C2C
❑ 357010 C2C
❑ 357011 C2C
❑ 357012 C2C
❑ 357013 C2C
❑ 357014 C2C
❑ 357015 C2C
❑ 357016 C2C
❑ 357017 C2C
❑ 357018 C2C
❑ 357019 C2C
❑ 357020 C2C
❑ 357021 C2C
❑ 357022 C2C
❑ 357023 C2C
❑ 357024 C2C
❑ 357025 C2C
❑ 357026 C2C
❑ 357027 C2C
❑ 357028 C2C
❑ 357029 C2C
❑ 357030 C2C
❑ 357031 C2C
❑ 357032 C2C
❑ 357033 C2C
❑ 357034 C2C
❑ 357035 C2C
❑ 357036 C2C
❑ 357037 C2C
❑ 357038 C2C
❑ 357039 C2C
❑ 357040 C2C
❑ 357041 C2C
❑ 357042 C2C
❑ 357043 C2C
❑ 357044 C2C
❑ 357045 C2C
❑ 357046 C2C

❑ 357201 C2C
❑ 357202 C2C
❑ 357203 C2C
❑ 357204 C2C
❑ 357205 C2C
❑ 357206 C2C
❑ 357207 C2C
❑ 357208 C2C
❑ 357209 C2C
❑ 357210 C2C
❑ 357211 C2C
❑ 357312 C2C
❑ 357313 C2C
❑ 357314 C2C
❑ 357315 C2C
❑ 357316 C2C
❑ 357317 C2C
❑ 357318 C2C
❑ 357319 C2C
❑ 357320 C2C
❑ 357321 C2C
❑ 357322 C2C
❑ 357323 C2C
❑ 357324 C2C
❑ 357325 C2C
❑ 357326 C2C
❑ 357327 C2C
❑ 357328 C2C

❑ 360101 GAR
❑ 360102 GAR
❑ 360103 GAR
❑ 360104 GAR
❑ 360105 GAR
❑ 360106 GAR
❑ 360107 GAR
❑ 360108 GAR
❑ 360109 GAR
❑ 360110 GAR
❑ 360111 GAR
❑ 360112 GAR
❑ 360113 GAR
❑ 360114 GAR
❑ 360115 GAR
❑ 360116 GAR
❑ 360117 GAR
❑ 360118 GAR
❑ 360119 GAR
❑ 360120 GAR
❑ 360121 GAR

❑ 360201 TFL
❑ 360202 TFL
❑ 360203 TFL
❑ 360204 TFL
❑ 360205 TFL

❑ 365501 OLS
❑ 365502 GTR
❑ 365503 OLS
❑ 365504 GTR
❑ 365505 OLS
❑ 365506 GTR
❑ 365507 OLS
❑ 365508 GTR
❑ 365509 ASR
❑ 365510 GTR
❑ 365511 GTR
❑ 365512 GTR
❑ 365513 ASR
❑ 365514 GTR
❑ 365515 OLS
❑ 365516 GTR
❑ 365517 ASR
❑ 365518 GTR
❑ 365519 ASR
❑ 365520 GTR
❑ 365521 ASR
❑ 365522 GTR
❑ 365523 ASR
❑ 365524 GTR
❑ 365525 ASR
❑ 365527 OLS
❑ 365528 GTR
❑ 365529 ASR
❑ 365530 GTR
❑ 365531 GTR
❑ 365532 GTR
❑ 365533 ASR
❑ 365534 GTR
❑ 365535 OLS
❑ 365536 GTR
❑ 365537 ASR
❑ 365538 GTR
❑ 365539 GTR
❑ 365540 GTR
❑ 365541 GTR

❑ 373007 EUS
❑ 373008 EUS
❑ 373015 EUS
❑ 373016 EUS
❑ 373021 EUS
❑ 373022 EUS
❑ 373205 EUS
❑ 373206 EUS
❑ 373209 EUS
❑ 373210 EUS
❑ 373211 EUS
❑ 373212 EUS
❑ 373213 EUS
❑ 373214 EUS
❑ 373215 EUS
❑ 373216 EUS
❑ 373217 EUS
❑ 373218 EUS
❑ 373219 EUS
❑ 373220 EUS
❑ 373221 EUS
❑ 373222 EUS
❑ 373223 EUS
❑ 373224 EUS
❑ 373229 EUS
❑ 373230 EUS

❑ 373399 EUS

❑ 374001 EUS
❑ 374002 EUS
❑ 374003 EUS
❑ 374004 EUS
❑ 374005 EUS
❑ 374006 EUS
❑ 374007 EUS
❑ 374008 EUS
❑ 374009 EUS
❑ 374010 EUS
❑ 374011 EUS
❑ 374012 EUS
❑ 374013 EUS
❑ 374014 EUS
❑ 374015 EUS
❑ 374016 EUS
❑ 374017 EUS
❑ 374018 EUS
❑ 374019 EUS
❑ 374020 EUS
❑ 374021 EUS
❑ 374022 EUS
❑ 374023 EUS
❑ 374024 EUS
❑ 374025 EUS
❑ 374026 EUS
❑ 374027 EUS
❑ 374028 EUS
❑ 374029 EUS
❑ 374030 EUS
❑ 374031 EUS
❑ 374032 EUS
❑ 374033 EUS
❑ 374034 EUS

❑ 375301 SET
❑ 375302 SET
❑ 375303 SET
❑ 375304 SET
❑ 375305 SET
❑ 375306 SET
❑ 375307 SET
❑ 375308 SET
❑ 375309 SET
❑ 375310 SET

❑ 375601 SET
❑ 375602 SET
❑ 375603 SET
❑ 375604 SET
❑ 375605 SET
❑ 375606 SET
❑ 375607 SET
❑ 375608 SET
❑ 375609 SET
❑ 375610 SET
❑ 375611 SET
❑ 375612 SET
❑ 375613 SET
❑ 375614 SET
❑ 375615 SET
❑ 375616 SET
❑ 375617 SET
❑ 375618 SET
❑ 375619 SET
❑ 375620 SET
❑ 375621 SET
❑ 375622 SET
❑ 375623 SET
❑ 375624 SET
❑ 375625 SET
❑ 375626 SET
❑ 375627 SET
❑ 375628 SET
❑ 375629 SET
❑ 375630 SET

❑ 375701 SET
❑ 375702 SET
❑ 375703 SET
❑ 375704 SET
❑ 375705 SET
❑ 375706 SET
❑ 375707 SET
❑ 375708 SET
❑ 375709 SET
❑ 375710 SET
❑ 375711 SET
❑ 375712 SET
❑ 375713 SET
❑ 375714 SET
❑ 375715 SET

❑ 375801 SET
❑ 375802 SET
❑ 375803 SET
❑ 375804 SET
❑ 375805 SET
❑ 375806 SET
❑ 375807 SET
❑ 375808 SET
❑ 375809 SET
❑ 375810 SET
❑ 375811 SET
❑ 375812 SET
❑ 375813 SET
❑ 375814 SET
❑ 375815 SET
❑ 375816 SET
❑ 375817 SET
❑ 375818 SET
❑ 375819 SET
❑ 375820 SET
❑ 375821 SET
❑ 375822 SET
❑ 375823 SET
❑ 375824 SET
❑ 375825 SET
❑ 375826 SET
❑ 375827 SET
❑ 375828 SET
❑ 375829 SET
❑ 375830 SET

❑ 375901 SET
❑ 375902 SET
❑ 375903 SET
❑ 375904 SET
❑ 375905 SET
❑ 375906 SET
❑ 375907 SET
❑ 375908 SET

- ❑ 375909 SET
- ❑ 375910 SET
- ❑ 375911 SET
- ❑ 375912 SET
- ❑ 375913 SET
- ❑ 375914 SET
- ❑ 375915 SET
- ❑ 375916 SET
- ❑ 375917 SET
- ❑ 375918 SET
- ❑ 375919 SET
- ❑ 375920 SET
- ❑ 375921 SET
- ❑ 375922 SET
- ❑ 375923 SET
- ❑ 375924 SET
- ❑ 375925 SET
- ❑ 375926 SET
- ❑ 375927 SET

- ❑ 376001 SET
- ❑ 376002 SET
- ❑ 376003 SET
- ❑ 376004 SET
- ❑ 376005 SET
- ❑ 376006 SET
- ❑ 376007 SET
- ❑ 376008 SET
- ❑ 376009 SET
- ❑ 376010 SET
- ❑ 376011 SET
- ❑ 376012 SET
- ❑ 376013 SET
- ❑ 376014 SET
- ❑ 376015 SET
- ❑ 376016 SET
- ❑ 376017 SET
- ❑ 376018 SET
- ❑ 376019 SET
- ❑ 376020 SET
- ❑ 376021 SET
- ❑ 376022 SET
- ❑ 376023 SET
- ❑ 376024 SET
- ❑ 376025 SET
- ❑ 376026 SET
- ❑ 376027 SET
- ❑ 376028 SET
- ❑ 376029 SET
- ❑ 376030 SET
- ❑ 376031 SET
- ❑ 376032 SET
- ❑ 376033 SET
- ❑ 376034 SET
- ❑ 376035 SET
- ❑ 376036 SET

- ❑ 377101 GTR
- ❑ 377102 GTR
- ❑ 377103 GTR
- ❑ 377104 GTR
- ❑ 377105 GTR
- ❑ 377106 GTR
- ❑ 377107 GTR
- ❑ 377108 GTR
- ❑ 377109 GTR
- ❑ 377110 GTR
- ❑ 377111 GTR
- ❑ 377112 GTR
- ❑ 377113 GTR
- ❑ 377114 GTR
- ❑ 377115 GTR
- ❑ 377116 GTR
- ❑ 377117 GTR
- ❑ 377118 GTR
- ❑ 377119 GTR
- ❑ 377120 GTR
- ❑ 377121 GTR
- ❑ 377122 GTR
- ❑ 377123 GTR
- ❑ 377124 GTR
- ❑ 377125 GTR
- ❑ 377126 GTR
- ❑ 377127 GTR
- ❑ 377128 GTR
- ❑ 377129 GTR
- ❑ 377130 GTR
- ❑ 377131 GTR
- ❑ 377132 GTR
- ❑ 377133 GTR
- ❑ 377134 GTR
- ❑ 377135 GTR
- ❑ 377136 GTR
- ❑ 377137 GTR
- ❑ 377138 GTR
- ❑ 377139 GTR
- ❑ 377140 GTR
- ❑ 377141 GTR
- ❑ 377142 GTR
- ❑ 377143 GTR
- ❑ 377144 GTR
- ❑ 377145 GTR
- ❑ 377146 GTR
- ❑ 377147 GTR
- ❑ 377148 GTR
- ❑ 377149 GTR
- ❑ 377150 GTR
- ❑ 377151 GTR
- ❑ 377152 GTR
- ❑ 377153 GTR
- ❑ 377154 GTR
- ❑ 377155 GTR
- ❑ 377156 GTR
- ❑ 377157 GTR
- ❑ 377158 GTR
- ❑ 377159 GTR
- ❑ 377160 GTR
- ❑ 377161 GTR
- ❑ 377162 GTR
- ❑ 377163 GTR
- ❑ 377164 GTR

- ❑ 377201 GTR
- ❑ 377202 GTR
- ❑ 377203 GTR
- ❑ 377204 GTR
- ❑ 377205 GTR
- ❑ 377206 GTR
- ❑ 377207 GTR
- ❑ 377208 GTR
- ❑ 377209 GTR
- ❑ 377210 GTR
- ❑ 377211 GTR
- ❑ 377212 GTR
- ❑ 377213 GTR
- ❑ 377214 GTR
- ❑ 377215 GTR

- ❑ 377301 GTR
- ❑ 377302 GTR
- ❑ 377303 GTR
- ❑ 377304 GTR
- ❑ 377305 GTR
- ❑ 377306 GTR
- ❑ 377307 GTR
- ❑ 377308 GTR
- ❑ 377309 GTR
- ❑ 377310 GTR
- ❑ 377311 GTR
- ❑ 377312 GTR
- ❑ 377313 GTR
- ❑ 377314 GTR
- ❑ 377315 GTR
- ❑ 377316 GTR
- ❑ 377317 GTR
- ❑ 377318 GTR
- ❑ 377319 GTR
- ❑ 377320 GTR
- ❑ 377321 GTR
- ❑ 377322 GTR
- ❑ 377323 GTR
- ❑ 377324 GTR
- ❑ 377325 GTR
- ❑ 377326 GTR
- ❑ 377327 GTR
- ❑ 377328 GTR

- ❑ 377401 GTR
- ❑ 377402 GTR
- ❑ 377403 GTR
- ❑ 377404 GTR
- ❑ 377405 GTR
- ❑ 377406 GTR
- ❑ 377407 GTR
- ❑ 377408 GTR
- ❑ 377409 GTR
- ❑ 377410 GTR
- ❑ 377411 GTR
- ❑ 377412 GTR
- ❑ 377413 GTR
- ❑ 377414 GTR
- ❑ 377415 GTR
- ❑ 377416 GTR
- ❑ 377417 GTR
- ❑ 377418 GTR
- ❑ 377419 GTR
- ❑ 377420 GTR
- ❑ 377421 GTR
- ❑ 377422 GTR
- ❑ 377423 GTR
- ❑ 377424 GTR
- ❑ 377425 GTR
- ❑ 377426 GTR
- ❑ 377427 GTR
- ❑ 377428 GTR
- ❑ 377429 GTR
- ❑ 377430 GTR
- ❑ 377431 GTR
- ❑ 377432 GTR
- ❑ 377433 GTR
- ❑ 377434 GTR
- ❑ 377435 GTR
- ❑ 377436 GTR
- ❑ 377437 GTR
- ❑ 377438 GTR
- ❑ 377439 GTR
- ❑ 377440 GTR
- ❑ 377441 GTR
- ❑ 377442 GTR
- ❑ 377443 GTR
- ❑ 377444 GTR
- ❑ 377445 GTR
- ❑ 377446 GTR
- ❑ 377447 GTR
- ❑ 377448 GTR
- ❑ 377449 GTR
- ❑ 377450 GTR
- ❑ 377451 GTR
- ❑ 377452 GTR
- ❑ 377453 GTR
- ❑ 377454 GTR
- ❑ 377455 GTR
- ❑ 377456 GTR
- ❑ 377457 GTR
- ❑ 377458 GTR
- ❑ 377459 GTR
- ❑ 377460 GTR
- ❑ 377461 GTR
- ❑ 377462 GTR
- ❑ 377463 GTR
- ❑ 377464 GTR
- ❑ 377465 GTR
- ❑ 377466 GTR
- ❑ 377467 GTR
- ❑ 377468 GTR
- ❑ 377469 GTR
- ❑ 377470 GTR
- ❑ 377471 GTR
- ❑ 377472 GTR
- ❑ 377473 GTR
- ❑ 377474 GTR
- ❑ 377475 GTR

- ❑ 377501 SET
- ❑ 377502 SET
- ❑ 377503 SET
- ❑ 377504 SET
- ❑ 377505 SET
- ❑ 377506 SET
- ❑ 377507 SET
- ❑ 377508 SET
- ❑ 377509 SET
- ❑ 377510 SET
- ❑ 377511 SET
- ❑ 377512 SET
- ❑ 377513 SET
- ❑ 377514 SET
- ❑ 377515 SET
- ❑ 377516 SET
- ❑ 377517 SET
- ❑ 377518 SET
- ❑ 377519 SET
- ❑ 377520 SET
- ❑ 377521 SET
- ❑ 377522 SET
- ❑ 377523 SET

- ❑ 377601 GTR
- ❑ 377602 GTR
- ❑ 377603 GTR
- ❑ 377604 GTR
- ❑ 377605 GTR
- ❑ 377606 GTR
- ❑ 377607 GTR
- ❑ 377608 GTR
- ❑ 377609 GTR
- ❑ 377610 GTR
- ❑ 377611 GTR
- ❑ 377612 GTR
- ❑ 377613 GTR
- ❑ 377614 GTR
- ❑ 377615 GTR
- ❑ 377616 GTR
- ❑ 377617 GTR
- ❑ 377618 GTR
- ❑ 377619 GTR
- ❑ 377620 GTR
- ❑ 377621 GTR
- ❑ 377622 GTR
- ❑ 377623 GTR
- ❑ 377624 GTR
- ❑ 377625 GTR
- ❑ 377626 GTR

- ❑ 377701 GTR
- ❑ 377702 GTR
- ❑ 377703 GTR
- ❑ 377704 GTR
- ❑ 377705 GTR
- ❑ 377706 GTR
- ❑ 377707 GTR
- ❑ 377708 GTR

- ❑ 378135 LOG
- ❑ 378136 LOG
- ❑ 378137 LOG
- ❑ 378138 LOG
- ❑ 378139 LOG
- ❑ 378140 LOG
- ❑ 378141 LOG
- ❑ 378142 LOG
- ❑ 378143 LOG
- ❑ 378144 LOG
- ❑ 378145 LOG
- ❑ 378146 LOG

❑ 378147 LOG
❑ 378148 LOG
❑ 378149 LOG
❑ 378150 LOG
❑ 378151 LOG
❑ 378152 LOG
❑ 378153 LOG
❑ 378154 LOG

❑ 378201 LOG
❑ 378202 LOG
❑ 378203 LOG
❑ 378204 LOG
❑ 378205 LOG
❑ 378206 LOG
❑ 378207 LOG
❑ 378208 LOG
❑ 378209 LOG
❑ 378210 LOG
❑ 378211 LOG
❑ 378212 LOG
❑ 378213 LOG
❑ 378214 LOG
❑ 378215 LOG
❑ 378216 LOG
❑ 378217 LOG
❑ 378218 LOG
❑ 378219 LOG
❑ 378220 LOG
❑ 378221 LOG
❑ 378222 LOG
❑ 378223 LOG
❑ 378224 LOG
❑ 378225 LOG
❑ 378226 LOG
❑ 378227 LOG
❑ 378228 LOG
❑ 378229 LOG
❑ 378230 LOG
❑ 378231 LOG
❑ 378232 LOG
❑ 378233 LOG
❑ 378234 LOG
❑ 378255 LOG
❑ 378256 LOG
❑ 378257 LOG

❑ 379001 GAR
❑ 379002 GAR
❑ 379003 GAR
❑ 379004 GAR
❑ 379005 GAR
❑ 379006 GAR
❑ 379007 GAR
❑ 379008 GAR
❑ 379009 GAR
❑ 379010 GAR
❑ 379011 GAR
❑ 379012 GAR
❑ 379013 GAR
❑ 379014 GAR
❑ 379015 GAR
❑ 379016 GAR
❑ 379017 GAR
❑ 379018 GAR
❑ 379019 GAR
❑ 379020 GAR
❑ 379021 GAR
❑ 379022 GAR
❑ 379023 GAR
❑ 379024 GAR
❑ 379025 GAR
❑ 379026 GAR
❑ 379027 GAR
❑ 379028 GAR
❑ 379029 GAR
❑ 379030 GAR

❑ 380001 ASR
❑ 380002 ASR
❑ 380003 ASR
❑ 380004 ASR
❑ 380005 ASR
❑ 380006 ASR
❑ 380007 ASR
❑ 380008 ASR
❑ 380009 ASR
❑ 380010 ASR
❑ 380011 ASR
❑ 380012 ASR
❑ 380013 ASR
❑ 380014 ASR
❑ 380015 ASR
❑ 380016 ASR
❑ 380017 ASR
❑ 380018 ASR
❑ 380019 ASR
❑ 380020 ASR
❑ 380021 ASR
❑ 380022 ASR

❑ 380101 ASR
❑ 380102 ASR
❑ 380103 ASR
❑ 380104 ASR
❑ 380105 ASR
❑ 380106 ASR
❑ 380107 ASR
❑ 380108 ASR
❑ 380109 ASR
❑ 380110 ASR
❑ 380111 ASR
❑ 380112 ASR
❑ 380113 ASR
❑ 380114 ASR
❑ 380115 ASR
❑ 380116 ASR

❑ 385001 ASR
❑ 385002 ASR
❑ 385003 ASR
❑ 385004 ASR
❑ 385005 ASR
❑ 385006 ASR
❑ 385007 ASR
❑ 385008 ASR
❑ 385009 ASR
❑ 385010 ASR
❑ 385011 ASR
❑ 385012 ASR
❑ 385013 ASR
❑ 385014 ASR
❑ 385015 ASR
❑ 385016 ASR
❑ 385017 ASR
❑ 385018 ASR
❑ 385019 ASR
❑ 385020 ASR
❑ 385021 ASR
❑ 385022 ASR
❑ 385023 ASR
❑ 385024 ASR
❑ 385025 ASR
❑ 385026 ASR
❑ 385027 ASR
❑ 385028 ASR
❑ 385029 ASR
❑ 385030 ASR
❑ 385031 ASR
❑ 385032 ASR
❑ 385033 ASR
❑ 385034 ASR
❑ 385035 ASR
❑ 385036 ASR
❑ 385037 ASR
❑ 385038 ASR
❑ 385039 ASR
❑ 385040 ASR
❑ 385041 ASR
❑ 385042 ASR
❑ 385043 ASR
❑ 385044 ASR
❑ 385045 ASR
❑ 385046 ASR

❑ 385101 ASR
❑ 385102 ASR
❑ 385103 ASR
❑ 385104 ASR
❑ 385105 ASR
❑ 385106 ASR
❑ 385107 ASR
❑ 385108 ASR
❑ 385109 ASR
❑ 385110 ASR
❑ 385111 ASR
❑ 385112 ASR
❑ 385113 ASR
❑ 385114 ASR
❑ 385115 ASR
❑ 385116 ASR
❑ 385117 ASR
❑ 385118 ASR
❑ 385119 ASR
❑ 385120 ASR
❑ 385121 ASR
❑ 385122 ASR
❑ 385123 ASR
❑ 385124 ASR

❑ 387101 GTR
❑ 387102 GTR
❑ 387103 GTR
❑ 387104 GTR
❑ 387105 GTR
❑ 387106 GTR
❑ 387107 GTR
❑ 387108 GTR
❑ 387109 GTR
❑ 387110 GTR
❑ 387111 GTR
❑ 387112 GTR
❑ 387113 GTR
❑ 387114 GTR
❑ 387115 GTR
❑ 387116 GTR
❑ 387117 GTR
❑ 387118 GTR
❑ 387119 GTR
❑ 387120 GTR
❑ 387121 GTR
❑ 387122 GTR
❑ 387123 GTR
❑ 387124 GTR
❑ 387125 GTR
❑ 387126 GTR
❑ 387127 GTR
❑ 387128 GTR
❑ 387129 GTR
❑ 387130 GWR
❑ 387131 GWR
❑ 387132 GWR
❑ 387133 GWR
❑ 387134 GWR
❑ 387135 GWR
❑ 387136 GWR
❑ 387137 GWR
❑ 387138 GWR
❑ 387139 GWR
❑ 387140 GWR
❑ 387141 GWR
❑ 387142 GWR
❑ 387143 GWR
❑ 387144 GWR
❑ 387145 GWR
❑ 387146 GWR
❑ 387147 GWR
❑ 387148 GWR
❑ 387149 GWR
❑ 387150 GWR
❑ 387151 GWR
❑ 387152 GWR
❑ 387153 GWR
❑ 387154 GWR
❑ 387155 GWR
❑ 387156 GWR
❑ 387157 GWR
❑ 387158 GWR
❑ 387159 GWR
❑ 387160 GWR
❑ 387161 GWR
❑ 387162 GWR
❑ 387163 GWR
❑ 387164 GWR
❑ 387165 GWR
❑ 387166 GWR
❑ 387167 GWR
❑ 387168 GWR
❑ 387169 GWR
❑ 387170 GWR
❑ 387171 GWR
❑ 387172 GWR
❑ 387173 GWR
❑ 387174 GWR

❑ 387201 GTR
❑ 387202 GTR
❑ 387203 GTR
❑ 387204 GTR
❑ 387205 GTR
❑ 387206 GTR
❑ 387207 GTR
❑ 387208 GTR
❑ 387209 GTR
❑ 387210 GTR
❑ 387211 GTR
❑ 387212 GTR
❑ 387213 GTR
❑ 387214 GTR
❑ 387215 GTR
❑ 387216 GTR
❑ 387217 GTR
❑ 387218 GTR
❑ 387219 GTR
❑ 387220 GTR
❑ 387221 GTR
❑ 387222 GTR
❑ 387223 GTR
❑ 387224 GTR
❑ 387225 GTR
❑ 387226 GTR
❑ 387227 GTR

❑ 387301 C2C
❑ 387302 C2C
❑ 387303 C2C
❑ 387304 C2C
❑ 387305 C2C
❑ 387306 C2C

❑ 390001 AWC
❑ 390002 AWC
❑ 390103 AWC
❑ 390104 AWC
❑ 390005 AWC
❑ 390006 AWC
❑ 390107 AWC
❑ 390008 AWC
❑ 390009 AWC
❑ 390010 AWC
❑ 390011 AWC
❑ 390112 AWC
❑ 390013 AWC
❑ 390114 AWC
❑ 390115 AWC
❑ 390016 AWC

❑ 390117 AWC
❑ 390118 AWC
❑ 390119 AWC
❑ 390020 AWC
❑ 390121 AWC
❑ 390122 AWC
❑ 390123 AWC
❑ 390124 AWC
❑ 390125 AWC
❑ 390126 AWC
❑ 390127 AWC
❑ 390128 AWC
❑ 390129 AWC
❑ 390130 AWC
❑ 390131 AWC
❑ 390132 AWC
❑ 390134 AWC
❑ 390135 AWC
❑ 390136 AWC
❑ 390137 AWC
❑ 390138 AWC
❑ 390039 AWC
❑ 390040 AWC
❑ 390141 AWC
❑ 390042 AWC
❑ 390043 AWC
❑ 390044 AWC
❑ 390045 AWC
❑ 390046 AWC
❑ 390047 AWC
❑ 390148 AWC
❑ 390049 AWC
❑ 390050 AWC
❑ 390151 AWC
❑ 390152 AWC
❑ 390153 AWC
❑ 390154 AWC
❑ 390155 AWC
❑ 390156 AWC
❑ 390157 AWC

❑ 395001 SET
❑ 395002 SET
❑ 395003 SET
❑ 395004 SET
❑ 395005 SET
❑ 395006 SET
❑ 395007 SET
❑ 395008 SET
❑ 395009 SET
❑ 395010 SET
❑ 395011 SET
❑ 395012 SET
❑ 395013 SET
❑ 395014 SET
❑ 395015 SET
❑ 395016 SET
❑ 395017 SET
❑ 395018 SET
❑ 395019 SET
❑ 395020 SET
❑ 395021 SET
❑ 395022 SET
❑ 395023 SET
❑ 395024 SET
❑ 395025 SET
❑ 395026 SET
❑ 395027 SET
❑ 395028 SET
❑ 395029 SET

❑ 397001 FTP
❑ 397002 FTP
❑ 397003 FTP
❑ 397004 FTP
❑ 397005 FTP
❑ 397006 FTP
❑ 397007 FTP
❑ 397008 FTP
❑ 397009 FTP
❑ 397010 FTP
❑ 397011 FTP
❑ 397012 FTP

❑ 399201 NOR
❑ 399202 NOR
❑ 399203 NOR
❑ 399204 NOR
❑ 399205 NOR
❑ 399206 NOR
❑ 399207 NOR

❑ 442401 OLS
❑ 442402 SWR
❑ 442403 SWR
❑ 442404 SWR
❑ 442405 OLS
❑ 442406 OLS
❑ 442407 OLS
❑ 442408 SWR
❑ 442409 SWR
❑ 442410 SWR
❑ 442411 SWR
❑ 442412 OLS
❑ 442413 SWR
❑ 442414 SWR
❑ 442415 SWR
❑ 442416 SWR
❑ 442417 SWR
❑ 442418 SWR
❑ 442419 SWR
❑ 442420 SWR
❑ 442421 OLS
❑ 442422 SWR
❑ 442423 SWR
❑ 442424 OLS

❑ 444001 SWR
❑ 444002 SWR
❑ 444003 SWR
❑ 444004 SWR
❑ 444005 SWR
❑ 444006 SWR
❑ 444007 SWR
❑ 444008 SWR
❑ 444009 SWR
❑ 444010 SWR
❑ 444011 SWR
❑ 444012 SWR
❑ 444013 SWR
❑ 444014 SWR
❑ 444015 SWR
❑ 444016 SWR
❑ 444017 SWR
❑ 444018 SWR
❑ 444019 SWR
❑ 444020 SWR
❑ 444021 SWR
❑ 444022 SWR
❑ 444023 SWR
❑ 444024 SWR
❑ 444025 SWR
❑ 444026 SWR
❑ 444027 SWR
❑ 444028 SWR
❑ 444029 SWR
❑ 444030 SWR
❑ 444031 SWR
❑ 444032 SWR
❑ 444033 SWR
❑ 444034 SWR
❑ 444035 SWR
❑ 444036 SWR
❑ 444037 SWR
❑ 444038 SWR
❑ 444039 SWR
❑ 444040 SWR
❑ 444041 SWR
❑ 444042 SWR
❑ 444043 SWR
❑ 444044 SWR
❑ 444045 SWR

❑ 450001 SWR
❑ 450002 SWR
❑ 450003 SWR
❑ 450004 SWR
❑ 450005 SWR
❑ 450006 SWR
❑ 450007 SWR
❑ 450008 SWR
❑ 450009 SWR
❑ 450010 SWR
❑ 450011 SWR
❑ 450012 SWR
❑ 450013 SWR
❑ 450014 SWR
❑ 450015 SWR
❑ 450016 SWR
❑ 450017 SWR
❑ 450018 SWR
❑ 450019 SWR
❑ 450020 SWR
❑ 450021 SWR
❑ 450022 SWR
❑ 450023 SWR
❑ 450024 SWR
❑ 450025 SWR
❑ 450026 SWR
❑ 450027 SWR
❑ 450028 SWR
❑ 450029 SWR
❑ 450030 SWR
❑ 450031 SWR
❑ 450032 SWR
❑ 450033 SWR
❑ 450034 SWR
❑ 450035 SWR
❑ 450036 SWR
❑ 450037 SWR
❑ 450038 SWR
❑ 450039 SWR
❑ 450040 SWR
❑ 450041 SWR
❑ 450042 SWR
❑ 450043 SWR
❑ 450044 SWR
❑ 450045 SWR
❑ 450046 SWR
❑ 450047 SWR
❑ 450048 SWR
❑ 450049 SWR
❑ 450050 SWR
❑ 450051 SWR
❑ 450052 SWR
❑ 450053 SWR
❑ 450054 SWR
❑ 450055 SWR
❑ 450056 SWR
❑ 450057 SWR
❑ 450058 SWR
❑ 450059 SWR
❑ 450060 SWR
❑ 450061 SWR
❑ 450062 SWR
❑ 450063 SWR
❑ 450064 SWR
❑ 450065 SWR
❑ 450066 SWR
❑ 450067 SWR
❑ 450068 SWR
❑ 450069 SWR
❑ 450070 SWR
❑ 450071 SWR
❑ 450072 SWR
❑ 450073 SWR
❑ 450074 SWR
❑ 450075 SWR
❑ 450076 SWR
❑ 450077 SWR
❑ 450078 SWR
❑ 450079 SWR
❑ 450080 SWR
❑ 450081 SWR
❑ 450082 SWR
❑ 450083 SWR
❑ 450084 SWR
❑ 450085 SWR
❑ 450086 SWR
❑ 450087 SWR
❑ 450088 SWR
❑ 450089 SWR
❑ 450090 SWR
❑ 450091 SWR
❑ 450092 SWR
❑ 450093 SWR
❑ 450094 SWR
❑ 450095 SWR
❑ 450096 SWR
❑ 450097 SWR
❑ 450098 SWR
❑ 450099 SWR
❑ 450100 SWR
❑ 450101 SWR
❑ 450102 SWR
❑ 450103 SWR
❑ 450104 SWR
❑ 450105 SWR
❑ 450106 SWR
❑ 450107 SWR
❑ 450108 SWR
❑ 450109 SWR
❑ 450110 SWR
❑ 450111 SWR
❑ 450112 SWR
❑ 450113 SWR
❑ 450114 SWR
❑ 450115 SWR
❑ 450116 SWR
❑ 450117 SWR
❑ 450118 SWR
❑ 450119 SWR
❑ 450120 SWR
❑ 450121 SWR
❑ 450122 SWR
❑ 450123 SWR
❑ 450124 SWR
❑ 450125 SWR
❑ 450126 SWR
❑ 450127 SWR

❑ 455701 SWR
❑ 455702 SWR
❑ 455703 SWR
❑ 455704 SWR
❑ 455705 SWR
❑ 455706 SWR
❑ 455707 SWR
❑ 455708 SWR
❑ 455709 SWR
❑ 455710 SWR
❑ 455711 SWR
❑ 455712 SWR
❑ 455713 SWR
❑ 455714 SWR
❑ 455715 SWR
❑ 455716 SWR
❑ 455717 SWR
❑ 455718 SWR
❑ 455719 SWR
❑ 455720 SWR
❑ 455721 SWR
❑ 455722 SWR
❑ 455723 SWR
❑ 455724 SWR

❑ 455725 SWR
❑ 455726 SWR
❑ 455727 SWR
❑ 455728 SWR
❑ 455729 SWR
❑ 455730 SWR
❑ 455731 SWR
❑ 455732 SWR
❑ 455733 SWR
❑ 455734 SWR
❑ 455735 SWR
❑ 455736 SWR
❑ 455737 SWR
❑ 455738 SWR
❑ 455739 SWR
❑ 455740 SWR
❑ 455741 SWR
❑ 455742 SWR
❑ 455750 SWR

❑ 455801 GTR
❑ 455802 GTR
❑ 455803 GTR
❑ 455804 GTR
❑ 455805 GTR
❑ 455806 GTR
❑ 455807 GTR
❑ 455808 GTR
❑ 455809 GTR
❑ 455810 GTR
❑ 455811 GTR
❑ 455812 GTR
❑ 455813 GTR
❑ 455814 GTR
❑ 455815 GTR
❑ 455816 GTR
❑ 455817 GTR
❑ 455818 GTR
❑ 455819 GTR
❑ 455820 GTR
❑ 455821 GTR
❑ 455822 GTR
❑ 455823 GTR
❑ 455824 GTR
❑ 455825 GTR
❑ 455826 GTR
❑ 455827 GTR
❑ 455828 GTR
❑ 455829 GTR
❑ 455830 GTR
❑ 455831 GTR
❑ 455832 GTR
❑ 455833 GTR
❑ 455834 GTR
❑ 455835 GTR
❑ 455836 GTR
❑ 455837 GTR
❑ 455838 GTR
❑ 455839 GTR
❑ 455840 GTR
❑ 455841 GTR
❑ 455842 GTR
❑ 455843 GTR
❑ 455844 GTR
❑ 455845 GTR
❑ 455846 GTR
❑ 455847 SWR
❑ 455848 SWR
❑ 455849 SWR
❑ 455850 SWR
❑ 455851 SWR
❑ 455852 SWR
❑ 455853 SWR
❑ 455854 SWR
❑ 455855 SWR
❑ 455856 SWR
❑ 455857 SWR
❑ 455858 SWR
❑ 455859 SWR
❑ 455860 SWR
❑ 455861 SWR
❑ 455862 SWR
❑ 455863 SWR
❑ 455864 SWR
❑ 455865 SWR
❑ 455866 SWR
❑ 455867 SWR
❑ 455868 SWR
❑ 455869 SWR
❑ 455870 SWR
❑ 455871 SWR
❑ 455872 SWR
❑ 455873 SWR
❑ 455874 SWR

❑ 455901 SWR
❑ 455902 SWR
❑ 455903 SWR
❑ 455904 SWR
❑ 455905 SWR
❑ 455906 SWR
❑ 455907 SWR
❑ 455908 SWR
❑ 455909 SWR
❑ 455910 SWR
❑ 455911 SWR
❑ 455912 SWR
❑ 455913 SWR
❑ 455914 SWR
❑ 455915 SWR
❑ 455916 SWR
❑ 455917 SWR
❑ 455918 SWR
❑ 455919 SWR
❑ 455920 SWR

❑ 456001 SWR
❑ 456002 SWR
❑ 456003 SWR
❑ 456004 SWR
❑ 456005 SWR
❑ 456006 SWR
❑ 456007 SWR
❑ 456008 SWR
❑ 456009 SWR
❑ 456010 SWR
❑ 456011 SWR
❑ 456012 SWR
❑ 456013 SWR
❑ 456014 SWR
❑ 456015 SWR
❑ 456016 SWR
❑ 456017 SWR
❑ 456018 SWR
❑ 456019 SWR
❑ 456020 SWR
❑ 456021 SWR
❑ 456022 SWR
❑ 456023 SWR
❑ 456024 SWR

❑ 458501 SWR
❑ 458502 SWR
❑ 458503 SWR
❑ 458504 SWR
❑ 458505 SWR
❑ 458506 SWR
❑ 458507 SWR
❑ 458508 SWR
❑ 458509 SWR
❑ 458510 SWR
❑ 458511 SWR
❑ 458512 SWR
❑ 458513 SWR
❑ 458514 SWR
❑ 458515 SWR
❑ 458516 SWR
❑ 458517 SWR
❑ 458518 SWR
❑ 458519 SWR
❑ 458520 SWR
❑ 458521 SWR
❑ 458522 SWR
❑ 458523 SWR
❑ 458524 SWR
❑ 458525 SWR
❑ 458526 SWR
❑ 458527 SWR
❑ 458528 SWR
❑ 458529 SWR
❑ 458530 SWR
❑ 458531 SWR
❑ 458532 SWR
❑ 458533 SWR
❑ 458534 SWR
❑ 458535 SWR
❑ 458536 SWR

❑ 465001 SET
❑ 465002 SET
❑ 465003 SET
❑ 465004 SET
❑ 465005 SET
❑ 465006 SET
❑ 465007 SET
❑ 465008 SET
❑ 465009 SET
❑ 465010 SET
❑ 465011 SET
❑ 465012 SET
❑ 465013 SET
❑ 465014 SET
❑ 465015 SET
❑ 465016 SET
❑ 465017 SET
❑ 465018 SET
❑ 465019 SET
❑ 465020 SET
❑ 465021 SET
❑ 465022 SET
❑ 465023 SET
❑ 465024 SET
❑ 465025 SET
❑ 465026 SET
❑ 465027 SET
❑ 465028 SET
❑ 465029 SET
❑ 465030 SET
❑ 465031 SET
❑ 465032 SET
❑ 465033 SET
❑ 465034 SET
❑ 465035 SET
❑ 465036 SET
❑ 465037 SET
❑ 465038 SET
❑ 465039 SET
❑ 465040 SET
❑ 465041 SET
❑ 465042 SET
❑ 465043 SET
❑ 465044 SET
❑ 465045 SET
❑ 465046 SET
❑ 465047 SET
❑ 465048 SET
❑ 465049 SET
❑ 465050 SET

❑ 465151 SET
❑ 465152 SET
❑ 465153 SET
❑ 465154 SET
❑ 465155 SET
❑ 465156 SET
❑ 465157 SET
❑ 465158 SET
❑ 465159 SET
❑ 465160 SET
❑ 465161 SET
❑ 465162 SET
❑ 465163 SET
❑ 465164 SET
❑ 465165 SET
❑ 465166 SET
❑ 465167 SET
❑ 465168 SET
❑ 465169 SET
❑ 465170 SET
❑ 465171 SET
❑ 465172 SET
❑ 465173 SET
❑ 465174 SET
❑ 465175 SET
❑ 465176 SET
❑ 465177 SET
❑ 465178 SET
❑ 465179 SET
❑ 465180 SET
❑ 465181 SET
❑ 465182 SET
❑ 465183 SET
❑ 465184 SET
❑ 465185 SET
❑ 465186 SET
❑ 465187 SET
❑ 465188 SET
❑ 465189 SET
❑ 465190 SET
❑ 465191 SET
❑ 465192 SET
❑ 465193 SET
❑ 465194 SET
❑ 465195 SET
❑ 465196 SET
❑ 465197 SET

❑ 465235 SET
❑ 465236 SET
❑ 465237 SET
❑ 465238 SET
❑ 465239 SET
❑ 465240 SET
❑ 465241 SET
❑ 465242 SET
❑ 465243 SET
❑ 465244 SET
❑ 465245 SET
❑ 465246 SET
❑ 465247 SET
❑ 465248 SET
❑ 465249 SET
❑ 465250 SET
❑ 465901 SET
❑ 465902 SET
❑ 465903 SET
❑ 465904 SET
❑ 465905 SET
❑ 465906 SET
❑ 465907 SET
❑ 465908 SET
❑ 465909 SET
❑ 465910 SET
❑ 465911 SET
❑ 465912 SET
❑ 465913 SET
❑ 465914 SET
❑ 465915 SET
❑ 465916 SET
❑ 465917 SET
❑ 465918 SET
❑ 465919 SET
❑ 465920 SET
❑ 465921 SET
❑ 465922 SET

Number	Operator
❑ 465923	SET
❑ 465924	SET
❑ 465925	SET
❑ 465926	SET
❑ 465927	SET
❑ 465928	SET
❑ 465929	SET
❑ 465930	SET
❑ 465931	SET
❑ 465932	SET
❑ 465933	SET
❑ 465934	SET
❑ 466001	SET
❑ 466002	SET
❑ 466003	SET
❑ 466004	SET
❑ 466005	SET
❑ 466006	SET
❑ 466007	SET
❑ 466008	SET
❑ 466009	SET
❑ 466010	SET
❑ 466011	SET
❑ 466012	SET
❑ 466013	SET
❑ 466014	SET
❑ 466015	SET
❑ 466016	SET
❑ 466017	SET
❑ 466018	SET
❑ 466019	SET
❑ 466020	SET
❑ 466021	SET
❑ 466022	SET
❑ 466023	SET
❑ 466024	SET
❑ 466025	SET
❑ 466026	SET
❑ 466027	SET
❑ 466028	SET
❑ 466029	SET
❑ 466030	SET
❑ 466031	SET
❑ 466032	SET
❑ 466033	SET
❑ 466034	SET
❑ 466035	SET
❑ 466036	SET
❑ 466037	SET
❑ 466038	SET
❑ 466039	SET
❑ 466040	SET
❑ 466041	SET
❑ 466042	SET
❑ 466043	SET
❑ 483002	SWR
❑ 483004	SWR
❑ 483006	SWR
❑ 483007	SWR
❑ 483008	SWR
❑ 483009	SWR
❑ 507001	MER
❑ 507002	MER
❑ 507003	MER
❑ 507004	MER
❑ 507005	MER
❑ 507006	MER
❑ 507007	MER
❑ 507008	MER
❑ 507009	MER
❑ 507010	MER
❑ 507011	MER
❑ 507012	MER
❑ 507013	MER
❑ 507014	MER
❑ 507015	MER
❑ 507016	MER
❑ 507017	MER
❑ 507018	MER
❑ 507019	MER
❑ 507020	MER
❑ 507021	MER
❑ 507023	MER
❑ 507024	MER
❑ 507025	MER
❑ 507026	MER
❑ 507027	MER
❑ 507028	MER
❑ 507029	MER
❑ 507030	MER
❑ 507031	MER
❑ 507032	MER
❑ 507033	MER
❑ 508103	MER
❑ 508104	MER
❑ 508108	MER
❑ 508110	MER
❑ 508111	MER
❑ 508112	MER
❑ 508114	MER
❑ 508115	MER
❑ 508117	MER
❑ 508120	MER
❑ 508122	MER
❑ 508123	MER
❑ 508124	MER
❑ 508125	MER
❑ 508126	MER
❑ 508127	MER
❑ 508128	MER
❑ 508130	MER
❑ 508131	MER
❑ 508134	MER
❑ 508136	MER
❑ 508137	MER
❑ 508138	MER
❑ 508139	MER
❑ 508140	MER
❑ 508141	MER
❑ 508143	MER
❑ 700001	GTR
❑ 700002	GTR
❑ 700003	GTR
❑ 700004	GTR
❑ 700005	GTR
❑ 700006	GTR
❑ 700007	GTR
❑ 700008	GTR
❑ 700009	GTR
❑ 700010	GTR
❑ 700011	GTR
❑ 700012	GTR
❑ 700013	GTR
❑ 700014	GTR
❑ 700015	GTR
❑ 700016	GTR
❑ 700017	GTR
❑ 700018	GTR
❑ 700019	GTR
❑ 700020	GTR
❑ 700021	GTR
❑ 700022	GTR
❑ 700023	GTR
❑ 700024	GTR
❑ 700025	GTR
❑ 700026	GTR
❑ 700027	GTR
❑ 700028	GTR
❑ 700029	GTR
❑ 700030	GTR
❑ 700031	GTR
❑ 700032	GTR
❑ 700033	GTR
❑ 700034	GTR
❑ 700035	GTR
❑ 700036	GTR
❑ 700037	GTR
❑ 700038	GTR
❑ 700039	GTR
❑ 700040	GTR
❑ 700041	GTR
❑ 700042	GTR
❑ 700043	GTR
❑ 700044	GTR
❑ 700045	GTR
❑ 700046	GTR
❑ 700047	GTR
❑ 700048	GTR
❑ 700049	GTR
❑ 700050	GTR
❑ 700051	GTR
❑ 700052	GTR
❑ 700053	GTR
❑ 700054	GTR
❑ 700055	GTR
❑ 700056	GTR
❑ 700057	GTR
❑ 700058	GTR
❑ 700059	GTR
❑ 700060	GTR
❑ 700101	GTR
❑ 700102	GTR
❑ 700103	GTR
❑ 700104	GTR
❑ 700105	GTR
❑ 700106	GTR
❑ 700107	GTR
❑ 700108	GTR
❑ 700109	GTR
❑ 700110	GTR
❑ 700111	GTR
❑ 700112	GTR
❑ 700113	GTR
❑ 700114	GTR
❑ 700115	GTR
❑ 700116	GTR
❑ 700117	GTR
❑ 700118	GTR
❑ 700119	GTR
❑ 700120	GTR
❑ 700121	GTR
❑ 700122	GTR
❑ 700123	GTR
❑ 700124	GTR
❑ 700125	GTR
❑ 700126	GTR
❑ 700127	GTR
❑ 700128	GTR
❑ 700129	GTR
❑ 700130	GTR
❑ 700131	GTR
❑ 700132	GTR
❑ 700133	GTR
❑ 700134	GTR
❑ 700135	GTR
❑ 700136	GTR
❑ 700137	GTR
❑ 700138	GTR
❑ 700139	GTR
❑ 700140	GTR
❑ 700141	GTR
❑ 700142	GTR
❑ 700143	GTR
❑ 700144	GTR
❑ 700145	GTR
❑ 700146	GTR
❑ 700147	GTR
❑ 700148	GTR
❑ 700149	GTR
❑ 700150	GTR
❑ 700151	GTR
❑ 700152	GTR
❑ 700153	GTR
❑ 700154	GTR
❑ 700155	GTR
❑ 701001	SWR
❑ 701002	SWR
❑ 701003	SWR
❑ 701004	SWR
❑ 701005	SWR
❑ 701006	SWR
❑ 701007	SWR
❑ 701008	SWR
❑ 701009	SWR
❑ 701010	SWR
❑ 701011	SWR
❑ 701012	SWR
❑ 701013	SWR
❑ 701014	SWR
❑ 701015	SWR
❑ 701016	SWR
❑ 701017	SWR
❑ 701018	SWR
❑ 701019	SWR
❑ 701020	SWR
❑ 701021	SWR
❑ 701022	SWR
❑ 701023	SWR
❑ 701024	SWR
❑ 701025	SWR
❑ 701026	SWR
❑ 701027	SWR
❑ 701028	SWR
❑ 701029	SWR
❑ 701030	SWR
❑ 701031	SWR
❑ 701032	SWR
❑ 701033	SWR
❑ 701034	SWR
❑ 701035	SWR
❑ 701036	SWR
❑ 701037	SWR
❑ 701038	SWR
❑ 701039	SWR
❑ 701040	SWR
❑ 701041	SWR
❑ 701042	SWR
❑ 701043	SWR
❑ 701044	SWR
❑ 701045	SWR
❑ 701046	SWR
❑ 701047	SWR
❑ 701048	SWR
❑ 701049	SWR
❑ 701050	SWR
❑ 701051	SWR
❑ 701052	SWR
❑ 701053	SWR
❑ 701054	SWR
❑ 701055	SWR
❑ 701056	SWR
❑ 701057	SWR
❑ 701058	SWR
❑ 701059	SWR
❑ 701060	SWR
❑ 701501	SWR
❑ 701502	SWR
❑ 701503	SWR
❑ 701504	SWR
❑ 701505	SWR
❑ 701506	SWR
❑ 701507	SWR
❑ 701508	SWR
❑ 701509	SWR
❑ 701510	SWR
❑ 701511	SWR
❑ 701512	SWR
❑ 701513	SWR

❑ 701514 SWR
❑ 701515 SWR
❑ 701516 SWR
❑ 701517 SWR
❑ 701518 SWR
❑ 701519 SWR
❑ 701520 SWR
❑ 701521 SWR
❑ 701522 SWR
❑ 701523 SWR
❑ 701524 SWR
❑ 701525 SWR
❑ 701526 SWR
❑ 701527 SWR
❑ 701528 SWR
❑ 701529 SWR
❑ 701530 SWR

❑ 707001 SWR
❑ 707002 SWR
❑ 707003 SWR
❑ 707004 SWR
❑ 707005 SWR
❑ 707006 SWR
❑ 707007 SWR
❑ 707008 SWR
❑ 707009 SWR
❑ 707010 SWR
❑ 707011 SWR
❑ 707012 SWR
❑ 707013 SWR
❑ 707014 SWR
❑ 707015 SWR
❑ 707016 SWR
❑ 707017 SWR
❑ 707018 SWR
❑ 707019 SWR
❑ 707020 SWR
❑ 707021 SWR
❑ 707022 SWR
❑ 707023 SWR
❑ 707024 SWR
❑ 707025 SWR
❑ 707026 SWR
❑ 707027 SWR
❑ 707028 SWR
❑ 707029 SWR
❑ 707030 SWR

❑ 710101 LOG
❑ 710102 LOG
❑ 710103 LOG
❑ 710104 LOG
❑ 710105 LOG
❑ 710106 LOG
❑ 710107 LOG
❑ 710108 LOG
❑ 710109 LOG
❑ 710110 LOG
❑ 710111 LOG
❑ 710112 LOG
❑ 710113 LOG
❑ 710114 LOG
❑ 710115 LOG
❑ 710116 LOG
❑ 710117 LOG
❑ 710118 LOG
❑ 710119 LOG
❑ 710120 LOG
❑ 710121 LOG
❑ 710122 LOG
❑ 710123 LOG
❑ 710124 LOG
❑ 710125 LOG
❑ 710126 LOG
❑ 710127 LOG
❑ 710128 LOG
❑ 710129 LOG
❑ 710130 LOG

❑ 710256 LOG
❑ 710257 LOG
❑ 710258 LOG
❑ 710259 LOG
❑ 710260 LOG
❑ 710261 LOG
❑ 710262 LOG
❑ 710263 LOG
❑ 710264 LOG
❑ 710265 LOG
❑ 710266 LOG
❑ 710267 LOG
❑ 710268 LOG
❑ 710269 LOG
❑ 710270 LOG
❑ 710271 LOG
❑ 710272 LOG
❑ 710273 LOG
❑ 710274 LOG
❑ 710275 LOG
❑ 710276 LOG
❑ 710277 LOG
❑ 710278 LOG
❑ 710279 LOG

❑ 717001 GTR
❑ 717002 GTR
❑ 717003 GTR
❑ 717004 GTR
❑ 717005 GTR
❑ 717006 GTR
❑ 717007 GTR
❑ 717008 GTR
❑ 717009 GTR
❑ 717010 GTR
❑ 717011 GTR
❑ 717012 GTR
❑ 717013 GTR
❑ 717014 GTR
❑ 717015 GTR
❑ 717016 GTR
❑ 717017 GTR
❑ 717018 GTR
❑ 717019 GTR
❑ 717020 GTR
❑ 717021 GTR
❑ 717022 GTR
❑ 717023 GTR
❑ 717024 GTR
❑ 717025 GTR

❑ 720101 GAR
❑ 720102 GAR
❑ 720103 GAR
❑ 720104 GAR
❑ 720105 GAR
❑ 720106 GAR
❑ 720107 GAR
❑ 720108 GAR
❑ 720109 GAR
❑ 720110 GAR
❑ 720111 GAR
❑ 720112 GAR
❑ 720113 GAR
❑ 720114 GAR
❑ 720115 GAR
❑ 720116 GAR
❑ 720117 GAR
❑ 720118 GAR
❑ 720119 GAR
❑ 720120 GAR
❑ 720121 GAR
❑ 720122 GAR

❑ 720501 GAR
❑ 720502 GAR
❑ 720503 GAR
❑ 720504 GAR
❑ 720505 GAR
❑ 720506 GAR
❑ 720507 GAR
❑ 720508 GAR
❑ 720509 GAR
❑ 720510 GAR
❑ 720511 GAR
❑ 720512 GAR
❑ 720513 GAR
❑ 720514 GAR
❑ 720515 GAR
❑ 720516 GAR
❑ 720517 GAR
❑ 720518 GAR
❑ 720519 GAR
❑ 720520 GAR
❑ 720521 GAR
❑ 720522 GAR
❑ 720523 GAR
❑ 720524 GAR
❑ 720525 GAR
❑ 720526 GAR
❑ 720527 GAR
❑ 720528 GAR
❑ 720529 GAR
❑ 720530 GAR
❑ 720531 GAR
❑ 720532 GAR
❑ 720533 GAR
❑ 720534 GAR
❑ 720535 GAR
❑ 720536 GAR
❑ 720537 GAR
❑ 720538 GAR
❑ 720539 GAR
❑ 720540 GAR
❑ 720541 GAR
❑ 720542 GAR
❑ 720543 GAR
❑ 720544 GAR
❑ 720545 GAR
❑ 720546 GAR
❑ 720547 GAR
❑ 720548 GAR
❑ 720549 GAR
❑ 720550 GAR
❑ 720551 GAR
❑ 720552 GAR
❑ 720553 GAR
❑ 720554 GAR
❑ 720555 GAR
❑ 720556 GAR
❑ 720557 GAR
❑ 720558 GAR
❑ 720559 GAR
❑ 720560 GAR
❑ 720561 GAR
❑ 720562 GAR
❑ 720563 GAR
❑ 720564 GAR
❑ 720565 GAR
❑ 720566 GAR
❑ 720567 GAR
❑ 720568 GAR
❑ 720569 GAR
❑ 720570 GAR
❑ 720571 GAR
❑ 720572 GAR
❑ 720573 GAR
❑ 720574 GAR
❑ 720575 GAR
❑ 720576 GAR
❑ 720577 GAR
❑ 720578 GAR
❑ 720579 GAR
❑ 720580 GAR
❑ 720581 GAR
❑ 720582 GAR
❑ 720583 GAR
❑ 720584 GAR
❑ 720585 GAR
❑ 720586 GAR
❑ 720587 GAR
❑ 720588 GAR
❑ 720589 GAR

❑ 745001 GAR
❑ 745002 GAR
❑ 745003 GAR
❑ 745004 GAR
❑ 745005 GAR
❑ 745006 GAR
❑ 745007 GAR
❑ 745008 GAR
❑ 745009 GAR
❑ 745010 GAR

❑ 745101 GAR
❑ 745102 GAR
❑ 745103 GAR
❑ 745104 GAR
❑ 745105 GAR
❑ 745106 GAR
❑ 745107 GAR
❑ 745108 GAR
❑ 745109 GAR
❑ 745110 GAR

❑ 755325 GAR
❑ 755326 GAR
❑ 755327 GAR
❑ 755328 GAR
❑ 755329 GAR
❑ 755330 GAR
❑ 755331 GAR
❑ 755332 GAR
❑ 755333 GAR
❑ 755334 GAR
❑ 755335 GAR
❑ 755336 GAR
❑ 755337 GAR
❑ 755338 GAR

❑ 755401 GAR
❑ 755402 GAR
❑ 755403 GAR
❑ 755404 GAR
❑ 755405 GAR
❑ 755406 GAR
❑ 755407 GAR
❑ 755408 GAR
❑ 755409 GAR
❑ 755410 GAR
❑ 755411 GAR
❑ 755412 GAR
❑ 755413 GAR
❑ 755414 GAR
❑ 755415 GAR
❑ 755416 GAR
❑ 755417 GAR
❑ 755418 GAR
❑ 755419 GAR
❑ 755420 GAR
❑ 755421 GAR
❑ 755422 GAR
❑ 755423 GAR
❑ 755424 GAR

❑ 769002 TFW
❑ 769003 TFW
❑ 769006 TFW
❑ 769007 TFW
❑ 769008 TFW
❑ 769422 GWR
❑ 769423 GWR
❑ 769424 NOR
❑ 769425 GWR

❑ 769427 GWR
❑ 769428 GWR
❑ 769430 GWR
❑ 769431 NOR
❑ 769432 GWR
❑ 769434 NOR
❑ 769435 GWR
❑ 769436 GWR
❑ 769437 GWR
❑ 769438 GWR
❑ 769439 GWR
❑ 769440 GWR
❑ 769442 NOR
❑ 769443 GWR
❑ 769445 GWR
❑ 769447 GWR
❑ 769448 NOR
❑ 769449 GWR
❑ 769450 NOR
❑ 769452 GWR
❑ 769456 NOR
❑ 769458 NOR
❑ 769459 GWR

❑ 777001 MER
❑ 777002 MER
❑ 777003 MER
❑ 777004 MER
❑ 777005 MER
❑ 777006 MER
❑ 777007 MER
❑ 777008 MER
❑ 777009 MER
❑ 777010 MER
❑ 777011 MER
❑ 777012 MER
❑ 777013 MER
❑ 777014 MER
❑ 777015 MER
❑ 777016 MER
❑ 777017 MER
❑ 777018 MER
❑ 777019 MER
❑ 777020 MER
❑ 777021 MER
❑ 777022 MER
❑ 777023 MER
❑ 777024 MER
❑ 777025 MER
❑ 777026 MER
❑ 777027 MER
❑ 777028 MER
❑ 777029 MER
❑ 777030 MER
❑ 777031 MER
❑ 777032 MER
❑ 777033 MER
❑ 777034 MER
❑ 777035 MER
❑ 777036 MER
❑ 777037 MER
❑ 777038 MER
❑ 777039 MER
❑ 777040 MER
❑ 777041 MER
❑ 777042 MER
❑ 777043 MER
❑ 777044 MER
❑ 777045 MER
❑ 777046 MER
❑ 777047 MER
❑ 777048 MER
❑ 777049 MER
❑ 777050 MER
❑ 777051 MER
❑ 777052 MER

❑ 799001 PTR

❑ 800001 GWR
❑ 800002 GWR
❑ 800003 GWR
❑ 800004 GWR
❑ 800005 GWR
❑ 800006 GWR
❑ 800007 GWR
❑ 800008 GWR
❑ 800009 GWR
❑ 800010 GWR
❑ 800011 GWR
❑ 800012 GWR
❑ 800013 GWR
❑ 800014 GWR
❑ 800015 GWR
❑ 800016 GWR
❑ 800017 GWR
❑ 800018 GWR
❑ 800019 GWR
❑ 800020 GWR
❑ 800021 GWR
❑ 800022 GWR
❑ 800023 GWR
❑ 800024 GWR
❑ 800025 GWR
❑ 800026 GWR
❑ 800027 GWR
❑ 800028 GWR
❑ 800029 GWR
❑ 800030 GWR
❑ 800031 GWR
❑ 800032 GWR
❑ 800033 GWR
❑ 800034 GWR
❑ 800035 GWR
❑ 800036 GWR

❑ 800101 LNE
❑ 800102 LNE
❑ 800103 LNE
❑ 800104 LNE
❑ 800105 LNE
❑ 800106 LNE
❑ 800107 LNE
❑ 800108 LNE
❑ 800109 LNE
❑ 800110 LNE
❑ 800111 LNE
❑ 800112 LNE
❑ 800113 LNE

❑ 800201 LNE
❑ 800202 LNE
❑ 800203 LNE
❑ 800204 LNE
❑ 800205 LNE
❑ 800206 LNE
❑ 800207 LNE
❑ 800208 LNE
❑ 800209 LNE
❑ 800210 LNE

❑ 800301 GWR
❑ 800302 GWR
❑ 800303 GWR
❑ 800304 GWR
❑ 800305 GWR
❑ 800306 GWR
❑ 800307 GWR
❑ 800308 GWR
❑ 800309 GWR
❑ 800310 GWR
❑ 800311 GWR
❑ 800312 GWR
❑ 800313 GWR
❑ 800314 GWR
❑ 800315 GWR
❑ 800316 GWR
❑ 800317 GWR
❑ 800318 GWR
❑ 800319 GWR
❑ 800320 GWR
❑ 800321 GWR

❑ 801101 LNE
❑ 801102 LNE
❑ 801103 LNE
❑ 801104 LNE
❑ 801105 LNE
❑ 801106 LNE
❑ 801107 LNE
❑ 801108 LNE
❑ 801109 LNE
❑ 801110 LNE
❑ 801111 LNE
❑ 801112 LNE

❑ 801201 LNE
❑ 801202 LNE
❑ 801203 LNE
❑ 801204 LNE
❑ 801205 LNE
❑ 801206 LNE
❑ 801207 LNE
❑ 801208 LNE
❑ 801209 LNE
❑ 801210 LNE
❑ 801211 LNE
❑ 801212 LNE
❑ 801213 LNE
❑ 801214 LNE
❑ 801215 LNE
❑ 801216 LNE
❑ 801217 LNE
❑ 801218 LNE
❑ 801219 LNE
❑ 801220 LNE
❑ 801221 LNE
❑ 801222 LNE
❑ 801223 LNE
❑ 801224 LNE
❑ 801225 LNE
❑ 801226 LNE
❑ 801227 LNE
❑ 801228 LNE
❑ 801229 LNE
❑ 801230 LNE

❑ 802001 GWR
❑ 802002 GWR
❑ 802003 GWR
❑ 802004 GWR
❑ 802005 GWR
❑ 802006 GWR
❑ 802007 GWR
❑ 802008 GWR
❑ 802009 GWR
❑ 802010 GWR
❑ 802011 GWR
❑ 802012 GWR
❑ 802013 GWR
❑ 802014 GWR
❑ 802015 GWR
❑ 802016 GWR
❑ 802017 GWR
❑ 802018 GWR
❑ 802019 GWR
❑ 802020 GWR
❑ 802021 GWR
❑ 802022 GWR

❑ 802101 GWR
❑ 802102 GWR
❑ 802103 GWR
❑ 802104 GWR
❑ 802105 GWR
❑ 802106 GWR
❑ 802107 GWR
❑ 802108 GWR
❑ 802109 GWR
❑ 802110 GWR
❑ 802111 GWR
❑ 802112 GWR
❑ 802113 GWR
❑ 802114 GWR

❑ 802201 FTP
❑ 802202 FTP
❑ 802203 FTP
❑ 802204 FTP
❑ 802205 FTP
❑ 802206 FTP
❑ 802207 FTP
❑ 802208 FTP
❑ 802209 FTP
❑ 802210 FTP
❑ 802211 FTP
❑ 802212 FTP
❑ 802213 FTP
❑ 802214 FTP
❑ 802215 FTP
❑ 802216 FTP
❑ 802217 FTP
❑ 802218 FTP
❑ 802219 FTP

❑ 802301 FHT
❑ 802302 FHT
❑ 802303 FHT
❑ 802304 FHT
❑ 802305 FHT

Coaching Stock

❑ 84 RAF

❑ 159 WCR
❑ 213 VSO
❑ 239 VSO
❑ 243 VSO
❑ 245 VSO
❑ 254 VSO
❑ 255 VSO
❑ 261 VSO
❑ 264 VSO
❑ 280 VSO
❑ 281 VSO
❑ 283 VSO
❑ 284 VSO
❑ 285 VSO
❑ 286 VSO
❑ 288 VSO
❑ 292 VSO
❑ 293 VSO
❑ 301 VSO
❑ 302 VSO
❑ 307 VSO
❑ 308 VSO
❑ 310 RAF
❑ 316 FSL
❑ 325 WCR
❑ 326 WCR
❑ 335 VTN
❑ 347 WCR
❑ 348 WCR
❑ 349 VTN
❑ 350 WCR
❑ 351 WCR
❑ 352 WCR
❑ 353 VTN
❑ 354 WCR
❑ 464 BOK
❑ 504 WCR
❑ 506 WCR
❑ 546 WCR
❑ 548 WCR
❑ 549 WCR

❑ 550 WCR
❑ 551 WCR
❑ 552 WCR
❑ 553 WCR
❑ 586 WCR
❑ 807 WCR

❑ 1105 MHR
❑ 1200 RIV
❑ 1203 RIV
❑ 1207 WCR
❑ 1209 OLS
❑ 1211 LSL
❑ 1212 RIV
❑ 1219 OLS
❑ 1221 WCR
❑ 1256 NRL
❑ 1375 BOK
❑ 1566 WCR
❑ 1644 WCR
❑ 1650 WCR
❑ 1651 RIV
❑ 1652 WCR
❑ 1655 WCR
❑ 1657 RIV
❑ 1659 LSL
❑ 1663 WCR
❑ 1666 WCR
❑ 1670 WCR
❑ 1671 RIV
❑ 1683 RIV
❑ 1691 RIV
❑ 1730 WCR
❑ 1813 RIV
❑ 1823 NYM
❑ 1832 RIV
❑ 1840 WCR
❑ 1859 SRP
❑ 1860 WCR
❑ 1861 WCR
❑ 1863 RIV
❑ 1882 WCR
❑ 1953 WCR
❑ 1961 WCR

❑ 2127 WCR
❑ 2903 NRL
❑ 2904 NRL
❑ 2915 NRL
❑ 2916 NRL
❑ 2917 NRL
❑ 2918 NRL
❑ 2919 NRL
❑ 2920 NRL
❑ 2921 NRL
❑ 2922 NRL
❑ 2923 NRL
❑ 3058 WCR
❑ 3066 RIV
❑ 3068 RIV
❑ 3069 RIV
❑ 3093 WCR
❑ 3096 BOK

❑ 3097 RIV
❑ 3098 RIV
❑ 3100 RIV
❑ 3105 WCR
❑ 3106 WCR
❑ 3110 RIV
❑ 3112 RIV
❑ 3113 WCR
❑ 3115 BOK
❑ 3117 WCR
❑ 3119 RIV
❑ 3120 RIV
❑ 3121 RIV
❑ 3122 RIV
❑ 3123 RIV
❑ 3125 RIV
❑ 3128 WCR
❑ 3130 WCR
❑ 3136 WCR
❑ 3141 RIV
❑ 3143 WCR
❑ 3144 RIV
❑ 3146 RIV
❑ 3147 RIV
❑ 3148 RIV
❑ 3149 RIV
❑ 3150 BOK
❑ 3174 WCR
❑ 3181 RIV
❑ 3182 WCR
❑ 3188 RAF
❑ 3223 RIV
❑ 3227 RIV
❑ 3229 LSL
❑ 3231 LSL
❑ 3232 WCR
❑ 3240 RIV
❑ 3247 WCR
❑ 3267 WCR
❑ 3273 WCR
❑ 3275 WCR
❑ 3278 RIV
❑ 3279 DBR
❑ 3304 RIV
❑ 3312 LSL
❑ 3313 WCR
❑ 3314 RIV
❑ 3325 RIV
❑ 3326 WCR
❑ 3330 RIV
❑ 3333 RIV
❑ 3340 RIV
❑ 3344 LSL
❑ 3345 RIV
❑ 3348 WCR
❑ 3350 WCR
❑ 3352 WCR
❑ 3356 RIV
❑ 3359 WCR
❑ 3360 WCR
❑ 3362 WCR
❑ 3364 RIV
❑ 3384 RIV

❑ 3386 RIV
❑ 3390 RIV
❑ 3395 WCR
❑ 3397 RIV
❑ 3426 RIV
❑ 3431 WCR
❑ 3438 LSL
❑ 3860 NYM
❑ 3872 NYM
❑ 3948 NYM

❑ 4198 NYM
❑ 4252 NYM
❑ 4290 NYM
❑ 4362 RAF
❑ 4455 NYM
❑ 4786 NYM
❑ 4817 NYM
❑ 4831 BOK
❑ 4832 BOK
❑ 4836 BOK
❑ 4854 WCR
❑ 4856 BOK
❑ 4860 WCR
❑ 4905 WCR
❑ 4912 WCR
❑ 4927 RIV
❑ 4931 WCR
❑ 4932 WCR
❑ 4940 WCR
❑ 4946 RIV
❑ 4949 RIV
❑ 4951 WCR
❑ 4954 WCR
❑ 4958 WCR
❑ 4959 RIV
❑ 4960 WCR
❑ 4973 WCR
❑ 4984 WCR
❑ 4991 RIV
❑ 4994 WCR
❑ 4997 WCR
❑ 4998 RIV

❑ 5000 NYM
❑ 5007 RIV
❑ 5009 RIV
❑ 5029 NYM
❑ 5032 WCR
❑ 5033 WCR
❑ 5035 WCR
❑ 5044 WCR
❑ 5125 WCR
❑ 5157 VTN
❑ 5171 WCR
❑ 5177 VTN
❑ 5191 VTN
❑ 5198 VTN
❑ 5200 WCR
❑ 5212 VTN
❑ 5216 WCR
❑ 5222 WCR
❑ 5229 WCR

❑ 5236 WCR
❑ 5237 WCR
❑ 5239 WCR
❑ 5249 WCR
❑ 5278 WCR
❑ 5292 RIV
❑ 5309 RIV
❑ 5366 LSL
❑ 5419 WCR
❑ 5482 DBR
❑ 5487 WCR
❑ 5494 RIV
❑ 5520 RRS
❑ 5636 OLS
❑ 5647 RIV
❑ 5756 WCR
❑ 5810 DRS
❑ 5888 OLS
❑ 5910 RIV
❑ 5912 LSL
❑ 5919 DRS
❑ 5921 RIV
❑ 5929 RIV
❑ 5937 RIV
❑ 5945 ASR
❑ 5950 RIV
❑ 5955 ASR
❑ 5961 RIV
❑ 5964 RIV
❑ 5965 DRS
❑ 5971 ASR
❑ 5976 DRS
❑ 5981 NRL
❑ 5985 RIV
❑ 5987 DRS
❑ 5991 LSL
❑ 5995 DRS
❑ 5998 RIV

❑ 6000 WCR
❑ 6001 ASR
❑ 6006 RIV
❑ 6008 ASR
❑ 6012 WCR
❑ 6014 WCR
❑ 6021 WCR
❑ 6022 WCR
❑ 6024 RIV
❑ 6027 ASR
❑ 6042 RIV
❑ 6046 DRS
❑ 6051 RIV
❑ 6054 RIV
❑ 6059 RIV
❑ 6064 ARS
❑ 6067 RIV
❑ 6103 WCR
❑ 6115 WCR
❑ 6117 ASR
❑ 6121 OLS
❑ 6122 DRS
❑ 6135 WCR
❑ 6137 DRS

❑ 6141 RIV
❑ 6158 RIV
❑ 6160 OLS
❑ 6164 OLS
❑ 6173 ASR
❑ 6176 DRS
❑ 6177 DRS
❑ 6183 DRS
❑ 6310 RIV
❑ 6312 WCR
❑ 6313 VSO
❑ 6320 RIV
❑ 6528 WCR
❑ 6723 WCR
❑ 6724 WCR

❑ 9005 RAF
❑ 9101 VTN
❑ 9104 WCR
❑ 9267 NYM
❑ 9274 NYM
❑ 9391 WCR
❑ 9392 WCR
❑ 9419 DRS
❑ 9428 DRS
❑ 9448 WCR
❑ 9481 NRL
❑ 9488 ASR
❑ 9493 WCR
❑ 9494 DBR
❑ 9502 VSO
❑ 9504 RIV
❑ 9506 DBR
❑ 9507 RIV
❑ 9508 DRS
❑ 9509 RIV
❑ 9516 NRL
❑ 9520 RIV
❑ 9521 ASR
❑ 9523 NRL
❑ 9525 DRS
❑ 9526 RIV
❑ 9527 ASR
❑ 9529 DBR
❑ 9531 DBR
❑ 9537 RIV
❑ 9539 ASR
❑ 9704 DRS
❑ 9705 DRS
❑ 9707 DRS
❑ 9709 DRS
❑ 9710 DRS

❑ 10204 3MP
❑ 10211 DBC
❑ 10212 FTP
❑ 10217 GWR
❑ 10219 GWR
❑ 10221 GWR
❑ 10225 GWR
❑ 10229 OLS
❑ 10231 OLS
❑ 10237 DBR

Number	Operator
10241	OLS
10242	DBR
10249	TFW
10256	OLS
10259	TFW
10260	OLS
10271	CRW
10272	CRW
10273	CRW
10274	CRW
10300	LNE
10301	LNE
10302	LNE
10303	LNE
10304	LNE
10305	LNE
10306	LNE
10307	LNE
10308	LNE
10309	LNE
10310	OLS
10311	OLS
10312	TFW
10313	LNE
10315	LNE
10317	OLS
10318	LNE
10319	GTL
10320	LNE
10321	LNE
10323	LNE
10324	LNE
10325	TFW
10326	LNE
10328	TFW
10329	OLS
10330	LNE
10331	LNE
10332	LNE
10333	LNE
10401	GAR
10402	GAR
10403	GAR
10404	GAR
10405	GAR
10406	GAR
10411	GAR
10412	GAR
10413	GAR
10414	GAR
10415	GAR
10416	GAR
10417	GAR
10532	GWR
10534	GWR
10541	GSW
10546	DBC
10547	OLS
10551	GWR
10553	GWR
10556	GSW
10563	GWR
10569	WCR
10584	GWR
10589	GWR
10590	GWR
10594	GWR
10596	GWR
10601	GWR
10612	GWR
10616	GWR
10661	OLS
10667	OLS
10698	OLS
10729	WCR
10733	OLS
10734	WCR
11006	DRS
11007	OLS
11018	OLS
11019	DBR
11028	DBR
11029	CRW
11030	DBR
11031	CRW
11033	DBR
11039	DBC
11046	DBR
11048	OLS
11054	DBR
11066	GAR
11067	GAR
11068	GAR
11069	GAR
11070	GAR
11072	GAR
11073	GAR
11075	GAR
11076	GAR
11077	GAR
11078	GAR
11080	GAR
11081	GAR
11082	GAR
11085	GAR
11087	GAR
11088	GAR
11090	GAR
11091	GAR
11092	GAR
11093	GAR
11094	GAR
11095	GAR
11096	GAR
11098	GAR
11099	GAR
11100	GAR
11101	GAR
11201	LNE
11219	LNE
11229	LNE
11241	LNE
11244	LNE
11277	LNE
11278	LNE
11279	LNE
11280	LNE
11281	LNE
11282	LNE
11283	LNE
11284	LNE
11285	LNE
11286	LNE
11287	LNE
11288	LNE
11289	LNE
11290	LNE
11291	LNE
11295	OLS
11298	LNE
11299	LNE
11301	LNE
11302	LNE
11303	LNE
11304	LNE
11305	LNE
11306	LNE
11307	LNE
11308	LNE
11309	LNE
11310	LNE
11311	LNE
11312	LNE
11313	LNE
11314	LNE
11315	LNE
11316	LNE
11317	LNE
11318	LNE
11319	LNE
11320	LNE
11321	LNE
11322	LNE
11323	TFW
11324	TFW
11325	TFW
11326	OLS
11327	GTL
11328	OLS
11329	OLS
11330	OLS
11401	LNE
11402	LNE
11403	LNE
11404	LNE
11405	LNE
11406	LNE
11407	LNE
11408	LNE
11409	LNE
11410	LNE
11411	LNE
11412	LNE
11413	LNE
11414	LNE
11415	LNE
11416	LNE
11417	LNE
11418	LNE
11419	LNE
11420	LNE
11421	LNE
11422	LNE
11426	OLS
11430	OLS
11501	FTP
11502	FTP
11503	FTP
11504	FTP
11505	FTP
11506	FTP
11507	FTP
11508	FTP
11509	FTP
11510	FTP
11511	FTP
11512	FTP
11513	FTP
11998	OLS
11999	OLS
12005	GAR
12009	GAR
12011	OLS
12012	GAR
12013	GAR
12015	GAR
12016	GAR
12017	CRW
12019	GAR
12021	GAR
12024	GAR
12026	GAR
12027	GAR
12030	GAR
12031	GAR
12032	GAR
12034	GAR
12035	GAR
12036	CRW
12037	GAR
12040	GAR
12041	GAR
12042	GAR
12043	CRW
12046	GAR
12049	GAR
12051	GAR
12056	GAR
12057	GAR
12060	GAR
12061	GAR
12062	GAR
12064	GAR
12066	GAR
12067	GAR
12073	GAR
12078	OLS
12079	GAR
12081	GAR
12082	GAR
12084	GAR
12089	GAR
12090	GAR
12091	GAR
12093	GAR
12094	CRW
12097	GAR
12098	GAR
12099	GAR
12100	GWR
12103	GAR
12105	GAR
12107	GAR
12108	GAR
12109	GAR
12110	GAR
12111	GAR
12114	GAR
12115	GAR
12116	GAR
12118	GAR
12119	CRW
12120	GAR
12122	OLS
12125	GAR
12126	GAR
12129	GAR
12130	GAR
12132	GAR
12133	OLS
12137	GAR
12138	OLS
12139	GAR
12141	GAR
12142	GWR
12143	GAR
12146	GAR
12147	GAR
12148	GAR
12150	GAR
12151	GAR
12153	GAR
12154	GAR
12159	GAR
12161	GWR
12164	GAR
12166	GAR
12167	GAR
12170	GAR
12171	GAR
12176	TFW
12177	TFW
12178	TFW
12179	TFW
12180	TFW
12181	TFW
12182	TFW

❑ 12183 TFW
❑ 12184 TFW
❑ 12185 TFW

❑ 12200 LNE
❑ 12201 LNE
❑ 12202 LNE
❑ 12203 LNE
❑ 12204 OLS
❑ 12205 LNE
❑ 12207 LNE
❑ 12208 LNE
❑ 12209 LNE
❑ 12210 LNE
❑ 12211 LNE
❑ 12212 LNE
❑ 12213 LNE
❑ 12214 LNE
❑ 12215 LNE
❑ 12216 OLS
❑ 12217 OLS
❑ 12218 OLS
❑ 12219 TFW
❑ 12220 OLS
❑ 12222 LNE
❑ 12223 LNE
❑ 12224 LNE
❑ 12225 TFW
❑ 12226 LNE
❑ 12227 GTL
❑ 12228 LNE
❑ 12229 LNE
❑ 12230 LNE
❑ 12231 LNE
❑ 12232 LNE

❑ 12300 LNE
❑ 12301 LNE
❑ 12302 LNE
❑ 12303 LNE
❑ 12304 LNE
❑ 12305 LNE
❑ 12307 LNE
❑ 12308 LNE
❑ 12309 LNE
❑ 12310 LNE
❑ 12311 LNE
❑ 12312 LNE
❑ 12313 LNE
❑ 12315 LNE
❑ 12316 LNE
❑ 12317 OLS
❑ 12318 OLS
❑ 12319 OLS
❑ 12320 OLS
❑ 12321 GTL
❑ 12322 OLS
❑ 12323 LNE
❑ 12324 LNE
❑ 12325 OLS
❑ 12326 LNE
❑ 12327 LNE
❑ 12328 LNE
❑ 12329 LNE
❑ 12330 LNE
❑ 12331 LNE

❑ 12400 LNE
❑ 12401 LNE
❑ 12402 LNE
❑ 12404 LNE
❑ 12405 LNE
❑ 12406 LNE
❑ 12407 LNE
❑ 12409 LNE
❑ 12410 LNE
❑ 12411 LNE
❑ 12414 LNE
❑ 12415 LNE
❑ 12417 LNE
❑ 12419 LNE
❑ 12420 LNE
❑ 12421 LNE
❑ 12422 LNE
❑ 12423 LNE
❑ 12424 LNE
❑ 12426 LNE
❑ 12427 LNE
❑ 12428 LNE
❑ 12429 OLS
❑ 12430 LNE
❑ 12431 LNE
❑ 12432 LNE
❑ 12433 LNE
❑ 12434 LNE
❑ 12436 LNE
❑ 12437 LNE
❑ 12438 OLS
❑ 12439 LNE
❑ 12440 LNE
❑ 12441 LNE
❑ 12442 LNE
❑ 12443 LNE
❑ 12444 LNE
❑ 12445 LNE
❑ 12446 TFW
❑ 12447 TFW
❑ 12448 LNE
❑ 12449 OLS
❑ 12450 LNE
❑ 12452 LNE
❑ 12453 LNE
❑ 12454 TFW
❑ 12458 OLS
❑ 12459 LNE
❑ 12460 LNE
❑ 12461 LNE
❑ 12462 OLS
❑ 12463 OLS
❑ 12465 LNE
❑ 12467 LNE
❑ 12468 LNE
❑ 12469 LNE
❑ 12470 LNE
❑ 12471 GTL
❑ 12472 OLS
❑ 12473 LNE
❑ 12474 OLS
❑ 12476 LNE
❑ 12477 LNE
❑ 12478 LNE
❑ 12480 LNE
❑ 12481 LNE
❑ 12483 LNE
❑ 12484 LNE
❑ 12485 LNE
❑ 12486 LNE
❑ 12488 LNE
❑ 12489 LNE
❑ 12513 LNE
❑ 12514 LNE
❑ 12515 LNE
❑ 12518 LNE
❑ 12519 OLS
❑ 12520 LNE
❑ 12522 LNE
❑ 12526 LNE
❑ 12533 OLS
❑ 12534 OLS

❑ 12602 CRW
❑ 12603 CRW
❑ 12604 CRW
❑ 12605 CRW
❑ 12606 CRW
❑ 12607 CRW
❑ 12608 CRW
❑ 12609 CRW
❑ 12610 CRW
❑ 12613 CRW
❑ 12614 CRW
❑ 12615 CRW
❑ 12616 CRW
❑ 12617 CRW
❑ 12618 CRW
❑ 12619 CRW
❑ 12620 CRW
❑ 12621 CRW
❑ 12623 CRW
❑ 12625 CRW
❑ 12627 CRW

❑ 12701 FTP
❑ 12702 FTP
❑ 12703 FTP
❑ 12704 FTP
❑ 12705 FTP
❑ 12706 FTP
❑ 12707 FTP
❑ 12708 FTP
❑ 12709 FTP
❑ 12710 FTP
❑ 12711 FTP
❑ 12712 FTP
❑ 12713 FTP
❑ 12714 FTP
❑ 12715 FTP
❑ 12716 FTP
❑ 12717 FTP
❑ 12718 FTP
❑ 12719 FTP
❑ 12720 FTP
❑ 12721 FTP
❑ 12722 FTP
❑ 12723 FTP
❑ 12724 FTP
❑ 12725 FTP
❑ 12726 FTP
❑ 12727 FTP
❑ 12728 FTP
❑ 12729 FTP
❑ 12730 FTP
❑ 12731 FTP
❑ 12732 FTP
❑ 12733 FTP
❑ 12734 FTP
❑ 12735 FTP
❑ 12736 FTP
❑ 12737 FTP
❑ 12738 FTP
❑ 12739 FTP

❑ 12801 FTP
❑ 12802 FTP
❑ 12803 FTP
❑ 12804 FTP
❑ 12805 FTP
❑ 12806 FTP
❑ 12807 FTP
❑ 12808 FTP
❑ 12809 FTP
❑ 12810 FTP
❑ 12811 FTP
❑ 12812 FTP
❑ 12813 FTP
❑ 12814 FTP

❑ 13227 WCR
❑ 13229 BOK
❑ 13230 BOK
❑ 13306 WCR
❑ 13320 WCR
❑ 13321 WCR
❑ 13440 WCR
❑ 13508 RAF
❑ 13581 RRS
❑ 13582 RRS

❑ 14007 SUP
❑ 14060 SUP

❑ 15001 SCS
❑ 15002 SCS
❑ 15003 SCS
❑ 15004 SCS
❑ 15005 SCS
❑ 15006 SCS
❑ 15007 SCS
❑ 15008 SCS
❑ 15009 SCS
❑ 15010 SCS
❑ 15011 SCS
❑ 15101 SCS
❑ 15102 SCS
❑ 15103 SCS
❑ 15104 SCS
❑ 15105 SCS
❑ 15106 SCS
❑ 15107 SCS
❑ 15108 SCS
❑ 15109 SCS
❑ 15110 SCS

❑ 15201 SCS
❑ 15202 SCS
❑ 15203 SCS
❑ 15204 SCS
❑ 15205 SCS
❑ 15206 SCS
❑ 15207 SCS
❑ 15208 SCS
❑ 15209 SCS
❑ 15210 SCS
❑ 15211 SCS
❑ 15212 SCS
❑ 15213 SCS
❑ 15214 SCS

❑ 15301 SCS
❑ 15302 SCS
❑ 15303 SCS
❑ 15304 SCS
❑ 15305 SCS
❑ 15306 SCS
❑ 15307 SCS
❑ 15308 SCS
❑ 15309 SCS
❑ 15310 SCS
❑ 15311 SCS
❑ 15312 SCS
❑ 15313 SCS
❑ 15314 SCS
❑ 15315 SCS
❑ 15316 SCS
❑ 15317 SCS
❑ 15318 SCS
❑ 15319 SCS
❑ 15320 SCS
❑ 15321 SCS
❑ 15322 SCS
❑ 15323 SCS
❑ 15324 SCS
❑ 15325 SCS
❑ 15326 SCS
❑ 15327 SCS
❑ 15328 SCS
❑ 15329 SCS
❑ 15330 SCS
❑ 15331 SCS
❑ 15332 SCS
❑ 15333 SCS
❑ 15334 SCS
❑ 15335 SCS
❑ 15336 SCS
❑ 15337 SCS

Number	Operator
❑ 15338	SCS
❑ 15339	SCS
❑ 15340	SCS
❑ 16156	NYM
❑ 17018	VTN
❑ 17019	SUP
❑ 17025	SUP
❑ 17056	RIV
❑ 17080	LSL
❑ 17090	VTN
❑ 17096	SUP
❑ 17102	WCR
❑ 17105	RIV
❑ 17159	LSL
❑ 17167	WCR
❑ 17168	WCR
❑ 17173	GWR
❑ 17174	GWR
❑ 17175	GWR
❑ 18756	WCR
❑ 18806	WCR
❑ 18893	WCR
❑ 19208	WCR
❑ 21096	SUP
❑ 21100	NYM
❑ 21224	RIV
❑ 21232	SUP
❑ 21236	SUP
❑ 21241	SRP
❑ 21245	RIV
❑ 21249	SUP
❑ 21252	MHR
❑ 21256	WCR
❑ 21266	WCR
❑ 21269	RIV
❑ 21272	RIV
❑ 34525	WCR
❑ 35089	NYM
❑ 35185	SRP
❑ 35317	SUP
❑ 35322	SUP
❑ 35329	SUP
❑ 35407	WCR
❑ 35451	SUP
❑ 35461	SUP
❑ 35463	SUP
❑ 35464	SUP
❑ 35465	SUP
❑ 35466	VSO
❑ 35468	SUP
❑ 35469	RIV
❑ 35470	SUP
❑ 35476	SUP
❑ 35479	SUP
❑ 35486	SUP
❑ 35508	SUP
❑ 35511	LSL
❑ 35517	SUP
❑ 35518	SUP
❑ 40101	-
❑ 40102	OLS
❑ 40103	OLS
❑ 40104	OLS
❑ 40106	OLS
❑ 40107	OLS
❑ 40108	OLS
❑ 40109	OLS
❑ 40110	OLS
❑ 40111	OLS
❑ 40112	OLS
❑ 40113	-
❑ 40114	OLS
❑ 40115	-
❑ 40116	-
❑ 40117	OLS
❑ 40118	OLS
❑ 40119	OLS
❑ 40204	EMR
❑ 40205	EMR
❑ 40207	-
❑ 40210	OLS
❑ 40221	EMR
❑ 40231	OLS
❑ 40402	DBR
❑ 40403	DBR
❑ 40416	DBR
❑ 40417	OLS
❑ 40424	OLS
❑ 40425	OLS
❑ 40426	OLS
❑ 40433	OLS
❑ 40434	DBR
❑ 40601	ASR
❑ 40602	ASR
❑ 40604	ASR
❑ 40605	ASR
❑ 40608	ASR
❑ 40610	ASR
❑ 40612	ASR
❑ 40616	ASR
❑ 40624	ASR
❑ 40625	ASR
❑ 40700	EMR
❑ 40701	OLS
❑ 40702	OLS
❑ 40703	OLS
❑ 40704	OLS
❑ 40705	OLS
❑ 40706	OLS
❑ 40707	OLS
❑ 40708	OLS
❑ 40710	OLS
❑ 40711	OLS
❑ 40713	OLS
❑ 40715	OLS
❑ 40716	OLS
❑ 40718	OLS
❑ 40720	OLS
❑ 40721	OLS
❑ 40722	OLS
❑ 40727	OLS
❑ 40728	EMR
❑ 40730	EMR
❑ 40732	OLS
❑ 40733	OLS
❑ 40734	OLS
❑ 40735	OLS
❑ 40737	OLS
❑ 40739	OLS
❑ 40740	OLS
❑ 40741	EMR
❑ 40742	OLS
❑ 40743	OLS
❑ 40746	EMR
❑ 40748	OLS
❑ 40749	EMR
❑ 40750	OLS
❑ 40751	OLS
❑ 40752	OLS
❑ 40753	EMR
❑ 40754	EMR
❑ 40755	OLS
❑ 40756	EMR
❑ 40757	OLS
❑ 40801	OLS
❑ 40802	OLS
❑ 40803	OLS
❑ 40804	OLS
❑ 40806	OLS
❑ 40807	OLS
❑ 40808	-
❑ 40809	OLS
❑ 40810	-
❑ 40811	-
❑ 40900	-
❑ 40901	OLS
❑ 40902	-
❑ 40903	OLS
❑ 40904	-
❑ 41004	-
❑ 41006	OLS
❑ 41008	-
❑ 41010	OLS
❑ 41012	OLS
❑ 41016	OLS
❑ 41018	OLS
❑ 41020	OLS
❑ 41022	ASR
❑ 41026	AXC
❑ 41028	OLS
❑ 41030	OLS
❑ 41034	OLS
❑ 41035	AXC
❑ 41039	OLS
❑ 41040	OLS
❑ 41041	EMR
❑ 41043	OLS
❑ 41044	OLS
❑ 41046	EMR
❑ 41052	OLS
❑ 41056	OLS
❑ 41057	EMR
❑ 41058	OLS
❑ 41059	OLS
❑ 41061	EMR
❑ 41062	OLS
❑ 41063	EMR
❑ 41064	EMR
❑ 41066	OLS
❑ 41067	EMR
❑ 41069	EMR
❑ 41070	EMR
❑ 41071	EMR
❑ 41072	EMR
❑ 41075	EMR
❑ 41076	EMR
❑ 41077	EMR
❑ 41079	EMR
❑ 41083	OLS
❑ 41084	EMR
❑ 41087	OLS
❑ 41088	OLS
❑ 41089	OLS
❑ 41090	OLS
❑ 41091	OLS
❑ 41092	OLS
❑ 41095	OLS
❑ 41097	OLS
❑ 41098	OLS
❑ 41099	OLS
❑ 41100	OLS
❑ 41102	OLS
❑ 41103	OLS
❑ 41104	ASR
❑ 41106	OLS
❑ 41108	OLS
❑ 41110	OLS
❑ 41111	EMR
❑ 41113	EMR
❑ 41115	OLS
❑ 41116	ASR
❑ 41117	EMR
❑ 41118	OLS
❑ 41120	OLS
❑ 41122	OLS
❑ 41124	ASR
❑ 41126	ASR
❑ 41128	OLS
❑ 41130	ASR
❑ 41132	OLS
❑ 41135	ASR
❑ 41136	ASR
❑ 41137	OLS
❑ 41138	OLS
❑ 41140	ASR
❑ 41144	ASR
❑ 41146	OLS
❑ 41149	OLS
❑ 41150	OLS
❑ 41151	OLS
❑ 41152	OLS
❑ 41154	OLS
❑ 41156	EMR
❑ 41158	ASR
❑ 41159	OLS
❑ 41160	-
❑ 41161	OLS
❑ 41162	OLS
❑ 41164	OLS
❑ 41165	OLS
❑ 41166	-
❑ 41167	-
❑ 41169	OLS
❑ 41170	OLS
❑ 41176	OLS
❑ 41180	OLS
❑ 41182	OLS
❑ 41183	OLS
❑ 41185	OLS
❑ 41186	-
❑ 41187	OLS
❑ 41189	OLS
❑ 41190	OLS
❑ 41192	OLS
❑ 41193	AXC
❑ 41194	AXC
❑ 41195	AXC
❑ 41204	EMR
❑ 41205	EMR
❑ 41206	EMR
❑ 41207	EMR
❑ 41208	EMR
❑ 41209	EMR
❑ 42003	-
❑ 42004	ASR
❑ 42005	-
❑ 42006	OLS
❑ 42007	-
❑ 42008	-
❑ 42009	OLS
❑ 42010	ASR
❑ 42012	ASR
❑ 42013	ASR
❑ 42014	OLS
❑ 42015	-
❑ 42016	-
❑ 42019	ASR
❑ 42021	OLS
❑ 42023	-
❑ 42024	-
❑ 42025	OLS
❑ 42026	-
❑ 42027	-
❑ 42028	OLS
❑ 42029	OLS
❑ 42030	ASR
❑ 42031	OLS
❑ 42032	-
❑ 42033	ASR

Number	Operator
42034	-
42035	-
42036	AXC
42037	AXC
42038	AXC
42039	OLS
42040	OLS
42041	OLS
42042	-
42043	OLS
42044	-
42045	ASR
42046	ASR
42047	ASR
42048	OLS
42049	OLS
42050	OLS
42051	AXC
42052	AXC
42053	AXC
42054	ASR
42055	ASR
42056	OLS
42057	OLS
42058	OLS
42059	OLS
42060	OLS
42061	OLS
42062	OLS
42063	OLS
42064	OLS
42065	OLS
42066	OLS
42067	OLS
42068	OLS
42069	ASR
42070	OLS
42071	OLS
42072	OLS
42073	-
42074	OLS
42075	ASR
42076	-
42077	OLS
42078	OLS
42079	OLS
42080	OLS
42081	OLS
42083	OLS
42085	-
42087	-
42089	OLS
42091	OLS
42092	-
42094	-
42095	-
42096	OLS
42097	AXC
42098	OLS
42099	OLS
42100	EMR
42101	GWR
42102	OLS
42103	-
42105	-
42106	OLS
42107	ASR
42108	ASR
42109	OLS
42110	OLS
42111	EMR
42113	EMR
42115	OLS
42116	OLS
42117	OLS
42118	-
42119	EMR
42120	EMR
42121	EMR
42122	OLS
42123	OLS
42124	EMR
42125	OLS
42126	OLS
42127	OLS
42128	OLS
42129	ASR
42130	OLS
42131	EMR
42132	EMR
42133	EMR
42134	OLS
42135	EMR
42136	EMR
42137	EMR
42138	-
42139	EMR
42140	EMR
42141	EMR
42143	ASR
42144	ASR
42145	ASR
42146	OLS
42147	OLS
42148	EMR
42149	EMR
42150	OLS
42151	EMR
42152	EMR
42153	EMR
42154	OLS
42155	EMR
42156	EMR
42157	EMR
42158	OLS
42159	OLS
42160	OLS
42161	OLS
42163	OLS
42164	EMR
42165	EMR
42166	OLS
42167	-
42169	OLS
42171	OLS
42172	OLS
42173	OLS
42174	-
42175	-
42176	-
42177	ASR
42178	OLS
42179	OLS
42180	OLS
42181	OLS
42182	OLS
42183	ASR
42184	ASR
42185	OLS
42186	OLS
42188	OLS
42189	OLS
42190	OLS
42191	OLS
42192	OLS
42193	OLS
42195	OLS
42196	OLS
42197	OLS
42198	OLS
42199	OLS
42200	ASR
42201	-
42202	-
42203	-
42204	-
42205	OLS
42206	ASR
42207	ASR
42208	ASR
42209	ASR
42210	OLS
42211	-
42212	-
42213	OLS
42214	-
42215	OLS
42216	GWR
42217	GWR
42218	GWR
42219	OLS
42220	EMR
42221	OLS
42222	-
42224	-
42226	OLS
42228	OLS
42230	EMR
42231	-
42232	ASR
42233	OLS
42234	AXC
42235	OLS
42236	OLS
42237	OLS
42238	OLS
42239	OLS
42240	OLS
42241	OLS
42242	OLS
42243	OLS
42244	OLS
42245	OLS
42247	OLS
42250	OLS
42251	-
42252	OLS
42253	OLS
42255	ASR
42256	ASR
42257	OLS
42258	-
42259	ASR
42260	OLS
42261	OLS
42263	OLS
42264	-
42265	ASR
42266	-
42267	ASR
42268	OLS
42269	-
42271	-
42272	OLS
42273	-
42275	ASR
42276	ASR
42277	OLS
42279	ASR
42280	ASR
42281	OLS
42283	OLS
42284	OLS
42285	-
42286	OLS
42287	ASR
42288	-
42289	ASR
42290	AXC
42291	ASR
42292	ASR
42293	ASR
42294	OLS
42295	ASR
42296	OLS
42297	OLS
42299	OLS
42300	OLS
42301	OLS
42302	-
42303	OLS
42304	-
42305	OLS
42306	OLS
42307	OLS
42308	OLS
42310	-
42315	-
42317	-
42319	OLS
42321	OLS
42322	OLS
42323	OLS
42324	OLS
42325	ASR
42326	OLS
42327	EMR
42328	EMR
42329	EMR
42330	OLS
42331	EMR
42332	OLS
42333	ASR
42335	OLS
42337	EMR
42339	EMR
42340	OLS
42341	EMR
42342	AXC
42343	ASR
42344	ASR
42345	ASR
42346	OLS
42347	-
42348	OLS
42349	-
42350	OLS
42351	OLS
42352	OLS
42353	OLS
42354	OLS
42355	OLS
42356	OLS
42357	OLS
42360	OLS
42361	ASR
42362	OLS
42363	OLS
42364	-
42365	-
42366	AXC
42367	AXC
42368	AXC
42369	AXC
42370	AXC
42371	AXC
42372	AXC
42373	AXC
42374	AXC
42375	AXC
42376	AXC
42377	AXC
42378	AXC
42379	AXC
42380	AXC
42381	ASR
42382	OLS
42383	OLS
42384	EMR
42401	EMR
42402	EMR
42404	EMR
42405	EMR
42407	EMR
42408	EMR

Number	Operator
❑ 42501	OLS
❑ 42502	OLS
❑ 42503	OLS
❑ 42504	OLS
❑ 42505	OLS
❑ 42506	-
❑ 42507	OLS
❑ 42508	OLS
❑ 42509	OLS
❑ 42510	OLS
❑ 42511	ASR
❑ 42512	OLS
❑ 42513	OLS
❑ 42514	OLS
❑ 42515	OLS
❑ 42516	OLS
❑ 42517	OLS
❑ 42518	OLS
❑ 42519	OLS
❑ 42520	-
❑ 42551	OLS
❑ 42552	OLS
❑ 42553	ASR
❑ 42554	-
❑ 42555	OLS
❑ 42556	OLS
❑ 42557	OLS
❑ 42558	-
❑ 42559	ASR
❑ 42560	OLS
❑ 42561	ASR
❑ 42562	ASR
❑ 42563	-
❑ 42564	OLS
❑ 42565	-
❑ 42566	-
❑ 42567	ASR
❑ 42568	OLS
❑ 42569	OLS
❑ 42570	-
❑ 42571	ASR
❑ 42572	OLS
❑ 42573	OLS
❑ 42574	-
❑ 42575	OLS
❑ 42576	ASR
❑ 42577	-
❑ 42578	ASR
❑ 42579	OLS
❑ 42580	-
❑ 42581	OLS
❑ 42582	-
❑ 42583	-
❑ 42584	EMR
❑ 42585	EMR
❑ 42586	EMR
❑ 44001	OLS
❑ 44002	-
❑ 44003	-
❑ 44004	ASR
❑ 44005	-
❑ 44007	OLS

Number	Operator
❑ 44008	-
❑ 44009	GWR
❑ 44010	OLS
❑ 44011	OLS
❑ 44012	AXC
❑ 44013	-
❑ 44014	-
❑ 44015	ASR
❑ 44016	OLS
❑ 44017	AXC
❑ 44018	OLS
❑ 44019	OLS
❑ 44020	OLS
❑ 44021	AXC
❑ 44022	OLS
❑ 44023	ASR
❑ 44024	OLS
❑ 44025	OLS
❑ 44026	OLS
❑ 44028	OLS
❑ 44029	ASR
❑ 44030	ASR
❑ 44031	OLS
❑ 44032	ASR
❑ 44033	-
❑ 44034	-
❑ 44035	ASR
❑ 44036	-
❑ 44037	ASR
❑ 44038	OLS
❑ 44039	ASR
❑ 44040	OLS
❑ 44041	EMR
❑ 44042	-
❑ 44043	OLS
❑ 44044	EMR
❑ 44045	OLS
❑ 44046	EMR
❑ 44047	EMR
❑ 44048	EMR
❑ 44049	OLS
❑ 44050	OLS
❑ 44051	EMR
❑ 44052	AXC
❑ 44054	EMR
❑ 44056	OLS
❑ 44057	OLS
❑ 44058	OLS
❑ 44059	OLS
❑ 44060	OLS
❑ 44061	OLS
❑ 44063	OLS
❑ 44064	-
❑ 44066	ASR
❑ 44067	-
❑ 44069	-
❑ 44070	EMR
❑ 44071	EMR
❑ 44072	AXC
❑ 44073	OLS
❑ 44074	OLS
❑ 44075	OLS
❑ 44076	-

Number	Operator
❑ 44077	OLS
❑ 44078	OLS
❑ 44079	OLS
❑ 44080	OLS
❑ 44081	-
❑ 44083	-
❑ 44085	EMR
❑ 44086	ASR
❑ 44089	OLS
❑ 44090	-
❑ 44091	-
❑ 44093	OLS
❑ 44094	OLS
❑ 44097	-
❑ 44098	OLS
❑ 44100	-
❑ 44101	-
❑ 45001	AXC
❑ 45002	AXC
❑ 45003	AXC
❑ 45004	AXC
❑ 45005	AXC
❑ 45018	WCR
❑ 45020	DBR
❑ 45026	WCR
❑ 46001	OLS
❑ 46002	OLS
❑ 46003	OLS
❑ 46004	OLS
❑ 46005	OLS
❑ 46006	-
❑ 46007	-
❑ 46008	OLS
❑ 46009	-
❑ 46010	ASR
❑ 46011	OLS
❑ 46012	OLS
❑ 46013	-
❑ 46014	OLS
❑ 46015	OLS
❑ 46016	OLS
❑ 46017	-
❑ 46018	OLS
❑ 48101	GWR
❑ 48102	GWR
❑ 48103	GWR
❑ 48104	GWR
❑ 48105	GWR
❑ 48106	GWR
❑ 48107	GWR
❑ 48108	GWR
❑ 48109	GWR
❑ 48110	GWR
❑ 48111	GWR
❑ 48112	GWR
❑ 48113	GWR
❑ 48114	GWR
❑ 48115	GWR
❑ 48116	GWR
❑ 48117	GWR

Number	Operator
❑ 48118	GWR
❑ 48119	GWR
❑ 48120	GWR
❑ 48121	GWR
❑ 48122	GWR
❑ 48123	GWR
❑ 48124	GWR
❑ 48125	GWR
❑ 48126	GWR
❑ 48127	GWR
❑ 48128	GWR
❑ 48129	GWR
❑ 48130	GWR
❑ 48131	GWR
❑ 48132	GWR
❑ 48133	GWR
❑ 48134	GWR
❑ 48135	GWR
❑ 49101	GWR
❑ 49102	GWR
❑ 49103	GWR
❑ 49104	GWR
❑ 49105	GWR
❑ 49106	GWR
❑ 49107	GWR
❑ 49108	GWR
❑ 49109	GWR
❑ 49110	GWR
❑ 49111	GWR
❑ 49112	GWR
❑ 49113	GWR
❑ 80041	RIV
❑ 80042	RIV
❑ 80043	WCR
❑ 80044	LSL
❑ 99025	WCR
❑ 99035	SUP
❑ 99040	SUP
❑ 99041	SUP
❑ 99080	SUP
❑ 99108	VTN
❑ 99120	SUP
❑ 99121	WCR
❑ 99125	WCR
❑ 99127	WCR
❑ 99128	WCR
❑ 99132	WCR
❑ 99193	WCR
❑ 99194	WCR
❑ 99195	WCR
❑ 99241	SUP
❑ 99304	WCR
❑ 99311	WCR
❑ 99312	SUP
❑ 99316	WCR
❑ 99318	WCR
❑ 99319	WCR
❑ 99326	WCR
❑ 99327	WCR

Number	Operator
❑ 99328	WCR
❑ 99329	WCR
❑ 99337	GSW
❑ 99348	WCR
❑ 99349	VTN
❑ 99350	WCR
❑ 99353	VTN
❑ 99354	WCR
❑ 99361	VTN
❑ 99402	WCR
❑ 99405	SUP
❑ 99530	VSO
❑ 99531	VSO
❑ 99532	VSO
❑ 99534	VSO
❑ 99535	VSO
❑ 99536	VSO
❑ 99537	VSO
❑ 99539	VSO
❑ 99541	VSO
❑ 99543	VSO
❑ 99545	VSO
❑ 99546	VSO
❑ 99678	WCR
❑ 99679	WCR
❑ 99670	WCR
❑ 99671	WCR
❑ 99672	WCR
❑ 99673	WCR
❑ 99674	WCR
❑ 99675	WCR
❑ 99676	WCR
❑ 99677	WCR
❑ 99680	WCR
❑ 99706	WCR
❑ 99710	WCR
❑ 99712	WCR
❑ 99713	WCR
❑ 99717	WCR
❑ 99718	WCR
❑ 99720	SUP
❑ 99721	WCR
❑ 99722	WCR
❑ 99723	WCR
❑ 99782	SUP
❑ 99792	SUP
❑ 99884	WCR
❑ 99953	SUP
❑ 99960	GSW
❑ 99961	GSW
❑ 99965	GSW
❑ 99967	GSW
❑ 99968	GSW
❑ 99969	GSW
❑ 99966	WCR
❑ 99968	VSO
❑ 99969	VSO
❑ 99991	SUP
❑ 99993	LSL
❑ 99995	SUP

NPCCS Stock

❑ 6260 NRL
❑ 6261 NRL
❑ 6262 NRL
❑ 6263 NRL
❑ 6264 NRL

❑ 6330 GWR
❑ 6336 GWR
❑ 6338 GWR
❑ 6340 LNE
❑ 6344 LNE
❑ 6346 LNE
❑ 6348 GWR
❑ 6352 LNE
❑ 6353 LNE
❑ 6376 COL
❑ 6377 COL
❑ 6378 COL
❑ 6379 COL
❑ 6392 COL
❑ 6397 COL

❑ 9393 LNE
❑ 9394 LNE

❑ 9701 NRL
❑ 9702 NRL
❑ 9703 NRL
❑ 9708 NRL
❑ 9713 NRL
❑ 9714 NRL
❑ 62287 NRL
❑ 62384 NRL

❑ 64664 AFG
❑ 64707 AFG

❑ 68501 AFG
❑ 68504 AFG
❑ 68505 AFG

❑ 72612 NRL
❑ 72616 NRL
❑ 72630 NRL
❑ 72631 NRL
❑ 72639 NRL

❑ 80204 SUP
❑ 80217 SUP
❑ 80220 SUP

❑ 82101 DRS
❑ 82102 GAR
❑ 82103 GAR
❑ 82105 GAR
❑ 82107 GAR
❑ 82109 OLS
❑ 82111 NRL
❑ 82112 GAR
❑ 82113 ATE
❑ 82114 GAR
❑ 82115 NRL
❑ 82118 GAR
❑ 82121 GAR
❑ 82124 NRL
❑ 82126 DRS
❑ 82127 GAR
❑ 82129 NRL
❑ 82132 GAR
❑ 82133 GAR
❑ 82136 GAR
❑ 82138 DBR
❑ 82139 GAR
❑ 82143 GAR
❑ 82145 NRL
❑ 82146 DBC
❑ 82149 OLS
❑ 82150 DBR
❑ 82152 GAR
❑ 82200 LNE
❑ 82201 LNE
❑ 82202 LNE
❑ 82203 OLS
❑ 82204 LNE
❑ 82205 LNE
❑ 82206 LNE
❑ 82207 LNE
❑ 82208 LNE
❑ 82209 LNE
❑ 82210 LNE
❑ 82211 LNE
❑ 82212 LNE
❑ 82213 LNE
❑ 82214 LNE
❑ 82215 LNE
❑ 82216 OLS
❑ 82217 OLS
❑ 82218 LNE
❑ 82219 LNE
❑ 82220 LNE
❑ 82222 LNE
❑ 82223 OLS
❑ 82224 LNE
❑ 82225 LNE
❑ 82226 TFW
❑ 82227 LNE
❑ 82228 GTL
❑ 82229 TFW
❑ 82230 LNE
❑ 82231 OLS
❑ 82301 CRW
❑ 82302 CRW
❑ 82303 CRW
❑ 82304 CRW
❑ 82305 CRW
❑ 82306 TFW
❑ 82307 TFW
❑ 82308 TFW
❑ 82309 CRW
❑ 92114 NRL
❑ 92159 OLS

❑ 92901 OLS
❑ 92904 WCR
❑ 92931 OLS
❑ 92939 NRL
❑ 95727 DBC
❑ 95761 DBC
❑ 95763 DBC

❑ 96100 VTN
❑ 96139 OLS
❑ 96175 WCR
❑ 96181 OLS

❑ 96371 EPX
❑ 96372 DRS
❑ 96373 DRS
❑ 96374 WAB
❑ 96375 DRS
❑ 96602 COL
❑ 96603 COL
❑ 96604 COL
❑ 96605 COL
❑ 96606 COL
❑ 96607 COL
❑ 96608 COL
❑ 96609 COL
❑ 99666 NRL

Service Stock

❑ 950001 NRL
❑ 960014 CRW

❑ 971001 NRL
❑ 971002 NRL
❑ 971003 NRL
❑ 971004 NRL

❑ 975025 NRL
❑ 975081 NRL
❑ 975087 NRL
❑ 975091 NRL
❑ 975464 NRL
❑ 975477 NRL
❑ 975486 NRL
❑ 975814 NRL
❑ 975974 AFG
❑ 975978 AFG
❑ 975984 NRL
❑ 977337 NRL
❑ 977868 NRL
❑ 977869 NRL
❑ 977969 NRL
❑ 977974 NRL
❑ 977983 NRL
❑ 977984 NRL
❑ 977985 NRL
❑ 977986 NRL
❑ 977993 NRL
❑ 977994 NRL
❑ 977995 NRL
❑ 977997 NRL

❑ 999550 NRL
❑ 999602 NRL
❑ 999605 NRL
❑ 999606 NRL

Right: *Owned by the Class 50 Alliance and operated by GBRf, Class 50s Nos. 50007 and 50049 sport full GBRf livery. The pair are usually based on the Severn Valley Railway and used infrequently on main line services. One such working was on 23 January 2020, when the pair operated 'top and tail' with former Caledonian Sleeper No. 10706 on a transit move from Laira depot to Long Marston. The train is seen passing Dawlish.* **CJM**

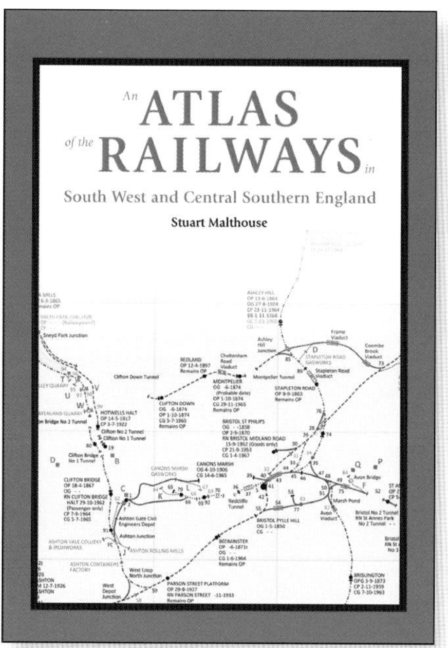

An Atlas of the Railways of South West and Central Southern England

Stuart Malthouse

This atlas gives an amazing insight into railway history in the south and west and is a labour of love, having taken many years to compile. The railways of the South West and Central Southern England are shown in astonishing detail.

Industrial railways are shown as well as passenger railways and each map is accompanied by a detailed key of the public and private railway systems with dates or operation and gauges, stations and topographical features, together with detailed opening and closing dates and name changes. A chronology of the public railway routes also accompanies each map, which includes independent public railways or independent private railways with public rail involvement.

The area covered extends from Cornwall in the South West to Hampshire in central Southern England, and as far north as Bristol and Swindon.

ISBN: 9780711038714
432 pages
£40.00

Rail Atlas of Great Britain & Ireland
15th Edition
Stuart Baker

The Rail Atlas of Great Britain and Ireland was first published in 1977 and now comes the release of its new 15th edition, proof indeed that the Atlas is one of the most successful and sought after railway titles ever published.

The Atlas is the most accurate, reliable and up to date guide to the current railway network in the British Isles. Lines open to all traffic and those used by freight only are differentiated as are single track sections. The maps also show preserved lines, freight terminals, LRT schemes, passenger stations, lines under construction and proposed lines.

This new edition as always has been fully revised and updated whilst retaining the convenient format established in previous editions. The mapping on each page overlaps with that on adjoining pages to make it easier to follow a long-distance route. Where appropriate, additional detailed inset maps have been drawn to show the complex railway developments in metropolitan areas such as London and Manchester.

The Rail Atlas of Great Britain and Ireland continues to be the essential work of reference for both railway enthusiasts and those working in the railway industry.

ISBN: 9780860936817
136 pages
£20.00